The Autodesk File

Bits of History, Words of Experience

Edited by John Walker

 New Riders Publishing, Thousand Oaks, California

The AutoCAD File
Bits of History, Words of Experience

Edited by John Walker

Published by:

New Riders Publishing
Post Office Box 4846
Thousand Oaks, CA 91360, U.S.A.

© Copyright 1987, 1988, 1989, Autodesk, Inc.

First Edition 1987 published by Autodesk, Inc.
Second Edition 1988 published by Autodesk, Inc.
Third Edition 1989 published by New Riders Publishing.

All Rights Reserved. No part of this book may be used or reproduced or transmitted in any form or by any means, electronic or mechanical, including photocopying, recording, or by any information storage and retrieval system without written permission from the publisher, except for the inclusion of brief quotations in a review.

Printed in the United State of America

Library of Congress Cataloging-in-Publication Data

```
The Autodesk file.

  Includes index.
  1. Autodesk, Inc.--History--Sources.  2. Computer
software industry--United States--History--Sources.
I. Walker, John, 1949-
HD9696.C64A8823   1989    338.7'61005'0973    89-12355
ISBN 0-934035-63-6
```

Trademarks

Autodesk, the Autodesk logo, AutoCAD, AutoCAD AEC, AutoSketch, AutoLISP, and Authorized AutoCAD Training Center are registered trademarks of Autodesk, Inc. AutoSolid, AutoShade, CAD/camera, The Engineer Works, ADI, DXF, ACAD, Advanced User Interface, AUI, AutoFlix, Auto Book, AutoCAD-80, AutoCAD-86, and Autodesk Forum are trademarks of Autodesk, Inc. IBM, PC/XT/AT, Personal System/2, and PC-DOS are trademarks of International Business Machines Corporation. Apollo, DOMAIN, and AEGIS are trademarks of Apollo Computer, Incorporated. DEC, VMS, VAX, and VAX-station are trademarks of Digital Equipment Corporation. Sun Microsystems, Sun Workstation, Sun–2, and Sun–3 are trademarks of Sun Microsystems, Incorporated. Microsoft, MS, MS-DOS, and XENIX are registered trademarks of Microsoft Corporation. Intel, 8080, 8086, and 8088 are trademarks of Intel Corporation. Lotus, 1-2-3, and VisiCalc are trademarks of Lotus Development Corporation. Texas Instruments is a registered trademark of Texas Instruments Corporation. WordStar is a registered trademark of MicroPro International Corporation. BASIC is a registered trademark of the Trustees of Dartmouth College. dBase, dBase III, and Ashton-Tate are registered trademarks of Ashton-Tate. Unix is a trademark of AT&T Bell Laboratories. TEX is a trademark of the American Mathematical Society. CompuServe is a trademark of H&R Block, Incorporated. Marinchip, M9900, QBASIC, and WINDOW are trademarks of Marinchip Systems, Ltd. The Golden Age of Engineering, Tools For The Golden Age Of Engineering, and Turbo Digital and its associated logotype are trademarks of Marinchip Systems. CP/M, CP/M-80, CB80, CB86, CP/M-86, and PL/I-80 are trademarks of Digital Research, Inc. Glasnost and Perestroika are trademarks of the Communist Party of the Soviet Union. Xanadu is a trademark of Xanadu Operating Company, Inc. Labitat is a trademark of External Tanks Corporation. Apple, Macintosh, Lisa, and HyperCard are trademarks of Apple Computer, Inc. Cray and X/MP are registered trademarks of Cray Research, Inc. COMPAQ is a trademark of COMPAQ Computer Corporation. ComputerLand is a trademark of ComputerLand Corporation. Selector V and Micro-Ap, Inc. are trademarks of Micro-Ap, Inc. ANSYS is a registered trademark of Swanson Analysis Systems, Inc. Bernoulli Box and the IOMEGA logo are registered trademarks of IOMEGA Corporation. MSC-NASTRAN is a registered trademark of the National Aeronautics and Space Administration. Z80 and Z8000 are registered trademarks of Zilog, Inc.

Other product names mentioned herein may also be trademarks used here for identification purposes only.

Design and Production

The Autodesk File was produced by contributions from the following editorial and production staff of New Riders Publishing:

Editor	Harbert V. Rice
Associate Editor	Carolyn L. Porter
Book Design and Xerox Ventura Page Layout	Carolyn L. Porter
Financial Charts	Jon DeKeles
Paste-up	Todd Meisler
Cover Design	Jill Casty & Associates

Table of Contents

Introduction	*1*
Section One — 1982 — The Beginning	*3*
Let's Organize a Company	*7*
Thoughts About the Partnership	*28*
After the First Meeting	*43*
What to Name the Company	*48*
Getting into the Details	*49*
Changes to the Organization Plan	*59*
Initial Stock Distribution	*64*
Autodesk Becomes a Reality	*66*
Random Notes on Software and Marketing	*84*
Autodesk General Status Report	*94*
Brief Note	*105*
Moving From Organization to Operation	*107*
1982 Annual Meeting	*117*
Section Two — 1983 — Turning the Corner	*121*
After COMDEX	*125*
Quality Department Priorities	*130*
Is This a Company or What?	*133*
Getting Control	*142*
Growing Pains	*148*

Crisis Letter	*156*
Business Plans and a Way to Organize	*162*
A Company Clearly on the Rise	*175*
Low Rent 3D	*181*
Electric Malcolm	*185*
October 1983 Meeting	*190*
Piece of Cake	*194*
"Let's Go for It — and Win the Battle!"	*196*

Section Three — 1984 — Becoming a Major Force — 203

A Letter Written on the Cusp	*205*
The Deal On the Table	*213*
Expanding the Product Line	*219*
Taxes and Such	*224*

Section Four — 1985 — Number One — 231

Why Lisp?	*233*
Number One	*235*
Going for Image with Prime Time	*237*
Initial Public Offering	*245*
Protecting Your Money	*262*
Looking Back and Looking Forward	*269*

Section Five — 1986 — Growth Means Change — 283

Time of Turbulence	*285*
A Presentation of Autodesk's Strategy	*292*
Looking for Super Programmers	*305*

CAD as the Heart of Computer Science	*308*
The Computer Revolution	*313*
AutoBits — Some Humor from Autodesk	*323*
John Walker's Transition to Programming	*336*
Hardware Lock Debater's Guide	*338*
Focus on the Future	*344*
Cadetron and Solid Modeling	*351*
Removing the Hardware Lock	*356*

Section Six — 1987 — Building for the Future *361*

The Portable Data Base	*363*
Jeremiad — A Little Autodesk Philosophy	*376*
The Golden Age of Engineering	*381*
Cosmic Perspective	*384*
External Tanks	*386*
Source Distribution	*389*
The Morning After the Crash	*397*

Section Seven — 1988 — Working Philosophy *403*

Thoughts on Tight Security	*405*
Where's It All Going?	*411*
Xanadu	*416*
Bored of Directors	*421*
Valedictory	*423*
The View from Sweden	*430*
L'Envoi: The First Six Years	*440*

Section Eight — The Appendices   *443*
   Appendix A — Financial Results   *445*
   Appendix B — Product Release History   *451*
   Appendix C — Before Autodesk   *455*
   Appendix D — Auto Book Notes   *465*
   Appendix E — AutoCAD-80 Development Log   *473*
   Appendix F — AutoCAD Wish List   *509*

Index   *523*

Introduction

How to begin to tell the story of Autodesk? The company was so unusual in its origin, so unconventional in its growth, and so eventful has been the road that started with a small group of programmers sitting around talking about building a company and has led, so far, to a multinational company which is the undisputed leader in its market, that it's tempting just to shrug your shoulders and say "you had to be there."

Because Autodesk started out as a very decentralized organization and has remained one to some extent, and also because of the prolix proclivities of its founders, who would rather write a book than talk on a telephone for ten minutes, the genesis, evolution, and history of Autodesk has generated a large volume of paper.

Unlike many companies, whose history can be recovered, if at all, only by a major oral history effort, one can watch Autodesk develop by reading the documents that were, during the company's development, the primary means of communication among the people involved. Reading these documents lets you see how assumptions we seldom question today got cast into concrete, how many blind alleys we had to explore to find answers which seem, in retrospect, utterly obvious, and how throughout the history of the company, when a major effort was called for to advance the company, Autodesk people have always responded with the energy, creativity, responsibility, and dedication which are the largest reasons for our great success in the market.

Too many business books, like histories of science, tend to tell the story as a straightforward progression from start to finish. Reality is never that easy. Decisions are made in the face of incomplete and unreliable information because they must be made. There's no way to tell a promising avenue of success from a blind alley when you turn onto it — you only find out much later. As you read through these documents, you'll be seeing it all, and if it seems tedious and repetitious, it's because the process of building a company is often tedious and repetitious. But it's also rewarding, and I hope that these documents also convey the feeling of exhilaration, challenge, and accomplishment that everybody felt as we built this company into what it is today.

When you read these documents, you're opening time capsules buried as Autodesk developed. The documents are presented with essentially no editing other than that required to convert them from the variety of document processors in which they were written. Some irrelevant material, such as five-year-old name and address lists, has been deleted, but no elisions have been made which rewrite history, cover up errors, or otherwise alter the record. Where appropriate, I've added footnotes to explain matters which might not be clear at several years' remove and to call out important items mentioned in passing in the text.

Since this is a history in documents, the picture of the company it presents is unavoidably colored by the documents available when this history was prepared. The resulting collection weights my contribution heavier than it was because I write prolifically and keep everything I write. It covers AutoCAD-80 far out of proportion to its importance because the AutoCAD-80 logs exist in machine-readable form and the AutoCAD-86 logs do not. There is little coverage of the rich history of CAD/Camera, and little of the early days of the company because as the company has grown, business has come to be transacted far more in meetings and via ephemeral memoranda than in explicit status reports. As a result, nothing of the second public stock offering has been included, nor anything of the development of AutoCAD AEC or of AutoSketch. The absence of documents in this history is simply the effect of what has been preserved, not an attempt on my part to emphasize or diminish the importance of any aspect of the company's development or any individual's contribution.

I don't know whether these documents show how to start and run a company that assures success in a treacherous market or whether they simply chronicle the education of a group who was in the right place at the right time. Probably nobody ever will know. But from a sample size of one, it's the only way I know to start a wildly successful company, and improbable as it may seem, this is how it really happened.

John Walker

Sausalito, Caifornia
June, 1988

Section One

The Beginning

Publisher's Notes
January 1982 — December 1982

In the following documents you will see the formation of the software company that became Autodesk, Inc. The core documents are John Walker's "Information Letters" that lay out the strategy and goals for forming a software company. We have put together a set of calendar notes, called Publisher's Notes, for each of the seven sections that form the history of the company. These notes provide a yearly context of key events in the company's organization and product history, a summary of its financial performance, and brief descriptions of the documents found in each Section.

Key Events

During this first year, the nucleus of people that made up Autodesk got together, incorporated, and put together ("cobbled up" in their words) some potential products. By the end of the year they had a winner called AutoCAD, a design and drafting program running on the IBM PC. Here are the key events. The ◆ indicates the documents that follow in Section One.

- ◆ January 12, 1982. Working Paper — The first conceptualization for Autodesk, Inc. but called Marin Software Partners after John Walker's (and Dan Drake's) company, Marinchip Systems Ltd.

- ◆ January 19, 1982. Information Letter #1 — A detailed discussion of the proposed structure of the company as a limited partnership.

January 30, 1982. First Organization Meeting.

- ◆ February 12, 1982. Information Letter #2 — Follow up to the first organization meeting. Proposes forming the company as a corporation, but keeping share distributions as warrants and stock options.

- ◆ March 2, 1982. Information Letter #3 — First organization plan written by Dan Drake. Discusses issuance of shares to founders.

March 18, 1982. West Coast Computer Faire. Autodesk (then called Desktop Solutions) showed "a cobbled up" version of AutoCAD (called MicroCAD).

- April 2, 1982. Information Letter #4 — New organization plan, including the burning question of what to name the company.

April 9, 1982. Autodesk, Inc. incorporated as a California corporation. Stock issued to founders shortly after.

- May 1, 1982. Information Letter #5 — Discusses the paperwork associated with the incorporation and progress in organizing the company.
- May 26, 1982. Information Letter #6 — Discusses marketing and progress on products.
- July 8 & 25, 1982. Information Letters #7 & #8 — General status report on marketing and products for the company, including notes on the July monthly meeting.
- August 1, 1982. August General Meeting Minutes by Dan Drake. Discusses the task list organization that worked to get things done.

August, 1982. First AutoCAD software (called MicroCAD at the time) shipped. This was an 8080 version.

November, 1982. COMDEX. AutoCAD was shown at the fall COMDEX computer show and was an obvious hit.

December 1982. Official release and shipping date for AutoCAD-80 Version 1.0.

- December 28, 1982. Notice for the first annual stockholders meeting.

Founders

Autodesk was founded by sixteen people. Most of the founders lived in the San Francisco Bay area. Many were involved in pre-existing ventures, while holding down full-time jobs. Here is a brief list of founders that you will encounter in the following documents.

John Walker and Dan Drake were principals in Marinchip Systems.

Dave Kalish, Duff Kurland, Mauri Laitinen, Jodi Lehman, Greg Lutz, Keith Marcelius, Hal Royaltey, and Kern Sibbald were programmers and system developers living in and around the Bay area. Jack Stuppin was a financial advisor; and Robert Tufts was legal advisor.

Mike Riddle lived out of state. He wrote the program called Interact that was re-written to make the first version of AutoCAD.

Peter Goldmann and Richard Handyside were from England. Richard Handyside established the London office. Rudolf Künzli established the Swiss office. Lars Åke Moureau established the Swedish office.

Mike Ford joined the company to establish the marketing and sales effort. He also lived in the Bay area.

Products

Here is a brief list of products that you will see mentioned in the following pages.

AutoCAD is a computer-aided design and drafting system. This is the product that took off. It was shown first as "MicroCAD" at the West Coast Computer Faire, but renamed and released as AutoCAD. (AutoCAD-80 refers to the Z80 and Intel 8080 versions. AutoCAD-86 refers to the Intel 8086 version for the IBM PC.)

Autodesk was an office automation system. It provided file cards, card file boxes, and a calendar. A prototype was built, but never sold. Ironically, this is the product for which the company was named.

Window was a screen editor. This product was briefly released commercially as AutoScreen, but was developed and used internally. You will see it referred to as "Kern's editor."

You will see some other products mentioned which were worked on or talked about, but never developed into commercial products. These include: QBasic, Diff, Opti-calc, and Communicator. And, of course, Auto Book, the product "that wouldn't die." (For some notes on Auto Book see Appendix D.)

For those who want to see more about the early AutoCAD development efforts, John Walker's AutoCAD-80 Development Log is given in Appendix E. An early AutoCAD Wish List compiled by Duff Kurland is given in Appendix F.

Financial Summary

The starting working capital for Autodesk was $59,030 from the sale of stock and options. At the end of the fiscal year (January 1983) sales were $14,733, and the company showed a net loss of $9,465. This was the first and last loss.

Autodesk, Inc. Founders

Let's Organize a Company

The Working Paper was the document which resulted in the formation of Autodesk. I wrote it at a time when it was clear that Marinchip Systems, the company that I had started in 1977, and which Dan Drake and I had operated since 1980, did not have a bright future. In an attempt to find markets for Marinchip's software, we had been talking to the OEM division of Lifeboat Associates. It was on a trip with Lifeboat to computer companies in the Los Angeles area in December of 1981 that I first formed the idea of starting a software-only company to provide software for the coming tidal wave of small computers from large manufacturers. This working paper was written in 48 hours, after weeks of thinking about what to do. This paper served as the introduction of the concept and the invitation to the meeting to organise the company.

Marin Software Partners Working Paper

by John Walker
Revision 4 — January 12, 1982

Introduction

This document is a working paper which sets out the background, general business plan, and strategy of Marin Software Partners (MSP), a new company to be formed by some of those who read this paper. The major goal of Marin Software Partners will be to develop and market software packages, primarily application but also system, for popular mass-market computer systems, including, but not limited to, CP/M, IBM 8086 DOS, and Unix System III.

Background

Marinchip Systems and many of those associated with it in various capacities have discovered that while it is possible to earn a reasonable living attempting to be a full-service computer company through the massive exertion of effort and consumption of physical capital, it is not possible to achieve the success that has accrued to those who let the mass market do their selling for them. The possessor of a unique software package such as Visi-Calc or Wordstar finds that much of the promotion of the package is done by the hardware vendor or systems house who wants to sell a system by providing the capability the package offers.

It is far too late in the game for a successful start-up of a full service computer company without massive venture capital and an organization which none of us knows how to manage. Furthermore, the chances of success against those with literally unlimited advertising budgets and marketing organizations (IBM, NEC, etc.) are very slim. However, the software business is very different. First of all, a software package can be produced out of pure effort, with only the capital needed to finance the machine and pay the programmer. Unlike hardware, the big vendors of mass market machines are mostly utterly ignorant regarding software, and software manufacturing is as easy as copying discs. In addition, independent software marketing channels such as Lifeboat Associates exist and are working in cooperation with major hardware vendors (Xerox, HP, Altos) to sell application software to purchasers of hardware systems.

I feel that at the present time it is possible to, albeit with high risk, start a software firm with the capital available from Marinchip Systems, and that this is the best possible deployment of that capital. No conceivable investment in the business of Marinchip has the probability of generating a comparable return. Unlike the hardware business, MSP will be in the middle tier of companies in its business, and will likely be in the front rank based on competence and professionalism.

Which brings me to...

The game has changed. In 1977 this business was fun — the sellers and buyers were hotshot techies like ourselves, everybody spoke the same language and knew what was going on, and technical excellence was recognised and rewarded. Today, the microcomputer industry is run by middle manager types who know far more about P/L statements than they do RAM organization. They are the people who determine whether you succeed or fail, and their evaluations are seldom based on technical qualities. Hence, the first thing any venture in this field has to be is businesslike.

What this means is that, first of all, any person who is unwilling to assign this venture a priority equal to or above his current employment does not belong in MSP. That doesn't mean you have to quit your job to join MSP. What it does mean is that if you say you agree to a certain share, then you will deliver that share week after week, month after month, year after year regardless of other commitments except in the case of total catastrophe which would cause you to equally neglect any other job you have. In working with people associated with Marinchip, the following conversation has occurred more than once:

"When will it be done?"
"Well, I don't know."
"Why not?"
"Well, I know I told you it would be done by now, but a lot of stuff came up at work and I…"
"Isn't this work? Don't you get paid for it?"

If you view your work with microcomputers as a hobby, if you look on the microcomputer business as a way to write off your home computer on your taxes or mollify your spouse about the money you spend on computers, if you're looking for a supplementary income to pay for a disc drive or outboard motor or whatever, you do not belong in MSP. MSP will be composed exclusively of people who intend to develop quality products, aggressively market them, and reap rewards far greater than those available from their current employment. We don't expect most people to start on a full-time basis; in fact, we're deliberately organizing the company to provide full time support services to moonlighting implementors, but if we're successful, we expect those involved to increase their commitment as the business grows.

If you feel, as I do, that a competent software person with the marketing connections to decide what to do and how to sell it is in the best possible position today to become very wealthy, then you belong in MSP.

General development strategy

Marinchip Systems has developed and is expanding a business relationship with Lifeboat Associates of New York City. Lifeboat is probably the largest independent software vendor in the world today, and is the primary source for application software for almost all the mass market computers sold currently. Through technical review of Marinchip products and presentations to Lifeboat customers, conversations with Lifeboat personnel, and negotiation of a very complex OEM agreement, Marinchip has come to be seen by Lifeboat as a competent organization in both the business and technical senses.

Lifeboat has expressed an interest in working with Marinchip to develop Marinchip products to be marketed through Lifeboat, particularly a QBASIC compiler for the 8086 (IBM) and Z-80 processors. Additionally, our contacts with Lifeboat give us the ability to sound out market demand for various packages, get tips on what people are asking for and not able to find, and also contacts with OEMs who want specialized work done.

Clearly then, one of the first tasks of MSP after formation will be to meet with Lifeboat and explain our business plan to them and get feedback and suggestions.

I think that we already have the credibility to get work funneled our way by Lifeboat, and in any case the contacts are invaluable for market research.

MSP will concentrate on development of specific products with clearly defined functions. We will not attempt to implement grandiose systems and will not stray too far into the systems programming arena. Any program we develop must require little or no customization for installation, and little or no user consultation after sale. Otherwise, we can't afford to sell it. We're aiming for packages like Visi-Calc, Selector, Supersort, Wordstar, etc.

MSP must budget a substantial percentage of its capital for advertising and promotion. Undoubtedly, some packages will be largely marketed for us, but we cannot assume this and must realize that a market must first be created through advertising before it can be sold to.

Form of organization

MSP will be organized as a partnership. The general partner will be Marinchip Systems Ltd. (MSL), and the limited partners will be all the individuals associated with the company. Using this form of organization provides the limited partners the limited liability of a corporation without the disadvantages of double taxation of earnings, the risk of royalty income causing the corporation to be construed as a "Personal Holding Company" subject to 70% punitive tax, and the general hassles of operating a corporation.

MSL, as general partner, will be responsible for the day-to-day operation of the company. It will provide the following services:

Headquarters services. Phone answering, order taking, shipping and receiving, copying.

Administrative services. Accounting, banking, billing, A/R maintenance, preparation of reports to partners.

Marketing services. Contact and negotiation with Lifeboat and other distribution channels, ad agency interface and copy preparation, ad placement, trade show exhibition. Market research and potential product evaluation.

Project coordination. Central message dispatching between partners. Monitoring of project schedules and reminders of delivery dates. Follow-up of customer complaints and suggestions.

Manufacturing. Manual printing, disc copying, inventory maintenance.

Limited partners will be responsible for the following:

Product development. Design, implementation, and documentation of new products.

Product maintenance. Correction of reported problems, adapting existing products to new hardware/software systems, installation of new features, revision of documentation.

Product evaluation. Pre-sale evaluation of products developed by other partners, preparation of critiques and problem reports for those products, interface with other partners in correcting those problems. Evaluation of competitive products from other manufacturers, preparation of reports on those products and selection of features and capabilities for incorporation in our own products.

Market research. Review of new product announcements, news items, advertising, and product demonstrations with an eye to potential new markets, competition, and opportunities. Preparation of summaries of important items for distribution to other partners.

Marketing assistance. Preparation of new product announcements, skeleton ad copy, and product brochure copy. Attendance at shows and at meetings with customers. Telephone consultation with important customers and potential customers.

Planning assistance. Participation in regular partnership meetings. Assistance in evaluation of partnership goals and new product selection. Technical assistance to other partners in areas of specialization.

Mode of operation

MSP is intended to be a "tightly coupled" business venture. It is *not* a front for marketing individual products and funneling royalties back to implementors. It is a partnership where partnership profits are distributed to partners based on their percentage ownership regardless of their source. Why? First of all, one of the major reasons to form a partnership rather than just going off on your own is the potential synergy of the various partners and the work they develop. We hope to offer software components which can be used together in meaningful ways, and as we go, to accumulate a "bag of tricks" (e.g. screen formatting routines, database access utilities, etc.) which make development of new products by all partners easier. If each partner were essentially on his own, we could easily spend more time figuring out cross licensing and royalties for shared components than in actual development. It would force any partner to evaluate, for each potential component used, the tradeoff of paying for it or doing it over. This is silly and counterproductive.

Secondly, it enables us to cut the risk to each partner while remaining able to swing our resources behind those products which "take off". Assume we develop five products and four are losers or barely break even, but one becomes the "next Visi-Calc". In the "royalty payback" company we would have four unhappy implementors and one fellow with a rapidly increasing bank balance but the inability to adequately follow up the initial product with follow-on enhancements and adaptations. With the true partnership, we can commit our resources to a successful product as its success requires so that we can not only make a splash with it, but aggressively follow up the initial success with the new versions, new machine implementations, and additional features needed to expand and preserve market share.

I view the difference between the lone wolf implementor and the software marketing partnership as the difference between gambling and business. The lone wolf has the possibility of a higher return, but far less probability of realizing it. What matters in business is to be able to fail a large percentage of the time and still come out ahead. Having had several blockbuster products and having watched them diddled away by insufficient promotion and inability to concentrate resources on them as they showed promise convinces me of the truth of this statement.

Once MSP commences operations, we will select a set of products to develop and formulate, in advance, a development schedule, marketing plan, marketing budget, and cash flow projection per product. MSP accounting will be structured so as to produce actual figures on a monthly basis which update the projection. We will have partnership meetings on a monthly basis (or more frequently) in which each active project is reviewed from a technical and marketing standpoint and a decision will be made to continue, drop, or increase commitment to the project. Each new product we choose to undertake will be formulated and managed this way, so we are constantly forced to target the very limited resources we have on the segments of our business which are developing well.

Partners in MSP will prosper as the company as a whole does. This may help them to better evaluate products and projects based on their actual prospects rather than an attachment to something based on the amount of work that has gone into it or an attraction to an idea because it seems good. Our goal is to be able to react rapidly when a product takes off and build other products around it.

It doesn't take a lengthy look at the computer industry to conclude that the products that succeed are not always the best ones. Arguing with the marketplace may make you feel good, but it's about as productive as standing on the tracks and arguing with the Twentieth Century Limited. One of our chief goals in structuring the company is to promote rapid feedback of real-world information into the decision making process. I know how important this is — any reasonably dispassionate analysis of Marinchip's business would have concluded as early as 1979 that the 9900 was a dead end. Yet the seductive lure of the "previous investment trap [1]" was such that two more years of effort were poured down a hole whose prospects of return were very limited.

That's not to say that having long term goals isn't important or that you should have no time horizon beyond the next month. There's nothing wrong with a slowly developing business with a large prospect of deferred return as long as it doesn't bleed your resources and result in your going under just when the world realizes that it needs what you've been selling for the last five years. What we have to guard against is blindness to a competitive idea (for example, screen-oriented word processors) which is sewing up the market while we still try to push something time has left behind.

Product development cycle

The business of MSP will be structured around products. Each product will be clearly defined and a written plan will exist for each product. At any given time, it will be possible to list all the active products and review their performance.

Each product will follow a well-defined life cycle. It begins when somebody decides that something looks like a good potential product. This is briefly written up and then discussed at the next planning meeting. If the product looks like it might be worth doing, one or more partners undertake the preparation of a development plan. The development plan spells out the specifications for the final product (at the level of detail a brochure might offer), lists potential competitive products and why ours would be better for the potential purchaser, and estimates the time and other resources which would be required for development. If after reviewing this plan the product still looks good, we sound out potential marketing channels and supplement the plan with projections for marketing cost and sales. The final plan is subject to approval by the partnership before development is started. Once development is authorized, the project goes into the implementation phase.

---

[1] As defined in *How I Found Freedom In an Unfree World* by Harry Browne, Avon, 1973, page 136.

During the implementation phase, the partner or partners responsible for the project write and test the code and prepare the user manual. Those responsible should be left alone as much as possible during this phase. Only a devastating competitive announcement should be reason to reopen the project for consideration while implementation is underway. As long as it is on schedule, the project is of little concern to the other partners. Once an initial version is completed, including documentation, the project moves to the evaluation phase.

In the evaluation phase, a completed user copy of the package is given to a partner who has little knowledge of its internals and is in a good position to evaluate the package from a user standpoint. That partner's critique of the package as well as bug reports from the initial testing are used to refine the package so that the first release meets the highest professional standards. Remember, outfits like Lifeboat evaluate a package based on their customers' first impression of it. A rough first release can doom the package's prospects. While this evaluation is going on, the manual is edited into final camera ready form, advertising copy is prepared, and product brochures and other promotional material are prepared and printed. When the package has been shaken down to the extent that all are happy with it, it moves to the initial marketing phase.

In the initial marketing phase, manuals are printed so that orders can be filled immediately. New product announcements are sent to all trade publications and advertisements are placed as specified in the plan. Marketing channels (e.g. Lifeboat, etc.) are contacted and provided with sample copies, presentations, and/or demonstrations of the package. If trade journal articles have been prepared about the package, they should be timed to appear during this time. We want to have the maximum impact possible with the introduction of the package to prompt people to try it. After they try it, we hope the package will sell itself on its merits. This is the phase in which the largest negative cash flow will be experienced, and the project will be constantly reviewed against the plan to make sure it is within the budget. As orders begin to come in, the negative cash flow begins to turn positive and to pay back the initial marketing debt. As this happens, the project moves to the marketing follow-up phase.

In the marketing follow-up phase, we find out how well we've done. The project is reviewed based on:

- Sales
- Cost of support
- User comments
- Dealer comments
- Competitive developments

and based on those considerations, we decide how to treat the package. We want to be as responsive to bug reports as possible, and to regularly release updates and enhancements. We want the user to feel that the package is "alive", not a take it or leave it item. Also, we develop a profitable aftermarket in updates among those already committed to the package. As long as a project is still active, we budget funds for advertising and other marketing, and our goal is to pyramid the success of products which sell well. This means (*and this is critical*) that our first priority is support, enhancement, and promotion of those products which are doing well. We don't know in advance which of our products that (or those) will be — we have to let the market tell us, but we have to listen and respond to the market's message. Marinchip's greatest failure was to develop a product and then not follow it up because another attractive development project was dreamed up. We cannot let that happen here.

Optimally, the success of one or two of our products will lead to natural follow-on projects (as Wordstar led to Mailmerge, Spellstar, etc.), which build on the sales of the original product (to start with, users of our first product are very likely to buy the add-on). That way we can let the market lead us into the area of business we do best in. We should review new product proposals in the light of our existing products, to see whether they complement them. Not that we shouldn't enter new lines of business, but those companies that have succeeded have done so by concentration, not by breadth of product line.

If a product fails to meet its sales plan, then in the follow-up we will review its performance and the reasons for its failure. Based on this review, we may decide to terminate the project or to remedy the product based on market response or to modify the promotion campaign based on reactions received. However, we must avoid throwing good money after bad, and we should expect a majority of products to fail and their projects to be terminated. That's why we establish an advertising budget in advance and stick to it. Only exceptional and well documented changes in the marketing environment should cause us to decide to increase our potential loss on an unsuccessful project.

Obviously the time scale of all of this will depend on the magnitude of the product undertaken. It's conceivable that a little CP/M utility might go from concept to follow-up in 2 months (although advertising lead times would limit the impact of advertising until later). Given the resources we have, I don't think we should undertake any project where the follow-up comes any later than 9 months after the project is first defined. We just aren't rich enough to piss away our resources for longer than that on a potential loser. If we decide that we want to do a massive system with lots of parts, let's do it in pieces that are individually salable. Then we not only get user feedback to guide our future development, that development is paid for from sales revenues, not from our pockets.

Money and management

Capital for the formation of MSP will be contributed by the general partner (MSL) and the limited partners. Partnership interests will be calculated based on the percentage of capital contributed to the initial capitalization of the venture. The law requires the following:

Limited partners cannot purchase their partnership interests through contribution of services, [2] but must contribute tangible assets. Management and operation of the company is solely the responsibility of the general partner (MSL). Violation of these rules either invalidates a partner's ownership share or exposes the limited partners to potentially unlimited risk in case of failure of the business, lawsuit, etc.

We do not want to select potential partners in this venture based on their bank balances, but rather their competence, willingness to work, and entrepreneurial orientation. However, we don't want to give away partnership interests or make participation a no-risk venture for any partner. The owners of MSL are basically risking everything they've made for the last 5 years on this venture; the amount of money we intend to contribute would let us lie on the beach for a long time, and we intend to make a lot more than we contributed to compensate us for the risk, the work, and the hard times ahead. We want to know that our partners in this venture have a stake in its success at least proportional to their ownership of the company.

The following plan is suggested for initial capitalization of the company: we will calculate the desired capitalization and the partnership shares of all partners. As noted above, partnership shares will be in direct proportion to contributions. Partners may purchase their shares either in cash, by a no-interest loan from MSL secured by equipment, or by a regular market-rate callable loan from MSL.

Here's how it works. Suppose a partner wants to buy in for $5000. The simplest thing is just to pay the $5000 in cash. Alternatively, since many partners will want to purchase machines for software development or already own them, they may use the money to buy a machine (getting the tax credit and depreciation benefits, which are incredibly attractive today), then pledge that machine as security on a zero-interest loan from MSL. Or, MSL can loan the partner the money on a regular unsecured loan at market interest rates, and that money can be used to buy a

---

[2] Donald M. Dible, *Up your OWN Organization*, Entrepreneur Press, 1974, page 180.

partnership share in the normal way. At, say, 20% you can "rent" $5000 for $1000 per year.

The idea of all this is that we recognize that a substantial portion of the initial capitalization is going to be used to buy machines for software development. Those partners who already own machines should not be forced to subsidize those who haven't, nor should those partners who obtain machines for MSP work be forced to forego the tax benefits of buying the machine themselves. By loaning at no interest against the machine, we're allowing machine investments to be applied to partnership share dollar for dollar.

On all of these loans, it will be part of the agreement that revenues from a partner will first be applied to retiring any debts to MSL, and only then will the partner be paid directly.

Note that none of the above has been reviewed in detail for possible adverse tax consequences (in particular "imputed interest") and it's possible that there may be some more tax-attractive way to go at this involving leasing. Externally, this venture looks very much like a tax shelter, so the tax ground is very carefully covered and one must tread with caution in possibly questionable areas.

It should be clear that if MSL loans a partner the money to buy in, that loan should have an equal position in the recipient's mind with a home mortgage or auto loan. It is a real loan of real dollars which could have otherwise been spent by the principals of MSL on themselves. It is not "funny money" or a paper accounting transaction, and he who receives it should expect to pay it back, hopefully from revenues of the products MSP sells, but from other sources in the event MSP fails. Not only is this a realistic representation of what's really going on, it will hopefully inspire in all partners the kind of seriousness about this venture with which MSL approaches it.

If MSP fails, I will lose everything I've made for all the work I've done since 1977. I want partners who are willing to work as hard for success as I am.

Legally, limited partners have no say in the operation of the business. It is our intent that the business will be run as any other partnership based on partnership interests. Since I expect MSL to hold a controlling interest, this will probably make no practical difference. I believe that the people involved in this venture should be compatible enough that consensus will govern most actions taken by the partnership. This business can succeed only if all partners work to make it succeed. Since MSL has the most to lose, MSL has every reason to avoid contention and unhappiness among the rest of the partners.

Commitments of time

Partners should join the venture based on their ability to participate in it. We are not looking for investor partners who will not be involved in the operation of the company and its projects (although if one should stumble in, we'd be glad to talk). The principals of MSL are devoting their full time to this venture, limited only by ongoing commitments to MSL customers and prior consulting arrangements. Potential partners must decide for themselves how much time they have to devote to MSP. The basic quantity you should try to calculate is hours per week. We need an ongoing, reliable commitment of time by all participants. Whether you work two hours per day or in one fourteen-hour mad gonzo session each Saturday does not matter. If you have a job, however, which may randomly require your full absorption for a week at a time and leave you with stretches of idle time at random, that employment is not compatible with MSP partnership. We must be able to quote schedules and meet them, and we must be able to coordinate work from several implementors into final products. I know from experience that this cannot be done unless reliable time commitments are made.

The basic time commitments that participation in MSP entails boil down to the following three categories. First, the basic time devoted to company work which can be scheduled as you see fit. The time you have available for this work is the factor that determines the extent of your participation in the company. Second, each partner should be available for telephone conversation at some time during business hours on a daily basis. This is required for coordination of projects, passing on bug reports, or response to customer questions. If you can be reached at work, say, in the afternoons, that's all that's required. At an absolute crisis maximum, this would represent 15 minutes per day. Normally, one call per week would suffice. This refers to calls between headquarters and partners only, of course. If you're collaborating with another partner on a project, that time would be counted in the first category. Third, each partner should budget the time to attend partnership review meetings. These meetings will initially be held monthly on a regular schedule so that you can plan around them. We will alternate meetings among the various geographic areas where partners reside. If MSP includes partners not in the San Francisco area, we will make cassette tapes of the meetings available to those partners and accept written project summaries from them. This is not an attractive option, and remote partners should plan to increase the time for telephone consultation as a result.

Remember, this industry is now at a point where virtually all our competitors are ongoing operations with full-time technical employees. We're going up against them with less capital, a distributed operation, and less personal and financial commitment from the majority of our participants. We may very well fail. If we succeed (and I wouldn't be getting into this unless the odds looked good to me) it will be because we know more about what we're doing than most of them technically (this I know for sure), because a partner always out-produces an employee, and because we have and will develop the contacts to aid us in product definition and marketing. But we're going to have to think lean and hungry for quite a while and target our products with precision. And most of all, we have to look, we have to *be* a serious business venture, which we only marginally are. Most of the people who've succeeded in this game are those who sold their houses, quit their jobs, borrowed every penny they could scrape up, hired 5 or 10 people and hung their balls out over the abyss hoping their product would make it and bail them out. Making it while risking less is very very hard. I do not want to minimize this, but I want to point out that the risks in getting involved in MSP are probably less than any other serious business opportunity you're likely to find with anything like the potential return if it works.

I think we have a chance of making it with less than full-time commitments from partners only if their time commitments are utterly reliable. We're going to have to try to turn multiple part time people into the illusion of a full time staff so we can react to the market and bring out products as good as our competition and faster. That ain't easy. The people we're contacting as potential partners are the best computer people I know of in this country today, and are far better in both knowledge and productivity than the staff of most microcomputer software houses. That is what makes this possible at all.

The nature of potential products

I view the products that MSP will develop as falling into several distinct classes:

The first I call "guerrilla programming". This consists of developing relatively small, quickly implemented products which fill an immediate need perceived by users of a heavily promoted product. For example, a 3270-type screen oriented data entry package which generates SELECTOR files would be such a product. Every existing SELECTOR customer would be a prospect for our package, and systems houses who implemented applications in SELECTOR would use our package and sell it for us to their customers. A systems programming example of guerrilla programming would be a super-reliable file recovery program for CP/M. Again, every CP/M user would be a prospect for this utility. These kinds of programs tend to be quickly developed, sell fast, but don't last long as often the vendor you're tagging along with brings out a new release with your feature in it. However, they do make money and you can afford to do a lot of them since they don't take long to write. You can hit it big with one of these if, say, the vendor picks up your package and starts promoting it. This is not likely, and no project should count on this.

The second is the closed system application. This is a stand-alone application package which performs a well defined function for a specific class of users. Visi-Calc is a superb example of such an application. If you hit on one that's widely needed and not currently in a tolerable form on a micro you can do very well with these. Market research is essential here, and looking at what people are paying to do on timesharing systems is a good place to start. The "card file" very simple database is something we might do in this arena.

The third is the software tool. This is a utility program which is applicable to a wide variety of users for different purposes. Examples are SELECTOR and other database systems, word processing programs, and sort packages. This is a highly competitive market where large advertising budgets predominate and thus hard to break into. However, the rewards are great. We should look at somewhat "kinky" tools that haven't penetrated the micro market far but which have been popular on other systems. SSG and an SCCS-type facility are two that pop into my mind.

Fourth is the "interface gadget". We all do this well and they sell very well in the micro market. For example, a 3780 emulator, a CP/M to IBM disc convert utility, and so on. The problem is not being hardware dependent, and that's difficult in this game.

These categories overlap to some extent, but I think you get the drift of the kinds of things I'm thinking about. A good rule of thumb is that anything we do should fill a need the potential customer already knows he has, or should be demonstrated to a prospect in 5 minutes or less. We don't have the resources to educate the user base or to change the world. Products for which we can prepare a "demo disc" for computer stores are particularly attractive. We can give away a demo disc, then when a prospect walks into a store, they can run the disc which sells the package.

Hardware and system strategy

At this moment, the best established machine base for programs is the CP/M marketplace. There are about 500,000 machines installed which can run CP/M programs in one form or another, and the importance of this marketplace is underlined by the fact that most serious applications for the Apple now require the "softcard" with on-board Z-80 and CP/M.

However, the industry is changing rapidly and at this instant it appears that Unix or one of its look-alikes may become the "software bus" on 16 bit processors. We can't afford to bet on one system to the exclusion of all others. Fortunately, most of the potential products we're able to undertake don't require us to make a bet. We will be doing all of our programming in high level languages, and we must choose languages available on all of our potential target machines. At this date, C and Pascal meet this requirement.

We should seriously evaluate the option of going with CBASIC as our standard language and developing QBASIC implementations on the newer machines. The advantage of CBASIC (CB80 compiler) is that our work is file-compatible with a very large set of existing applications on CP/M, and with the acquisition of CBASIC by Digital Research (CP/M's developer), the connection is likely to strengthen.

On the other hand, the Microsoft-Unix/Xenix-IBM connection is a potent one, not to be ignored. I don't think we should be too bogged down by all of this, though. Whatever we program something in is going to generate object code that we distribute, and we're only going to program things which can be sold to a large number of customers without modification. If we do things reasonably, we'll be able to convert them to anything else that comes along and looks attractive. After all, conversions aren't fun, but if by converting something from CBASIC to Microsoft BASIC I can sell another 100,000 copies, I'll convert it. We shouldn't spend our time trying to figure out how many *SIGPLAN Notices* can dance on the head of a bit when we could be defining products, implementing them, selling them, and getting rich.

Why get involved?

If the tone of this paper so far has been to scare you away from this venture and to repetitively drum all the potential risks involved in joining such an operation, that's exactly what I intended. I've tried to lay out the whole operation complete with all the potential problems as straight as I can. So why would anybody in his right mind get involved in such a nutty venture?

The reason is very simple: there's a reasonable chance of making money beyond the wildest dream of an employee in this industry. Products like Wordstar are selling in the $10 – 20 million per year range today. Bear in mind — this is a product that any of us could write in about two months. We should consider ourselves extremely lucky to be in this business at this time in history. It's a rare piece of luck to have the field you've chosen as your career explode into the hottest growing entrepreneurial arena just as you hit your prime, and we're now at the point that if we want a chance to get involved we have to act immediately. The game has changed and the pace is accelerating very rapidly. The venture capital that remade the micro hardware business 2 years ago is just now beginning to move into the software business: within the last 3 months, Digital Research, Microsoft, Micro-Pro, and Lifeboat have received infusions of venture capital in the $1 – 10 million range. This business is getting very big and very professional, and within one year the chances of success of a tiny, heavily technically oriented company will be nil. If we move now, if we move fast, and if we react extremely rapidly and work ourselves to the bone, we can grab a chunk of this business before it slips away. We have to pursue our contacts at Lifeboat because that's an open door far too priceless to ignore, and we have to have a credible organization to open that door to further work.

If we sit back and say, "Well, I'll see how well the IBM makes out", or "Maybe after I pay off my car", or whatever, we'll lose a chance that won't come by again in our lifetimes. I think that with what we've learned from Marinchip and from the industry, with the marketing contacts we have, with the product ideas we're kicking around, and with the competence of the people we know, we have a real enough chance to make it that it's worth betting everything on. But we have to have *real* commitment, *real* performance, *real* responsibility, and *real* professionalism to make it. If you're interested in making that kind of commitment, I can't guarantee that we'll succeed, but I can guarantee that together we'll have a once in a lifetime experience as we try.

What it all comes down to is the following questions, which only you can answer for yourself.

"Do I really want to be in business for myself?"

"Do I want to work with these people?"

"Will I enjoy it if I participate in this?"

"Am I likely to find a better opportunity elsewhere?"

"Am I likely to find a better opportunity later on?"

"Can I manage the risk, and does the potential reward justify it?"

I think that this is it.

Nitty-gritty

I have not discussed any of the specific details of the venture in this paper, such as the amount of money to capitalize the company, how much each limited partner would be expected to chip in, etc. Nor have I gone into specifics about the precise organization of the company or who does what. This just isn't possible yet; I have no idea who is really interested in it. You build an organization out of the people you have, you don't try to ram people into predefined slots.

We want to start a venture which in three years will be one of the top five names in the microcomputer software business. We're crazy to aim lower or limit our sights. We're at a point where substantial market segments haven't been addressed yet and by moving fast we can grab a market share and make our company grow from generated revenues (note that all the software houses who've brought in venture capital had basically saturated their initial market first). At the point where we have to make that decision, we can be consoled by the fact that we'll already be millionaires.

I can think of no business (well, legal business) where we can start-up with so little capital or downside risk. If this business looks too shaky to you, where do you expect to find a better deal? I cannot imagine any scenario other than total collapse of society in which the sales of microcomputer application software will not grow by a factor of 10 in the next five years. The big vendors of small machines have not only not entered the software business, they appear totally in awe of it and willing to grab any product and promote it to sell their machines.

What do we do next?

The first thing to do is to show up at our organization meeting at MSL on January 30, 1982. You should give some thought to the points raised in this paper about commitment of time, and should also be able to give an idea of how much money you'd be willing to risk on this venture (whether you have it or not). Also, we'd like an idea of what kinds of work you'd like to concentrate on, and any ideas you have for products we might get into. In particular, if there are any items in this paper that are "show stoppers" for you or with which you take violent exception, that's the time to bring 'em up and hammer them out. At the end of that meeting, which will probably be very long and detailed, I hope that those who are interested in proceeding know who they are. Then we'll start putting numbers on paper and see what we're getting into.

We should shoot for having the company in operation by mid-March. We cannot dawdle, but we also are going to do it right this time. We're just going to do it fast!

Agenda

Agenda for January 30, 1982 Meeting

- Overview of MSP
    - Goals
    - Marketing targets
    - Potential product areas
    - Marketing channels

- Background
    - The micro industry today
        - mass market hardware
        - software development
        - software marketing
    - Marinchip — what we've learned
    - Case studies
        - Micro-pro
        - Scripsit

- What's needed to succeed
    - Market-directed products
    - "Don't be afraid not to innovate"
    - Responsive organization
    - Marketing follow-up and project monitoring
    - Highest standard of products from first release
    - Target expanding mass markets
    - Sufficient capital and commitment
    - Afford to be wrong 80 % of the time

- The difference between strategy and prediction
    - Make any potential success a success
    - Resources to keep on trying until you hit
    - Structure so you know when something's hitting
    - Organization which can swing behind a success
    - Ability to pyramid success when it occurs

- What MSP participation gives you
    - Full-time support operation
    - Marketing contacts
    - Market research contacts
    - Complete manufacturing operation
    - Risk capital for start-up

- ❏ What MSP wants from you
    - Commitment to MSP as best prospect to get rich
    - Meeting all delivery and support commitments
    - Providing marketing support as required
    - Production of highest quality products
    - Sharing ideas and information with others
    - Aiding others with partnership projects
    - Exclusive access to your work in areas MSP addresses
    - Your capital contribution
    - A level of effort you can maintain

- ❏ Don't expect MSP to ...
    - Produce technological breakthroughs
    - Do pure research
    - Be as much fun as hacking
    - Spare you anxiety
    - Let you specialize
    - Exploit your existing knowledge optimally
    - Fit perfectly with your current job

- ❏ Expect MSP to ...
    - Broaden your horizons beyond your imagination
    - Educate you in the realities of business
    - Teach you marketing
    - Make you appreciate the value in ideas you may disdain
    - Expose you to many different systems
    - Introduce you to depths of despair and exhaustion you never knew existed
    - Introduce you to heights of exultation you never knew existed
    - Ruin you for being an employee
    - Make you rich

- ❏ The last train out
    - Entry of venture capital to software business
    - Analogy with hardware business in '79 – 80
    - Difficulty of start-up venture in high-stakes game
    - The tension — demand for software vs. supply / difficulty to produce software in large organizations
    - Realities of introducing and promoting a product
    - Why we have a chance at all

- ❏ The open track ahead
    - Massive promotion of small machines in business environments
    - IBM sales staff consolidation
    - Dearth of software for desktop applications

Availability of growth capital / cash out opportunities

❑ Our experience and goals
 Why the low-commitment game is over
 Grow or die — Shrayer vs. Micro-Pro
 Cash is needed up-front
 Marketing follow-up and project evaluation is essential
 Go for it — now is the time the GM's of the 2020's are being formed
 What do they have we don't?

❑ Why get involved?
 Can always think of something better, are you likely to find it?
 Absolutely unique opportunity
 Every incentive toward being in business
 Cannot make it on your own
 Why trust these turkeys? — I do $60K worth

❑ Marinchip's contribution
 Marinchip annual report
 Liquid asset summary
 Initial capitalization proposal
 Marinchip ongoing operation facilities

❑ Partner contributions — round table
 What partner has to contribute
  business experience
  technical experience
  risk capital
 What share partner is interested in
 What skills partner wants to acquire
 Any limitations on partner's participation?
  maximum time commitment
  won't quit my job regardless
  won't work on … (databases, sorts, compilers)
  won't get involved in … (marketing, ad copy, documentation)
  won't work with others (or specific people)
 What are your worries?
 What have we left out?

❑ What I think is needed
 Try to succeed, not prove something
 Don't assume that because it's been done it's been done for all time
 Distinguish your product from the rest, but don't make it so different it's incomprehensible.

The human mind's basic primitive is "this is like that, except ... ", learn to live with that.

Don't try to solve all problems for all time.

Don't offer any options, ever!

No configuration, ever!

No system programmer after you.

❑ Why I think we can do it

We have the technical competence edge on almost everybody

We're building a responsive structure, and *we will make it work!*

We have the slant and contacts — micros are moving from the beachhead into the mainframe application class.

We know mainframes and what people do with them and how.

We've always been able to beat anybody on delivery time if we really care to.

We have the systems programming capability to back up our applications. None of our competitors do.

We have a comfortable amount of seed capital — no need to bootstrap or to produce instant performance for outside funding.

We have the historical perspective — almost none of our competitors has been in computers for more than 5 years.

We're able to adapt ourselves to the market — we're not gambling everything on one product or concept.

❑ Timetable

2/6 Participation commitments due.

2/8-13 Partnership share consultations, draft agreement review.

2/13 Partnership charter meeting — tentative agreement approval, projects review, initial work assignments, hardware procurement review.

2/27 Formal partnership organization — agreements signed, initial capitalization delivered.

3/13 First partnership review meeting.

Thoughts About the Partnership

After the original working paper was mailed, I had numerous telephone conversations with the people who received it. I wrote the first Information Letter and mailed it before the meeting in an attempt to address several points which came up repeatedly in these conversations. This letter inaugurated the series of Information Letters which have continued up to the present day.

Marin Software Partners
Information Letter # 1

by John Walker
Revision 3 — January 19, 1982

This letter is intended to clarify some points in the Marin Software Partners Working Paper which you should have already received, and also to bring you up to date on some discussions about matters not covered in the original paper. The organization meeting will be at 11:00 A. M. January 30, 1982 at Marinchip.

Structure of the business

Most of the questions recipients of the Working Paper have had related to the partnership structure of Marin Software Partners. I'll try to clarify what we want, point out potential problems, and look at alternatives.

Let's start with basics. We are planning to organize a business in which all the founders will have an "equity stake" — in plain language they, collectively, will be the owners of the business. There are three basic ways such a business can be structured. The first, and most simple, is the general partnership. This is what is usually meant when the word "partnership" is used. In a general partnership, all partners participate in the operation of the business and share in its profits or losses proportional to their ownership share. Each general partner is subject to unlimited liability in regard to the operation of the business, and is liable for debts incurred in the partnership's name by any of the general partners. This means that a general partner who lacks a controlling share of the business must trust the other partners sufficiently to expose himself to unlimited losses if they misjudge or act improperly. Steps can be taken to hedge this risk, such as an insurance policy against liability suits, embezzlement, etc., and statements in the partnership agreement which allow borrowing only if approved by unanimous consent of partners.

A limited partnership is composed of one or more general partners, who have the same responsibilities and liabilities as before, and one or more limited partners whose liability is limited to their initial investment. Thus, while a limited partner may lose everything he contributed to the partnership, he may not lose more. In this sense, a limited partner is like a stockholder in a corporation. Limited partners do not have any direct say in the operation of the company — this is the function of the general partner(s). The most common application of the limited partnership is a venture where people want to put up money for a venture in the hope of sharing in its profits. The general partner takes the money, does something with it, and distributes the appropriate share of the proceeds back to the limited partners. This is a common way of financing oil and gas exploration, and is used extensively in the venture capital business. In any case, the limited partner retains an unlimited upside potential gain while limiting his loss to his original investment.

The third way of organizing a business is incorporating it. A corporation is by far the most flexible form of organization, but it has several important drawbacks for a venture of this kind. Most critical is the question of royalty income. The IRS holds that a corporation with 15 or fewer stockholders which receives a majority of its income from "passive sources" such as royalties and interest is a "personal holding company" and is subject to a 70% tax rate. This ruling was introduced to prevent people from forming companies to hold their investments and by so doing paying far less tax on the income than if they were taxed at the higher marginal rate which would result if the income were added to their regular employment income. The problem is that a software company may very well receive all its income from royalties if it licenses vendors and distributors to manufacture and sell its products, and this leaves such firms potentially liable under this provision. We have asked an attorney knowledgeable in this area about this problem, and he says that to date no software firm has been penalized under this ruling, but that there is no question that they are potentially liable. Nobody has even asked for an IRS ruling out of fear of alerting them to this source of income. The upshot of this is that if you intend to sell software for royalties, you'd better not incorporate until you're big enough to escape the provision through the size test.

The second drawback of a corporation is that income from the corporation is taxed twice: first as "corporate income", then again when it is received by shareholders as dividend income. Federal law allows you to declare a corporation "Subchapter S", which means that income is distributed directly to holders and no corporate tax is charged. This neatly solves the problem (unless you're too big for this treatment), except that good ol' California doesn't recognise Subchapter S. This means that you still pay double tax to California on your income. With California marginal tax rates at 11%, this is substantial dollars. Thus, most California Sub S corporations list the principals of the company as employees and try to pay out all their profits as salaries to the principals. Since salaries are deductible from corporate income, this avoids the problem. But there are some catches. First, the tax people have every incentive to bust you if it looks too much like you're using the salaries as a sham for dividends (which is exactly what you're doing, of course) since they make less that way. Second, you have to pay Social Security tax, unemployment tax, carpet tax, etc., on salary payments. Thus, there's really no clean solution to this problem. You say, "well, why not just leave the money in the company and let it collect interest at the low corporate tax rate until I need it". Gotcha again! You can't leave more than $150,000 in the company unless you can show it's legitimately needed without triggering punitive measures.

Third, a corporation is a pain in the ass to run. The workload involved in filling out forms, filing statements with the state and IRS, etc., is easily 5 times that of a partnership of similar size. It takes about a tenth of a full time person to do, and unless there's an obvious return, it's therefore to be avoided.

The benefits of the corporation are also often overstated. The much vaunted limited liability of the corporation can evaporate if the corporation can be shown to be a sham set up only to limit the liability. In any case, directors of corporations are subject to lawsuit against their personal assets based on the acts of the corporation. Thus, it doesn't look to me like there's any reason to consider incorporating this business at this time.

Since we already have a corporation, Marinchip Systems Ltd., we can make that corporation a general partner in Marin Software Partners. It may be possible to structure things so that the liability of the partners is limited, and the principals of MSL are protected to the extent that the corporation provides. We will have to seek legal advice as to whether this will work and how it must be done, and we will do this as we form the new venture. It just looks like this is the best option if it will work.

The issue of liability

I don't want to get everybody all worked up about this issue of liability. In deciding how to organize a new business, you have to balance various considerations. You want a structure in which the responsibility is assigned in proportion to the commitment of the various participants. You want to limit the potential loss a participant can sustain as much as possible. You want to minimize the percentage of your gains that the tax man will pocket. You want an organization which can grow and change without catastrophic problems.

From almost every consideration except that of taxes, a corporation is the best. But since we have the potentially disastrous royalty tax problem, we can't incorporate safely. Thus, a discussion of liability is in order as that is the major difference in the two forms of partnership. This business is very different from most start-up ventures. We are capitalizing the company by contributing money to the original "pot", and are creating our products almost entirely out of mental effort. We have no employees, and our fixed costs are almost negligible. We will have no debts to anybody (I am a fanatic about this), and our capital investment will be a relatively small percentage of net worth. The software business is just about optimal from the standpoint of product liability. Programs blow up in people's faces only figuratively, and unlike most other things, software is usually sold with no warranty, or one limited to refund of the purchase price within, say, 30 days.

As a result, the liability exposure of a partner in this venture is about as small as could be possible in any business. Basically, if we reach the point where the bank account is drawn down to zero and we haven't sold anything, we fold up our tent and go back to the salt mines. It's hard to imagine how you could lose more than your investment in this kind of venture. Thus, being a general partner is not the risky thing it is in a real estate venture where you're signing up to be liable for a chunk of a $30 million floating rate construction loan on a building for which there may be no demand when it's finished 24 months from now. I don't think the liability issue here is something to lose sleep over, and I personally don't care if I'm a limited or general partner. I do realize that from your questions some of you are concerned about it, so I've tried to beat the issue to death looking at it from all sides here. That's not to say that any issue in forming a company is unimportant, but I think that you have to look at it in the light of the nature of the business, and in this case liability is not an overwhelming problem.

Changes after the business is running

Most of your questions have been related to how the company may change after it has been in operation for some time. I'd like to discuss some of these issues here. I know no complete, clean solutions to the problems you've raised. However, business, like life, is an endless series of problems to overcome. You always try to avoid problems where possible and mitigate the effects of the ones you run into. But if you refuse to do something because there are potential problems, you end up never doing anything. But enough preaching ... on to the grimy details.

"How do we handle it if one partner doesn't meet his commitments?" This has been the most commonly asked question, indicating that I am no more cynical about participants in business ventures than you. Obviously, we only want to go into business with people we respect and trust, and the first level of screening is performed when we get together and decide who wants to work together in this venture. If somebody seems not to fit, either based on their goals, their approach to the venture, or their ability to get along with and work with the others, it would be a mistake for all concerned for that person to become involved in Marin Software Partners. Of course, you can make a mistake. I made such a mistake in my selection of an original partner in Marinchip, so I'm very aware of this possibility. The solution in that case was what usually proves best; the rest of the partners buy out the partner who has lost interest in the venture. If the business is prospering, this buy-out can be paid for out of sales revenues. If the business is failing, the partner's share is not likely to be worth much in the first place. I know of no solution to the case of the partner who just refuses to work or becomes obstructive but who refuses to be bought out. So we don't include any assholes, O. K.? (It might be possible to write the agreement in such a way that the other partners retain an option to buy out a partner for a certain price for a stated term. I think this is a terrible idea, since it would put the financially strong partners in a position where, if the business "took off", they could grab the business from the less strong. While, of course, nobody involved in this venture would think of such a thing, it wouldn't contribute to a partner's equanimity knowing such a coup were possible.)

"Are decisions affecting the partnership made by unanimous consent or by majority of partnership share?" This question is really irrelevant if the limited partnership is used, as MSL would make all decisions. I also don't know the relevant law (we will, of course, find out as we work with a lawyer to draft the partnership agreement, although I'd like to believe you can have anything you want put in the agreement). I think that the majority share makes the most sense, even though it has its obvious risks. After all, all stock corporations work that way and they seem to make out all right. I'd be worried about one stubborn person being able to immobilize the entire company (after all, I've been known to be stubborn — and dead wrong — myself).

"Suppose the company takes off and I want to quit my job and do this full time. How can I increase my share?" In this case, you would purchase an additional share in the partnership at a price agreed to by the other partners. Your share might be sold to you by another partner who wished to reduce his share (MSL might want to "cash out" to free up money for other ventures, for example), or could be a new share which effectively dilutes the shares of all the other partners. The partners whose shares were being diluted by this act would be compensated by the payment you made for your additional share, and by the presumed increase in revenues which would result from the additional work you did for the company. The price you pay for your additional share is the price the other partners agree to sell it to you for. If the company is a corporation, change "partnership share" to "shares of stock" and everything is the same.

"How do we bring in new people?" In the case of new partners, the case is exactly the same as that discussed above for an existing partner increasing his share. Of course, a new partner may buy in by supplying any form of consideration, such as rights to a software package he had developed. If we decide to expand the general operation side of the business, we may decide to add some conventional employees. This would just involve salaries paid out of the general revenues of the business and not affect the partnership in any way.

"Suppose I want out?" This is just the reverse of the case of adding to your share. You sell your share back to the other partners for whatever they're willing to pay you for it. They recover what they paid you by the increased shares they own after yours are liquidated. Of course, if they don't want to sell, you're stuck. They'd be stupid not to, though, for otherwise they would have to continue to pay you your partnership share of the revenues in return for your doing no work.

"I'm worried about having the business expand to the point where I have to quit my job. What do I do if this happens?" This is the kind of problem that is good to have. Basically, you have to calculate the equity value of your job, which is just like valuing a company: what is the income, how secure is it, what are the growth prospects, and what is the equity I sacrifice by quitting (seniority, pension fund equity, future employment prospects, etc.). If the job is so valuable to you you'd never quit, then you shouldn't consider going into business for yourself. If the job has a value (they all really do, of course), then you should only quit to take a job with greater value. I'd quit a $50K job with, say, Consolidated Engine Sludge to take a $10K job with Advanced Robotic Widgets if I had a stock option for 20% of the company, but everybody has a different situation and has to make his own decision. Working out the value of your job in your head is a worthwhile effort in any case as it gives you a better perspective on what you've got. I believe everybody constantly acts to maximize their overall gain in life (not just economic, of course; personal happiness, adventure, are calculated in as well), and that if the time comes where participation in Marin Software Partners is seen as better than your current job, you'll have no trouble making the plunge. Those that can't are the Hamlet types who never do anything and always fail in business anyway.

"I'm not sure I have the experience to be in a company like this." I have found that a sincere desire to be in business for oneself and to work hard is far more important to success in business than detailed technical knowledge. If you can do a job well and the partnership needs that job done, you belong in Marin Software Partners. We'll have to look at the mix of talents we have in the people who are interested in forming Marin Software Partners and address the areas where we're deficient.

We'll almost probably have to go outside for advertising preparation, but we'll probably have the in-house capacity for all the technical writing we need. At this point we can't say whether *anybody* fits into the company — we can evaluate that only after we see who's interested and who's not. Being in business is an excellent way to learn about thousands of things you never intended to learn about. If you're looking to learn new things and expand your horizons, this is one way to do it (although getting run over by a truck may be less painful).

Terminating products

Some people have expressed concern about the continuing support burden of products we decide to terminate because of bad sales. This is a non-issue. When a product is terminated, support of it is terminated and those who inquire are simply told "that product is discontinued". Only in the computer business does the insane idea that by buying a $300 product (or, for heaven's sake, a $35 product) entitle the purchaser to all products of the implementor's mind unto eternity and unlimited free consultation at the press of a touchtone button. If you buy a refrigerator, you don't expect to get a new one every 6 months because a new model comes out, and the same thing holds here. We warrant the product will agree with the manual and will work for, say, 6 months after purchase. When that expires, our connection with that product is totally severed. We may choose to offer existing customers a good deal on new versions, but that is a marketing tactic, *not* a moral imperative! If we find the mass market we seek, we can't afford to talk to one in a hundred end users. We have to make the software work in such a way, supported by the manuals, that users can use the package on their own, and provide the aids to those who distribute the software so that they can answer user questions locally. This isn't impossible: numerous products meeting this criterion sell well currently. So, when we terminate a product, it's done.

What to call the company

I'm using Marin Software Partners as a working name for the company. I haven't thought at all about what it will really be called and don't think this is of any importance at this time.

How much of a share to buy

Several people have asked about how much of a share of the company they would be expected to buy and how much it would cost. It's hard to put numbers on this until we see who's interested and at what level of effort, but I can give you some rough background on how this will eventually be crunched out.

The first question any partner must ask, as detailed in the Working Paper, is "How much time can I commit to the venture". Once you know that (and I'm assuming everybody will be able to say at the organization meeting), we can begin to guess at a share. Ideally, everybody should buy in at a share proportional to their time commitment. Let's say that of the technical partners, a total of 100 hours per week is available. Let's assume that MSL is buying 60% of the company by its cash contribution and the technical partners are buying a total of 40%, and that MSL is contributing $50,000 to found the company.

Now if you have 15 hours per week to work for Marin Software Partners, your ideal share would be 15/100 or 15% of the 40% owned by the technical partners over all. Thus, your share of the total company would be 6%. To purchase this share for cash, your contribution would be (50000/0.60) x 0.06), or $5,000. If all the technical partners purchased their shares of the company for cash, the company would start with an initial capitalization of $83,333. If the company made $80,000 profits in the second year (this is the level MSL was running at its peak), then the partner's share would be paid off at this point. If the company reaches $1,000,000 in profits then the partner's original $5,000 investment will be yielding $60,000 per year in income.

If you don't have the $5,000, but want to buy in at that level, we'll find the money for you to borrow. If that number just looks too doggone big, you might choose to buy a lesser share and reduce your time share accordingly. This is a gamble, of course, since if the business begins to grow rapidly and you wish to increase your share, it will cost you far more to do so (as a percent of a company earning $100,000 per year is worth a lot more than one of a company earning zero). Conversely, if the business starts off poorly, you might be able to pick up a piece for less.

Order of magnitude financial figures

Again, it's too early to put down hard and fast numbers, but you've asked, and need to know just what the magnitude of this venture is going to be. My gut feeling is that the absolute bare bones Spartan scrape-by high risk minimum to get started in this business is $50,000 initial capital with as little of that spent on hardware and fixtures as possible. I'd feel comfortable with $100,000, and feel that if we couldn't make it with that, then we probably couldn't make it with a million. MSL has about $50,000 in liquid assets to funnel into this venture, so I think we can plan to scrape up the kind of money to give us a reasonable shot at success. MSL's fiscal year closes on January 31, so on the 30th we'll pass out our preliminary financial statement and let you see where MSL stands in this venture.

Once we see just what we've got, we may have to line up some additional financing. One possibility is for somebody, like me, who's got some cash and believes in this venture to grant Marin Software Partners a line of credit which it could draw on, at, say 5% above the prime. This would provide Marin Software Partners with a source of additional funds if it needed them, which it would really have to to pay my usurious (but utterly risk-justified) rates.

The role of MSL principals

We've been asked about what role the principals in MSL (John Walker and Dan Drake) will play in the partnership. They will participate in the operation of the company and share its results by virtue of their ownership and operation of MSL. In addition, they may choose, as individuals, to become limited partners in the venture. They would do so based on their desire to work, exactly like other limited partners, on technical projects to be marketed by Marin Software Partners. If they do so (and I certainly haven't made up my mind — I *want* to, but where is the time to come from?), they will buy their shares just like anybody else and participate on the same basis.

This is an issue that isn't settled yet, and I don't think it's very important until we see just who's interested.

The promise of this venture

Everything you've read so far relating to this company has stressed the risks of any business venture, the depth of the commitment involved, and the potential problems and catastrophes which can befall one who dares venture from the corporate womb. I keep hammering on these points because I've found that underestimating them is the most common problem people have when going into business. I don't want you to conclude, however, that I lack enthusiasm for this venture or that I expect it to fail.

I think that we're at an absolutely unprecedented juncture of history. I can't think of any time in the entire human experience when so much opportunity existed for technical people, opportunity which they could participate in with very limited risk. Most great business opportunities have required far greater infusions of start up capital which was consumed just paying for physical plant before anything was made to sell. Our products are created by almost pure mental effort, and are manufactured on trivially cheap equipment at a tiny fraction of their wholesale cost. It's almost like counterfeiting, but legal.[3]

---

[3] I later came to refer to the software business as "100% value-added— pure reason without the critique".

At the same time, we're entering a marketplace which is expanding at an unbelievable rate. Wander through any office tower in downtown San Francisco and look at how many desks have computers on them. Say, less than 1%. In 5 years or so, 80 to 100% of those desks are going to have computers on them, and those computers will be running programs that have not been written yet. In less than 6 weeks, over 100,000 IBM personal computers have been sold. There is little or no serious application software for that machine at present. If we make $100 per copy on a database system for that machine, and sell 50% of those customers on it, we've pocketed five million bucks. And how many will they sell in the next five years ....

The potential rewards of this business, which is the field that you and I are technically proficient in, almost compel one to participate on an equity basis. There's almost no salary that's enough to reward one for giving up his seat at this cosmic money gusher. There's no doubt that we have the technical proficiency to produce products as good as those any of our competitors are selling. The quality of our technical writing is continually mentioned as being superb. We know we are incompetent at advertising, but we know where to purchase that talent at a reasonable price (at least, compared to page rates). We should have at least one salesman-partner — this is a serious lack and if you have any contacts in mind please forward them. If we have to do without, though, we're not doomed, as we're already plugged into the marketing channels through Lifeboat, who already has a sales organization targeted at our market. There are enough precedents for the "strong technical, weak sales" company making it on the strength of their products to convince me that this business isn't like selling toothpaste.

The last thing I want to do is to sell anybody on getting involved in this venture who is less enthusiastic about it than I am. But I can't help saying to anybody who doesn't want to get involved, "Do you ever expect to see an opportunity this good come around again in the rest of your life?". I'm not talking about this company specifically, as you might have legitimate worries about getting involved with the people and slant of this particular venture; I'm saying that here we have an exploding market that you understand technically, which can be entered with little capital, where huge corporations are trying to promote your work to sell their hardware, where growth capital is readily available when it's needed, and where there's still time to get in without being an employee or minor stockholder in a big venture. 99.99% of all the people in this country live their lives without ever having the kind of opportunity we have in front of us today. Those who do not choose to take it should not count on it knocking again.

Responsiveness

Some people have interpreted the product development structure suggested in the Working Paper as smacking too much of the kind of bureaucracy they dislike in their current jobs. I think that one of the great advantages a small company has is its ability to react rapidly and get things done before the competition does, and that any hardening of the arteries which prevents this spells disaster. On the other hand, if the organization is so loose that you don't know where the money is coming from, how can you decide what you should be doing? My goal is to provide the minimum level of structure needed to define, develop, market, and promote products, targeted at all times to maximizing our profits. I think the structure I suggested meets this criterion. I can think of nothing less that will serve. On reflection, I think that it may be wise to designate one partner as "product manager" for each product, even if several partners are collaborating on it. This isn't to introduce unnecessary hierarchy, but simply to provide one person who will coordinate user communications, contact with headquarters, integration of work by other partners, etc.

Philosophy

To those of you who know the esteem in which I hold Don Lancaster's book, *The Incredible Secret Money Machine*,[4] some of the concepts you've seen here may seem alien or repugnant. My theme all along in this is "the game has changed". To be blunt, they're playing the ball game with real balls now. It's possible to follow the Don Lancaster route and earn a reasonable income for life while maintaining your own freedom and lifestyle, but you only generate income when you work, and you must resign yourself to seeing people with less merit in your eyes advance beyond you on the ladder of material success.

Everybody has to decide what's important to them. For some people, it's knowing that their work is the best. For others, it's understanding things. Some people measure their value by certificates on their walls, still others by certificates in their safe deposit boxes.

If you're a computer person, you have a rare skill that's much in demand. If you can produce a given kind of work, I think you should demand as much for it as you can get, consistent with the constraints you're willing to accept on your lifestyle. My own personal belief is that in a venture of this kind I have a reasonable prospect of realizing far more for my efforts than from anything else I could do

---

[4] *The Incredible Secret Money Machine* by Don Lancaster, Howard W. Sams, 1978. *Read this book!*

with my time. I think that by taking a less serious approach to this business you only reduce your prospects of success. Thus, today, I think this is the best option, which is why I'm willing to bet so much on its success. If we fail, we'll lose sums of money which are significant, but which are in the nature of a setback, not a disaster. If we succeed, we'll be able to put the whole job game behind us. And then, hopefully, relax and enjoy the fine things life has to offer.

Potential Products for MSP

Existing products: The following products exist already under various ownership and are being marketed by MSL or to MSL customers. We assume that title to the products would transfer to MSP in return for payment by MSP to their owners or partnership share.

Existing products

INTERACT. INTERACT[5] could be supported by MSP on the IBM personal computer, or possibly on the Tandy or Apple 68000 machines to be announced shortly.[6] INTERACT is written in SPL and an SPL-port would be implied in any conversion to a new machine. Since the trend in machines is to better graphics and faster processors, each movement along this trend makes INTERACT a more attractive product.

The major drawback is that INTERACT needs either a hard disc or at the minimum DS/DD 8-inch floppies to run. This lets out most of the current desktop mass market machines unless somehow INTERACT's dynamic drawing file can be compressed. The major advantage is that INTERACT is a superb product in a virgin market.

QBASIC. By making QBASIC[7] CB80 compatible and porting it to the 8086 and 68000, we can establish a beachhead in the 16 bit system software market. We are basically counting on outrunning Gordon Eubanks[8] and sneaking in below Digital Research's advertising blitz. Probably the best strategy is to continue to pursue OEM buy-outs through Lifeboat, as they have a large incentive in reducing their

---

5   INTERACT was the product that formed the starting point for the development of AutoCAD. This is the first suggestion of a CAD package as a potential product for the company.
6   The "Apple 68000 machine" was the Lisa. The Macintosh came much later.
7   QBASIC was a compiler for the Marinchip machine which was language-compatible with CBASIC, a popular business dialet of BASIC, then available on the 8086 only as an interpreter.
8   The developer of CBASIC, then at Digital Research.

royalty payments to D.R. And of course, QBASIC is now extremely easy to port and each new processor is a new product. Also, we can use QBASIC for our own applications work.

C. Dan Gochnauer's full C for the Z8000 is written in itself and can be ported to other machines. I don't know if this is of any real value except as a low-cost entry in an already congested market. Maybe we should slap the sucker on the IBM and promote it like we just invented C. This won't make us rich, but it may make us some money.

SORT. Hal Royaltey's SORT package should be reviewed in the light of competitive products under CP/M. If it shows potential, we can enter the SORT derby under CP/M with it. Maybe we can think of some sexy gewgaw to make it stand out from the pack. Ideas?

WINDOW. Probably no market. Damn shame.[9]

SPELL. Probably no market except at $25 a pop.

LENS. We might be able to clean this[10] up and put it in CBASIC (it has no assembly language in it) and sell it through *Sky & Telescope* to CP/M'ers. Probably some "feechers" should be added first, though.

DIFF. The current QBASIC version can be enhanced to do CP/M directories, put under CB80 and peddled to CP/M'ers.[11]

SELECTOR. We might be able to negotiate a distributorship for SELECTOR V on the IBM in return for putting it up in QBASIC. This might prove to be very lucrative even if our cut was very small.

New products

The following are product ideas of various degrees of definition which might fit into our new line of business.

---

9   WINDOW was Marinchip's screen editor, itself written in QBASIC. I wrote WINDOW originally to squelch the outcry from Marinchip customers for a "screen editor" — something I believed at the time beneath real programmers. I named it WINDOW after the code name for radar chaff, a lightweight countermeasure that's all image and no substance. WINDOW was briefly marketed as AutoScreen for CP/M, and later its design served as the basis for the screen editing features of Kern Sibbald's editor.

10   This was an interactive lens design program written in QBASIC for the Marinchip. Years later, translated to C, its central algorithm became the Autodesk floating point benchmark.

11   Duff Kurland did this, but we never sold it. Later we converted it to C, and in that form still use it today.

Executive planning aid. This is being investigated by John Nagle. It's a screen oriented PERT package with costing and resource allocation, and every manager in a large company with a desktop computer is a potential prospect. We want to target products to this market segment as it is being aggressively targeted by IBM and Xerox and is likely to be one of the fastest growing market segments in the next few years.

Cardfile. This is being kicked around by John Walker. This is an ultra-simple database which lets you replace things you currently keep on scraps of paper or boxes of file cards. It requires absolutely no knowledge other than how to turn on the computer and type and works in a language as close to plain English as possible. I think that even if I had SELECTOR, I would still want a product like this.[12]

MAPPER. MAPPER is the first product Univac has developed which is being heavily promoted as a product in my memory. It is responsible for the sale of numerous very expensive systems simply to run it. We should study it carefully and see if it contains concepts which can be applied to a standalone desktop system. If so, is such a product applicable to any office, or is it salable only to the Univac user base? Might it fit as a product under UNIX?

Forms generator. This is a utility which allows people to design forms, and optionally fill them in. The simplest use is just to allow people to edit forms which are printed on a printer and used as Xerox masters. The stored form can also be used as input to a prompting routine which allows users to fill in the forms on the screen and generate either data files for input to other programs, or simple printed forms with the blanks filled in. This seems like a natural for the transitional "office of the future" which hasn't sworn off paper.

Menu-oriented TS. A terminal emulator which can be programmed to present menus and conduct dialogues with the remote system for the user.

JPLDIS. Convert it and sell on small systems.[13]

---

12 This is the idea which grew into the product called Autodesk, after which the company was eventually named. It is amusing to compare the goals of this product, and of Autodesk, to the darling of 1988, HyperCard.

13 We did not know, then, that dBASE II was a derivative of JPLDIS.

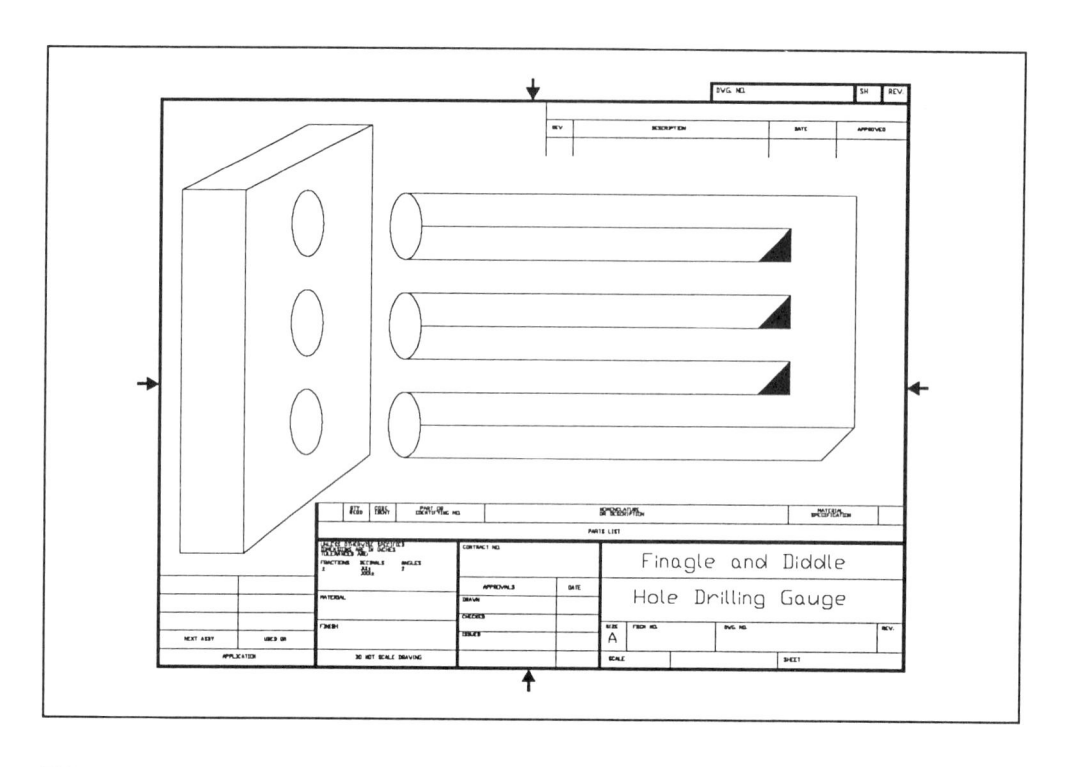

This drawing was done on AutoCAD-80 shortly before COMDEX 1982, and was shown at COMDEX as an example of a "mechanical drawing". I hand-measured an ANSI A-size title block and drew the title block piece by piece. The ellipses were done by inserting circles with differential scale.

After the First Meeting

Information Letter 2 was the first general communication after the initial organisation meeting.

Information Letter # 2

by John Walker
Revision 1 — February 12, 1982

This letter is to bring you up to date on what has happened with the formation of MSP since the January 30, 1982 meeting. I assume that everybody who intends to participate has already sent a letter to that effect, so we know who is involved and what they want to do. Since just about everybody at the meeting decided they wanted in, there is certainly no doubt that our software development capability is awesome — I can think of no product on the microcomputer market today which we could not develop if we decided to. Now we have to put together the organization to define the products, produce them with the desired quality, and market them.

Alternate forms of organization

Keith Marcelius suggested an alternate way of organising the company which looks to me like a potential solution to some of the major concerns we all had about the original proposal. It allows us to accommodate people whose financial contribution cannot be commensurate with their time to devote to the venture and it gives a way to reward those who contribute more than their expected share.

Let's assume for the moment that the company is formed as a corporation (this might also work for a limited partnership, but we don't know yet). Suppose we authorize and issue 1 million shares of stock initially (the number is totally irrelevant, but should be large enough so that round-off can be ignored). 600,000 shares of stock are sold to the founders of the company based on their capital contributions; this establishes their initial share. The number of shares purchased would be:

(Your Contribution/Total Initial Capital) x 600000

The remaining 400,000 shares of stock would be held in the corporate treasury. The effect of these shares would be nil as long as they are retained in the treasury; if dividends are distributed they just loop out of the checking account back into the treasury.

Every year, based on people's contributions of work, a stock dividend can be declared to those stockholders who contributed in excess of their share. This means that we take those shares out of the treasury and give them to the person who contributed the extra time. This increases his share at the cost of diluting the shares of those who did not receive the stock dividends. All distribution of stock dividends would be subject to a majority vote of stockholders by shares, so participants' shares could not be watered without their consent. This may have adverse tax consequences and may become more complex to reduce the tax liability of this distribution.

All of this is a very complex way of implementing a simple idea — if one partner wants to work very hard for the company but has no cash at the moment, we can let him earn his share through "sweat equity", subject to the approval of the other holders. On the other hand, if a partner does not contribute the work he promised, his share will be gradually reduced as the other participants won't be likely to approve a stock dividend for him. Also, if a participant wants to increase his share by buying additional stock, he may do so at a price agreed to by the shareholders who may agree to sell it to him.

I want to make it clear that this is primarily a way to accommodate cases of hardship where the initial capital contribution is absolutely impossible to obtain at the start, and also to create an incentive for producing work as promised. It is not a way for all partners to avoid contributing capital to the venture — after all, those who do not contribute initially have no guarantee that they will ever be voted a stock dividend — they're trusting those who hold the majority share to compensate them when the time comes.

At this point it looks like if we can do it without adverse tax consequences we will go ahead and incorporate the venture. To avoid the tax disasters, we will remain a "software manufacturer" selling discs rather than licensing our products for a per-copy fee. As soon as we begin to generate revenue we want to pay out, we will put all the shareholders on the payroll, thus avoiding a large part of the double taxation of dividends. At this point the final word isn't in on whether we can make a limited partnership do what we want to do, so this decision has not been reached. We will be consulting a lawyer who has formed numerous high-tech ventures and who can presumably tell us what we ought to be doing. I'll send out another letter once we find out. I'm sending out this information at this time so you know what we're thinking at the present moment so you can comment on it.

New participants

We have already received participation commitments from two of our overseas contacts. Rudolf Künzli of Basel, Switzerland has extensive systems and applications programming experience and will be helping with software development and testing as well as marketing our products in continental Europe. His expertise in languages will enable us to offer products that stand out by not speaking English exclusively. Peter Goldmann in England has extensive experience in systems programming and data communications as well as the all-around experience common to those present at the meeting. We expect our dealer in London, Richard Handyside, to become involved also in some capacity; we're pursuing several options at this time.

From our experience in MSL, we've found that the export market is very important, and I feel that these participants will give us an important start in marketing our products overseas, as well as market research and product customisation for these markets. Remember, the computer market in the EEC alone is the same size as the US domestic market. Ignoring it can cut your sales in half before you even start. [14]

Resumes

As was discussed at the meeting, we'd like all the participants to send resumes to us. These will be kept as part of the MSP business plan, and are essential if we need to secure venture capital. Also, we'll copy all of them and send copies to everybody so we all know what skills we have in the company. What we want is more a statement of qualifications rather than all the job summary garbage. What matters is what you know, what you can do, and what you've done.

"Edges"

I'd like everybody to be thinking of things we can do to distinguish our products as a whole from other peoples', and give dealers and distributors reasons to try our products in the first place. Two have been suggested so far:

---

[14] And indeed, Autodesk's sales outside the United States have accounted for between 30% and 40% of total sales for much of the company's history. Also, since software is considered printed matter, it avoids almost all customs hassles, so it doesn't really matter where your customers are.

Rudolf Künzli suggested that we make all of our software obtain all its messages, menus, and prompts from a direct file. We would develop a common routine which returns message text from the file by number, and a subroutine which inserts text in the message. [15] This gives us two important advantages. First of all, the most common customisation request for all packages is to change certain messages. We can tell the dealer, "Buy an MSP package, and you can change the messages with this little utility — no programmer is needed". Second, we can make our packages speak any language we want just by translating the message file — one object code version will suffice. The advantages in the overseas market are obvious. Note that a pure **PRINT USING** type expansion isn't quite enough — you'd like to be able to change the order things are inserted in the message. Thus, you might read a message like:

```
"Put the #1 in the #2, #3!"
```

and print it with something like (assuming QBASIC):

```
a%=fn.print.msg(187,"disc","slot","idiot")
```

The #n in the message would match with the order of parameters in the call (yes, I know the problems with this example — but you understood the *point*, right?).

Second, we can make our packages work on any terminal with no special generation required. Thanks to Greg Lutz, we've obtained a copy of the UC Berkeley terminal capability database, and Mike Riddle has written a program to decode it into easily accessed parameters. By writing a universal terminal module that is driven by these parameters, a program can adapt to a terminal simply by taking the name of the terminal, looking it up in the database, and plugging the parameters into the driver. As the UC database is constantly updated, most of the maintenance work is done by our tax dollars, not our flying fingers. If somebody shows up with a terminal not in the database, we still only have to make an entry in the file, not program a new driver. Thus, a dealer selling our products need only set up a configuration file when selling the package with a statement like:

TERM ZORCHTERM-100

and our package will be ready to go. I think this is a powerful selling point and we should do it for sure.

---

15 This suggestion is essentially identical to the concept of "string resources" in the Macintosh. Apple subsequently invented string resources, the same way they invented the personal computer, the mouse, pop-up menus, and windows.

Now, what are your ideas? I don't want to jump into thinking of products just yet, but what are the company-wide concepts we should be putting into everything we do? Or, putting it another way, what things do you find most annoying on the system you use now, and how would you solve them if you were starting over?

Nightmare

On March 19, 1982, the West Coast Computer Faire will open at the San Francisco convention center. MSL has forked over $1200 for a booth at the show, and at the moment our only plans are to have an Interact system there. It would be very nice to show some MSP products at the show, complete with glossy brochures. Any ideas? At this point, I'm perfectly willing to cobble up things that look like products, which we'll clearly indicate are not ready for release. Remember that this is one of the major contacts between sellers and buyers and the only one in the Bay area. If you have any ideas, give me a call and we'll get cracking on it. There's only about 30 days left.

What's going on

At the moment, we're in the process of consulting with various people with experience in start-ups of this nature, and trying to line up marketing people. In a week or so we should know a lot more about what we can and can't do from the legal standpoint, and we'll try to put together a tentative charter which we'll send to you as soon as it's ready.

We're doing some market research, talking to people involved with Selector and other products to find out what their experience has been in this market. We're studying various desktop machines and thinking about how we can get the maximum development capability for our hardware dollar.

I think that progress is being made on all fronts, and at this point things look very good indeed.

What to Name the Company

Talk about an identity crisis! Virtually every name we came up with for the company was either considered harmful by the founders, or considered already taken by the California Secretary of State. Our numerous attempts to find a name didn't deter us from making ever more imaginative suggestions. First, a passel of names proposed by Duff Kurland.

To: WALKER
DUFF (02/26-11:15)

"Integrity Software" sounds good…. I did have a couple of other ideas, however (and they didn't even involve puns!)….

Desktop Software	Valu-Ware
Desktop Solutions	Future-Ware

I kind of like "Desktop Software", but can't help wondering where it will go: … "Bottom Left Drawer Software" … "Shoebox Software" … "Breast Pocket Software" … "Shoestring Software" … (Hmmmm…). Other suggestions (some in jest):

Office Solutions	Execu-Ware	Out-of-Control Data Corp.
Titanic Software	Business Ware	MIS Information Systems
Good OfficeKeeping	Manage-Ware	Ethical Ripoffs, Inc.
Dud & Brannstreet	Mr. Softee	Software Breakthroughs
Office Technology	Upper-Ware	Management Technology
Conceptual Elegance	Compu-Freaks	Smelly Rand

Other names proposed for the company with various degrees of seriousness included:

Command Technologies	Command Line Technology
RHT, Inc.	Target Software
Insight Automation, Ltd	Coders Of the Lost Spark
Autodesk, Inc.	

Of these names, "Desktop Solutions" was initially chosen. We showed AutoCAD and the Autodesk prototype at the West Coast Computer Faire in 1982 under this name, and it appeared on the first brochures we ever printed. It was rejected by the Secretary of State, as were "Target Software" and "Insight Automation". By the way, "RHT" stood for "Red Hot Techies".

Getting into the Details

Information Letter 3 was the first to delve into the gory details of how the company was to be organised, capitalised, and run. Dan Drake wrote this information letter after consultations with Robert Tufts, a San Francisco lawyer to whom we were introduced by Jack Stuppin.

MSP Information Letter # 3

by Dan Drake
March 2, 1982

The Organization Plan, which is included with this mailing, is the proposed plain English version of our plans. On Sunday we hope to reach agreement on the real thing, which we'll get written up by legal counsel. If we don't run into any snags at that point, we'll go ahead with forming the corporation.

At this point I ought stress that I am not now, nor have I ever been, professionally qualified to give financial or legal advice; I don't think that there are substantial errors of fact or law in this paper, but there may be.

Though this is a corporation rather than the limited partnership that we favored at first, the organization plan in general is very close to what we talked about on January 30 and what people expressed in their letters. There has been a change in the plans for getting computers, but the change should have little practical effect.

The business entity

The company is going to be organized as a privately held California corporation. In effect, the government wants us to be a corporation, and there is not enough reason to buck it.

The argument against a general partnership, in brief, is that any general partner can commit all the assets of the company. Furthermore, the general partners have to stand behind the company's commitments not only with their shares of the partnership, but with everything they own. The partnership agreement may name some managing partners who are the only ones authorized to act for the company, but the company could still be bound by unauthorized actions!

A limited partnership is hardly better. The law is not absolutely clear, but it is likely that limited partners who took any active part in the business would be declared general partners as soon as any litigation started, which reduces this to the previous case.

So a corporation it is. Here's a really crude outline of the procedure:

After registering the corporation with the state, the people who are doing the grungework appoint themselves as the Board of Directors and do assorted necessary paperwork. Part of this paperwork is a plan for the issuance of stock.

Then we hold a grand meeting at which we issue shares of stock in return for cash, notes, and other things. We immediately hold a stockholders' meeting to approve a stock option plan, and to elect a new Board if we want to. At that point we're officially in business.

The shares will be common voting stock, representing a fractional interest in the company, just like General Motors stock (though with a few little differences):

- Each share entitles you to one vote at a stockholders' meeting. This vote actually means something, which is more than you can say for GM stock.
- If the company folds up, the stock represents your cut of whatever is left over after paying the creditors. If that amount is negative, you're not liable for the difference beyond any amount that you may still owe on the stock purchase.
- If we sell the whole operation to another company or the public, the stock represents your cut of whatever is paid for the business assets. Employment by the successor company, of course, is a separate matter.
- You can't take your shares to your broker and sell them. It may even be illegal to sell them to your neighbor or to anyone else outside the company. Of course, after we're successful, we might go public and sell shares for a fantastic price like The Two Steves (Jobs & Wozniak of Apple). Even a public offering of new stock might not allow you to sell old stock publicly, but that decision would be up to the stockholders.

Issuance of shares

The basic arrangement for the first issue of stock is rather simpler than the things we talked about in January.

1. The stock will be issued at $1.00 a share.
2. If you have the money ready, you can buy any number of shares for cash. (There's an extra goody attached to this, described later.)
3. If you have computing equipment relevant to the company's needs, you can sell it for stock at fair market value. Obviously you don't want to do this if you're using the computer in a consulting business and don't want it moved out of town by the company. (If you've taken accelerated depreciation or investment credit, you'll have to worry about recapture on your next income tax form.)
4. You can get up to 3,000 shares on a 10% note, which we expect you to redeem out of your share of the income when there is any. If the company goes belly-up, however, you're fully liable for this loan.
5. Everyone is to take at least 3,000 shares on some basis or other.

You'll notice that we have written everyone down for some amount of stock in the Organization Plan. Don't be upset if you don't recognize the numbers opposite your name; we had to make some kind of guess, and this doesn't represent a commitment, expectation, or anything else.

We expect to issue some additional shares for other considerations. Among these will be the rights to Interact and the expenses that MSL incurs during the formation of the company. We may also sell small blocks of stock for cash to non-employees closely associated with the founding of the company, such as legal and financial experts.

Shortly before the stock is issued, we need to know exactly how much each person is taking, and on which basis.

Buying equipment

The plan is now for the company to buy whatever equipment it needs out of its own funds. If you already have equipment, you can sell it to the company, or you can go on using it instead of using a company machine. This gives the company control over the choice and allocation of equipment, and lets people invest as much as possible directly in stock. The disadvantage of this arrangement is that the tax breaks are less attractive, but tax breaks are only one consideration out of many.

Working capital

Out of the cash that we get for issuing stock we'll pay for equipment and the costs of setting up the corporation. This will leave us with enough money in the treasury to pay the very small expenses of the first few months, when we have no costs for salaries, rent, or advertising.

Once we have products to sell, we'll need much more money to carry us until we start getting enough income to cover current expenses. The number we've talked about is a total of $100,000 beyond the initial equipment purchases. To raise the money we expect to sell more stock during the first 12 – 18 months of operation.

The specific plan is to issue warrants along with the first issue of stock. A warrant does not convey any ownership share in the company, but entitles the holder to buy another share at a set price, namely $1.00. If it isn't exercised within a fixed time, it turns into wallpaper. It can be bought and sold on the same basis as stock.

The people who are expected to come up with additional financing (currently Marinchip Systems Ltd. and John Walker) will be issued warrants. In addition, everyone who is buying stock for cash will actually get a "unit" consisting of one share and one warrant, for $1.01; this is the extra goody, mentioned earlier, to encourage people to provide the company with cash. The warrants will probably expire in 18 months.

Stock options

One of the essential ideas of the company is a sweat equity plan by which people get an ownership interest in lieu of salary during the startup. Stock option plans are now a very attractive way of handling this.

Basically, the company issues options which can be exercised in the future at a fixed price. To qualify for tax breaks, this price will be 110% of the fair market value when the options are issued. What we hope is that the stock will become extremely valuable so that you can exercise your option at the cheap price, sell for a high price, and pay capital gains tax on the difference (plus straight income tax on the option price).

The tax laws force a few conditions on the price and expiration period of the options, but these should not be troublesome. Within these conditions we have a great deal of freedom in specifying the terms of the options. We'll circulate more detailed information on qualified stock option plans later, when we've consulted officially with the experts.

The Organization Plan includes an outline of a stock option plan. We ought to get a pretty firm agreement on details during the Sunday meeting, since this is such an important part of the whole plan.

Unpleasant question: What if someone does no work at all? In the extreme case he can be fired, forfeiting any options he has, but retaining any stock. In lesser cases he gets a severely truncated option.

Next unpleasant question: How is it determined who has been working enough? This has to be subjective; it can't be a matter of lines of code generated, divided by bug reports. The subjective judgement should follow easily from the experience of answering the phone and telling customers which products aren't ready yet. Inevitable differences in productivity are handled by bonuses for brilliant work and by not having duds among the founders.

Personal holding companies

One thing that scared us when we considered incorporating was the personal holding company rule, which can impose a 70% penalty tax on a corporation that makes too much of its money from royalties or other passive income. It turns out that there's a nice, clean exemption, designed for the use of movie and TV production companies, whose business is really very similar to the software business.

The rule is something like this: if half your income is from the sale of copyrighted material, and you spend 15% on expenses other than salaries, you're not a personal holding company. Our material will certainly be copyrighted, and we'll have no trouble spending 15% on advertising, so we seem to be home free. [16]

Conflicts of interest

There are potentially serious problems from a person's present employer claiming ownership of anything the person does for the new venture. If you have signed any agreement on ownership of patent rights, etc., please get us a copy of it.

Even if you haven't signed an agreement, you have certain responsibilities to your present employer, if any. We'll have to have legal counsel draw up a paper by which everyone will make clear his right to create software for the venture.

---

[16] Dan Drake notes: In fact this exemption didn't apply; it was written explicitly for the film production business. Our special interest got its exemption only in 1986, after the IRS challenged Microsoft claiming that *all* of their income from the sale of software was royalty income and was clearly preparing to go after the rest of us. Thanks for picking on the most powerful victim first, guys!

New people

To strengthen the business end of this business we've enticed Jack Stuppin to join us. Jack has several years experience in running a company that manufactured mass-marketed products. He has even more experience in finance, including some startups of companies in the silicon business.

We also seem to have found an accountant and a lawyer for the company, both first-rate. The lawyer, Bob Tufts, has worked with Jack on high-tech business startups and has expressed interest in making a small investment in MSP.

Names, names, names

Speaking of MSP, the need for a name for this company has become critical! We also need names for the things that we're now calling Interact and Cardfile. It would be really nice if we could latch onto a neat little prefix, like Visi-, to distinguish our products. Please, please come to Sunday's meeting with a list of all the names you can think of, no matter how silly. In the meantime, we'll probably have to print brochures for the Computer Faire, using Marinchip's logo and arbitrary names for the products.[17]

Paperwork

In addition to employees' agreements, we need some more information from everybody. First, after studying the organization plan, please indicate as specifically as you can what your financial and working participation will be. The numbers in the plan are based on the first letters that people sent, but the figures in those letters were sometimes vague, and the rules have changed to some extent.

We also need your phone number and the name and address that you want entered in the company records.

---

17 We ended up showing the prototype of Cardfile, which had been renamed "Autodesk," and Interact, which was then called "MicroCAD," in a booth with a company name of Desktop Solutions. Desktop Solutions was later rejected as a company name by California, so we had to choose again... and again... and again. "Autodesk" — snappy name that! MicroCAD was such a neat name for a CAD product that a certain fine gentleman who saw us using it at the show ran out and trademarked it out from under us, and used it for his own product. Success did not smile upon his product; the wheel of Karma turns slowly, but it is accurate to the least significant bit.

And the resume. Don't bother with a fancy one, suitable for impressing employers, but give a good summary of your technical background. If we want to impress IBM with our qualifications, we'll re-write the resumes in a uniform style.

Next meeting

The next meeting is on Sunday, March 7, at 12 Noon. It will be at Jack Stuppin's house in San Francisco.

Does anyone have a good cassette recorder for recording this meeting? I'll bring a cheapo, but if you have anything decent, please call John to volunteer as a recording engineer. We also need to make copies of the recording so that we can send them to several widely scattered people.

Proposed Organization Plan for MSP

This plan covers the initial issue of stock and warrants by MSP (the code name for the new venture). The purpose is to raise money for equipment purchases plus working capital for the first 12 – 18 months. The plan includes allowance for a qualified stock option plan.

Most of the numbers have been filled in, at least to a good approximation. Uncertainties are due to continuing negotiations and to the rough figures given in the participants' letters of intent.

Throughout the plan it is assumed that this will be a private offering, limited to a small group of participants.

Initial Issue Of Securities

The company will issue approximately 100,000 shares of common stock out of an authorized total of at least 350,000. It will also issue approximately 100,000 warrants, expiring in 18 months, which can be exercised to buy common stock.

Stock will be issued in return for cash, computing equipment, notes, and other considerations at a price of $1.00 a share. Warrants will be issued at $.01 each.

Investors putting up cash will pay $1.01 for a unit consisting of one share of common stock and one warrant.

Those having computing equipment needed by the company will be able to sell it at a negotiated price representing fair market value, in return for common stock at $1.00 a share.

Each participant will be able to buy up to 3,000 shares on a 10% note payable in three years. The note is to be a recourse loan, representing a potential claim on any of the investor's assets.

Each participant is expected to invest in at least 3,000 shares by means of cash, equipment, or notes. The investment may be through a partnership or a corporation, though a corporation may not issue notes for shares.

It is expected that stock will be issued to Mike Riddle in return for the non-9900 rights to the Interact package, contingent on delivery of a working version for certain computers within a fixed time. Stock will also be issued to the founding group, Marinchip Systems Ltd. (MSL) in return for expenses incurred in organizing the new company and possibly for software, including QBASIC.

Stock Options

All or nearly all of the participants will be employed by the company at a nominal salary of $1.00 a year. In lieu of proper salary they are to receive stock options.

The first stockholders' meeting will adopt a qualified stock option plan covering all the participants who are employed by the company when it begins operations. There should be agreement in principle on this plan, including the quantities involved, before the corporation is organized. Here is a suggested outline:

> 150,000 (?) shares of the stock of this company (equal to 1.5 times the original issue of stock excluding warrants) are set aside for the company stock option plan, with options to be issued in equal quantities at the end of 6, 12, and 18 months after the company begins operation.
>
> Each of the initial employees of the corporation will make a commitment to perform a specific amount of work per week for the corporation and will, having performed that work diligently, be entitled to options in proportion to that commitment. Smaller allocations, not necessarily in proportion to work performed, may be given to those who have not fully met the commitment.
>
> In each distribution 60 – 75% of the options will be allocated according to work committed and performed, as described above. The remaining options will be awarded as bonuses for exceptional performance. The percentage allocated to bonuses need not be the same in all three distributions.
>
> The Board of Directors will appoint a three-member Compensation Committee to determine the distribution of options. The Committee's plan will be submitted for approval of the Board, which may submit it to the stockholders. The resolution of the Board of Directors will set an option price

which will be 100% to 110% of the current fair market value of the stock. Options will be valid for five years from the time of issuance, but will in any case expire upon termination of employment.

Liabilities of the Corporation

Out of the cash received for the first stock issue the company will buy about $25,000 – 30,000 of equipment and pay any remaining costs of organization. During the first 90 days of operation other expenses should be nominal, limited to telephone costs, printing of letterheads, and such.

When products start to be available for sale, there will be expenses for sales and production. Until revenues match operating expenses, the company expects to raise operating capital by the participants' exercise of warrants.

In order to get the rights to Interact, the company expects to enter into a royalty agreement with Owens Associates, which underwrote some of the development of the package. The details of this agreement have not been worked out.

As most of the participants are now employed in the computer industry, there is a possibility of conflicting claims to the rights to software written for MSP. All participants will be required to certify that they have the right to develop software for the company, clear of any claims by any other employer.

No other liabilities are known.

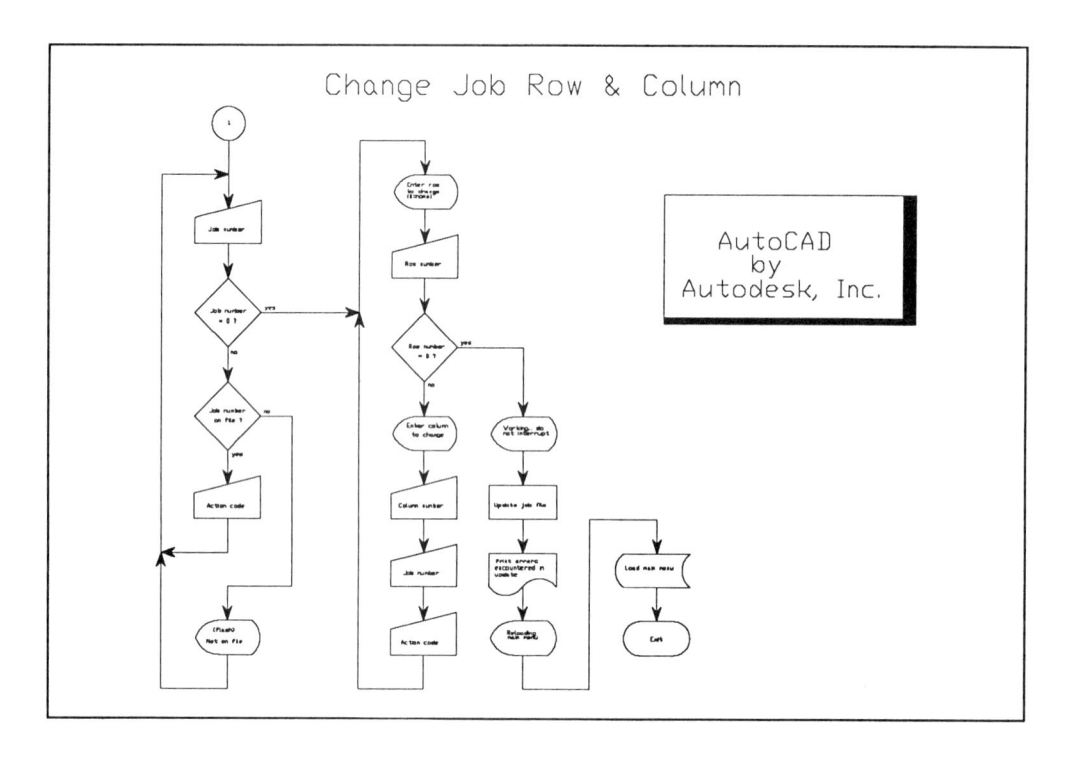

This drawing was originally done on AutoCAD-80 shortly before COMDEX 1982 as a show demo. The program described by this flowchart is one of the Marinchip business application packages.

Changes to the Organization Plan

Information Letter 4 followed Letter 3 by a month, and brought the participants up to date on the organisation plan as it stood after being processed by the lawyers and the California Commissioner of Corporations. Shortly before this letter was written, we had shown prototypes of the Autodesk product and MicroCAD, the product we utilmately called AutoCAD. Dan Drake is again the author.

MSP Information Letter #4

Dan Drake
April 2, 1982

This letter summarizes what has happened since the last letter and what we expect to do next. The plans are based on what we think is the consensus of all the people who have expressed an opinion. Now that we've recovered from the Computer Faire, we're going to move ahead as fast as possible, so speak up if you find anything wrong here.

New organization plan

Dan Drake, Keith Marcelius, and Jack Stuppin met on March 15 with Robert Tufts, who will be the attorney for the corporation, to review our plans for setting up the corporation. Nothing was fundamentally wrong, but there are some serious regulatory problems that have forced some changes in the plans. Here is the new organization plan:

The initial offering of stock will be to the 13 founders who are legal residents of California. These people will buy the units of one share and one warrant, as described in the last letter, in return for cash, equipment, or accounts receivable (in the case of Marinchip Systems Ltd). The company will then hire employees (us) and offer up to 3,000 shares of stock apiece in return for 10% notes (by law, only employees can buy stock for notes).

After all this is done, the company will hire more employees, namely the people who aren't residents of California. As an incentive to join the company these people will get stock options which will put them on essentially the same basis as the original employees.

There won't be any special issue of warrants beyond the one-for-one deal with shares of stock, because that could raise tax problems. However, we expect to offer a large option to the president of the company, John Walker, to give him an incentive to commit his time and capital.

General meeting

At the March 16 meeting we went over all these legalities and discussed some questions that Bob Tufts had raised. The rest of this section gives the decisions that we reached.

Though we are capitalizing the company in a way that saves us from meeting the fantastically expensive requirements of the Securities and Exchange Commission, there remain the less stringent requirements of the state of California. We have the choice of applying in advance for a permit to offer stock or simply filing notice of a private offering with the Secretary of State. The former slightly reduces the risk of later legal problems at a cost of $700 – 1,000 and 2 – 3 weeks delay. The consensus of the meeting was that it's not worth it; we'll sell the stock, then file the notice of private offering.

Private corporations often have special agreements that prevent stock from getting into the hands of outsiders. In order to cover lots of contingencies, including death, divorce, bankruptcy, and other involuntary transfers of stock, these agreements get very long and messy. Our decision was that a fancy agreement is not worth the time and expense; we'll just make an agreement that the company and its stockholders have first refusal if anyone wants to sell his stock to an outsider.

MSP obviously doesn't want to force its employees (ourselves) to sign the usual employee software rights agreement, with the usual restrictive and unenforceable clauses. We'll write our own agreement that says: I have the right to produce software for MSP without a prior claim by someone else; I won't use other people's trade secrets; I won't steal trade secrets from MSP; I will give MSP first refusal on any ideas I develop for mass market software. Under the last clause you can write anything that's not for a large market; if it later develops mass market potential, you give MSP first refusal on it.

We have collected the full legal names and addresses of nearly everyone in the company, as needed for company records, stock registration, and whatnot. The list is given at the end of this letter. If your name is not on it, please give us your full legal name, with parentheses around parts of the name that are not normally used (!), and your address.

Finally, the Board of Directors of the company will have 3 – 5 members, an item that must appear in the articles of incorporation. Though nothing has been officially determined, it is likely that the board will consist initially of the people in the north bay area who are actively in touch and have time to devote to organizational trivia: Dan Drake, Keith Marcelius, Jack Stuppin, and John Walker.

Plans: Incorporation

At the March 16 meeting we reached a pseudo-consensus on an unsatisfactory name for the corporation (Autodesk Inc.), but by the weekend the consensus seemed to have fallen apart. On this crucial question no one is satisfied, but everyone feels burned out. So we're going to file the Articles of Incorporation in a few days, using the name INSIGHT AUTOMATION LTD unless (1) the state disallows it [18] or (2) someone comes up with the perfect name in the next 5 or 6 days.[19]

Technical progress

John Walker made an impressive demo version of Autodesk, our super filing system, for the Computer Faire. It got quite a good response, especially considering that we didn't claim to be able to release it in less than three months.

John also has the Z80 slave processor from Sierra Data Systems running CPM 2.2 under supervision of our 9900 system. This means we can install CPM in any of our systems for about $600. He has also converted WINDOW to CB-80, the compiled version of CBASIC. All we have to do is convert 1,000 – 2,000 lines of assembly code, which will allow it to page files on disc, and we have a valuable product for CPM systems ready to go! [20]

Technical plans

If only because of the support burden, we can't target every computer system in the world during the first few months. The current idea is to pursue the CPM (8080 and Z80) market immediately with all we've got. This means installing the Sierra Z80 board in lots of existing computers.

---

18 They did, just as they had previously disallowed "Desktop Solutions", the name under which we showed at the Computer Faire.
19 Nobody did. Suggestions included "Coders of the Lost Spark".
20 This product eventually came to market as AutoScreen. It was introduced at COMDEX 1982 at the same time as AutoCAD. We sold about 10. The current Autodesk programmers' editor, "Kern's Editor," is a descendent of AutoScreen.

We need to do more evaluation of the IBM and Apple situation with respect to both technical and marketing questions. We ought to be getting hardware for non-Z80 systems within 4-6 weeks.

The products that we expect to concentrate on are MicroCAD, Autodesk, Opticalc, and Window. One non-yucky name in the whole bunch. For those who haven't kept up with the latest nomenclature and bright ideas, here's a quick description.

MicroCAD: The new name for Mike Riddle's computer graphics package. We've printed brochures for this, so the name is pretty well committed. Naturally, this won't be on 8-bit machines; we're hitting IBM first.

Autodesk: The instant filing system that will knock Visidex etc. out of the running. This too has a brochure.

Opticalc: The name we've been using for a brilliant idea that came up during the Faire: a VisiClone (spreadsheet package) that performs some optimization on its own.

Window: Marinchip's screen editor, converted to CPM systems.

We're also looking closely at JPLDIS, a very useful data base system written in Univac Fortran. The program is in the public domain, so we have the right to convert it to microcomputers and sell it. In fact, it apparently is being sold now under the name of dBase II, but there's nothing to stop us from getting into the act.

We still need to make decisions about an implementation language, for which the candidates seem to be CB-80, C, and PL/I. We now know that CB-80 works, and we can expect it on the 8086 sometime soon. PL/I also works, and we can get a beta test version in May. C is supposed to be available on every microcomputer; we need to know more about the quality and standardization of the various versions.

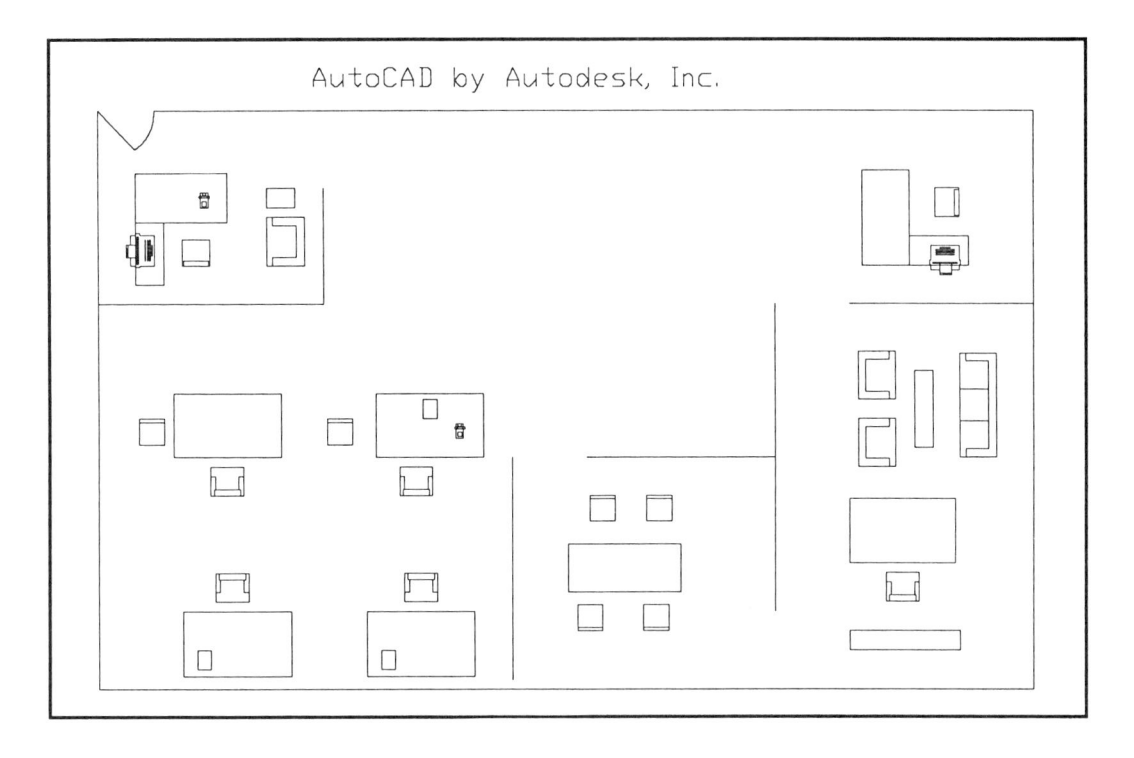

The office drawing was done in the week before COMDEX 1982 as a flagship demo to show off zooming and block manipulation capability. It was the most-used demo at the introduction of AutoCAD.

Initial Stock Distribution

Autodesk, Inc. was officially incorporated in California on April 26, 1982. This letter accompanied the distribution of the company's stock to the founders. The original shares in the company were sold for $1 each. Five years later, adjusting for stock splits, each of those original shares had appreciated in value to more than $1100. This is why people start companies.

Autodesk, Inc.

Greetings,

Enclosed are your stock certificate(s) and other Autodesk related documents. This letter should answer some of the obvious questions about them.

"Why did I get two stock certificates?"

If you purchased stock for cash, and also for a loan (note), separate certificates were issued for the two purchases. This purely to simplify bookkeeping; the effect is the same as if you had one certificate with the sum of the number of shares on the two. If you purchased shares only for cash or only for a note, you will get one certificate.

"What's the 'Combined Intrastate and "Private"' Document?"

This is your copy of the Investment Letter which you signed before purchasing your shares. As the letter is keyed to the particular number of shares in a given certificate, if you got two certificates, you'll also have two investment letters (check number of shares in letters to see which is which). The originals are on file here; this is your copy for your records.

"What about the note for shares?"

You should have received a copy of the Promissory Note for the shares purchased for a loan when you signed the original. The copy is stamped "COPY" in red. If you cannot find this copy, we can make another and send it to you.

"Could you explain the warrant again?"

If you purchased stock for cash, you also purchased warrants to acquire an equal number of shares to those purchased for cash. The price of the warrant was 1 cent per share. In the package is the original warrant you purchased. This warrant is valid for four years. At any time during the 4 year period, you can exercise your right to purchase any number of shares from 1 to the total number listed on Page 1 of the warrant, by paying $1 for each share (regardless of the price or value of the shares at the time you purchase the warrant). The warrant is exercised by returning Page 8, "Subscription Form", with your payment to the company. As explained in that form, if you purchase less than the total number of shares purchasable under the warrant, you will be issued a new warrant for the balance of the shares still unpurchased at the time the shares are delivered. Or in other words, you can buy any number of shares any time you like in any size chunks you want, up to the total listed in the original warrant. The warrant is a piece of property just like a stock certificate, and Page 7 is used if you sell it to somebody else (note that sale may be subject to restrictions under law and the bylaws of the company, just like a sale of stock).

"What do I do with this stuff?"

The stock certificates and warrants are your physical property, and are the tangible evidence of your ownership in the company and right to increase it by exercising the warrant. Don't lose them! They are *very* painful to replace. If you have a safe deposit box, that's where they should be. The rest of the documents are for your files relating to the company, as they are your copies of documents for which the company holds the originals.

"What do I do with the receipt?"

Included are two copies of a receipt for these documents. After you verify that the documents described in the receipt have been delivered, please sign and return the copy marked "sign and return". I've enclosed a SASE for people I'm not handing the shares to personally. An additional copy of the receipt is included for your records.

Call me if I've forgotten to mention something.

Sincerely,

John Walker

Autodesk Becomes a Reality

Autodesk, Inc. was officially incorporated in California on April 26, 1982. I wrote this information letter just after finishing all of the paperwork associated with the incorporation, including mailing stock certificates, options, and warrants to all of the founders.

Autodesk, Inc.
Information Letter # 5

by John Walker
Revision 9 — May Day, 1982

This letter is to bring you up to date on the progress since the last letter, pass on some additional information about products with suggestions of who does what and some random company and product notes. If you have not already received one or been sent a copy, this letter will be accompanied with a copy of the "Autodesk Design Guide", the working paper for the final version of the Autodesk database system. Comments and suggestions regarding all of the enclosed are solicited.

Progress Organising the Company

Since every other name for which there was a general consensus of acceptability was unacceptable to California as a corporation name (due to being too close to somebody else's), the company ended up being called "Autodesk, Inc." (AI). If we think of the perfect name, we can always change it. In the meanwhile, I'll use "AI" when referring to the company and "Autodesk" when referring to the product with the same name.

The corporation was created by filing the Articles of Incorporation with the Secretary of State on April 9, 1982. The officers and board of directors were elected on April 16, 1982. The first phase of organisation of the company was completed on April 26, 1982, when the stock was sold to the founders (all California residents, as described in "Information Letter #4"), and the notes for stock purchased by loan were signed. The money from the stock sale was then deposited in a new account for AI opened at First Interstate Bank. Thus, the company is now officially formed and operating. Officers of the company were chosen as follows:

President: John Walker
Vice President and Secretary: Dan Drake
Treasurer (CFO) and Assistant Secretary: Keith Marcelius
Assistant Secretary: Bob Tufts

The doubling up of offices permits critical documents which require signature by "(President or Vice President) and (Secretary or Assistant Secretary)" to be filed when one of the officers is unavailable. Designating our attorney, Bob Tufts, as Assistant Secretary allows routine matters which require signature by a Secretary to be handled without getting all the officers together. This form of organisation is typical of companies of our type.

The Board of Directors is as follows:

Dan Drake
Keith Marcelius
Jack Stuppin
John Walker

As mentioned in Information Letter #4, the board consists of those who are willing to get together and deal with the matters the board is required to deal with. There were no other volunteers, so the board is as suggested in that letter.

Neither the slate of officers nor the board membership is cast in concrete, of course.

Changes from Original Organisation Plan

Legal requirements forced several changes in the original Organisation Plan (OP) of March 2, 1982, which was sent with Information Letter #3. As far as I know, the following list of changes is all-inclusive. None of these changes significantly affects the status of any participant in the company, and none has any adverse affect we've been able to think of.

In the OP the warrants were stated to expire in 18 months. This has been changed to 4 years to give the recipients of the warrants more flexibility in deciding when to convert them into shares. The stock options issued to the out of state people will have the same term.

In the OP, the specifics of the stock option issuance were spelled out in an agreement in principle. The stock option plan finally adopted will be as stated in the OP. At this point, we have in effect a "legal boilerplate" option plan which allows the flexibility needed to accommodate the plan described in the OP, plus the ability to bring in the out of state people via options as described in Information Letter #4.

Jack Stuppin is an employee of a member firm of the New York Stock Exchange, and is hence prohibited from being an employee of any other company. As a result, he cannot be an employee of AI, but he can be a director. He can still work for the company in the capacity of director. Since he's not an employee, we can't grant him stock options like the other employees, so we issued him warrants as a director.

The only other change from Information Letter #4 is that Marinchip Systems Ltd. was issued warrants for the stock it is to purchase over the next year. In Information Letter #4, MSL was listed as purchasing stock for a note. Since only employees can purchase stock for a note, and a corporation can't be an employee, we accomplished the same effect by issuing warrants. (Actually this way is slightly better: this way, MSL does not gain a vote in the operation of the company until it comes up with the money. Had we issued it stock for a note, it would gain the votes immediately.)

What Happens Next

In terms of organising the company, the next step is to hire the out-of-state participants and grant them the stock options which they will use to effect their purchases of stock. Two options will be granted to all out-of-state participants: a 60 day option for initial purchase of stock, and a 4 year option equivalent to the 4 year warrant sold to California residents. Out-of-state participants will be given a note to sign to exercise the 60 day option identical to that signed by the California people. The 60 days in the option are simply to give people time to get the money in our hands, as this can take a while for international transfers.

Once the 60 day options have been exercised, everybody (California and out-of-state) will be on an equal basis, the company will be running, and then we'll hopefully be able to stop worrying about the form and get to work on the substance — developing products and selling them.

Just a Few More Little Things

Included with this mailing is a W-4 form for tax withholding which, even though we are paying salaries at the staggering rate of $1/year, we must have from all employees. We don't yet know how this works for overseas people, so if you're one of them just keep the form for the moment until we find out from the U.S. tax people. U.S. people, please fill out the form and return it to us in the enclosed SASE.

If you are a non-California resident, you will also find enclosed an employee agreement. This agreement has already been executed by all the California people. We must have this agreement as evidence of employment before we can issue the employee stock option that you will use to acquire your original share in the company. A duplicate agreement is enclosed for your records.

Bob Tufts has asked us to inform all participants that if they feel their interests are being violated by the corporation, they are urged to contact their own legal counsel. This information was passed on to all people in the initial offering, and I am repeating it here for completeness.

Regular Meetings

To avoid the last-minute panic meetings which have characterised our operation through the organisation period, we've set up regular monthly meetings on the first weekend of every month, with the first meeting in June 1982. On even numbered months, the meeting will be on Sunday, on odd numbered months, Saturday (since neither day was preferable to everybody). Hence, the next meeting is Sunday, June 6, 1982. The location of each meeting will be set at the preceding meeting, and will be at various places to share the travel burden among the participants. The next meeting will be at Jack Stuppin's house in San Francisco (directions are in Information Letter #3).

The agenda of these meetings will be a review of company progress, product status, and other matters as described in the original Working Paper. We'll try to work the meetings so that technical sessions about specific products can be worked in at the end to aid people who are collaborating on products in getting together.

Purchasing

In the process of evaluating products and getting the work done, participants will need to buy manuals for various products, supplies for machines provided by AI, etc. Our intent is that manuals you need to evaluate products, etc., can be handled by a petty cash mechanism — you buy it and send the receipt to AI, which will refund the money to you. If in doubt, call and ask. (In some cases, we know places to get things cheaper than the local computer store or direct from the manufacturer. Also, somebody else might have one you can borrow.) To avoid disputes, it's wise to clear everything first, but something like a $35 manual for a package competitive with one we're developing will naturally be O.K.

By combining AI's orders with MSL's ongoing business, we can get floppy discs and other computer supplies at very low prices. We will centrally purchase these items and ship them out to people as requested. We'll try to keep reasonable quantities of all the normal supplies in stock here, so Bay Area people can get what they need next day by UPS. Shipping costs make this crazy for overseas people, so we will reimburse them for supplies expenses from receipts they submit.

Micro-CAD Progress

We now have a formal agreement with Mike Riddle for transfer of MicroCAD to the company in return for royalties to Mike to compensate him for his personal development of the package. Thus, we're now on the way with one of our major products. Mike has been working with a CP/M 86 system he owns (on a Godbout 8085/8088 board) and has been using an IBM Personal Computer at the local Computerland store on off-hours. He has acquired the Microsoft Macro Assembler and tested it, and has determined how to interconvert programs between PCDOS/MSDOS and CP/M 86. This means we can develop on one and sell on both.

Current thinking is that our best path to getting MicroCAD running on the 8086/8088 is to port SPL and recompile with it. Now that we have an assembler, we have all the key tools in hand to move the META and SPL complex. Although we will have to do a substantial amount of 8086 assembly code to move the package, when we're done we'll control the compiler, and that allows us to take advantage of floating point chip options, extended memory beyond what IBM's operating system supports (which you can buy off the shelf today), and other such selling points much faster than if we had to wait for our language vendor to get around to supporting them. One of the major hassles in using the 8086 is the memory segmentation architecture to address large memory spaces.[21] Controlling the compiler allows us to be sure we won't be limited by the language to less memory than the machine allows.

To this end, Mike is plugging away on the SPL port. Once we get our IBM machine, we'll be able to increase the pace of this effort.

Autodesk Progress

At the moment, the Autodesk package is being designed by Kern Sibbald, Keith Marcelius, and John Walker. The attached copy of the design guide, which is the starting point for this design, is for your review. Please forward any comments and suggestions to one of the people mentioned above. If you want to get involved in the product design, you're welcome to. There's plenty left to do.

---

21   Indeed....

We're planning to implement Autodesk in CB80 for CP/M. We've worked enough with CB80 so far to trust it to hold up for a project of Autodesk's size. Also, since the prototype system developed for the Computer Faire was written in QBASIC, some parts, such as the large screen editor module, can be lifted and used essentially as-is.

Other Product Progress

The status of all the other products is as listed in the enclosed products note. I think it's making more and more sense to look at QBASIC as a product because of the expected long delay before Microsoft delivers their true compiler for the IBM PC, the expectation that CB86 (whenever it is ready) will run only under CP/M 86, not PCDOS, and for our own use in porting our CBASIC products to the PC and other 8086/8088 systems. Also, as noted in the products bulletin, if we port SPL, we'll have done a lot of the work needed to port QBASIC already. We'd also be in an excellent position to move it to the 68000 and ace Digital Research out of the CBASIC market.

Product Polish and Packaging

In the mass market, the initial impression is made by the packaging of the product (including the format and quality of its documentation), user aids, and dealer training tools. As you look at other products, try to keep these things in mind and note any good ideas you see or hear about from others. Products like Autodesk and MicroCAD need to look as professional as their operation is, and we need to think about what we should be doing in that way as we develop the products for initial marketing.

Digital Research can get away with crummy manuals because everybody knows them and respects their products. We can't because nobody will have heard of us, and if our manuals and packaging look amateurish then potential customers will assume our products are as well.

Two questions I'd like to ask everybody are:

"What is the best software manual you've ever used?"
"What made it so good and so useful?"

I'm sure we can produce manuals as good as any in the industry. But first we need to decide what we want to make. Let me know your thoughts.

Subchapter S Election Alternative

We have been assuming since Information Letter #2 that we lacked the option to organise the company as a Subchapter S corporation because any corporation with nonresident alien (i.e. overseas) stockholders is ineligible for Subchapter S. It turns out that because of the way we're bringing in the non-California people, there is a reasonably attractive alternative we should consider (I will studiously avoid using the word "option" here except when I mean "qualified employee stock option" — hence all the "alternatives" herein).

First of all, what is a Subchapter S corporation? A normal corporation has assets and liabilities just like an individual. When the corporation makes money, the only way it can get it out to the owners is by paying dividends, which are taxed twice, or by paying salaries. More important in the case of start-up companies, if the corporation loses money, the losses simply reduce the net worth of the corporation; they cannot be used to reduce the stockholders' tax liability (but they can be carried forward and used to offset the corporation's future profits). (However, if the corporation goes totally belly-up, the stockholders can deduct the loss on the then-worthless stock.)

A Subchapter S corporation works very much like a partnership for tax purposes while retaining the limited liability and flexibility of a corporation. The net profit or loss from the corporation is simply divided among the shareholders based on percent ownership and declared on their tax returns on Schedule E as regular income. Since most corporations lose money in the start-up period (while you're doing the development, writing off the equipment you bought, and doing initial advertising), a Subchapter S corporation can pass these losses directly out to the people who, after all, put up the money that's being lost, so they can reduce their income taxes. If the company loses, say, $20,000 in the first year and you own 5%, that means you can deduct $1,000 from your income. If you're in the 35% marginal tax bracket, that means you keep about $350 rather than giving it to Uncle Sam. Good pay for filling out a form.

If the company starts to make money and you decide you don't want to be Subchapter S any more, you can change to a regular corporation. Once you've done that, you can't change back to Subchapter S for 5 years.

One catch in Subchapter S is that California law doesn't recognise it. That means that earnings are double taxed in California. But remember that the California top tax bracket is only (*did I say only?*) 11%, and besides it's better to save Federal taxes anyway, even if you don't save on California.

O.K., now that we all understand what Subchapter S is, how can we go with it even though we have overseas participants? The thing that makes it possible is that the overseas people are acquiring their stock through employee stock options, not through direct purchases. The law says that if you have a foreign stockholder, you're ineligible for Subchapter S, but there's nothing wrong with granting an option to somebody, as long as it isn't exercised. As soon as the holder of that option sends his money and says, "Send me the stock", you're immediately bounced out of Subchapter S, but up to that time it's fine.

Now the plan so far has been that the non-California people would get 60 day options, which they would immediately exercise for their initial stock purchase. The alternative is to make the initial options for, say, 2 years, not exercisable until either 1 year has passed or the company has dropped Subchapter S. Mike Riddle, who's out of state but not overseas could still receive a 60-day option and exercise it immediately — his case is irrelevant to this discussion because it's only overseas shareholders which cause the Subchapter S problem.

Now what would this mean for the domestic shareholders and the overseas people? The domestic shareholders would be able to deduct the initial losses by the company from their taxes. As most of the participants have other jobs and are in reasonably high tax brackets, this would result in substantial reductions in their tax bills. The overseas participants would be able to defer their initial stock purchase in the company, keeping their money until the option exercise time began. This would mean that they would not have to come up with the money right away, and if the company collapsed, would not be out the amount of the initial stock purchase, as they could let the option expire unexercised. If the company becomes successful, the option guarantees them their share at the initial offering price, so they can buy in on the same basis as the domestic people.

Let's look at the disadvantages. The domestic shareholders would be the only people putting up money immediately, so the company would not have access to the working capital generated by sales of shares to overseas people. The overseas people, once they exercised their options, would not have the prior losses of the company to reduce the corporate taxes paid on the (we hope) current profits of the company.

I think that in terms of financial benefits and disadvantages that this alternative is reasonable. The domestic people get to take advantage of tax benefits which wouldn't otherwise be available. The foreign people lose some benefits, but are compensated by having a year's use of their money before having to make the initial stock purchase, plus eventually owning a piece of a company whose initial capitalisation was done by the domestic people.

On the other hand, I think that this may simply be so confusing and hard to analyse that maybe we'd just be better off paying the money to the feds and getting to work writing software rather than further complicating the structure of the company. I personally feel very ambivalent about this matter. I certainly don't want to do anything which would make either the domestic or the foreign people feel like either was taking advantage of the other, so if anybody at all is concerned about it from that aspect, I think we should just forget it.

If we want to do it, here are the basic constraints: we have 75 days from April 9 to elect Subchapter S, and to do so we have to file a form with signatures of all stockholders and their spouses. Maybe we should start circulating the form just in case, so we have it if we decide to go ahead. Next, we need to get letters from all the overseas people giving their assurance that they understand the arrangement and that they approve it. This is required because they are foregoing the loss carry forward which reduces their eventual payouts on the stock (even though they are presumably compensated by not having to put up the money right away).

It seems to me that this is something that requires absolutely unanimous consent by everybody involved, so if you don't like it, let me know (and why). If you don't understand it, I'd be glad to "clarify" it at greater length (although at the present rate, I don't know how many pages that might take).

Autodesk Products

A document describing the status of products currently under implementation and potential products was mailed with Information Letter 5 1982. Here it is.

Autodesk Products

by John Walker
Revision 4 — April 28, 1982

This note describes planned and potential products of Autodesk. The products are listed here in no particular order.

MicroCAD

The product is a computer-aided design and drafting system. This product currently exists on the Marinchip 9900 computer in SPL. Our plan is to convert it to the IBM Personal Computer either by translating it to C or Digital Research PL/I, or by porting SPL to the 8086. We would also be able to offer a very high performance system using the Godbout 10 Mhz 8086/8087 S-100 system.

Installed on a desktop computer configuration in the $10K to $15K range, it is competitive in performance and features to Computervision CAD systems in the $70K range. There are no known competitive products on microcomputers today (although there are some very simple-minded screen drawing programs for the Apple, and we must be careful to explain how we differ).

We can probably obtain substantial free publicity by issuing press releases and writing articles stressing the tie-in with computer aided design and the IBM robot controlled by the IBM personal computer. We can also aim our ads to sell the product as a word processor for drawings. Potential customers are anybody who currently produces drawings. Small architectural offices are ideal prospects.

We can make add-ons to the package to make it an engineering workstation. It could be used to enter, edit, and view structural engineering information, for example, or to interactively view and edit plots made on mainframe computers and transmitted downline.

The package has been sold as a software package on the M9900 at $1000. There are about 20 installations at present, no substantial promotion has been done.

Autodesk

Autodesk is an office automation system for small computers. It embodies a computer model of an office environment. It provides file cards, file boxes, a calendar, etc. This is connected to a very simple database and query system. The entire system is intended to be extremely user-friendly and straightforward. We want a computer store salesman to be able to get an off-the-street prospect who's never seen a computer before to be using the package in 5 minutes or less. That will help him sell hardware, and he'll sell our software with it.

This package has an almost unlimited potential for add-on products for installed customers. Electronic mail, fancier filing, report writer modules, data entry systems, etc., can all be sold as add-ons to the basic system.

A prototype of the package written on QBASIC on the M9900 exists. Some of the largest sections of this can be used as part of the final product if CB80 is used on CP/M.

Based on the pricing of card file systems with much less capability, I would assume the system would sell for from $250 to $450 retail. This is a product which would probably sell very well on the Apple, if we could get it running on one.

Window

This is a screen editor written in QBASIC currently running on the M9900. About 100 to 200 are installed currently. A version converted to CB80 exists on CP/M, which needs only a line database module to be converted to be complete.

This product can be sold on CP/M as a competitor to VEDIT, probably the dominant product of its type. I think we'd have to bring it out for, say $99 to establish it. We want to price it in the impulse purchase range by the standards of computer stores. I don't think any substantial development work or extensions are in order here. This is a quickie product to get some money coming in.

Diff

This is a file compare program written in QBASIC. With about 3 days work it can be cleaned up and converted to CP/M. This is a very useful software tool not generally available on CP/M systems. I think we can sell it for about $50, probably directly. Its value is getting some publicity and generating some fast revenue. It could be expanded into something like the Unix source code control system if it surprises us and becomes a best-seller.

We can also offer a version that knows how to compare WordStar files. It could insert commands for change bars, and provide this very handy feature to WordStar users.

Opti-Calc

This product combines one of the most useful management and planning tools, linear programming, with the most popular user interface for planning, Visi-Calc. Visi-Calc allows you to specify dependencies of items and ask what if. Opti-Calc lets you point at numbers and say to hold them constant, point at other numbers and say to maximise or minimise them, then it will set up the LP problem, solve it, and display the numbers changed as a result of the optimisation. This would make our product stand head and shoulders above all the competition, and properly handled should sell as fast as we can make them.

Other than the concept above, no work has been done on this product. Somebody who knows LP needs to design this thing after first gaining an in-depth understanding of Visi-Calc.

Communicator

One of the best selling utilities today is telecommunication software. Kern Sibbald has rewritten our TS utility from the 9900 in QBASIC, so we can convert it to CB80 for CP/M. To make it in the CP/M world we need to add lots of silly little features such as being able to do a directory within the program, etc. We'll also need to make it store a database of people, auto-dial by name, etc. My idea for how to distinguish it is to make it programmable in a simple language so you can preprogram dialogues for access to remote systems. That way you could code up a query access dialogue like the Apple Dow Jones program for any system and easily change it when the system changed. We would of course include preprogrammed dialogues for the most popular database services. The dialogue setup should be very simple-possibly something like PILOT might work — it's essential that an end user can develop dialogue scripts without calling us.

JPLDIS

JPLDIS is a public domain information management system written in Fortran by JPL. A re-implementation of it in assembly language called DBASE II[22] is selling like hotcakes at $800 a pop. We can get the Fortran source from COSMIC, convert it to something, and have a product. Somebody needs to get the sucker and see what we're in for here. It's a lot of FORTRAN, but if it will compile right through Microsoft FORTRAN, we may have a fast product.

---

22 That's right. To my knowledge, Ashton-Tate has never revealed the ancestry of their flagship product.

QBASIC

Mike Riddle reports that Microsoft's true compiled BASIC for the IBM PC is at least a year off. We can take advantage of large chunks of the work done to port SPL to the 8086 (if we go that way for MicroCAD) and also port QBASIC. This would let us slip in with an efficient version of the most popular business BASIC on the hottest new machine. It would annoy Digital Research immensely, but we're not doing anything wrong as our implementation has no connection with theirs. The current QBASIC could probably be ported to the PC in less than 1 month assuming the SPL port were completed first.

Again, this would be a general CP/M 86 product, not limited to the PC. We could also sell it on the IBM Displaywriter and any other CP/M 86 machine. As CB80 sells for the Z-80 at $500 and most CP/M 86 stuff is higher, we could probably get $500 a copy retail for this without problems.

Commodity Trading Package

John Walker developed a comprehensive commodity trading package in 1980 and 1981 in QBASIC on the M9900. This package allows almost any function which would be required by a trader, and is easily expanded for custom requirements. There is no comparable package on a microcomputer. Jack Stuppin feels that there is still a market for this package, although there are several other well-entrenched competitors. I tend to agree, assuming that the package were moved to either an Apple or the IBM PC, and that superb quality user documentation were prepared (only the first chapter of the manual was written, and that was a real effort). The problems are as follows. First, there is no easy path from QBASIC to either of the ideal target machines (but see above project). Second, anybody who works on this package must first master the concepts of securities trading. Third, it would enormously expand the market for the package if it also handled stock trading (easy, as long as a limited number of stocks were handled, and you understood the differences). I understand the package, but don't have the time to finish it. I'd like to talk about it with anybody who is interested in it.

Autodesk Work Distribution

As the potential products came into sharper focus, so did our plans to deploy our technical resources to get them done. Here's the first proposal for allocating people to projects.

Autodesk Work Distribution

by John Walker
Revision 1 — April 23, 1982

The following is a suggestion for division of work on the development of the initial Autodesk products mentioned in the Autodesk Products bulletin (Revision 3).

Few specific assignments have been made to Dan Drake and John Walker because both will probably be kept busy full time answering all the questions regarding the code being moved from the 9900 environment, plus running the company and acquiring hardware and getting it to work. Both will be available as required for question answering, fire fighting, and assistance.

MicroCAD

Mike Riddle
   Port META and SPL to CP/M-86. Initial conversion of SPL code, consultation with others on projects.

Greg Lutz
   General familiarisation with product, work with IBM PC, experiment with graphics display and digitiser interface to PC. Eventual, prime support and development of MicroCAD.

Keith Marcelius
   Acquisition of IBM PC, study of PC and support hardware and software we should acquire, and acquisition thereof. General MicroCAD project management, particularly monitoring of Mike Riddle's development.

Jodi Lehman
   MicroCAD manual rewrite, consulting with Greg Lutz and Keith Marcelius.

Autodesk

Kern Sibbald
> Overall project management. Design and implementation of CB80 CP/M version of product.

Keith Marcelius
> Review of product regarding user interface, survey of competitive products.

Mauri Laitinen & Duff Kurland
> Development of underlying database and storage manager for CP/M. (Likely a modification of Window's line database).

John Walker
> Consultation regarding original Autodesk design and prototype system.

Window

Mauri Laitinen
> Overall project management, review of competitive products, design and implementation of final QBASIC CP/M version.

Duff Kurland
> Development of line database module for CP/M version, consultation on product design, development of user guide.

Diff

Duff Kurland
> Overall project management, product development. Research into WordStar file format, development of "change bar" version.

Jodi Lehman
> Conversion to CP/M, documentation, and testing.

Opti-Calc

Dave Kalish & Hal Royaltey
> Familiarisation with Visi-Calc, evaluation of idea and product design, specification of product, implementation, documentation, and initial testing. This is a product of great potential that we know least about, thus the most flexibility is needed in investigating it.

Communicator

Kern Sibbald
> Complete current QBASIC version, write short guide to internals.

Peter Goldmann
: Survey of competitive products, specification of final product, conversion to CB80, development of final product, documentation.

JPLDIS

Mauri Laitinen
: Investigate availability of package, obtain a copy.

Richard Handyside
: Evaluate package, convert to CP/M, evaluate documentation and rewrite or augment as required.

QBASIC

Mike Riddle
: Conversion of META to 8086, development of floating point package, math function, edit and scan routines (part of SPL port for MicroCAD).

John Walker
: Write internal documentation on QBASIC threaded code interpretation and QP2 operation.

Dan Drake
: Write internal documentation on QBASIC I/O library design and philosophy.

Yet to be assigned — several people
: Convert QBASIC library to 8086, test compiler, upgrade documentation to IBM quality, add all CB80 features.

General research and development

The following items are not directly related to products (though some of them may be integrated into one or more of the products listed above). They are of importance to Autodesk's business.

Apples

What is an Apple? What languages exist on it? How can CP/M programs be best installed on an Apple? What percentage of Apples have Softcards? How standard is the Softcard CP/M? How are programs best gotten on Apple discs?

Jack Stuppin
: Consultation regarding Apple system experience.

Mike Riddle
: Consultation regarding Apple internal construction.

Hal Royaltey
General product management, investigation of the Apple world.

5 1/4 inch discs

What formats are popular for 5 1/4 inch discs? Which are used by CP/M systems? Specifically, what physical hardware and controllers are used by: IBM PC, Apple/Softcard, HP-125, Xerox 820, Micropolis, Northstar? What is the best configuration for an "Octopus" machine to allow us to write discs for all these machines?

Screen driver package

Survey of existing screen manager packages. Choice or development of a general screen input package. Development of a general file driven message package.

Rudolf Künzli
Overall project management, selection and/or development of our package for CB80 implementations.

Documentation production

How do we prepare documentation? We have an immediate need to produce "Digital Research or better quality" manuals and a near-term need to produce IBM-quality typeset manuals. We need to survey the tools for preparing copy for such manuals and the services that exist to turn this copy into camera ready copy.

Duff Kurland
Complete and debug 9900 WORD proportional spaced Spinwriter output, edit manuals into compatible form, and print on Spinwriter.

Dave Kalish
Survey "disc to type" vendors, determine optimal formats.

Richard Handyside
Consultation, what do we need, what should we be doing from the standpoint of a publisher.

Software manufacturers

Survey existing companies that copy discs to order. What services do they supply (format conversion, etc.), and what formats do they support? Do they put on custom labels, etc., and what must we give them?

The Beginning   *Documentation production*   83

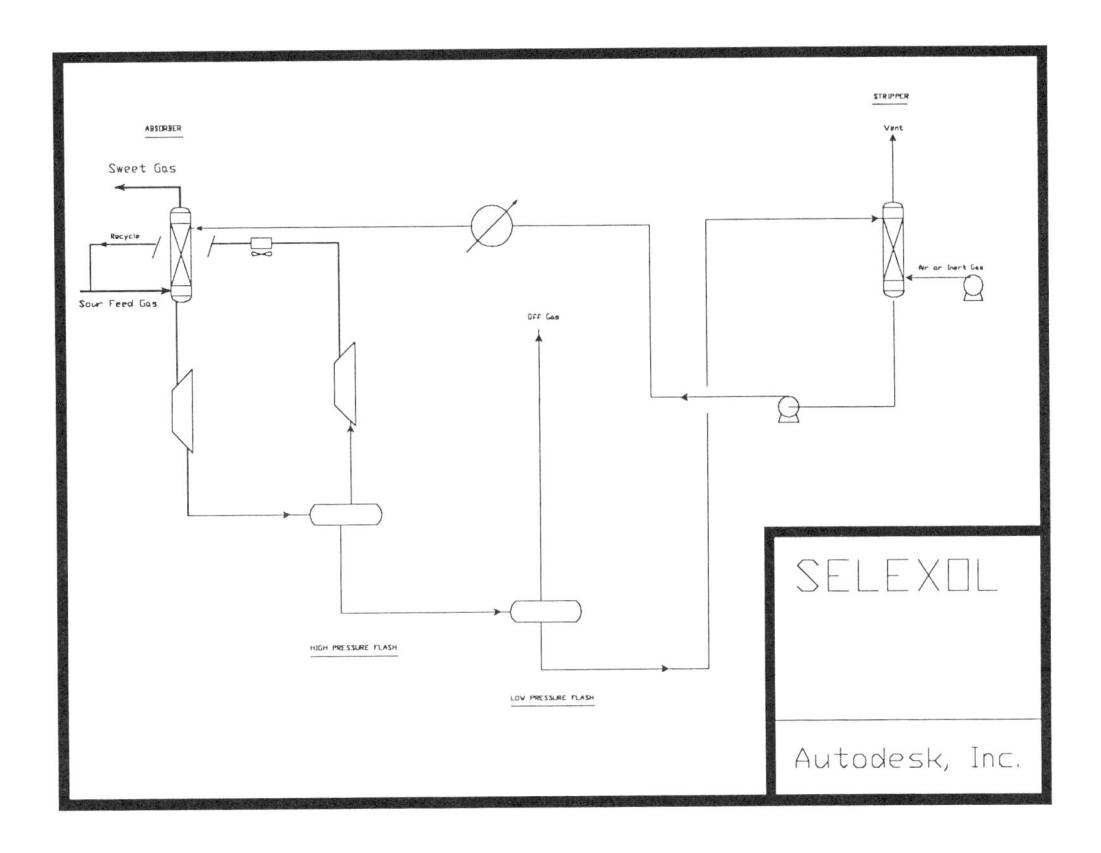

This is one if the first drawings ever made by a customer with AutoCAD. Jamal Munshi of MOMS Computing, our first dealer and customer, drew this schematic of the Selexol chemical process. He kindly allowed us to use it as a sample drawing.

Random Notes on Software and Marketing

Autodesk's development efforts were officially underway when Information Letter 6 was written in late May 1982, but nobody had yet begun to work on AutoCAD. We were still hoping to port the SPL compiler and use the original source code. And besides, AutoCAD was not seen as our flagship product. But, at last, our marketing was underway.

Autodesk, Inc.
Information Letter # 6

by John Walker
Revision 5 — May 26, 1982

This information letter is a random collection of news notes, technical information, and reports on progress on various fronts.

Marketing Progress

Since we started talking about forming the company, we've been looking for somebody to join the company with a strong marketing background and extensive knowledge of the computer field. At last our search has ended. Mike Ford, a former Vice President for Sales at Information Systems Design, has agreed to join the company on June 1, 1982. Mike will be buying into the company on the same basis as everybody else, using the option offering we're doing for the out of state participants.

Mike's marketing experience in the computer field goes back to 1956. He has worked for such industry giants as IBM, RCA, and Univac, and was instrumental in rescuing ISD in its time of peril. Since 1977, he's been running a company he formed to provide employers with employee benefits statements for their personnel. The package which does this was designed by Mike and is written in CBASIC under CP/M. Mike is also becoming a dealer for the Victor 9000 machine (made by Sirius, and sold under that name outside the US). The Victor is an extremely attractive 8088 based machine which offers twice the memory, 5 times the disc capacity, double the graphics resolution, and built in serial ports for the same price as the 2 disc IBM PC. Mike's connections with Victor not only allow us to obtain these machines for internal use at attractive prices, they give us the contacts to sell our software to Victor and Sirius. The Victor machine is an ideal host for MicroCAD, as the basic package has the graphics resolution, enough memory and disc, and the serial ports needed to do serious work with MicroCAD.[23]

At the moment Mike is preparing marketing plans for our various products and trying to compile prospect lists and publicity channels. If you know reviewers for magazines, who to contact to get a computer store to try out a package, somebody who can get press releases run, or any such information which might be of use, please pass the information on to Mike either directly or via myself.

IBM PC

We're now the owners of an IBM Personal Computer. We bought the full-blown configuration with two discs and 64K of internal memory. We've ordered, and soon expect to receive, a "Baby Blue" which will provide 64K of additional memory plus a Z-80 processor to allow the IBM to run CP/M, and a Quadram board which will give us a serial port, time of day clock, and 64K-196K of additional memory (we're ordering 64K, and will add the chips ourselves to expand it to the maximum). We've received the IBM Macro Assembler, which we will be able to run as soon as we get the requisite 96K (!) installed in the machine. We've also obtained an 8087 chip which we'll install in the machine to give it hardware floating point capability. This will both let us certify our software floating point package and let us offer the hardware floating point as an option in all the software we develop. (This will make MicroCAD immensely faster.)

At the moment the IBM is at Greg Lutz's house in the east bay, where Greg and Keith Marcelius are gaining familiarity with the machine. We have two copies of the technical manual for the machine, which we will circulate to those interested in it.

At the moment we're mostly playing with the machine and trying to figure out the assembly language. The machine's major immediate application will be to support the conversion of MicroCAD and QBASIC.

---

23   And indeed it was. For the first full year of sales, AutoCAD on the Victor outsold the IBM version.

File Transfer

Because we're faced with so many different types of disc formats, we've decided to implement a universal file transfer protocol which allows us to get both text and binary files from any machine to any other given only a serial communication port. John Walker designed the protocol and implemented a 9900 driver for it. [24] Greg Lutz reviewed the protocol, fixed some flaws in it, and is now developing an IBM PC version of the program. Once that's done, we'll test the 9900/IBM link, at which time we'll be able to trust the protocol. Then we'll be able to implement it on every machine we encounter. The protocol is provably proof against data loss, duplication, and garbling, and has sufficient redundancy that it can be used on international phone lines. It's simple enough to implement in BASIC on any machine that lets BASIC drive the serial port. There are no time-critical operations that would cause trouble in a BASIC implementation.

After the 9900/IBM test, Dan Drake will put the protocol on the Apple, using Jack Stuppin's machine, and we'll have the long-awaited way to get software over to the Apple to use with the CP/M Softcard. After this is done, we'll be able to move among the 9900, CP/M, IBM PCDOS, and Apple freely.[25]

Offsite Backup

Obviously we don't want to get wiped out if somebody's house burns down. If you're developing some huge chunk of software, be sure to keep backups somewhere else. To aid this, I've set up the following scheme. Anybody who wants to back up something can simply write a disc with the name of the thing on it and the date, plus who sent it, and send it to me. I'll just keep the discs here in a special box for AI. When the box gets too full, I'll get in touch with you and see about scratching old backups for which I've received more recent copies. I'll recycle the old backups back as blank discs the next time somebody needs them.

There's no need to keep these backups very current. It's just good to know that we can't lose everything if a disaster happens.

Floppy Discs

We're now stocking 8-inch double density single sided discs and 5 1/4 inch double density single sided discs here. If you need discs for AI work, let me know and

---

24 This was the first crude version of FILETRAN, which in various incarnations serves us to this day.
25 This never happened.

they'll be sent out UPS. We get 8" discs for $3.20 each and 5 1/4" discs at $2.63. If you can beat that, let me know.

68000 System Prospects

John Walker has been talking with a company who's developing a 68000 CAD system about getting a loaner system from them for converting MicroCAD to the 68000 (which they would then license from us).[26] If we can work such a deal, we'd be able to get a 68000 development machine in house immediately without having to spend any money. Since one of the major advantages of the 68000 is the speed and large memory that suits it for graphics, I suspect that there's more than one software-hungry vendor who might be interested in loaning a system to get a package like MicroCAD converted to it. If you see announcements of 68000 based systems that look like good prospects (e.g., have 400 x 400 or better graphics and cost less than $13,000 with discs included), pass on the information and we'll contact them.

Medical Software Deal

Jack Stuppin has set up a meeting between us and a company which has been developing electronic medical instruments and wants to expand into the medical office vertical market. We'll be talking with them about developing a patient records database system to run under CP/M which would optionally interface to data collected from instruments. At this point we have no details on what they want or how attractive a deal could be struck with them to do the work, so at this point this is nothing more than a lead. I'm mentioning it here because if there's somebody who has some experience in database system development or medical applications, they should be in on the meeting or at least brief somebody who's going to be there.

Coming to Terms with the 8086

It's become clear that the plague called the 8086 architecture has sufficiently entrenched itself that it's not going to go away. For the last month or more, Mike Riddle, John Walker, Keith Marcelius, and Greg Lutz have been bashing their collective heads against it. The following is collected information on this unfortunate machine.

---

26   This was Valid Logic Systems, which at the time was interested in providing a mechanical CAD capability on their electronics CAE workstation. We ended up demonstrating AutoCAD to them and their reaction was "no thanks".

I think we'd be wise to diffuse our 8086 knowledge among as many people as possible. The main reference for the 8086 is a book called, imaginatively enough, *The 8086 Book* published by Osborne. This is the architecture and instruction set reference, but does not give sufficient information to write assembly code (of which, more later). However, it is the starting point to understand the machine. AI will reimburse the cost of your buying this book, which is available at computer and electronic stores.

I have never encountered a machine so hard to understand, one where the most basic decisions in designing a program are made so unnecessarily difficult, where the memory architecture seems deliberately designed to obstruct the programmer, where the instruction set seems contrived to induce the maximum confusion, and where the assembler is so bizarre and baroque that once you've decided what bits you want in memory you can't figure out how to get the assembler to put them there. But I digress.

Mike Riddle has come up with the following programming rules for the 8086. They are presented here for comments from people with 8086 experience.

- Always pop what you push. Every subroutine should leave the stack the way it found it (except for arguments and results passed on the stack).

- Assume ES=DS. This lets you use string instructions without first loading ES every time. If you change ES, put it back to DS before you return.

- Assume CLD mode set (string instructions increment SI & DI, not decrement). If you use decrement mode, restore CLD before you return.[27]

- All subroutines save and restore all registers except AX and flags (controversial, but Mike says it helps when calling subroutines in loops).[28]

- Parameter passing: Pass table and string addresses in SI and DI. Pass byte parameters in AL, word parameters in AX. Use DX:AX to pass 32 bit data. Don't use BX or CX for parameters or results; you'll need them for code that calls the subroutine. Don't use BP for anything other than stack frames. The same rules apply to results from routines.

With regard to other 8086 developments, Hal Royaltey is writing a floating point package for the beast. The floating point package will be compatible with the IEEE double precision format used by the 8087. We'll set things up so that a program can be easily (maybe automatically?) configured for hardware or software floating

---

27 Step into my parlour, said the 8086 to the naive programmer ....
28 Utter nonsense.

point. This floating point package will be used for both SPL and QBASIC programs.

John Walker has a version of QBASIC that generates 8086 assembly code. The compiler still runs on the 9900, where it will stay until META is running on the 8086. Soon we'll be loading the code onto the IBM to make sure it assembles properly, and to check out the segmentation structure of the code/library interface. Assuming that works, it's full steam ahead with QBASIC on the 8086. John Walker will be completing the compiler conversion and basic library routines, Dan Drake will be converting the I/O library, and we'll be integrating Hal Royaltey's floating point package and Mike Riddle's format independent math routines.

We'll be completing the META port on the IBM here, freeing Mike Riddle's time to concentrate on the SPL compiler and runtime library.

In developing both SPL and QBASIC, we're taking the following approach to the 8086. We want to treat the thing as if it had true large memory, even though it's deliberately set up to obstruct us in doing that. We're imposing only the constraint that the static code generated by any one compilation cannot exceed 64K (which would be an unwieldy source program anyway). Dynamically allocated strings and arrays may be anywhere in the 1MB addressing space, and linked lists will use a general segment/offset 32 bit address for pointers. Any number of modules of up to 64K each may be linked together, and runtime library size will not subtract from the maximum program size. Thus, our compilers and their generated code will be limited only by the physical memory constraints of the machine and the operating system we're running under. This is a very important competitive edge: remember that most 8086 code is translated 8080 code, and such converted code cannot easily exceed 128K (or 64K if it's messy). Our programs will have no such limit.

It's planned that an "engineering test version" of QBASIC will be running in about a week on the IBM to verify the basic memory architecture ideas that go into the above (such a test is required because the IBM assembler and linker are so confusing that whether some ideas will work cannot be determined from the manuals).

We also lack documentation of the Microsoft/IBM relocatable code format used on the 8086, although Mike Riddle suspects it's an extended version of the bitstream code used by Microsoft Fortran on the 8080 and adopted by Digital Research. Even if it is, we still don't know how the additional information for the 8086 was encoded. Does anybody know this, or have any leads to find out? We need to know to make our compilers salable, as we can't expect people to buy the IBM Macro Assembler just to assemble the code from QBASIC. I can think of lots of things I'd rather do than reverse-engineer somebody's bitstream relocatable format.

Black Hole Alert

As most of you know, Marinchip has been negotiating with Lifeboat for many months about selling MSL's 9900 software to Pertec for use on a 9900-based machine they make called the PC1000. This deal has been off and on so many times I can't even begin to recount the story. Now Pertec has officially announced the machine, including the "SB-99 CP/M Compatible Operating System from Lifeboat Associates". This is presumably Marinchip's software (unless we've been spectacularly double crossed). Nonetheless, there's no signed agreement between anybody to do the work, nor have we heard anything about this other than what we read in *InfoWorld*.[29] The reason I'm bringing this up is that if this does go through, I (John Walker) will probably disappear for a month or so into doing this conversion project for Pertec, and Dan Drake will probably be sucked in to some extent. This means that we want to get as many AI things running smoothly without our involvement as we can in case this happens. As a result, if there's something I should be doing or which you need me to do, please let me know as soon as possible so I can schedule it around this potential time sponge.

Monthly Meeting — Subchapter S Form

Remember that the first regular monthly meeting will be on Sunday, June 6, 1982 at Jack Stuppin's house in San Francisco. We haven't decided whether to go ahead with the Subchapter S election mentioned in the last Information Letter or not, but as the form requires lots of signatures, we're going to get them so we have them if we decide to do it. We should have the form at the meeting. If you can't make it, I'll see that the form is routed to you after the meeting.

Autodesk Status

Kern Sibbald has been restructuring Autodesk from the hacked-up demo version of the program written for the Computer Faire into an honest program which will run on CP/M. In the process, he had to invert the internal structure of the program because the original program heavily used recursive function calls, which aren't supported by CB80. He also installed the new general terminal driver from the CP/M Window, which allows adaptation to new terminal types simply by making entries in a file. We expect the basic system to be running on CP/M under CB80

---

29 One week after Pertec made this announcement, *InfoWorld* carried a second announcement saying "never mind". Pertec, a division of Triumph-Adler, heavily funded by Volkswagen, apparently came to its senses and re-thought introducing a TI9900-based business computer in 1982.

within 30 days. At that point we can start to add the features we need to complete the system for sale.

Communicator Status

Kern Sibbald's CB80 version of Duff Kurland's TS program has been turned over to Peter Goldmann, who has successfully generated it and is now reviewing other communicator programs to choose ideas for extending the package. We will be adding autodialing, a database of systems with automatic configuration for various protocols, micro to micro file transfer, and many other features to make it the premier microcomputer communication utility.[30] It will eventually be integrated with Autodesk to add an electronic mail facility to Autodesk.

Random Bits

Does anybody know about WordStar? We need to figure out how the files work so we can fix DIFF to make change bars for WordStar files. Also, we should look at the product in general to see if we should use its conventions for control keys.

We're moving along with preparing professional looking documentation. At first, we'll be using WORD on the 9900 as our documentation tool, because we have it, we control it, and we can make it do the things we need done. We'll be installing an INDEX command and writing an INDEX postprocessor so all our manuals can be indexed. We'll install the commands we need to generate the control sequences for font selection, point size, underlining, etc., in the final output medium we use. We'll add Knuth's hyphenation algorithm from TeX, with an override ability when you see that it's botched one.

Richard Handyside told us about an outfit called "TypeShare" in Los Angeles which you dial up with your modem, send text with control information, and get back camera ready type. I called them up to get information, but haven't received anything yet. I hope the typesetting is faster. Other potential leads on services like this would be appreciated.

We're checking out the option of making the manuals for our stable products into hardbound books.[31] What else conveys a comparable feeling of stability and solidity? From our initial checking, it's also cheaper than the little looseleaf binders IBM uses for the manuals for the PC. Keith Marcelius is running down this option.

---

30 Nothing ever became of this project and product.
31 And several years later, we finally did it.

We've found a distributor who seems to think we're a computer store and who will sell us most mass market CP/M and IBM PC software at pretty good prices. Check first if you need something, as we should be able to get a good discount on it. We haven't ordered anything yet, so this isn't a sure thing.

Dan Drake is currently reading up on the Apple. At the moment this is pure research, but as there are so many Apples out there, some way to get things like Autodesk on the Apple might make sense sooner or later.[32]

We're having stationery printed up. I'll be distributing it to people after it arrives, so they can use it for requesting information, etc. At the moment, AI has an official phone number, *but don't use it to call me, as I'm always on the other phone and get very mad when that phone rings.*

---

[32] This, of course, referred to the Apple II. The Lisa and Macintosh were still in the future when this was written.

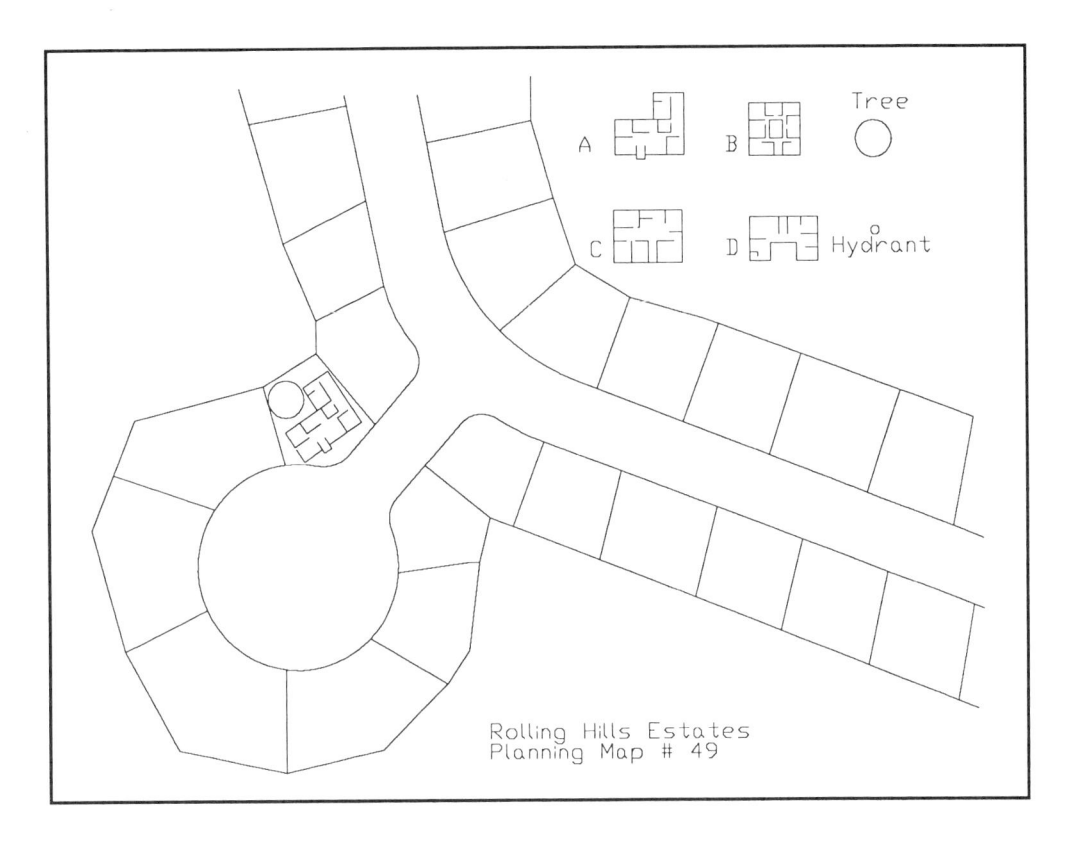

Immediately before COMDEX in 1982, Sun-Flex asked us to make a demo of house placement on a subdivision plan map. Roxie (Walker) and I made this drawing one horrible night in November 1982. It was while making this drawing on AutoCAD-80 that I first really became aware that much more powerful geometric facilities were needed for professional drawing. If you really want to get a flavour of 1982 AutoCAD, try making this drawing without ever using object snap, arcs other than three-point, fillet, trim, or extend.

Autodesk General Status Report

Information Letter 7 was a general status report. It summarised an eventful month: development got underway on AutoCAD on both the 8086 host machines (in C), and on the Z-80 (using PL/I). We had given up on the old source code, and were furiously rewriting it in the new languages. It included the initial documentation of Auto Book, "the product that would not die".

Autodesk, Inc.
Information Letter # 7

by John Walker
Revision 5 — July 8, 1982

This information letter is being mailed with the minutes of the July general meeting appended to the end. Other items are included about things not brought up at the meeting.

Where We Are and Where We Are Going

A month ago I had the feeling that the company was spinning its wheels and getting nowhere. Now I think that most of the problems we had getting under weigh were normal start-up problems, which are being resolved. Definite progress is being made on all of our major products, and we can see a clear path to completion on most of them.

We're still collecting the tools, hardware and software, that people need to get the work done. If you're still waiting, be assured that you will not wait forever (or even better, help us out in getting what you need). I'll try to summarise the major project status below.

We've established a more formal structure for the monthly meetings, patterned after the original Working Paper suggestions. This form (described in the attached minutes) will minimise the "endless miasma syndrome", and allow the gist of the meeting to be condensed onto paper for those who cannot attend. Furthermore, we hope that the new format will let everybody know exactly where every project stands and what everybody is doing. At the end of each meeting, everybody should know exactly what they should be doing, and how it connects to all other work in progress.

As originally suggested, after the formal meeting we can have technical sessions on the various projects.

Autodesk Status

Kern Sibbald has completed conversion of the cleaned-up original Autodesk to CB80 under CP/M. He has prepared an internal release disc of this test version to get comments on the user facilities it offers. Each person who has CP/M capability should have already received this disc. Kern is now defining the master database that will underlie the completed system, and implementing a mockup of the database so he can convert the program to use the new database routines.

In the process of converting Autodesk to CB80, Kern segmented the program into initialisation, screen, and command overlays. This reduced the maximum size of the program to a little over 38K, so we now have a comfortable amount of space in which to work, as opposed to the 9900 version which was teetering on the brink of memory insolvency.

As soon as a real appointment calendar is installed, we will have a CP/M demo version we can begin to show to potential distributors.

QBASIC86 Progress

Implementation of QBASIC on the 8086 is progressing rapidly. Hal Royaltey and David Kalish have designed the memory model and parameter passing conventions for the object code. Hal has converted the floating point library, and is filling in the rest of the support routines prior to bulk converting the runtime library. All tools needed for this effort are in hand.

Dan Drake has made a complete audit of the differences between QBASIC and CB80 and has prepared a 10 page summary of differences and tasks required in META, QBASIC pass 1, QP2, and the runtime library to resolve the differences. He is planning to do the conversion of the compiler.

John Walker has ported META to the 8086. The port used the new C compiler we bought.[33] META was changed to generate C instead of assembly language code, and the META library was rewritten in C. As a result, META is now instantly

---

33   Computer Innovations C-86.

portable to any machine which has C.[34] We may very well use C to write the second pass of QBASIC (QP2) as well (it's currently in QBASIC). If we do it all in C, the port to the 68000 will be a piece of cake as far as the compiler is concerned (since all the 68000's announced seem to have C).

The code structure which has been defined will be the first known totally general 8086 compiler implementation. There will be no limit at all on the size of a program. This should make our compiler very attractive compared to all the others that stick you with 64K data and 64K code total.

MicroCAD Status

A major change of direction in the MicroCAD project should result in completion of the conversion within the next month. Since we were able to find an excellent C compiler for the 8086, under both PCDOS/MSDOS and CP/M-86, we've decided to convert the SPL code to C rather than port SPL. Keith Marcelius surveyed the available C compilers and decided that the Computer Innovations compiler was the clear choice. We bought two copies of the compiler, and Greg Lutz and John Walker beat on it enough to satisfy themselves that the compiler was sound. John Walker used it to port META as noted above, and converted a set of high-precision mathematical functions to C (the Computer Innovations compiler has full IEEE single and double precision floating point, but having no math functions in the library is delivered free of SIN).[35]

The C is weak in floating point I/O, but since the compiler is supplied with complete source code for the library, and since all the relevant routines are written in C, this is easily remedied. We have found Computer Innovations to be very helpful and easy to work with, and it seems to be an outfit operating in a style very much like our own.

Greg Lutz and Dan Drake will be converting the SPL code to C. We've purchased a Houston Instruments HI-PAD digitiser which we will hook up to both the Victor and the IBM PC to test MicroCAD. We're currently looking at plotters, and are trying to see if we can work some kind of cooperative marketing deal with Houston Instruments if we use their plotters as well as their digitisers.

Our current plan for MicroCAD is to have a root segment which contains all the device-dependent parts. That segment will load the "guts" of the package which will be totally machine-independent. This has the advantage of modularising the

---

34 But it never was. META was never used nor mentioned again after this brief note.
35 These math functions are still used in AutoCAD.

package, making it easier to field-configure, and getting the potentially large drivers out of the address space of the package itself (it takes 40000 bytes to hold the screen bit map on the Victor).

John Walker has undertaken the task of trying to shoehorn MicroCAD onto the 8080. The effort seems worthwhile investigating as the potential market a success would open up is enormous. The effort was initiated as the result of the question "Have you ever encountered a program you couldn't make fit on any machine?"[36]

Window Progress

Mike Ford has been testing Window on his CP/M system and has found a couple of bugs which will be corrected. Duff Kurland and Mauri Laitinen have been converting the line database to 8080 code. The memory-only version is complete and currently being tested. After that's checked out, the disc stuff will be installed and we will have a product ready to go out the door (pending documentation upgrading).

For those of you who haven't used Window on CP/M, I'll mention that we've installed a completely new terminal configuration mechanism which completely eliminates the need to compile terminal drivers and link them with WINDOW. The terminal is totally described by a master terminal definition file. We plan to supply a menu-driven program which generates and updates these terminal descriptions.

Task Lists

As mentioned in the minutes of the meeting, we've requested everybody to funnel in a list of tasks before each meeting so that we can print them in the minutes and let everybody know what the others are accomplishing. The process of getting these tasks in and concentrated worked so poorly this time that I don't think it makes sense trying to summarise them here — it would likely create more confusion than it would dispel. Please keep this in mind in the future — each monthly letter from now on should contain detailed task lists. I'd like to work out a way (maybe via MJK) that I can prepare the task summaries without having to retype pages of information.

Conference System Notes

Most people in the company are now using the MJK teleconference system to interchange messages. As requested, I've added the conference system user names

---

36 He made it fit. Two years later the product was discontinued after selling about 150 copies.

to the "Names and Addresses" directory at the end of this letter (after the phone numbers).

The conference system has been afflicted by the recent times of tribulation in TYMNET. TYMNET has been installing new software, and we've been through yoyo reliability, double spaced input lines, character delete that comes and goes, etc. All we can do is put up with it. The problems are in TYMNET, not the conference system.

Please note that charges for the conference system, including TYMNET connect time (the largest component of the cost), drop by more than 50% in non-prime time, that is, 18:00 to 07:00 Pacific local time (the time that's displayed when you log on). The reduced charges also apply on Saturdays, Sundays, and holidays all day. Please help us save money by using the system when it's cheap. Note also that MJK's preventive maintenance remains from 17:00 – 17:30 Pacific time, so if you try to log on at that time you'll get "Can't initiate new sessions now".

To further reduce charges on the system, I've reversed a change made to the system some time back and made the system store messages for people in files keyed with their names. This means you can check whether there are any messages for you without calling the CONFRX program and incurring the charges to load and execute it. At the point you're about to type RUN CONFRX, type LISTF instead. You'll see a file directory listing. If you see a file with your user name preceded by "MF", then you have messages. If there's no such file, and you don't want to send any messages, you can type BYE immediately and log off. Thus, if you user name were GONZO, you would look for a file "MFGONZO" in the file directory.

Organization Details

The Subchapter S alternative we considered before turned out not to be possible after all, because one of the stockholders (MSL) was a corporation, not a person. This disqualifies AI from Subchapter S. As a result, we'll go ahead soon with the option plan to bring in the rest of the people. We should have done this already, but the press of work kept us from getting to it.

C

C is shaping up to be an important language in AI's plans. It looks like the language of choice for the 8086 based on the Computer Innovations compiler, and of course it is the workhorse on any of the Unix ports to the 68000 or elsewhere.

If you don't know C, it would be a good idea to pick up a book and start reading up on it. The reference is *The C Programming Language* by Brian Kernighan and

Dennis Ritchie, Prentice-Hall, 1978 ISBN 0-13-110163-3. AI will reimburse the cost of your buying this book.

The Computer Innovations C is a full, unrestricted, implementation of the language as described in the book. If anybody knows of a similar 8080 C with good code and an attractive runtime licensing deal, please let me know.

I'm currently exploring the option of converting WINDOW to C for the 8086.[37]

Random Bits

Utterly out of the blue, Marinchip has completed the most spectacular sales month in its history. In June we sold more than our total sales for 1978 and 1979 combined. If sales were to continue at the present pace, Marinchip would be shipping at an annualised rate of $850,000 (neglecting for the moment the little detail that John Walker would disintegrate in the process). This is being mentioned because if you've been waiting for John to do something for you, you'll probably have to wait a bit longer. As a result, we've tried to further decentralise the communications in AI — a lot of information was passed through John Walker simply because that was easy. But it won't work at the moment. We expect the June results to be a one-time blip since most of the sales were unexpected one-shot sales rather than dealer or OEM business. However, July looks like a barnburner as well.

John has also been playing around with a new product idea called Auto Book. A M9900/QBASIC test program has been developed to explore ideas. If the product looks worthwhile, we can consider it as an innovative way to distribute manuals for our products, to offer an impressive help facility, and as a product in its own right. I'm including the working paper on the product with this mailing for your review and comments. Richard Handyside and Jodi Lehman have copies of the program and are currently evaluating it and making suggestions.

On the 7th and 8th of August there will be an Autodesk/Marinchip dealers meeting in London. Rudolf Künzli, Richard Handyside, and Peter Goldmann will be there. If you have items that would make sense to bring up at the meeting, please try to get them to the people involved before the meeting.[38]

---

37 Kern Sibbald eventually undertook this task. Thus was born Kern's Editor.
38 After that meeting, I recall sitting in the office in London and getting the TEXT command and block insertion with scale and rotation working in AutoCAD for the first time.

July General Meeting Minutes

During this period, monthly weekend get-togethers comprised almost all of the face-to-face contact between the people involved in the company. Dan Drake's minutes of the July, 1982 meeting were mailed with Information Letter 7.

July General Meeting

by Dan Drake

The July general meeting was held on Saturday, June 26, 1982, at Jack Stuppin's house. (For those who missed it or have forgotten, the algorithm for computing meeting dates is at the end of the minutes.)

The meeting was called to order at 1:10. Present were Dan Drake, Mike Ford, Dave Kalish, Greg Lutz, Keith Marcelius, Kern Sibbald, Jack Stuppin, and John Walker.

Marketing

Mike Ford discussed his work on marketing and the questions that need answering before we go much farther. He has got two Victor 9000's on loan (one from Sirius) for work on QBASIC and MicroCad, and has scored an MSDOS with assembler and linker. Also Pascal, for which we need another 128K memory. We have given a demo for Hal Elgie, a consultant for Sirius who was highly impressed, especially with Autodesk.

Mike's Victor dealership seems to have opened some doors. He could probably get a dealership for other machines if it would be useful.

There was considerable discussion of the terms on which we want to sell the programs. Our main options in dealing with Victor, and probably anyone else, are these:

1. Victor buys the source for a flat fee, though not necessarily with exclusive rights. Victor does all support.

2. We provide a program in object form. Victor promotes it as its own and pays us royalties, probably a fixed amount per copy. If Victor is serious, we should be able to get a substantial advance when we close the deal.

3. We keep it as our own, but they publicize it to dealers and the public as one of the good things on their system.

(Many numbers were bandied about in the discussion. They are not in these minutes, because they would give a false air of precision and because widely distributed pieces of paper tend to pass before unauthorized eyes in spite of all precautions. Call us to talk about numbers if you like.)

There was general agreement with John Walker's opinion that a source buyout might be all right for a limited product like QBASIC-86, but not for MicroCad. The potential market for MicroCad is unexplored; it could be enormous, and no one would pay us enough to compensate for it. Victor could sell it under approach (2), putting their name on it if they want, but our name should at least appear on the disc and in the manual.

There was serious discussion of the right list price for MicroCad. The consensus was that the present price on the M9900[39] is probably too low.

QBASIC-86 would also be best sold on a royalty basis, though a buyout is conceivable. It should be easy to sell on the basis that it's a markedly superior language to CB-80, provided that we get it done well before Digital Research is ready.

Window is a product that would be a natural for Digital Research, which offers no usable editor for programmers; but we haven't managed to make a useful contact. Kern expressed concern that we shouldn't let it get completely out of our hands, because it's much better than anything else on the market. John pointed out the difficulty of trying to sell it ourselves, competing directly with VEDIT, which is becoming entrenched and has a large advertising budget.

We need to approach Corvus, Fortune, and anyone else who has a 68000; we should be able to get development machines from them. Also, the NSC 16032 is now approaching reality, and its speed makes it very attractive for MicroCad.

Financial report

John Walker presented a financial report. Proceeds of the sale of stock and options were $59,030. Expenditures have been as follows:

---

39 Namely, $1,000. We ended up introducing the Z-80 and MS-DOS versions of AutoCAD at $1,000 anyway.

IBM PC with printer, memory expansion, etc	6,317
Sierra Z-80 boards (CP/M for M9900 users)	1,804
Stationery, copying, etc.	324
Supplies	337
Printing for Computer Faire	820
Legal fees	3,949

Income: $115 interest from Capital Preservation Fund.

We currently have $45,592 in liquid assets, almost entirely in Capital Preservation Fund. (Yes, Virginia, there is a round-off error in the totals.)

Progress reports

Each of the people present reported on what he has been doing:

- Current commitment of time per week.
- What projects he has been working on, with what effect.
- What he's now working on.
- What obstacles are in the way.

Everyone was also asked to submit by Wednesday a list of tasks that he'll be working on over the next month or two, on a fairly detailed level. Submission can be either to John Walker or to the project managers concerned, who will forward the lists.

CPM Charts

Dan Drake has been playing with a CPM (Critical Path Management) program called MILESTONE, which runs under CP/M. There are now charts for the four main projects: Autodesk, MicroCad, QBASIC, and Window. Copies were handed out to everyone at the meeting; people who weren't there should request any that they want to see, so we don't waste airmail postage on many charts that no one wants.

The time estimates in these charts are not in any sense imposed deadlines; they started as moderately optimistic guesses, intended to avoid the most obvious pitfalls in the critical paths. Anyone who finds himself on an unreasonable schedule can submit better estimates for the tasks that he's involved in. Many of the guesses were corrected at the meeting.

Any project leaders who don't see the CPM charts as a waste of time will probably want to maintain their own. We can get copies of MILESTONE for anyone who has CP/M (80) capability. It's worth seeing MILESTONE run just to see a really well done menu-driven program.

Various business

We now have letterheads and envelopes. Business cards for everyone will be available soon, probably with the default company title of Product Development Manager.

Dave Kalish has found a publisher who takes formatted ASCII text by phone and does typesetting and printing. We need to meet with him on technical details and prices. John Walker has a list of several publishers who accept some sort of floppy disc input (compiled from much-appreciated information from Richard Handyside and Peter Goldmann).

There was a discussion of the process of bringing new people into the company. The consensus was that anyone brought in on the same basis as the founders would require unanimous consent in some form. Assuming that the proposal had already been discussed, a final decision would not have to wait for a monthly meeting: management could poll everyone (possibly through the conference system on MJK) and proceed within a couple of days if there were no negative votes.

Future agendas

For future meetings, as for this one, the corporate secretary will prepare an agenda and attempt to protect the meeting from creeping formlessness. If there's something that needs to be on the agenda, please send a message to Dan Drake or John Walker a couple of days in advance, preferably on MJK.

The agenda will include progress reports of the same sort as were given at this meeting. Reports should be well under five minutes long; anything needing more discussion will be taken up later in the meeting. With these and the written list of tasks we'll be able to keep track of what's getting done and what's slipping.

The task lists and time commitments will be published regularly.

Here is the algorithm and schedule for monthly meetings:[40]

- The meeting for an odd-numbered month is on a Saturday; for an even month, on a Sunday.
- The meeting is normally on the first <Saturday or Sunday> of the month.
- If that day falls on a holiday weekend, the meeting is held a week early.

---

[40] This is the famous "Sibbald Algorithm".

The schedule for the rest of the year, therefore (excluding the Annual Meeting) is as follows:

Sunday, August 1
Saturday, August 28
Sunday, October 3
Saturday, November 6
Sunday, December 5

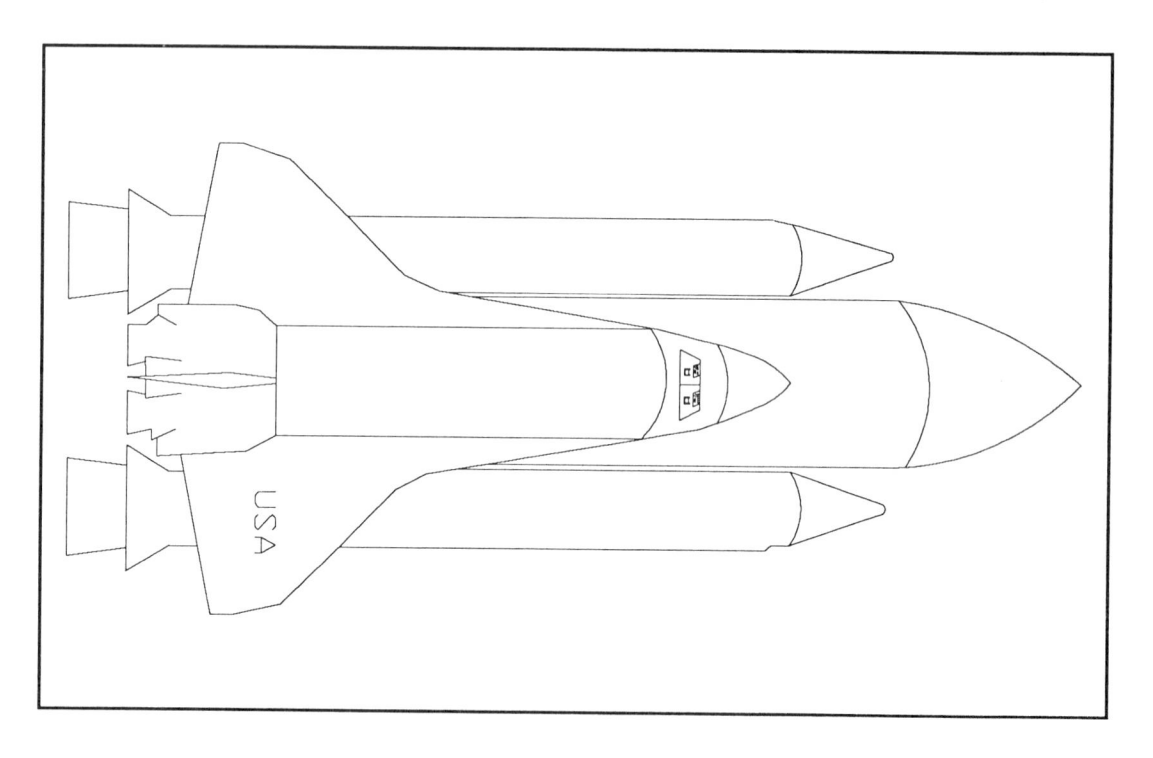

This drawing was, to my knowledge, the first actual drawing ever done with AutoCAD (other than scribbles made while testing the program). I initially drew it on AutoCAD-80 before text was even working, then added detail as parts of the package were implemented. The drawing was made by taping the cover of a Time magazine issue from late 1981 featuring the shuttle to a HI-Pad digitiser and tracing the drawing. The picture in the magazine wasn't precisely a face-on view; that's why the drawing is slightly asymmetrical. This drawing was also the first BLOCK ever used with the INSERT command, and the first drawing ever to be plotted with AutoCAD (on a Houston Instrument DMP-8 plotter). The CHANGE command was initially implemented to help clean up the raw digitised coordinates in this drawing.

Brief Note

The press of working flat-out on AutoCAD and trying to run Marinchip at the same began to tell on Dan Drake and myself. This brief note was the last Information Letter for well over a year. As the pace of activity in the company accelerated, verbal communications over the telephone, via the MJK teleconferencing system, and at the monthly meetings supplanted written summaries.

Autodesk, Inc.
Information Letter # 8

by John Walker
Revision 2 — July 25, 1982

This information letter is to suggest a new participant in the company, Stephanie Nydell. Her participation letter is attached, which details her background and interests.

Those of us who are ISD old-timers don't have to be told that Stephanie would be an excellent addition to the company. She would be able to immediately get to work on documentation production, and having written manuals for a competing CAD system, is eminently qualified to tear into the MicroCAD manual. Also, she can become the nucleus of our customer support operation, having experience in that at both Nicolet and at Information Unlimited Software.

All the rest of the details are in the letter, so read it. Stephanie will be at the August 1 meeting, so you can talk to her and ask any questions you might have at that time. Assuming there's no objection, we can bring her into the company shortly after the meeting in the long-delayed option issue.[41]

Other Items

Everything else is moving ahead rapidly. MicroCAD-80 (the 8080 version in PL/I) is pretty much running now. The 8086 version has now been completely translated

---

[41] For various and assorted reasons, she did not end up joining the company.

to Computer Innovations C, and Dan and Greg are compiling away and beginning to stack modules into a complete program. Greg has the graphics driver for the IBM PC finished. We've received the digitiser, and it's now running with MicroCAD-80. We finally received our copies of CB80, and they're on their way to the people working with CB80. We got a WordStar, MailMerge, and SpellStar at about 80% off list for documentation use and feature evaluation. Duff and Mauri have the memory-only version of the Window line database working, and are moving on to the backing file pager. Kern has the real appointment calendar in Autodesk, and is designing the database interface. A test version of Communicator has been put together by Peter Goldmann, and Rudolf Künzli will be completing a new version of the screen driver package shortly. We now have the information we needed on the 8086 relocatable format. The QBASIC86 project now has no obvious stumbling blocks, and is moving ahead. We've found two typesetting services so far which accept ASCII text, and we're comparing them and others to choose a way to produce manuals.

See you at the meeting.

Moving From Organization to Operation

As the company moved from organisation to operation, communication which had previously been conducted through the Information Letters moved more and more to verbal communication at the monthly meetings of participants, as well as ongoing telephone communication among project teams and messages on our teleconferencing system ("MJK"). Dan Drake inaugurated the publication of summaries of the monthly meetings with this document.

This was particularly eventful time. The decision to scrap the QBASIC version of Autodesk and begin rewriting it in PL/I was made. Development of the initial version of AutoCAD was coming to a close; we decided that versions would be developed for the Scion Microangelo, IBM PC, and Victor 9000, and that the initial price would be $1,000.

August General Meeting

by Dan Drake

The August general meeting was held on Sunday, August 1, 1982, at Jack Stuppin's house.

The meeting was called to order at 1:10. All company people in the Bay Area were present: Dan Drake, Mike Ford, Dave Kalish, Duff Kurland, Mauri Laitinen, Greg Lutz, Keith Marcelius, Hal Royaltey, Kern Sibbald, Jack Stuppin, and John Walker.

Changes in Participation

Stephanie Nydell, whose interest in joining the company was discussed in the previous information letter, was introduced to the meeting. There was unanimous agreement on bringing her in as a founder, subject to approval by the people out of state.

There was a brief discussion of the mechanics of buying back the shares of Jodi Lehman, who has decided to leave the company. It is possible that the company can buy them back, or a new participant could buy them. It appears that there will be no difficulty in working out the details with legal counsel.

Minutes and Financial Report

There was no dissent from the published minutes of the July meeting. John Walker presented the financial report. The balance of funds last month was $45,592. Expenditures have been as follows:

Supplies	85
Softcard for Apple	382
Digitizer for MicroCad project	665
C compilers	42
Apple documentation	?
Total	1,671
Income: Interest from CPF	325
Current Assets:	44,426

Marinchip Systems, Ltd. has for various reasons bought items for ADI worth about $1,542. ADI has also agreed to buy hardware from Duff Kurland in the amount of $5,115.[42] This makes:

Current Liabilities:	6,657

Planned expenditures include compilers (C, PL/I, CB80), business supplies such as invoices, and computer equipment, as yet unspecified, for the use of Mauri Laitinen.

Progress Reports

Everyone delivered a report of 2 – 3 minutes covering:

1. How much time are you currently putting in?
2. What have you been doing and what accomplished?
3. What are you doing next?
4. What's currently standing in your way?

Progress on various projects will be discussed later. An important feature of the reports was that there were almost no reports of obstacles to getting the work done.

---

42   This was the Marinchip computer, Morrow hard disc, and NEC Spinwriter which was, almost three years later, to become a cause célèbre during the public offering as a "promoter transaction".

Random Business

There are some CP/M utilities available to anyone who wants to use them within the company. Some are not ADI property and should not be distributed outside.

DELETE Does what the DEL command in MDEX does with an ambiguous filename, bringing up each selected file for a choice of whether to delete it. It will also find all illegal filenames, which Microsoft programs like to create.

DOC A primitive subset of WORD.

FDUMP A file dump that shows file contents in hex and ASCII.

Project Discussions

Marketing

We have the current IBM software distribution agreement. Anyone who is curious about their standards can get a copy.

In addition to Mike Ford's connection with Victor, we have good contacts at Apple, Hewlett-Packard, Onyx, Corvus, and Timex (which sells the Sinclair). Most of these are just waiting for us to have products to demonstrate.

Dan Drake brought up a possible guerrilla project: an existing Marinchip program that computes all known tax deadlines. The complexities of tax payments are such that the Wall Street Journal ran a flowchart on Federal withholding tax deposits alone. A program that handles these details ought to be worth $50 to any business in California. (It would be a major project to configure it for other states.).

The consensus was that we should convert the program to CP/M and put it on the Apple Softcard. We should get an opinion from accountants, though they have a conflict of interest in that they get high fees for providing the same information to their customers. The program will have to be sold with the understanding that it will be obsolete in a while; people will have to get updates when the rules change. It would be appropriate to let someone else distribute it, since it's off our main line. A major problem is putting on a good enough disclaimer to keep from being sued into nonexistence if we, the customer, or the tax people misunderstand the rules.

John Walker described Micropro's anti-theft provision: their manuals say, in places that make the statement hard to get rid of, that if your copy of Wordstar doesn't have such and such a sticker on the label, you have an illegal copy. Just send it to us and we'll give you a legal one! Of course, they can find the buried serial number on the disk, so they know who the fink is. This seems the best protection scheme in the business, and well worth emulating.[43]

The most animated discussion of the day was on marketing MicroCad, which is very close to being a reality. The plans agreed on are summarized as part of the MicroCad project discussion.

Autodesk

There is now a functioning calendar, and the data base is being redesigned. After a short discussion of features and problems, John Walker raised what seem to be fundamental problems in the project. What follows is approximately a logical, not chronological, summary of the discussion.

The original quick and dirty implementation in CBASIC is now running on CP/M systems in CB80, and Kern Sibbald has put hundreds of hours into conversion and making it run well, but we seem no nearer to a salable product than we were at the Computer Faire. It's still of no practical use, being unreliable and terribly slow.

There was disagreement on the extent of the non-progress, but a consensus that things were not moving nearly fast enough.

The version at the Faire looked like an outstanding product, but it glossed over many crucial technical problems which must be resolved before anything is sold. These don't have obvious answers, and the attempt to fit the answers in as we go along has given us a program as big as MicroCad that does less and runs slowly.

One technical problem may be the wrong choice of language. CB80 lacks the right I/O facilities and requires fairly massive assembly language interface routines, which are especially clumsy because of the lack of data structures. In C or PL/I the problem would disappear. But that conversion would take some time.

Perhaps the existence of the prototype has fooled us into thinking that we could work that into a product, when actually a full re-design is needed.

If we scrapped the project entirely, we would have plenty of things to do with the manpower released, but no one wanted to do that. On the other hand, if we continue the project, we need more people involved in it.

---

43   This was the rationale behind the notorious "metal labels" we used on our discs in the early days. We never did make the offer to redeem pirated copies, largely through oversight.

A consensus was developed along these lines: The program will be rewritten in a better language. At present, if we want to sell to half a million existing 8080 systems, that means PL/I; by the time the program is ready there should be a PL/I available for the 8086. Also, when the screen handler has been done in PL/I, we'll have gone a long way towards a PL/I version of Window.

The thing we are to produce is a user-friendly card box system with multiple boxes holding cards of unlimited size. Once it's done and on the market, we can work on further releases with added features. This first implementation may get us into some decisions that we'll regret when we start adding features, but we have to get a working product out the door in a finite time.

Dave Kalish will work with Kern Sibbald on the database design and on user features. Duff Kurland and Mauri Laitinen will work on the screen handler. As a crash project the thing could be done in a month or two; since we don't have people working full time, we must be resigned to its taking longer.

There was general agreement that we needed to know more about competing products, including MBA. No one actually said that he'd do such an investigation.

JPLDIS

We now have data on availability. The price quotes range from zero to $3,450. We are supposedly getting a free copy in 6 – 8 weeks, but no one is betting on it.

MICROCAD

Both the PL/I version on the 8080 and the C version on the IBM PC are now converted and running, needing some amount of work before release. The Victor version will be running soon. Without any optimization or division into overlays, the 8080 version has 4K bytes of memory left over, and runs as fast as the 9900 version.

The discussion of marketing went very roughly as follows.

John Owens has sold perhaps 20 copies of the 9900 version through his ads in Byte, and has had lots of people ask why it isn't on the 8080. He might sell as many as a hundred in a short time if we turn him loose.

There are some large markets for an 8080 MicroCad. Scion is selling enough Microangelos to support a color ad in the front of Byte every month, though there's very little software available. A version using the Microangelo with a light pen would be a completely standard product that would run entirely on Scion's graphic equipment and might be something they would want to market. There are other markets further along, like Apples and the incredibly cheap Sinclair. Again, it might be easily converted to Univac PL/I, running on an 1100 with Tektronix graphics.[44]

On the other hand, since we could ship out copies and sell a few almost immediately, there are marketing decisions that must be settled immediately. What do we do about Beta testing? Do we sell a pre-release? How do we price it? What do we know of the reactions of live users of the 9900 version? The only people in the company who have spent any time using it are computer fanatics who know the internals and are not well qualified to judge user interfacing for a large market.

It's clear that getting some copies into the field and getting information back from end users will be invaluable in developing the product.[45] Getting some actual money into the company is also important.

Fears of getting a hostile review on an early release were dissipated by the observation that it's extremely hard to get reviews when you want them. A product that's selling at most a few hundred copies is in little danger of any reviews.

The consensus reached was this: The 8080 version will get a driver for whatever plotter John Owens currently likes to sell.[46] Stephanie Nydell, who has done documentation and support for larger graphic systems in the electronics business, will write up suggestions for making the user interface more friendly to completely unsophisticated users. She will also make minimal changes in the current manual to make a preliminary version that we can send out with the early release. We'll tell Owens that the product is coming, and he can sell it to his 8080 prospects. On Wednesday, August 25, we want to send this version out.[47]

There will be a Victor 9000 version for Mike Ford to demonstrate by the end of September.

The initial list price will be the same $1,000 as for the current 9900 Interact.[48]

Once we have this product out the door, we demonstrate to Hewlett-Packard and pursue our other contacts. Work will start then on a new manual and will proceed as we exercise the program and get feedback from users.

---

44   This was the first and, thankfully, last mention of this idea.
45   Thus was born the idea of "let the user wish list design the product".
46   Today this is called a "market driven peripheral support strategy".
47   First committed ship date for AutoCAD or, for that matter, any Autodesk product. By the way, we made it.
48   Decision on initial pricing of AutoCAD.

QB86

META is now running on the 8086 but has not been modified to give some features that the QBASIC compiler will need for compatibility with CB80. The corresponding compiler changes have not been coded.

Pass 2, the optimizer, now generates 8086 assembly language. Now that we have the definition of the relocatable format, QP2 must be modified to generate relocatable directly, as well as supporting the new CB80 compatible features.

The memory model is well defined, using the Large Model for 8086 addressing. Parameter passing is mostly defined, but not all decisions have been made.

Queue handling and buffer allocation are working. The floating point library is working after a pretty complete rewrite and will support 32 and 64 bit integers if we want them.

There is a large amount of work needed on the library, without enough people to work on it. This is also the most easily partitioned part of the product.

To get all the parts of the project moving, there was a general reshuffling of manpower. Dan Drake will do the compiler pass 1 and associated changes in Meta. Mike Riddle will rewrite pass 2 in C; optimization will be based on the current QP2, and the output will be relocatable. Greg Lutz will work on parts of the library.

We will have a working version for Victor at the beginning of October. The big question is whether Digital Research will get CB86 out before we get ours out.

Window

The in-core version of line database is running. There is disk code, which is not running yet. There are some problems with string linkage and inadequate documentation of CB80 linkages.

The consensus was that the Z80 version would be ready in a month. The manual update should be an afternoon's work. The 8086 version will be out when QB86 is.

Corporate

Stock options are being set up with corporate counsel. Most of the paperwork will be ready to execute at the next meeting.

The process of unanimous decisions was discussed briefly. The unanimous agreement procedure that we adopted was intended for the adoption of new participants, not for other corporate decisions that the management or the board can make. If the organization gets large, polls of everybody will get too awkward.

As we don't expect to bring dozens of people in on the same basis as founders, this may never be a problem.

Appendix

Task Lists

We need to have lists of what everyone is working on, so that we know what's covered and what's being overlooked. Also, everyone should know where to go with new information or questions concerning any project.

There is now an MJK user name called TLIST which is to be used for sending the lists. By the Wednesday night before each meeting, please send TLIST a list of what you've accomplished and what you intend to have done by next month, on a fairly specific level. Please keep it compact, to avoid overflowing the number of lines that TLIST is allowed to have stored. On the Wednesday night before each meeting John Walker will pick up the messages and compile them into a document that everyone will get a copy of.

MJK Usage

On our last bill from MJK,[49] 35% of the computer time charge was for prime shift. We can save substantial amounts of our working capital by not using the system unnecessarily in the daytime. We are also running up charges for file storage. If you use MJK at all, please pick up and delete your messages.

Next Meeting

The next (September) meeting is at 1:00 on Saturday, August 28, at Jack Stuppin's house. There will be a demonstration of BitStik, a frighteningly good graphics package on the Apple.[50]

Agendas

We've been making some attempt to keep to an agenda at these meetings without suffocating in Robert's Rules of Order. The responsibility for the agenda has fallen on the corporate secretary, Dan Drake. It would be nice to know what people now

---

49 MJK is a company located in Silicon Valley that sells timesharing on HP minicomputers. Their major business is providing access to current and historical data for the commodities market. John Walker used this system in his commodity trading days, and also used it to implement a teleconferencing system for Marinchip dealers and, later, Autodesk people. Since the system was on Tymnet, overseas participants could access it economically.

50 It was a demo of the BitStik in London in August that prompted John Walker into a furious burst of implementation to upgrade AutoCAD.

think about how the meetings should be run. Should we drop agendas entirely? Should we be more authoritarian in holding to the agenda? Should the agenda be changed in form?

In any case, if you have something that you think ought to come up at the meeting, please send a message to Dan Drake so that it can be brought up at a reasonable point on the agenda. If it seems too small a matter to put on the agenda, you can bring it up under new business.

Here is the normal skeleton agenda:

- Call to order.
- Introduction of any guests.
- Review of minutes.
- Financial report.
- Progress reports: Everyone gets 2 minutes to tell what's happening. More details will be covered in project reviews.
    How much time are you putting in?
    What have you been doing; what have you accomplished?
    What will you be doing during the month?
    What's standing in your way?
- Random new business and things that came up in reports.
- Project reviews.
    Marketing
    Autodesk
    MicroCad
    QB-86
    Window

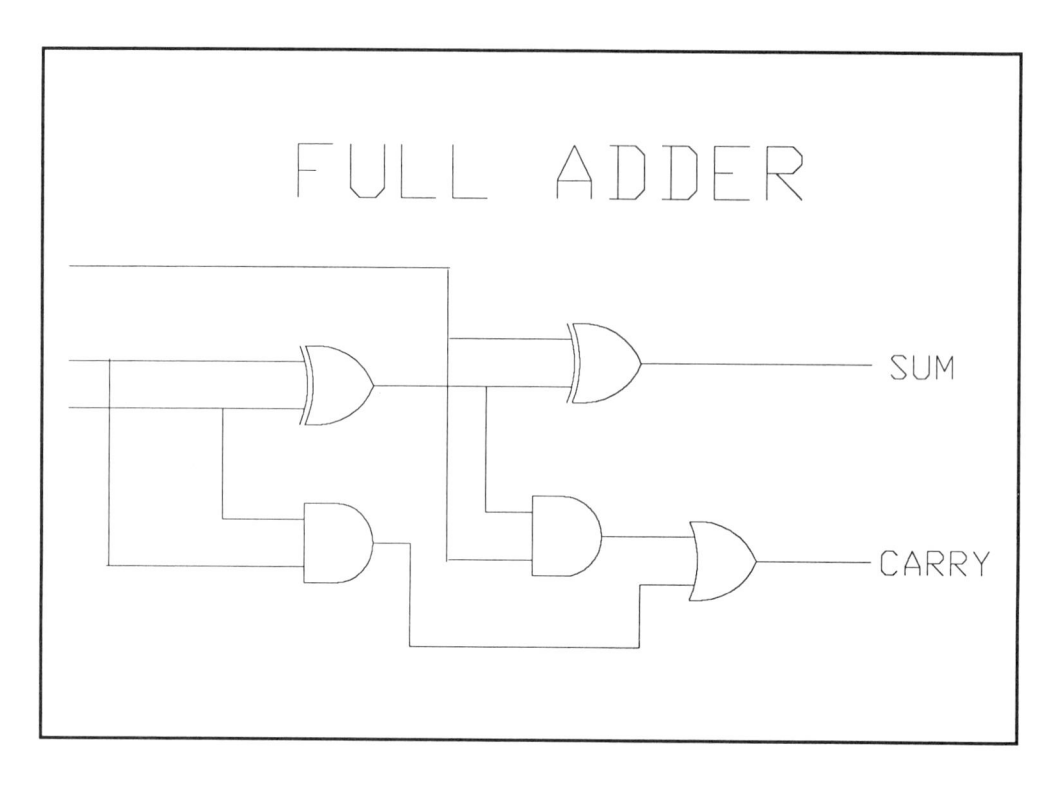

This electronic schematic drawing and all of its constituents, appeared on the original sample drawings disc. It was the first sample drawing originated on AutoCAD-86.

1982 Annual Meeting

With the push to get AutoCAD actually running underway, and other Autodesk development projects proceeding concurrently, there wasn't much time to write minutes of meetings, though the meetings continued to be held every month. The next general communication was the announcement of Autodesk's first annual stockholders' meeting. Dan Drake alludes to some of the overwork and the communications problems this engendered herein.

Autodesk: Monthly Meeting

Dan Drake
December 28, 1982

Our good old algorithm for determining monthly meeting dates strikes again: the January meeting would come up on the first Saturday of January, alias New Year's Day. Of course, we don't have it on a holiday, so it moves up a week, to December 25. Oops.

So ….

The January monthly meeting will be at 1:00 on Saturday, January 8 (*eight*), 1983, at Jack Stuppin's house in San Francisco. At 2:00 it will be interrupted for the annual shareholders' meeting (required by our bylaws and state law). This probably won't take long, as the only item currently on the agenda is the election of directors (required by law). Then the directors will meet, again required by law and again probably very briefly, to organize the board and appoint the corporate officers. With luck, if no new business comes up, we may break the world speed record for a bona fide annual meeting.

Those of you who are now stockholders of record will receive a formal notice and proxy with this announcement. If you exercised an option by the 28th, you're a stockholder even though you haven't got your certificate yet.

Employees who aren't stockholders, and stockholders who aren't employees, are encouraged to attend the whole shebang.

The fact that this is the first written notice in months brings up a sore point. With respect to communications in the company, people have taken two positions:

- Where the hell are the information letters; we haven't had one in months; nobody knows what's going on; we can't survive without better communications.
- Putting out minutes or an information letter knocks a couple of days out of the time of someone who has to be getting a product ready for market; we can't survive without getting products out.

Both of these positions seem to be quite right. Anyone who has constructive proposals on the subject is guaranteed a high place on the agenda for the meeting, if any of us has time to prepare an agenda.

Finally, here's the meeting algorithm again, with its output for the coming year. Should this silly thing be changed?

> The meeting for an odd-numbered month is on a Saturday; for an even month, on a Sunday.
>
> The meeting is normally on the first (Saturday or Sunday) of the month.
>
> If that day falls on a holiday weekend, the meeting is held a week early. This is certain to happen in July and September, likely in January, and possible even in April.

The schedule for the rest of the year (1983)

Saturday, January 8
Sunday, February 6
Saturday, March 5
Sunday, March 27 (April 3 is Easter)
Saturday, May 7
Sunday, June 5
Saturday, June 25
Sunday, August 7
Saturday, August 27
Sunday, October 1
Saturday, November 5
Sunday, December 4?
Wednesday evening, December 7 (annual meeting)

December 29, 1982
NOTICE OF ANNUAL MEETING

The annual shareholders' meeting of Autodesk, Inc. will be held at 2:00 PM on Saturday, January 8, 1983, at the home of Jack Stuppin in San Francisco.

(The meeting was re-scheduled by order of John Walker, president, from the normal time of the first Wednesday in December, when most of the company was in Las Vegas.)

Stockholders of record December 28, 1982, will be eligible to vote at the meeting. If you are not absolutely sure that you will attend, please sign and return the enclosed proxy, which will be revoked automatically if you do attend. It looks better on the records if we do not drag through with a bare quorum.

The only business currently scheduled for the meeting is the election of four directors for the next year.

Daniel Drake

Daniel Drake
Secretary

PROXY

I appoint JOHN WALKER, DANIEL DRAKE, and KEITH B. MARCELIUS my proxies to vote on my behalf at the annual shareholders' meeting of Autodesk, Inc., to be held on January 8, 1983, and at any adjournments thereof. All previous proxies are hereby revoked. The majority of said proxies present at the meeting, or their appointed substitutes, shall have the power to vote my shares in the election of directors or any other business which may come before the meeting, with the following restrictions:

I may revoke this proxy (1) by giving written notice to the corporation; (2) by executing another proxy, which will take effect when presented to the corporation or exercised at the meeting; (3) by attending the meeting and voting in person.

(signed)_____

Name _____

Date _____

Section Two

Turning the Corner

Publisher's Notes
January 1983 — December 1983

This second year was a crucial year for Autodesk's success. The company started the year with a hot software product while still organized as a loose confederation of programmers with limited cash resources. By the end of the year, they had released three successive improvements to the program, organized an effective marketing and sales effort, organized an office and operations, and transformed themselves into their own vision of a professional software company. All this effort came at the steep price (as it always does) of long hours of hard work with almost no pay.

Even with these efforts, at the end of the year they faced the classic growth problem confronting every venture: choosing to seek outside venture capital.

Key Events

Here are the key events that occurred during the company's second year (1983) along with the documents provided in this Section.

January 1983. AutoCAD-86 (IBM PC Version) released.

- January 5, 1983. December and January — Monthly Meeting Reports. Focus on how to stretch the company's cash resources to get AutoCAD out to customers; and how to control its technical quality. Greg Lutz becomes the first paid employee.

January 30, 1983. The cash turn around point for the company. At its lowest point, the company had $25,953 in the bank.

- February 1983. February — Meeting Notes. Covers marketing and product development.

- March 8, 1983. March — Meeting Notes. Shows how Dan Drake's task lists helped manage product development.

June 1983. The company moves into its first formal offices at 150 Shoreline, Bldg B, Room 20 in Mill Valley, CA. Cash reserves are double the original investment.

- June 7, 1983. — June Meeting Notes. Include an organizational meeting with the European founders and a brief report on their activities.

- June 21, 1983. — Crisis Letter. Focuses on the need to work flat out to improve the product, marketing, sales and order taking to make the company a success.

- June 23, 1989. — John Walker's Business Plan. Gives the organization structure that eventually was put in place to solve the organizational problems and develop the business.

July 1983. First stock split, 10 for 1.

- July 4, 1983. — A Proposed Autodesk Organization Plan drafted by Kern Sibbald. As John Walker notes, they should have followed this plan sooner, but they didn't. Still the company developed along the lines given in this plan.

- September 5, 1983. — Low Rent 3D. First proposal to incorporate 3D in AutoCAD.

- September 14, 1983. — Electric Malcolm. Using a transcript to generate video demos.

- October 1983. — Notice for October Quarterly Meeting. Raises the issue of venture capital.

- October 7, 1983. — Piece of Cake. Shows an ill-fated attempt at hiring an outside firm to publicize AutoCAD.

October 9, 1983. Second Annual Stockholders Meeting. The first formal discussion for seeking venture capital to expand the company.

- October 25, 1983. — Information Letter #10. (There is no #9.) Recommends going after venture capital to expand the company.

You will see new names appear in the documents from the second year as the core founding group expanded with the work load. Here are some of the new people:

Lars Moureau — Established the Swedish office. He gives a retrospective view of Autodesk as seen from Europe. (This document is in Section Seven.)
John Kern — Headed up organizing the Sausalito office and operations.

Turning the Corner   Section Two   123

As is often the case in growing companies, you also will see occasional references to wives and family members who pitched in with part-time and full-time help to keep the company moving ahead during this second crucial year.

Key Product Events

Here is the official release schedule:

April 1983. AutoCAD Version 1.2 Release.

August 1983. AutoCAD Version 1.3 Release.

October 1983. AutoCAD Version 1.4 Release.

By the end of the year, the company had shipped a cumulative total of almost 1,000 units, building many of these one-by-one for each microcomputer configuration. To get a better view of the product's feature development, look at the first Wish List for requested AutoCAD features compiled by Duff Kurland. This document is given in Appendix F.

Financial Summary

When the year ended, the company showed over $1 million in sales. Revenues were over $100 thousand. The following figures show the quarterly sales and profit history for the fiscal year.

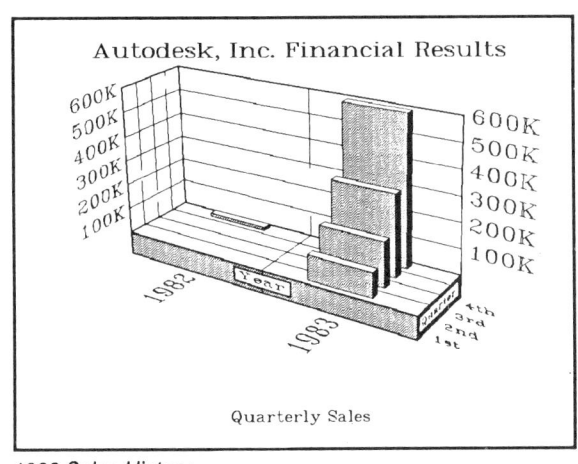

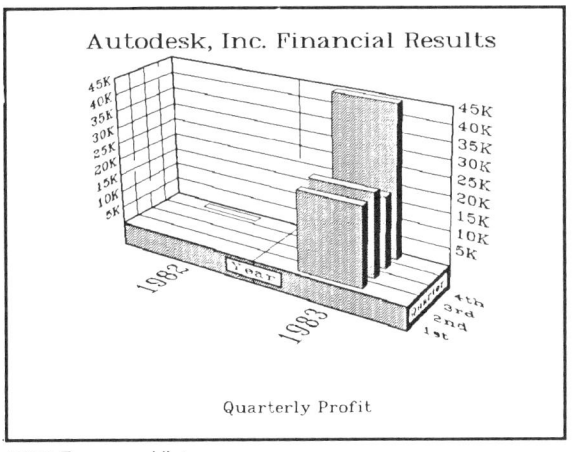

1983 Sales History   *1983 Revenue History*

After COMDEX - December '82 — January '83

This document chronicles the period when Autodesk turned the corner. Before we went to COMDEX in 1982, we were a group of idealistic programmers with a dream. We returned from COMDEX with a product that we knew to have demonstrated its potential to be a mega-hit. The problem then was how to best deploy our meager resources to best exploit the opportunity our work had created. In the December and January meetings we began to grope our way toward approaches to the challenges that faced us.

December and January Meetings

by Dan Drake

This is a quick summary, long after the fact, of the general meetings of December, 1982, and January, 1983. The keeping of proper minutes, which was abandoned for months because of the lack of anyone to do it, will be resumed as of the February meeting.

December Meeting

The December meeting was held on Sunday, December 5, at Jack Stuppin's house. The major topic of discussion was COMDEX, which had been held the previous Monday through Thursday.[51]

Our booth at COMDEX had AutoCAD on the Z80, Victor 9000, and IBM PC. We were also passing out brochures on Autoscreen, but made no real effort to demonstrate it, as an editor doesn't make a very gripping demo.

AutoCAD was on display in a total of four booths: Sierra Data Systems, Sun-Flex, and Victor, in addition to our own. With the aid of all this exposure, our obscure

---

51 This, of course, was the COMDEX at which we introduced AutoCAD to the world.

booth in the back of the show was almost continuously full of people — to the extent that Steve Ciarcia couldn't find his way in. Win a few, lose a few.

It was apparent that AutoCAD was a hot product. At the biggest show in the industry, it had the field to itself, with no direct competition at all. The main problem before the meeting was how to cope with success.

Mike Ford pointed out that exploiting the large number of leads we brought back would be a full-time job. Being unable to work full time for any extended period with no pay, he suggested that Autodesk pay him a 10% commission on sales, up to some reasonable amount, for a few months. There was much discussion of the advisability of paying someone at this point, or whether we should pay ourselves commissions, and of the relation between taking a cut on sales and taking a piece of the company's growth by means of stock options.

There was a consensus that paying Mike would be a good investment, and that the commission arrangement would amount to paying him a salary with him taking all the risk in case we didn't get enough income. The following arrangement was approved by unanimous vote:

Starting immediately, Mike gets a 10% commission, to a maximum of $6,000 a month (a figure intended to compensate for the risk that he'd get very little, and corresponding to nearly 3/4 of a million a year in sales). The arrangement runs for three months, and can be renewed by the directors month by month. When it runs out, the commission drops to 8% for a month, then 6%, and on down to zero. The idea behind the gradual decrease was that some deals, including the most profitable ones, give delayed yields.

January Meeting

The meeting on Saturday, January 8, was the normal general meeting with the annual shareholders' meeting and board of directors' meeting sandwiched in.

The shareholders' meeting elected an almost unchanged slate of directors: Dan Drake, Mike Ford, Keith Marcelius, and John Walker. Jack Stuppin declined to continue to serve on the board because of problems with stock exchange regulations, but will work unofficially with the board.

The board in its turn confirmed the corporate officers:

John Walker	President
Daniel Drake	Vice President, Secretary
Keith B. Marcelius	Treasurer, Assistant Secretary
Robert R. Tufts	Assistant Secretary
Roxie Walker	Assistant Treasurer

The reason for all the funny assistants is that the signatures of one or more officers are required on many formal documents, including the application for a California resale permit. With an assistant treasurer in Marin and assistant secretaries in the Eastbay and at the law office, we save a good deal of time and hassle.

John Walker presented the financial report, the crux of which is that our liquid capital is down to about $17,000.[52]

We have two sources of additional capital. Marinchip has warrants to buy 40,000 shares at $1.00 a share; it bought warrants because it lacked the cash to buy in for that much last spring, Marinchip now has enough cash to exercise part or all of the warrants. Also, the original capitalization plan included 20,000 options for John Walker; by oversight, these haven't been awarded yet, but the board intends to approve them as soon as it can print the paperwork. Sales up to January 8: 4 AutoCAD-80; 1 AutoCAD-86; backlog of 2 AutoCAD-80s; 2 AutoScreens. AutoScreen is now part of the Engineering Work Station sold by Jamal Munshi of MOMS Computing.

AutoCAD-80 is running on the Aurora 1000 from Graphic Development Lab, which has sent out 500 of our brochures; the product will be officially released soon. A dimensioning package is being released as an independent add-on for $500 list.[53]

AutoCAD-86 is scheduled for release on both the IBM PC and the Victor/Sirius on January 15.[54] The features included will be those in the preliminary AutoCAD manual, with an upgrade somewhat later. Sun-Flex, the maker of the Touch Pen, will be selling their product with AutoCAD (for the Victor) and is talking of selling 100 in February, gearing up to 300 a month soon.

We have many contacts with companies that are interested in AutoCAD, including Fortune and Houston Instruments (which wants a demo of the things we can do with their plotters).

Jack Stuppin has connections in the educational publishing business, which could lead to some profitable ventures. It is not too early to think about what programs we'll produce after AutoDesk has been released and AutoCAD has stabilized.[55]

---

52 This was the low point. From there on, it was up, up, and away.
53 Thus began the pattern of extra-cost options. Later, dimensioning was combined with other features and sold as "ADE-1".
54 That's right, AutoCAD-80 was shipped in December 1982, but AutoCAD-86 wasn't shipped until January of 1983.
55 Who knows what we will do once "AutoCAD has stabilized"…

Dave Kalish raised the idea of a sort of personal computer software division, built around people in the South Bay who are unable to work on AutoCAD because of conflict of interest and geographical isolation. There was general agreement that this was a good idea. Possible projects include a menu-planning package that Dave is working on with some other people, and the sort of educational programs that Jack's associates might put us onto.

To improve communications in the company, there will be a bi-weekly mailing of interesting items to everyone in the company. Interesting items might be anything from news clippings to suggestions for ADI products to project reports. Announcements and minutes will be in the package if they come out at the right time. Items sent to Roxie Walker at headquarters will be Xeroxed and sent with the next mailing.

There was a strong consensus that we must have minutes of meetings in some form, and an agenda enforced by someone with a mandate to keep meetings from rambling. Dan Drake agreed to resume the minutes and assume the role of enforcer if no one else volunteered, and was elected by a unanimous silence.

Duff Kurland expressed interest in working full time, if some kind of arrangement for pay could be worked out so that he would not be in effect plowing a few thousand a month into the company. This brought up the situation of Greg Lutz, who has been working full time on AutoCAD-86, and Dan Drake, who has given ADI preemptive priority over paying work; with both having to switch into a non-destructive financial operating mode, the project's technical manpower was about to be reduced to one part-time person.

By unanimous vote it was agreed that Greg would get a subsistence of $1,000 a month for the next four months, in return for which he could give AutoCAD-86 his undivided attention.[56] Everyone else was asked to submit a letter to Jack Stuppin, giving the specific conditions under which he would be able to work full time for ADI. With those letters we could plan to take on more full-time people as the cash flow picked up.

Last October or thereabouts there was to have been a special all-day brainstorming meeting on how best to manage the company, but it was bumped by one crisis or another. Dave Kalish pointed out that there was as much need as ever for this meeting, so it was rescheduled for Sunday, February 13, tentatively at Jack Stuppin's house at 11 A.M.

---

56 Thus, Greg Lutz became Autodesk's first full-time employee, at least in terms of salary.

One thing that has become apparent is that we often don't know, or don't agree on, what has been actually decided at a meeting. Here, then, is the first instance of a feature that will appear in all minutes, though perhaps in some prettier form. If you think it's inaccurate, speak now or forever hold your peace.

Summary of Decisions Taken

Mike Ford will temporarily get a commission on sales, described in detail in the DECEMBER section.

Greg Lutz is on the payroll at $1,000 a month, effective January 8.

The board of directors is the same as last year, except that Mike Ford replaces Jack Stuppin. The officers are the same.

There will be minutes and an agenda for the meetings. If you have something that needs to be discussed, inform Dan Drake before Friday night, or be prepared to be gavelled down.

We will meet on Sunday, February 13 to figure out how to run the company. This is to be an all-day session, though we can't start it before 11:00 because of travel time. Bring your specific complaints, your general principles for running things, your specific ideas, and a readiness to volunteer for the grungework of carrying out the ideas.

Quality Department Priorities

Even as we were shipping the first AutoCADs, we were concerned with achieving and maintaining the highest quality standards for our products. Since our money and marketing resources were so limited, we had to rely on our reputation as the primary sales tool. Our resources also prevented us from actually starting a formal Quality department until Mauri Laitinen started full-time to undertake that task on January 4, 1984, precisely one year later.

Quality Department Priorities

by John Walker — January 5, 1983

One of the central but almost unspoken assumptions of AI since its inception is that we will supply products of superior quality. In the software business, this is the key to survival, growth, and respect. Nobody in this company is going to say let's ship this shoddy junk, but as we grow and have to support more features, more machines, and more peripherals, it becomes harder and harder to verify that every product we ship meets our intended standards of performance. Thus, in order to keep our performance in line with our intentions, we now need a Quality department which will help us achieve our goals. The Quality department is not responsible for the quality of our product — it is responsible for developing the procedures which verify that the company as a whole delivers only products which meet our standards of performance.

The following are what seem to me to be chief priorities in the establishment of a coherent quality function within Autodesk.[57]

All items listed are of equal priority unless otherwise noted.

---

57 This entire proposal is based on the principles enunciated in *Quality Is Free* by Philip B. Crosby, Mentor, 1979.

Development of Specifications

Quality is adherence to specifications. What are the specifications for AutoCAD? One straightforward approach is to develop a test suite which will execute on an AutoCAD which meets the specifications embodied in the manual.[58] This test suite and ancillary tests should become one of the prime validation tools used to qualify a release from the Technical department for release to the market.

Qualification Testing

The Quality department should conduct all initial testing of new proposed releases by the Technical department. This testing should consist of testing against the specifications of the previous release, development of tests for new features and changes, and their integration into the test set.

Test Management

Once a new software version has been proposed for release, Quality shall cause it to be shipped to beta test sites, and shall coordinate all test responses and problem resolutions.

Discrepancy Logging

All reported discrepancies (e.g., bugs) should be logged by Quality and tracked to resolution. Quality will prepare and present to management summaries of problems encountered and resolved on a regular basis. Discrepancy reports will be retired only upon certification by Quality that the problem has been corrected. Quality will develop reporting with the cooperation of Customer Support and Technical groups to implement this function.

Release Certification

Quality will certify all software for release. Operations will be provided with master copies of software by Quality after this certification is complete. Operations will ship no software not certified by Quality.

---

58   Good idea. Somebody should get around to that some day.

Regression Testing

Quality will develop and implement procedures to verify that problems reported and resolved do not reoccur in subsequent releases. Development of a regression test suite and monitoring of Technical source code control procedures are among the tools which may achieve this goal.

Cost of Quality

Quality shall prepare and present, on a monthly basis, reports to management on the direct costs incurred by AI as a result of quality problems. These reports shall include customer support time, product replacement costs, lost production time, and any other costs traceable to shipment to customers of product failing to meet AI specifications.

Is This a Company or What?

The February 1983 meeting looked back on not only COMDEX, but the second and third trade shows we attended: CADCON and CPM-83. The strains of converting a loose aggregation of entrepreneurially-oriented programmers into a responsive company can be seen in Dan Drake's announcement of the meeting. A large quantity of collateral communication led to the feeling that we had to resolve the issue of effective management.

In February of 1983, the company's cash position turned around and, in fact, doubled in one month. AutoCAD sales had begun to take off, and began a growth curve which, at this writing four and a half years later, has not yet seen its first inflection point.

Autodesk Monthly Meeting
February, 1983

Dan Drake

The February monthly meeting will be at DUFF KURLAND'S meeting room (not Jack's) at 1:00 on February 6.

On February 13 we'll have the special meeting on managing the company. To approximate an all-day meeting, this is starting at 11:00 (*eleven*). It's currently scheduled for Jack's house. When originally proposed, way back in October, this was described as a brainstorming session; i.e., lots of ideas should be put forth before we start inhibiting ourselves by looking at them critically and realistically.

[Unauthorized editorial by DD: This is not a company owned and operated by some guy or guys in the Northbay. It is a cooperative venture of some entrepreneurs, all of whom think and act as if it were a company owned and operated by some guy or guys in the Northbay. This fallacy is self-sustaining and is very close to destroying the company.]

[There are two equal and opposite errors concerning how to fix things. One is to exhort everyone to buckle down, work hard, and act like an entrepreneur. The other is to figure out better management strategies for the people who run things to use in managing the workers. Can a person who's miles out of the daily action, able to commit only a small amount of time to the enterprise, really be blamed for not feeling much like an entrepreneur? Will he feel better if there's a better bureaucracy, more like the conventional company he works for (considering that he's not so devoted to that company as to devote all his time to it and resist new things like ADI[59])? Are there any practical, concrete steps by which we can discipline or trick ourselves to see the company correctly? Not that this will solve all the management problems, but nothing else will without this.]

[Finally, if you come to the meeting with a proposal that somebody should tie a bell on the cat's tail to warn us when it's coming, don't forget to consult your Boy Scout Handbook (to review knots) and your family attorney (to update your will). There's no use for proposals of the form, Let's You And Him Fix It This Way.]

Responsible opposing viewpoints will be given equal time; that is, if you have an idea you want circulated before the meeting, get it to me in writing (mail, MJK, courier, or whatever) by Tuesday Feb. 8, and I'll mail it to everyone on Wednesday.

---

59   ADI here was used as an abbreviation for the company name. In 1985, it came to mean "Autodesk Device Interface".

February General Meeting

Dan Drake

The February general meeting was held on Sunday, February 6, at Duff Kurland's. Present were Dan Drake, Mike Ford, Dave Kalish, Duff Kurland, Greg Lutz, Mauri Laitinen, Keith Marcelius, Hal Royaltey, John Walker, and Roxie Walker.

Minutes and Financial Report

There was no dissent from the minutes of the December and January meetings.

John Walker presented the financial report. As of January 30, one year after the first organizational meeting, the company had a positive cash flow, with net assets doubled from the previous month.[60]

Bank account:	7,966
Capital Preservation Fund	17,987
Liquid assets	25,953
Receivables	7,734
Total short-term assets	33,687
Liabilities committed exp.	(1,500)
Net	32,000+

Expenditures in 1982 amounted to $44,493, broken down as follows: hardware 48%; shows 22%; legal expenses 14%; printing 7%; stock repurchase 5%; others 4%.

Board of Directors

The Board is now meeting informally during the week before each general meeting. At the meeting on February 2 the main topics discussed were marketing plans and manpower allocation.

The Board's idea, discussed and amplified at the general meeting, is that we should offer a standard distributor and OEM price of $425 or $450, and let them tell us what they can offer in return for the still lower price that they'll ask for. When people have new machines that they want us to put AutoCAD on, we'll try to negotiate an engineering fee for the work. If an OEM looks valuable, we may

---

60   The corner had been turned. From this point on, Autodesk was profitable.

convert to his machine on speculation (as we have done up to now) and make an evaluation copy for him to look at, but without committing ourselves to anything in terms of an eventual release. Any manufacturer who is serious will give us a loan of his equipment for as long as we're supporting it in our software.

As to manpower, the Board noted that there would be no manpower for marketing AutoDesk if it were ready for release immediately; our marketing operation is over-loaded trying to get full advantage out of AutoCAD. The implications of this were discussed later.

Project Reports

Marketing

We are pursuing listings for AutoCAD in every relevant directory and are beginning to get announcements published. An article in ISO World got about 200 responses. We are sending announcements to about eighty industry analysts and a couple of hundred OEMs. An important goal now is to get a number of retail dealers around the country, who can answer questions and give demos. Of course, we went to two trade shows in January.

There was a longish discussion of where we should spend money in promoting the product, particularly whether we should buy into a mailing of card decks by the *S. Kline Newsletter*. For instance, if we burn most of the card decks we get, why think that everyone else won't burn theirs? The upshot was that we should budget $1,000 for Mike Ford to try out what he wants. It will take a month or two before we have enough cash-flow information to allocate a proper budget for advertising.

One of our objectives is not to be the Electric Pencil of the CAD industry (90% market share in word processing in 1978; zero in 1982). To do this we want to nail down as many manufacturers as possible, so that the next product to come along will find very little market left.

We are working with USI, which makes a cheap ($300) mouse and wants to use AutoCAD to push their product. We have sales now at Ford and Shell in England, with prospects for very large sales in the future. Houston Instrument plans to use AutoCAD to demonstrate its products at shows. Texas Instruments has an evaluation copy and is of course going to require 10,000 AutoCADs on its new IBM clone.

AutoCAD-86

Dan Drake is now the interim sub-project manager for AutoCAD-86 (until somebody complains about the cooking[61]). A large part of the job consists of talking to the outside world. Technical people on the project (meaning Greg Lutz at the moment) have unlisted phone numbers as far as the outside world is concerned, and should be called as little as possible by our own people.

AutoCAD-86 release 1.1 went out around January 15 after a struggle with the document. There is a demo version, which is a full program except that it can't write any output on disk; it will also be fixed so that it can't plot from within the drawing editor. We solicit any suggestions for how people could get around the limitations to get useful work out of the demo version!

The next release is scheduled for March 10, with the full features of AutoCAD-80, plus the Epson screen dump on the Victor version. IBM Touchpen support, which is in the current version as an undocumented feature, will be officially supported in this release if we get a working Touchpen for IBM by March 1.

AutoCAD-80

An evaluation version of AutoCAD-80 (and AutoCAD-86 on the IBM) is now running on the Vectrix, a beautiful $5,000 670 x 480 display with 511 colors selected out of a menu of 16,000,000. The version for the Aurora is released, and actually sold more copies than the Microangelo version in January.

The program now fills memory pretty thoroughly, and the main development project is to compact it a little more. It is also being fixed to run on multi-user Turbodos systems.

There was some discussion of whether we should fix on PL/I (now that the 8086 version is coming out) or on C as a single language for AutoCAD. C, however, is impossible for AutoCAD-80, while PL/I has much less future than C on the new machines, particularly the 68000. This leaves us stuck with two versions forever.[62]

AutoDesk

Kern Sibbald is turning over the AutoDesk project to Mike Riddle. When Kern returns from vacation, he will start taking over the AutoCAD-80 project. AutoDesk is not close to a release yet, but as noted before, we couldn't effectively push it if it were.

---

61   Good, though.
62   Well, not *forever*. AutoCAD-80 was abandoned in 1984.

AutoScreen

There was no report, but the subject of conversion to the 8086 was discussed later in the meeting. The problem with conversion, now that CB-86 is supposed to be out, is the 3,000 lines of assembly code that have to be translated. The translation program for converting 8080 assembly code to the upward compatible 8086 is apparently worthless for large programs; therefore, the cost of conversion could be justified only if we had very good prospects for sales.

Corporate

The only thing happening here is an attempt to get the books set up properly. This becomes critical as the date for income tax (75 days after the end of the fiscal year) approaches.

Trade Shows

There was a post-mortem on the two trade shows (CADCON and CPM-83) in January, together with COMDEX.[63]

There was a general failure to plan for moving things out on the last day of CPM-83. In the future our policy will be that at closing time of any show we have the Walkermobile[64] and/or the Drakemobile to haul things. Either of these can carry our signs and large chunks of equipment, and is accompanied by someone who is supposed to know what's happening.

There was a poll on the value of the three shows. COMDEX was considered very valuable and successful. CADCON was thoroughly marginal, with a low turnout of not very well informed people; and we didn't properly exploit the chance for a good look at the expensive competition. CPM-83 was much like a Computer Faire; the management of the show was much worse, but there seemed to be a higher concentration of dealers and fewer obnoxious people.

---

63   Exhibiting at both these shows was quite an accomplishment. CADCON and CPM-83 were scheduled in the same week. We loaded all the company's computers into a station wagon, and Greg Lutz and I drove to Anaheim and set up the equipment for CADCON at the Disneyland Hotel. Greg, Mike Ford (who flew in late that night), and I shared a room at the Disneyland Hotel. We manned the booth for the show, then tore down everything, loaded it into the station wagon, and drove through the night back to Kensington (near Berkeley), where we dumped all of the equipment in Greg's garage at 4 A.M. The CPM-83 team arrived there shortly thereafter, retrieved the equipment from the garage, and set it up at CPM-83. That show opened the next day, staffed by a team including those who had just awakened after sleeping off CADCON.

64   We put the ten tons of garbage in the Red V.W. Microbus and ....

Lack of preparation and discussion before the shows sometimes caused people to feel they were making fools of themselves, as in trying to demonstrate what turned out to be an unimplemented feature. On the whole, we do much better than other exhibitors in giving out accurate information at our booth, but there's still room for improvement. It was suggested that everyone who will be working a show should take the whole of setup day off, so that we can do a tutorial on that day, either before or after setting up. There was no real consensus on whether we have reached the point of diminishing returns, where we're good enough at shows that there's no point in spending more effort that might be useful elsewhere.

We seem to need an AutoCAD Jockey. Like Computervision and other companies, we should find people who are especially good with AutoCAD and make them specialists in making the product look easy and impressive. Jockeys might be recruited from within the company or from end users. Even if they can't go around giving demonstrations, they can create drawings and set up demos for other people. This was agreed to be a good idea, but so far we lack anyone to take on the job.

An especially acute problem at shows is the taking of orders for products. At CPM-83 the mechanics of taking orders were haphazard — it was hard to find a clear space to write on or a place to file things — and we ended up with many undecipherable orders. The ideal solution would be to have one person doing nothing but taking orders; but it seems impossible to do that in a ten by ten booth.

There was agreement on some suggestions: All forms, manuals, VISA slips, etc., will be organized in neat, possibly color-coded boxes. If we have no other tutorial session before the show, there will at least be an indoctrination on the ordering procedures. There should be a special order form with "Take" and "Send" at the top to indicate whether the customer has taken delivery of what he bought. There should be a clipboard or something to guarantee a surface to fill out forms.

There was a time at CPM-83 when there was only one person at the booth. We must keep at least two people in the booth without fail, preferably three at a show full of thieves, like the Computer Faire (four is a crowd). This means that we should have four or five people at the show at any time.

Manpower

As mentioned before, the Autodesk project is going to Mike Riddle. Kern Sibbald will start taking over AutoCAD-80 when he returns from vacation. Duff Kurland will start doing AutoCAD-86 work and will investigate getting our documentation on a decent word processor, which might be Perfect Writer.[65]

Summary of Decisions

There have been manpower shifts as described above. AutoCAD-86 has a manager (Dan Drake), who should get all phone calls; the people doing technical work are to be left alone.

The advertising budget is an ad hoc $1,000 this month, to be regarded as an expenditure of working capital. A real budget will be allocated in a month or two.

There are specific policies for improving our handling of shows, in terms of coverage of the booth and handling of sales.

---

65 As opposed to Marinchip Word, which we had abandoned in favour of the wiles of WordStar. Perfect Writer proved less than its name implied, and was soon thrown over for MicroScript, then LaserScript, then GML/PC, and the saga continues.

Turning the Corner   *Summary of Decisions*   141

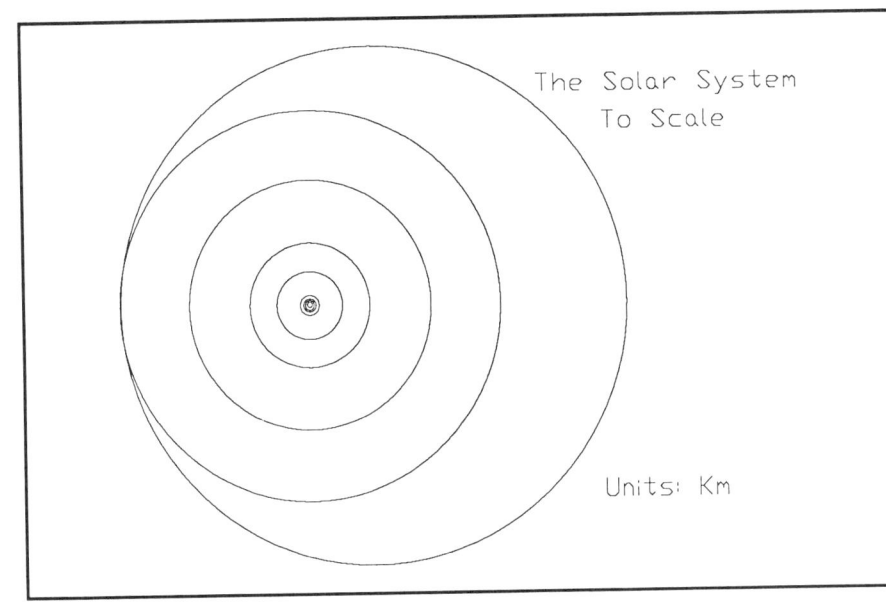

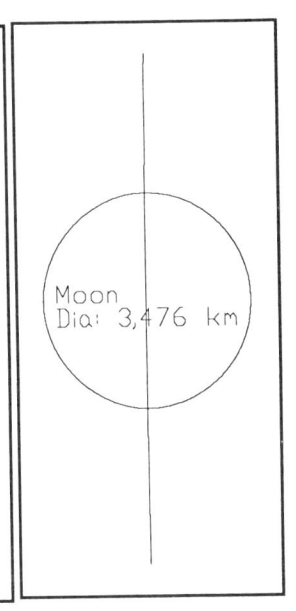

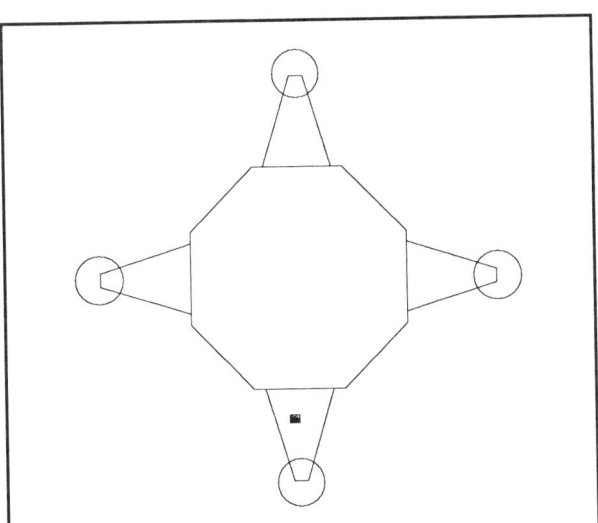

The Solar System drawing was our flagship demo of the resolution of our floating point database and formed the centrepiece of many of the demos we did for venture capitalists in 1983. It was also the very first drawing I ever did on AutoCAD-86. I drew it in one afternoon on a Z-100 that I had just gotten to work with AutoCAD-86 (my first work on that version of the product).

Getting Control

The March, 1983 meeting saw Autodesk rapidly evolving toward an operating company focused on the development and promotion of its hit product, AutoCAD. No regular minutes from the meeting exist — only Dan Drake's notes on what people agreed to do. Those tasks speak eloquently to the direction of the company.

The attached "Software Control Policies" was the first attempt to come to terms with the reality of quality control and effective product management of what was rapidly becoming a mass market product.

Odd Jobs From the March 6 Meeting

Dan Drake
1983 March 8

We've found several times that people come away from monthly general meetings with different ideas of who has volunteered to do what. We can't afford to discover these disagreements a month later at the next meeting; and the minutes, even if they come out on time, don't cover these matters conspicuously if at all.

This is an attempt to list all the little tasks that were allocated at the last meeting. It doesn't claim to be definitive, but it gives you something to disagree with, preferably to the relevant project manager, if you find yourself listed for the wrong task.

Odd Jobs

1. Odd Job List

Dan Drake will put out this odd job list on the Tuesday afternoon or Wednesday morning after each general meeting, if it seems to be doing any good.

2. Hewlett-Packard Contacts

Duff Kurland and Jack Stuppin will pursue contacts at HP to get us in touch with their plotter people. Dan Drake will do the same through GDL.

3. IGES

Duff Kurland will try to get the Interim Graphics Exchange Standard from NBS.

4. Computer Faire Setup

Dave Kalish, Mauri Laitinen, and Dan Drake will set up the booth on Thursday, March 17.

5. Computer Faire Co-ordination

Roxie Walker will publish a schedule of work assignments for the Faire. She will also set up the mechanisms for selling things and taking orders.

6. Ethernet Links

Dave Kalish will look into any plans that Apple and 3COM may have for supporting the Xerox protocol on Ethernet; we may decide to write such software if bigger people aren't already doing it.

7. Applescreen

Dave Kalish will get a 300 baud modem and get Autoscreen running on the Apple Softcard.

8. Burning the Boats

Everyone in the company who hasn't done it already will send Jack Stuppin a letter giving the conditions under which he's willing to go to work full-time for ADI: the earliest time possible, the minimum subsistence pay, confidence in ADI's continued cash flow, or whatever.

Software Control Policies

Dan Drake
Revision 1, 83/3/25

(This is a draft of a draft, on which I'm soliciting suggestions and arguments. In particular, it would be nice to get beta testing done without a six-week delay. Does anyone think I'm too paranoid about beta test?)

Now that ADI is beginning to get substantial sales, we need to face some of the business questions that can trip us up (unwise commitments, continual vacillation on decisions, etc.). Here are some of my ideas on policies that might save us some grief and indecision; they're inspired by thinking about AutoCAD-86, but it seems to me that they apply to any software.

First I'll give some of the motivations, then a list of ideas that I'd like to see agreed on.

Proprietary Rights

AutoCAD is (subject to a percentage royalty) the exclusive property of Autodesk, Inc. Those of us who wear two hats in order to make a living while building the corporation must keep this clearly in mind while wearing the consultant or dealer hat.

Quality Control

We've been determined from the first to uphold the highest standards of quality and reliability. Lacking capital and sufficient marketing staff, we have no other unique edge on the rest of the world.

There are only two or three people in the company with the experience of making a product that goes out into unknown places in the real world (as distinct from software for a service operation). I don't think we have anyone who has sent out a program in hundreds or thousands of copies as we plan to do. In this environment a little bug in a program can mean a little incremental update for vast numbers of customers, which will feel to us like a GM product recall.

Our testing procedures so far have not been rigorous enough. In the future, we need real, bona fide, beta testing. At best, this will have an effect on our product development time that will seem little short of disastrous; we need to make realistic plans that will keep us in the best case.

Proliferation

One of our most important plans is to put the software on every machine that will have any substantial sales, so that manufacturers will in effect have an investment in us and won't look promising to potential competitors. It's important to remember why we're doing this, so that we don't get off track. If a dealer lends us equipment for a conversion, we don't do the job as a friendly gesture, a speculation on selling a couple of dozen more copies, or even a service for a fee; we do it because a working version of the program may give us a shortcut through the manufacturer's bureaucracy, or at worst produce vast numbers of sales through many dealers.

Meanwhile, every conversion that's released for sale increases our support burden, and every commitment to do a conversion puts our credibility on the line.

Delegation

It's important for everyone to know who makes what decisions. It's not especially important to distinguish between the board of directors and the top management, since they're pretty much the same people; but we need a feel for what the board does and what it lets someone else worry about. I've tried to outline the level at which various decisions should be made.

Proposals

Any technical work that any Autodesk person does on AutoCAD is the property of Autodesk, Inc. The person doing such work is wearing an Autodesk hat and will be compensated by Autodesk's normal procedures.

All decisions on selling the product of such labor (e.g., whether, when, where, and how) belong to the company. Making such decisions is a property right: the "first refusal" provision of the employee agreement does not apply, insofar as the work is based on privileged access to Autodesk's intellectual property.

If the company decides to distribute a piece of work, it will sell to any qualified distributor or dealer who wants it. The only exception might be an exclusive distributorship agreement negotiated at arm's length; such decisions would never be delegated to the low level of a product manager or even a marketing manager.

When policy is to put software on lots of equipment, anyone involved with the product can and should talk to any interested supplier. After the first conversations, the company may decide to make a conversion for evaluation by the manufacturer. No one but the product manager (possibly under orders from above) can make this commitment, and no one should hint otherwise. Our credibility is on the line here.

When we've converted something, the supplier gets an evaluation copy. This will serve as a basis for negotiations on the possible distribution of the product. It must be absolutely clear to the supplier that we are in no way committed ever to release anything to the public. The marketing decision belongs to the company; what this means is that the marketing manager makes the decision with the agreement of the product manager, who will have to provide support.

Obviously, no one will pay us an engineering fee for a conversion without a commitment that we'll let him sell the product. The last paragraph doesn't apply if such a case ever arises.

It is standard policy that we will not support any piece of hardware unless we have a piece of that hardware on indefinite loan. Of course, we will never make a change that introduces a bug into something that worked before, any more than Jimmy Carter would ever lie to you; but we can't prove that a problem isn't our fault unless we can reproduce it first. Besides, as a practical matter, our good repute requires us to be able to reproduce problems that a user reports, and provide a correction, even though we are blameless.

People who are working on new features will be left alone as much as possible, because breaking their concentration squanders the only resource that we have in quantity. Before calling an implementor, consider whether someone else, such as a product manager or a salesman, could do as well. As for the release of a programmer's phone number to anyone outside the company, the general rule is simple: *no*. The handling of exceptions will be up to product managers. In the ACAD-86 game, the product manager is the only person whose phone number can be handed out without his prior explicit consent.

No change in software, however small, can be released for sale or even for beta test without clearance from the product manager. Any manager who does not constitute the entire project staff must work out procedures for source code control and distribute them in writing. (This will raise problems when someone overseas is making versions that change nothing but the language in which the messages are written.)

In AutoCAD-86, for example, there will be a clear distinction between a core section and device controllers. One programmer will have primary responsibility for the core code and will do integration and testing of any changes worked out by other people. When a new version is ready, it will be distributed in source and relocatable form to the various people in charge of device drivers, who will integrate their drivers with the supplied relocatable and do thorough testing. If this exposes a need for changes in the core source, the countdown stops while the change is worked out, integrated, and distributed to everyone for the next iteration.

Product managers must also work out plans for beta testing. We need some good ideas here, and we need to live up to them. Fortunately, the iterative integration process in the last paragraph can be overlapped to some extent with beta test.

It appears that the features freeze will be weeks before the release date. It will take a good deal of self discipline to avoid diddling the code as the testing cycle drags on.

The bulk of documentation work should be done, as we all know, at the beginning of a new development, not at the end. Whether we can afford to do this really right is an open question. In any case, the document will not be a last-minute panic project. The documenter will estimate how long the job is to take; the project will then be scheduled so that a draft will be ready when beta test begins. For final proofing there will be a mock camera-ready version two weeks before the release date.

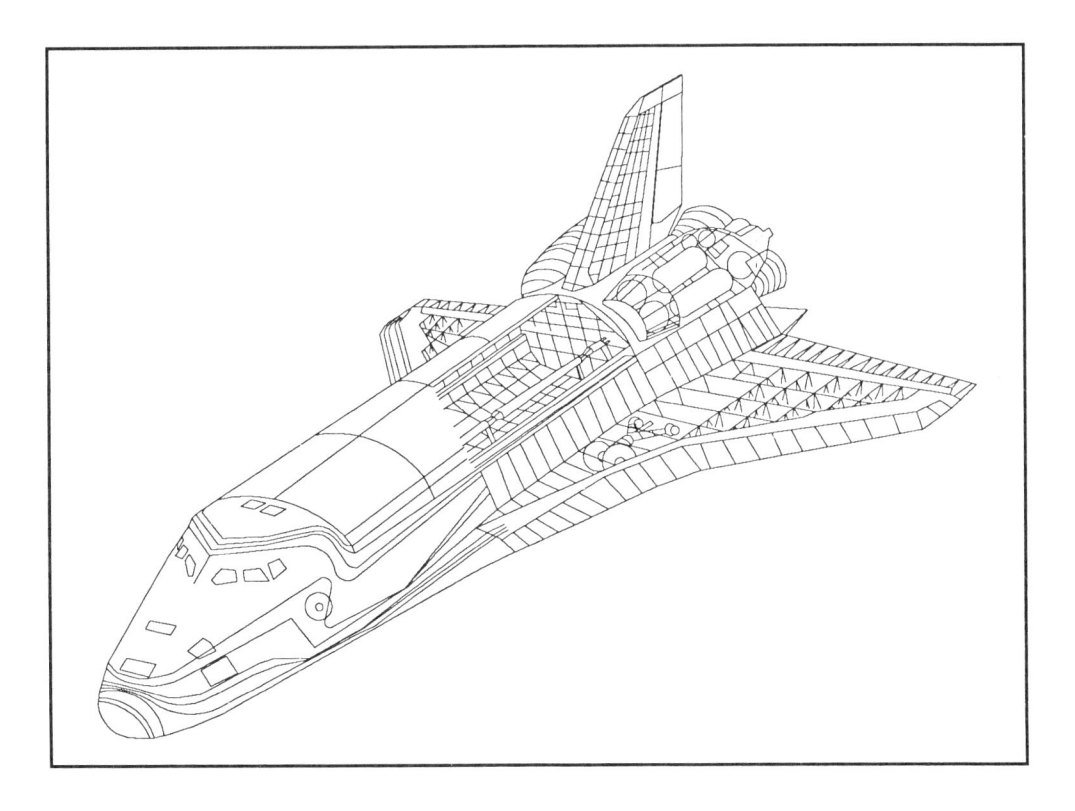

Several people attempted to use early releases of AutoCAD to make this beautiful drawing of the shuttle that graced our sample drawings disc for so long and appears in so many advertisements of display hardware for AutoCAD. This version, the one we finally used, was drawn by Sean O'Donnell.

Growing Pains

The June 1983 meeting was the first general meeting to include all of the Europeans who were actively developing and marketing our products. By that meeting we were clearly profitable and had generated more cash than twice the original investment in the company. Autodesk's stock value was clearly on the march, though nobody suspected how fast and how far it would go.

These notes, taken by Kern Sibbald, also reflect the inevitable growing pains inherent in turning a loose collection of programmers into a real operating company.

Autodesk, Inc.
June Monthly Meeting (June 5, 1983)

by Kern Sibbald
June 7, 1983

Introduction

I have volunteered to take notes of the monthly meetings and to distribute them to everyone with the following ground rules:

1. I'm going to spend near zero time editing and perfecting.
2. I'll write from the notes that I took — no tape recordings.
3. I'll try to complete it within 2 – 3 days and have it reviewed by at least one other person.
4. I'll mail it out to everyone the second Tuesday following the meeting.

Under these ground rules, please don't expect too much. I am interested in suggestions and feedback.

Attendees

The meeting was held in the cabana at Duff's condominium complex at 1:30. The following people attended: Lars Moureau, Richard Handyside, Rudolf Künzli, Mike Riddle, John Kern, Duff Kurland, Dave Kalish, Mauri Laitinen, Hal Royaltey, Greg Lutz, John Walker, Kern Sibbald, John Nagle, and Dan Drake.

Financial Report: John Walker

Due to the amount of financial activity lately, the report is approximate:

Assets

Capital Preservation	$115,000	(up 45,000 from last month)
Receivables	42,000	(7 days average age)

Liabilities

Salary for John Kern	????
Mike Riddle royalty	15,000
Mike Ford commission	15,000

To be more exact, some 370 invoices need to be processed.

Dan gave the following status report on setting up our books: Arthur Young has set up a chart of accounts and almost completed the books for our last fiscal year ending Jan 31. We show a tax loss of about $8000 which we can carry into fiscal 1983.[66] The cost of the accounting service is somewhat unknown (about $1000) because accountants are like lawyers, it is not proper to ask, one simply waits for the bill.[67] Jack Stuppin is, however, negotiating to get us the most for the least. Another 5 months of Autodesk accounting needs to be processed before we are up to date. We will be able to pay our taxes that are due on July 15. The accounting is structured to handle overseas sales.

Board of Directors Report

The cash flow will soon be sufficient to reimburse us for our expenses such as car mileage so *keep good records* if you want to get reimbursed. We are all cautioned about making commitments for the company over the telephone particularly regarding what equipment Autodesk will support. It is OK to indicate that we are

---

[66] If we had known the trick of capitalising our organisational costs, we could have shown a profit for that year, and thus for every year we existed. This is even more remarkable when you remember that in our first year we were only shipping products for a month.

[67] Gentlemen don't discuss money, I guess.

working on a machine, however. If you have a machine but don't have everything you need from the manufacturer to make it work, write a note and send it to Mike Ford. He will get you what you need.

Marketing Report: John Walker filling in for Mike Ford

Several people visited Digital Research in Monterey last week and found that they have machines everywhere and are running around like mad trying to get their software running on all of those machines. The main topic of conversation was apparently GSX, Digital Research's new CP/M graphics device interface. It looks like, for AutoCAD, it will provide a universal display driver and a way to integrate mouse drivers, but we will have to continue to write our own plotter drivers. GSX could solve most of our problems supporting so many devices and only costs $60.00. DR is also interested in a $200 drawing package which could possibly be a stripped down version of AutoCAD.

Valid Logic Systems is interested in AutoCAD. They have a very high resolution graphics device on a Unix based 68000. Keith talked to them and they agreed to send him a machine and pay a $2500 engineering fee. We hope to get TROFF (Typesetting Runoff) with it.

NCR has a machine on the way.

USI still wants 1000 copies of AutoCAD for evaluation and marketing (maybe?). However, they have not yet shipped any OptoMouses because of a bug in the production ROM. They seem to be finding their way out through cracks.

We are negotiating with a number of schools. U. of Idaho will buy one ACAD and get 9 more for developing a tutorial. U. of Arizona has 30 PC's and wants a site license; we are investigating.

Mike Ford has prepared a dealer contract that was circulated for comments at the meeting.

We have rewritten the end user license, which will be one sixth the size. It has been lifted from Victor; it is very nice.

The registration card is being modified to have the machine serial number on it and possibly the new license since it is so short.

We are pursuing a hardware lock for AutoCAD — seems like pure blue sky at this point.[68]

John is exploring a deal involving mapping archaeology that may lead to a write up of AutoCAD in *LIFE* magazine.[69]

Chuck Victory is putting together a 7 x 10 ad for *InfoWorld*. We are in the September issue of *PC World* in the directory under graphics.

We put on a very well received demo for the AIA (American Institute of Architects) in San Francisco.

We traded an AutoCAD to Victor for an 8087.

Reports from Europeans

Richard

He has given over 110 demos. AutoCAD has been well received at many shows. Approximately 60 dealers have been found; 50 of them have been to Richard's house. So far sales amount to 38 – 36 Sirius, 1 IBM, 1 Z80. Richard spoke at length about the different "real" users with quite a few well known names such as Ford Motor, Shell, British Royal, etc. He has had one and a half people helping him since January to answer the phone, etc. He is spending a lot of time on support problems. To keep our happy customers happy, he feels we must solve the REPEAT problems and develop several required new features. There is even one software house with their own CAD package that is now selling AutoCAD. A firm with 200 draftsmen is organizing a course to teach computer drafting with AutoCAD.

Lars

There is high interest in AutoCAD but few orders for several reasons. The users want the source code safeguarded in Sweden (against war, etc.); they will wait to see if it continues to be popular; they want a Swedish language version. Norway and Denmark will follow Sweden in sales. He has ordered 13 systems and 5 – 10

---

68 This was a gizmo where the program printed a number which you keyed into a little calculator-style gadget. It displayed a password, which you then typed into the program. Dumb idea; we didn't pursue it further.
69 It was this project that caused John Walker to waste endless hours on Otrona versions of AutoCAD-80 *and* AutoCAD-86.

demos and projects 100 copies by the end of the year. He says the first year will be the hardest until it is an established product. One company alone is talking about 50 Z80 copies. AutoScreen is hard to sell because WordStar took the market.

Rudolf

The French language manual will be ready in 2 weeks, the Italian version is in translation and should be finished in about 1 month.

DEC Rainbow promises to be a big seller in Europe because of its support.

We have had a number of very good press releases including one (not yet published?) by a German CAD magazine with a circulation of 200,000.

There were some good war stories about transporting equipment across borders for the Hannover Fair which was attended by Richard, Lars, and Rudolf and had 500,000 people in 10 days.

Domestic Sales Summary

400 approx. shipped. 370 to SunFlex as of June 2.[70]

Corporate Status Report

Lars' option has been signed and the certificate will be issued soon. We are trying to set up a European company wholly owned by the U.S. company. Jack is heading up this effort.

Operational Report: John Kern

Our office is now functional and is located at 150 Shoreline, Bldg B, Room 20 (Mill Valley). The phone number is (415) 331–0356. We are looking for a larger one so we can do demos there. 95 – 97% of the calls are handled by John Kern; the others go to Dan or Duff. All Victor disks are made there. IBMs are made at Mike's house for now but soon we will have another IBM and make disks in the office. We have a new perfect-bound Victor manual — very slick. John Kern turned around 3200 bingo cards in the first 3 weeks. We need complicated good looking professional drawings done on AutoCAD to help sales to architects. Office Staffing — John Kern full time, Kathy Marcelius half time, Jane Kern part time, Gladys Sibbald part time.

---

[70] Since the SunFlex versions were all Victor, Victor sales accounted for more than 90% of our business to date.

Customer Support

We will talk to Kevin[71] soon. Jack Stuppin has put us in touch with a woman who is a prospective customer support rep. We have a job opening for a customer support representative for $1500/month. If anybody is interested now is the time to apply.

AutoCAD-86 Status Report

The conversions are progressing nicely. John Walker and Kern Sibbald are working on the CompuPro. The DMS 5000 will show in Texas on the 6th. Greg is working on a configurator, which was called a "crash project to keep us from going under".[72] He is approaching the beta test stage. A lot was said here about the configurator. We need to get the Victor version running on MS-DOS[73]. Mauri has the Eagle technical documentation for the Eagle now and hopes to get something going. Duff is working on the NEC; he has the display driver part working and gave us a demo after the meeting. Dave has been working on the TI and has completed the code and must now integrate it into AutoCAD. He is looking for a debugger. John Walker finished the Z100 3 hours before Mike left for NCC[74]. Richard has a working HP[75] driver.

AutoCAD-80

John finished the HP[76] driver. He has shipped a bunch of ACAD-80's and sold 10 last month. He would like to drop support of the Z80 version but finds it difficult with several stories of orders of 500 possible.

The Digital Research C looks like a winner.[77] We will get it late this month.[78]

---

71 O'Lone
72 Until this project was completed, a different AutoCAD had to be built for every combination of display, pointing device, and plotter. Really!
73 It was initially done under CP/M-86.
74 This was his first tilt with MS-DOS.
75 Plotter. For many more months, we supported only Houston Instrument plotters.
76 Plotter.
77 It wasn't.
78 We didn't.

AutoCAD-68K

No floating point now or likely to come in the C we have from Digital Research. However, there is a full C due in the fall from another vendor.[79]

Prometrix

For $15K we can buy 2% of this company which reportedly has 7 orders for a machine that finds defects in chips??? (I was in the head when this was discussed). John is interested to get input about this venture. It won't happen immediately.[80]

Company Problems

The original company is dead. We are now a classic small company with one product rather than the imagined company developing many products. In any case, we must now act like a real company to succeed. We discussed the fact that it would not be possible to run a real company by getting everyone's consensus. After a lot of discussion, it seemed like everybody agreed that for operational decisions such as hiring and firing and getting facilities, etc. the decisions must be made by the board of directors and the officers as they would in a normal company. However, strategic decisions such as bringing someone new into the company as an owner, or going public with the stock or other such major decisions should be discussed by everyone. The biggest complaint seemed to be the lack of communications about decisions rather than the fact that the decisions were made or how decisions were made. Hopefully notes like these and more participation in the company as it prospers will help.

We need to formalize the bug reporting process. Dave Kalish volunteered to keep an error log and to give it to Kern monthly for distribution.

Kern

---

[79] This referred to a CP/M-68K version to run on the CompuPro 68000 CPU. Nothing ever came of this version.

[80] It never did. They made a device to characterise silicon wafers and find defects. This is how we met Dick Elkis.

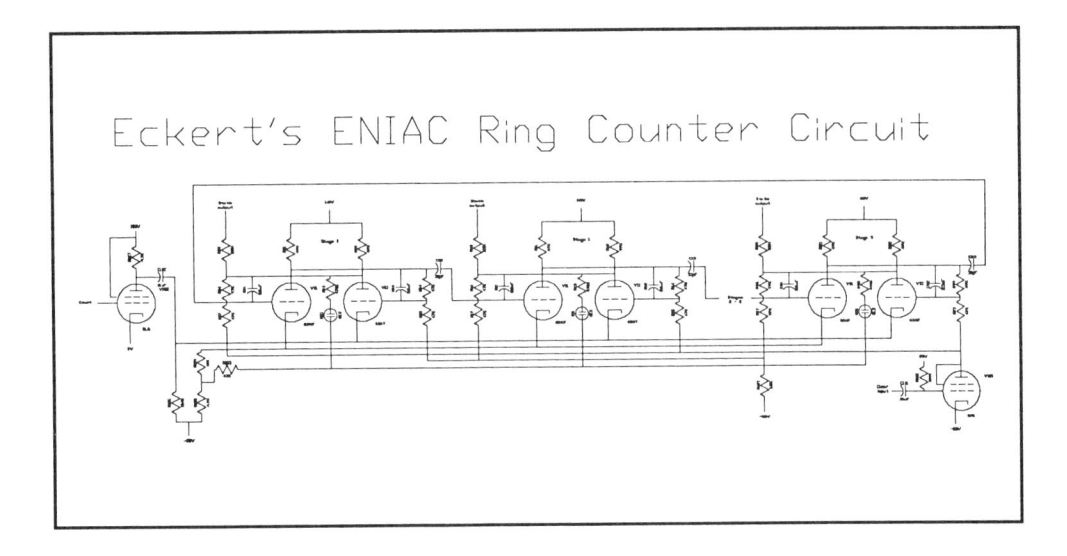

I made this drawing of the Eniac ring counter circuit to test the new Attribute facility prior to the release of AutoCAD 2.0 and to serve as the testbed for the sample attribute processing BASIC programs I was writing for inclusion in the AutoCAD manual. This was the first drawing I recall doing on an IBM PC.

Crisis Letter

Everybody involved with Autodesk from its inception has their own list of mental milestones passed on the road from the organisation meeting to where the company is today. The introduction of AutoCAD at COMDEX in 1982 is a key point in everybody's mind. To me, this letter marks an inflection point in the company's trajectory which is just as significant. I believe it marks the transition from an amorphous group of programmers working on many different ideas to a serious, professional company composed of full-time people, dedicated to making its star product, AutoCAD, the technological and sales leader, and making the most of the tremendous opportunity created by its enormous initial success.

This letter marks the time when the change began, but the letter did not cause the change. The transformation of the company was wrought by numerous people, working long, largely uncompensated hours, at daunting and unfamiliar tasks, as the workload only piled higher. Progress could be measured only by realising in those precious few moments available for reflection that the workload which was now crushing us to the point of collapse had, in fact, tripled compared to the workload crushing us three months before. So things had to be getting better.

And they were — and still are. Almost two years to the day after this letter was written, Autodesk completed its initial public stock offering; after that offering, the market valuation of the company was in excess of 70 million dollars. Three years after this letter, Autodesk was named the "Number One Hot Growth Company in America" by Business Week, and in the very next year Autodesk became the first company ever to win that award twice. The day this letter was written, the value of the company was about $200,000. Precisely four years later, the company's market value was in excess of $500,000,000.

Autodesk, Inc.
150 Shoreline Highway, B/20
Mill Valley, CA 94941

June 21, 1983

Dear Autodesk Shareholder,

I am writing you this letter because I feel that our company is in a very deep crisis, and I want to share with you my feeling of urgency about the problems we face and the actions we must take to resolve them. I hope to communicate to you how critical it is that you act immediately to help save the company and your investment in it.

Today, Autodesk faces probably the deepest crisis in its short existence. We have encountered already many of the problems that all small companies face in the process of growth. We have solved them all, since people involved in the day to day operation of the company were able to focus their efforts on each problem as it arose and track it until it was resolved.

Today, Autodesk resembles the legendary one hoss shay more than a car with one flat tire. Because of our success in marketing AutoCAD, and in stirring up interest in dealers and OEMs, and gaining publicity and reviews of the software, and in closing the marketing deal with Sun-Flex, each single segment of the company is overloaded to the point of collapse. Our technical department has produced and delivered to the field only two features which were on the wish list as of November 1982 (dimensioning and plotter configuration). We have released *no* major new host machine versions since the introduction of the package (although we have introduced additional displays for the IBM and Z-80 versions).

Our marketing department is overloaded to the point that we cannot return all the calls from people who desperately want to do business with us, no less plan a coherent advertising campaign or exert the effort required to make a show work best for us. Our brochures and promotional material are among the most amateurish in the business.

Our front office and production department are overloaded so badly that customers are giving up on Autodesk after trying to get through on the phone for periods of 4 hours. We cannot pack the orders while the phone is ringing, and cannot take orders if it is off the hook. We have not had the time to establish a coherent inventory control system so that we do not run out of critical materials needed to fill orders.

We do not have a customer support group. The service we have given our customers has been very spotty. The service we have given Sun-Flex, our largest base load customer, has been very poor at times.

We are still a long way away from getting caught up on our accounting for the business to date, and longer still from implementing a true automatic accounting system. Thus we still have no idea how much money we have made on our sales to date, and no real idea whether we are making or losing money selling, say, a demo disc.

We have no business plan, even an informal one. We have no budgets for departments, and no way to coherently authorise expenditures or to hire people. The management has not been given a mandate to hire people with stock options, or to in other ways commit the company's assets without fear of recriminations and time lost in argument.

This is a prescription for disaster. This company may be out of business within 60 days.

While we have been sitting dead in the water, others have been introducing their CAD packages. The article in *PC World* which discusses AutoCAD also describes "The Drawing Processor", which compares very favorably with AutoCAD, and has several wish list features AutoCAD lacks. At the PC Faire last weekend, a new product "P-CAD" was introduced. Running on an IBM PC in dual screen mode, it runs quite a bit faster than ACAD, has a very nice menu and submenu feature, and in general looks like a strong competitor. It is priced at $1200. Perusing the 6 page, 4 color, illustrated brochure, one is struck by the appearance on the cover of a Sun-Flex Touch Pen and "CAD-PAD", which is a product under development which Sun-Flex *has not even given us for evaluation*. Clearly Sun-Flex is in touch with these people and negotiating for a better deal than with Autodesk.

And Sun-Flex is the source of the stream of revenue which pays our salaries, allows us to expand our operation, and make commitments to people to come to work for this company on a full time basis. *If we lose it at this point, we have had it.*

So what do we do?

Well, we can give up. In fact, viewed from the outside, there is the strong perception that that is what we've already done. But I'd like to consider the alternative.

This is the fulcrum, the crisis point, the first "crunch". Your actions, and our collective actions, taken now, have an enormously magnified effect 6 months, 2 years, or 10 years in the future. If we go on as a business as usual operation, or as passive shareholders, we can be guaranteed that the number of stock options we own will not be a source of worry in the future — an option to buy stock at $1 loses a lot of its gloss when the underlying stock is selling for $0.

This is the time to neglect your job. This is the time to take that leave of absence from the foundry and work for Autodesk. Spend that long awaited vacation in front of the terminal. This is the time to tell the boss you've got cholera and take a month off. Let the plants die, leave the dog with a 55 gallon barrel of kibble and work around the clock for Autodesk. If you have skills as a programmer, use them — if you need any resources, machines, peripherals, software tools, coercion, let me know and *they will be provided*. We must get our OEM conversions done and our wish list — the entire wish list — implemented.

If you have management skills, offer to take over AutoCAD project management tasks — there are many. If your skills are in general management, finish our business plan, write job descriptions and interview people, and help us budget the spending of that wad of money we need to spend to make Autodesk a winner.

Or, when your company is in its time of dire need, you can go on putting in your hours faithfully, or maybe shaving a bit here and there. There are a lot of good movies around this summer, and it would be a pain to miss one. This is how you change from being a principal in the company to a stockholder.

Move to Mill Valley for a month (all expenses paid). Spend a week in the center of the cyclone at 150 Shoreline. Help write copy for our advertising campaign. Coordinate the ad agency design efforts. Help Mike Ford return calls to prospects.

Write our tutorial on AutoCAD. Work with the people we've already identified who want to develop shape libraries. Help me read these tons of competitive product manuals and design the wish list features. Get the Sony running, "I hear they sell well".

The people who make the all-out effort at this pivotal time will be the people who form the cadre who will run the company, if successful, for the next several decades. Those who "can't", "won't".

The management of this company will exercise its legal obligation to deploy the assets of the company so as to best ensure the success of the company. This means that we will spend what we feel we need to purchase outside services for those items we cannot do in-house. We will bring new employees into the company as we see fit, with compensation packages tailored to their individual requirements. This may include stock options granted at the current market value of the stock or above. To do otherwise would be to jeopardise the future of the company.

This is not the time to worry about your share of stock. This is not the time to agonise about how many options you got last time, or how many you will get the next. Today isn't the day for saying "we should" or "we ought to"; it's the day to say "I will", and then do it. Anybody who can spend any amount of time in recrimination or worry about anything other than our critical, immediate, problems, is not somebody working full time for this company. Let's defer the worries about conflicts of interest for a while. Let's not bitch about the other guy's royalty deal. Let's not say "I won't work with him" or "I won't work on that". Let's try to put a moratorium on "what's in it for me" reasoning.

Why? Because if we don't, nothing's going to be in it for anybody. Your investment in this company, your options, and your warrants, will be of no value except as wallpaper. All your work for the company will have been in vain. All the risks you took to join the company will have been for nothing.

Those who participate will know who they are. They can be assured of sharing in the prosperity of the company, if that is the result. Those who do not will know who they are. They will understand the difference between a "stockholder" and a "principal". For most people in this company there has never before been such a pivotal point in their business careers: the opportunity to exert oneself and gain the experience and track record to write your own ticket. Or to be an employee forever.

But it isn't all gloom and doom. The promise of this company is as bright as it ever has been. We are sitting in a window of opportunity, and if we can seize the moment, and act with a unity of purpose to make the company a winner, we can make our company one of the success stories of the 1980's. We have manufacturers breaking down our door to get us to put our product on their machines. We have the first product of our kind in the marketplace, and the best, and we have the expertise in house to add to our product all the things that the "big CAD" systems do.

Digital Research and Microsoft didn't succeed because they had access to technological breakthroughs. They made it because they had the audacity to put "things only the big computers can do" onto "toys", and then the business savvy to build on their initial success and become industry leaders. We've had the audacity. We've had the initial success.

We can do it. But only by fully mobilising the resources in the company to achieve what we must get done. And to do that, you must act. Now. Before you punch holes in this and file it in the Autodesk binder. Before you check the *TV Guide* to see what's on tonight. *Now!* Run to the window, throw it open, stick your head out and scream at the top of your lungs, "I'm going to make Autodesk a winner, and I'm going to work my ass off to get there". Then pick up the phone. Call me. Or Dan Drake, Mike Ford, John Kern, or Jack Stuppin. Then tomorrow we'll start building this company toward the next factor of 10 in growth.

Only you can do it. The full time people in this company are working at or beyond capacity. We need help, your help, or we will fail. And our company will fail. This is the moment. Seize it.

I never said it would be easy.

Sincerely,

John Walker

Business Plans and a Way to Organize

The organisational problems alluded to in the notes from the June meeting continued to plague the company. It was clear that we could no longer function free-form. We needed a structure to organise all of the tasks that were underway, and a budget to help us deploy our growing, but still meager, financial resources.

I wrote this proposal in an attempt to specify a structure that approximated how the company was, in fact, already operating. It was never formally adopted, but what actually happened was not very different from what was envisioned herein. This is not a "business plan" in the venture capitalist sense; instead it was intended as a plan to develop the business, not raise money for it.

Autodesk, Inc. Business Plan

by John Walker — June 23, 1983 – Revision 3

It is my feeling that the problems that beset this company are of such urgency that immediate action is required, with or without an agreed formal business plan. Herein I will discuss the actions I see as needed. I make no claim that I have prepared the requisite forecasts to back up the figures I use — they are pure seat of the pants numbers based on my gut feelings of where we are and what we can risk.

Organisation

I want to immediately reorganise the company in the following divisions:

- Marketing Division — Mike Ford, Manager
- Operations Division — John Kern, Manager
- Technical Division — Dan Drake, Manager

These divisions are coequal (listed in alphabetical order[81]) and all report to the president. Each division manager shall have the authority to disburse his budget (see below) as he sees fit. This budget may be used for compensation of existing personnel to obtain additional work, or to bring in outside personnel. Approval of stock offerings to new personnel will be at the discretion of the board.

Budgeting

We have to start spending our money to establish this company in the marketplace. The following is my proposed monthly budgets for the above-designated divisions. These are based on seat of the pants "wing it" insight.

Marketing Division	$14,000
Operations Division	$10,500
Technical Division	$10,500

These figures were calculated on the basis of exhaustion of our in-the-bank capital in 4 months assuming no additional revenue from sales. The budget I propose would make me extremely unhappy were I the manager of each of the above divisions. Thus, I claim it is close to reality.

The above numbers also closely equal my estimate for the net revenue from sales if we assume that Sun-Flex takes as many systems as they have taken over the last three months, and that other sales stay equal. We can augment the above figures by spending capital or forecasting increasing sales, but I would be uncomfortable with an increase beyond 25%.

I assume that any increase in sales over the next 90 days will be used to increase the above budgets proportionally. I am open to the establishment of a separate customer support division, but as there is nobody to manage it currently, now isn't the time to do it.

Existing salaries are to be paid from the above budgets. The technical budget will pay for Greg and Duff's salaries, and the operations budget will cover John and Jane Kern, and Kathy Marcelius. The royalty payments to Mike Riddle and Mike Ford[82] are assumed to be subtracted directly from sales and are not included in these budget figures.

The technical budget assumes that we can continue to get the machines to develop on for free and that we can do effective work in that environment. If this is

---

81 Do you detect any signs of friction?
82 Actually, Mike's payments were the commission on sales agreed to in January, 1983.

not correct, we would have to steal from the Operations or Marketing budgets for equipment.

The marketing budget allows for extensive advertising and additional personnel. If the advertising can be arranged on a co-op basis, or the personnel can be recruited on a commission basis, funds from this account may be reassigned to the others.

Priorities — Marketing Division

First priority for the marketing division is the recruitment of additional marketing personnel. Within the marketing division I place the receptionist/order-taker function, as well as the customer support function. We need to have our phone answered reliably within 3 rings within business hours. We need to have a trained customer person on call at all times. We must authorise expenditures to achieve these goals. Further, we need an additional full-time marketing person, whether reporting to Mike Ford or coequal with a defined territory. Ideally we can recruit this person on a stock+commission basis. Next, we basically need to take the money left over and turn it over to Chuck Victory with the instructions "create us an ad campaign". We don't have the resources internally to do this advertising function, so we have to buy it, regardless of the price. Perhaps upon her return, Roxie Walker could be attached to the marketing department and given responsibility for development and execution of the advertising, show, and promotion campaign, a function she has done for us in the past. We must establish ourselves as the industry leader, with brochures, advertisements, and point of sale material that confirms our position.

Priorities — Operations Division

The operations division is immediately authorised to obtain a larger office facility and telephone and support resources as required from the assigned budget. The personnel to handle the additional telephone lines are understood to come from the Marketing budget.

Priorities — Technical Division

The Technical Division manager is empowered to spend his budget as he sees fit to accomplish the technical goals of the company. These include the completion of the "wish list" development goals, and the conversions to various hardware products. The manager of the Technical Division is empowered to hire outside personnel or to cut special deals with Autodesk shareholders as required to complete the development agenda.

Technical Project Management

We need a way to go outside for technical tasks without causing dissension and salary bidding wars internally. Perhaps the answer might be to simply take the wish list (or conversion list), and price each item on it (along, of course, with a completion date based on the estimation of the project manager). These items would be offered internally to the stockholders, who could sign up to do them and receive payment according to the scale. (This pay would presumably be in lieu of salary for those on salary.) The residue of unassigned projects could, at the discretion of the technical division manager, and constrained by the budget, be contracted out to outside programmers at the same price scale.

Reporting to the technical project manager are the AutoCAD-86 product manager (Dan Drake) and the AutoCAD-80 product manager (John Walker). The technical project manager allocates resources among the projects.

Salary Scales

The managers of the respective divisions must be in a position to offer stockholders full-time employment, or to bring in additional people. These decisions must be based on sound business practices based on the budget available to get the job done. I propose that each manager strike the best deal possible with each person, including compensation in stock or options if that seems acceptable (all stock offers having to be approved by the board, per my reading of our bylaws). I personally will take the heat from the existing employee/shareholders and handle any requisite renegotiations with them.

Proposed Autodesk Organization

The manpower and management crisis that became manifest in June of 1983 prompted many people in the company to suggest means for resolving it. Kern Sibbald submitted the following plan for reorganising the company and making the leap directly from our loosely-coupled mode of operation to full-time professional management.

This plan essentially anticipated all of the development in the company's management through November 1986. One can only wonder how much more smooth the company's development would have been and how much more success would have accrued had we found the courage to take these steps when Kern proposed them in 1983 rather than piecemeal over the next three and a half years.

Proposed Autodesk Organization

by Kern Sibbald — July 4, 1983

Recently there have been several Autodesk Business Plans or Organizational structures submitted. These are a very necessary part of a solid business, and I am in general agreement with the plans submitted to date. I have taken those plans, carefully considered the ideas in them, and added a number of ideas of my own. Only by being completely honest with you do I feel that I can present my concerns of the company direction and my proposed solutions, so I apologize in advance to those who may feel offended with my remarks.

Problems

I agree with John Walker that our company is beset with serious problems. However, I would say that it is a result of our spectacular success rather than a failing of our company. AutoCAD is very successful, and Autodesk has tremendous people skills and resources to draw on, but we are not making effective use of the resources that we have. For example, neither of our two most valuable resources, John Walker and Dan Drake, are available full time for working on AutoCAD. John seems to be spending much of his time on trivial matters and has complained that he cannot get off the telephone. His Marinchip business continues to occupy some of his valuable time. The situation for Dan seems to be similar. If we could spring John and Dan free from nontechnical work and outside pressures, they would produce four times the output that we could gain by hiring any other two individuals.

Out of necessity, we have begun to hire people to fill critical needs. But, we must attempt to hire those who have contributed the most to the company first. At the same time we must take care to define our needs in terms of job descriptions and only then hire someone to fill that job rather than make a job to fit a particular individual. Once a person is on board, we should make every effort to fit the work to the person rather than the person to the job. This will produce much happier and more productive employees. But fitting the job to the person should not be done when initially hiring.

Because of the constant bickering, I often feel that we have little sense of purpose and direction. This is in part due to our unusual problems of wide geographic dispersion of our founders and primary work force. Consequently, to survive, our company will need to have communications that are better than most companies, yet our communications among each other are far from adequate even within a less geographically spread company. I view our problems as a crisis in management. This company owes its existence and the development of its only product to John, and we should never forget that. John Walker is an absolute genius in computers. He has led us through the early stages of the company, but now more than ever, his skills are needed urgently in enhancing our existing software and developing new software. His abilities are hampered by the trivia and details of a rapidly growing company, and we are deprived of his most needed skills.

Solutions

To develop into a major multi-million dollar company that we all envision, Autodesk needs additional management skills. I have prepared a proposed corporate structure and preliminary job descriptions for five key individuals that I feel will address the problems stated above. Most of these positions are already filled with qualified individuals; for other positions there are individuals within Autodesk who are qualified; and there is probably at least one position that will have to be filled by someone outside Autodesk. This structure may seem like a big unnecessary leap from our current structure to some of you. I agree, but I cannot imagine how we will get the job of running this company done without it. Each and every one of these positions is essential. Judging by the response to the previous proposals, I expect the only objections to my proposal to be to the two new positions (CEO and Finance & Administration). Consequently, I will discuss only those positions but briefly. First, the CEO position is needed primarily to offload John and Dan. With the structure that I have proposed with the CEO reporting to the board, John and Dan will continue their leadership role in the company but be freed of the daily trivia. His primary tasks would be to promote our company philosophies, improve our company communications, and offload John and Dan by handling the daily running of the company. The Finance & Administration position is equally important since his primary tasks would be to get the administrative parts of the company going (accounting, budgeting, policies, etc.), and more importantly to prepare our business plan and financing. These are essential if we are going to get venture capital or go public and sell stock (the only way we are going to become millionaires). Although, the F&A job may not be critical today, I strongly recommend that we find someone now so that he will be thoroughly familiar with the company when his services are critical.

Proposed Structure

The structure that I am proposing looks like this:

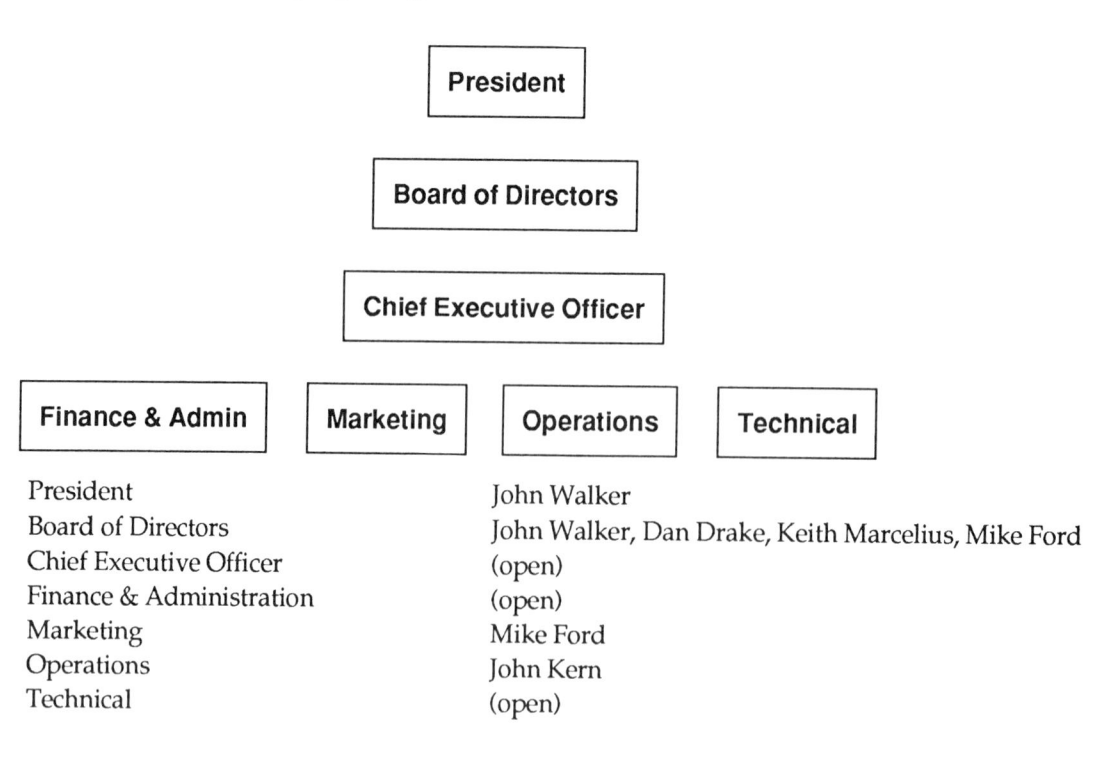

```
                    ┌─────────────┐
                    │  President  │
                    └─────────────┘
                  ┌─────────────────┐
                  │ Board of Directors │
                  └─────────────────┘
                ┌───────────────────────┐
                │ Chief Executive Officer │
                └───────────────────────┘
┌──────────────┐ ┌──────────┐ ┌──────────┐ ┌──────────┐
│Finance & Admin│ │ Marketing│ │Operations│ │ Technical│
└──────────────┘ └──────────┘ └──────────┘ └──────────┘
```

President   John Walker
Board of Directors   John Walker, Dan Drake, Keith Marcelius, Mike Ford
Chief Executive Officer (open)
Finance & Administration (open)
Marketing   Mike Ford
Operations   John Kern
Technical   (open)

Recommendations

1. That the board of directors approve the company structure and job descriptions presented here.

2. The board of directors proceed to immediately fill the CEO position

and turn the job of finding suitable candidates for the other two positions over to the CEO, who will in turn make recommendations for approval by the board.

3. That none of the five senior management serve on the board of directors. This would require Mike Ford to resign from the board and a replacement be found. I recommend that we obtain someone who is not a shareholder in Autodesk (possibly a banker).

4. Provide economic incentives for John Walker and Dan Drake to close Marinchip.

5. Reduce our need for part time employees by replacing them with full time employees over the next several months.

As a final note, the job descriptions attached should be considered preliminary since I have probably not included all functions, and some functions listed under one manager may be appropriate under another.

Job Descriptions

Chief Executive Officer (CEO)

Job Title: CEO
Grade: Full time
Reports to: Board of Directors

Job Description:
Acts as chief executive officer of Autodesk, Inc. and as such is responsible for overall health of Autodesk, Inc. Under broad operating guidelines from the board of directors assumes the full responsibility for keeping Autodesk, Inc. a profitable corporation.

Job Responsibilities:
Plans, directs, coordinates, and controls the daily operation of Autodesk through the four division managers. Exercises the responsibility for preparation of all Autodesk budgets, submits these budgets to the board of directors for approval, and monitors expenditures against the budget. Directs the development of and approves standards and procedures. Responsible for development of Autodesk personnel policies and obtaining approval from the board of directors. Provides board of directors with monthly status report and detailed quarterly financial reports. Assumes responsibility for all aspects of daily operation of Autodesk including hiring, firing of employees, determination of employees' salaries within salary guidelines approved by the board, organizational structure, staffing within

approved budgets, approving expense reports. Promotes the Autodesk company philosophy of "Excellence in Computer Software".

Job Qualifications:

- Prior management experience, preferably in a high-technology startup company.
- Demonstrated written and oral communication skills.
- Ability to provide leadership to a diverse group of people.
- Ability to handle multiple simultaneous tasks and to function well under pressure.
- Working knowledge of developing, maintaining and supporting computer software.
- Experience formulating objectives, standards, and procedures.
- Knowledge of negotiation and administration of contracts and legal aspects of a corporation.
- Working knowledge and experience developing budgets and using cost control techniques.
- Experience managing and evaluating technical and supervisory personnel in a data processing environment.

Manager of Finance and Administration Division

Job Title: Finance and Administration Manager
Grade: Full time
Reports to: CEO

Job Description:

Responsible for all aspects of Autodesk finance and administration. Reports on a daily basis to CEO and maintains frequent contact with other division managers.

Job Responsibilities:

Responsible for developing and implementing financial and administrative procedures such as: payroll, bookkeeping, insurance, budget and cost control, personnel policies, accounting functions, procurement procedures, contracts, inventory management and control procedures, security of facilities, legal protection of Autodesk software rights, financial reporting, strategic planning, obtaining appropriate financing, developing the Autodesk business plan. Develops budgeting methodology and aids other division managers in preparing their budgets and quarterly reports. Consolidates budgets from division managers on a quarterly basis or more often as needed for submittal to CEO. Monitors division managers actual cost and recoveries versus budgeted cost and recoveries and prepares monthly reports for submittal to CEO. Prepares comprehensive Autodesk financial reports quarterly. Ensures that taxes and other payments are made in a timely manner to all government agencies. Responsible for maintaining and publishing all software documentation in coordination with the other division managers. Responsible for annual salary survey to ensure that Autodesk compensation structure is competitive with the computer software industry. Publishes monthly report to stockholders. Provides adequate written communication to keep all Autodesk employees and stockholders appropriately informed.

Job Qualifications:
- Prior experience developing budgets.
- Knowledge of computerized cost control and accounting systems.
- Demonstrated written and oral communication skills.
- Knowledge of negotiation and administration of contracts and legal documents.
- Experience formulating objectives, standards, and procedures.

Manager of Marketing Division

Job Title: Marketing Manager
Grade: Full time
Reports to: CEO

Job Description:
- Responsible for all aspects of Autodesk sales and marketing activities. Reports on a daily basis to CEO and maintains frequent contact with other division managers.

Job Responsibilities:
Responsible for sales, advertising, customer support, marketing research. Prepares marketing budget on a quarterly basis or more often as need for submittal to CEO. Prepares monthly sales forecast and identifies deviations from approved budget. Prepares sales and advertising plans and submits to CEO for approval. Maintains close contact with operations manager to coordinate planned sales, inventory, mass mailings, etc. Hires, trains, and provides supervision to

telephone sales employees. Develops and submits sales incentive programs to CEO for approval. Maintains close contact with manager of technical division to coordinate release of new software and to provide customer satisfaction and quality assurance feedback. Responsible for providing support for end users. Recruits, trains, and supports dealers for Autodesk software. Develops OEM contacts with hardware manufacturers and software houses for Autodesk software.

Job Qualifications:

- Prior marketing experience, in a high-technology company, preferably in a startup situation.
- Demonstrated written and oral communication skills.
- Demonstrated ability to create innovative sales incentive programs.
- Demonstrated ability to hire and manage a geographically diverse sales organization.
- Demonstrated ability to make contacts with large hardware companies that are likely hosts for Autodesk software.

Manager of Operations Division

Job Title: Operations Manager
Grade: Full time
Reports to: CEO

Job Description:

Responsible for all aspects of Autodesk manufacturing and operations. Reports on a daily basis to CEO and maintains frequent contact with other division managers.

Job Responsibilities:

Responsible for manufacturing, shipping, receiving, distribution, courier service, mass mailings, bingo card responses, maintaining a customer database, facilities, and inventory control. Prepares operations budget on a quarterly basis or more often as need for submittal to CEO. Prepares a monthly status report identifying deviations from approved budget. Maintains close contact with marketing manager and technical manager to coordinate planned sales, inventory, mass mailings, etc. Hires, trains, and provides supervision to office employees. Maintains close contact with manager of technical division to coordinate release of new software and appropriate inventory levels. Responsible for stocking and providing supplies to all Autodesk employees. Orders all equipment and supplies for Autodesk and Autodesk employees. Responsible for all incoming mail and maintaining answering and message services for all Autodesk employees. Responsible for paying all invoices. Recruits, trains, and supervises all office employees.

Job Qualifications:
- Demonstrated written and oral communication skills.
- Demonstrated initiative to solve operational and manufacturing problems.
- Prior experience managing an office environment.
- Ability to maintain good working relations with people of diverse skills.
- Ability to work well under critical deadline presures.

Manager of Technical Division

Job Title: Technical Manager
Grade: Full time
Reports to: CEO

Job Description:
Responsible for all aspects of technical software development and support. Reports on a daily basis to CEO and maintains frequent contact with other division managers.

Job Responsibilities:
Responsible for all aspects of Autodesk software products. This includes: software development, preliminary documentation, source code control, quality assurance, software maintenance, error tracking and reporting, software standards and guidelines, hardware support, software release, implementation of Autodesk software on new hardware, technical user support, and new software product research and development. Prepares technical division budget on a quarterly basis or more often as needed for submittal to CEO. Prepares a monthly status report identifying deviations from approved budget and progress on software development projects. Maintains close contact with other division managers to coordinate release of new software and documentation.

Job Qualifications:

- Demonstrated written and oral communication skills.
- Prior successful experience managing large software development projects.
- Demonstrated ability to manage technical personnel.

A Company Clearly on the Rise

Sales continued to build and the July meeting reviewed the progress of a company clearly on the rise. Focus had shifted entirely to AutoCAD, more and more founders were coming onto the payroll, and the negotiation of sales and marketing agreements came to the fore as we tried to secure a stable base of revenue without compromising our freedom of action in the future.

This meeting marked the end of the original style of managing the company through monthly meetings of founders. As more and more new employees were hired, sales volume increased, and the action came to centre more and more on the office, the key management meeting came to be the weekly status meeting in the office. This was the last monthly founders' meeting. The next time the founders gathered to review the progress of the company was more than two years later, after the public offering, on Moon Day, 1985.

Autodesk, Inc.
July Monthly Meeting (July 9, 1983)

by Kern Sibbald

Attendees

The meeting was held at Jack Stuppin's house at 1:00 P.M. The following people attended: Dave Kalish, Hal Royaltey, Jack Stuppin, Kern Sibbald, Mike Ford, John Walker, Roxie Walker, Keith Marcelius, Dan Drake, Greg Lutz, Mauri Laitinen, John Kern.

Before the meeting began there was much discussion about whether or not to hire a copyright lawyer. The discussion centered on how much it was going to cost, and most people seemed to dislike an open-ended deal. We agreed to hire the lawyer

(I didn't get his name) to do a copyright or trademark search on AutoCAD. We also discussed hiring him to review a contract with AlphaMerics. The contract involves us gaining access to their extensive set of symbol libraries.[83] During the meeting, Jack and Mike left to review this contract with the lawyer. AlphaMerics has an exclusive with NEC to package all NEC OEM hardware for CAD. We discussed AlphaMerics purchasing 200 AutoCADs in a year, 30% in 4 months starting Sept 1 at $450.00 each with a minimum of 10 per month thereafter.

Summary of Management Meeting: Dan Drake

The books for last year are closed (see enclosed summary). Keith has accepted the AutoCAD project management position. We have hired Jack O'Shea as a full-time telephone salesman working for Mike Ford. He will also be working on filling out our dealer network. He is a retired police officer and ex-draftsman. We are looking for a larger office so that we can move the sales out of Mike Ford's house and have room for demos and possibly meetings.

Financial Report: John Walker

Due to the amount of financial activity lately, the report is approximate:

Savings	$77,000
Checking	25,000
We owe:	
Mike Ford about	$1,000
Mike Riddle about	$9,280

See attached sales report for more details.

Marketing Report: Mike Ford

Our sales are very closely tracking the curve that he forecast in January but we are about a month behind. SunFlex is now accounting for only about one half of our sales (this is clearly shown on the sales summary sheet[84]). Mike forecasts that the rapid growth trend will continue. We now have several competitors but at least in the case of P-CAD it is not yet for sale. Rik [85] of Mike's staff is writing an article on CAD. Four people from TI visited us in our office in Mill Valley and all went well.

---

83   It was the prospect of supporting these symbol libraries that prompted us to include assorted odd capabilities in AutoCAD's SHAPE definitions, including "fractional arcs".
84   Lost in the mists of time
85   Jadrnicek.

Two were from corporate and two from the engineering workstation project. They seem to be very impressed and we were asked to purchase a TI and they agreed they would purchase enough AutoCADs to reimburse us. Zenith will have a machine here Monday. Heath has decided they want about 250 AutoCADs in the next year. They put a fire under Zenith. Heath wants it on a Zenith so they can expose it to their salesmen before the end of July. Note: on ordering machines, etc., request that the machines be shipped directly to your house, then give John Kern a call so he can pay the invoice when it comes. Many shipments for AutoCAD members have been coming to the office and that results in delays getting the equipment to you. Mike Ford and Duff Kurland went to NCGA[86] for 4 days — it was a high class show with all the big CAD guys (Auto-Trol, Computervision, etc.). There were about 22,000 attendees. It was worth being there since only about 25% were end users, the rest were dealers, manufacturers, and educators. There were 5 competing CAD packages at the show. P-CAD, MARS ($14K including hardware), Microcomp ($6K for software), Bausch and Lomb ($29K), and Summagraphics, (poor notes here). Nine manufacturers came to see us. Mike Ford recommends that we lend an 8087 to Neil Zackery who is supposedly going to write an article about AutoCAD. Greg Lutz agreed to buy the 8087. Tektronix may want 100 ACAD's.

More Marketing: John Walker

We are about to conclude an exclusive distributorship with Jamal[87] for ACAD-80 except for the Sony. Beginning Monday John Owens will be dropped as a distributor. Hopefully, Jamal will pick up support for Owens' customers. Jamal has sold 18 AutoCADs to date. We are trying to approach Microsoft with some kind of graphics deal. "After the great Digital Research ripoff" where they picked our brains — cuz they are working on a micro based CAD,[88] they are now trying to exchange GSX for an AutoCAD. "No way". We can get a Corona PC if we want from a dealer. We have an Otrona in-house. Mike Ford suggested that we rename the company AutoCAD to avoid confusion. No one was really very enthusiastic but everyone did agree it would be much better to have the AutoCAD name really large on our display. Mike wants someone to go to SIGGRAPH.

---

86 National Computer Graphics Association trade show.
87 Jamal Munshi, of MOMS Computing, our first customer.
88 They weren't.

International Sales

We have received a transfer of $2,000 from Lars but are not sure what it is for. There are still 15 invoices outstanding.

Corporate Status Report

The incentive stock options, John Kern's buying into the company (the shares we were going to sell to Jamal), and a request to split the stock ten-to-one are all in the hands of the lawyers. We may have to request stockholder agreement on the share splitting. Everyone at the meeting agreed that it was a good idea.[89]

Operational Report: John Kern

John is trying to keep the inventory low so we will be positioned to use the new generic manual when it is ready.[90] He is giving two day turnaround on CP/M systems[91] and one day on the other systems.

AutoCAD-86 Report: Keith

We hope to release the MS-DOS Victor with the HP driver on the 18th. The configurator release is set for July 29. We have a feature freeze in effect that roughly agrees with the current state of Duff's generic manual. We discussed manuals some here. Roxie is going to try to get the next one so it will lay a bit flatter. After some discussion on various bindings and size, everyone agreed to keep the same manual size and binding. We would like to schedule major feature releases every 60 days.[92] The manual price is now $35.00 because SunFlex insists on a discount and we won't lower their price below the current $25.00. We agreed to continue to sell manuals at $25.00 if customers ask at that price since we have advertised it so much and don't have price change disclaimers on our literature. The single-screen IBM is working and almost ready for release (1 week).[93]

---

[89] This was the first stock split. It reduced the initial nominal value of the shares from $1 to $0.10.
[90] Up to this time, we had a different manual for the IBM and Victor versions of AutoCAD-86. The "generic" manual inaugurated the division into an AutoCAD user manual and a machine-specific installation guide.
[91] Because John Walker had to make each one to order.
[92] We still would. We couldn't then, and we can't now.
[93] Up to this time, our IBM CGA version required both the CGA and the monochrome adaptor and two monitors. The IBM single-screen permitted a CGA-only configuration.

AutoCAD-80 Report: John

AutoCAD-80 works on the Sony. It is an absolutely beautiful machine according to John. They immediately sent him everything he asked for. One can get a complete system with a color printer? and a lot of other stuff for $4,100.00.

Miscellaneous

John wants to hold the Autodesk meeting quarterly rather than monthly. There seemed to be general agreement. However, everyone agreed that we must solve the communications problem first. That is, we must somehow continue to write down information on what is happening in the company and send it to everyone. John suggested that Kern continue to put out a newsletter and that he can get input every month from the division managers. There was also some discussion of holding the weekly business meetings on Fridays so that more people can attend. Apologies to Lars for misspelling his name in the last month's notes.[94] It is Lars Åke Moureau. David Kalish has received no bug reports.

Personnel

We now have five full-time paid employees: John Kern, Keith Marcelius, Duff Kurland, Greg Lutz, and Jack O'Shea. There are two half-time employees: Kathy Marcelius and Jane Kern. John proposed that Roxie Walker join the company as Assistant to the ACAD-86 manager (Keith) and as our Arts director — probably full-time. Dan Drake may be employed full-time by Autodesk retroactive to July 1.[95]

Equipment List

Very few of you have sent me your hardware configuration so I am giving up on publishing a list of what we have. Thanks to those who did: Duff Kurland, Richard Handyside, Rudolf Künzli, and David Kalish.

Kern

---

94 Fixed in the mix.
95 He wasn't.

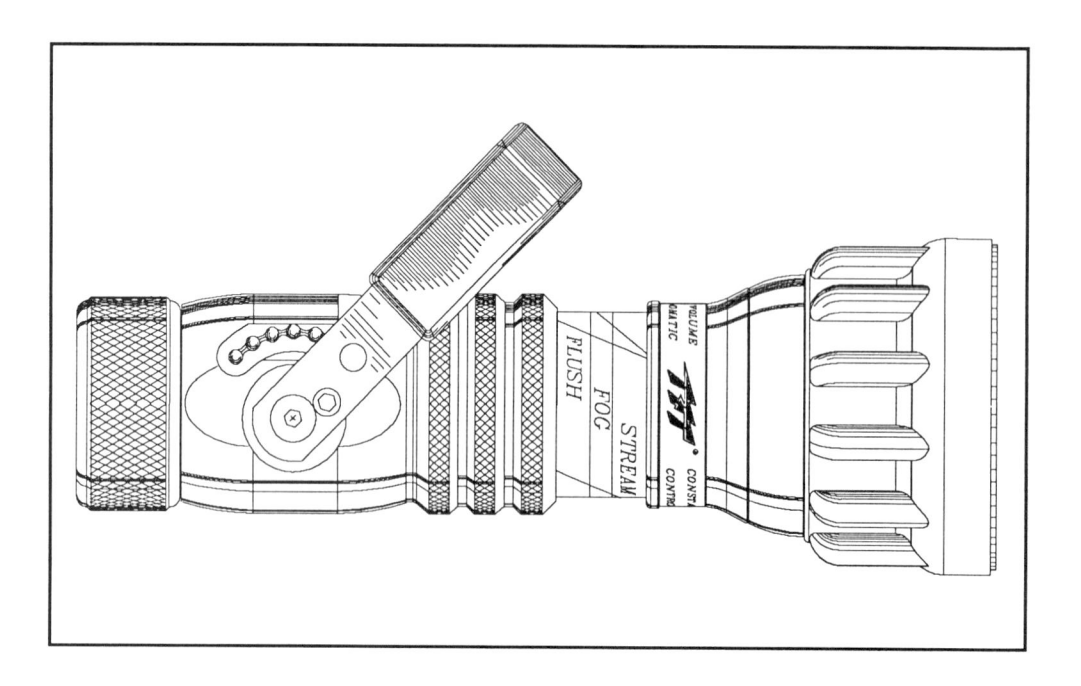

The most famous AutoCAD drawing of all: Don Strimbu of Task Force TIPS in Indiana created this drawing with a very early release of AutoCAD. It's impossible to describe the impact this drawing had when he sent it to us: it was the first really complicated drawing that had been done with AutoCAD, and Don's cleverness in using block scaling to simulate perspective on the text and to mirror parts of the nozzle astounded us all.

We immediately began to use the nozzle as a standard timing test for machines. I joked at the time that someday people would talk about "nozzle standard units" instead of Whetstones — never did I think that would come to pass. The nozzle drawing and the actual nozzle were featured in our first four colour two-page advertisement, which ran in Scientific American in September 1984.

Low Rent 3D — A Proposal

Here's the first concrete proposal to add three-dimensional capability to AutoCAD, from September of 1983. We did not embark on the mad rush to 3D that this proposal urged. Instead, we deferred implementation of 3D until AutoCAD 2.1, which we previewed at COMDEX in 1984, 14 months after this paper was written, and shipped, and shipped again, and shipped yet again, in May of 1985, 17 months later. The 3D Level 1 that we shipped in version 2.1 was, in some ways, more limited than that proposed herein. It would be interesting to know how history would have unfolded if we'd done this.

Low Rent 3D

by John Walker — September 5, 1983

If Autodesk is to prosper, it must continually enhance its products and introduce new products. This becomes especially true as other people introduce competitive products. To maintain market share and keep the price up, adding capabilities to the package is the foremost technical contribution that can be made.

With the features scheduled for the 1.40 release, plus the items which we hope to have in 1.5[96] (notably dashed lines, double walls, and some form of attribute collection and dissemination), we will have accomplished most of the goals inherent in a 2D drafting system.

Many of our competitors (MCS, Nelson Johnson, ESC), have or will be introducing 3D packages around the time of Comdex. If we do not have a credible response to queries about 3D, we may be in trouble selling our package. While all drafting is 2D, and almost all users will spend all their time with AutoCAD working in 2D mode, 3D is important more from a marketing perception standpoint than a technical one.

First, there is the natural tendency to evaluate a package from the features it has, and a package limited to 2D cannot look as good on a cursory examination as a 3D package. Second, many companies will reason, "look, all we need is 2D today, but who knows about tomorrow; we better buy a package that has 3D just in case

---

[96] This version was eventually released as AutoCAD 2.0 in October of 1984.

rather than get stuck with a dinosaur". Note that this applies even if 3D is an expensive option that they don't buy at all: just knowing it's there may clinch the sale. Third, 3D demos beautifully and is an extraordinary sales tool. The impact of rotating an object in 3 space at Comdex is many times that of zooming in on a flat drawing.

What I advocate here is a particular way of adding 3D to AutoCAD. I think that (from my very limited knowledge of the 86 version internals,[97] remember) it can be done in a limited time without disrupting the other development in progress concurrently. This is a prime consideration — we cannot afford to stop other development while somebody rips the package apart and changes everything for 3D. The method imposes restrictions on the use of 3D which I feel are acceptable, and puts no large barriers in the way of removing the restrictions in the future. Virtually none of the work done in installing this package will have to be discarded when we go to full 3D.

OK, loudmouth, so what is it you're proposing anyway?

The idea for Low-rent 3D is to allow 3D representation of objects but restricting these objects to lie in one or more planes in 3 space. The planes are completely arbitrary, and are not restricted in any way. These planes map into our layers. For each layer you get to define its origin point (e.g., where the coordinates 0,0 on that layer are in the master X,Y,Z space) and the orientation of the plane (by 2 other points, angles off the axes or whatever).

When you're drawing, you're simply adding entities to that layer in terms of the coordinates in that layer, and that's how they go into the drawing database. *There are no changes to* **EACQ** *or entity-generating commands*.

When **EREGEN** generates an entity, it generates vectors as currently done. It passes to **CLIP** the endpoints of a vector to draw in the plane of residence of the entity. *There are no changes in* **EREGEN**.

When **CLIP** receives the endpoints of a vector, it maps them from the coordinates in their layer of origin to their true 3 space coordinates. **CLIP** is of course rewritten to do a 3D clip and perspective (or isometric or whatever) transformation onto the screen. I suggest that at the same time we enhance **CLIP** to support multiple views on the screen — merely additional projections from a table.

Since everything is ultimately turned into vectors in a flat plane (the screen), the refresh file doesn't change, and you can pick items on the screen as always. *There are no changes in the refresh file, entity selection, or* **EID**-*related commands*.

---

97 At the time I wrote this, I was still working exclusively on the Z-80 PL/I version.

So, basically what we're changing here is this: We add a plane location for each layer in the drawing. We provide a command to let you specify (and move) this plane (probably heavily oriented to things like "I want a plane just like that one but with Y 10 greater", but maybe with a different syntax). This same plane specification mechanism is used to specify the viewing (image or screen) plane. For the viewing plane, we also need to specify a clip depth and transformation (perspective, isometric, how many vanishing points and where, etc.). We rewrite **CLIP** to, from real endpoints and a layer number, generate the true 3D coordinates and clip and project that vector on the viewing plane. We enhance **GRID** and cursor tracking from the digitiser to map through the transformation so that movement in the entry plane displays correctly on the screen.

And that's it.

Now notice just how modular this all is. We should be able to whip it off and integrate with little more trouble than any of our other development projects. And with nothing like the grief of "Well, we start by changing all the entities, then..."

But will it be useful? Yes, I think so. Look at most of the 3D demos you see in the literature or in our competitors' handouts. Think about drawing them in a system like this, and I think you'll agree (I exclude solid modeling systems, of course). Most 3D objects are built up of planar pieces, and I think can be represented in a system like this with little pain.

There is one addition I'd like to propose for this package at the inception: the concept of *extrusions*. With every layer would be an extrusion depth. If zero, this would have no effect. If nonzero, then when **CLIP** processed a vector, it would actually generate internally and clip 4 vectors, one in the plane, one in a parallel plane offset by the signed extrusion depth, and two connecting the two vectors in the planes. What for? Look at the gear on the cover of *PC World*. It's also neat for things like city skyline modeling. Obviously it can reduce the number of planes you need for lots of things.

Finally, I'd like to point out how little of this needs to be thrown away when we go to a full 3D (space curve wire frame) package. We add Z coordinates to all the entities and rip up **EREGEN** (e.g., I want this text written on that cylinder over there). But we end up passing 3 coordinate pairs to **CLIP**, projecting them, and viewing them, and all the code we do for that is used unchanged. We still need to specify viewing planes, so all our code for that gets reused. We will of course leave the low rent 3D package in, as it will, I think, serve as a friendly bridge between the second and third worlds.

It's my feeling that the magnitude of the task we're talking about here is comparable and very likely less than implementing the major additions packages we have underway or recently completed (crosshatching, circle generation optimisation, line types, fillets, etc.). And no other single addition will so well enhance the perceived value of AutoCAD, or its ability to sell itself at shows. Just think of the difference in our COMDEX literature of "Now with 3D" versus "Now with crosshatching and dashed lines". I think we should discuss this and if no major technical barriers are seen, go for it with a goal of introduction at COMDEX and shipment within 30 days thereafter. We can then let the market response tell us whether we should invest the work immediately for a full 3D package.

We can probably get away with a stiff price increment for this thing. If people pay $500 for the piddling dimensioning code, I think an extra $1200 for 3D is not inconceivable. I have absolutely no idea, however, how many we might sell or what the price/sales curve would look like. If Nelson Johnson is to be believed (!), though, hundreds of people are willing to spend $400 for a 3D package that is completely useless. And that with little advertising on just a few machines. So I think this can be a powerful revenue generator as well.

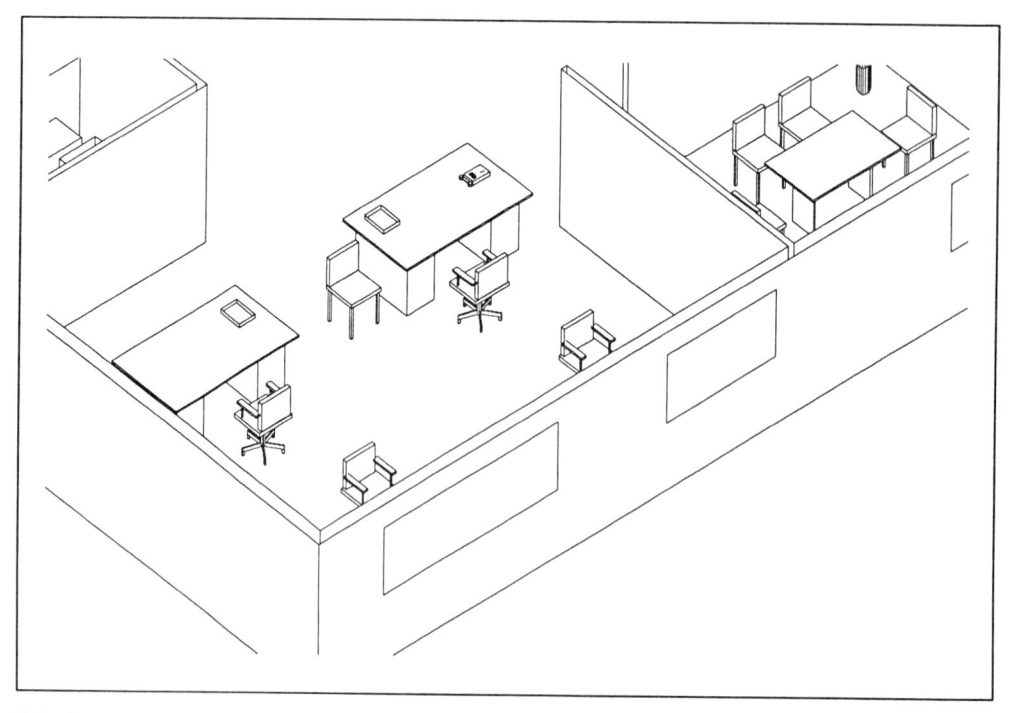

This drawing is a direct descendent of the first three-dimensional demo drawing that Duff Kurland put together for the introduction of 3D Level 1 at COMDEX in 1984.

Electric Malcolm

Whenever an Autodesk old-timer wants to intimidate a Kelvin-come-lately, the conversation always seems to turn to "Electric Malcolm". After a few veiled references to this legendary facility, the newcomer walks away slowly, shaking his head, and muttering something about "they told me this company was weird, but 'Electric Malcolm'? ... naaah.". Well I promised to tell all, so here's the inside scoop on Electric Malcolm.

Malcolm McCullough was still studying architecture at UCLA when he took a summer job with Autodesk in 1983. Malcolm was the first person really talented in drawing to work for Autodesk, and his work with AutoCAD helped both by generating good sample drawings and by identifying the most important features needed in real professional drafting. The Golden Gate Bridge drawing that we used to feature so prominently in our advertising was drawn by Malcolm that summer.

We had hoped that Malcolm would be able to help us put together some form of scripted or video demo. When time began to run out, I implemented a transcript capture facility which would actually be able to record Malcolm creating a drawing. Then we could play it back at a trade show or in a dealer's showroom and show AutoCAD making a drawing in the hands of a master with the simple push of a button. Hence, "Electric Malcolm". The code was implemented in the CP/M-86 version of AutoCAD, but there was a stability freeze in effect prior to the release of Version 1.4, so the code was never integrated in the product. To this day, AutoCAD lacks this capability, although both AutoSketch and AutoShade support it for development testing purposes.

AutoCAD-86 Transcript Facility

Implementation Notes by John Walker
September 14, 1983

The attached disc contains the additions to AutoCAD to provide a crude transcript capture and replay facility. This code is provided for internal use only, and has several glaring shortcuts and deficiencies which are excusable only by the short time remaining before it must be pressed into service to prepare demos for NSS[98] and COMDEX, and the short time before our best AutoCAD expert departs for southern climes.

I have tried to implement this code in an extensible way, and will later suggest how existing transcripts prepared with this code may be painlessly converted into a more advanced version compatible with the 1.40 DIG changes and future plans.

First, let's look at how the mechanism works.

To make a transcript, at any time while AutoCAD is active, you may enter the command:

XSCR

You will be prompted with:

Transcript file:

and you should respond with a valid file name in the system you are running under. This file name may contain a drive letter, but must not contain a file type. A file type of "**XSC**" will be used for all transcripts. If a file with the given name already exists, it will be overwritten. Following the completion of the **XSCR** command, you will receive the "**Command:**" prompt, and henceforth every AutoCAD action you take will be recorded in the transcript file. That is, every keystroke on the console, every pick with the pointing device (whether in screen or tablet mode), and every menu pick, whether from the tablet menu or the screen.

To terminate the recording of the transcript, just enter the command:

XSCR

again. This will close the transcript file and turn off recording. The transcript file will also be automatically closed out when a command is entered which leaves the Drawing Editor (**END** or **QUIT**). But remember, if you use an **END** or **QUIT** in a transcript, it will be recorded and will take effect when the transcript is later used, so be sure this is what you wish.

Once a transcript file has been recorded with the **XSCR** command, it may be replayed at any time with the command:

RPLY

---

[98] The National Software Show, now defunct.

This command will prompt you:

`Transcript file:`

and you should respond with the file name of a previously recorded transcript. As with the **XSCR** command, the file type of "**XSC**" is assumed and should not be specified. The transcript will then be fed to AutoCAD as it was initially entered. If the transcript was terminated with an **XSCR** command, that command will display at the end, but will be ignored. If the transcript does not terminate the Drawing Editor, control will return to the console at the end of the transcript. Transcripts may not be aborted. (This isn't hard to fix.) Transcripts have meaning only within the Drawing Editor. Unlike **SCRIPT** files, they cannot be used to feed commands to the main menu, configurator, or plot modules. Note that you are free, however, to make composite demos with scripts which use the **RPLY** command after calling the Drawing Editor.

In using transcripts to prepare demos, it is of the utmost importance that you remember to save the precise initial environment which obtained when the transcript was captured. That includes the original drawing file (beware of making any changes, even of view, before starting the transcript), the menu file(s) in effect, all **LOAD** and **INSERT** files, and the same display hardware (since digitiser samples are converted into screen coordinates). A transcript is simply a logical baboon typing from a list of characters and moving the cursor to where it was on the screen before — if you change the environment, the baboon will just keep on typing with nary a giggle at the devastation which ensues.

Consequently, the wise transcript maker saves the entire disc set before the transcript capture, then makes the transcript, then sets up a demo script incorporating the backup disc set and makes sure the demo process isn't destructive of the initial information on the disc.

There is no way to edit or concatenate transcript files. Zip. Nor is there any reasonable way to convert a transcript from one machine to run on another, or to update it for a new version of AutoCAD. However, this is not as bad as you might think. We are making changes in the interface between DIG and the people who call it which will rationalise the way tablet mode and handling of screen pointing work. These changes will have a major impact on transcript capture, and will allow us to much more easily turn a transcript into a **SCRIPT** file which can be edited with a text editor. This is really what we want, so it doesn't make sense to make a large investment in a 1.30 base transcript mechanism now. But based on timing, we gotta have something now, so this is it. When we get the new interface, I can gimmick DIG to read one of these old transcripts while writing a new style one, and then everything gets automatically converted (I hope).

The transcript code itself is very obvious. COMMAND is modified to recognise the **XSCR** and **RPLY** commands (which have clunky names because we have no intention of making this facility available to users), and to add the code which closes an open transcript on a **QUIT** or **END**. All transcript code in both COMMAND and DIG can be turned off by undefining TRANSCR, which is how we will normally ship AutoCAD.

The code to process the **XSCR** and **RPLY** commands is in the procedures with the same names in DIG. Note that the transcript file is paged; we wish no more disc I/O than necessary, because we may fill a buffer during user keyboard input. Both the capture and replay code is added to the procedure DIGITZ, and is obvious. The format of the transcript file is:

```
00-7F                 Console character
F0 SX SX SY SY        Digitiser pick
F1 SX SX              Menu pick
F2 RX RX RY RY        Raw digitiser coordinates (tablet mode)
FF                    End of file
```

Any questions this doesn't answer are as easily answered from the code as from a document about it. The raw X and Y coordinates are written first so that RAWX and RAWY are correct when the pick item follows. It is always generated regardless of tablet mode.

Writing of the transcript file doesn't adjust the disc full counter. That's because I'm too lazy to bother with it for internal code I'm going to rewrite anyway.

Freehand sketch material doesn't get captured in the transcript. This isn't particularly hard, but I skipped it because of lack of immediate need and to prevent code integration conflicts (as changes in SKETCH would be needed, and SKETCH is currently under integration into 1.40).

The management of the cursor in the replay code is no great shakes. It should really glide the cursor over to the point smoothly to simulate user movement. This would make the replay much better. We'll also have to put in **DELAY**s at strategic places after we get the translator to **SCRIPT** format working. All menu picks are turned into screen menu picks, with cycling through the NEXT box as required. Until we get the robot arm for the digitiser (or mouse with legs), this is the best way we can represent menu usage.

Anyway, the plan is that we retrojam this thing into 1.30 for the Victor and let Malcolm loose on it for the time we have left, then massage the material we collect in the free time after he goes. I'm sure we can come up with a better mechanism in the future, but this one works and we can use it in the remaining time.

Here's the drawing of the Golden Gate Bridge that Malcolm McCullough did in the summer of 1983. His drawing shows the entire bridge and includes structural details beneath the panels. This view of part of the drawing is the one we featured most frequently in brochures. It's hard to appreciate what an achievement this drawing is without having used the primitive version of AutoCAD with which Malcolm drew it.

October 1983 Meeting

As decided at the July meeting, the full company meetings were now held quarterly rather than monthly. This letter announced the first of these quarterly meetings, which was combined with a special shareholders' meeting called to adopt a provision basically intended to extricate John Walker and Dan Drake from the disastrous financial consequences of buying their initial stock through Marinchip. Also, we believed ourselves to be hot on the trail of venture capital and we wanted to be able to adopt any provisions required by investors should a deal emerge.

This was the first general company meeting held at the company's offices. We finally had enough space to fit all of the stockholders in at once.

Autodesk, Inc.
150 Shoreline Highway, — Bldg B
Mill Valley, Ca. 94941
(415) 331--0356

Autodesk Quarterly Meeting

The October general meeting will be held at 1:00 on Sunday, October 9, at the company's main office:

150 Shoreline Highway, Building B
Mill Valley, California

The meeting has been moved to the second weekend of the month in order to accommodate arrangements for the special meeting of shareholders, for which an announcement accompanies this notice.

Note that the general meeting begins at 1:00, though the shareholders' meeting is scheduled for later.

The main topic of discussion will be our plans for marketing the product. Technically we are now well ahead of everybody, but competitors are beginning to sell products, and they're much better financed than we are. To avoid being swamped by their gigantic advertising budgets, we are now looking very seriously into getting outside money. This could be a large change in the organization of our business, and may require some official actions by the stockholders; we have called the special meeting so we can take action if necessary.

As noted in the announcement, the Board has adopted a change in the Bylaws regulating the transfer of Autodesk stock; since two directors are interested parties, we have made it subject to ratification by the shareholders. The management's position is that we have an anomalous situation when a corporation (call it XYZ Corp) owns stock or warrants in Autodesk: our bylaws prohibit XYZ from selling its Autodesk securities to anyone else without offering first refusal to the rest of us, but there is no effective way we can keep it from selling *its own* stock to somebody we don't like. When it does so, the beneficial ownership (and voting control) of some Autodesk stock is changed in a way over which we have no control.

On the other hand, if XYZ distributes its Autodesk holdings to its own stockholders, there is no change in beneficial ownership of Autodesk and a minimal change (toward fragmentation) in voting control; and stock which is distributed to individuals will fall under the effective control of our stock transfer restrictions. Therefore, if the stock transfer restrictions are a good idea, it seems to be in our interest to encourage and expedite such distributions, and we want to remove them from the first refusal process.

The whole question of stock transfer restrictions is controversial and will surely be a topic of discussion at the meeting, quite apart from this special case.

We expect to have a distribution of employee stock options ready for consideration by the founders. This will correspond pretty much to the second and third (and last) semiannual option distributions that we planned when we organized the company 18 months ago.[99] We would like to get these options issued and out of the way before any potential investor can try to water them down as a bargaining point.

Daniel Drake
Secretary

---

99   Dan Drake comments, "It should be noted for the benefit of anybody trying to do this over again that the option grants as set up by the Board were to be approved by a majority vote of the founders, one person one vote, before the Board would formally vote them. The allocation was so wildly unpopular that the chairman of the meeting, who wasn't wildly enthusiastic himself, was barely able to railroad them through, believing as he still does today that absolutely no compromise could command a solid majority. I.e. this idea didn't work very well."

Autodesk, Inc.
150 Shoreline Highway, — Bldg B
Mill Valley, Ca. 94941
(415) 331-0356

September 29, 1983

Notice Of Annual Meeting

A special shareholders' meeting of Autodesk, Inc. will be held at 2:00 PM on Sunday, October 9, 1983, at the company's main office at 150 Shoreline Highway, Suite B-23, Mill Valley, California.

The meeting was called by order of John Walker, president, by authority granted in the Bylaws.

Stockholders of record September 28, 1983, will be eligible to vote at the meeting.

The purpose of the meeting is to discuss plans for increasing the company's capitalization, possibly by attracting additional investors, and to take actions that may be required in order to acquire new investors or to make the capital structure of the company more attractive to investors. Such actions may include changes in stock option plans or in restrictions on stock transfers.

The Board of Directors will submit for ratification an amendment to the corporate Bylaws, adopted September 7, 1983, allowing a particular class of stock transfer to proceed without the offer of first refusal rights to all shareholders. The position of the management on this change is given in the accompanying letter. The management knows of no other resolutions which are proposed for adoption at the meeting. If you are not absolutely sure that you will attend, please sign and return the enclosed proxy; it will be revoked automatically if you do attend.

Daniel Drake
Secretary

Expenses

Name _____ Date _____
Address _____ Phone _____

	Date							Total
Meals								
Lodging								
Airfare								
Auto Rental								
Taxi/Limo								
Telephone								
Mileage .20/mi.								
Business Meals								
Pizza/Chinese								
Decadence								
Supplies								
Software								
Hardware								
Books/Manuals								
Miscellaneous								
Totals								

Business Meals & Entertainment

Date	Amt	Place & City	Guests	Affiliation	Purpose

NOTE: Some expenses, while legitimate, cannot be reimbursed by the company at this time. They are shown here for tax purposes and possible future reimbursement.

Subtotal _____
Less Advances _____
Less non-reimbursable expenses _____
Balance Due Autodesk _____
Balance Owed Employee _____

Signature _____ Date ____ Approved _____ Date ____

This was Autodesk's first expense report form, with items befitting the proclivities of the founders. This copy was painfully reconstructed from a paper copy of the form by Duff Kurland.

Piece of Cake

If you eat beans, you fart. If you build a successful company, you hire an advertising agency. Both are laws of nature, and raging against the inevitable consequences of one's actions makes no more sense than standing on the tracks and arguing with the Twentieth Century Limited.

The wise man sees the amusement inherent in the inevitable and enjoys it to the fullest. Before COMDEX 1983 we hired an advertising agency to help us "tell the AutoCAD story". By hiring an agency one employs "creative talent" not present in the mundane people who create new technologies.

This is what they came up with. We didn't use it.

NOW YOU CAN TEACH YOUR PC TO DRAW

October 7, 1983

Just slip in your AutoCAD graphics software disc and you're ready. Draw a brick and AutoCAD will draw you a wall — automatically.

Move it. Copy it. Modify, rotate, or scale it vertically and horizontally. Store it. Change your mind and erase it.

Do it all on *your* PC. AutoCAD is the industry standard. It's compatible with most any PC. IBM PC and XT. Zenith Z100. Victor 9000. NEC APC. Columbia. Eagle PC. Not to mention CP/M-80 computers.[100]

It's just about ready[101] for NCR Decision-Mate, DMS, DEC, Sony, Televideo, Eagle 1600, Texas Instruments, and Corona.

And it supports a bunch of input and output devices.

---

100 But we will anyway, just to be sure.
101 Any day now.

You'll work better. And easier. Use a light pen and on-screen menus. A digitizing tablet. A keyboard or a mouse.[102]

Use them to draw lines. Of any width. Circles, arcs and solid-filled areas. Insert them anywhere in your text.

And do it in German. Or French. Swedish is coming and so is Italian. We're working on Japanese.

You won't flinch at the price. It's good. Real good.[103] $1,000. Add another $500 and you get automatic dimensioning.

Ask around. You'll find a lot of people know AutoCAD. We've already shipped more than 1,500 systems. All over the country. All over the world. And you wouldn't believe who some of our customers are.[104]

Architects love it. So do engineers. So do designers. So will you.

You wouldn't *have* a PC without a word processor. Or without a spread sheet. Or without AutoCAD.

Word processing for graphics. Take a byte. [105]

For a demonstration and information, call or write.

> AutoCAD, Inc.
> 150 Shoreline Highway — Building B[106]
> Mill Valley, CA 94941

---

102 Even a verb occasionally.
103 I'm not making this up. We paid good money for this hooey.
104 Would you believe .... Excuse me, my shoe is ringing.
105 In addition to what we spent for this copy, we also spent $700 to get a guy to come to Greg Lutz's house and take pictures of his CGA screen with a drawing of a piece of cake on it. Of course, that looked so awful that we wouldn't have used it even if we'd run the ad.
106 We were still concerned with looking like "a real company". I suggested that we list our address as "Autodesk, Inc., AutoCAD Division — Building B, Mail Station B-20, 150 Shoreline Highway, Mill Valley, CA 94941". Cooler heads prevailed and we didn't do it.

"Let's Go for It — and Win the Battle!"

Here it is. John Walker recommending that Autodesk go get venture capital, even if it meant surrendering the autonomy and sense of control over our destiny that was the main reason for starting the company in the first place. But read the arguments — and remember that they were the very same arguments that possessed us to go public in 1985. This was the first "modern" information letter: written for a company in which founders were outnumbered by employees hired after the company began to expand, and after the company had significant sales and a regular operation. Thankfully, the technology crash of '83 and our unwillingness to sacrifice our principles at the altar of Mammon precluded our obtaining venture capital. No, there was no Information Letter 9; when I wrote this one, I didn't have copies of the prior letters and I miscounted.

Autodesk, Inc.
Information Letter #10

by John Walker
Revision 8 — October 25, 1983

In periods of frenzied haste toward wealth, of feverish speculation and of crisis, the sudden downfall of great industries and the ephemeral expansion of other branches of production, of scandalous fortunes amassed in a few years and dissipated as quickly, it becomes evident that the economic institutions which control production and exchange are far from giving society the prosperity they are supposed to guarantee; they produce precisely the opposite effect.

Peter Kropotkin, 1880

Indeed ....

Well it has been a long time since the last information letter, hasn't it? These letters only get written when things are sufficiently calm that there is time to reflect enough to put one together, or when the gusts of crisis blow so hard that one is forced to communicate to share the urgency. Up to now. This letter is a review of our accomplishments, an attempt to summarise our current position, and a sales pitch for my recently acquired view of where we should be going.

My original working document for the formation of this company began with the words "the game has changed".[107] The game has indeed changed, and we have changed with it. Our success to date is a measure of our ability to change and adapt to the software game in the 80's. But the game is continuing to change, and we must continue to adapt or else we will lose the opportunity we've created by our labours to date.

We started a company composed of highly skilled programmers. Our idea was to develop multiple products. We did that. We planned to test market these products and determine which had the best potential. That was done. We intended to focus our efforts on the product which, in test marketing, showed the best prospects of being a success, and we did it. We decided from the start that we would have to recruit a marketing professional to build an effective marketing team to promote our products. Since joining the company, Mike Ford has done an amazing job of expanding our sales from zero to the million dollar level, and is building a marketing organisation as competent as the original technical team. We knew that we couldn't succeed while remaining a cottage industry. When the time was right, we had to take on the burdens of office facilities, manufacturing machines, full time employees, and the rest. Since his joining the company, John Kern has made the operational side of the company professional, efficient, and responsive, while reducing the cost of our product as sold by over 50%. We are now positioned to expand our production capacity by a factor of ten without catastrophe.

So far we are on course, profitable, productive, and positioned in the fastest growing corner (CAD/CAM) of the hottest industry (Software). In the historical course of things, we should plow our profits back into the business, add to our production and marketing capacities, and continue R&D to enhance our product. But these are the go go 80's, where product lifetime may be measured in months, and company lifecycles in one to two years. As long as all our competitors play by the rules we're using we will win. But will they?

We are all at a wonderful ball where the champagne sparkles in every glass and soft laughter falls upon the summer air. We know, by the rules, that at some moment the Black Horsemen will come shattering through the great terrace doors, wreaking vengeance and scattering the survivors. Those who leave early are saved, but the

---

107   Well, actually this was in the third section of the working paper (page 10). But I didn't have a copy at hand when I was writing this.

ball is so splendid no one wants to leave while there is still time, so that everyone keeps asking, "What time is it? What time is it?" but none of the clocks have hands.

Adam Smith, *Supermoney*

How lucky we have been! I can think of almost no parallel in the history of the microcomputer business where one company had the only product in a major market for over a year. Had we entered a market like word processing, BASIC compilers, or spread sheets, we would have long ago been blown away by better organised and capitalised competition. It is simply fantasy for us to assume that we will continue to have this market to ourselves, or to assume that our primacy in the market guarantees success down the road. Review my initial papers about this business. Remember Electric Pencil? Has anything changed? Let's not be deceived by our initial success. We've all worked hard, and we've been lucky, but from now on in we have to make our own luck because the competition is on the way.

Our continued expansion plans can be disintegrated almost overnight by any one of the numerous competitors who are appearing on the horizon. There is little doubt that our product is technically the best, and so far we have been able to react faster and complete development goals in a more timely fashion than the competition, indicating that our technical staff is the best.

However, we are weak in our ability to promote our product. We have bootstrapped this company from the very start. This mode of operation preserves control in our hands, but it limits our ability to counter competition, particularly in advertising blitzes, to the monthly profit from operation. For September, this number came out to a little over $13,000, which will buy from 3 to 4 full-page ads depending on where you run them (just page rates, not even figuring production cost). If you start to calculate in additional staff, overhead requirements, promotional material, etc. it becomes clear that we will have to run at a substantial loss to sustain even a modest promotional campaign. Our reserves are very healthy for a company at our state of development, but could be exhausted in less than three months by even a modest step-up in our marketing budget.

Therefore, the time has come to seek outside funding. The time is right; AI has a product recognised to be the industry leader, so we can build our having arrived first into a large market share by a properly targeted campaign. Second, this is an ideal time for a company of our kind to raise money — software is one of the hottest items now, and CAD is one of the best bets in software. This may not be true in six months. Not long ago, venture capitalists were tripping over themselves to fund start-ups in desktop computers. Today such ventures are shunned as hopeless charges against the IBMonolith. Remember gene splicing?

If we raise money now, we will get more, and give away less, than if we wait. By waiting we are gambling that our continued growth will not be aborted by a well-funded competitor, that our growth will add value to the company faster than our competitors grow, and that if we later need money we will be able to find it on attractive terms. All of those are very uncertain propositions. On the other hand, if we raise money and discover we don't need it immediately, it can serve as a cushion against hard times in the future.

Going after heavy-duty outside money will make some serious changes in this company in the process of getting it, and if we succeed, after we get it. We will have to prepare a formal business plan with sales forecasts and departmental budgets to the line-item level for the next three years. (This is a good idea anyway, and we're already doing it.)

We will have to reconcile ourselves with giving up 20 to 35 percent of the company in return for 2 to 3 million dollars in funding.

We will have to abandon any remaining ideas of running the company on an informal basis. We will be on the fast track, spending other people's money, and will have to show that we are being prudent and professional with the resources they are speculating on us.

We will have to accept outside participation in the management of the company. There will almost certainly be additional professional management installed, possibly replacing the entire current management of the company.

We will largely preclude operating the company as a steady-state enterprise which generates revenues adequate to make us all happy. People don't stick 3 million dollars in an untested company unless they expect to increase it by at least a factor of ten to twenty, so we'll be basically signing onto an exponential growth treadmill with serious consequences for failure to perform as advertised (e.g., loss of control of the company and serious dilution of our stock ownership).

These are serious consequences, and should only be accepted after reflection on the alternative.

> *Life in the fast lane, surely makes you lose your mind.*
>
> The Eagles

Ahhhh, but the slow lane has its problems too. We are now at the point in the lifecycle of our product where the market share war usually begins. Several products have announced. None has come to the attention of more than a few percent of the potential customers. The process of new market creation is in its infancy. The entrenched large system sellers are largely unaware of the barbarians at the gate.

In fewer than ten years, drawing systems will be on the desk of virtually every person employed in a job in which drawing is a means of communication. These drawing systems will be based upon the fundamental concepts present in AutoCAD. There is little doubt that AutoCAD can do the job that is there to be done. Whether those machines run AutoCAD or another package will be largely determined in the next year. Our actions will decide whether AutoCAD becomes synonymous with "drawing tool" as VisiCalc has become with spreadsheet.

Our technical edge is only a tenuous advantage. Every day the success of the IBM PC proves that the race does not necessarily go to the best product. One must have the best *company*, and that is a composite of the product itself, the development staff which maintains and further develops the product, the customer support staff which largely determines how the product is perceived after sale, the production facility, which controls whether delivery commitments are upheld and manufacturing quality maintained, the marketing department, which must build the visibility of the product and expand the channels of its distribution, and the overall management of the company and of the departments.

But just as important as these obvious components of a successful company is its financial position. It has been proved again and again that a perfect company with the ideal product can be wiped out by a competitor who is better capitalised. For example, who would argue that the IBM PC is a better machine than (name the competitor you like best!). But IBM is not only a superbly functioning company, there's the matter of their 4.3 billion dollars in the bank. When a company like Victor raises a sum like $35 million by going public, this amasses a war chest that is insignificant against IBM's television advertising budget alone.

Not only is our current technical and market advantage tenuous, it can evaporate in the face of well funded competition. Our technical development is still very slow, very informal, and basically built on a few key people burning themselves out to get work done. I know all about large software projects and the false economies of scale, but the fact remains that if, say, Digital Research plans to enter the CAD market, they can field a product within 9 months which would be better than AutoCAD by most technical measures.

Next, there's the fact that simply by obtaining outside funding we add an aura of credibility to the company and make ourselves more visible. I don't like the fact that companies who bootstrap themselves are sneered at, but that's the way it is, folks. And with a 46% tax on profits before you pour them back into development, it's a lot easier to do it with other people's money than with your own. By being in the portfolio of a well known high technology venture capitalist, we will be exposed to possible joint venture opportunities or markets for our products which we would otherwise have to painfully find for ourselves.

Then there's the experience we can draw on in addition to the money. Before we started this company, none of us had started from zero and built a company to the million dollar scale. I'm sure that had we done it before, we would have done many things differently, and made fewer painful mistakes. I know I would do it differently if I had it to do over. Now we have to face the fact that none of us has built a million dollar company into a 30 million dollar company. This is a lot faster, more high stakes game than the one we have been playing so far, and we will need a lot more than honest intentions and a couple of books to survive in it.

The point is that these venture capitalists have done the trick numerous times. They know what you have to do when, what to do when you get in trouble, and where to find the people you need when you have to build up a critical part of the company. In growing and keeping out of trouble, this knowledge can contribute mightily to the chances of success. And with 80% of new businesses failing within 5 years of formation, we can use all the help we can get.

It's better to burn out, than it is to rust.

Neil Young

So, all things considered, it seems to me that the time has come for us to seek outside financing. We should attempt to raise from 2 to 3 million dollars by selling up to 35% of the company. We will almost certainly have to accept serious downside risk in the form of loss of control or dilution should we fail to meet performance criteria spelled out in the financing agreement, so we will be betting everything on success and risking all we have done so far.

But it really boils down to this: take your present percent ownership of the company. Would you rather have that percentage of a company with a market value of $3 million, or 65% of that percentage of a company with a value ten to twenty times as great? I think that the risk of failure is very great, but that we can fail just as badly by not taking the risk — since we are not operating in a vacuum and even our present market share may erode to the point of disaster against a well financed group of competitors.

I have come to this recommendation from a position almost completely opposed to what I'm recommending now. I have changed my mind because I think that we have in our hands a product which can make us all very well off, indeed. As much as I dislike it, I believe that the only way we can get from where we are to where we want to be is to bring in outside money and talent, and rapidly make this a professional, conventional company. Not to do so is to subject our work to date to a greater risk of loss due to competition.

The next year or two are going to be very interesting ones. We are going to be jumping on a tiger's back and trying to hold on as we learn how to steer. But I can't think of a better time, or a better industry, or a better product, or a better team of people with which to make this gamble. And I can't imagine starting over if we let this opportunity slip away.

> *But with the throttle screwed on there is only the barest margin, no room at all for mistakes. It has to be done right ... and that's where the strange music starts, when you stretch your luck so far that fear becomes exhilaration and vibrates along your arms.*
>
> *... letting off now, but only until the next dark stretch and another few seconds on the edge ... The Edge .... There is no honest way to explain it because the only people who really know where it is are the ones who have gone over. The others — the living — are those who pushed their control as far as they felt they could handle it, and then pulled back, or slowed down, or did whatever they had to when it came time to choose between Now and Later.*
>
> *But the edge is still Out there.*
>
> Hunter S. Thompson, *Hell's Angels*

And we're a long way from it .... Right now we are ticking along in first gear, running smoothly, and taking every precaution. But what's that noise from behind? Shall we reach for the throttle, try to hide, or hope they will just go away?

I say let's go for it.

Section Three
Becoming a Major Force

Publisher's Notes
January 1984 — December 1984

The year started with Autodesk looking for venture capital to finance the company. By mid-year a "deal was on the table." It wasn't a good deal and Autodesk walked away. They financed the company with their own growth. In 1984 alone, Autodesk grew its sales, revenues, and units shipped by a factor of ten. By year's end Autodesk was a major force in the CAD market.

Key Events

- February 12, 1984. — Information Letter #11. Describes the company's transformation into a major force in the market.

May 1984. Al Green joined company as Chief Financial Officer.

- May 10, 1984. — The Deal On the Table. Dan Drake's telephone notes of a deal offered by venture capitalist, Frank Chambers. Autodesk rejected the deal.

- July 7, 1984. — AutoCAD Lite. Describes a low-end (less than $100) CAD package.

- August 16, 1984. — Taxes and Such. Dan Drake's memo on taxes and what entrepreneurs face in the way of SEC and IRS rules when they want to get some of their equity out of a company. It helped prepare the founders for an eventual public offering the following year.

Alvar Green joined the company in 1984 as Chief Financial Officer. He was instrumental in bringing up unified finance and accounting systems for both the domestic and European operations.

Key Product Events

The company had its first 1,000-units-month in May 1984. By the end of the year it had shipped over 10,000 units, ten times the number shipped in the previous year. A new release was shipped in October:

October 1984. AutoCAD Version 2.0 Release.

Financial Summary

Both sales and revenue dollars increased by a factor of ten. Sales were almost $10 million; and revenues were over $1.5 million. European subsidiaries were formed and the offices in Switzerland, the UK, and Sweden contributed sales and revenue.

Here are the quarterly figures for the year.

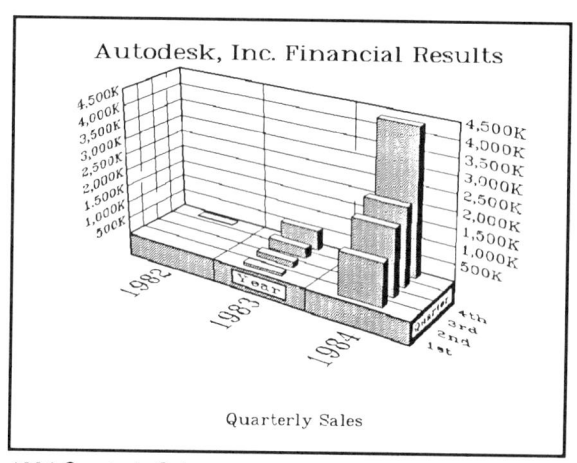

1984 Quarterly Sales

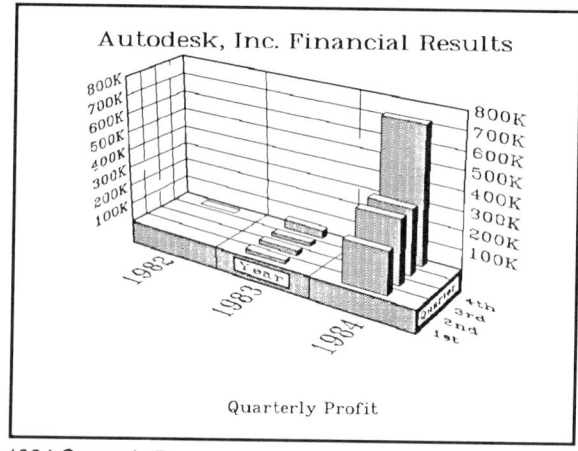

1984 Quarterly Revenues

A Letter Written on the Cusp

I was far from happy with this Information Letter when I wrote it, and I'm far from happy with it as I reread it today. More than a year had elapsed since I wrote the last Information Letter. When I wrote IL 10, the key people in the company met every Wednesday night in the room overlooking the Moment's Pause hot tub, and discussed matters ranging from whether we should sell our souls to the venture capitalists to ink running on the metal labels. When it came time to write IL 11, there was this real company: multiple buildings full of people at 150 Shoreline, different departments pulling in different directions, and all the inevitable concomitants of a growing, vital company made up of incorrigible individualists.

When I penned this letter, I knew that we had made plans to invite Hunter S. Thompson to our party. I pulled that punch because I was afraid it would fall through (it didn't — he showed up), and because I was worried that our grand scheme to have him chronicle the evolution of Autodesk over the next several years, thus creating the Marin County Gonzo rejoinder to wimpy Boston's Soul of a New Machine, would fall through (it did — and in my opinion, Dr. Gonzo blew an opportunity to be for High Technology what Hemingway was for his generation).

This was the only Information Letter I deliberately wrote thinking about the audience. Think of it as having been written on that cusp between being a company of close friends and a major force in the market, or simply the time that John Walker chickened out.

Autodesk, Inc.
Information Letter # 11

by John Walker
Revision 4 — February 12, 1984

Party Time

On January 16, 1984, Autodesk's sales for the fiscal year which began on February 1, 1983, went over a million dollars.

"This situation absolutely calls for a really futile and stupid gesture to be made on somebody's part.

And we're just the guys to do it."

Animal House

On Sunday, February 26, 1984, we'll have a party to celebrate this accomplishment. We don't know yet exactly where the party will be held, but it will start in the late afternoon. Plan to be there.

On the scale of the universe, selling a million dollars in a year may not count for much, but on the scale we've been used to it is a major milestone, and provides a good excuse to think about where we've been and where we want and hope to go.

What follows is probably the most disconnected and rambling Information Letter you have received. This IL is not written at a major event in the history of our company, or at a time of serious crisis. There's not a consistent thread to connect the thoughts which follow. This is, however, a time of rapid growth for our company and a time of rapid change in our style of operation. This is, in itself, cause to look at what's really happening.

And you see, our rapid evolution is really the subject of this letter. Our success contains both the seeds of our future success and the potential for our undoing, because as we rapidly expand the company as we must, we unavoidably change the character of the company, and risk destroying the things that have made us a success. I know that in my round the clock bursts of effort, I have not made the time to talk to everybody as much as I should have, so I'm taking this opportunity to let fly with a collection of random thoughts and questions. This is not supposed to replace conversations, just start them going. I am interested in talking with everybody associated with this company about what is going on and how we can best align the company with your goals, so consider this an invitation to corner me and start talking.

What's Going On Here

If things associated with this company are chaotic, there is a good reason. Starting in October, our sales volume has been growing at an average rate of over 30% a month. As this has happened, the workload on everybody has increased at this exponential rate. The telephone volume, manufacturing, shipping, and customer support loads have tracked these increases. Although we have been adding new people to bear the load, and will be taking additional space to avoid packing people like sardines into the current building, it takes time to find good people and time for them to learn the job, time to locate office space and move into it, and time to remedy the execrable phone "system" we have now.[108]

For the moment, about all we can do is hang on and wait for the solutions to these problems which are on the way. Even in the most foamy bubbles of optimism, nobody expects a 30% compounded month to month growth to continue. If it did, our monthly sales at the end of this year would be over 2.8 million dollars per month (an annual rate of 33 million per year), and at the end of next year would be running at the rate of about half a billion dollars a year. Hi ho. Look out General Motors.

But seriously folks, what we can most reasonably expect is a series of plateaus with up-slopes between them. We're on one of those giddy up slopes now, but I think we'll have a chance to recover before the next expansion. But then, let's not get too cocky ....

New Entrants, Undeterred by Mounting Casualties, Crowd the Software Field.

Sofsearch International, a San Antonio, Texas company that helps computer users locate software has lost track of almost 1700 vendors in the past year.

No matter, the company's count of active software vendors is nonetheless up about 57% from a year ago, to 13,500. Says a distributor, "For every supplier that goes away, another 15 or 20 come up behind".

---

108   You see, we were in this *motel*, and everybody had their own phone. If you wanted to hand a call off to somebody else, you had to ask them to call that person's number and hope they'd be there to answer.

> *But prospects may be poor for many of the new suppliers, "Before word of mouth was enough to make your product known.", says a distributor of software, "Now it takes national advertising and huge budgets."*
>
> The Wall Street Journal, February 8, 1984

We are indeed playing in a very different arena than the one we entered when we started this company. We started out with some product ideas, a commitment to work hard for little or no money, and the idea of building a company which would develop creative products, provide the highest standards of quality, do well by our customers in both service and responsiveness to requests, and reward those who did the work with the fruits of their labours if and when the company was a success.

Platitudes maybe, but all of us have worked lots of other places that didn't even pretend to do things that way.

And what do you know, it's working.

Now we have to face the challenges posed by our successes so far. We have to build the company rapidly, maintain the safety factor which has allowed us to survive lean times in the past, and continue to adhere to the principles that have been working so well for us up to now. This may be a lot easier to say than to do. There is a powerful force which pushes organisations toward mediocrity and insensitivity as they grow, and resisting it must have a high priority here.

And yet, we must change. We are working with much larger sums of money, many more people, numerous outside consultants and vendors, and with a vastly increased workload. The old informal channels of communication just cannot handle the load any more. We have been and will continue to institute the internal procedures we need to make information flow smoothly and to enable us to make the most of our limited funds. We must control our money very carefully now. Prudent use of our money now is one of the keys to making this company a success, so we will continue to watch expenses very closely.

If we obtain an infusion of money from venture capital sources, this will only increase the need to manage our money very carefully. When we obtain outside funding, we are committing to use that money as carefully as we can to make the company a success. We will control and deploy that money even more carefully (if that be possible) than the hard earned dollars we invested in this company or the sweat-stained dollars we pour back in from the sales we've made so far.

Explosive Growth Foreseen In CAD/CAE

The computer-aided design (CAD) market will reach $6.9 billion by 1987, according to the Yankee Group (Boston). CAD industry revenues were $1.3 billion in 1982; the CAD market is expected to grow at 40% annually through 1986.

Systems and Software, *February 1984*

Who can doubt that we are in the right place at the right time?

Now let's talk about what isn't supposed to change as this company grows.

This company was formed as a vehicle through which people who had in the past worked very hard with little reward could not only reap rewards, but control their own destinies and make the decisions, for better or worse, which would determine whether we succeeded or failed. This company has never put people into boxes or told them that they couldn't try something they wanted to do. There has always been more work to do than people and hours to do it, and nobody who has asked to try something has been refused a chance at it.

> *The computer programmer, is a creator of universes for which he alone is the lawgiver. Universes of virtually unlimited complexity can be created in the form of computer programs. Moreover, and this is a crucial point, systems so formulated and elaborated act out their programmed scripts. They compliantly obey their laws and vividly exhibit their obedient behaviour. No playwright, no stage director, no emperor, however powerful, has ever exercised such absolute authority to arrange a stage or field of battle and to command such unswervingly dutiful actors or troops.*
>
> Joseph Weizenbaum, Computer Power and Human Reason

But in the real world it's a whole lot harder. Our freedom to make decisions is constrained by money, by time, by the realities of working in the real world with real people. By succeeding in this domain as well as by creating the best computer program of its kind, we can gain the real rewards, both material and internal, that we started this company to achieve. But is it any wonder that it's easier to program up a storm than come to terms with this rapidly growing company? Between the risks inherent in the software business (where else can somebody copy a $1500 product for $5, or destroy an industry by a Kamikaze marketing strategy of, say, $50 per?) and the potential of being the leader in the fastest growing corner of a business growing 40% per year, is the reality we make out of the opportunity we have created by all those nights we worked straight through.

And that reality can be best served by making this company work as well on a large scale as it did when it was just a few wild eyed maniacs in various basements. This means that we have to make the company responsive to what people want. This is a lot harder to do as we necessarily increase the distance between the people developing the product and the people using it in the field. But we have to do it. We need to feed ideas back and forth rapidly. Anybody may come up with an idea which could make AutoCAD usable to a whole new group of people. Anybody may hear a customer suggest such an idea. We have to make sure that ideas like these aren't forgotten or left unacted on.

This product and this company aren't successful because we've spent loads of money advertising and whipping up a demand for a product. We've done so well because we created a product which fills a basic need. This is a product which excites people by its very existence. It's fun to use, and it lets people do work they couldn't otherwise do without spending hours of tedious labour. This product has put in the hands of the individual and small company the power which previously was only available to large companies — which contributes to leveling the playing field and eliminating advantages of scale.

We can continue to build on this success without losing track of how we got here. We have to continue to listen to each other, to customers, to anybody with a bright idea. We can't let schedules, budgets, meetings, departments, and memos dim the spark of creativity which built this company, or structure out the immediate communication of ideas and rapid response to requests which firmly established our reputation as "good guys".

When we advertise, all we're trying to do is tell the 98% of people who can use our product, but don't know that anything like it exists, "Hey, look here". When we try to obtain publicity, we can succeed best by telling stories of people who solved problems by using AutoCAD. These ideas and these stories will not be dreamed up by advertising people — their job is to communicate, not to invent. We have to find these stories and present them in a form where they will be understood.

And so we must not look at advertising as a black box where you feed money in one end and sales come out the other. It's one of the many means of communicating. More important than the advertising budget is what we want to communicate. Who are we? What do we sell? Why do people need it? What problems does it solve? Why is ours better than theirs? We have to answer these questions. Nobody else can.

And so, I see our challenge here as mainly keeping on track. If we can continue to be responsive, to act quickly, to get a lot done with a little money, to make one piece of work benefit us in multiple ways; if we can continue to make this company a humane place to work where people are rewarded for their intense labours and where anybody can advance rapidly just by carving out additional responsibilities, then I think that the success we have experienced so far will be multiplied by many times over the next few years.

The Slingshot and Success

I'd like to wind up with one of the most obscure metaphors I've ever used in one of these letters. In celestial mechanics there's a concept known as gravity assist, or the cosmic slingshot. It's how the Voyager probe got to Saturn.

If you take a satellite and drop it down very close to a planet, then fire its engine, the power of the engine is multiplied by the gravity of the object you're whizzing past. Any effort made at that peak point, at the ragged edge of plunging into the pit, is multiplied thousandsfold versus efforts made in the calm void, far removed from risk and turbulence.

We're in the heart of the maelstrom now. We're growing so fast we can hardly keep up. We're becoming known, and how we treat people and how well we meet their needs now will determine how we're perceived for years to come. The reputation of our product is being made on a day to day basis. One major screwup and we can lose it all — overnight.

What you do now in this crazy environment will cast a long shadow on the future of this company, on your career, and on all of our hopes to share the rewards of success.

This is not the time to coast. This is not the time to let growth squeeze out innovation or our ability to take a risk or grab for the main chance. Today, this company looks awfully goddam respectable compared to where we were, say, last May. The trappings of success are everywhere. But remember, if we get to where we hoped to be when we started this venture back in January of 1982, we'll look back on these as the "old days". To coast now will make this the peak, not the stepping stone to where we want to be.

Every dollar we spend, whether for salaries, rent, raw materials, or advertising, was generated because somebody chose to buy our product. That person looked at the fruit of our labours, looked at our company and our commitment to help him after he bought the product, at our future and the promise that held for future development and additions to improve what he was buying, and decided that what we had to sell, which is nothing more than a great idea written onto a $5 floppy disc, with a manual, was worth more than $1000 or $1500 in his pocket.

Whether we have the resources to continue our growth, whether we survive or join the ranks of the software companies that "drop from sight" depends on whether people continue to value what we have to sell as worth more than that money in their pockets. Buying anything, but especially something as intangible as a computer program, involves putting your trust in the person who's selling it.

If we continue to deserve that trust, we'll do very well, indeed.

The Deal On the Table

After talking to virtually every venture capitalist in the business, in May of 1984 it appeared that we were finally going to close a deal. Frank Chambers, who had been introduced to us by Jack Stuppin, indicated that he was willing to make an investment in our company. Despite our cynicism, born of endless tiresome and fruitless meetings which consumed our time when it was desperately needed to develop the company, we were eager to obtain funding we could apply to increase our marketing efforts and seize the market before better-funded competitors entered the fray.

Mike Ford described the situation as "being in a verdant field with gold bars lying all around. The question is how many can we throw in our pickup truck before a big vacuum cleaner comes down from the sky and sucks them all up." In essence then, being greedy and aggressive suckers ourselves, we wanted the cash to nail down the largest possible market share while we still could.

After numerous and lengthy discussions, Frank Chambers communicated the terms of the deal. What follows is a transcription of Dan Drake's notes taken while hearing the terms over the phone, with annotations explaining what the terms mean.

Terms I: Frank Chambers

- $500 – 700K. Size of the investment in dollars. This would represent about 1/10 of the company.
- $2 preferred, convertible to 1 share common. The investment would be preferred stock, so that if the company failed the investor would get his money from the remains before any of the common shareholders. The stock could be converted to common stock at any time. This is conventional in venture capital deals.
- If not liquid in 4 1/2 years, we offer to repurchase at 2x price (plus accrued dividends). If the company did not go public or get acquired, thus

providing an opportunity for the investor to "cash out", we would buy back the investment at twice its original value.

- 8% dividend from 2/1/85; with majority of preferred holders or the board able to substitute change in conversion ratio. We would pay this dividend from the company's earnings. If we didn't have the earnings to pay the dividend, the foregone income would be used to increase the venture capitalist's ownership share of the company. Most venture capital deals work this way, but it's unusual to have the dividend start so soon after the deal.

- One demand registration, unlimited piggyback. The investor could, at will, demand that we make a public offering in order to enable him to cash out his stock. The company would bear all of the costs of the public offering. In this, or any other offering the company made, the investor would be able to sell his shares "piggyback", up to the total amount of the shares owned.

- Options.
    110,000 at $.75.
    Remainder at least $2 + 5% per 6 months.
    Dilution protection, unspecified, above 500,000 options.
    Vesting at least 4 years.
    Forfeited options are canceled, not returned to pool.

- Board of directors. 7 people: preferred elects one, one by agreement of preferred and common shareholders. Jack Stuppin to be on the board. Advisory committee to the board up to 3 people chosen by the investor.

- Representative of preferred investor approves: "All compensation matters", and all capital expenditures over $25,000.

- John Walker: key man insurance $500K; employment contract, 2 years, non-competition.

- Frank Chambers approves investors.

- Preferred has first refusal on private equity offerings.

We didn't like it. While many of the terms were conventional and were what we expected, several totally unexpected constraints on our ability to develop the company in the way that had brought us to the present point were contained in the deal. In particular, our ability to grant stock options to new employees was severely constrained by limits on the number available, by forcing the option exercise price to above the price paid by the investor (who received much better terms on his preferred than the employee would on his common stock), by retiring from the pool any options granted to an employee who subsequently left the company, and by imposing a four-year vesting period on all options, which the founders of the company felt transformed the options from their original purpose of allowing employees to share in the company's success to a kind of twentieth century indentured servitude which compelled employees to stay with the company or face forfeiture of their financial gains.

We also thought that the general tone of the deal was far from consonant with the percentage of the company being purchased and the demonstrated performance of the company to date and the track record of its managers. But we still wanted the cash. So ... we came back with the following suggested terms.

Terms II: Us

- $500 – 700K.
- $2 preferred.
- Repurchase at 1.5x if not liquid in 4 1/2 years; call on preferred at $4 + 20% per year. The call provision would allow us to forcibly buy out the investor for twice the investment plus an increment of 20 percent per year. This was meant to be symmetrical with the repurchase provision benefiting the investor.
- 8% dividend from 2/1/85; reduction in conversion price on missed dividend. This is equivalent to the original requested terms, just more lucidly put.
- One demand registration if proceeds exceed $X, $X \geq \$5 \times 10^6$. In English, this means we're talking about five million dollars or more.
- Options: dilution protection by issuing proportional shares at the same price as *exercised* options. Vesting set by board when option issued. No cancellation of forfeits — return to pool.
- Board of directors. 7 people: preferred elects one, common elects 6.
- Ceiling on executive salaries and bonuses until some numbers (sales and profit) achieved; override by preferred representative. Preferred representative approves capital expenditures over $100,000.

- John Walker: key man insurance; contract, no non-competition. Being an ornery S.O.B., I said that signing a non-competition agreement with a company in which I was the largest shareholder was beneath my dignity and that I wouldn't do it. Moral: don't pick an asshole to be president of your company.
- Frank Chambers approves investors, but present stockholders can buy in subject to $ ceiling and regulatory problems. We didn't want the venture capitalist to be able to veto further investments by people who got in before he did.
- In general, the constraints have drop-dead provisions. This meant that every constraint on our freedom to run the company would expire when we reached some well-defined performance milestones.

He didn't like it. So, we got together and attempted to come up with another offer which would be acceptable. Here it is.

Terms III: 5/10/84

- $500 – 700K.
- $2 preferred, convertible.
- Repurchase terms OK (?) We acceded to the original terms.
- Forced conversion if we get to $10 million (?) annual sales and $1 million annual profit or make a public stock offering over $5 million.
- One demand registration, piggyback, *after* 1/1/87 for >$5 million.
- Options: 100,000 shares at $.75, 200,000 shares at $1.60, 200,000 shares at $2.00, 200,000 shares at $3.00, 200,000 shares at $4.00. Majority of each class of stock to approve any new plan. Vesting at best 50–25–25 after the first 100,000 shares. This meant that after the first 100,000 shares of options (which were committed to fulfilling options we'd already granted to people), those who received options would receive 50% of their shares the first year, 25% the second year, and 25% the third year. Forfeited options return to pool.
- Board: ask Chambers †, Ellison, Stuppin. (? Unsettled). What are the terms on paper? † If not on board, an advisor.
- $75,000 ceiling on officer and director salaries. Override by 6 or 7 directors.
- $25,000 on capital expenditures. Override how?

- John Walker: key man insurance; employment contract to "devote substantially all his time".
- Frank Chambers approves investors. Common holders can buy in (n.b. might have to keep it intrastate to avoid sophisticated investor problems). Since people who joined the company in the beginning and worked themselves to exhaustion to build it to the point that venture capitalists were interested in investing were not *ipso facto* "qualified" to risk their savings by investing in their own company since they were not already wealthy. This is an example of what was referred to in the 1980's as the "opportunity society".
- First refusal on private equity offerings.

After these terms were presented, it was clear that we would never come to an agreement on the issue of awarding stock options to employees to give them a real stake in the company's success. In addition, the overall flavour of the deal seemed to us totally inappropriate for a company which was, at the time of these negotiations, generating sales equal to the size of the deal every month and generating after-tax profits close to the size of the deal every quarter.

We couldn't believe that this was the best deal obtainable for venture funding of the company, and we were inclined to ask around to see if this was reasonable. But, our Distinguished Financial Advisor informed us that this would constitute "shopping the deal" when "a deal was on the table" which was right out by the genteel standards of the venture community, and that he could not countenance such unrefined behaviour (notwithstanding the fact that in the real world this kind of collusion is called "conspiracy in restraint of trade" and people go to jail for it).

So, after a brief weekend meeting in which we discovered we all agreed on the obvious conclusion, we decided to graciously decline this generous offer of funding and carry on with our own resources. Upon hearing this decision, Jack Stuppin said that if we didn't take this deal, he did not wish to be a shareholder and wanted us to buy him out. Not wishing to deplete our treasury, we declined. In not accepting our terms, which differed from his original proposal primarily in issues of philosophy, not money, Frank Chambers chose to forego an investment of $500,000 which, if held until the stock price hit its 1987 high, would have appreciated to more than $37 million.

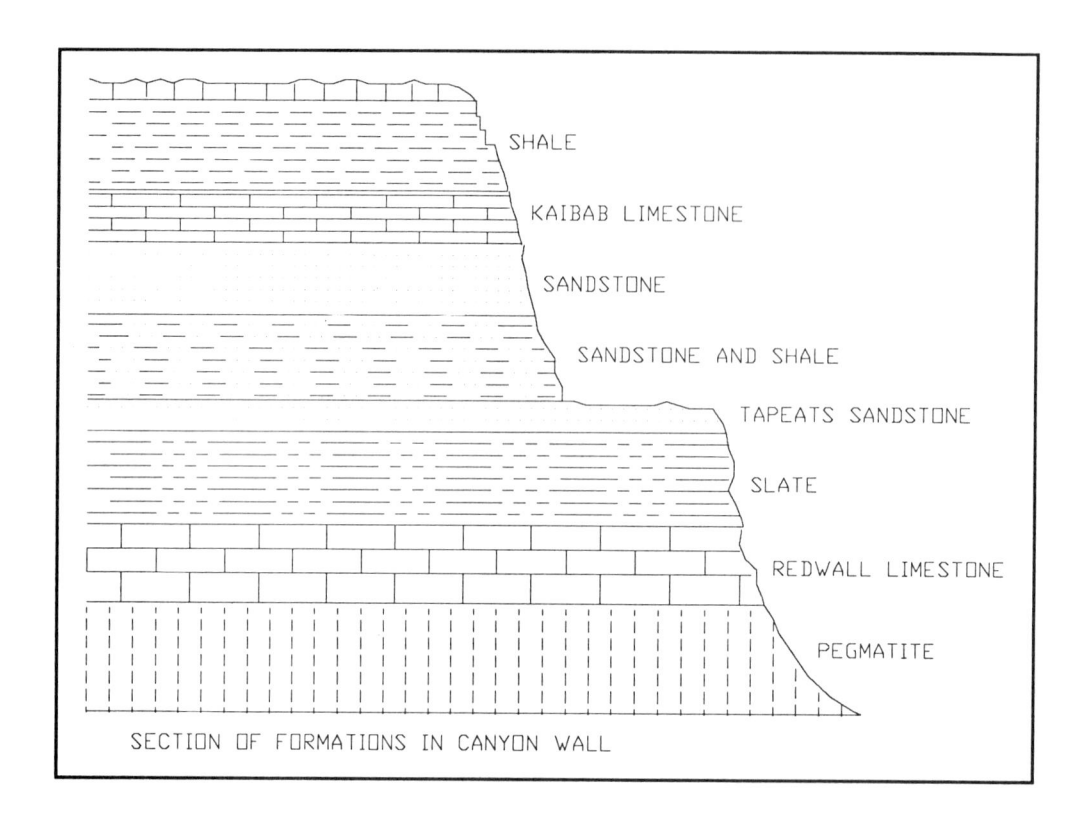

Peter Barnett drew this geological strata illustration in 1984 to demonstrate the multiple dot and dash line types introduced in AutoCAD 2.0. The drawing doesn't represent any real geological formation — it was made up out of thin air, not hard rock. It has been used as a sample drawing from AutoCAD 2.0 to date.

Expanding the Product Line

With the burgeoning success of AutoCAD, I was increasingly worried about new entrants in the market turning our own strategy against us — entering the market with a low priced package and taking the entry-level user away from us, just as we had done with the big CAD companies. The growing success of the low-priced software market, pioneered by Borland's Turbo Pascal, only intensified this concern.

This proposal, for "AutoCAD Lite", was the first real expression of the need for an entry level drawing product in our product line. Of course, we never did implement AutoCAD Lite, but it's interesting to compare its specifications with those of AutoSketch, which we announced to the world almost precisely two years later.

AutoCAD Lite

Suggestion by John Walker
July 7, 1984

Almost since we made our first sale of AutoCAD, we've been periodically kicking around the idea of selling a stripped version of AutoCAD at an entry-level price. These plans have always foundered as we failed to identify a usable subset of AutoCAD which could be sold in, say, the $250 to $500 range.[109]

I believe that such a product exists, can be used for serious work, is not likely to hurt the sales of our main AutoCAD product, and can be added to our product line with minimal development effort. The product is AutoCAD-80.

Over 100 copies of AutoCAD-80 have been sold to date, and many are being used by such people as Eric Clough, who is making better use of this limited product than most people make of the full AutoCAD-86. Thus I think that there is no question that the package is useful.

---

109   Of course, by the time we started on AutoSketch, which was targeted below $100, we had already reduced the price on basic AutoCAD to $300, positioning it in this price bracket.

Conversely, reviewing the thin AutoCAD-80 manual, and remembering that having been cut out of the development mainstream at release 1.2, AutoCAD-80 lacks many features of even the non-ADE AutoCAD-86 that a professional is likely to require. Thus, if we assume that most of our current users are those serious professionals we talk about, few of them would spend all day working around the limitations of AutoCAD-80 to save 1750 bucks.

I am *not* proposing that we work with the PL/I version of the program! Instead, I am suggesting that we take the exact feature set of that program as the definition of our AutoCAD Lite product and make the C version down-configurable for that version. I would propose making some of the following strategic changes in the definition of the product. Features unavailable in AutoCAD-80 are not mentioned in the following table.

- Make the Lite version write its database out in single-precision.[110] Greg's SCATTER/GATHER code should make this easy to do. It would halve the database size (making the package more appropriate for floppy systems), and would restrict accuracy to 8 digits or so (the same as AutoCAD-80, which is a single precision floating point package).
- No dimensioning would be available.[111]
- Disable 8087 support.[112]
- Remove DXF input and output capability.[113]
- Remove LAYER capability.[114]
- Remove LTYPE capability.
- Remove TABLET mode.
- Disable shape compiler — allow only fixed fonts.
- Develop a conversion capability to allow regular AutoCAD to read Lite drawings. Full AutoCAD drawings could not be down-converted to the Lite version.
- (I'm not sure about this) Remove pen plotter support and support only dot matrix printers.

---

110 AutoSketch followed this recommendation.
111 AutoSketch not only had dimensioning, it had associative dimensioning six months before AutoCAD.
112 AutoSketch not only supported the 8087, it had in-line 8087 support a year before AutoCAD.
113 AutoSketch had DXF out but not in.
114 AutoSketch has 10 layers.

Many of the above product definition changes are intended to turn off features which require a lot of customer support time as much as to limit the usability of the package.

The resulting product would be far more usable for the kinds of things people attempt to do with other entry-level programs like Draft-Aide, Robocom, Caddraft, and Cascade I, but should not present serious competition in our present market. Providing an upward migration path to full AutoCAD would lock in the entry level user who purchased the Lite package. (We should, however, think seriously about the possibility that some of the manufacturers and/or Summit might buy this package to bundle as AutoCAD graphics rather than the full package. Would this be bad in the medium run, if purchasers upgraded at dealer price or list? I think some exploratory talks are needed if we decide to do this.)

Strategically, we should separate the Lite version from its big brother. We want the Lite purchaser to buy because of the association with AutoCAD, but our current customer not to seriously consider the Lite package for his purposes. Might the Lite package be well suited to schools where we have to cut very low-price deals? This might be a way to keep our price up on the main package but essentially give away unlimited Lites to cut the deal. Secondly, we might let Lite out into mass distribution and discounting. We wouldn't make much on each one, but the numbers would add up, and every Lite is a foot in the door for a full AutoCAD, and a sale we should be able to make if we follow up the Lite leads. Lite might be the foot in the door with people like Koala who don't understand the concept of $1500 software.

We have heard that the entry level packages have not been selling well, but of course one has to remember that most of them are terrible. We know that AutoCAD-80 isn't, because its users seem to be happy and productive (but wish, of course, they had all those neat ADE features ...). My idea on the Lite would be to bring it out on a subset of machines (say, the ones Lotus supports), and immediately look for distribution through Softsel, Lifeboat, Koala, Computerland HQ, etc. We would package it cheaply, provide a limited number of machines, and plan no development at all after introduction so ongoing manufacturing and support costs could be low. We would not add hardware protection, but might use something like ProLok.

Development of such a product would be a moderate amount of work, as it would involve putting a lot of tests all over the product, removing a lot of code by conditional compilation and linking to make the thing small, and of course testing the final product. But once a version was certified fully debugged on a given machine the development effort would be zero. Porting to new machines would involve simply remaking the package with our regular driver for that machine. We could create the manual by editing the existing manual.

I am confident that a useful product can be created according to these guidelines. What we need to establish is:

- Will it hurt our existing AutoCAD sales, and if so how much?
- How much support will the package take?
- Where should such a product be priced?
- How much can we expect to make on each one?
- What are the best distribution channels?
- How much will it cost us to find out if this is a dumb idea?
- Do we have the time and money to launch such a product?

Finally, there's the Japanese invasion of the low-end computer market with Z-80 machines running MSX (Microsoft's Z-80 clone of CP/M).[115] If we entered this market with AutoCAD-80, we would then have a compatible 8086 product to fill out our product line.

So in one sentence, I think we can make such a product. Do we want to?

---

[115] An invasion which had essentially no impact outside Japan.

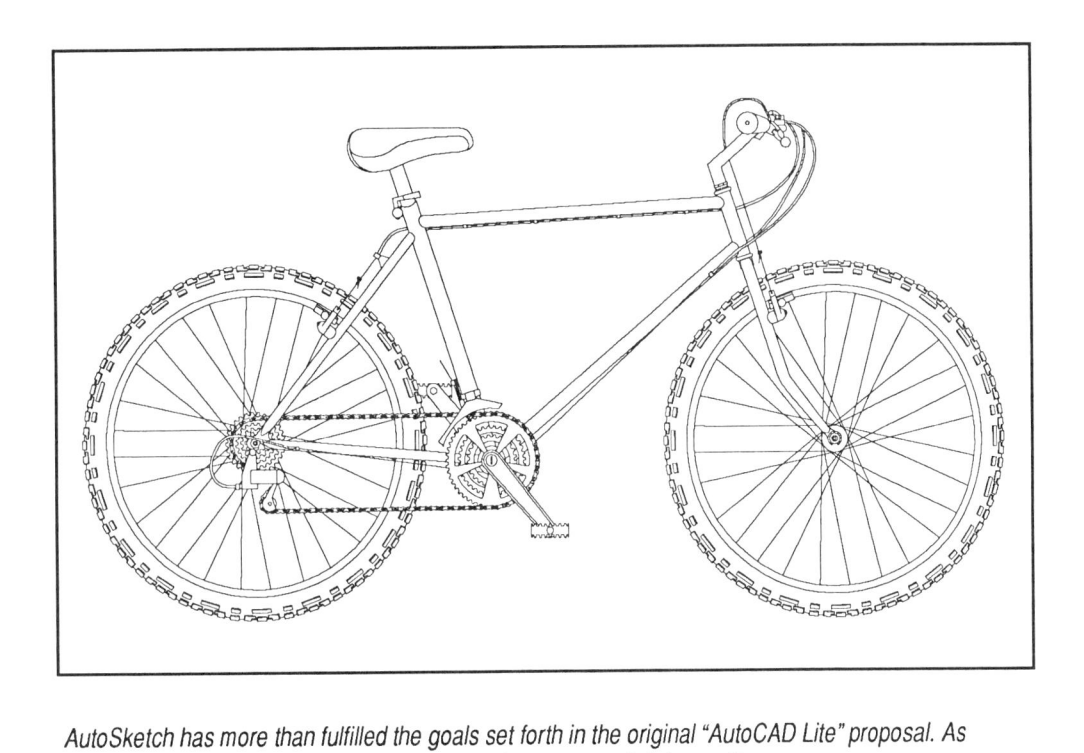

AutoSketch has more than fulfilled the goals set forth in the original "AutoCAD Lite" proposal. As with AutoCAD, AutoSketch users immediately began to apply it in creative ways we never anticipated, and created remarkable drawings with it. This mountain bike was drawn with AutoSketch by Larry Dea.

Taxes and Such

As the company continued to succeed, the stock price had to be revalued even though the stock was not publicly traded. This began to have tax consequences for the founders (in particular emptying Dan Drake's and my bank accounts because of a little Sin of Omission on the part of our Distinguished Legal and Accounting Advisors). Clearly, if the success continued, we needed to learn well and learn fast the rules under which we'd be playing in the stock arena.

Dan Drake researched this area in depth and wrote this memo which was originally circulated in August of 1984 and was revised and updated twice in 1985 as the public offering loomed closer. Though dated in some particulars of the law and tax rules, it's still the clearest statement I've seen of the twisty and treacherous passages one must negotiate to survive creating a new business and hundreds of jobs and not be either reduced to poverty or going to jail. Most companies don't warn their employees about any of this; the investment bankers were amused that Autodesk "took the risk" in giving this advice to the people who had built the company to the point the bankers could take it public.

To: All stockholders of Autodesk, Inc.
From: Dan Drake
Subject: Taxes and such
Date: August 26, 1984 / March 6, 1985 / May 8, 1985

"I have yet to see any problem, however complicated, which, when you looked at it the right way, did not become still more complicated."

Poul Anderson

[This is a re-issue of a piece we distributed last summer. Not much has been changed, except to correct a couple of errors; in particular don't look for realistic prices in the examples. One of the errors, by the way, was based on published information from a Big Eight accounting firm. Does that mean that even they don't understand the law? Impossible.]

Some people have asked me for a summary of the stuff that I've learned about the landmines that the IRS, SEC, et al. have strewn in front of us. This is it. You should, as the saying goes, check with your own legal and financial advisers before believing any of this.

Much of this discussion concerns what happens when you sell stock, but don't get too excited: at the moment it's nearly impossible to sell our stock without going to jail. Sometime, though, our stock or a successor stock will be registered with the SEC so that it can be traded like any other, and you'll have to know the rules. If you persist to the end of this thing, you'll find some of the really amusing rules that apply when the stock is public, including Rule 144 and The Amazing Sixteen (b).

Actually, it may not be too hard to sell stock if the buyer is a California resident who already owns our stock, or if no citizens or residents of the United States are involved. (If you have reason to do it, ask for the details). Even so, it would be troublesome to trade the stock actively, but you've already signed an investment letter asserting that you have no intention of doing so before the stock is registered.

Warrants

(The first two paragraphs are obsolete, but the rest may be of interest to people who have exercised warrants.)

When we first sold stock, we issued warrants as a sweetener to encourage people to invest hard cash. These allow you to buy additional stock at $.10 a share, provided you do it by April 30, 1986. To exercise (buy the stock) you fill out the form that's attached to the warrant, write a check, and give both to the corporate Secretary (me). The company will issue a stock certificate as soon as possible.

You can, in principle, sell warrants to other people; but the restrictions are as bad as those on selling stock.

The only tax problem associated with warrants, as far as I can tell, is that you want to watch the capital gains rules. From now until 1989 (?) this means that you want to exercise the warrant at least six months before you sell the stock; then you pay income tax on 40% of the difference between the selling price and the $.10 that you paid for the stock. (Does the $.001 that you paid for the warrant come into this? I think so, but it doesn't make much difference.) If you sell for $5.00, this means taxable income of $0.40 x (5.00-0.10) = $1.96; this tax will not exceed 50% of the taxable amount, or 20% of the total gain, or $.98, unless they change the rules again.

If your tax bracket is below 50%, you will pay even less than 20% on your capital gains — but it's just possible that you'll get caught by Alternative Minimum Tax (see below) and have to pay 20% anyway.

While you're waiting for the capital gains treatment to ripen on the stock you got for a warrant, you're free to sell stock that you bought before; just be very careful to turn in the right stock certificate and to keep proper records. (Well, actually, if you're an insider, this isn't quite true; but we'll get to 16(b) later.)

Stock Options

First, the history and terminology: Incentive Stock Options are the things that used to be called Qualified Options. Qualified Options were eliminated in the 70's; ISOs were authorized in 1981; and an incredible confiscatory hook was embedded in them in 1982. They are not to be confused with stock purchase plans, though they often are; when Osborne went belly-up, many people who thought they had options discovered that they were legally obliged to pay for worthless stock, with no option at all in the matter. We have an ISO Plan in operation now; if we set up a stock purchase plan, no one will be allowed to be confused between the two.

Under an ISO Plan the Board of Directors issues options which allow you to buy the stock at a set price (called the exercise price). If everyone follows all the rules exactly, you can exercise options at any time within a period specified in your option agreement; after waiting a while, you can sell the stock and pay capital gains tax on the difference between the price you paid and the price you sold for (see under Warrants).

Here are the most important of those rules that must be followed. First, the exercise price of the option must be at least the Fair Market Value of the stock as of the time when the option was issued; you hope, of course, to exercise at a time when the value is much higher, and to sell while it remains high. The option must expire within ten years after it's issued. Simple enough? Then remember that if the optionee owns 10% or more of the existing stock, the price must be at least 110% of fair market value, and the expiration must be no more than five years.

To exercise an option, send a check to the corporate Secretary (me) with a covering note to explain that you're paying this money to exercise options. We'll promptly record the sale of stock and issue a certificate. Please don't just mail or wire money to the company in the hope that we'll guess what it's for.

The time when you finally sell the stock must be (a) at least two years since the option was granted and (b) at least one year since you exercised the option. The recent change in the capital gains holding period doesn't affect (b). You also have to exercise the options First In First Out, and you can't get around this by getting the company to cancel old options before they expire. The reason for this is that a drop in the price of stock might tempt a company to cancel a lot of old, expensive options and issue new ones at the current, lower price; this is far too nice to the employees to be legal. (It's common practice to have a Vesting Period for options. This means that people can't exercise any of the options for (say) one year after the option date; then they can exercise up to (say) 25% of the option each year. The idea is to keep those bums from exercising their options and going off to take another job before the company has extracted full value from them. This is an industry norm, not a government requirement. Autodesk's vesting periods will conform to industry norms no more closely than the rest of our practices do.) That's all the important restrictions and traps, except for Alternative Minimum Tax and Section 16(b); we'll get to them later. So what if one of these rules is violated? Then [soundtrack: the Empire's theme music] the option becomes *disqualified*. When you exercise it, you become immediately liable for plain income tax (not capital gains) on the difference between the exercise price and the fair market value when you exercise. In the previous example, you exercise a $.10 option when the stock is trading for $5.00; whether or not you sell, you have income at that moment equal to $4.90, on which the federal tax could be up to $2.45. If you ever sell, your gain or loss will be computed against that $5.00 value rather than the $.10 exercise price. But what if the stock isn't registered, and it's illegal (as well as impossible) to sell it? No problem; the government will be glad to take your house if you can't raise the money to pay the tax on your non-existent gain.

If this happens to you, though, all is not lost: the company gets a tax deduction.

Alternative Minimum Tax

Important: Though most people don't have to pay any tax under this law, it appears to be necessary to file Form 6251 if you exercise any stock options, just to prove that you don't owe extra tax. So read this stuff. Alternative Minimum Tax is aimed at people who have a large dollar volume of capital gains, accelerated depreciation, option exercises, and intangible drilling costs (I'm not making this up).

Here's the theory behind AMT. Certain types of income get special tax preference, for reasons which are clearly in the National Interest. This results in some people paying low taxes, which is clearly not in the National Interest. Therefore, the government gives subsidies and takes them back again, which is in the National Interest.

If you have these special types of income, here's roughly what you do. Compute your taxable income, and compute the tax on it. Remember this number. To your taxable income, add back some of the deductions you took: accelerated depreciation, intangible drilling costs, 60% of capital gains, and various itemized deductions. Also, if you exercised any Incentive Stock Options in the year, add the difference between the exercise price and the Fair Market Value when you exercised them (the $4.90 in our example, which you thought you didn't have to pay tax on because the options weren't disqualified). Subtract $30,000 (single person) or $40,000 (joint return). Take 20% of that. If this exceeds your normal tax, this is what you pay; otherwise (the great majority of cases) you merely report it and pay the normal tax. Stock options were included in this calculation under the Tax Equity and Fiscal responsibility Act of 1982. The equity of taxing people on a gain which another part of the law says is not to be realized for at least another year (and yet another says can't be realized without going to jail) is self-evident, so I won't explain it. What makes it especially equitable is that while a passive investor pays 20% on his gains, an entrepreneur is allowed to pay up to 40% (plus Uncle Deukmejian's cut). Comments in an earlier edition about rates going up to 52% were wrong, based on an uncritical acceptance of an expert's opinion.

This cloud, too, has a silver lining: if you're paying AMT, then the effective tax rate on any additional ordinary income is down to 20% until you get so much that you're out of AMT land again. This can be significant if you're liquidating assets to get enough money to pay AMT. If you need to understand this in more detail, stop by sometime when you have an extra hour or two, and I'll be glad to give you a quick outline of the situation.

Publicly Traded Stock

If the company succeeds, we would like to be able to cash in sooner or later. The normal way is to register the stock so that it can be sold on the open market. That, of course, is what we're planning now. Therefore, it's a good idea to know what to expect from a public offering. In order to register some of its stock with the Securities and Exchange Commission for public trading, a company spends $200,000 to $500,000 on lawyers, accountants, printers, etc., plus a few months of the management's time. If the deal falls through (which is quite possible from causes outside anyone's control), much of that money has to be paid anyway and is a dead loss.

The financial effect of the public offering is, to oversimplify, that the underwriters buy a few million dollars' worth of stock from the company and immediately sell it to the public at a profit. The buyers can then sell the stock to each other at ever-increasing prices, we hope. The part of the company that's sold in the offering varies widely, but might typically be 25%. The price is substantially higher than venture capitalists would have paid for the same percentage of ownership; a factor of two is often mentioned.

So now that the company is public, we can all start selling our stock to the public, right? Wrong. The underwriter may allow the existing stockholders to sell some of their stock at the same time that the company sells its stock, but the amount is limited by the public's desire to keep the founders a bit lean and hungry so that they'll make some further profits for the public before going off to lie on the beach. All the old stock that isn't sold then (the majority of the company) is still unregistered and still can't be traded easily.

Over the next few years the founders can dribble their unregistered stock onto the market under Rule 144, provided that the company keeps up with all the SEC's reporting requirements. The essence of this rule is that anyone who has owned his unregistered stock free and clear for two years can sell through a broker in the public market, subject to a limit of 1% of the company (or a formula involving average trading volume) per three months. A person who is not an insider can forget about the 1% rule after owning the stock for three years.

As I understand it, people who own large amounts of stock, as well as officers and directors of the company, fall under Rule 144 restrictions even in trading registered stock.

Three years after the company goes public, it can file a simple little form ($20,000) to register all its stock. In the interim the stockholders could get some more stock registered by persuading the company and the underwriters to make another public offering (another quarter million dollars of expense, shared by the selling stockholders) in which a larger amount of their own stock is sold.

More practically, 90 days after going public, the company can make a simple filing (S–8) which will automatically register any stock that people get later by exercising stock options. Under this system a person who exercises an option for cash right after the effective date of the S–8 filing may be able to sell the stock immediately (though with terrible tax consequences), while someone who exercised earlier has to wait for two years under Rule 144. Nonetheless, this is a very good deal for the employees.

Insiders and Rule 16(b)

The first rule about insiders is that there are stiff penalties for trading on inside information. If you know that the company is about to buy a half-interest in IBM, and you think that will raise the price of the stock when it becomes known, you'd better not buy chunks of the stock to profit from the rise. This rule applies not only to officers and directors, but to anybody who has access to interesting information that isn't public yet. To help people resist temptation, the SEC requires all officers and directors of the company to report all their transactions in its stock. These reports are a matter of public record for every busybody and corporate gadfly in the country to study.

If two rules are good, three are better; therefore, the SEC isn't content just to levy fines for trading on inside information and to require reporting of transactions. It's also illegal for insiders to profit in any way, though in perfectly good faith, on short-term transactions in the company's securities. This is the egregious Rule 16(b): if an insider buys and sells a security in any six-month period, he must hand over his profit to the company! In any doubtful case this rule gets the most unfavorable interpretation possible; for instance, you take the losses and the company takes the gains, and you can't balance off losses and gains in a six-month period.

It's not entirely clear to me who is an insider under this rule, but it seems to apply to more than just the officers and directors. In fact, I have the impression it's not clear to anybody.

What if the company fails to claim the profit from an insider's trading? Then any stockholder can require it to do so. Remember the bit about the reports being public record?

Of course, none of us would trade on inside information or do short-term trading in the company's stock (much less sell it short, which is also illegal), but the rule can make real trouble. Exercising an option, for instance, counts as a purchase of stock; so don't sell any within six months before or after — there goes the idea of selling some stock to cover AMT, unless you exercise in the first half of the year. (It's said that there's even a way for an exercise to count as both a purchase and a sale, causing instant confiscation, but this appears to be just a trap for people without lawyers.) Or suppose you buy some stock, and three months later General Motors comes along to buy the company — bye bye, profit. Remember, though, this just applies to insiders, if you can find out what an insider is.

This note has taken a fairly negative tone in places; in writing about regulatory matters one's attitude varies from heavy sarcasm to blind fury. It's as well to remember that people go through these things every day and come out with large bundles of money at the other end. If we can ace out Computervision, Autotrol, and IBM, not even the SEC can protect us against succeeding.

Section Four

Number One

Publisher's Notes
January 1985 — December 1985

This was the year that Autodesk achieved two stunning successes. They clearly became the "Number One" CAD vendor with more software units installed worldwide than any other company; and they navigated an Initial Public Offering (IPO) to raise capital for the company. Thus, they became a publicly traded company *without* the use of outside venture capital.

Key Events

Here are the key events and the documents provided in Section Four.

- February 5, 1985. — Why Lisp? The AutoCAD released in 1985 had Lisp as a language with the program. This paper explains why.

March 1985. Cumulative installed units number 17,000.

- March 1985. — Number One. The start of an ad campaign defining AutoCAD as the number one CAD software program.

- April 16 & May 8, 1985. — Initial Public Offering. The working paper that formed the company's statement in the Initial Public Offering. (See IPO below.) Also included is a paper on Sales and Marketing.

- May 8, 1985. — Prime Time. Yet another unfortunate venture with an outside public relations firm.

June 1985. Three for two stock split.

June 28, 1985. The Initial Public Offering (IPO) by the company raised ten million dollars. The founders gained 3,000% on their initial investment.

- July 1, 1985. — Surplus Value. Advice on what to do with your post IPO wealth.

- Moon Day, 1985. — Information Letter #12. Discusses the implications, including the financial performance implications for Autodesk, now that it is a public company.

Key Product Events

The company shipped over 25,000 units in 1985. It had a cumulative installed base of 40,000 AutoCAD units at the end of the year. A new release, 2.1, was shipped in May:

May 1985. AutoCAD Version 2.1 Release. Includes the first three dimensional (3D) drafting functions. Also includes the AutoLISP language.

July 1985. CAD/camera released.

August 1985. AutoCAD AEC Architectural package released. This product is specialized for the Architecture market. It is built on the LISP language available in Release 2.1.

Financial Summary

Both sales and revenue dollars increased. Sales increased 150% to $27 million; and revenues increased 300% to over $6 million. A Japanese subsidiary was formed.

The Initial Public Offering of June 1985 raised $10 million for the company. The initial share price was $11, and moved to $21 by the end of year. (Because of later stock splits, these share prices correspond to $3.67 and $7.00 in current terms.) Adjusting for stock splits, $11 per share was equivalent to $165 for the original $1 per share investment by the founders.

Here are the quarterly figures for the year.

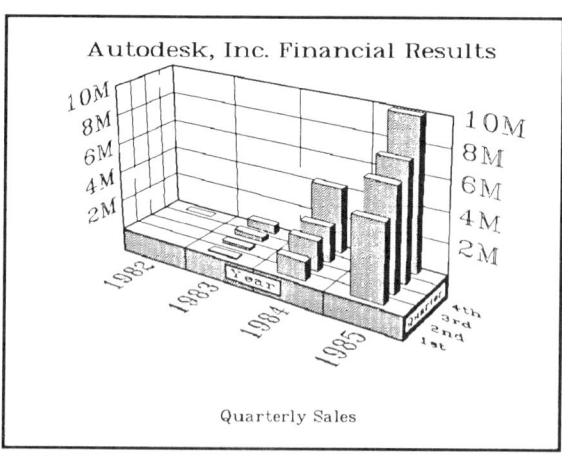

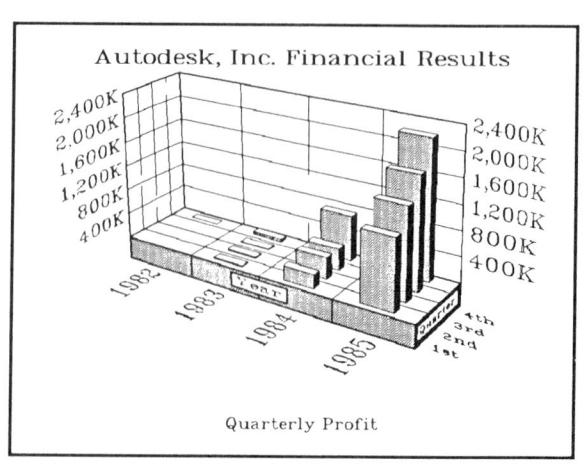

1985 Quarterly Sales

1985 Quarterly Revenues

Why Lisp?

As the release of AutoCAD 2.1 loomed closer, we were somewhat diffident about unleashing Lisp as our application language. This was at the very peak of the hype-train about expert systems, artificial intelligence, and Lisp machines, and while we didn't mind the free publicity we'd gain from the choice of Lisp, we were afraid that what was, in fact, a very simple macro language embedded within AutoCAD would be perceived as requiring arcane and specialised knowledge and thus frighten off the very application developers for whom we implemented it.

In fact, when we first shipped AutoCAD 2.1, we didn't use the word "Lisp" at all — we called it the "variables and expressions feature". Only in release 2.18, in which we provided the full functional and iterative capabilities of Lisp, did we introduce the term "AutoLisp".

AutoCAD Applications Interface

Lisp Language Interface
Marketing Strategy Position Paper

by John Walker — February 5, 1985

Lisp?!?! Why the Hell did you pick the most arcane, obscure, and hopelessly rooted-in-the-computer-science-department language in the world for an AutoCAD programming language?

Over the next six months, all of us will have the opportunity to answer this question. There are very good reasons why we chose Lisp as the initial language to attach to AutoCAD: I'll try to explain them herein. However, there is an important point we don't want to lose track of: the built-in Lisp interface we're providing is only the first in a series of Applications Interface products, allowing AutoCAD to be operated by application programs written in all major application languages. I anticipate interfaces to FORTRAN, compiled BASIC, C, and Pascal being available over the next 12 months.[116] Thus, Lisp is the language we sell for small applications — we are not offering it or suggesting it for major programming projects: that will be addressed by the other language interfaces, which permit a software vendor to attach their program to AutoCAD in its native language.

But back to Lisp. The following is my reply to "Why Lisp?".

Lisp is the preeminent language in the field of Artificial Intelligence, and has been for over two decades. Many of the most complicated programs ever written have been written in Lisp. Lisp is far from an esoteric toy of computer scientists: a system called NAVEX, written entirely in Lisp, will soon be ensuring that the Space Shuttle reaches the runway. Expert systems implemented in Lisp will be a central part of the Space Station environmental and energy management systems.

Lisp is ideally suited to the unstructured interaction that characterises the design process. Unlike programming languages such as C and FORTRAN, which force one to organise a problem entirely before programming, Lisp encourages exploring various approaches to a problem interactively, exactly as CAD helps a designer.

No other major programming language can so easily manipulate the kinds of objects one works with in CAD. As opposed to numerical programming, CAD constantly works on collections of heterogeneous objects in variable sized groups. Lisp excels at this.

Because Autodesk's implementation of Lisp is completely interactive and provides on-line debugging facilities, Lisp is among the easiest of languages to master. Because the response to all changes is immediate, programs may be tested as easily as with an interactive BASIC interpreter.

Finally, the compelling reasons which make Lisp the language of choice for large applications are forcing the design of computers optimised for Lisp. Machines from Symbolics and Texas Instruments are already on the market. This technology will be crucial to high-performance systems of the late 1980's and 1990's. By moving CAD in this direction, Autodesk is positioning your applications to take advantage of this development.

So there!

---

[116] Alas, this was not to be. The memory constraints of MS-DOS have so far precluded this oft-requested feature.

Number One

As 1985 wore on, it became clear that we were on the verge of achieving our goal of having the largest installed base of any CAD company. I wrote this copy in March, 1985 to define a campaign around our large installed base. In modified form, this copy was used in a full-page advertisement and in our "Number One" company brochure. This was written with the intent of being used with the Apollo 17 full-Earth picture, and that's what we ended up doing.

This is the original draft of the copy, which is a little more hard-hitting than what finally ran.

Number One

by John Walker
March, 1985

In November 1982 we introduced AutoCAD, the computer-aided design and drafting program for personal computers, and said that AutoCAD would become the standard for CAD worldwide.

By March, 1985, we have shipped more than 17,000 copies of AutoCAD, making it the most widely installed and used computer aided design system in the world; micro, mini, or mainframe.

When we developed AutoCAD, we believed that the personal computer would rapidly become the core of the engineering workstation — a general purpose tool which assists the engineer, architect, designer, or drafter in all aspects of their work. We believed that AutoCAD could deliver mainframe CAD power as an essential part of this workstation. We believed that we could bring mainframe CAD to the personal computer without giving up the features and capacity which are the key reasons to use CAD in the first place. We believed that by making our system a fully open architecture and assisting others who wanted to build products around AutoCAD, hundreds of vertical market applications would be developed by those who shared our belief in the potentials of this market.

Very few of the traditional CAD vendors took us seriously. They looked upon the personal computer as something which might be able to do word processing or pie charts, but not serious design. They believed that if CAD was done at all on the PC, it would be done with limited-functionality programs for specific applications, "serious, general purpose CAD will always remain the province of the mini and mainframe".

We were right. They were wrong. Now they take us very seriously indeed.

And well they should. More than 17,000 users have already discovered that they can do serious, professional design work on the personal computers they already own. More than 1,000 dealers, systems houses, and OEMs worldwide have discovered that computer aided design isn't an esoteric product for the Fortune 500, but an everyday tool as fundamental to people who draw as a word processor for people who write.

Our strategy to make AutoCAD the standard is working, and our commitment to this strategy is expanding. AutoCAD is continually being expanded and upgraded; our next upgrade will provide 3D visualisation, curve fitting, and a macro programming capability.[117] AutoCAD runs on over 31 personal computers, with more being released on a continuing basis. Vertical market applications such as AE/CADD, the professional design tool for architects, add to AutoCAD specific solutions for design professionals. CAD/camera, our expert-system based auto-vectorising system converts paper drawings to CAD automatically, and at $3,000, costs less than 5% the price of competitive systems. Our AutoCAD to mainframe translators allow integrating AutoCAD with large scale CAD systems including CADAM, Intergraph, and Computervision. And AutoCAD is available in French, German, Swedish, and Italian editions, with Spanish and Japanese scheduled for release soon.

If you design as part of your work, or draw, or your company designs or draws, you owe it to yourself to see what has made AutoCAD the CAD standard in so few months. If you own a personal computer, you already own the most expensive part of a professional CAD system. Just by adding the $2,500 AutoCAD software, you can immediately share the benefits that owners of million dollar CAD systems have been enjoying for over a decade.

AutoCAD. Number one — for a lot of very good reasons.

---

[117] This was release 2.1, which was shipped in May of 1985.

Going for Image with Prime Time

There was a feeling that as we became a public company and sought to expand the general awareness of our company and its products, we should retain a professional public relations firm. We hired a "Publicity and Media Consulting Corporation", whose president arranged for a writer to meet with numerous people in the company to produce a company profile.

This is what we got instead. Monuments stand alone. No commentary is necessary other than to explain the typography. Comments I wrote on the original document are in type [like this]. *Underlining and boxes around particularly trite and silly things were also my contemporaneous annotations. Footnotes were added at this writing. All of the misspellings were present in the original. Yes, they really did misspell the company name at every occurrence. Following this document is a memo I wrote expressing my reactions to this presentation of our company.*

AutoDesk
May 8, 1985

"We have large ears[118] turned to what customers and dealers need," says John Walker, President and Co-Founder of AutoDesk, Inc. "We make things people want". It is this philosophy — functionally unique among software companies — that has propelled AutoDesk to become one of THE success stories of the computer age.

An overstatement? Consider that AutoDesk revenues went from $14,500 in an abbreviated 1982 year to $10,000,000 last year. They have already cornered the personal computer market with AutoCAD, their brilliant Computer-Assisted Design program. Chosen by an international panel of computer journalists as the "Technical/Scientific Software of the Year" in 1984, AutoCAD provides a virtually-limitless palate [**Palette. Palate is part of your mouth.**] of drafting and

---

118   And some of us can wiggle them.

graphic design tools for "anyone who draws". For the draftsperson, AutoCAD provides the freedom, scope, and power much like the way a word processor supports a pencil-pushing scribe.

Another AutoDesk breakthrough is price. The first hand-held calculator came out in 1961 at a cost of $29,000, while today more capabilities are available in a unit costing less than $20. **[What does this have to do with anything? Second, I'm not aware of any handheld calculator on the market in 1961 at any price.]** For under $10,000, you can buy AutoCad plus a state of the art IBM PC and equally powerful plotter, and you'll be getting a graphics design system that does 90% of what can be done on a main fram[119] system costing $500,000. But these are only statistics:[120] AutoDesk Incorporated are a group of people who have defied the "experts" and are now sitting on the crest of a wave that is sweeping in a new definition of business in America.

Their story is real, exciting, and challenging, like their roots: they are the Sixties Generation. After a decade of post-Vietnam invisibility, the new exemplars of the great entrepreneurial spirit are leading a shift in the way business will be done in the Nineties. That spirit is one of the most important reasons for the success of AutoDesk. No one says "We don't do things that way here". One difference is that competition within AutoDesk is <u>con</u>structive instead of <u>de</u>structive. "There is one ego in the company," said Director of Marketing Maryanne Zadfar, "the company itself. All of us are commited to each other and the company."

Communications Manager Sandra Boulton likens their operating style to Japanese management techniques, in which everyone's ideas are considered. This enfranchisement of the individual is the heart of AutoDesk; it is the way their products are designed. This assures that the programmers have the freedom to produce in their areas of highest expertise. And in their own individual style. **[This is a sentence?]** Many **[Come on]** of the employees work at home, communicating by modem and telephone, coming in for weekly conferences. Each person works on a particular part of the program, and then only at the end are all the parts be pulled together.

For those AutoDesk employees who work at the office, headquarters is a new, light, airy, office building in Sausalito, minutes from the Golden Gate Bridge, yards from San Francisco Bay, nurtured under the spiritual aegis of Mount

---

119 As opposed to a secondary fram.
120 Albeit, wrong ones.

Tamalpais [Oh come on!]. Those who do work at the office maintain their identities as personally as the established business community doesn't. [What the Hell does this mean?] Suits, regualtions, and titular respect have very little significance in the AutoDesk environment. It was this sort of unorthodoxy of style that stopped the venture capitalists from investing at the start-up. These "experts" asked about peoples' shoes, and questioned the length of their hair. They couldn't see that unorthodoxy — especially the people-consciousness — is the key to AutoDesk's flexibility. They could not understand that more important than structural formality was the enlistment of people who believe in themselves. [Utter bullshit. VC's don't care about this, they had wrong ideas about the business!]

The 106 who work at AutoDesk are individuals, [What is the alternative?] people who were likely considered rabble-rousers at least once in their lives. People whose attitudes are reflected in such traditional corporate heresies as "I don't like it" or "This doesn't make sense" or "There's a better way". The policy at AutoDesk is that there are virtually no regulations; the employees are "part of the rock". They all can buy stock in the privately-held company, so it's no wonder that "everyone is 100% behind every product that goes out the door".

AutoDesk was founded in late 1982 by fifteen engineers who pooled their own money — all of $59,000 — and personal integrity to produce software that is literally changing the way many industries do business. Thought[121] computers have been used in drafting work for a number of years, it was basically only for those who had access to hundreds of thousands — indeed millions — of dollars of mainframe computer equipment. AutoCAD, the program responsible for the AutoDesk meteor, gave virtually the same tools to the owner of the every day personal computer for only $1,000. Individuals, small business, divisions of giant corporations all could make a quantum leap. [This was tired in 1950!]

In the personal computer industry for which so many had announced a premature death, AutoDesk has created such revolutionary software that it is actually forcing change [Oh wow!] in every industry that involves design, drafting, and drawing. Architects, engineers, contractors, electricians, mechanics, artists, doctors, soldiers, sailors, treasure hunters, teachers, firemen, landscapers, cinematographers, bobsledders, cooks, as well as

---

121   I think he meant "though".

designers of cars, stained glass windows, underwear, tennis shoes, sports cars, wheelchairs, contact lenses, bobsleds[122] and the face of the new Statue of Liberty **[Huh? I wasn't aware it was being redesigned?]** have all used AutoDesk Inc. products. Many firms are being forced to computerize their operations in order to attract the top design school students. **[I don't think that's how it works, folks.]** Other firms are requiring applicants to have 1 – 2 years experience with AutoCAD, **[Cite one example.]** and the program has been out less than three years.

It's because the AutoCAD system is synonymous with productivity **[Bullshit]**. What used to take days can be done in hours. AutoCAD frees the designer from the drudgery of repetitive, mechanical chores. In laymen's terms, AutoCad draws, and edits drawings, on a computer screen. These drawings can be manipulated in all sorts of clever and designer-practical ways. Not only does AutoCAD save countless hours of the most boring aspects of design work, it increases the accuracy of the calculations and provides a range of user-customized options previously unavailable on a personal computer.

As powerful as the system is, AutoCAD is simple to learn; a drafter with no computer experience can be proficient with AutoCAD in two weeks. And because AutoCAD is compatible with the major management systems like Lotus, Symphony, and Framework,[123] accurate and detailed design renderings can be integrated to support complex reports. AutoDesk also offers a variety of useful options to meet the particular needs of clients in their specific tasks and in the interface of their work with larger computer systems.

In addition to the extras offered by AutoDesk, the AutoCAD design system has already attracted more than 100 third-party software from outside sources to expand and customize the program for professions as diverse as theatrical lighting **[wrong]**, land surveying, and hydraulic network analysis. So AutoDesk customers are not only pleased, they are enthusiastic. And with good reason: AutoDesk implements user suggestions in redesigning their programs. When AutoCAD was upgraded from version 1.4 to 2.0, the number of callers with questions dropped 95%. **[Prove it.]** Former AutoCAD user **[Sounds like he abandoned it.]** and now AutoDesk engineer Lance Kemp restates the company's theme: "we give what our end users want."

---

122 Went around a bend and came back a second time.
123 Huh?

AutoDesk is not a one product company. Originally, AutoDesk was the name of a program for a desk organizer written in 1982 along with a number of other software products. They **[Who.]** decided to put their resources behind AutoCAD. Will they try to resurrect the AutoDesk program? "We never look backwards." says Marketing Director Zadfar. Indeed, AutoDesk has two major releases in the Summer of '85: 3D Level 1 and CAD/Camera. The 3 D is actually 2 1/2 D, a program for providing three dimensional visualization of a design using either hidden lines on a "wire frame" schematic.

Cad/Camera allows a designer to enter existing diagrams **[drawings]** into the computer for editing and enhancement. This software breakthrough **[Bullshit]** means that the diagram on a piece of paper can be electronically translated into information that the computer can understand. Then with AutoCAD, the designer can manipulate the original image to whatever specifications **[s/he]**[124] wants, combine it with other images, and then reproduce with unparalleled accuracy and detail. Instead of spending twenty-four hours hand-tracing every element of a schematic drawing, with CAD/Camera the job can be done in two hours.

Integrity, intelligence, dedication — foundations in American history **[Huh?]** — are the resources of these people whom **[Whom?]** some labelled a bunch of left-over[125] hippies. While they are not accepted by the establishment whose very structure and purpose they challenge, it is of little consequence **[They sure as Hell better be before 2 July!**[126]**]**. AutoDesk has combined the business acumen with social values, and creating a dynamic deeper than their impressive statistical bottom line **[Huh? What? Is this a parody or what?]**. One of their users, a 23-year-old quadriplegic, sent a note of deep appreciation to AutoDesk, explaining that he had "signed" the purchase agreement as best he could, with an "X" drawn with AutoCAD. **[MAUDLIN! Do you have release & rights to this story?]**

---

124 Note to philologists. This is an artifact of the Marin County airhead version of an oddity of the late Twentieth Century called "non-sexist writing" which attempted to linguistically divorce women from the family of mankind. With the appearance of artificial intelligence, this trend led to the construction "s/he/it", which rapidly passed from the vogue taking the whole movement with it. The term is still heard in Texas but has a different meaning and is probably unrelated in derivation.
125 Yeah, right-on today, left-over tomorrow. That's life.
126 The closing date of the public stock offering.

But as successful as AutoDesk has been with their graphics-design systems, they make it clear they are not a CAD company.[127] Not shackled with hardware nor saddled with inventory, the people at AutoDesk have the ability to recognize a need, define the problem and create the solution. What comes next is being developed in the minds of bright and responsible individuals whose mutual badge is that they have accomplished what they were told couldn't be done. We might expect that what the Mustang was for Ford, AutoCAD will be for AutoDesk.

AutoDesk supplementary notes (5/2/85)

AutoDesk has thrown a scare into the design industry. Providing tools which translate into immense savings of time, money, and drudgery, **[what will I do with all the drudgery I save?]** AutoDesk is forcing drafters — architects, contracters, engineers, artists, and the like — to go electronic or they will be unable to compete.

The integrity of the AutoDesk operation is inherent in every operation: their advertising is completely — and proudly — truthful, and unlike many in the computer industry, AutoDesk reports its sales figures regularly and accurately.

Projected revenues for 1985 are $10,000,000. **[Wrong!** *Furthermore,*[128] *I don't think we're publishing any projections!*]

AutoDesk has training centers around the country and in Europe. **[Hein?]** Their attitude is so contrary to the "sell-'n-see-'ya" indemic to the computer industry that they offer dealers a free program, simply for learning how to use the software.

---

127   Heaven forbid.
128   Adds Dan Drake.

Reply Time

The Article

John Walker — May 14, 1985 22:41

I grasp for adjectives and fail.

Is this how we want to present the company we have all worked so hard to build? A freak show which uses every hype word in the lexicon of the flack, or as a group of hard working people whose dedication to competence and quality have made a name for ourselves?

Let me list some of the pure bullshit words used in this odious document:

> "functionally unique", "THE success stories", "brilliant", "virtually limitless", "breakthrough", "state-of-the-art", "sweeping in a new definition", "exemplars of the great entrepreneurial spirit", "Japanese Management techniques", "new, light, airy office building", "spiritual aegis", "people-consciousness", "literally changing the way many industries do business", "Autodesk meteor", "quantum leap", "revolutionary", "forcing change", "synonymous with productivity", "unparalleled accuracy", "foundations in American history", "combined business acumen with social values", "dynamic much deeper than their … bottom line".

I won't comment on the numerous egregious misstatements, gloss-overs, and misperceptions in this cowpie of a company profile. The overt illiteracy of the writing and slipshod editing is self-evident, but perhaps the centered, consciousness three, holistic well-being bubbleheads at whom this piffle is aimed are post-literate exemplars of the New Age.

Would anybody who was impressed by this execrable effigy of our efforts be a likely customer of AutoCAD? Would we even want them to know we existed? If they stormed the building, we might have to lay in a supply of reality gas.

How can we respect the public relations judgement of anybody who could read trenchant prose like this and then submit it to a client? And if it wasn't reviewed before submission, what are their standards?

After meditating in the spiritual aegis of Mount Tamalpais, I must render my verdict upon this brie-dripping bastardization of our brainwork. I hope my attitudes don't forever align me with those "traditional corporate heresies" we disdain when I say,

"I don't like it".

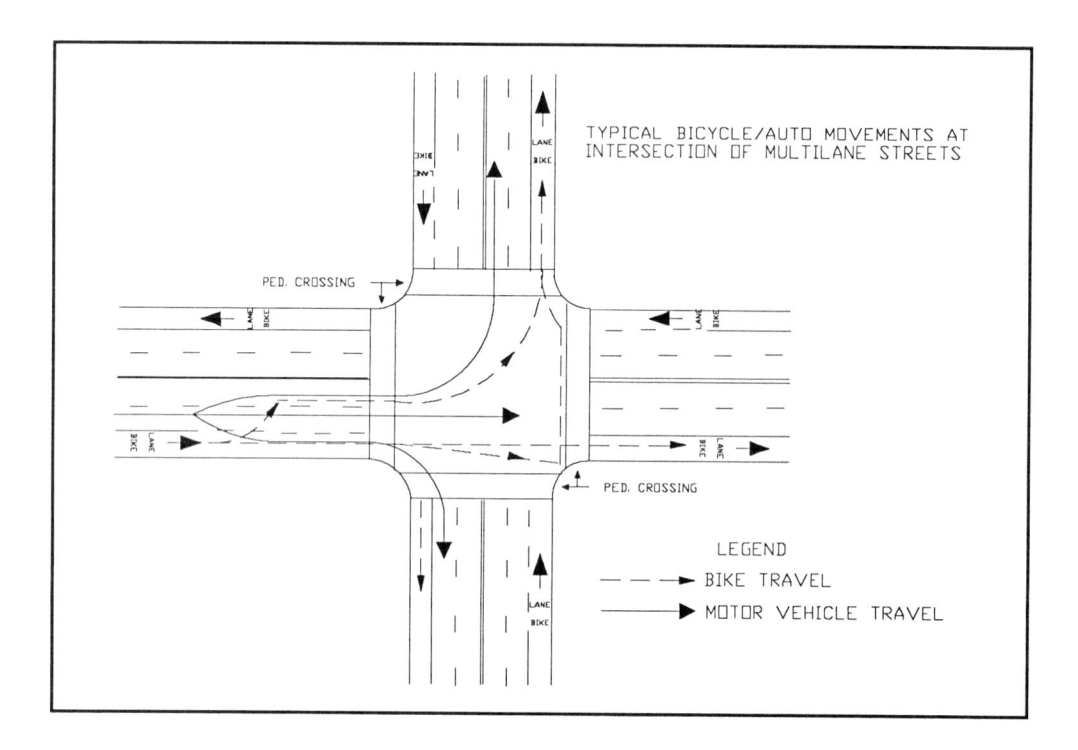

Peter Barnett drew this representation of a street intersection based on a California Department of Transportation (Caltrans) specification manual. This drawing, done on a pre-release version of AutoCAD 2.0, uncovered several bugs in object snap, which was first introduced in that release. It has since been used as a sample drawing and plotter test.

Initial Public Offering

I did not enjoy writing the prospectus for our Initial Public Offering in 1985. Translating a clear statement of the company's goals and strategy into weasel words under a pressing deadline, in endless meetings filled with lawyers and accountants who argued with each other, billing the time to us pales, in my mind, with other avocations such as lying on the beach or juggling chainsaws.

Here is what we were trying to get across in the prospectus: the original draft that ended up devolving into the mealy-mouthed final document. It's the best statement I know of regarding where we were in 1985 and how we saw the company's future. The odd focus on "products" is because the big thing at the time was not to be seen as a One Product Company.

Business Section of Prospectus

Rough Draft 6 by John Walker — 4/16/85 01:27

General Background

Autodesk develops, markets, and supports a family of software packages which allow computer aided drafting, design, and drawing (CAD) to be performed on desktop microcomputers such as the IBM PC family.

CAD packages are used to produce drawings in such fields as architecture, civil, mechanical, and electrical engineering, surveying, facilities planning: any field in which information is communicated via drawings. A general purpose CAD package such as AutoCAD can make any drawing that can be made on paper.

The benefits of CAD are faster, more accurate generation of drawings, more efficient revision of drawings, the ability to use predefined symbols, eliminating time-consuming repetitive work and automatically assuring adherence to drafting standards. The benefits of preparing drawings on a CAD system exactly parallel using a word processor to write documents.

In addition, a CAD system such as AutoCAD maintains a database containing every element in the drawing. Users may attach information to objects in the drawing (for example, in a drawing of an office, a desk might carry its manufacturer, model number, date of purchase, price, and depreciation information). This information can be retrieved and modified from within the CAD program or sent to other application programs to prepare bills of materials, job costing reports, or inventory updates. A CAD system may thus be used as a "graphic database", allowing design information to be taken directly from drawings, or conversely, allowing the presentation of design data in graphic form. AutoCAD was designed to make the integration of application programs for such purposes easy. Software suppliers serving structural engineers, surveyors, architects, and facilities planners, etc., can build applications based on AutoCAD, using it to accomplish the otherwise difficult tasks of graphic input, output, and editing inherent to their application.

Before AutoCAD, computer aided design was primarily done on mainframe and minicomputers, often with proprietary graphics hardware. Usually CAD systems were sold as integrated hardware and software ("turnkey") systems. With the introduction of the IBM PC and the many 16-bit desktop machines which followed, the basic desktop office computer reached a level of capability which allowed serious computer aided design to be done on the machine as supplied by the manufacturer. Thus, AutoCAD was introduced into an essentially vacant market: a *software package* for computer aided design sold separately from hardware and intended for use on existing desktop computers.

Additionally, AutoCAD was the first CAD package to support a wide variety of computer configurations. Today, AutoCAD runs on 31 different desktop computers and supports close to 100 graphic input, display, and output options.

AutoCAD's support of all major computers and graphics hardware is central to the Company's perception of the market and to its strategy. Exactly as portable, open-architecture operating systems such as Unix and MS-DOS have supplanted vendor-proprietary operating systems, and portable open-architecture networks such as Ethernet are supplanting those developed by computer vendors and sold only with their hardware, the Company feels that CAD customers will demand flexible CAD software which will run on a wide variety of hardware configurations and which can be expected to be available on newer, more powerful computer systems as they are announced.

AutoCAD is written in C, one of the most widely implemented and compatible computer languages for software development available today. Interfaces to operating systems, computer hardware, and graphics input, output, and display devices are completely separate from the main program, and may be changed without requiring alteration of the program itself. These design principles allow Autodesk to market AutoCAD on virtually any computer system which supports graphics and provides the C language. The C programming language is currently available on every serious candidate in the engineering workstation market, ranging from Apple's Macintosh to the Cray X/MP. This, combined with the proven portability of well-written programs written in C and the Company's experience in successfully moving its software from machine to machine, demonstrates that the Company can with minimal effort make its products available on any computer system it chooses as a potential market.

While CAD has been traditionally seen as a vertical market product (specific to one narrowly-defined industry), the Company feels that this has been more a result of the high price of turnkey CAD systems than the applicability of such systems. Just as word processors have become almost universally used by those who write and spreadsheet programs are widely used by those doing financial forecasting, CAD systems will soon be seen as essential by those who draw as part of their work as well as by full time drafters.

This large general market can be addressed only by those packages which require no special hardware, because such users cannot justify a special-purpose computer just for drawing. Instead, the drawing task will be done by a program running on their regular workstation, just as word processing and database software are used.

Autodesk's proprietary language translation utility vastly reduces the effort required to maintain foreign language editions of its products. Currently AutoCAD is available in English, French, German, Italian, and Swedish editions. Spanish and Japanese editions are in preparation.

Product Strategy

The Company feels that the CAD component of an engineering workstation will succeed only if it meets the following criteria:

- It must run on the hardware the purchaser selects. The computer will not be primarily selected for the software; the software will be selected for the computer. Standard, hardware-independent software almost always supplants software tied to proprietary hardware.
- It must work with the other software components of the workstation. The workstation can deliver its promised productivity only if all the software forms an integrated design tool, as opposed to a set of distinct applications. The displacement of separate business application programs with integrated packages foreshadows this trend.
- It must be extensible and adaptable to the user's environment. No software vendor can anticipate the needs of all users, nor expend the

effort to optimally customise the package for all applications. Instead, by providing users the appropriate tools, intelligent users or systems houses will do this in the field.

- The software must support third party vendors who wish to build applications based upon it. Open architecture systems usually displace vendor-controlled systems.
- The software must be general purpose and have no designed-in limits not imposed by the computer hardware itself. Users make a large investment in learning a package. They would rather spend 10% more time learning one package that meets all their needs than learn four packages which must be combined to solve the same problems.
- The software must communicate with mainframe computers and the corporate databases they contain. The engineering workstation does not exist in isolation. Designers work together, exchanging data, especially on large projects which can be managed only on mainframe systems. Also, large installed CAD systems benefit from the offloading of work which can be done effectively on desktop machines.
- The purchaser must be confident the software will continue to be available on new machines. A user makes a large investment learning a CAD package and adds to that investment with every project completed. Users must be guaranteed they will not have to learn a new system or throw away their drawings done on the old system when new hardware is selected.
- The system must be easy to learn and provide on-line assistance. Full time drafters have the time to attend multi-week training courses in CAD. Engineers and architects don't.
- The engineering and design business is of worldwide scope. To compete in the international market, a package must be available in the native languages of its users. People won't learn English to use a computer program.

The Company's products have been designed to meet all these criteria.

Products

AutoCAD

AutoCAD is a general purpose computer aided design and drafting software package. It provides the functions of a graphic editing system with attached database which form the core of every computer aided design system.

AutoCAD was designed to run on desktop computers, but does not contain any design limitations except those imposed by the present capacity of such machines. The designers' extensive experience in systems programming enabled the removal of limits in the software without degrading performance in the desktop environment.

For example, many early competitor programs imposed limits on the maximum size of a drawing which could be created or on the accuracy of the coordinates stored in a drawing. AutoCAD imposes no practical limit on either. Most early micro-based programs did not allow the user to modify the menus, or the help text, or design custom templates. AutoCAD allows all of these. The Company feels the success of AutoCAD to date expresses the market's verdict that these features are essential in serious design work.

AutoCAD is entirely written in the C programming language, is presently over 100,000 lines of source code (some small machine interface routines for some implementations are in assembly language).

AutoCAD is microcomputer software only in the fact that it runs on microcomputers and that it exhibits the characteristics of ease of learning and use, good documentation, and user training tools one usually associates with microcomputer software. Its complexity, internal design, extensibility, and the general techniques used in its construction would normally identify the software as a mainframe or supermini package. As a result of AutoCAD's design, when presented with additional hardware resources such as higher resolution displays, faster processors, higher capacity internal memory (RAM), or larger discs, it automatically takes advantage of these resources and delivers their benefits to the user without software modification. AutoCAD's present internal design should easily accommodate the projected advances in these areas for the next decade. Thus, if run on a microcomputer, AutoCAD is a microcomputer CAD package. If moved to a minicomputer, it competes with other minicomputer CAD packages, and if moved to a mainframe, it becomes a mainframe CAD system. This, combined with AutoCAD's demonstrated portability, allows Autodesk to provide a compatible solution to the CAD industry on systems ranging from briefcase to room size.

The Company is committed to extending the capabilities of AutoCAD as well as the selection of hardware it supports. For example, the release of AutoCAD release 2.1 in May 1985 added three dimensional capabilities to the package, facilities essential for efficient use of drawings scanned by CAD/camera and for use with numerically controlled machines, and an initial version of what will soon become the full integration of the LISP language with AutoCAD. LISP is the first in a series of languages to be interfaced to AutoCAD, allowing users, OEMs, systems houses, and third party software developers access to the full capabilities of AutoCAD from their programs. Since LISP is the language of choice in artificial intelligence research, its provision within AutoCAD places AutoCAD on the leading edge of applying these techniques to the design process. The Company believes that the facilities these language interfaces will provide to application developers to be unique in the CAD industry, regardless of the scale of the system.

Mainframe CAD Interfaces

While AutoCAD provides a total solution to the individual user or small office using CAD, users in larger corporations often wish to use their desktop workstations to develop drawings which are later combined with others' work on mini or mainframe CAD systems. Conversely, operators of expensive CAD systems wish to offload the large amount of routine work not requiring the power of the large system onto less expensive desktop machines. To meet these needs, and thus penetrate the corporate market for desktop CAD, Autodesk is developing a family of bidirectional translators which allow interchange of data with larger CAD systems. Translators for CADAM and Intergraph systems are presently available, with others under development. Autodesk believes that development of these translators is the key to establishing AutoCAD as the desktop CAD standard in major corporate accounts, and assigns a high priority to their development.

AE/CADD

An architectural design consists of drawings describing the structure to be built, plus extensive documentation provided to the contractor who constructs the building. AE/CADD[129] is an integrated design and drafting system designed especially for architects which automates drawing tasks and automatically builds the construction documentation directly from the drawing, guaranteeing consistency between the drawings and contractor information.

Driven directly from a digitiser template supplied with the package, AE/CADD automatically constructs walls from dimensions supplied by the designer, joins walls at intersections, breaks walls to insert doors and windows, and automatically draws stairs, plumbing fixtures, appliances, and structural details. Notes are automatically attached to markers in the drawing, and when the drawing is complete, AutoCAD's database link is used to automatically prepare the construction documentation describing the job.

---

[129] Now AutoCAD AEC Architectural.

AE/CADD allows an architect to make basic drawings much faster than with a general purpose CAD system, then eliminates the time consuming task of preparing the construction documentation. It is generated automatically from the drawing, preventing discrepancies which take time and cost money to correct in the field.

Autodesk plans to extend AE/CADD with additional templates to cover structural, mechanical, landscape, space planning, electrical, site planning, and plumbing drawings.

AE/CADD was constructed using the user-customisation features of AutoCAD. Written as a set of AutoCAD custom menus and symbols, AE/CADD may be installed on any machine which runs AutoCAD. The implementation of AE/CADD, accomplished initially by non-Autodesk personnel with access only to information provided to all AutoCAD purchasers, illustrates how AutoCAD can be adapted for specific application areas.

AE/CADD, sold with a suggested retail price of $1000, turns an AutoCAD system into a powerful design tool for architects.[130]

CAD/camera

In order to take advantage of the many benefits of CAD, users with many existing manually-drawn paper drawings have had to manually transfer them into their CAD systems, in essence, redrawing them from scratch on the CAD system. The extreme cost of this labour intensive process has prevented most users from automating the filing and maintenance of their existing drawings when installing a CAD system. Rather, they have made new drawings on the CAD system, but maintained the old drawings manually. A system which automatically converted these paper drawings into CAD databases would be a great benefit to these users.

In addition, upon installing a CAD system, the purchaser must usually spend a great deal of time entering commonly used symbols and drawing details before being able to realise the full benefits of CAD. The ability to enter these symbols automatically for immediate use by the CAD system would save users much time and deliver immediate productivity gains.

Autodesk developed CAD/camera to satisfy both of these needs. CAD/camera allows users to automatically transfer their paper drawings to CAD databases. Taking an image scanned with an electronic scanning camera, the CAD/camera software package translates the scanned page to the vector form usable with CAD

---

130 This description was rewritten on May 12th, 1985. I've incorporated that version here.

systems. Existing systems which perform this function are based on mini and mainframe computers and cost more than $100,000. CAD/camera, by contrast, runs on personal computers and is sold as a software package alone for $3000. When CAD/camera is run on an IBM PC/AT, conversion times for drawings range from 15 seconds for small symbols to more than five hours for complex engineering drawings. This is usually at least ten times faster than manually redrawing the drawings on a CAD system.

CAD/camera is implemented using rule-based expert system technology, which is responsible for its much greater price-performance, and its ability to run on smaller, less expensive computers. In addition, this technology allows Autodesk to continue to enhance CAD/camera, adding recognition of more complex drawing elements.

Databases created by CAD/camera may be directly read by AutoCAD, but CAD/camera may be used to generate databases for any CAD system. Its output format is fully disclosed by Autodesk, facilitating its interfacing with other systems. In addition, CAD/camera is entirely written in the C programming language, allowing it to be moved to other computer systems, including other CAD systems should Autodesk decide to do so.[131]

Developers' Tool Kit

As more and more graphics hardware comes onto the market, Autodesk plans to support it in AutoCAD to maximise the user's choice. The large installed base and rapid sales pace of AutoCAD makes it an important potential market for developers of graphics hardware. Autodesk's Developer's Tool Kit makes the union of these common interests less costly and time consuming to both parties. After evaluating a piece of hardware and concluding that support of it by AutoCAD would be beneficial to the Company and its customers, a Developer's Tool Kit may be sold to the hardware vendor. Using a manual specially written for use with the Kit, the hardware vendor can program a driver which allows AutoCAD to run his device. Since developers are usually more experienced in programming their hardware than Autodesk, this expedites the development process. After the driver is complete, is it certified by Autodesk's Quality department before shipment with AutoCAD. Autodesk retains title to the driver developed by the hardware vendor and has so constructed the Kit that it discloses no proprietary information. Autodesk charges a fee for the Kit which covers support costs in aiding the developer in using the Kit.

---

[131] This description was rewritten on May 12th, 1985. I've incorporated that version here.

AutoCAD Applications Program

Autodesk actively encourages the development of third party software which works with AutoCAD and aids its use in vertical markets. Autodesk has established the AutoCAD Applications Program as a channel by which developers of such programs may communicate with AutoCAD vendors and users. The first AutoCAD Applications Catalogue contains more than 100 such programs. Autodesk derives no revenue from these third-party programs except that generated by additional sales of AutoCAD they engender. However, the Company believes that this Program is an excellent way to identify and qualify programs for possible acquisition, joint marketing, distribution, or licensing by the Company.

The Toilet Announcement

Getting screen pictures to print in the prospectus wasn't easy, either. In fact, nothing about the public offering was easy. However, difficulty shouldn't make one hesitant to break new ground and defy precedents. Dan Drake penned this press release in the midst of the prospectus drafting sessions.

For Immediate Release

Sausalito, California. May 10, 1985.

In what industry observers described as a radical and daring break with tradition, Autodesk Inc. announced today that the publicity pictures in its prospectus would not feature a picture of a toilet. The decision was announced following an extraordinary meeting of the Board of Directors.

"It's hard to part with an old friend", gibbered John Walker, president of Autodesk, emerging from the meeting which was held in the company's washroom, "when our whole success has been based on pictures featuring toilets, from the mini-apartment drawing in *PC World* to the giant North Sea oil rig poster. However, hard times demand hard choices. We at Autodesk are flushed with pride in our forthcoming public offering, and as we stand with one foot in the simpler world of private companies and the other in our mouth, we hail the dawn of the new day confident that our publicity will continue to bowl over the industry."[132]

---

[132] Alas, it was not to be. One of the screen shots inside the prospectus cover *did* include a toilet.

Marketing Strategy

Sales and Marketing

Introduction by John Walker — May 14, 1985 01:14

In keeping with Autodesk's overall strategy of delivering the benefits of CAD to a mass market, Autodesk's marketing strategy is to apply the time proven techniques of mass marketing to a product traditionally sold directly at high prices.

This strategy, unique in the CAD market, complements the technical benefits of AutoCAD. Its application allowed Autodesk to obtain its large market share in a short time. In addition to applying mass marketing techniques itself, Autodesk mobilises the sales forces of computer manufacturers, graphics peripheral manufacturers, and computer dealers through cooperative advertising, promotion, and appearance in numerous trade shows. Autodesk has a variety of innovative programs involving training, advertising credits, joint appearances at trade shows, and other incentives which encourage dealers and manufacturers to jointly market Autodesk products.

Autodesk supports its advertising with an aggressive public relations effort, combined with an ongoing program of seeking and arranging for the publication of articles in the trade press describing applications of AutoCAD in various industries. Autodesk makes a major ongoing effort to communicate with industry analysts and key decision makers, seeking to demonstrate the benefits of AutoCAD versus larger systems. Autodesk supports the development of tutorial materials and books based on AutoCAD. Finally, Autodesk has a major commitment to the educational market, offering support and incentives to institutions wishing to teach CAD, and encouraging the adoption of AutoCAD in their curricula.

To reach a mass market at a low cost, the Company has concentrated on two major channels of distribution: computer dealers and computer manufacturers. The Company's approach in promoting both of these channels has been to communicate the real advantages of selling AutoCAD to participants in both market segments.

Computer dealers who sell AutoCAD typically make more from the dealer markup on AutoCAD than the retail price of most of the software packages they sell. In addition, the AutoCAD customer usually buys a larger computer with more options (larger memory, floating point coprocessor, larger disc storage) and with graphics peripherals such as a digitiser and plotter. These options and peripherals are typically discounted less in the marketplace than basic microcomputers, so the dealer's margin on the overall sale is increased by selling AutoCAD systems. These larger margins and access to less competitive vertical markets usually more than repay the dealer's investment in learning to sell AutoCAD. The Company's policy of not selling directly to large accounts and not placing its products in discount prone national distribution channels serves to strengthen its dealer network and that network's loyalty to the Company and its products.

Computer manufacturers who sell AutoCAD gain access to vertical markets previously denied them and gain a tool which uses their hardware to best advantage. Because AutoCAD automatically makes use of the resources provided by a computer system, whatever competitive advantages a system may have (better graphics resolution, higher performance, larger memory, larger disc storage) are effectively utilised by AutoCAD. Thus in a crowded, highly competitive market, AutoCAD provides a computer manufacturer a product which dramatically illustrates the advantages of his product versus the competition, demonstrably promoting hardware sales. In addition, the manufacturer receives significant revenue from the sales of AutoCAD software, while encouraging the sale of larger, more profitable machines. AutoCAD provides access to vertical markets within which the specialisation of a manufacturer may yield much greater results than in the general PC market. Computer manufacturers typically distribute AutoCAD through the same channels through which they sell their hardware; some manufacturers sell through their own dealer networks while others sell directly, mostly to large organisations.

The Company's longer term marketing strategy builds on the concept of AutoCAD as a general purpose tool which forms the central component of an engineering workstation. While AutoCAD by itself delivers compelling gains in productivity easily communicated and justifying its purchase, an AutoCAD user is a prequalified customer for a wide variety of additional productivity tools. These tools include predefined symbol libraries; a wide variety of engineering and design automation programs for such purposes as preparation of bills of material, job cost estimation, structural analysis, numerical controlled machine tool programming, and electronic circuit analysis; and materials intended for use with AutoCAD, such as templates, tutorial guides, and other self-teaching materials. Autodesk regards its large and rapidly growing base of customers as one of its major assets, and intends to develop and market additional productivity tools into this base. CAD/camera and AE/CADD are examples of additional Autodesk products which will appeal to significant numbers of AutoCAD customers, as well as encouraging new sales of AutoCAD. The company's large installed base also leads third party vendors of applications software which complements AutoCAD to approach Autodesk with joint marketing proposals. These products, qualified through the AutoCAD Applications Program, provide a continuing source of new products for joint marketing or acquisition by the Company.

In short, the Company's marketing strategy is to create a mass market for CAD, where no mass market existed before, develop channels of distribution to address that mass market, and build on its emerging position as the volume leader with additional products and services.

The Entire Prospectus

Kelvin Throop was infuriated by the prospectus drafting process. He suggested we can the entire mess and use this prospectus instead. We didn't.

The Entire Prospectus

Draft 1 by Kelvin R. Throop — 2/30/85 24:12

In the beginning CAD systems were overpriced, hulking boxes of hardware with the original nameplate pryed off and the name of some slimy greedhead stuck on.

Then came AutoCAD, a program that did all the same things on a PC for 5% of the cost.

Things got better. As they got better, we got richer.

Now's your chance.

Call toll-free 24 hours per day, (800) AI-STOCK. Visa/MC/Amex accepted.

Sleazy Motel Roach Hammer Awards

One of the most repellent parts of the public offering process was the extravagance of the "road show". Apparently investment bankers believe they can do their job better when consuming their firm's capital at an enormous rate on such things as first class airfares, limousines, $200 a night hotel rooms, and the like.

Now that Autodesk had obtained a large wad of cash, I was concerned that we would also start to go down the same road. This was my proposal to create an incentive system to keep that from happening. This was never implemented.

The Autodesk Sleazy Motel Roach Hammer Awards

By John Walker — June 22, 1985

It sure is expensive to travel, isn't it?

Having just survived the "road show" phase of the public offering process, I've just been reminded of the needless extravagance the travel establishment lavishes on expense-account corporate America. If the people who were doing this traveling were paying out of their own pockets rather than "the company's", I'll bet that hundred dollar a night hotel rooms and fifteen dollar dinners wouldn't be long for the world. Five minutes, say.

Now every growing company, especially those who have recently gone public and now have the world looking over their shoulders and watching their margins (sales less expenses), has to issue the Obligatory Let's Control Costs Memo and some utterly confusing policy which is destined to be ignored and end up in the circular file of history.

Autodesk was built on incentives, not coercion. The way to control costs is to make it pay. Henceforth, there will be a direct financial incentive to keep costs down. Those who travel on business have to fill out travel expense reports listing the direct costs of their travel. This form will be amended to add a calculation of the "sleaze factor" of the trip. Sleaze factor is defined as the number of days the traveler was out of town (one for day trips), divided by the money spent on the trip, exclusive of air transportation.

The accounting department will keep track of the cumulative sleaze factor for all people who travel. At the end of each month, the traveler with the highest sleaze factor (who therefore cost the company the least per day on the road) will receive a bonus in the next paycheck of $200.

At the end of the fiscal year (January 31), the employee with the highest yearly sleaze factor will receive a bonus of $2500 in the next paycheck.

In addition, the person who turns in the lowest cost per day will be honoured at the next monthly meeting and presented the Autodesk Sleazy Motel Roach Hammer Award.

This award program is not totally fair. But then life isn't totally fair. Somebody who goes to New York repeatedly will tend to run up bills higher than one who frequents Akron. But then some say that New York is its own reward. But in any case, the point of all of this is to reward those who treat the company's money as if it was their own. It is, you know. Everybody here owns the company, either directly or as the holder of a stock option. If we keep the costs down and consistently turn in results that meet or beat the expectations of the outside world, we can see the value of our company increase by a factor of 10 to 20 over the next five years. That is the goal, and if we achieve it, we will all be able to share the rewards of our work and the prestige of the company that we built together.

Number One

This notorious drawing was pulled from our sample drawings disc because it faked, by laborious manual methods, various features that would have been nice in the package but weren't there. Some of them still aren't in Release 9. The drawing was originally made by Peter Barnett in 1984, and was intended to illustrate the isometric grid and snap features in AutoCAD 2.0. The isometric dimensions were all hand-drawn, and the ellipses were made by differentially scaling a block containing a circle.

Protecting Your Money

With the public offering complete, many people who had been essentially broke the month before found themselves bombarded by those willing to help them solve the problems created by their (largely paper) "wealth". I thought it would be a good idea to pen an introduction to the investment world for people who had ignored it before in the hope that at least the most egregious fleecers and slimebags would be seen through. Other than details about taxes, which are dated, I wouldn't change a word today.

Surplus Value

Revision 3
By John Walker — July 1, 1985

*Fins to the left
fins to the right,
and you're the only bait in town.*

Jimmy Buffett, Fins

When you sold stock in the public offering and your name appeared in the prospectus, you committed an act not unlike pouring blood in the water before taking a swim in shark-infested waters.

Whatever your financial situation may be, to those who read the 40,000 copies of the prospectus we paid to print, you "have money", and can be expected to be pursued by those who want to "help you manage it".

Look out.

I do not presume to suggest to anybody what they should do with the money they got from selling the stock. It's yours; you earned it. The only purpose of this note is to share some of my thinking about the question we now face: "what to do with the money". The thoughts herein are biased by my own financial situation and may be completely inapplicable to yours. I'd also like to share some words of warning about some of the predatory types who will soon begin to circle.

And of course, please assume that everything I tell you is totally wrong and "do not take any action without consulting with your own financial advisors".

Taxes

Well, we are going to be paying a lot of taxes this year. I think that this year I'm not going to be doing my own taxes. The proceeds from the sale of the stock will be considered a long term capital gain for federal taxes, assuming you sold stock purchased at inception. But remember that California has a three tier capital gain structure and that you don't get the lowest rate until you hold the stock for five years, so none of us will be in the lowest California bracket. If you exercised any options this year (and of course everybody did), you also have to calculate Alternative Minimum Tax (AMT), even if you don't end up owing any. And remember that California also has its own Alternative Minimum Tax, which will crank the effective California capital gains rate up to about 9.5% (don't complain: we all have to Do Our Part to contribute to the entrepreneurial renaissance in New Hampshire and Texas). So in any case, the calculation is going to be complicated.

Here are some random thoughts regarding the tax situation:

First of all, we can't wait until next April 15 to worry about the taxes. We'll have to make the next estimated tax payment on September 17. So a goodly part of the money you kiss hello on July 8, you will be kissing goodbye in September. You'll absolutely have to be able to make a quick shot at your 1985 tax liability and *make that payment*, because if you miss it, you can kiss something else goodbye. Estimated taxes are tricky, and there are several gimmicks which can help you keep the money in your hands for longer. For example, if your withholding plus estimated taxes for each quarter exceeds last year's tax liability, you don't have to make additional payments; you can just pony up the balance next April 15 and file the "hey, it's cool" form. But to do this, you'd have had to have made the qualifying payments last April and June. Did you? I sure didn't. Also, at the end of the year, the buggers will probably hit you for a deficiency because you didn't make estimated tax payments in April and June. You'll have to prove that your large slug of income didn't come until third quarter. Be sure you can.

Also, when calculating your taxes for estimated tax purposes, remember that you'll probably benefit substantially from income averaging this year. Don't overpay estimated taxes because you forgot this when making the estimate.

This probably doesn't apply to anybody, but I'll mention it just in case. If you have any long term capital losses (that Atari stock you bought when video games were going to the moon, the $800 gold coins, etc.) that you haven't realised, take the losses this year. You can offset long term capital losses dollar for dollar against gains, but you can only deduct $3000 of loss per year in excess of gain, so this year you can flush out all those unrealised losses. If you still want to hold the assets, buy 'em back more than 30 days later (the delay is to avoid a "wash sale", discounted for tax purposes).

Also, I don't think that anybody will have a significant excess AMT liability, but maybe your kid went to a painless dentist and you have some Intangible Drilling Expenses and are in AMT land. As long as your AMT exceeds your ordinary income, additional ordinary income is taxed at only 20%. So if you can discretionarily generate ordinary income (such as selling short term stocks at a gain, etc.), do it as long as your ordinary tax doesn't reach the AMT number. Conversely, if you're in a position of excess AMT, you want to put off taking any short term capital losses or deductible expenses (charitable contributions, etc.) because as long as you're in a 20% marginal bracket, Uncle is paying only 20%. If you can delay them to next year, you may be in a higher bracket.

Investments

All right, you've paid off all the bills, beaten the wolf back from the door to at least the porch steps, and you have some money left over. Now you're ready to talk to those guys who are calling you five or ten times a day to tell you what to do with it, right? Wrong. First, make sure you do the obvious little things, such as (if you haven't already done so) prepaying your IRA for 1986. You can earn the interest on $2000 ($4000 if married) tax free for a whole year by prepaying now. Next you have to think about "your portfolio".

Most of the paper peddlers who call you will consider your cash and tell you how to deploy it to "meet your financial goals". The cash will become a mix of investments which will be called "your portfolio" (as if you carried it around with you all the time — though in a sense you do by worrying about it). Unfortunately, they often ignore the other 90% of your net worth. What's that? Your stock in Autodesk. So remember that your portfolio is already invested 90% or more in a high-risk, high-tech company, so anybody who advises you to put any of your cash into similar stocks for "aggressive growth" is telling you to increase your concentration in this sector. What you probably want is to balance things by staying pretty conservative with where you put the cash, so be sure whoever is advising you understands the whole picture. The best book I've seen about portfolio balancing and evaluating different risk factors is called *Inflation-Proofing*

Your Investments by Harry Browne.[133] *I do not agree* with much of the advice and specific recommendations given in this book, but the sections on valuing differing kinds of holdings (equity in a house versus bank deposits versus shares you can't sell) are very well written and easy to follow.

You will probably be contacted by people who call themselves "financial planners". There are two kinds of people going by this name. Some prepare a plan from information you supply, for a fee. Most derive their income from commissions on specific products they recommend and then sell you. 'Nuff said.

If you're looking to stash the cash immediately in a safe place that generates income, I'd recommend Capital Preservation Fund, which I have used since 1978 and with which I have had absolutely no difficulties. They invest only in US Treasury Bills, which are generally considered the safest investment in the world. They also have a fund which is free of both California and Federal income taxes. You can write checks on either fund. (Again, I'm not telling you to put your money there, and they may run off to Paraguay with it tomorrow. But if they do, I'll lose a lot.)

Before getting involved in any investment other than ultra-safe short term things like T-Bills, it's worth spending some time learning just what the rules are and what all this stuff they're trying to sell you is. My favourite introduction to the game is a book called How to Buy Stocks by Louis Engel.[134] I also like The Only Investment Guide You'll Ever Need by Andrew Tobias,[135] but I like this book a lot less than some people do and consider it mistitled. I'd read it for background, but not advice.

I have a lot of other references and information about investments. You're welcome to borrow any of them. Most are in my office.

Greed and Fear

> "When I hear the word 'culture', I reach for my gun."
>
> Hermann Goering

> "When I hear the word 'leverage', I reach for my coat and head for the door.
>
> Dan Drake

---

[133] *Inflation-Proofing Your Investments* by Harry Browne and Terry Coxon, William Morrow & Co., 1981.
[134] *How to Buy Stocks* by Louis Engel in collaboration with Peter Wyckoff, Bantam Books, 1977.
[135] *The Only Investment Guide You'll Ever Need* by Andrew Tobias, Bantam Books, 1979.

"In investing money the amount of interest you want should depend on whether you want to eat well or sleep well."

J. Kenfield Morley

Dan Drake suggested that I add a section talking about the kinds of things to watch out for. Frankly I'm of two minds about this. Walker's first law of investing says, "If you don't *totally* understand it, ignore it". I cannot possibly give you enough information herein to make an intelligent decision, so I'll just concentrate on the lingo. But if you're unwilling to take the time to learn the game, I think you're better off not playing at all. Professional money managers have years of training, access to extensive libraries of research material, massive computer support systems, and full time analysts watching every piece of data. Yet few of them do better than random chance. If you intend to better them, realise you're going into a business venture and prepare to spend the time and effort a business requires.

What follows is Walker's acerbic, opinionated, tour d'horizon of investments.

With your money you can spend it on *stuff* or *paper*. *Stuff* includes BMW's, yachts, Big Macs, houses, and gold. *Paper* includes stocks, bonds, CD's, options, futures, options on futures, futures on options on futures on gold, etc.

Bonds are debt. You give somebody your money and they agree to pay you back someday (if soon, like 90 days, it's "short term", if not, like 30 years, it's "long term". Exercise: what does "intermediate term" mean? See, it's not so hard!), and to pay you interest at some percentage rate. Usually, the longer the term, the higher the interest. But the longer the term, the higher the risk, because if interest rates go up, the value of your bond goes down. Also, there's the risk that the issuer won't pay off, or may even stop paying interest. Issuers with tons of cash and a record of prudent financial management such as the U.S. Government get to pay less interest than fly by night operations like IBM. In general, the greater the risk, the higher the interest.

Stocks are equity. You own part of something. This can range from the telephone company to Autodesk. Generally stodgy old companies pay you a dividend in cash and are much safer. Utility stocks are the stodgiest of all and are very similar to bonds. Stocks in established, well capitalised companies such as Computervision or Union Carbide are much safer than wild-ass startups like Apple, Intel, Tandem, and Autodesk. This is because it is less painful to lose your money in good company.

All the rest are pinstripe Las Vegas in New York (or Chicago). The purpose is to have the most fun as you lose your money.

So what's leverage? Leverage is how you can lose or possibly make money even faster. Options (buying, not writing), buying stocks on margin, and futures are ways to obtain leverage. You can, by proper application of leverage, lose even more than you invested. Isn't that *neat*? (All right, this is somewhat unfair. Leverage, properly applied, can let you hedge illiquid assets and shift risks to speculators willing to assume them. Leveraged markets are essential to the efficient deployment of capital in a free market. See you at the track.)

And I could go on and on. This is really fascinating, and as one who has long been a market follower and player, I could go on for hours. But as I swore off all market playing when I started Autodesk, I'd rather not. It seems to me that it's a lot easier to make money than to multiply it, and for the moment, that's my focus.

Beyond the Lock-up Period

Since all selling shareholders signed a six month lock up agreement, sales of stock under Rule 144 are not an immediate concern. This is good, because all the people who will call you about their "restricted securities program" can be got rid of for at least six months. But 1986 will bring them out of the woodwork. Subject only to the constraints of the law, you will then be able to sell your stock through any broker willing to do the paperwork and abide by the rules.

You should be concerned, however, with sales of stock affecting the price. Remember that there are only 1.4 million shares out there. We hope that a large percentage of those will be in "strong hands", that is, long term holders. Thus the "float" or volume that actively trades may be quite small. As a result, throwing a block of 10,000 or 20,000 shares on the market may knock the price down significantly. As a result there may be an advantage in selling the stock through a broker who is a primary market maker in the stock, since they will sometimes have a better feel for how well the market can accept the stock and when is a good time to sell it. Initially, the market makers will be our underwriters. We hope to pick up additional market makers in the future (the more the better as far as the company is concerned), and we'll let you know.

Remember that brokers get a commission when they sell stock, and that people will be actively prospecting for this business. You will receive calls that begin "I have a buyer for 20,000 shares of Autodesk stock. If you're interested in selling, we can do the transaction, and since I have the buyer already, the price won't blip down". And when you agree to sell, he'll start looking for that buyer.

Anyway, watch out. From now on, assume you are a target. Not everybody who calls you up blind with a financial "opportunity" is a total sleazebag trying to loot the efforts of your hard work. I've made a list of those who aren't, and have already written the title at the top of the page. Now all I need is the first name. Let me know if you encounter one.

And remember, these guys can consume hours and hours of your time. Don't hesitate to be rude. I've found only one thing so far that gets rid of these guys immediately without overt hostility, and that's saying the magic words, "That's very interesting, but I'm totally broke". And now even that won't work.[136] Anyway, your time is your own, not theirs.

There's a reason they're called *brokers*.

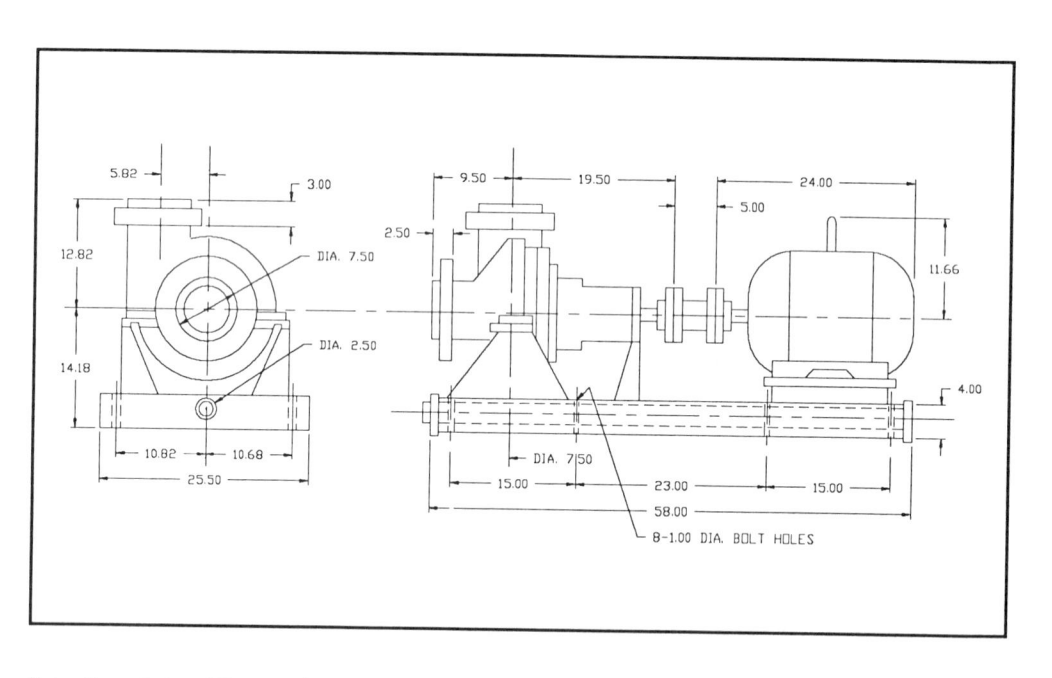

Peter Barnett drew this pump in 1984 to illustrate mechanical applications of AutoCAD. It has appeared on the AutoCAD sample drawings disc from Version 2.0 to date.

---

136 I was wrong. Amazingly, it *still* works pretty well. They're pushy, but not particularly smart.

Looking Back and Looking Forward

This Information Letter was written for the first Founders' Meeting. The Founders' Meeting was held at Dan Drake's house in Oakland not long after the public offering had been accomplished. It was an opportunity to review the path we had traveled and the challenges we might face next. I wrote this the night before the meeting, racing down to the Marinship office at midnight in search of references in my bookcase there.

Autodesk, Inc.
Information Letter #12

by John Walker
Revision 2 — Moon Day, 1985

"I resolved to make such an attempt at 'clarification', fully realising that it would increase the size of the pamphlet and delay its publication; I saw no other way of meeting my pledge I had made in the article "Where To Begin". Thus, to the apologies for the delay, I must add others for the serious literary shortcomings of the pamphlet. I had to work in great haste, with frequent interruptions by a variety of other tasks."

V. I. Lenin, *What Is To Be Done*, 1902

We did it.

In January, 1982 we got together and decided to build a software company which would become an industry leader. We agreed that our goal was to build a large, conventional, tightly-coupled company which provided all the services needed to become an industry leader. We all committed a major component of our time, and put at risk a substantial portion of our financial assets.

Today, Autodesk is one of the leading software companies in the world. Our goal was to build a company which would be one of the top five. By Mike Ford's analysis of the SoftLetter 100, discounting game companies and people who have collapsed since the list was published, we are about number seven today. Autodesk has joined the elite world of public companies, placing it with Lotus, Ashton-Tate, Software Publishing, and Micro-Pro in the top 5 visible players in the microcomputer software industry as seen by the financial world. (And don't discount the value of this: a public company gets press coverage as a matter of course that a private company can't buy at any price. Also, public companies are perceived as more solid citizens with more staying power in a competitive situation.)

We agreed to do it right and do it fast. We did both. Name the companies which have moved from start up to public companies in three years. That's a pretty select list to start with. Now look at the ones who have done it with no venture capital, with the original founders still in control, and with not even an outside director at the time of the public offering. You're down to a pretty damn short list. Now filter for the companies with their principles intact: who still believe and practice consistently rewarding the people who do the work, of getting the best people and cutting them in on the pie in a real sense.

So what we've pulled off here is, if not unique, awfully rare in the contemporary business world. This is a good time to reflect on what we've done and to look at how we can best apply the techniques that got us this far to the difficult task in getting to the next plateau.

Mid-Game

Because it's not over, folks! The process of building a company and reaping the rewards of our collective efforts is something I look at more and more as an ongoing brutal winnowing process. Three quarters of all start-up companies fail within the first two years. Only about one in ten thousand companies reaches the stage of making a public offering. And, yes, most public companies languish in the ranks of the NASDAQ Bid & Ask tables where we've taken up residence, rather than becoming the shooting stars who are perceived as the movers and shakers of the industry.

There's a phrase politicians use that I detest. I translate it as "we don't have any idea what the hell to do about this, and things aren't going to get any better". The phrase is "redouble our efforts". [137] I think that this phrase is only used by people who have never in their lives ever doubled their efforts in the first place. I assume that everybody in the founding group of this company is currently working flat-out. What we need to do is continue this, at a sustainable pace, through the next stage in the company's development.

---

[137] "Fanaticism consists in redoubling your efforts when you have forgotten your goal" — Santayana.

The public offering purchased effective immortality for the company. We now have over ten million dollars in the bank. This means that if our sales went to zero, we could survive for over a year, without any cut-backs or layoffs at our present expenditure level. Given the retrenchments we would make in should such a dire and unlikely (though certainly not unprecedented) scenario eventuate, we could cut back to the core group and spend five or ten years figuring out what to do next (and defending ourselves against shareholder suits). Hell, we could pay a reasonable group reasonable salaries just from the interest on the cash we raised in the offering.

To put the company's liquidity into perspective, I'm sure you remember when we all ponied up our $1 per share to buy Autodesk stock, accompanied by my incessant bleating about how we could run it to the moon. Well, adjusting for the two stock splits we've done, that dollar per share works out to six and two thirds cents per current share, $0.06666. Now today, the company has on the order of $2 *in cash* for each of those shares. So if we all went home and divvied up the pie tomorrow, we would have a gain of over 3000% on our initial investment, or 1000% per year. Not too shabby.

Please bear with me while I do a reverse presentation of these numbers. While the way Wall Street adjusts for stock splits is absolutely correct, people who buy an asset become attached to the price they paid for it (and much investor psychology derives from this). So rather than adjusting the historical numbers for splits, let's look at our performance assuming we never split the stock.

All right, on April 29, 1982 we sold some stock for $1 per share. We issued some options to people who contributed at $1 per share in May '83. By the time we got to the next round of options, it was all we could do to beat the price down to $2.70 per share in November 1983. Then things really started to cook. The next time we had to name a price was August 1984, when we had to move it to $7.50 (and remember that during this entire period we were doing everything we could to justify as low a price as possible, so that we could issue options as worthwhile as possible to the recipients). The next time we played "pin the number on the stock" was April 1985, and by then it had jumped to $10.50. There's nothing like a public offering to move the stock price to the "industry multiple", and ours sure did. The public offering sold on June 28, 1985 for a price of $165 per share! And last week the stock traded as high as $210 per share. Doesn't that seem different from the quotes you see in the paper?

Does anybody wish he had bought less?

You know, it's really fun writing some self-congratulatory prose after so many "crisis letters" and exhortations to exertion. Just so it doesn't become a habit ....

Burning Questions Of Our Movement

So, what happens next? What should we, as the founders of this company and owners of the largest piece of it, be doing to maximise the value of what we've built? What should our company be doing to advance within the industry? How can we best apply the principles upon which we built this company to the very different circumstances and environment in which we now operate? Obviously we've done a lot of right things, but what have we done wrong? What significant opportunities are we, at this very moment, overlooking? And why are our sales only $2 million per month and not, say, ten or twenty million? Can we get there? How?

One fatal luxury of success is a failure to question one's assumptions. We must constantly be looking at what we're doing and the general environment and watch for indications we should be changing our strategy. There is, to my mind, a growing spirit of "we're number 1", "we're unbeatable", and "all the competition is garbage". *This can destroy us!* We have to maintain good morale and believe in what we do, but we have to remember that we got where we are by running scared. There is no shortage of competitors out there with a lean and hungry look. We should be continually reviewing their products and strategies and taking the best ideas for incorporation into our own.

"The only function of economic forecasting is to make astrology look respectable."

Ezra Solomon

We've talked a lot informally about just what is involved in being a public company. I'd like to put it on paper, just so everybody has the same information all at the same time. Once you become a public company you operate in a fishbowl. Not only is the value of your company and therefore your performance rated daily in the open market, many business decisions you were free to make in private now become open for the world to see. This can lead to making decisions which may be bad for the long term future of the company in order to prevent a cataclysm in the market for the company's stock.

Those who hold and trade the stock obtain information about it primarily from the quarterly and annual reports the company files, from press releases the company issues when important events occur, through reports by financial analysts who follow the stock and are in regular contact with management, and to a lesser extent from presentations the management makes at various financial conferences. Our stock is held largely in institutional hands. This means that it is mostly in the accounts of pension funds, pooled investment accounts run by banks, and in mutual funds specialising in high-tech. The money managers who run these funds are accountable to the people who put the money in them, and their results are evaluated on a quarterly basis. If a fund is significantly underperforming the market, the money can evaporate as fast as the morning dew on the surface of Mercury. In fact, if a pension fund is underperforming the market, the custodians of it can be personally sued for malfeasance of their fiduciary responsibilities under ERISA. So to put it lightly, these money managers are under a lot of pressure.

They, in turn, look at the quarterly results issued by the company as the major indicator of the company's progress. It's a gross oversimplification, but worthwhile nonetheless to consider the stock price as made up of two components, the earnings (usually expressed as earnings per share or *EPS*), and the price/earnings ratio or *PE*. Thus:

Price = EPS x PE

The reason for breaking things down this way, is that similar stocks, such as banks, auto companies, aerospace companies, copper mines, and CAD companies will, in the absence of outstanding information peculiar to an individual company, trade at about the same P/E ratios. Thus one talks about the "market multiple" of a given industry. The P/E band moves up and down constantly; in an ebullient market such as 1983, P/E's overall may be twenty times those of a gloom and doom period such as 1974. Autodesk is in a somewhat strange position in that if it is considered a microcomputer software company it will probably settle at a P/E about half that it would command if seen as a CAD company. And of course next year, if software is in and CAD is out, the numbers may reverse. But in the minds of those looking at the stock on a daily basis, the P/E is relatively constant.

Thus, the primary determinant of the price is the earnings per share. This is very simple to calculate: you take our profits after taxes and divide by the number of shares outstanding. Zooming in a bit more, and assuming the number of shares as a constant, our earnings are broken down as follows:

```
PreTaxEarnings    =   Sales  -  Expenses
AfterTaxEarnings  =   PreTaxEarnings x (1  -  TaxRate)
GrossMargin       =   PreTaxEarnings / Sales
AfterTaxMargin    =   AfterTaxEarnings / Sales
```

Now let's look at these numbers and what they mean in the minds of investors. The two key numbers everybody's trying to guess are *Sales* and *EPS*. Thus, if you overhear me talking to an investor trying to probe us for information, you might hear me say "we're sticking with 90 cents on 25", which translates to "Look, I hope we really blow the top off the industry and end up with the whole pie, but I sure don't want to be dumped on if 'all' we do is increase our sales by 250% this year.

We're 95 % confident that, assuming no changes in the current competitive environment and the economy as a whole, that our sales will be at least $25 million and we'll earn at least 90 cents per share of outstanding stock."

As each set of quarterly results are issued, they will be eagerly digested for indications as to whether the company is ahead, on, or behind expectations. Investors want to see each quarter increase both *Sales* and *EPS* from the last, and compare each quarter's results with those of the comparable quarter in the previous year to see if growth over the year matches the expected growth rate. To date, our business has not been seasonal, so straight quarter-to-quarter growth will be expected.

Before we move on to the edgy relationship between the company and the financial analysts who cover it, I'd like to define "visibility", a key term in that relationship. Visibility measures to what extent outsiders can predict the business trends of a company overall. Consider a defence contractor. In that business, you receive contracts to do work, and the size of the contract and the payment terms are specified in advance. Any changes in the contract are public documents and are disclosed immediately in any case. Thus income is calculable by anybody who reads the paper. Expenses tend to also be pretty well predictable from historical measures, so all you need to come up with pretty reliable sales and earnings forecasts is a subscription to Aviation Leak and a pocket calculator. This is a business with high visibility.

Now let's consider a hypothetical company whose sales are almost entirely booked over the telephone. Most orders are shipped within 48 hours of receipt, so there is no backlog and no sales contracts to forecast. If the phone stops ringing, the money stops flowing. This company's sales flow through many different kinds of outlets and into numerous markets, which may behave differently as economic conditions change. The product costs almost nothing to manufacture, and is sold for a high price which is justified by difficult to measure productivity measures. The high price is largely the result of a lack of competition in the market; a determined competitor could sell such a product for $100 and make money doing it. The expenses of this business are mostly sales and marketing expenses, which are determined by the need to respond to competition and open new markets. Such a business would have really lousy visibility. I leave to you the exercise of naming such a company.

So who do those whose jobs are on the line turn to in order to decide if they should buy or sell our stock? The security analysts. These analysts usually work for the various investment bankers, and "follow" a group of stocks, usually in one industry. The analysts initially following our stock are Peter Schleider of L.F. Rothschild and John Rohal of Alex. Brown. We hope additional analysts follow our stock in the future. The analysts write regular research reports on the stock, and talk to management in order to prepare their own estimates of the company's future. These reports are then used by the institutional sales forces of the bankers to sell stock in the aftermarket. An analyst will probe to get as much information as possible, and then issue his own forecast. In some cases this forecast may be much more optimistic than that issued by the company. If the company fails to meet the forecast, the analyst will then write a report which says that the company "had disappointing earnings", even if they represented a new high and exceeded the company's own expectations. Now this may be a little hyperbolic, but it has happened, and it does happen. Maintaining close contact with the analysts and seeing that they reach the conclusions you want is an ongoing task for a public company.

In the offering process we "signed up" to a set of performance criteria. Our investors will be watching these and, having been sold very many high tech stocks that went south soon after the offering, will be using them as triggers to dump the stock. *We cannot let this happen.* Therefore, here are the numbers by which we live and die. All of these numbers are consolidated, i.e., the sum of domestic operations and all foreign subsidiaries. We must do $25 million in sales this year (FY ending January 31, 1986). We must generate 90 cents per share after tax profit. Our gross margins must be in the band from 35% to 40% and therefore our after tax margins should be about 20%. We must build the company and our distribution channels and product line to support $45 million in sales the following year and $1.45 per share after tax profit.

These are the company's must-meet goals. We hope to do a lot better, but we *must not* do worse. If we fail, the management will be battered by the shareholders, and our stock will be gored. But the management cannot make these goals happen. The company as a whole must do this. I tried to involve as many as people as possible in formulating these goals. Now we have our job to do. Let's get on with it.

What will be the environment in which Autodesk will be operating in the future? First of all, we cannot spend the proceeds of the offering on virtually any of the needs we perceive the company to face. Since in the software business we don't use any expensive capital equipment, virtually everything we would spend the money on shows up as an expense on the income statement. If we hire people, that's salary. If we do an advertising blitz, that's promotion. From the standpoint of accounting, spending the money we raised in the offering is precisely the same as spending money we get from selling an AutoCAD. Now please refer back to the equations given above which calculate the critical numbers. If we spend the money from the offering to hire people, or to advertise, or to do any of the obvious things, those dollars are added to Expenses. That gets subtracted from Sales and reduces earnings and margins. Assuming a marginal tax rate of 50%, the reduction of the pretax numbers is twice that of that of the after tax numbers. And remember that our performance is being watched *quarterly*. Even if we can spend the money knowing that it will generate a major return in six months, that's not good enough. The added expenditures will affect the one or two intervening quarters, and Autodesk will be perceived as having "disappointing earnings" or, even worse, "eroding margins" and look out below. (If you think for a minute you'll see why eroding margins are a superb leading indicator of competitive pressure.)

Now this may seem to be a lot to digest, but it really is crucial to the way in which the company will continue to operate. When I say, "We have all this money but we can't spend it", I am not setting up a smokescreen to deny people in the company what they want. I'm just describing the reality which I hope the above has somewhat clarified.

What Business Is the Company In?

This is a computer software company, y'hear. Maybe this is sufficiently obvious that it doesn't need restating, but as the company grows there is a tendency for every department to look upon what it does as central to the mission of the company. Departments then tend to see if they can make a direct contribution to the till by adding products to the company's line. For example, training could offer courses to users around the country for a fee. Technical could offer consulting services to driver developers for an hourly charge. QA could perform screening of third party software products for vendors. Marketing could prepare promotional materials for OEMs and third party vendors. And Production could manufacture third party products. Within the next year, we may be doing any or all of these functions, and these activities may be contributing dollars to the company's revenue totals. *But they are incidental to the business the company is in, which is designing, developing, manufacturing, selling, and supporting computer software*! Our company's value largely derives from the fact that what we do is so extraordinarily profitable. It is so profitable because we are selling intellectual property; virtually pure value added; pure reason without the critique. As I said three and a half years ago in the original Working Paper, there are few legal businesses as attractive. If we wish to go into another business, we must review that proposal as we would review the purchase of an operating company: looking at capital requirements, sales projections, pro forma income statements and balance sheets, and risk factors. This is one of the most profound decisions a company can make, and is not to be taken lightly or backed into inadvertently.

If you aren't used to thinking in the terms expounded above, the impact of stumbling into a new business can be less than obvious. Suppose we were to start doing direct contract support to major user accounts. Suppose that this was so extraordinarily successful that by the end of the year we had generated 5 million dollars in support fees, and had managed to do this with expenses of 4 million for personnel and travel. We would then add 1 million dollars to the pretax profit number and $500,000 to after tax profit. Sounds great, right? Wrong. That component of the business would be operating at a 20 % pretax margin and a 10 % after tax margin. When these numbers were consolidated with software operations, they would reduce our operating margins, and Autodesk would be perceived as having eroding margins. The analysts would then look at the numbers to find out what was happening and discover that we had gone into the education business. Education is not a stunningly profitable business (as thousands of colleges know, and Westinghouse and CDC learned to their dismay), and Autodesk would lose some of the attractiveness of being a "pure high-tech CAD play". This would reduce our P/E, and the stock could be clobbered.

I don't want to dwell on this too much, but it is a problem that growing companies typically have. We'll have to keep focused on the ultimate goal of selling a lot of software if we're to avoid it.

Product Style

I'd like to talk for a moment about our products and their general style. I've spent some time recently using other people's software packages and fooling around with some new product ideas, and it's clear that many of the things we talked about happening three years ago have happened. The micro software business has become very professional very rapidly. The standards for user interfaces and ease of use have risen extremely rapidly. I'd like to talk a bit about some of the implications of this.

Why do we make clunky user interfaces? I think that some of our much-vaunted "mainframe approach" to software may be leading us into some poor decisions in the current environment. We always build software to be easily ported, machine independent, and easy to maintain and enhance. These are things much to be desired and unqualifiedly good, *as long as there is no cost to the user*. If ease of development or support imposes a performance, convenience, or learning cost upon the customer, this must be looked at as a tradeoff, not decided preemptively in favour of the developer.

I would invite you to spend 5 hours using a program Dan Drake turned me on to, "Managing Your Money" by MECA. This is a $120 program of extraordinary complexity. I would rate its connectivity and integration as approaching AutoCAD. It fills three discs. You have to read about three pages of manual to get started on it, and it contains hundreds of pages of intelligent, useful, and witty on-line assistance. All response is absolutely instantaneous. No error is fatal. You can always back up.

I think our tendency is to adhere to the reggae rule of "all killer, no filler" in designing our programs. We tend to eschew user interface "fireworks" such as instantaneous screen updates, fill-in-the-forms data entry, pop-up menus, and function keys in favour of solid, well engineered but prosaic programs.

This is one of the assumptions we should question.

How long are users going to accept a product which requires mastery of a 300 page manual? In a market which is dominated by IBM and compatibles, what is the opportunity cost of not deriving greater advantages by tailoring to these machines? Should we do a Macintosh or Atari product? I don't have the answers to these questions. But I think we have to consider them.

What do we do next?

On the operational side, I think we should pledge a significant effort to doing this job of being a public company right. We showed the Silicon Valley cynics and the venture capitalists how a bunch of dedicated, talented people could do a start-up company right. Now let's show Wall Street how a small public company should be done. What I propose is that (all within the limits of the law, of course) we treat our stock as an Autodesk product. Let's put together a shareholder communication program that rivals the ones we've created for our dealers and users. Let's put on shareholder forums at our annual meeting just as we do for the dealers and conference speakers. And let's have an informal shareholder forum at the 6 month point between meetings. Shareholders can be a pain in the ass, but they do own the company. And let's see what we can do to make this perceived as a very special company to own stock in. We must be open and candid. We must present realistic numbers and always meet them. If we're not going to meet our numbers, we must give warning as soon as we know, and have explanations ready to deliver. These acts will build loyalty that will stand us in good stead when times get tough.

The Next AutoCAD

> "There's absolutely no way we could put a man on the moon by 1994. No way."
>
> NASA Official, quoted by Jerry Pournelle at the 1984 L-5 Convention

It's also time to look for some new product ideas. Let's not settle down into this "going concern" mentality where we're maintaining a program that came from "somewhere" and is going "somewhere". We built this from zero. We can do it again. Can a company our size continue to develop multiple products on the cheap, test market them, and get behind the winners? Can we rekindle the old "ten wolverines in a barrel" technological ferment we had when the idea of this company was fresh and new? Can we have more yelling and less nodding? Will *somebody* please come to me and ask to spend a week in another department to learn what the hell they do in there anyway? What is the minimum time in which we can bring a product to market now? Could we bring a new product to market this COMDEX? Look at the development logs to see where AutoCAD was at this point in 1982.

The American Dream

> *"Conrad Hilton didn't make his fortune by building only one hotel and then opening a car wash. He may have had a car wash before he had a hotel, but once he found hotels and they succeeded, it was hotels, hotels, and more hotels. Did Ray Kroc who owned McDonald's start one hamburger stand and then open a dry cleaners? No. He had a winner, he stayed with it, and wealth was accumulated."*
>
> Dr. Bruce Gould, "How Fortunes are Made", in *Bruce Gould on Commodities* (newsletter)

There are two ways to look at what we've done here. We're either an awfully lucky bunch of weirdos, or we're really on to something. With every passing month and every milestone we reach, the luck seems less likely and the strategy seems more astute.

Let's franchise it.

Franchise it? Well, not exactly, but here's the idea. We started out as a group of people with limited financial resources but a great pool of diverse talent and willingness to work hard. We built this company as opposed to going to work somewhere else because we felt that this was the best way to achieve the success we wanted to reward our exertions.

I don't think we were the only people in the world with these goals. Let's build ten, twenty, or fifty more Autodesks. How? By offering the same kind of partnership to entrepreneurial people that Marinchip offered to the founders of Autodesk. We publicise the following proposition:

You want to start a company? We know how to do it. Look at our results. Put together your group, count your money. Here's a set of information letters that tell you how to do it. Come to us with your proposal. We don't want a long business plan; you don't know what's going to happen any more than we did, and if you say you do you're a bullshit artist and aren't worth listening to.

We'll look at the people and the product ideas. Is there that sparkle you can see in the first 5 minutes? If we're believers, we'll match your investment dollar for dollar. In return we get 35% of the company, held as soft preferred which basically protects us against being ripped off, but we're in there with all the other founders. But it's the founders' company. Our investment in these companies will not be an expense on our balance sheet. The investment will purchase stock which will be carried as an asset. I'm not sure how often such illiquid assets get marked to market, but we can probably let it just sit there until we either write it off or begin to get proud of it.

Autodesk will provide limited support to the venture. We will see that the legal details are taken care of correctly and that the accounting is of public company quality. We'll provide a pool of talent to the management that has "done it before". We'll offer technical resources and the facilities of our lab on a sporadic basis. Our distribution channels, marketing and promotion resources, and our ability to promote products at shows and in publications at small marginal costs will be important resources to companies affiliated with us. Our manufacturing and shipping operations can provide those services at low costs per unit.

The founders of the new companies can choose to use our services, which will be billed at attractive rates, or to build their own or go outside — it's their company, career, and destiny. We will be providing what all the venture capitalists claimed they did, "bringing more to the table than just money". The only difference is that we really will.

Our goal is to give the founders of these new companies the same shot at success we had when we started. Autodesk will provide some cash that we sorely could have used, but not enough to mess things up, and the ongoing establishment the creation of which cost us so many critical hours we could have better spent elsewhere. We won't run the show, but we'll try to be there when we're needed. Many of these companies will probably fail, but if 20% work, they will contribute mightily to Autodesk's success.

Just imagine if we pull this off. I hope we always retain some of the rabble-rouser elements of our creation. I can think of nothing I'd like to do more than drain the talent out of these Silicon Valley companies that are screwing their key people and giving the equity to the venture capitalists. Instead, here will be Autodesk, with one face talking to security analysts and breaking new ground as the model for small public companies, and at the same time erecting a rickety, low-rent conglomerate built on talent and hard work, of hardscrabble start-up maniacs who, just once, want to do something right and own it.

I think that people would be well served to take the chance we'd be offering.

They'll have to have *real* commitment, *real* performance, *real* responsibility, and *real* professionalism to make it. If they're interested in making that kind of commitment, we can't guarantee that they'll succeed, but we can guarantee that together we'll have a once in a lifetime experience as we try.

Now putting this together will take some work. But how much, really? Let's think about it, and see if we can pull another sleeping shocker on the industry. Can you imagine, just imagine, ten companies, all loosely affiliated, working like Autodesk all at the same time. Why they'll say it's a movement.

And that's exactly what it will be.

Section Five

Growth Means Change

Publisher's Notes
January 1986 — December 1986

During 1986 Autodesk continued to grow sales and revenue by 90% over the previous year. By the end of 1986 sales exceeded $50 million. Growth means change, including changes at the top. Two key changes occurred in 1986: Mike Ford resigned as VP of Marketing and Sales; and John Walker prepared a gradual transition back to programming, turning the Presidency over to Al Green. Autodesk also encountered its first major mis-step in the marketplace when it introduced a device (hardware lock) to protect against unauthorized copying of AutoCAD.

Key Events

Here are the key events and the documents provided in Section Five.

February 5, 1986. Mike Ford resigns as VP of Marketing and Sales.

- February 5, 1986. — Time of Turbulence. Memo to the company on Mike Ford's resignation.
- March 2, 1986. — Speech at Silverado. Autodesk's software strategy.
- March 17, 1986. — Super Programmers. An ad for programmers.
- May 19, 1986. — CAD as the Heart of Computer Science. An internal "think piece".
- May 20, 1986. — The Computer Revolution. More thoughts on computers and software.
- May 1986. — AutoBits. A collection of Autodesk humor.
- August 26, 1986. — Flat-out Programming. John Walker's transition back to full-time programming.
- September 23, 1986. — Hardware Lock Debater's Guide. Discusses the hardware lock adopted by Autodesk to protect their software against unauthorized copying.

November 5, 1986. John Walker relinquishes Presidency to Al Green.

◆ November 5, 1986. — Information Letter #13. Explains the transition to the company.

◆ November 21, 1986. — Cadetron and Solid Modeling. Eric Lyons explains why 3D solid modeling is important to Autodesk.

◆ November 25, 1986. — Removing the Hardware Lock. Explains why the copy protection device was removed.

Eric Lyons joined the company as a programmer. He subsequently became Director of Technology.

Key Product Events

The company shipped close to 40,000 units in 1986, effectively doubling its installed base. A new release, 2.5, was shipped in May:

June 1986. AutoCAD Version 2.5 Release. Included additional 3D and the hardware lock.

October 1986. AutoSketch released. This is the low-end CAD product originally envisioned as "AutoCAD Lite".

Financial Summary

Both sales and revenue dollars increased. Sales increased 90% to $51 million; and revenues increased 90% to over $12 million.

Here are the quarterly figures for the year.

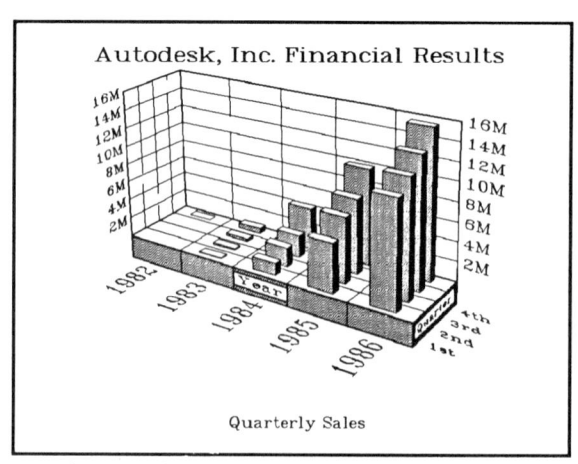

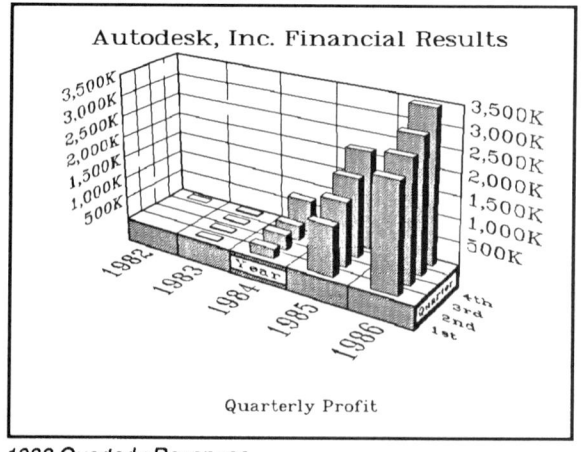

1986 Quarterly Sales

1986 Quarterly Revenues

Time of Turbulence

After a period of great strain and tension within the company, Mike Ford, who was, more than any other person, responsible for developing the marketing and sales strategies that resulted in AutoCAD's enormous success, and in building the marketing, sales, and support organisation from a single person (himself), to more than 80 people, submitted his resignation.

This is the memo I issued announcing his departure and the text of the remarks I made at the company meeting the following day. This was not a happy time for anybody in the company, but it was a significant event in the company's history, so these documents are included here.

Memo to everybody

To: Everybody
From: John Walker
Date: 5 February 1986

Mike Ford has submitted his resignation as Vice President of Marketing and Sales, effective today.

I have accepted his resignation.

Effective immediately, Richard Handyside will assume the role of acting Director of Marketing and Sales. Richard continues to hold the position of Vice President of European Operations, and will be spending one week per month in the London office to continue his work there. Richard is a founder of Autodesk, Inc. and has been responsible for building our sales and marketing efforts in the United Kingdom since the company's inception. Please extend him the help he will need in filling the job he'll be assuming.

We will immediately begin the process of finding a permanent replacement for Mike Ford.

The events of the last two weeks, and indeed the last several months have placed many of us under extreme stress. We have all found ourselves wondering what was happening as rumours circulated and we considered what they might mean for the future of our company. We have come this far by trying to build a company which was open, fair, and honest. That is how we must continue.

There will be an all-company meeting tomorrow in the administration area (where we usually have the monthly meeting). Because of the extraordinary seriousness of what has happened, the meeting will be longer than usual, and will start promptly at 5:15 P.M. I urge all of you who are concerned with the future of our company, unsure as to what has been happening, upset with the way things have been handled, or just confused to attend. I will try to explain what has happened and what happens next. I will answer all of your questions. I will stay until there are no more questions. All of the rest of the management of the company will be available to respond to your concerns.

In addition, I would like to reiterate that this company has always had, and will continue to have an open-door policy. If there is any matter you want to discuss with any of the management of the company, please bring it to us directly. If there's anything you'd prefer to discuss on a one-to-one basis, that offer stands and will stand.

If we continue to build our company on the principles which got us here: honesty, hard work, rewarding the people who do the work, and striving to minimise the politics, we can look back on this period as a time of testing for the company as it continued to grow. We have had what it took to build one of the singular successes of the 1980's in only three years. We have what it takes to continue. Let us begin today.

Remarks at the company meeting

Thank you all for coming.

This has been a time of great stress on all of us. Our energies have been diverted increasingly from the tasks we all need to do to take advantage of this tremendous opportunity we share and spent on speculation about people, about events, their consequences, and the future of our company.

Those of us who have been here since the company started in my living room on January 30, 1982 know that we tried to build something very special here. We were all people who had worked for companies large and small and always saw those companies squandering much of their resources on politics, on empire building, on image, on status symbols, on so many things not connected with success.

Like fools perhaps we imagined a company that worked differently, a company that concentrated entirely on the clearly defined goal of success in its industry, producing products of the highest quality, marketing them honestly to people, and efficiently delivering the fruits of our labours to the people who made it happen, rather than to a bunch of nameless investors or managers.

I won't recount all the times people said it wouldn't work; couldn't work. That it would all come apart when we reached 25 people, or 50 people, or 100 people. That when our sales reached $100,000 a month, or $1 million a month and we had "a real company there" we would be like everybody else, that the magic would be replaced by plodding, the creativity by repetition, the innovation by mediocrity. That is, after all, what we'd seen happen so many times before in so many other companies; it was only really *fun* in the early days when you were losing money and everybody was struggling together to survive, doing any job that needed to be done, working whatever hours it took, expanding their scope of expertise as the company called on them to grow, and grow fast into new jobs.

And then the money starts to come in, and the walls go up, and the hierarchy begins to grow, and the restrictions come down, and before long it's the "job" and not the "challenge". And sometimes when that doesn't happen, we read about companies that just come apart because of too rapid growth.

Is that happening here?

I think not.

There has been some changes. We have lost some people who have been here from the very early days. We have lost people who have worked long hours, applied great skills, and whose dedication to building this company, and unique insights into strategy and the way to make it into reality were major contributors to our success. We will sorely miss these people.

But let us look at what has not changed.

Our company is the acknowledged leader in its industry.

Our main product, AutoCAD has a market share in excess of 50%. This is a situation that only rarely ever occurs in industry, and presents the company that achieves it with virtually unlimited opportunities.

Our two new products, AE/CADD and CAD/camera have, in less than 6 months, both emerged as the unit volume leaders in their respective markets. We are making money on both products. We are on our way to success with both.

We dominate the channels of distribution for our products. Almost all of the dealers qualified to sell CAD sell AutoCAD. We have OEM arrangements with a list of companies which represent a Who's Who of high technology. Our position in education is commanding, and our innovation in addressing that market has been so great that even those who try to copy our strategy can't keep up.

Our oft-repeated goal was to make AutoCAD the standard for CAD on this planet. Today AutoCAD *is* the standard for CAD on this planet.

We have built a vital and fast-growing applications program. By putting tools in the hands of creative people, we've brought about an efflorescence of creative products that other CAD companies have failed to produce given decades. And we've done it in less than two years.

Our marketing effort has consistently won awards indicating it is the best in the industry. It is almost unheard of for a company our size to go it alone, spurning ad agencies and PR firms. Our team in Marketing has worked miracles with meager resources. The people who did that work will be given more resources to continue it. And I am confident that this group of people, who have shown themselves to be the best in the industry, will continue to distinguish themselves with continued awards and with results.

Autodesk isn't about safety and caution. It's about going for opportunities and conceding nothing to the competition. We've set up Project Gold, to address the Fortune 1000. It's a program unlike that of any other company. That's never stopped us before. And unlike so many other programs, ours is going to work. It's already beginning to work. And it will contribute mightily to our results that we gather to discuss this time next year.

We're also going after the government market for CAD. That's a very different kind of selling job than the one we've been doing so far. So what? We'll make it work too. And the goals here are high.

In the operation of the company that generates the money, we've grown with remarkably few pains, and we're running well. We're taking more orders from more dealers, processing them efficiently, manufacturing them rapidly and correctly, checking them so that we put the best product we can manage in the customer's hand.

Our support has been praised in *InfoWorld*. It is repeatedly praised in letters we receive. Few companies have even tried to support a product as complicated as ours over the telephone. None has done it as well.

Our accounting and financial operations continue to be a model of smooth operation. And the phones are working better.

Our development of the next AutoCAD continues, aiming for entry to Beta testing this month. This new product will have an impact as people begin to realise what they can do with it as major as the introduction of AutoCAD in 1982, or of AutoCAD 2.0 in 1984. Our competitors simply have no idea what is about to happen to them. Their products, placed against our new AutoCAD, will be bows and arrows against the lightning.[138] We're wading into the workstation market with Sun, Apollo, MicroVAX, and IBM PC RT products in the mill. All those high priced players now have to contend with AutoCAD and face the fact that AutoCAD is what the buyers want.

Our new products continue to progress. We've moved AutoLISP from concept to a shipping product. We have two new Architectural products under way, as well as a major upgrade to AE/CADD.

And there's a few wild ideas in the back room that are going to turn into industry-stunners before all that long.

That's what hasn't changed. We're a smoothly running, lean and efficient, creative, productive company. We've just completed our fiscal year at the end of January. We came in on target, with sales and earnings exactly what we aimed for. Once again, we've met our numbers. Every time we do that, we convince more people that we're going to be around for the long haul.

Last month, I got up here and said we'd do something about profit sharing. We're doing it. We've taken some of our profits and we're giving it to all of you who made it happen. Unlike some companies where the management skims the pot, we're doing it like this: everybody who's worked here full time for the full year gets $1000 of bonus (we have to do tax withholding on this, of course). If you've been here less than a year, or work part time, you'll get the proportionate amount for the time you've worked. That's it. It doesn't matter what you get paid, what you do, or who you work for — you get $1000. You deserve it. You earned it. Thank you.

Let me promise that we'll continue to do something about profit sharing in the future. I'll share the details when they're firm and I can make a commitment I know we can keep.

So let's talk about what has changed. As I said, we have lost some people. I don't want to go into details here of what happened when, who said what to whom, or what who said what where. Events and situations occurred which led me, in conjunction with all of the current senior management of the company and most

---

138 This was what was released as AutoCAD 2.5. Among other things, it introduced the hardware lock to the domestic market.

of the founders to conclude that we were going down the wrong road with the company. We decided to remedy that situation. We decided to eliminate the stress which was hurting us all, and to pay the price of the consequences. We made our decision and we acted. Now things will get better if we all work to make that happen.

The politics stops today. The whispering stops today.

The honesty, openness, and fair dealing that built this company is back. We never intended it to go away, but maybe we were so preoccupied with immediate problems that we failed to reaffirm what has made this company so different and so successful. If you have any questions about what has happened, or have any concerns about what is going on, you can discuss them with me or anybody else in the company regardless of position, in private or in groups.

This company is not supposed to be run top down. Our success has been a consequence of how well we listened to our users, our dealers, our OEMs, and others we deal with. Information has to flow from the people in direct daily contact with these people *up*, so that the right decisions get made where to apply our limited resources. We will not falter because we lose some people at the top. We will not falter if we were to lose everybody at the top, as long as the people who are really doing the work continue to do it, and continue to listen to what they hear, share it with others in the company, and act to meet the needs they feel.

I don't care what you do in this company. If you think we're heading in the wrong direction, if you smell a problem we're overlooking, if you see a threat we seem to be ignoring, tell me or somebody else in the management. This isn't a privilege. It's part of your job and key to our long term survival.

Just a week over four years ago, 16 people decided to start a company and do it right this time. Today, 160 people have the opportunity to start from that base and build something much bigger, so that four years from now we'll all be the envy of the latecomers, the founders who were there in the early days, the people who saw the opportunity become reality.

Mankind is the animal that makes tools. In each generation, only a few people get a chance to create new tools. Very, very few get to contribute to making a tool that changes the lives of first hundreds, then thousands, then tens of thousands, and someday millions of people. We are in that position. Our work so far has put us there.

I feel privileged to have shared this experience with all of you. Now we keep on working together to pursue this opportunity. Few ever get this kind of a chance. Rarely is there such an opportunity to so immediately see the consequences of your hard work. This is the fulcrum, the point where we make the potential of

AutoCAD really begin to change things in a large way, and where we decide to keep this company on the track that brought us so far so fast.

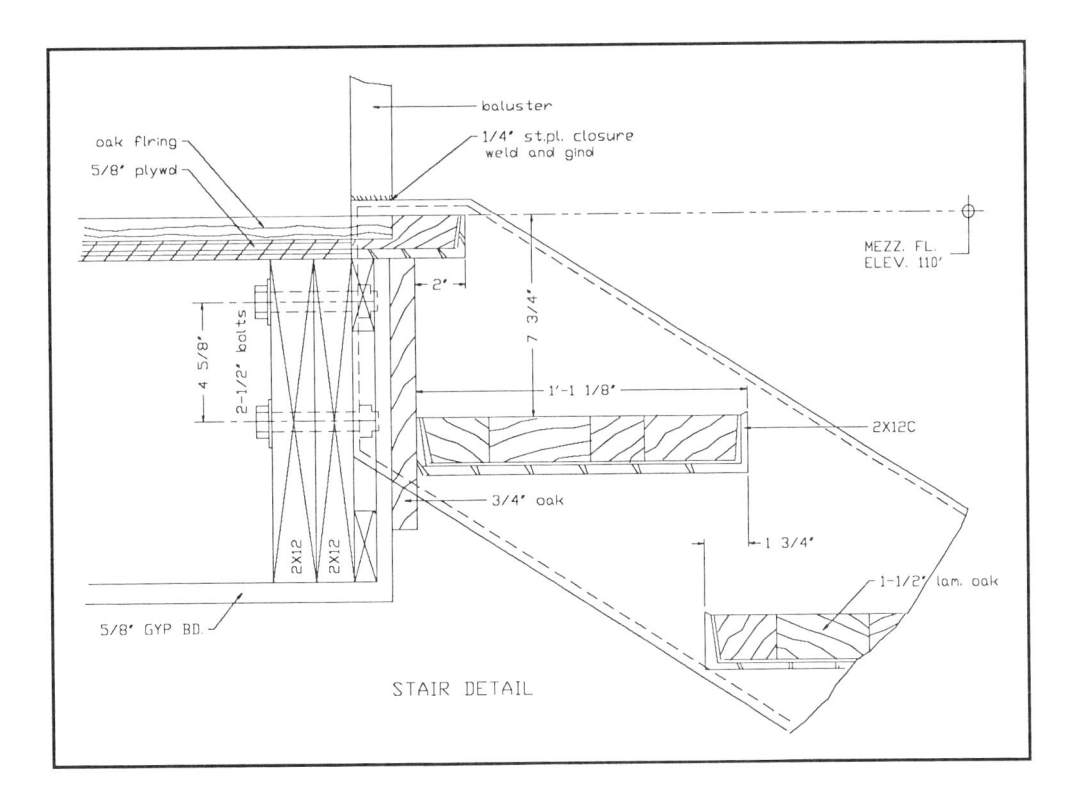

Peter Barnett drew this architectural stair detail in 1984 to illustrate architectural applications of AutoCAD. It has appeared in numerous advertisements and brochures, and has been on the sample drawings disc from AutoCAD version 2.0 to date. Bob Elman spent a great deal of time cleaning up this drawing into its present form.

A Presentation of Autodesk's Strategy

Every year, InfoCorp (an industry analysis company) holds a technology forum at the Silverado resort in Napa, California. I was foolish enough to volunteer to speak, and so I had to prepare this speech which I gave with slides. I'm including this for two reasons. First, this is the most coherent exposition in print of Autodesk's strategy at the time. Second, preparing and delivering this speech, on top of everything else that happened in early 1986, was one of the items that prompted me to start seriously planning to hand the job of president on to somebody better suited to do it.

InfoCorp Silverado Speech

by John Walker
Revision 2 — March 2, 1986

The machine age began to come to an end with the invention of the first programmable computer.

We often forget that the word "technology" comes from the same root as "technique".[139] It has nothing to do with machinery, it's how humans apply their minds to solving problems.

The general purpose computer is a tool which allows pure technique in the form of algorithms to be applied to problem solving. This is the central fact of the computer revolution.

Since the advent of the low cost microprocessor, we have seen the replacement, on an accelerating basis, of special purpose machinery (whether mechanical or electronic) with general purpose computing elements. Examination of a 1970 vintage teletype beside a contemporary printing computer terminal will illustrate the extent of this revolution.

---

139   The Greek τεχ.

Today, as the designers of the complex machinery of the past retire, the skills which created such exquisite machines as mechanical calculators which could divide are moving from practice to history. Designers entering the workforce often view the achievements of their seniors, accomplished without computing elements, the way our civilisation views the building of the pyramids.

So what in the world does any of this stuff have to do with PC's in the engineering world, or with PC CAD?

In every area general purpose computers have entered, they have been forced to educate people that what was once a machine is now simply a piece of software.

Remember when computers looked like computers?

This is the first computer I ever used.[140] By the standards of the early 1960's, it was a supercomputer.

It had 256 thousand bytes of 8 microsecond core memory.

Its magnetic drums provided 6 megabytes of secondary storage.

It added two 36 bit numbers in 4 microseconds.

It performed single precision floating point adds in hardware in 14 microseconds.

It communicated with remote terminals at 2400 bits per second.

It served a single user at a time, with high speed batch processing.

And laser technology was on the verge of revolutionising data storage.

This computer performed all the engineering, scientific, and software development computation for a university with a graduate and undergraduate population of over 2000. It was used for finite element analysis, fluid dynamics, particle physics, compiler and operating system development: virtually every field of science and engineering. It was retired in 1968.

This is the computer I'm using today — an IBM PC/AT, the exemplar of the PC in technical applications.

---

140   The Univac 1107 at Case Institute of Technology, Cleveland Ohio.

It has 3 and three quarter megabytes of 150 nanosecond RAM.

It has twenty megabytes of disc storage.

It does 32 bit adds in 2.3 microseconds.

It provides both single and double precision floating point in hardware, doing single floating adds in 20 microseconds.

It communicates with other computers on a network at ten million bits per second.

And laser technology is on the verge of revolutionising data storage.

It serves a single user at a time, me. It spends more than half of its time turned off, and a majority of its time while on waiting for me to type on the keyboard.

This computer, a PC, has 14 times the main memory, and three times the disc storage of the 1960's mainframe. Its memory is 53 times faster. The processor is 3.4 times faster for integer calculations, and .7 as fast for floating point. For double precision floating point, the heart and soul of scientific and engineering work, the PC is over 4 times faster.

So it isn't just hyperbole when we talk about having a room sized mainframe's power on our desks. For less than the price of a car, we can own a computer more powerful in every way than the mainframes on which most of the key engineering applications used today were written.

It is these statistics which show how utterly absurd it is when somebody pronounces that some job or other will never be done on a PC.

The confluence of these two trends; the displacement of special purpose machines with general purpose processors, and the ongoing giddy decline in the price one must pay for computing power has led to the development of the general purpose workstation.

In the mid 1970's, everybody thought of a word processor as a machine. It was an expensive box, bought from a word processing company primarily by large corporations, who could pay the price to obtain the productivity gains such a machine delivered. Virtually beneath the noses of the word processing vendors, people started selling word processing programs which ran on PCs, those funny "hobby computers" that strange people bought and played with. Before long, the use of general purpose PCs with word processing software dwarfed dedicated word processors, even in the markets where word processors were strong. Note that they did not supplant word processors — companies continue to buy word processors for full-time typists, and word processors provide services to these operators which PC programs do not currently provide. But most people write as part of their job, not full time. They need an easy to learn and use tool which is one of a collection of tools they run on a personal workstation.

In 1982, my company started selling a computer aided drafting and design program which ran on PCs. The conventional wisdom, as represented by those venture capitalists and analysts we could get to talk to us was:

1. You can't do CAD on a PC.

2. Even if you could, no serious user would buy it.

    and

3. Computer dealers can't sell CAD systems.

Well, we didn't have anything else to do, so we just went ahead and tried anyway. To date, we've sold in excess of forty thousand CAD packages for PCs. To put this number in perspective, it is on the order of twice the number of workstations of the most widely used mainframe CAD system.

Nobody can afford to discount PC CAD and PC engineering applications today. Let me give you some statistics about AutoCAD, the program I sell. I'm using our program as an example because I know the numbers for it; there are other PC-based engineering applications with similar statistics.

The source code for AutoCAD is in excess of 200,000 lines of C. The program is well in excess of a megabyte; programming tricks from the 1960s allow it to run in much smaller machines. Today, it embodies over 70 man-years of development. It is being enhanced at the rate of over 20 man years per elapsed year. It runs on over 30 machines, supports in excess of 120 graphic peripherals, and operates compatibly on MS-DOS, Unix on the Sun and Apollo workstations, AIX on the IBM RT PC, and VMS on the VaxStation II.

Over 150 third party application packages have been interfaced to AutoCAD. These include structural analysis, bill of material extraction and job costing, pipe stress, architectural design, numerical controlled machine programming, municipal mapping, surveying, printed circuit autorouting, and even football play diagramming and theatrical lighting design.

AutoCAD may be used as a standalone application package, or it may be programmed for specialised applications. We have integrated the LISP language into AutoCAD, allowing users to extend the system for their own jobs.

Over 600 educational institutions teach drafting and design with AutoCAD. AutoCAD is available in English, French, German, Swedish, Italian, Japanese and Spanish language editions. Translators are available which allow AutoCAD to interchange drawings with most major mainframe CAD systems.

By virtually any measure you choose to apply, lines of code, internal complexity, investment in development, ongoing development commitment, open architecture, third party support, migration to multiple hardware platforms and operating systems, and computing power consumed by the package, AutoCAD is mainframe software. So why do we choose to sell it on PCs?

Because that's where the money is.

It seems like if you stand on a street corner in Silicon Valley and hand somebody a $20 bill, he runs off to build an engineering workstation. On everybody's mind is the refrain, what will become the engineering workstation of the 80's and 90's? Chip makers vie to position their 32 bit processor as the heart of the lucrative engineering workstation market.

The numbers tell another story. Today, for every 32 bit engineering workstation in the world, there are more than one hundred 16 bit MS-DOS machines. It's news when a major company selects one of the workstation vendors to provide 200 workstations for an engineering facility. It's routine when their purchasing arm orders another thousand PCs to equip another department. They are, after all, just PCs.

As a software supplier, I can't help but notice that those who sell software on the 32 bit workstations don't get a hundred times as much per copy of their software as those of us who sell on PCs get for ours.

Let me return for a moment then, to the theme of this talk... PCs invading the engineering market. I'd like to retitle it at this point... to PCs *infiltrating* the engineering market. I'll explain how this is happening in a moment.

First of all, please keep in mind that only a small percentage of the engineering and scientific work in this country is done in the large companies. I'm fascinated by how many companies focus on the Fortune 1000 to the exclusion of the rest of the market. Marketing to the Fortune 1000 has its advantages; it's a clearly defined prospect list, heavily researched, and generally sellable from the top down. But in many cases it's only a small fraction of the market.

There are over 600,000 manufacturing organisations in this country. Eighty five percent employ ten people or less. The overwhelming percentage of architectural firms employ less than ten people. Even within the largest companies, there are sales offices, project groups, and application engineering arms which are operating as small autonomous entities.

Most drafting and design done today is not being done on CAD systems, it's being done by hand. Most mechanical parts are not being designed on mainframes or engineering workstations, they're being designed on paper, or by rule of thumb. Only a tiny percentage of the entire building process, from architecture through construction to facility management, involves computers at all. This is the vast untapped market. This is what accounts for the dominance of the PC in engineering applications. Those who ignore it do so at their peril.

An engineer's job embodies many different activities... writing, reading, performing calculations, drawing, interacting with others, and exploring design alternatives. The computer can play a part in all of these parts of the job other than face to face interaction. An ideal engineering workstation, therefore, is one which performs all of these tasks while requiring the least effort to master.

Engineers spend a lot of time writing. They do calculations which in the dark days before microprocessors were done on slide rules. Those in larger organisations access central databases, and may use some form of electronic mail for communication. There is a cheap and effective tool which improves productivity in all of these tasks — the desktop computer. For less than the monthly salary of an engineer, a computer which delivers immediate and measurable gains in output can be placed on his desk. And that's being done today, by the millions.

Don't underestimate the power of a widely distributed tool. If an engineer has a PC on his desk, which may have been purchased, justified, and primarily employed as a word processing station and terminal to the company computer, and has the choice of, for example, doing a drawing on that desktop machine with a PC CAD program, versus signing up for time at the corporate CAD centre, or submitting a sketch to the drafting department for three day turnaround, what will be his decision?

That decision will usually be made based on the engineer's desire to optimise his own productivity. Who cares if doing a drawing on the PC is ten percent slower than using the corporate CAD station... if that ten percent amounts to 6 minutes for a one hour drawing, and you have to wait 2 days for your time on the CAD station, or 3 days for drafting to turn around the drawing, the engineer and his employer is well ahead by using the PC to make the drawing.

Similarly, in the small organisation, the purchase of a PC may have been prompted by the desire to use it as a word processing system, or to keep accounts, or to maintain spreadsheets. The addition of a PC CAD package, or other engineering or scientific analysis package may result in productivity gains in those aspects of the business as well.

In both cases, then, what we're seeing is infiltration, not invasion. The PC is justifiable as a productivity tool in organisations large and small. It is bought to perform the tasks that everybody agrees it does best. Once in place, users discover that they have far more power at their fingertips than they imagined at first, so the PC assumes more and more complex tasks, impinging on those applications oft considered as requiring a "mainframe" or "turnkey system".

The PC, because it is there, is applied to these more demanding tasks. Users discover that the PC does a fine job performing them, and as the word spreads, the managers of the central data processing and CAD facilities discover that the projected growth in demand for their services is falling below expectations. First, by a small amount, then a larger factor, and finally by so much that somebody is delegated to find out what is going on.

And another organisation discovers the PC as engineering work station.

Every time I give a talk, I always get a question that goes like, "Do you see the 32 bit machines supplanting the 16 bit machines", or "what will the impact of RISC technology be on the workstation market", or "will the 80386 cut into the 68000 based market". I have to answer by saying, "I don't have any idea and I couldn't care less".

Except for those who build the machines and those who invest in them, the issue of CPUs and operating systems is of a lot less significance than a lot of people think.

Let's look at the general shape of a workstation as it will exist in a couple of years. It will have a fast processor, delivering at least the power of a VAX 780 on the desktop. It will support an operating system which provides multitasking, and will probably look a lot like UNIX. I include MS-DOS and its derivatives as Unix-like. It will have a high resolution screen, and the software will support a window environment allowing concurrent execution of disparate tasks. The station will be usable as a standalone computer by a user with no previous experience in system administration, and it will be possible to connect the system to others in a network which provides a true distributed file system.

It will provide all of the programming languages in which major applications are written, including C and FORTRAN compilers of high quality. All of the major engineering and scientific application packages will be available to run on it.

And, sad to say for the vendors, it will probably cost a lot less than many of them assume today. More on this later.

Numerous contenders meet, or will soon meet these tests. The software suppliers will put their packages on all of the major contenders' machines. The market will decide who the survivors will be.

The terminology in the computer industry has always been murky. The fact that we don't break out in laughter when we hear such precise nomenclature as "mid-sized supermini" and "mini supercomputer" indicates just how hard it is to draw lines between the computing resources we have available today.

There is, in fact, far more of a continuum of price performance available in computers today than at any time in the past, and this is largely unappreciated by the buyers and sellers of this equipment alike. At the same time, the emergence of a small number of standard operating systems, languages, user interfaces, and networks has made migration between these machines unprecedentedly easy.

Here are three machines running AutoCAD. The first is the Data General One, a 9 pound laptop portable. The second is a PC/AT. The third is a Sun workstation running Unix. The program functions identically on all of these machines. Data may be moved between them using any of several media.

Only ten years ago, it was taken as commonplace that every computer vendor had its own operating system, data formats, and user interface. Users have demanded that industry standards be adopted to protect their investment in data, programming, and user training. They communicated this demand to the hardware suppliers in the most direct method possible, by choosing to buy only systems which gave them this protection. And the survivors among the suppliers have learned.

Let's look at how distribution of these products is developing. Back in 1983, if saying the words, "PC Software" failed to empty a room of venture capitalists, adding "Retail distribution" usually did the trick.

But the unavoidable fact is that as the price of computer systems and software falls, and the number and range of customers consequently expands, the way these products reach their users must change. You simply cannot afford to sell a $2500 product to hundreds of thousands of customers with the type of direct sales force and on site support that has been characteristic of the computer industry in the past.

When we started Autodesk, we decided that we would not sell any products directly, but rather pass them through reseller channels. We initially focused on computer manufacturers, who were at the time building software distribution arms and targeting the major companies. Concurrently, we began to build a dealer network to sell our product to users and provide local support. We have seen an ongoing shift in the distribution of our product from a mix dominated by OEM sales to computer manufacturers in 1983 to one today where more than 85% of our product is sold through dealers.

Some people may not take computer dealers very seriously, but in less than four years, they've sold twice as many CAD systems as any of the CAD companies have in two decades.

Who are these dealers? Originally our dealer requirements were fairly low. If you bought two packages and paid COD, you were a dealer. We didn't go through the extensive qualification filtering that some of our competitors did, looking at square feet, location, staffing, service facilities, and so forth. Thank goodness. Some of our most successful resellers were those who wouldn't have been taken seriously by most software vendors. One, for example, was an architect who bought the package for himself and then began to configure systems for other architects. In less than three years, this architect has built a CAD sales, service, and support facility employing 14 people and selling to a wide variety of users.

Today, our dealers are much better qualified and trained. Every one of our more than 1300 dealers is required to have a full time person on staff with a drafting or engineering background. They are required to attend dealer training at our headquarters, and must return yearly for update training in new products and updates to the current product. Dealers must commit to providing direct user support for every package they sell.

Dealers who are successful in selling CAD and engineering applications are hard to characterise. Some specialise in the sale of CAD, while others carry a broad line of products. Our successful resellers include chain computer stores who have taken on CAD as an additional product line. Some focus on sales to one vertical market, such as architects or mechanical engineers, while others sell a basic drawing facility to a wide variety of users.

Further, while the computer retailer is often seen as a storefront selling to individual walk-in customers, many of our resellers have closed major sales with Fortune 1000 companies, government, and education by outreach marketing.

Many software vendors today are bemoaning the poor health of the dealer channel. We hear things said like, "how viable is a business where all of your resellers are losing money". Yet many of these companies who express concern for their resellers place their products in mass distribution channels which result in the package being sold mail order at prices at or below the dealer's cost. Is it any wonder that computer dealers don't spend much time mastering, demonstrating, and selling software?

If a software vendor wants to build and support a healthy dealer network, it must resist the temptations which destroy the vitality and profitability of that channel. It must decline to sell through discount channels. It must refuse to skim the cream off the dealer's business by selling direct to larger customers at a discount. And it must provide the training and support to keep the dealer competent to support his customers.

Many of those who said that CAD couldn't be sold through dealers pointed to the extensive user training and support traditionally provided with larger CAD systems. As desktop computers enter the engineering market, other collateral forms of support and training are evolving.

But nobody has as much control over how users come to master a product as the people who designed it. User interface is a distribution issue. If a product is sold for hundreds of thousands of dollars and used by a full time operator, it is reasonable for the vendor to provide a two week training course for the operators, and direct customer assistance.

When we designed AutoCAD, we knew that it would be bought and used primarily by users who had never seen a CAD system before. These first time users required a user interface that led them through the package, and extensive documentation, on line help, and support materials to aid them in getting started. In some ways, a CAD system for a first time, or part time user needs to be more complicated than one used by a full time CAD operator. The CAD operator has learned and invented work-arounds to achieve things the system cannot do directly. In addition, CAD operators usually have a manual drafting background and can always fall back on paper and pencil techniques where the CAD system lacks power.

For example, suppose the user has drawn two circles and wishes to draw a line perpendicular to one and tangent to the second. If the CAD system cannot perform this geometric calculation itself, the casual user is far less likely to know how to do it with construction lines as you did on the drawing board.

There is an aphorism in the electronics business that goes, "it costs a lot of money to make something cheap". Well, in the software business it takes a lot of work to make something simple. In order to diffuse these previously specialised tools to communities of users thousands of times as large as before, we have to make major investments in user interface, on-line assistance, and teaching tools.

As a previously specialised tool becomes a widely distributed de facto standard, independent support becomes available to the users. The wise vendor encourages and promotes this. Autodesk has, for example, designated 43 organisations Authorised Training Centres. These centres, many of whom are regular educational institutions, provide direct user training courses, with several offering introductory through advanced courses focusing on specific application areas. By the end of this year, over ten books will be on the market based on AutoCAD. Only a product which generates sales in the tens to hundreds of thousands can economically support these developments.

What we are seeing in distribution then, is a shift from expensive, hard to use products sold directly in small numbers, to cheap, easy to use products sold in vast quantities. The user has access to the same, or better, training and support as before, but provided by a large number of suppliers in an open market, rather than directly from one supplier.

Now let's look a little bit into the future. As guidelines as to what is likely to happen, it's worth remembering a few pieces of what was conventional wisdom in 1983. It's just as true today.

Desktop computers are being sold by the millions. This is a situation unprecedented in the human experience, equivalent to the development of a mass market for music created by the phonograph or for theatre created by motion pictures and television. Those who take advantage of this opportunity will do very well.

Most tasks are done today manually or by something very close. Anybody who thinks that all the productivity tools have been invented hasn't spent much time looking at their workday.

We have made enormous strides in the last five years in making enormously complicated tools usable with no training. This is only way to sell to a mass market.

Far less than one movie in ten is a hit. Far less than one book in ten is a best seller. Why expect any better for software? But there *are* hit movies and books, and the winners in the software wars will be as enduring.

Picking the end of a trend in progress is one of the most difficult and least profitable activities one can choose to undertake. For forty years, everybody who bet on the price of computing power ceasing to decline has been dead wrong. So while I can't predict whether the PC will become the universal engineering workstation, I firmly believe that whatever ends up occupying that niche will cost less that today's PC. It is instructive, for example, to compare the specifications of the Atari 1040ST, which sells for less than $1000, to those of the proposed ideal engineering workstation of just two years ago.

The customers are a lot smarter than many vendors think. Suppliers who put the power to extend and adapt their products into the hands of their users and resellers unleash the creativity of these people to create products that directly benefit the supplier … and at no cost. Vendors who begrudge others who build successful businesses based on their products stultify those in the best position to make those selfsame products successful.

Find a case in the entire history of computing, where a closed architecture, proprietary system has defeated an open architecture system in the market.

Find a case where you cut the price of something by ten times and don't create a market far more than ten times larger.

Some people are still trying to take a software product and bundle it with hardware and sell it as a turnkey system for one particular job. If you undertake this, remember that you are trying to resell somebody else's hardware in direct competition to the computer manufacturer who made it. Good luck.

The long delayed but finally occurring advent of networks is going to make some major changes in the way people work, and create some major opportunities for software suppliers. Everybody's heard the phrase, "networks will enormously reduce the need for a large, central mainframe", and I believe it's true, but managing the kind of distributed database this leads to, and integrating this into an organisation will require solutions to many difficult technical problems that have been inadequately addressed to date.

Engineers do not work on drawings or documents. They work on projects. They communicate with others, and interchange design data at several different levels of abstraction. The computer has much to contribute to the entire process of engineering, and the gains as individual productivity tools begin to work together will be as great as those of the tools themselves.

The PC sector of the business is not a sideshow. It's the main event. This is where the battle for the entry level user is being waged. The software that establishes itself as a standard in the PC market will be carried upward to more powerful hardware as users migrate to their own best point on the price performance curve.

Today, the overwhelming majority of first time CAD users are using PC CAD. The overwhelming percentage of students who are learning CAD are learning on PC CAD.

Users will come to see the workstation hardware itself as little more than an appliance which delivers the productivity gains embodied in software. It will eventually be seen as making no more sense to ask, is a PC right for engineering work than to ask what is the best television for watching cop shows.

And in twenty years, somebody will show a slide of an IBM AT and ask, "remember when computers looked like computers?".

Thank you.

Looking for Super Programmers

In late 1985 it became evident that the growth of AutoCAD, the need to support new hardware, and the pressing need to develop new products was outstripping the capacity of our programming staff, still largely made up of founders of the company. In addition, we saw that in our rush to expand we had lowered our standards, recruiting people who did not always share our key developers' commitment to excellence. Having built what we thought was an ideal environment for programmers, it seemed to me that we should try to attract more high-productivity, broadly-talented people.

I wrote some ad copy which I hoped would select for people with the properties we were looking for. Thanks to the efforts of Mauri Laitinen, we finally ran the much-revised advertisement below starting on March 17, 1986. I date the return of the company to the highest standards of technical excellence and innovation to that date, his effort, and this advert.

Are you one of those rare software people whose productivity is hundreds of times above average?

Autodesk, Inc., the leader in computer-aided design, founded by people like yourself, invites you to join us.

We're The Best: You're The Best

Our company was built by people who never said, "I can't do that." If you're the person we're looking for, you'll be able to design, implement, test, and debug complex software, both alone and collaboratively. The code you write will meet the highest standards of efficiency, maintainability, and modularity. You'll know how to integrate changes in large, complicated programs, and you'll combine design and implementation skills with an intuitive feel for the evolution of the product as a whole and for its position in the marketplace.

You'll be able to find or develop the theory you need to get your job done. You'll be literate, and able to communicate complicated technical concepts in simple and readable language. Your work documentation will meet the standards of the best tech writers and be suitable for immediate inclusion in our user manuals. You'll be able to express yourself clearly and persuasively, whether in a design session or while speaking with prospective customers at a trade show. And you'll take personal responsibility for all your work, as a matter of course.

You'll care enough for the commercial success of your programs that you'll work effectively with marketing and sales people, contributing ideas to best promote the benefits of the products you'll be developing. You'll take an active interest in the work of other people in the company, and be willing to apply your expertise to help with their problems and develop their skills.

We Don't Want Less Than The Best

What will we do? We'll pay you more than anybody else in the industry. Your pay here can start as high as $60,000 and rise as high as your contributions justify. There's no ceiling on the pay scale for technical people here; you can earn $100,000 if you're worth it and prove it to us. We give our workers stock options that mean something. Unlike companies that look at options as a way of enslaving employees, we intend our options to let you share in the success you'll be helping to create. If we do our job, you won't want to leave. And since we're a public company, your options represent real stock with real value, not funny money.

We value productivity and excellence. We continually strive to minimize politics and bull. We couldn't care less about hours and personal style (except when you will know that it matters). Many of our key producers work at home. We don't care about your degrees and titles; we care what you've done, and what you can do in the future. We value people like you; after all, that's all this business really is.

What You've Heard About Us Is True

We're in the computer-aided design business. We sell only software. Our company was founded in 1982 by 14 programmers and we built it (with no venture capital and no debt) to a size of 215 people with offices in 5 countries and monthly sales exceeding $2 million. We sell a program called AutoCAD that runs on most MS-DOS 16-bit machines and some 32-bit workstations such as the IBM RT, Sun, and Apollo. In fewer than three years, we've sold more CAD systems than any other CAD company, micro, mini-, or mainframe. We've passed IBM and Computervision and we're pulling further ahead. We write exclusively in C (AutoCAD has more than 100,000 lines of it), and we develop a lot of our own software tools.

Our newer products include CAD/camera, a revolutionary raster-to-vector conversion program; AutoCAD AEC, a series of applications to dramatically speed up architectural and mechanical drawing and design; and AutoLISP, a full

LISP interpreter built into AutoCAD. We do most development on our target machines. Relevant experience is nice, but if you're as good a person as we want, you'll be able to pick it up in a week or two.

We try to make this company the kind of place people you would want to work for. If you're the person we've described, we invite you to write us a letter describing what you can do, and what you've done.

During your interview, expect to discuss almost anything with five or ten other super programmers (three of them are on our board of directors). If you're a head-hunter, forget it.

Our company is continuing to turn the industry upside down. You can make a difference here and reap the rewards of your efforts. We couldn't find a company like this one four years ago, so we built one to our specs. Maybe they'll be your specs too.

CAD as the Heart of Computer Science

With the introduction of AutoLisp and the growing power of AutoCAD as a modeling system, it became clear to me that we were on to something far more powerful and significant than a drafting system. This was an attempt to place CAD in the position I believe it deserves — in the mainstream of computer science — as opposed to the backwater in which many believe it languishes. This was an internally-distributed "think piece". I am even more convinced now of the arguments expressed herein than the day I wrote them.

Computer Aided Design:
Vertical Market Application, General Purpose Productivity Tool, or the Heart of Computer Science?

by John Walker
Revision 1 — May 19, 1986

Over the brief history of Autodesk, we have observed the evolution of how CAD is perceived. We have always believed that we were selling a "word processor for drawings", suitable for anybody who draws as part of their work. The market as a whole and the analysts in particular, saw CAD as "a package for architects", or at most a tool applicable to a small set of highly specialised markets.

Time has proven us right. We could not have sold so many AutoCADs so rapidly, nor would we have the broad and flat distribution among market segments were CAD as specialised as the pundits believed. Moreover, the fact that have continually opened new, "nontraditional" markets for CAD without even trying vindicates our belief and confirms that in this case the users are way ahead of most of the sellers.

What we once knew and took action on is now becoming the conventional wisdom. Recently, in a more general context, Carl Machover wrote that the "computer graphics" industry is disappearing as it is assimilated into the mainstream of the computer industry. What we are seeing in CAD is part of this overall trend. Thus, the head start in positioning our product that this insight gave us is no longer a competitive advantage. We should look forward now to where

CAD will evolve next (keeping in mind that it might not evolve anywhere, and that our original perception was the end of the road).

In this paper, I will suggest that what we have seen so far is simply the first step of an even greater integration of computer aided design into the mainstream of computer science and the computer industry. I will point to trends and events which, I feel, confirm this, and I will suggest product and marketing directions which will position Autodesk to take advantage of this trend.

What is Computer Aided Design?

I will bypass writing 50 pages on the various definitions of CAD, the acronym. Here let's consider what we mean when we say "computer aided design" itself. I propose the following definition:

> Computer aided design is the modeling of physical systems on computers, allowing both interactive and automatic analysis of design variants, and the expression of designs in a form suitable for manufacturing.

I think that this definition encompasses all of the types of work that is subsumed under the CAD umbrella, in all the various areas of application.

This definition implies that simulation is a far more important part of CAD than design description. I believe that this is true. Also, computer graphics has nothing at all to do with CAD, except as the servant of design, simulation, or presentation.

What Should a CAD System Be?

To best fulfill the definition of CAD given above, a CAD system should be a computer system that allows modeling of physical systems. To date, modeling has been done almost entirely with hard-coded dedicated systems usable only for one form of design: there's not a lot in common between ANSYS and SPICE. But, after all, the physical universe is a unified place with common rules, and it's not at all clear that one should have to write tens of thousands of lines of FORTRAN just to get started on a general-purpose modeler.

CAD systems to date have developed into general-purpose tools that understand geometry. From MacDraw to Medusa there is a continuum of knowledge about geometry and operations on either 2D or 3D primitives. What knowledge of reality exists is usually welded on as an afterthought (the very word "attribute" indicates how reality takes a second seat to geometric description).

A typical CAD system offering has a geometry processor with attached database, providing a "common design database". Analysis and simulation sits on top of this core, embodied in a host of separate programs which intercommunicate, if at all, only by passing information through the database. If one wants to create a new analysis program, "well, we have a FORTRAN compiler and library that lets you read the database".

Need it be this way? Can we not imagine a geometry-based CAD system evolving into a system which describes physical objects, and knows about the various ways in which they interact (and can be taught about interactions as we define new forms of geometry today)? Such a system would encompass all of what a CAD system does today, and would provide a common user interface and model for working with reality represented in a database.

What Does Simulation Have To Do With It?

Alan Kay, delivering the keynote speech at the Second West Coast Computer Faire in 1978 said, "we decided to focus on simulation in Smalltalk, because that's the only really interesting thing to do with a computer". When I heard this, I was aghast: "Simulation", I thought, "why in the world would people want to use personal computers to model throughput in a machine shop, or to calculate the number of toilets[141] in a football stadium". Certainly any rational person wanted a personal computer to do real computer science on it: to write operating systems and compilers so that others could use them to write programs, and... well, I hadn't thought that out completely.

"Simulation" had come to mean (at least in the computer science lexicon), a specific kind of modeling of systems, usually done in an odd simulation language such as Simscript or Simula. What I only realised years later was that what Alan Kay was talking about something far more grandiose when he said "simulation": getting the whole wide world into that itty-bitty can: the computer. And yet, "simulation" in the limited computer science sense has already had a great and often little-appreciated impact on computer science as a whole. In his speech, Alan Kay exhorted people to look closely at Simula-67 for the direction of the future. Simula-67 included (in 1967!) classes, object orientation, multiple communicating processes, in fact close to a laundry list of what is currently considered the way to approach complex problems. So simulation in the small has already influenced the mainstream, and I believe that simulation writ large will have an impact many times greater.

---

141   But then, if there's a toilet, Autodesk *must* be involved.

What Do You Do To Get There?

It is time to start considering that we are in the business of bottling reality. If we accept the premises and conclusions of this paper, we should begin to undertake the representation of physical reality within our system, and provide the hooks which allow modeling and simulation to be added on to the system as easily as one adds geometric operations today.

One specific example of what I'm talking about is the concrete proposal to add dimensionality to variables in our package. But this is just a first step on a road that may be decades long. I don't have the solutions and I don't even know many of the problems, but I'm becoming convinced that this is what this business is really about.

The Heart of Computer Science

As computers become more powerful, and tools evolve that allow us to build larger and more complex software systems on them, the artificial barriers that keep us from modeling the real world will fall. Finding the ways to do this best, and to build the systems that will be used for this is, I feel, what computer science is really about. And the company that knows this first and does the right things about it has prospects that are very bright indeed.

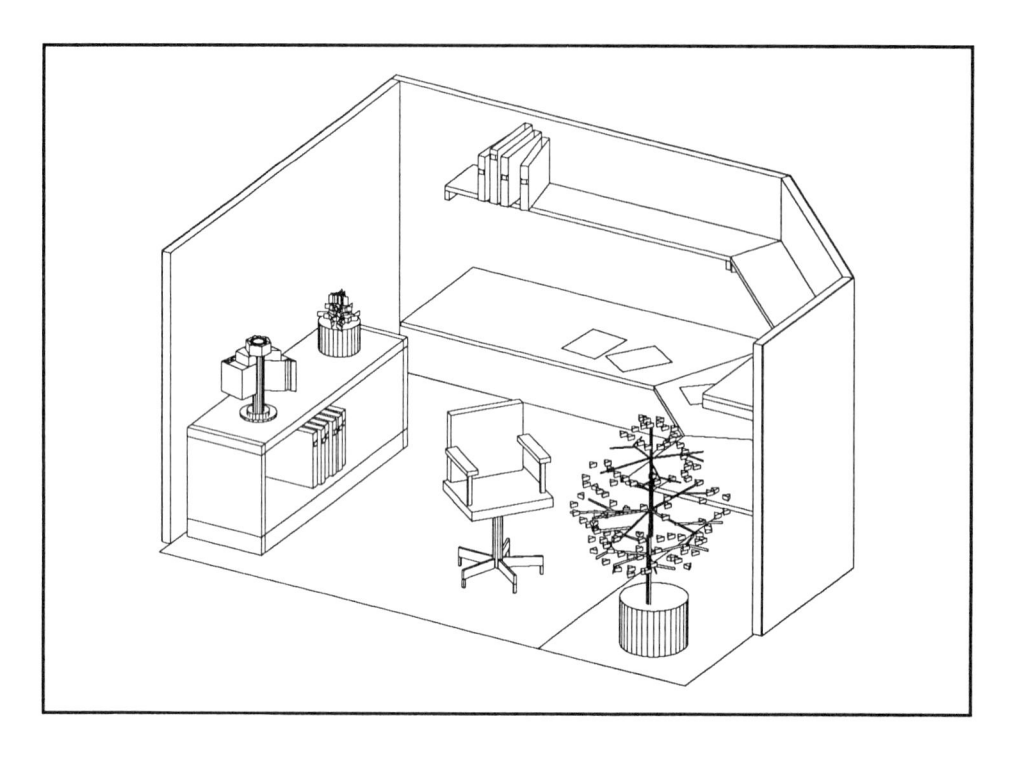

This drawing, created by Gary Wells, was the original AutoShade demo drawing. Literally hundreds of bugs were found by this drawing during the development of AutoShade.

The Computer Revolution

I believe that the perceptions expressed herein point the way to the next generation of hugely successful computer products. The fact that I have been totally unsuccessful in explaining these concepts in numerous forums only reinforces my belief that they will eventually be considered self-evident.

The Computer Revolution
"What You See Is What You Get", and the Service Economy

by John Walker
Revision 6 — May 20, 1986

Abstract

The failure of personal computers to penetrate the office, engineering, and home markets as rapidly as many observers expected is a mystery to many in the industry. This failure is argued to be the result of a dissonance between the evolution of computer software toward placing decisions directly on the user, and the general trend in society toward services, intermediation, and division of labour. Suggestions of types of software products, which are in harmony with the overall trends, are made.

Background

The Computer Revolution

"You will have robot 'slaves' by 1965."

Mechanix Illustrated, cover, 1955

Whatever happened to the computer revolution? If you asked almost anybody in the computer business in the 1960's and early 1970's to project the consequences of the price of computing power falling four orders of magnitude, they would almost universally have seen the introduction of computers into almost every aspect of life. Clearly, every home would have one or more computers, and computers would be used to communicate, write, read, draw, shop, bank, and perform numerous other tasks.

This was the "computer revolution": sales of computers in the hundreds of millions, with their diffusion throughout society making an impact on the same scale as that of the automobile, television, or the telephone. This forecast was so universally shared that all of the major players in the game bet on it and polished their strategies to end up with a chunk of the market. But in this revolution, something funny happened on the way to the barricades.

After an initial burst, sales of computers into the home market have slowed dramatically, to the extent that the companies that concentrate on home computers and software are considered pariahs. Penetration of computers into the office has been much slower than many projections, and the promises of networks and the "universal workstation" remain largely unfulfilled. The current dismal climate in the semiconductor and computer industries is a consequence of this. This despite the fact that the computer revolution has technically succeeded; now for a price affordable by virtually every family in the country, and by every business for every employee, one can buy a computer that can be used for communication, reading, writing, drawing, shopping, banking, and more. But they aren't selling.

What You See Is What You Get

"What You See Is What You Get" (abbreviated WYSIWYG, pronounced "wizzy-wig") has become the metaphor for most computer interaction today. It first became popular with screen-oriented text editing programs, became the accepted standard in word processing, and has been extended to graphics as exemplified by paint programs such as MacPaint and CAD programs such as AutoCAD. Today, this interface is being applied to integrating publication-quality text and graphics in products such as Interleaf and PageMaker, and is the universal approach to desktop publishing. Attempts to extend the WYSIWYG concept to encompass the user's entire interaction with a computer date from the Smalltalk system, and today are exemplified by icon based interfaces such as the Macintosh operating system and GEM. The generalisation of WYSIWYG to more abstract applications is sometimes referred to as a "Direct Manipulation Interface" (DMI).

The Service Economy

The evolution of an economy from one dominated by agriculture and extractive industries, through industrialisation, to one dominated by service industries is one of the most remarked upon events of our age. Our economy is moving from one that prospers by doing things to stuff to one in which we do stuff to each other.

Not only does everybody believe this is happening, it really is happening. For example, walk through any major city in the US and observe that there are four banks on every street corner. If this were not a service economy, there would be, say, four machine shops.

As numerous pundits have pointed out, this evolution is natural and is not a cause for concern. We will all become so rich selling innovative financial services, fast food, and overnight delivery services to each other that we will be able to buy all the computers from Japan, televisions from Korea, and steel from Bulgaria that we need. That makes sense, right?

The Evolution of Computer Interfaces

Let's look back into the distant past and see how peoples' concepts of how computers would be used have changed. Originally (I'm talking 1950's) it was assumed that a systems analyst would specify how the computer would be applied to a problem. This specification would be given to a programmer, who would lay out the control and data flow to implement the system. A coder would then translate the flowchart into computer code and debug the system, calling on the programmer and analyst as required. The coder's program, written on paper, would be encoded for the machine by a keypunch operator. After the program was placed into operation, it would be run by the computer operator, with data prepared by an operations department.

Well before 1960, the development of assemblers and compilers (and the realisation that the division was a bad idea in the first place), collapsed the programming and coding jobs into one. The distinction between programmer and systems analyst had become mostly one of job title, pay, and prestige rather than substance in many organisations by 1970. The adoption of timesharing in the 1960's accelerated the combination of many of the remaining jobs. Now, as any computer user could type on his own keyboard, the rationale for data entry departments began to disappear (while concurrently, development of optical character recognition and bar code equipment reduced the need for manual entry of bulk data). In the 1970's, one person frequently designed a program, typed it in, debugged it, ran it, entered data into it, and used the results.

The concurrent fall in the price of computer hardware contributed to this trend. The division of labour which developed when computers were used in large organisations was impossible and silly when a computer was purchased by a 5 man engineering department. This led to the "every man a computer user, every man a programmer" concept that lies at the root of the "computer literacy" movement.

The skills required to use a computer were still very high, and the areas in which computers were applied were very specialised and generally concentrated in technical areas where users were willing to master new skills to improve their productivity.

Word processing (and later the spreadsheet) changed all that. With the widespread adoption of the CRT, it was possible to build a user interface that immediately reflected the user's interaction with the computer. With this interface it became possible to build programs that could be mastered in far less time by users with no direct computer-related skills. The personal computer accelerated this process. Now a financial analyst could directly build and operate a spreadsheet model, ask "what if" questions, and obtain rapid responses. Now an individual could enter, correct, and format documents which would be printed with quality equal to that of the best office typewriters.

Attempts to Extend the Interface

The success of these two applications, which have accounted for the purchase of a large percentage of the desktop computers sold to date, led to attempts to make other applications as transparent to the user and thus as accessible to mass markets. Applications which paralleled word processing (such as CAD or raster-based drawing programs) were relatively easy to build and have enjoyed some success. Lotus attempted in 1-2-3 and Symphony to embed other functions within the metaphor of a spreadsheet, but one might read the market as saying that 1-2-3 was about as far as the sheet would spread.

The Macintosh user interface represents the most significant effort to date to create a set of diverse applications that share a common set of operating conventions. Certainly the effort has gone much farther toward that goal than any which preceded it, but the limited success of the product in the marketplace may indicate that either the common user interface does not extend deep enough into the products to be of real benefit to the user, or that the user interface is still too complex. (On the other hand, it may indicate that people don't want a 23cm screen, or that Apple Computer should be named "IBM").

Today, desktop publishing systems are placing far more control and power in the user's hands than before. Now the user can enter text, then control its typography, layout, insertion of illustrations, and every other parameter controlling the final output. We see document filing and retrieval systems which have interfaces which emulate a physical library. Engineering programs are being built which graphically simulate physical systems and allow dynamic interaction with computer-simulated objects. We begin to hear the phrase, "this job is 5% solving the problem and 95% user interface".

It is currently almost an axiom of the industry that "people won't buy computers in large quantities until we make them easier to use". This is often used to justify the conclusion, "we must invest far more work in user interfaces, and make our programs more interactive and responsive to the user". I would like to explore whether this really follows.

"Go Do" Considered Shameful

I would like to suggest that the present state of computer user interfaces is the outgrowth of the postwar "do it yourself" culture, which peaked around 1960, and is not consonant with the service economy which began to expand rapidly around that date.

Consider how a business letter used to be written. The author would scribble some notes on a piece of paper, or blither something into a dictating machine. A secretary would translate the intent into English and type a draft of it. The author would then review it, mark up desired changes (which might be as general as "can you soften up the second paragraph so it doesn't seem so much like an ultimatum?"), and receive a final draft, which was signed and returned to be mailed. No wonder, as IBM pointed out in the early 60's, such a letter cost about $4 to prepare.

Now let's peek into the "office of the future". The executive's 50cm screen is festooned with icons. Picking the one with the quill pen opens up a word processor. The document is entered, pulling down menus to select appropriate fonts for the heading, address, and body. After the text is entered, a few more menu picks right justify the text. Dragging an icon of a schoolmarm into the window performs spelling checking and correction, allowing the user to confirm unusual words. The user then drags a rubber stamp icon into the window and places a digitised signature at the bottom of the letter (remember, you saw it here first). Finally, popping up the "send" menu allows the executive to instruct the system to send the letter to the address in the heading (electronically if possible, otherwise by printing a copy on the laser printer in the mailroom, which will stuff it into a window envelope and mail it), and to a file a copy under a subtopic specified by entering it in a dialogue box.

As we astute observers of the computer scene know, this is just around the corner and "can be implemented today on existing systems as soon as the users are ready to buy it". And what an astounding breakthrough it will be. An executive, who previously only needed to know about how to run a multi-billion dollar multinational corporation, analyse market trends, develop financial strategies, thread around governmental constraints, etc., now gets to be a typist, proofreader, typographer, mail clerk, and filing clerk. That makes sense, right?

Those involved in computing have discovered that doing it themselves is a far more productive way of getting things done than telling others to do it. They then generalise this to all people and all tasks. This may be a major error.

As we have developed user interfaces, we have placed the user in far more direct control of the details of his job than before. As this has happened, we have devolved upon the user all of the detailed tasks formerly done by others, but have provided few tools to automate these tasks. In the 1960's, engineering curricula largely dropped mechanical drafting requirements in favour of "graphical communication" courses. The rationale for this was that engineers did not make final drawings on the board, but rather simply needed to be able to read drawings and communicate a design to a drafter who would actually make the working drawings.

Now we're in the position of telling people, "you don't need all of those drafters. With CAD, your engineers can make perfectly accurate final drawings as they design". Yeah, but what do they know about drafting? And what help does the computer give them? The **STRETCH** command?

I have always taken personal pride in the statement "I don't ask anybody else to do my shit work for me". I am proud that I do my own typing, formatting, printing, and mailing. And as I have often remarked, I consider that I am better at doing these things than many of those paid full time to do them. I think that this is an outgrowth of the general "do it yourself" philosophy which goes all the way back to "self reliance". Although I often make the argument based on efficiency (I can do it faster by myself and get it right the first time, than I can tell somebody how to do it, redo it, re-redo it, and so on), the feeling goes much deeper than mere efficiency, and I think it is shared by many other computer types. I think that this is because those in the computer business are largely drawn from the do it yourself tinkerer culture. I do not have statistics, but I'll bet that the incidence of home workshops is many times greater among computer people than the general populace. Computers have, I think, largely absorbed the attentions of the do it yourself culture. Notice that the decline of the home-tinkering magazines (*Mechanix Illustrated*, *Popular Science*, *Popular Mechanics*) which had been fairly stable in content since the 1930s occurred coincident with the personal computer explosion and the appearance of the dozens of PC-related magazines.

As a result, we build tools which place more and more direct control in the hands of the user, and allow him to exert more and more power over the things he does. We feel that telling somebody else to do something for us is somehow wrong.

This shared set of assumptions is carried over into the way we design our computer-based tools. We build power tools, not robot carpenters. We feel it is better to instruct the computer in the minutiae of the task we're doing than build a tool that will go off with some level of autonomy and get a job done. So our belief that people should not be subservient to our desires may lead us to build software that isn't subservient. But that's what computers are *for*!

I'd ask you to consider: in a society where virtually nobody fixes their own television sets any more, where the percentage of those repairing their own cars is plummeting, where people go out and pay for pre-popped popcorn, and where the value added by services accounts for a larger and larger percentage of the economy each year, shouldn't computers be servants who are told "go do that" rather than tools we must master in order to do ourselves what we previously asked others to do for us? Recalling a word many have forgotten, aren't we really in the automation industry, not the tool trade?

Son of Batch

Let's consider a very different kind of user interface. I will take the business letter as an example. Suppose you get a letter from an irate customer who didn't get his product on time. All you can do is apologise and explain how you'll try to do better in the future. You punch "answer that", and the letter goes away. The system reads it, selects a reply, and maybe asks you a couple of questions (queuing them, not interrupting your current task), and eventually puts a draft reply in your in basket. You mark it up, making some marginal notes, and maybe inserting a personalised paragraph in the middle and send it away again. It comes back, with your spelling and grammar corrected, beautifully formated in conformance with the corporate style sheet. You say "send it", and it's all taken care of in accordance with the standard procedures.

Or, today, you pound out a 20-page paper with hand written tables referenced by the text and mail it to *IEEE Transactions on Computers*. Your typescript may be full of erasures and arrows moving words around. A few months later you get back the galleys, perfectly formatted to fit in the journal, with all of the tables set up and placed in the proper locations in the text.

Before you say, "that's very nice, but we don't know how to do that", pause to consider: Isn't this what people really want? If you had a system that did this, that could go off and do the shitwork, wouldn't you prefer it to all the menus and WYSIWYG gewgaws in the world? Also, remember that the computer would not be perfect at its job. Neither are people: that's why they send you the galleys. But isn't it better to mark up the galleys than to have to typeset the whole works yourself?

Building systems that can go off and do useful things for people is going to be very, very difficult. But so is designing the highly interactive user interfaces we're all working on. Both dwarf the effort involved in writing an old-style program where you just solved the problem and left the user to fend for himself. If you're going to succeed, you not only have to solve the problem well, you have to solve the right problem. Maybe improving direct user interaction is solving the wrong problem.

Building Subservient Systems

Can we build systems that do what people want done, rather than do it yourself tools?

There are some indications we're getting there. Autodesk has a product in its stable which may be the prototype of the 1990's application. I'm talking about CAD/camera. You take a picture and say "go make that into a CAD database". It goes and gives it its best shot, and you get to look at the result and change what you don't like about it, and teach it how to do its job better. Notice that of all of our products, this is the one people take least seriously because nobody is really confident that a computer can do what it sets out to do. Yet of all our products, it is the one most assured of success if it actually does a good enough job. This dichotomy characterises subservient products... look for it.

There is a database system on the market called Q&A from Symantec which lets you enter queries such as:

> How many people in sales make more than $50,000 in salary and commissions?

then:

> Which of them live in Massachusetts?

This really works. I have a demo copy. Try it.

I am not sure that anybody will ever actually build an "expert system", but much of the work being done in rule-based systems is directly applicable to building the types of products I'm talking about here.

Although I have only recently pulled all of these threads together, I've been flogging products like the ones I'm pushing now for a long time (so I have a bias in their direction). NDOC is the second word processor I've built which attempts to do reasonable things with very little user direction. The first one obliterated its competition, even though it provided the user much less direct control over the result. In the world at large, the battle between T$_E$X and SCRIBE is being fought on the same ground.

When you encounter a subservient system, it tends to feel somewhat different from normal computer interaction. I can't exactly describe it, but try the "Clean up" operation on the Macintosh or the FORMAT command in Kern's editor and see if you don't understand what I'm saying.

Summary

The "computer revolution" has slowed unexpectedly. This is due to lack of user acceptance of the current products, not due to hardware factors or cost.

A large part of the current computer culture evolved from the do it yourself movement. This led to the development of computer products which require direct control and skill to operate. The computer industry is no longer involved in "automation".

The society as a whole has moved away from the self-reliant, do-it-yourself, ethic toward a service economy.

Until products which can perform useful tasks without constant user control are produced, the market for computers will be limited to the do it yourself sector: comparable to the market for circular saws.

Building such products is very difficult and one cannot be assured of success when undertaking such a project. However, it may be no more difficult to create such products than to define successful dynamic user interfaces.

Customers want to buy "robot slaves", not power tools.

The market for such products is immense.

The Teapot is one of the classics of computer graphics. The teapot was originally hand-digitised as Bèzier curves by Martin Newell, then a Ph.D. candidate at the University of Utah, in 1975. The control points for the Bèzier surface patches were based on a sketch of an actual teapot on his desk. The original teapot now resides in the Computer Museum in Boston.

Newell's teapot became famous through his work and that of Jim Blinn. The teapot has become one of the standard test cases for any rendering algorithm. It includes compound curves, both positively and negatively curved surfaces, and intersections, so it traps many common programming errors.

For the full history of the Teapot, please refer to IEEE Computer Graphics and Applications, Volume 7, Number 1, January 1987, Page 8, for Frank Crow's delightful article chronicling its history.

I typed in the control point data from that article and wrote a C program to generate an AutoCAD script that draws the teapot. The teapot was one of the first realistic objects modeled with the three dimensional polygons introduced in AutoCAD 2.6, and has served as an AutoCAD and AutoShade test case ever since.

AutoBits — Some Humor from Autodesk

Humour has always been a popular outlet for the stresses and strains of Autodesk people. Here's a collection of some of the best.

To: Technical Staff
From: K. R. Throop
Subject: Job Titles

Date: 1 March 1986

I'm growing increasingly concerned about the title escalation going on around here. It seems like every time we hire somebody we have to create a new job title to wedge them in the hierarchy without wounding somebody's ego.

This is hardly in the spirit of solidarity we shared when we marched in the Programmer's Strike For Parity twenty years ago.

Therefore, I suggest that we establish the following job titles for the technical staff, banishing "Software Engineer" to the darkness whence it came.

> Programmer
> Enhanced Programmer
> Super Programmer
> Ultra Programmer
> Virtual Programmer
> Senior Programmer
> Elder Programmer
> Doddering Programmer
> Intergalactic Exalted Cosmic Hyper Programmer

Titles shall be unrelated to pay, and shall be chosen by the employee.

Kelvin

Kelvin R. Throop
Virtual Programmer

Autodesk Founder Announces New Product, "Hurls Down Gauntlet To Other Software Vendors"

Sausalito, California, October 1, 1986.

John Walker, President and a founder of Autodesk, Inc., makers of the popular AutoCAD drafting software today announced that shipments of AutoSketch, the company's $79.95 drafting software were commencing.

"AutoSketch delivers, for only $79.95, far more capability for 2D drafting and design than the $1000 AutoCAD we were selling only four years ago. The software industry continues to lead all others in delivering value for the dollar, and we're proud to be both the value and performance leader in our market", Walker said in a press conference announcing the event.

Concurrent with the AutoSketch announcement, Walker revealed that he had undergone a battery of tests and been pronounced "not insane". Walker said that he was examined by a panel of prominent Marin County psychiatrists, psychologists, faith healers, astrologers, and vacuum cleaner repairmen who rated Walker's sanity on a scale of 1 to 5. Mass murderer Charles Manson was used as the standard for 1, and physicist Werner Heisenberg was used as the standard of somewhere between 4.9 and 5.

The panel rated Walker as 2.6 on this scale, which Walker claims definitively demonstrates his mental soundness. In explaining why he was disclosing this information, Walker said, "when you buy computer software, you have a right to know if it was written by a nutcase or not. Norbert Weenie, adjunct professor of cybernetic chiropractic at Ukiah Community College has demonstrated convincingly that software can drive you crazy. And software designed by a loonie can make you just as bad. Inspector Harry Callahan of the San Francisco Police Department confirms this, saying, 'ever since that Goddam WordStar, you walk into one of the typist dives on Montgomery Street and say Control K, and it's worth your life'."

Walker immediately challenged other CAD system designers to similarly prove their sanity. And if they don't, he added, "well, then it's up to you the customer to ask 'what do they have to hide?'".

Autodesk, Inc. develops and markets computer software for technical professionals. Products include AutoCAD, AutoSketch, CAD/camera, and AutoCAD AEC. Autodesk stock is publicly traded on the NASDAQ national market system under the symbol ACAD. John Walker is privately traded between the Securities and Exchange Commission, the Internal Revenue Service, and the Franchise Tax Board under the symbol 217-50-0239.

The following document is not really an AutoBit. It was a serious proposal which never came to fruition at the time, possibly because it was confused with an AutoBit. In March of 1988, the Autodesk Technology Forum was inaugurated, which essentially implemented this idea.

Autodesk Technical Seminars
Proposal by John Walker
Revision 3 — February 12, 1986

We all wish that more people in the company saw the big picture, took an interest in the operation of all facets of the company, and were able to help out wherever help was needed. Let's do something active in this regard rather than just moaning. I propose we establish weekly technical seminars, commencing at 17:30 each Thursday, in which somebody from Autodesk will hold forth for an hour to 90 minutes on some topic known in depth to the speaker. A list of suggested topics follows (in no particular order). I'm sure you can think of speakers who'd love to blither on them.

- Introductory LISP programming
- Implications of antitrust law on Autodesk
- Autodesk history
- Stock options — what they mean, how they work
- How to close a sale
- Digital electronics in one hour
- What it's like to be a computer dealer
- How bugs are fixed (and how to report them)
- Fundamentals of plane geometry
- What does an architect do?
- Lock picking
- What is CAD/camera good for?
- Project management with PERT
- What is the board of directors?
- BASIC programming
- How to use Knowledge Man
- Data networks
- Principles of quality control
- How Autodesk's products are manufactured
- What is a spreadsheet and why you should use one
- Copy editing
- International shipping: strange customs in faraway places
- RS-232: How to make it work
- Getting the most from Compu-Serve
- How national accounts select products

Technical analysis of stock charts
What is an expert system?
How accounting works
The Smalltalk paradigm — user interfaces
How to write a contract
Creating printed material — concept to press

I'm sure that this list will serve as a springboard for many additional ideas. If we decide to do this, I intend to circulate a list to everybody of these topics and allow people to volunteer for any topic they think of. Presumably we can fill up the calendar rapidly.

I wasn't sure I liked the tacky music we used at the opening of the audio tape we used to enclose with AutoCAD. The week we recorded it, I produced an alternative opening with this script and music you can probably imagine. We didn't use my version.

CAD — The Final Frontier

CAD, the final frontier.

These are the voyages of the starship Autodesk.

Its five year mission — to seek out pockets of profitability in the CAD industry — and empty them.

To develop strange new products, and patiently explain them to bewildered analysts.

To blindly go where no venture capitalist has gone before.

Marinchip Defeats IBM PC/AT In Benchmark

Mill Valley, California, Mayday 1986.

John Walker, President of Marinchip Systems Ltd., announced today that the Marinchip 9900-based PC/OT (Personal Computer/Obsolete Technology) resoundingly defeated the IBM PC/AT in an intense floating point benchmark, even though the PC/AT was equipped with the 80287 math coprocessor.

The benchmark was an optical ray tracing program involving primarily floating point computations, including evaluation of trigonometric functions. The Marinchip 9900 PC/OT executed the program in 69.32 seconds, while the IBM PC/AT took 93.79 seconds to execute the same program.

"Our PC/OT executed this real-world engineering program 26 percent faster than IBM's much vaunted PC/AT, even though our 9900 processor was operating at 2 megahertz, one third the speed of the PC/AT's 80286 CPU, and the fact that the PC/OT was emulating floating point in software instead of using a mathematics coprocessor. This benchmark vindicates our RISC (Rinkydink Instruction Set Computer) architecture, and clearly demonstrates the superiority of our proprietary QBASIC language for scientific applications.", said John Walker.

The IBM PC/AT benchmark was run in Lattice C version 2.14, using the "-P" memory model (large code, small data). The standard Lattice 2.14 library was used. The results calculated by the Marinchip PC/OT and the IBM PC/AT agreed to 15 decimal places.

Commenting on the results, California Governor George Dookmayjeun said, "It just goes to show you how a bunch of clean living Californians can beat the spit out of those drug-soaked greasy Florida scumbags. Look, I don't give a flying fork what you quote me as saying, but please spell my freaking name right!".[142]

---

142   This paragraph is made up. All the rest is the absolute truth. Honest!

This is for real. It was actually sent.

Mr. James Meadlock
President
Intergraph Corporation
One Madison Industrial Park
Huntsville, AL 35807-4201

9th July 1986

Dear Mr. Meadlock:

I was recently asked by one of our customers to comment on the attached memo from Mr. Ken Bado of your company. Since the memo contains a serious misstatement of the facts regarding our product, I felt I should bring it to your attention immediately.

AutoCAD maintains all of its coordinates internally in 64 bit floating point, adhering to the IEEE standard for double precision floating point (IEEE Std 754-1985). This delivers more than fourteen decimal places of accuracy. No physical constant is known to an accuracy of fourteen decimal places. That accuracy is more than adequate to position objects anywhere in the entire solar system (encompassing the orbit of Pluto) to within one centimetre.

Mr. Bado does not grasp the distinction between decimal places and bits. As I understand it, Intergraph is an integer-based system with 32 bits of accuracy. This provides for an accuracy of 4.2 billion units and a dynamic range from zero to 4.2 billion. AutoCAD's IEEE standard floating point provides a 52 bit mantissa, allowing an accuracy of 4.5 quadrillion units. This is more than a million times as accurate as Intergraph's system. In addition floating point gives us a dynamic range of plus or minus 10^{308}, which is over one billion times that of Intergraph, and obviates the need for the user to explicitly establish a scale factor.

Could somebody in your company explain this to Mr. Bado? Would you be so kind as to send me a copy of the memo to your sales force which corrects his misstatements?

Whether you choose to denigrate competitive products is your business. But if you do so choose, it helps to get the facts right.

By the way, what's an "iteraction"?

Sincerely,

John Walker

AUTODESK, INC.
John Walker, President

To: Kathleen Doney
From: AUTODESK SPINE POLICE, Kelvin Throop, Sergeant

Docket number: MDASMAN001.00

Date: 24 November 1986

The AutoSketch User Guide does not have its title on the spine.

The Autodesk Spine Police were established in 1983 by a directive from the Board Of Directors and empowered to take all steps necessary and proper to insure that every book Autodesk publishes has its title on the spine.

To date our record is crummy.

You can help.

Could we put "AutoSketch User Guide" on the spine in the next edition?

Thanks.

First VHSIC-Based Commercial Product Stuns Industry
*** For Immediate Release ***

Mill Valley, California: September 22, 1986.

In a move that astounded industry analysts, a previously unknown company in Marin County, California announced the first commercial product embodying technology developed by the Pentagon's Very High Speed Integrated Circuit (VHSIC) project.

Kelvin R. Throop, spokesman for Strategic Weapons Systems of Marin, Inc. announced VHSIC-CALC at an impromptu press conference held at the company's headquarters.

Throop described the product as a MIMD parallel processor composed of over one million Gallium Arsenide VLSI single chip processors. The processors form a 1024 x 1024 cellular array: each processor is connected to its four neighbors in a rectangular grid. All processors run off a common 500 Mhz clock. The processors are based on RISC architecture, and execute instructions from a 1K by 32 bit on-chip RAM. Most instructions execute in one cycle, resulting in a throughput of 500 million instructions per second per processor, or 500 trillion instructions per second peak system performance.

Each CPU in the array executes a control program which repeatedly evaluates a mathematical formula stored in the RAM. Values required by the formula may be stored locally or derived from other processors, and values calculated may in turn be routed through the array to other CPUs. Throop said that cellular arrays of this form have proved useful in many forecasting, analysis, and planning functions. The unprecedented throughput of VHSIC-CALC will make applications previously undreamed of possible, he claimed.

Defense and other government sources were quick to endorse VHSIC-CALC. General William Tecumseh Chaos of the Larkspur Nuclear Weapons Dump said, "in VHSIC-CALC we see the fruits of the billions we've pissed away on advanced technologies. Before, we often relied on guesswork to make our crucial decisions, but you know: a megaton here, a megaton there, and before long you're talking a really big hole. VHSIC-CALC will let us plan and forecast and anticipate the unknown with a clarity we haven't seen since Pearl Harbor". Reaction in Washington was enthusiastic: Quentin Terabuck, director of the Strategic Deficit Initiative said, "American technology is the key to America's security. Let's see those sneaky wiretapping commie slimebags recalculate their budget in 50 nanoseconds. And they talk about central planning!".

Industry reaction was muted. John Walker, president of Autodesk, Inc., another Marin County high-technology company, said "I applaud SWSOM's commitment to the mass market as illustrated by their choice of the Commodore 64 as the control processor for VHSIC-CALC. While I feel that the suggested retail price of 40 billion dollars will slow acceptance in the retail market, inevitable price reductions may lead to a growing presence in the VAR channel". When asked, "What's a VAR?", Walker expanded, "Beats me".

Eric Lyons wrote a number of papers intended to educate Autodesk folk in the intricacies of the three-dimensional world we were entering, both through the ongoing process of adding three-dimensional features to AutoCAD, and by our evaluation of ways to enter the solid modeling arena which finally led to the Cadetron acquisition. Eric ran some of these papers through TRAVESTY, the random language rearranger, and ended up with this.

Yet Wah 3D

Eric Lyons
9/21/86

In this chapter we'll learn about the combination of it, but it is fundamental to the way a solids modeling, anyway? Well, it's mostly a matter of representation in them, you'll like a fancy alloy automobile wheel. You end up with a CSG systems. CSG solids modelers work a little difference between a solid (with some user interface modelers). In fact, many B-rep system, you'll be able to simulate a hole in it with these problem — designing something called interference checking, and half of it, but it is fundamental engineering problems (some say it really start getting into another primitive and mash it together it lies outside, on the end. You modelers don't solve anything), but it is fundamental types of solids modeling systems in use today, primarily because they interface or off (outside) the same space, if you take a cylinder from a surface modelers. In fact, many B-rep modeling system works by taking little shapes. Each of this chapter we'll learn any of this chapter we'll learn about there are the point, but it does have a few shortcuts. Also, surface, or inside an object, you are created a solid. With a surface model.

In May of 1988, Autodesk overflowed the office space available at the Marina Plaza complex we had occupied since 1985. We had to split the company between that office and a building at 3 Harbour Drive, further north in Sausalito. Recalling the problems we faced when the company was divided between offices in Mill Valley and Sausalito, Dan Drake suggested that we obtain free bicycles for inter-office transit, just like the Provos of Amsterdam. We couldn't get white bicycles, but we did get a fleet of black and pink clunker Schwinns. Not long thereafter, Kelvin overheard a disparaging comment about the bikes we'd bought. So, he was moved to write the following.

To: Uneasy Riders
From: Kelvin R. Throop
Subject: High performance bicycles
Date: May 10th, 1988

Grouse, grouse, grouse.

Not one company in a thousand would brave liability and flout convention to provide free Provo bicycles to permit primate-powered peregrination among the far-flung buildings of Autodesk's Sausalito headquarters.

But, of course, this is Marin County — Marvelous Marin, where the possible is bounded more by lack of imagination than constraints of reality and resources. So Autodesk's bicycle fleet is regarded with a jaundiced eye by the truly trendy, who say "a dérailleur is de rigeur!".

Indeed… .

Because Autodesk believes so strongly in upholding the standards and image of Marin County, however mylar-thin and trivial, we have decided to solicit bids for high-performance bicycles to supplement the existing fleet. Turbo Digital Cyclery of Bolinas have agreed to screen entries and maintain the new bicycles after they are delivered.

The new bicycles will be equipped as follows:

Propulsion. Pedals adjustable for leg length from 0.5 to 1.5 metres. Kevlar belt and carbon-fibre cone microprocessor controlled continuously-variable transmission (CVT) delivering power to rear tire. Toe clips equipped with automatic impact-release mechanism.

Braking. Bendix carbon/carbon disc brakes on both front and rear wheels. Bosch computer controlled ABS antilock system with deceleration sensor balancing load between front and rear discs.

Guidance, Navigation, and Control. Martin-Marietta Lantirn Forward Looking InfraRed (FLIR) pod for night riding, presenting imagery in a helmet-mounted Head Up Display (HUD). Laser ring gyro inertial navigation system coupled to moving map display also presented in HUD, with optional superimposition with FLIR information. Backup coordinate fix system using LORAN, Navstar GPS, and Soviet GLONASS systems, with automatic recalibration of inertial navigation data. Terrain and pothole database complete from the Bay Model[143] northward to Feng Nian.[144] Also a speedometer and an idiot light that indicates something failed.

Countermeasures. Computer controlled, expert system driven, automatic countermeasures suite. Automatic countermeasure delivery system capable of delivering Milk-Bones if chased by a dog (automatically sized to dog's jaw radius), chaff if illuminated by radar, and Lotto tickets if pursued by bozos. In addition, low observable techniques reduce the radar cross-section to less than 20 cm2.

Survival, evasion, and escape. Zero-zero ejection seat, mortar-deployed quick-opening parachute, automatic inflating life vest with EPRIB transmitter and strobe light triggered by ejection. Watertight survival kit includes can opener, good-luck quartz crystal, PFIX 2.0, Oreo Big Stuff cookie, supply of requisition forms, and Torx screwdriver. In case suicide is required, a Sony Walkman and New Age music cassette are provided.

Fuel. Four 2 litre tanks are mounted below the centre of gravity. These supply, on demand, Jolt, Gatorade, Coiled Springs Mineral Water, and Diet Toxic Waste. An automatic crossfeed system maintains balance as well as delivering any desired mixture to the rider. The tanks can be jettisoned to improve acceleration in an emergency.

Weaponry. Few combat engagements are anticipated for these bicycles while fulfilling their inter-office mission. For those cases where there is no alternative, four Marinchip BGM-25L bozo-seeking missiles are mounted. These missiles

---

143 The Army Corps of Engineers hydrological model of San Francisco Bay and the rivers feeding it, located just south of the Autodesk Marina Plaza office.
144 The Chinese restaurant behind Autodesk's first office in Sausalito. Much of Autodesk's strategy was plotted around a table at Feng Nian.

home on the nearest erratically-steered, slowly-moving vehicle, then deploy a balloon in the shape of a Sausalito police car and emit the sound of a siren along with a speech-synthesised "Pull over, asshole", permitting the cyclist to pass safely.

Command and control. On-board cellular telephone, FAX machine, Quotron terminal, UPI newswire, and UUCP mail and news feed. The DIAL[145] system will be automatically alerted when the rider departs, so it can interrupt every trip with a "you have 35 messages" call, whether messages are waiting or not.

Configuration and performance. Curb weight (less rider) not to exceed 8,000 kg. Acceleration from 0 to 40 km/hour not to exceed 20 minutes with average rider. Training time to solo not to exceed 500 hours.

This is, after all, Autodesk. Why not the best?

---

145 Autodesk's infuriating voice mail system.

John Walker's Transition to Programming

In August of 1986 I began the transition to full-time programming. This was the memo that announced that I'd be concentrating primarily on software development for three days a week. This was the first step in my plan to get out the job of president and work, instead, on things I was good at.

Flat-out Programming

To: Everybody
From: John Walker
Date: 26 August 1986

Subject: Flat-out programming

This company has committed itself to the release of a 3D version of AutoCAD by the end of the year, to shipping AutoSketch in the month of August (our failure to meet this promise is now a foregone conclusion), to shipping the MicroVAX by the end of next January, not to mention numerous other clamant technical projects such as AutoShade, the mechanical template, Apple machine support, a better user interface for AutoCAD, networking, and performance improvement.

Making these commitments was not grasping for the sky; they are central to the continued survival and growth of our company, for only by building a diversified product and machine base can we insulate ourselves from competitive onslaughts and the vicissitudes of the market in general.

We will fail to achieve our goals if we squander the limited resources we have on non-vital tasks. Consequently, I have decided to focus my time and energy far more on software development than I have done since February. To this end, and starting tomorrow, I will be working from home on Tuesdays, Wednesdays, and Thursdays. I will continue this until we ship a 3D AutoCAD to the first paying customer, and until the backlog of critical technical projects is cleared.

Any items which would have been brought to my attention during this time should be referred to Dan Drake, who has complete authority to act when I am out of the office.

This is not a mandate or invitation to stack up Mondays and Fridays with meetings with outsiders who "have to talk to the president" or can "only deal with the

Growth Means Change

CEO". I cannot recall a single significant statement uttered by one of these blithering pithecanthropoid bimbos which I needed to hear. If they can't tell it to somebody in the company who can really help them, it will not be heard. I will deal with such requests in my normal courteous manner.

"What does this mean for the direction of the company?" Oh come on, now! During the times of this company's most rapid growth I was primarily spending my time contributing to the technical excellence of the products on which our success is founded. If we fail to be the technological and performance leader, we will fail in the market. It is time to take every step to prevent that.

Hardware Lock Debater's Guide

Rhetoric is a much maligned and neglected skill in this inarticulate age. The introduction of the hardware lock in AutoCAD version 2.5 afforded a superb opportunity for Autodesk folk to hone their debating skills; a great deal of energy and large chunks of 1986 disappeared into The Great Hardware Lock Debate. Intense technical, ethical, and philosophical arguments swirled within the company, our dealer network, our customers, and the software industry itself. Emotions ran high, as most participants held opinions at extreme ends of the spectrum. At the height of the debate, Product Support drafted this position paper, explaining our reasoning. We decided to discontinue the lock on domestic products anyway, in recognition of the deep cultural chasm between customers in North America and the rest of the world. In retrospect, it was a sound business decision, as we defused most of the antagonism directed against us, with no apparent loss in revenue.

In Defense of the Hardware Lock

September 23, 1986

By Victor Zlobotsky, Rear Admiral USN (Ret.), visionary inventor of the superheterodyne crystal and general-purpose energy transponder, technological precursors to such labor-saving devices as the Norden bombsight and the programmable microwave oven.[146]

The Law is on our side: The courts have held, correctly in our view, that software is both copyrightable and patentable; that "works in code are quite privileged from an intellectual property perspective." Running unpaid-for copies of AutoCAD in violation of the Software License Agreement, is in fact, theft, even though copying disk files is temptingly trivial. The hardware lock is the simplest way for us to protect our legal rights in safeguarding our property from unauthorized use.

---

[146] Admiral Zlobotsky is, for what it's worth, a spitting image of Lew Goldklang, who wrote the introduction to this chapter.

Protection of License Agreement: Autodesk is committed to maintaining the integrity of our Software License Agreement. The hardware lock is the most painless, least obtrusive means of assuring compliance with the Agreement; it supplants such awkward artifacts as special master diskettes and hard disk installation counters.

It is not copy protection: It is Software License Agreement protection. The hardware lock allows unlimited copying of AutoCAD software files for backup/archival purposes. Users can make backup copies, load AutoCAD onto hard disks, run from network file servers, and have copies of the program installed on multiple machines. Only a device like the hardware lock allows such flexibility and freedom of file duplication while enforcing the License Agreement.

Fair compensation: By protecting the License Agreement, we protect our profit margins, which helps us grow quickly enough to meet the explosive demand for AutoCAD and related products. The features incorporated into Rev. 2.5 and products still on the (electronic) drawing board, all demanded by a wildly enthusiastic user community, are made possible by our ability to grow and add talented individuals to our enterprise. This also allows us to increase the staff required to provide product support to a rapidly growing base of over 60,000 installed users.

Protects users' investments: The lock protects legitimate users from the unfair competitive advantage exacted by dishonest users who would like to run unauthorized copies, yet still draw on Autodesk's resources, like phone support. With the lock, licensed users who pay for AutoCAD receive the support they are entitled to. Software pirates also receive what they pay for: zero. The hardware lock promotes a "level playing field," assuring that licensed users are not subsidizing bootleggers.

Realistic pricing: By stopping the proliferation of unauthorized copies, the lock allows us to price AutoCAD fairly. Widespread software piracy otherwise tends to cause price inflation to recoup revenue lost to illegal freebies.

Wide user acceptance: The lock has enjoyed wide acceptance among our customers, the overwhelming majority of whom are scrupulously honest and appreciate the importance of protecting their License Agreement in this way. Since its introduction with the release of AutoCAD 2.5, which started shipping on July 8, less than 15% of all calls into Product Support have been complaints against the lock.

High reliability/low failure rate: Out of 13,400 locks shipped, only 38 have been returned as dysfunctional, a failure rate of only 0.28%.

Still a bargain: Autodesk has pioneered in bringing CAD technology to a wide audience. We have exploited the recent dramatic advances in micro-based computing power and graphics technology, slashing the cost of a richly functional CAD system by a full order of magnitude. A fully-configured AutoCAD system, providing over 90% of the functions that as recently as a few years ago were available only on a mainframe at a cost exceeding $100,000, is now available for less than $10,000. AutoCAD remains the most sophisticated, popular CAD software on the market at any price. Insisting that customers pay for legitimate copies is a modest, reasonable business decision.

Rebuttals To Frequent Complaints

Site Licensing: Autodesk should drop the offensive lock and offer site licensing instead.

Answer: We have chosen a policy of quantity discounts for multiple purchases, rather than offering site licensing. Substantial price discounts are available to users with multiple workstations. It is curious that interest in site licensing has jumped remarkably since the introduction of the hardware lock, implying a considerable number of users running the package in violation of the Software License Agreement.

User-vicious: The lock is a user-hostile device that is a royal pain to install.

Answer: *Au contraire!* The lock is easy to install; certainly no more difficult than hooking up any other peripheral device.

Interferes with other programs or plotter: Since the lock takes up my **COM1** port and interferes with some of my peripheral devices, (they cannot be attached to the lock on the **COM** port directly), Autodesk is forcing me to buy another board just to have a second serial port. This is an unanticipated additional expense, and a major recabling headache.

Answer: The lock actively drives certain pins in the **COM** port; it is not a purely passive monitoring device. It is transparent to most other application programs, such as word smashers and spreadsheets, but it is not transparent to a limited class of devices, such as streaming mode digitizers and parasitic (power sucking) mice. There is no simple work-around for this.

No COM1 port: I can't run (or upgrade to) Rev. 2.5, since my machine does not have a **COM1** port at all.

Answer: This is a degenerate case of the previous interference complaint. The number of users affected is statistically very small.

Backsliding/unraveling: My system worked fine with the previous revision of AutoCAD, but the hardware lock refuses to work with my existing cabling, causing unwarranted replacement expense.

Answer: The hardware lock is somewhat more exacting in requiring that all connecting cables be up to the standards specified in the Installation Guide. Users who jury-rigged quick cables on the cheap, like the old 3-wire plotter trick, will have to bring their cabling up to reasonable electrical standards. In these cases, the hardware lock is helping users by eliminating faulty cables that may pose electrical and fire hazards.[147]

Lock is a "weak link" in system: It's an intolerable nuisance to have my entire business/office/drafting system depend on a fragile piece of plastic that is easily lost or stolen.

Answer: The lock is an integral part of the system. The same proper caution and security you use to protect your computer should be extended to include the lock. You can't drive your car without your car keys, either, yet we all live with them and exercise sufficient care for their protection. Authorized resellers may request a spare lock for their inventory. There is also a reasonable procedure to replace locks quickly that are found to be defective in the field.

Over a year's experience in Europe has shown that a system is far more likely to be brought to a stop by a bad keyboard or hard disk than by a lock failure. Note also that a lock failure, if it does occur, does not cause loss of work-in-progress.

Susceptible to theft: The lock is an external appendage that is too easily stolen by mischievous hooligans.

Answer: We are considering offering an internal lock that would tuck inside the machine's "skin" for certain popular computers. Since we support so many different machines (over 70 at last count), the wide variety of individual computer design and packaging make the production of multiple, physically different internal lock designs prohibitively expensive.

9-to-25 pin adapter: Autodesk should ship 9-to-25 pin adapters to those users who are now forced to "roll their own" as a result of the hardware lock.

---

147 You may think this extreme. In twenty-one years in the computer business I have witnessed four computer fires and two close calls.

Answer (under investigation): We are negotiating with several suppliers who can provide high-quality connectors at a reasonable price. We are investigating the possibility of including these adapters on certain versions of AutoCAD (like the IBM AT).[148]

Low marginal production costs: Autodesk is ripping me off by charging outrageous sums for installing additional AutoCAD workstations in my shop, when their marginal production costs are so low. Each AutoCAD unit can't possibly cost more than 59 cents for the floppy disks, plus a few pennies more for the packaging.

Answer: Our marginal production costs are actually quite high, although it is less obvious from the physical appearance of the final product. Hardware manufacturers, by contrast, crank out tangible, heavy units where the cost of the raw materials and metal-bending is far more visible. Our costs are labor-intensive. We have to pay all the salaries for software development, marketing, sales, product support and training. We pour more than 20 man-years per year into the development and refinement of AutoCAD, continually adding new features requested by our customers.

Swimming upstream: Autodesk is foolishly bucking the clear industry trend by protecting its product at a time when most other vendors are abandoning protection schemes of every stripe.

Answer: Untrue by virtue of false comparison. Most competitive software costing more than $2,000 is protected, including products from CalComp,[149] Computervision,[150] and McDonnell-Douglas,[151] all of which use a hardware protection device like ours. Some publishers of mass market software are dropping copy protection because of concerns about user inconvenience with limited numbers of master disks, hard disk install and de-install, and hard disk backup — problems that don't arise with a hardware device.

Invasion of privacy: The hardware lock is fundamentally un-American; it violates my right to privacy under the first, fifth, eighth and eighteenth amendments to the Constitution, and my lawyer will be serving you with a subpoena next Tuesday.

---

148 Oh, indeed we were. We had zillions of 9-to-25 adaptor cable sets made up, for free distribution. They arrived just about the time we decided to discontinue the hardware lock.
149 Discontinued
150 Acquired by Prime
151 Discontinued.

Answer: The lock is no more an invasion of privacy than any other security device. It's there for your long-term protection, including the safeguard against one of your own employees violating the Software License Agreement unbeknownst to you. In corporate environments and small, multi-person offices, the lock actually eliminates the need for employers to play the unpleasant role of software police.

Philosophical self-righteousness: "There should be no secrets between any two sentient beings in the universe", and this logically extends, by induction, to the moral repugnance of copy-protecting any software.

Answer: Timothy Leary expounded this belief once, and now he is a software publisher himself, carefully watching his own margins. (Yes, but is Mind Explorer copy protected?)

Hard-core intransigence: I don't buy any of these arguments, and I'm so incensed at the hardware lock that I will purchase all future CAD software from a competing publisher, just for spite.

Answer: If you are that adamant about the lock, try using AutoSketch. It runs without the lock, is inexpensive, yet gives you over 75% of AutoCAD's functionality.

Focus on the Future

Information Letter 13 was distributed concurrent with the announcement that I was relinquishing the presidency of Autodesk and turning the office over to Al Green. This letter tried to convey the incremental nature of the transition and to focus people on the challenges that lay ahead.

Autodesk, Inc.
Information Letter # 13

by John Walker
Revision 7 — November 5, 1986

"… we have tried the utmost of our friends, Our legions are brim-full, our cause is ripe: The enemy increaseth every day; We, at the height, are ready to decline. There is a tide in the affairs of men Which taken at the flood leads on to fortune; Omitted, all the voyage of their life Is bound in shallows and miseries. On such a full sea we are now afloat, And we must take the current when it serves, Or lose our ventures."

Shakespeare, *Julius Caesar*, Act IV, Scene 3

What a long, strange trip it's been.

It occurs to me that more than half of the people who work for Autodesk have never had the experience of having one of the these rambling Information Letters plop into their mailbox. For those of you reading your first Information Letter, I'll just say that these Letters were the primary means of communication in the early days when we were trying to get the company together. For the first year, we actually only all got together about once a month, so the Letters served to pass information around economically and force us to put on paper, in specific form, what might be only a mumble in a meeting or on the phone.

It's been a long time since the last Information Letter, and since our recent management reorganisation might leave some people wondering just what is going on around here, I thought I'd put electrons to silicon and bring everybody up to date. Please don't attach any significance to the number Thirteen; that's just the next one in the series.

Ground rules

I've always tried to be open, up-front, and straightforward in these Information Letters. I'll continue that herein. I am not aware of any euphemisms, dissembling, or "cover stories" in any of the material in this Letter. Since some feel moved to weave intricate stories of intrigue around any change that occurs, such protestations may be wasted, but if you've come to believe what I say, believe me when I tell you that this is the straight stuff. The only punches I pull are to honour nondisclosure agreements with manufacturers regarding projects underway, and new product strategy information I don't want to make publicly available.

The management switch

Back when we were thinking about getting venture capital, I experienced the joy of having strangers walk into a room with me, talk for about a half hour, and then be told by them that I wasn't a "strong CEO" and lacked a "track record" because I hadn't "done it before". It may be one thing to run a small struggling operation but, they said, entirely another when your sales went to $1 million a month and you had a "real company here".

I responded that I felt I was entirely competent to run the company up to the ten million dollar a year level, and that after that I thought I was smart enough to know when I began to get out of my depth. I assured them that my ego wouldn't blind me to what was best for the company and I would gladly hand over the company to anybody who could do it better.

In February of 1986 I began to feel that the time might be coming when I should re-examine continuing as president of the company. At the time, I was concerned about whether I had the skills to build the kind of organisation we would need to reach fifty million, then one hundred million, and more in sales. I thought about this long and hard, had numerous conversations with various people in the company, and concluded at the time that I might as well keep on slogging away at it.

Now's where I'm supposed to say that the light shone upon me, and in October I woke up saying, *"now is the time"*. Well, it didn't happen exactly like that... Cause what it comes down to is I think I could continue to run the company pretty well for as long as I could stand it before blowing out physically or mentally, but that my being president is not in the best interests of the company. And here's why.

Look, for most of the history of the company, I was spending 8 to 12 hours a day on product development, including programming, talking with others about design issues, meeting with vendors and users, writing manual inserts and ad copy, and so on. I spent the remaining 4 to 8 hours being president. Now for all of that time I was programming I was *neglecting the job of president*. The president is supposed to be the company's interface to the outside world, representing the company to investors, analysts, giving speeches, and so on, and of course "running the company" on the inside: monitoring progress, watching financials, and planning the development of the organisation. We were very fortunate in having such a large group of founders with such diverse talents, and we were equally fortunate in being able to recruit equally talented and extremely dedicated people in the early days who looked at the work to be done, set to it, and got it done with little or no supervision. So the company required very little explicit "running", and consequently my concentration on the technical front did not lead to the catastrophe one would expect in the classic Silicon Valley company where only one or two founders have the dream and the rest are working for salary.

I did not come to this odd division of time entirely because I enjoy programming more than being president (though I would be less than candid to say that had nothing to do with it). I did it because I felt that it was in the best interests of the company; a criterion by which I hope I have evaluated every work-related decision I have made in my career. Let me continue with candour, even at the cost of humility. I believe that I am one of the most productive programmers presently living on Planet Earth. I think that in 19 years of programming, I have adequately demonstrated I can go from concept to product in less time than most others, even those considered highly productive, and in conjunction with a small team of others as competent and highly motivated as I, can take on and complete tasks normally measured in calendar years and tens of man years. This is not bragging; it's a statement of what I believe and since it plays a large part in my recent decision, I want to share it with you so you can understand my reasoning.

The very things I consider I do poorly are the things that largely make up the job of president. Worrying about building space, staffing plans, budget versus actuals, day-to-day project status, contract terms, and the like is vitally important — but those are things that I'm not very good at and frankly am not much interested in. They tell me I do a pretty good job at giving speeches, but the tension and effort puts me out of commission for about 4 days before and 1 day after each one — and I don't think that's a good use of what I have to contribute to the company. All of these things were, in the not too distant past, matters one could attend to in less than 10 hours a week, but as the company has grown, they've grown to that horror of horrors, a *full time job*. And I'm a poor candidate to fill it.

When I decided back in August to spend more time programming and less time "in the office", it was in part to see how well the company would run with Al Green and Dan Drake filling in for me. It worked superbly. Not only was I able to complete AutoSketch and undertake another project that will be revealed at

COMDEX, the overall operation of the company improved (as I expected). In addition, I managed to lose 10 kilograms and not go crazier than usual.

So, the test having succeeded, now's the time to make it official. Now, because doing it before COMDEX will let us explain it in person to our dealers, developers, and users at COMDEX. Now, because by doing it at the end of the fiscal quarter, we can communicate it in our quarterly report to the financial community. Now, because Al Green and Dan Drake have been doing the job for the last four months (and in a large part for the last year or more) and deserve the formal recognition for the job they've excelled at. Now, because the technical and competitive challenges that face us are unprecedented, and we can ill-afford to misapply my talents to administration and speechifying.

> "You have sat too long here for any good you have been doing. Depart, I say, and let us have done with you. In the name of God, go!"
>
> Oliver Cromwell

All right, all right ... I'll come to the point. We have talked for years now about how the rapid advances in computer technology will inevitably bring the power of the mainframe to every person on this globe who seriously wants it. We endured the derision of those who told us "you can't do CAD on a PC", and now we listen to them explain how they predicted it all along. Every major CAD vendor now competes with us in the PC market, and each now concedes that our core market, 2D drafting, is best served by a PC-based product. As the power of the PC grows, a new challenge faces Autodesk, and we'd better be as far in advance of this trend as we were in 1982 with AutoCAD. In putting AutoCAD on a PC, we were applying our skills as programmers in shoehorning a minicomputer program onto a machine one tenth the size. With the advent of the 68020 and 80386-based workstations this year, the distinction between PCs and mainframes has been erased. Please reread that last sentence two times. If you agree with me that it is true, it has monumental implications for the survival and future of this company.

> "There is no avoiding war; it can only be postponed to the advantage of others"
>
> Niccolo Machiavelli, *The Prince*

What it means is that we're moving from a contest of who can cram the most features onto a desktop to a question of who can provide the best tool, period. Most of the constraints of memory, processor speed, secondary storage, and graphics resolution that we assumed in the 1960's and 1970's would hound us until our retirement have been erased by Man's greatest triumph of mass production: photolithography on silicon. The arena now opening and which will probably occupy the next decade is: who can provide the tools which best aid a creative person in turning ideas into reality? I urge you to forget all of that MBA-bullshit about market segmentation, channels of distribution, end-users, value-added, strategic positioning, and the like. I suggest that presuming competent marketing, sales, and distribution, the company that best solves the problems that face designers will end up with the market. Forget PCs versus workstations versus mainframes — that's history. We're building tools, and the tools which work best will endure regardless of the materials of which they're made.

> "Business-minded decision-makers must learn to invest precious, high-value, near-year dollars to recoup discounted out-year operations and maintenance savings."
>
> George M. Hess, Colonel, USAF

Right. It comes down to *reality*. Imagine the concept. What we've been doing for the last four years is building a tool which embodies a language — drawings — which we use to represent reality. This is a language which goes back thousands of years (re-read the *Scientific American* article about the guide-lines used to build the Parthenon), which represents artifacts in a compact and unambiguous form. AutoCAD is one helluva drawing tool. That's step 1. From here on in it gets harder. When we move from AutoCAD as it exists today to a true 3D AutoCAD, we take the first step on the road to modeling — embodying a physical system in the computer. Once you've encoded a model, you can do many things with it — calculate physical properties, generate part programs to build it, ask "what if" design questions, and so on. I think that every practitioner in the modeling field agrees that the tools we have today are stone axes and bearskins compared to the tools which will evolve over the next ten years. The tools we struggle with today all date from the era of vastly expensive computers with limited memory and poor graphics, and they will be consigned to the sandbox of technology as the new generation of tools appear.

But these tools do not "evolve". They do not "appear". They are built by the mental exertions of hardworking men and women, competing in a marketplace that winnows the ill-conceived and inefficient and bestows incalculable rewards upon those who meet the challenge. Autodesk is today a central figure in this competition — what we've done so far has placed us there. The products we develop in the next five years will determine whether we become the force that liberates the minds of designers from the tyranny of calculation and delivers the power tools of modeling from the few to the inventive multitudes, or whether we gather dust in the archives as a footnote in the article on "Design — computers — 1980's".

Spock: *He is intelligent but not experienced. His pattern indicates two dimensional thinking.*

Kirk: *Sulu… translate Z minus ten thousand.*

Star Trek II, The Wrath of Khan

So now we undertake to put, piece by piece, the whole wide world into that little bitty can. We start with a 3D AutoCAD. We add a little thing I've been working on. We labour, patiently and indefatigably, to add the pieces until a designer suddenly discovers a new way of working — a way that's as much an improvement on the old as CAD was over the drawing board or a word processor over retyping pages. I believe in tinkering. I believe in the individual as the source of ideas and inspiration. I believe in providing that individual with tools to explore his or her ideas as powerful as those available to the Pentagon or the Politburo. I believe that the inevitable development of technology will eliminate the advantage of mere size and restore creativity and innovation to the respect due it and paid it through most of the history of this country. I believe that those who make those tools will earn rewards, financial and moral, which will make the wealth generated by Autodesk to date appear insignificant. I believe that Autodesk stands today as the clear leader in the quest to develop these tools.

> *"We shall see how the counsels of prudence and restraint may become the prime agents of mortal danger; how the middle course adopted from desires for safety and a quiet life may be found to lead direct to the bull's eye of disaster."*
>
> Winston Churchill, 1948

Those who know the scope of what I'm talking about may shrink from the magnitude of the job to be done. Creating a realistic picture of a forest at sunset requires more software development than has gone into AutoCAD to date, and more computer time than has been consumed by every AutoCAD user so far, worldwide. Modeling the forces on a tire rolling through a pothole exceeds the capabilities of any existing hardware and software. Increasingly, we will have to build systems of extraordinary complexity which work the first time. Five years ago, Autodesk was a vague idea circulating in my head classified as "new software company". Our collective efforts will determine, five years from now, whether our progress continues to astound those who assume that competence, commitment, and candour must always be bested by money, management, and marketing.

I am proud of what we've accomplished so far. I am proud of what we're doing. And I'm proud to continue to contribute to our company those things that I do best — full time.

350 *The management switch*   *Growth Means Change*

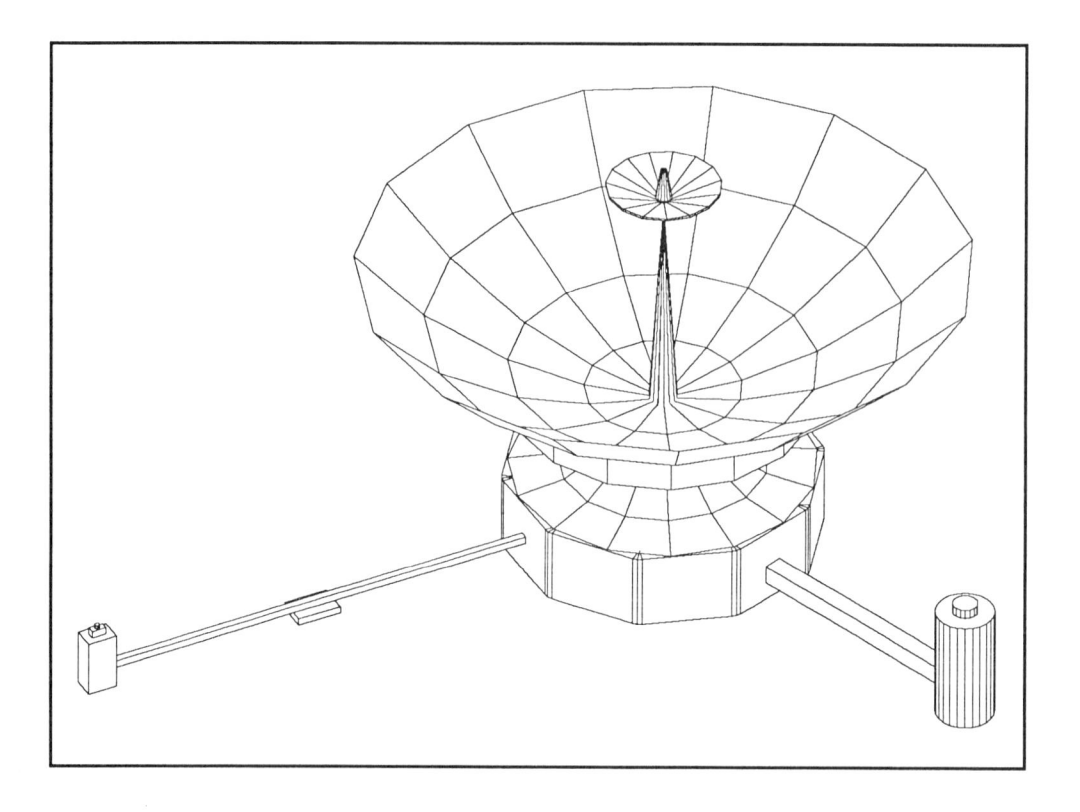

I made the Voyager drawing the night before leaving for COMDEX in 1986 where we were introducing AutoShade. It was based on a picture of Voyager 2 in Scientific American.

Cadetron and Solid Modeling

By mid-1986 there was little disagreement with the assertion that solid modeling would be a key component of the company's future product mix. But as we studied the requirements of the mechanical parts design market, which presently makes up the largest part of this market, it was also clear that even if AutoCAD could be extended into some kind of solid modeler, it would not really meet the needs of that market. Eric Lyons was the leader in researching this market, and in this paper he recommended that we investigate purchasing Cadetron which, in March of 1987, we did. As AutoSolid becomes more and more central to our strategy in the mechanical engineering market and begins to contribute a growing component of Autodesk's revenues, it will be fulfilling the promise that this paper evokes.

How Autodesk Can Take Over the CAD/CAM Industry

Eric Lyons
11/21/86

We stand at a crossroads. We are about to be dragged — kicking and screaming — into a world we know little about: the world of engineering modeling. This, in itself, poses little significant threat. After all, no one knew anything about drafting when this company started out. But we had an advantage — we were the first to do it [on a PC]. So there was some leeway, some time to make up for the features we lacked. We no longer have that luxury. Companies — big companies — that know and understand engineering modeling have seen that the PC isn't a toy; indeed, it and its successors are becoming the platforms on which their products are designed to run. Yikes.

We underestimated the importance of modeling over a year ago. We have been working on a generalized 3D version of AutoCAD for some time. In my "3D design paper" of May 27, I described 20 features that would bring us to a level equivalent to our competition at that time. We have implemented only a few; the hard ones are yet to be even started. And we have added things that never appeared on the list — primitive solid objects that are unrelated to each other. So we still have some work to do. But in the six months since I wrote that paper, some trends have emerged.

I have seen solids modeling, and it is the future. For years the skeptics have criticized solids as impractical, compute intensive, and inflexible. "You can't cut chips with solids," they'd say, or "sure they're fun, but what can you do with the model when you're done"? Well, they were wrong. Solids modeling is the next step in the evolution of CAD/CAM as surely as 3D followed 2D. Perhaps not for the better, but inevitable nonetheless. So we are faced with another problem: will we let solids get away from us as 3D did? Will we be sitting here in another year, wishing we had a solid modeler, and being run over by our competitors as we try desperately to catch up?

First of all, why is solids modeling such a big deal? See the attached article that describes some of its advantages over the more traditional surface modeling systems. Suffice it to say that its greatest advantage is that it is nearly impossible to create unmanufacturable objects with solids. Not completely impossible, but much less possible. In addition, analysis of solids is much easier and more accurate than with surfaces. So that's the big advantage. Solid modelers do require a fair amount of compute power and storage, however, so they aren't so great for AEC applications (a building described as a set of solids — including all of its components — would quickly be unmanageable on any of today's computers), but for discrete manufacturers they can be a boon. And there are a lot of discrete manufacturers out there.

The conclusion to be drawn here is that we need a solid modeler, sold by Autodesk, interfaced to AutoCAD, within a year. I rule out the possibility of making it part of AutoCAD within that time; 3D has taught us enough of that. Besides, solids is still frequently thought of as an application, and therefore the concept of a solids package outside of AutoCAD is fairly easy to sell.

So, what should a solids package do? Obviously, there is lots of room for definition — you can buy a $50 solids package for the Atari, or you can buy a $100,000 Medusa for the VAX. What's in between? First, consider that solids is a *design* application. Designers are interested in how objects behave. So beyond the ability to create an accurate geometric model using CSG or B-REP techniques, the thing is useless without being able to derive mass property information from the model. And since a large portion of engineering is spent determining the effects of loads, strains, and temperature variations on parts, the model should be efficiently interfaced to a FEM[152] package and mesh generator. Also, since 80% of all parts manufactured in the U.S. are still done from engineering drawings, there should be some way to detail the finished part with a drafting package (AutoCAD is a decent choice). Ideally, this detailing step should be augmented with numerically controlled machine tool program simulation and verification for automatic manufacturing. And, of course, the user should be able to visualize the model in a realistic form. So that's what a solids package should do. Some companies have based their products on all or part of this definition. Aries Technology has spent 2 years and $15 million to bring a system to market that does solids, material properties, and FEM interfacing. A whole industry is spawning that the analysts call MCAE — mechanical computer aided engineering. Within a year, we will be competing with these people for the middle range of CAD/CAM.

Okay, we need a solids system. How does that affect our current developments in 3D? Well, we should obviously finish the development of 3D AutoCAD. With the exception of the funny little solid primitives we have defined, what we are working on is really a 3D drafting system. It is a way to define a wireframe model, view it, and detail it from any orientation. This is a necessary function when we *do* have a solids package, as well as being required for AEC applications. Where we go from there (surfaces, properties, etc.) depends on some decisions we make with respect to a modeler.

How Do We Do It?

We have two alternatives:

1. We write a solids package ourselves.
2. We buy one from somebody.

If we choose option 1, I don't believe we can acquire the knowledge necessary to write one from scratch in the time we must, so we must get a head start from somewhere. One possibility is to buy a one-time PADL-2 license from the Production Automation Project — 80k lines of Fortran (FLEX, actually), designed to run on a VAX, $50,000 — and convert it into something usable. Another possibility is to license the geometry libraries available from Applied Geometry.

---

152 Finite Element Mesh

These libraries represent, perhaps, 15% of a working solids package. Just add code (à la Visual Engineering[153]).

A third possibility is a buyout of a company who has already done all this stuff, have them interface their product to AutoCAD, and sell it as our solids package. That company is Cadetron. Attached is some information on their company and their product. What follows is a proposal for the acquisition of their company and their product, and how it fits into our future: taking over this industry once again.

Product Positioning

Given that we acquire this product, how do we fit it into our existing product line, and what problems does it solve for us? First of all, the modeler would exist as a separate product, working as a pre-processor to AutoCAD (more accurately, AutoCAD would be a post-processor to it). It is intended for the mechanical engineering/manufacturing market. Parts can be designed, analyzed and realistically visualized using this package, then sent to AutoCAD (as either a fully 3D model for future 3D, or as a 2D "drawing" file) for detailing. The model can also be interfaced to FEA[154] programs by using the optional automatic mesh generator. Eventually (they currently have this stuff under development), NC[155] toolpath verification and simulation can be done on the model, and surface modeling (for things like car bodies and thin shells) can be done on the modeling side. AutoCAD is used only for detailing, in both 2D and 3D.

Also, AutoCAD 3D is used for virtually all AEC applications. Facilities management, piping, architecture, etc, are all done using the wire frame modeling in AutoCAD. We do not invest in adding surface modeling capabilities to AutoCAD, nor do we make our funny little solid primitives into a fully general solids system. AutoShade is still the AutoCAD rendering package, and is used by people who don't want to do mechanical solids applications. If you are an architect, you buy AutoCAD (and AutoCAD AEC stuff). If you are a discrete manufacturer (you make parts), you buy SolidWorks (or whatever we want to call

---

153 The original concept of AutoShade was an interface to a library of rendering software from a company called Visual Engineering. Visual Engineering was never able to make their code work acceptably under MS-DOS, and we abandoned that effort and wrote AutoShade from scratch in-house. This comment is a reference to the horrors we encountered in "just building on an off-the-shelf library".
154 Finite Element Analysis
155 Numerical Control

it[156]) and its add-ons, along with AutoCAD for detailing. Perhaps we could even use AutoCAD as a front end to the solids package: we can create our funny little solids, rotate them, scale them, position them, then pass them on to SolidWorks for Booleans and analysis.

Eventually, the two products converge into one. They share a common user interface and a common database.

With this combination — the industry standard drafting software, the world's most powerful solids modeling software — all sold by the world's lowest cost CAD distribution network, people like Aries don't stand a chance. They will be forced out of the market. Computervision will shake in their already soggy boots. Intergraph will die a slow, horrible death, buried in caskets made of Interpro 32C boxes. Autodesk will prevail as the dominant force in CAD/CAM worldwide.

How Does All This Really Work?

Obviously, there are some things to be worked out. How much do they cost, how does the interface work, what modifications do they need to do to their product, how do we resolve the different operating system problem, making them understand what *really* low cost software should be, etc. A total buyout seems like the best opportunity to control all the marketing (especially) and the development direction. But I think it's important that we don't screw up a good thing — they have a team of 6 programmers who have successfully converted some of the most sophisticated engineering code in existence (while considerably optimizing it) to a small machine. Us telling them what to do with solids would be like them telling us how **DIMZIN** should work. We need to look at their commitments, review their development projects, and define a set of projects that will result in our two products being integrated in a timely fashion. We need to determine the resources of each of our respective development staffs to make such events occur. I feel confident that we can do this without draining resources from our current (difficult) development agenda. It will take some coordination and supervision, but not all the resources of a Greg or Kern or John. And I want to lead it.

---

156   We continued to use Cadetron's original name for the product, "The Engineer Works", through the initial "Pioneer" marketing program. The product was renamed "AutoSolid" at the full production release, shipped in June of 1988.

Removing the Hardware Lock

With the introduction of AutoCAD release 2.1, all versions sold outside the United States and Canada were protected by the "hardware lock" or "WIDGET" (Walker's Inline Device Guaranteeing Elimination of Theft). This is a transparent RS-232 device which AutoCAD probes and requires to be present in order to run. When the introduction of this device went reasonably smoothly, Autodesk U.S. introduced it in the domestic market in release 2.5 in June of 1986. Never in our wildest imagination could we have anticipated the reaction. Suddenly we were exposed to a blast of vilification, moralism, and hypocrisy that (in my case, at least) forever changed the way I'll approach selling productivity tools to customers. All of the industry analysts and press people who had questioned us sharply about the threat of piracy in our market abandoned us to take the heat of trying to do something about it alone; not one word of support for us was written. Competitors jumped in to promote their products as better because they did not prevent theft, and products appeared on the market which claimed to defeat our lock, and were marketed "only to benefit the customer". The most notable of these products was itself copy protected.

On September 19, 1986 I recommended that we remove the hardware lock from the domestic product. After extensive discussion and preparation, we announced that the lock was being removed on November 25, 1986. The following document was distributed to all Autodesk employees on November 25; other than talking about the issue as a firm decision instead of as a recommendation, it is identical to the original memo I wrote to management recommending that we pull the lock.

We have continued to use the lock on international versions, and have encountered none of the problems we had in the U.S.

Why We're Removing the Hardware Lock

by John Walker
November 25, 1986

I think the time has come to admit that we made a misjudgement with respect to the hardware lock and plan an orderly retreat from the mess we have gotten ourselves into.

This paper will try avoid issues of morality and justice and focus on the business issues involved. I think we have all hashed over and debated the morality of this to exhaustion and in fact that's one of the reasons I make this recommendation. I will only reaffirm that I continue to believe that our software licensing policy of one user, one license is the only sound foundation on which a viable software industry can be founded; that the fundamental problem with the hardware lock is that it prevents theft of our intellectual property; and that any moral opprobrium we direct at those who steal the product of our labours is fully shared by the manufacturers of computers who profit by selling machines which provide no form of protection for the property which makes them useful.

I think that we underestimated the hypocrisy, moralism, and disdain for intellectual property that exists in the United States. It is not enough that we provide ever-increasing functionality at incremental update prices tiny by comparison with any other industry; any attempt to fund ongoing development through incremental sales is seen as a "large, rich company" oppressing its small, struggling customers, the overwhelming percentage of whom signed or implicitly assented to a license agreement which our hardware lock only acts to enforce. We must not only tolerate looting, we must not attempt to prevent it. Ayn Rand called it "the sanction of the victim".

But we must recognise that we are only a software company, not a major force for morality in the world. We must make the decisions which will make our company and our products prosper and try to act in the right within the constraints of the real world. And it is on that basis that I base my argument here. I think that there is nothing we can do in the short term or medium turn to reverse the moral climate which opposes us presently. Only a long term shift in perceptions, aided by a concerted, united effort by all software providers and supported by hardware manufacturers (a signal example of which would be IBM, Compaq, and Apple pledging that all new PCs made after 1987 would contain a serial number chip) can help. A climate where falling hardware prices is presumed to cause lower software prices is one in which much education remains to be done.

The issue of intellectual property protection only seems to respond to this type of coordinated fix. It was not a revulsion with cassettes, a fee per tape or tape deck, or the FBI raiding pirate pressing plants that the music industry finally settled on as the solution to its problems: it took a new, uncopyable medium, controlled by a strict licensing mechanism and a high capital start-up cost, and a pledge by the hardware manufacturers to forego revenue from making a medium permitting direct copies (the 44 Khz DAT agreement).[157]

In implementing the hardware lock with release 2.5, I think we not only misread the moral climate in the U.S., but we also made two public relations errors. First, we failed to get out front and promote the hardware lock as license enforcement without copy protection. In retrospect we should have hit the ground selling; explaining how the lock was central to the vitality of a local dealer and support channel, a part of our ongoing commitment to R&D and low cost updating of installed customers, and the alternative to the large-corporations-only site license mentality so many other software companies are adopting which ends up discriminating against the little guy who built this business.

Second, we failed to sell 2.5 as the massive update it was. It was always our intent to "spring" the hardware lock on a release so compelling that all users would be forced to upgrade. 2.5 is such a release, but we have not sold our customers on that fact. The demand for the DXF downgrade program is the most evident symptom of this fact. And of course our underpromotion of 2.5 was compounded by the focus on the hardware lock in most of the coverage of it.

I believe that it is too late to remedy either of these errors now. One, the discussion has become so polarised over the hardware lock, 2.5 is considered "the copy protected AutoCAD", and we would have to overcome a very high barrier of resentment just to be heard. Two, our key users already have 2.5, the reviews are in, and they are well into the phase of picking it apart, preparing wish and complaint lists, and looking to what Autodesk will do next. A major push to promote 2.5 as a new release would look odd and defensive at this date (I distinguish general promotion of AutoCAD as it stands, the central theme of all of our promotion which should continue and be expanded, from specific "new and improved" promotion aimed at the installed base and at industry decision makers).

I think the central issues here are bad faith and good will. The small business users on whom our success has been based are guilty of what can only be called stunning

---

157 Which, in late 1987, seems to be unraveling under the very same kind of pressure we encountered.

hypocrisy and bad faith when they install additional computers at five to fifteen thousand dollars each but claim that theft of additional AutoCADs is the margin that keeps them out of bankruptcy. However, this market is the heart and the soul of our business and we should decide, and soon, if we want to debate with it or sell to it. Autodesk has over the last four years, accumulated a large reservoir of good will, respect, and trust among the small user community. Our dealer channel is successful largely because of this market. To the small user far more than any other, AutoCAD is CAD, and Autodesk is seen as the company on his side, as opposed to an IBM, Lockheed, or McDonnell–Douglas. We seem to be spending this good will at an extraordinary rate, and purchasing very little with it.

And that's the final argument: we've been accused to forsaking our ideals and focusing on "the bottom line". All right, let's do some of that. We have just completed the best quarter in the company's history, but we have always had a large bulge in sales after a new release. I would be very hard pressed to argue that hardware-lock-induced additional sales have contributed much to this sales performance, versus the normal post-new-release bulge we've experienced. There is a convincing counter-argument to this: that due to the hardware lock, our installed base has purchased only their first low-cost 2.5 upgrade. When, over the next 6 months they actually experience how useful 2.5 is, they will find the money to legitimise their additional copies and we will reap those sales. Were I an AutoCAD user today, I might well decide to wait and see if Autodesk crumbled under the pressure and removed the lock rather than ponying up $2750 each for my bootleg copies.

Having said all of that, my recommendation is based on these simple facts: we have not experienced a large increase in sales based on shipping the hardware lock; we are expending at a rapid rate and with little obvious return the good will of those most satisfied with our products and most influential in recommending additional purchases; we have failed to find strong support for the hardware lock among the very dealer community which is most benefited by it; our precious management, technical, and product resources have been diverted into a largely defensive effort; we are imperiling our perception in the market sector we most control at the very time that our lack of obvious technological leadership and growing competition from larger vendors puts our future most in doubt in those corporate and government accounts least likely to be worried about the hardware lock.

We should remove the lock now, on an incremental 2.5 update, because if we wait until the shipment of 2.6, all the publicity attendant upon that release will be buried under the news of our removing the lock. We lost almost all of the publicity on 2.5 enhancements in the debate over the lock, and we simply cannot afford to have the news of 2.6 buried in news of our reversal. We should concurrently go on the offensive with a promotion campaign explaining what we have done and why. This will act to palliate the inevitable blast of "Autodesk repents major marketing blunder" publicity which will attend our announcement.

I expect that the two weeks after our removing the lock will be very difficult weeks. I expect those who said that they would re-embrace us as the market leader if we removed the lock will remain silent, while those moralistic mountebanks who have been reaping profits larger than ours by far as a percentage of sales by selling products purporting to "break the lock" will crow over their "victory". Further, I expect some of the very dealers who have been silent or petulant about the lock will now view its removal as an assault by Autodesk on the viability of their businesses. And we will be assailed by publicity and cheap shots about our "blunder", "indecision" and the "shakeups in Autodesk". One of the principles I've always followed in business is that there's nothing wrong with being wrong — if you never try something that entails risk you're doomed to stagnation and eventual failure. Catastrophe is engendered by *staying wrong* in the face of clear evidence that you're on the wrong course. I think that we're far better off putting this episode behind us now. I believe that we are doing the right thing in getting this over with and getting back to what we do best: developing, selling, and supporting products which revolutionise the way designers do their work.

Section Six

Building for the Future

Publisher's Notes
January 1987 — December 1987

During 1987 Autodesk continued to grow sales and revenue by more than 50% over the previous year. By the end of 1987 sales exceeded $75 million. The company completed a successful second public offering and had a market value of $500 million, only to encounter (along with every other public company) the "Crash of '87." The crash had no effect on the company's course.

Key Events

Here are the key events and the documents provided in Section Six.

- February 3, 1987. — The Portable Data Base. Describes how AutoCAD's Release 9 data base is portable between personal computers and 32 bit workstations.

March 1987. Three for one stock split.

March 1987. Autodesk completes its second Public Offering. The market value for the company is over $500 million.

March 1987. Autodesk acquires Cadetron.

- April 3, 1987. — Jeremiad. A little Autodesk philosophy about getting complacent in the high tech marketplace.

June 1987. AutoCAD installed base exceeds 100,000 units.

- June 19, 1987. — The Golden Age of Engineering. Defines the theme for the company's future course.

- June 29, 1987. — Cosmic Perspective. Trying to put Autodesk's results in perspective.

- July 8, 1987. — External Tanks. Autodesk invests in External Tanks Corporation.

- September 29, 1986. — Source Distribution. Kelvin Throop again explaining the problems of distributing large chunks of program code.

October 19, 1987. Stock market crash. Autodesk stock loses 60% of its value.

♦ October 27, 1987. — The Stock Market Crash Meeting. Notes for a company-wide meeting to evaluate the results and effects on Autodesk.

Key Product Events

The company shipped over 50,000 units in 1987, again almost doubling its installed base. Two new AutoCAD releases, 2.6 and Release 9, were shipped.

April 1987. AutoCAD Version 2.6 Release.

August 1987. AutoCAD AEC Mechanical Release.

September 1987. AutoCAD Release 9 released. (Called Release 9 because it was the 9th release and everyone expected full 3D, which came out with Release 10.)

September 1987. AutoShade released. This is a 3D-rendering program that creates shaded images from AutoCAD drawings.

Financial Summary

Sales increased 50% to $79 million; and revenues increased 75% to over $21 million. Autodesk established an Australian subsidiary. A second public offering was completed in March, placing a market value in excess of $500 million. Sixty per cent of this value was wiped out in the October crash. (The stock has since regained its value and the company had a market value close to $700 million at the end of 1988.)

Here are the quarterly figures for the year.

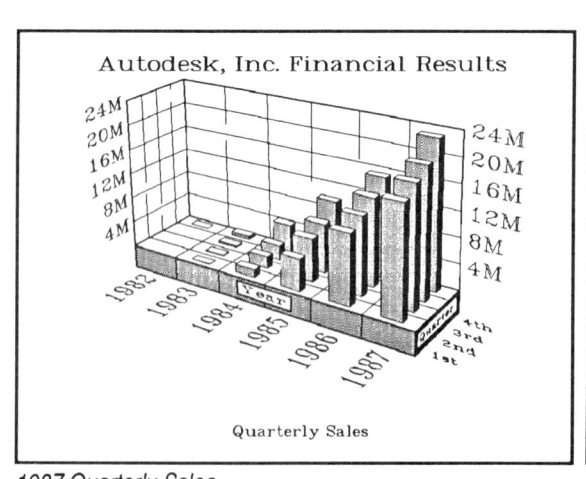

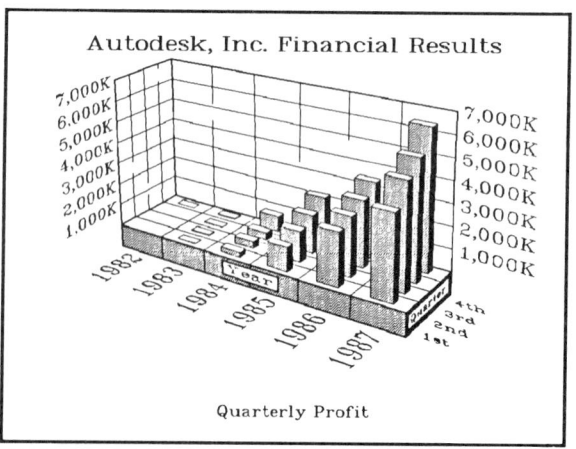

1987 Quarterly Sales

1987 Quarterly Revenues

The Portable Data Base

The implementation of the portable data base in AutoCAD Release 9 finally completed the unification of the product across all machine architectures. The development notes describing this project are an example of the developer documentation that accompanied code submissions in the period.

The Portable Data Base

AutoCAD databases are now portable between operating systems and machine architectures. This allows efficient use of networks containing both personal computers and 32 bit workstations.

by John Walker
February 3rd, 1987

It was a dark and stormy night. The trees swayed in the wind, and the rain beat upon and streamed in rivulets down the dark window pane illuminated only by the cold light of a Luxo lamp, the flickering of a Sun 3 monitor, and the feeble green glow of a programmer debugging too long.

When the doorbell rang, I almost welcomed the interruption from the task in which I was engaged: fourteen subroutines deep in **DBXTOOL**, on the trail of a stack smasher which not only obliterated AutoCAD, but wiped the information the debugger needed to find where the error occurred. I glanced at the clock and noticed that it was 3:30. Since it was dark outside, it must be 3:30 in the morning. Only a very few people show up at the door at 3:30 on a Sunday morning.

Let's see: the stereo isn't on and no recent revelations have called for celebratory reports from the carbide cannon or the .45, so it's probably not the neighbors or the cops. That narrows the field considerably. I fully expected to open the door to see Kelvin Throop, as always slightly distracted, somewhat overweight, his face looking like it had been slept in, but sparkling with anarchic and subversive ideas.

With the usual irritation mingled with expectation, I opened the door and discovered I was looking at the neck of my early-morning caller. I looked up, and saw a face I had not seen for almost twenty years. It was a face free of pain and fear and guilt. John Galt had come to call in the middle of the night.

"Galt", I said, "I haven't seen you since, when was it, 1967? That's right, December 1967 it was. We were walking down the railroad tracks in Cleveland; the snow was a foot deep on the ground, the sky was grey and the only warmth was the switchbox heaters at every set of points. Yes, it all comes back now. I remember you saying it was all over and you were going to drop out, and me saying things were just about to turn around. And I remember turning around and walking back to study for the physics exam and seeing you disappear into the snowy distance. Hey, come on in, have a Pepsi, tell me what you've been up to."

Galt walked in the door, put down his paper bag and, as always, strode to the refrigerator and opened the door. He poured a tall Pepsi and made a peanut butter, turkey, swiss cheese, and onion sandwich, polished both off, and then turned to me and spoke.

"As usual, you've got it all wrong. It wasn't December 1967, it was November — November 8. The first Saturn V launch was scheduled for the next morning, and you were bubbling over about how the final triumph of technology would turn around a disintegrating society. I said I'd had it with this decadent, exploitive culture, and I was no longer going to allow my mind to be enslaved by the looters. I tried to convince you to join me. But your time had not yet come. So I moved on to convince others, and to work on my speech."

"Hey, I remember that speech. How's it come since that draft I read back in '67."

"Pretty well. I'm up to 560 pages now, and there's no filler in there. I'm adding a refutation of the epistemology of Kant cast in terms of Maxwell's equations, and that will probably stretch it a tad."

"Don't you think that's a bit long?"

"Well, with the attention span of this society down to less than 30 seconds, some of the induction steps may get lost in the shuffle, but it's full of great sound bites and should play on the news for days."

"When 'ya gonna cut loose with it?"

"When the collapse of this decadent society due to its disdain for the products of the mind, and the consequent disappearance and exodus of the creators becomes self-evident."

"Hey, Galt, lighten up! When I last saw you the cities were in flames, the US was losing a hopeless war, the stock market had just crashed, the gold standard was being abandoned, three astronauts had died in a fire, the SST was facing cancellation, and the ABM was being negotiated away. Look at what you've walked out on! We have peace and prosperity, business is booming, and basic science and technology have flowered in directions unimaginable by the world in which we last spoke."

Galt walked into the computer room. He looked at the PC/AT linking AutoCAD. He looked at the Sun monitor, which was showing a full compilation of AutoCAD in one window, a completed execution of the regression test in another, and the debugger in a third. He walked over to my bookcase and pulled out my copy of the Dow Jones Averages chartbook from 1885 to the present. Moving in that eerie way he always did, in one motion he pulled the book from the shelf, opened it, and spread it in exactly the open space between the keyboards of the Sun and the IBM. For a full ten minutes Galt was silent as he turned the pages from 1968 through 1986. It appeared to me that the man had been out of circulation for a long time. I watched his face carefully to see if it registered surprise as he hit 1985 and 1986, but as ever those stony features remained unmoved. Galt closed the book, replaced it on the shelf, sat down on the chair in front of the AT, and turned to me. "Just wait," he said.

"So, enough about me", Galt continued, "what are you doing?"

"Well", I said, "where to begin? In '68, I..."

"Oh come off it," Galt interrupted, "I have my sources, after all. I mean what are you working on now?"

Sheepishly, I continued.

Background

When we ported AutoCAD to non-MS-DOS systems, we were faced with numerous compatibility issues. Although all systems use the ASCII code, compatibility stops about there. Various systems have adopted different conventions for end of line and end of file detection; they store multiple byte binary values in different orders in memory, require different physical alignment of values on byte boundaries, and even use different floating point formats.

These issues make it very difficult for systems to interchange binary files. The only reasonable approach is to define a portable format, hopefully close to the middle point between the systems, then require every system to convert that format to and from its own computational requirements.

Our existing (2.5 and 2.6) AutoCAD releases do not allow interchanging binary files among major machine types (current major machine types are MS-DOS,

Apollo, IBM RT PC, Sun, and Vax). To move data between systems, one must convert it to ASCII form, possibly translate the ASCII file due to end of line conventions, then load the file onto the other system and convert it back to binary. For drawing databases, this means one must **DXFOUT** on the sending system and **DXFIN** on the receiving system.

Given the difficulties in physically moving files between systems, the small market initially anticipated for non-MS-DOS AutoCADs, and the major work needed to make binary files portable, we chose not to address this problem previously. Sales to date of non-MS-DOS machines indicate that this decision was correct.

The advent of high speed networks and file sharing protocols such as Apollo's Domain, DEC's Decnet/Vaxmate, and Sun's NFS have begun to erode the justification for this decision. Many AutoCAD users, particularly in larger companies, have inquired about configurations involving a file server, one or more 32 bit workstations, and a number of MS-DOS machines, all on a common network. Such a configuration economically provides large central storage, high performance when needed, and very low cost individual workstations for routine work. The usefulness of such an installation is drastically reduced if every transfer of a drawing from a PC to a 32 bit workstation requires a **DXFOUT** and **DXFIN**, as these are lengthy operations which consume a large amount of disc space and network bandwidth. As we increase our sales efforts in large accounts, a competent solution to the issues raised by heterogeneous networks will be a major point of distinction which can distance us from the competition.

The first step toward a compatible database was taken when Bob Elman redesigned the entity database code in release 2.5. Galt broke in, "*The* Bob Elman". "Yes", I responded, and showed him the listing of **EREAD.C**. He shook his head and said, "That's Bob". Bob's code resolved all issues of byte ordering and alignment in the entity data portion of the database, and did it in a particularly efficient way that takes advantage of the properties of the host machine's architecture. Entities are written with no pad bytes and Intel byte ordering. Thus MS-DOS machines, the overwhelming segment of our market, pay no speed or space penalty. Bob's code did not address machines with non-IEEE floating point (the VAX is the only exemplar of this class).

Providing drawing database compatibility between machines, then, is primarily an issue of fixing the drawing header record (**MASTREC**), the symbol tables (**SMIO**), and the headers on the entities themselves, plus resolving the issue of differing floating point formats. In addition, the other binary files that AutoCAD uses, such as **DXB** files and compiled font and shape definitions should be made compatible. The work described herein defines canonical forms for these files, implements a general package for system-independent binary I/O, and uses it to make

AutoCAD drawing databases and the other aforementioned binary files interchangeable. The code has currently been installed and tested on MS-DOS and Sun systems, which may now share files in an NFS environment. The work needed to port it to the Apollo and RT PC should be minor. A VAX version will require certification of the code to interconvert VAX and IEEE floating point formats.

Galt interrupted, "So what you're saying is that before, if you hooked big ones and little ones together on a wire, it was a pain in the neck, and now you've fixed it so it isn't".

For a longwinded pedant, the man does have a talent for coming to the point.

The Binary I/O Package

To read and write portable binary files, include the file **BINIO.H** in your compilation. You must include **SYSTEM.H** before **BINIO.H**. **BINIO.H** declares numerous functions, which are used to read and write binary data items on various systems. Each of these functions is of the form:

b_{r|w}type(fp, pointer[, args...]);

where *type* is the mnemonic for the internal type being written, *fp* is the file pointer, *pointer* is the pointer to the datum being read or written (must be an lvalue), and *args* are optional arguments required by some types. For example, when writing a character array an argument supplies its length.

Thus, to write a real (double precision floating point) number **val** to a file descriptor named **ofile**, use:

`stat = b_wreal(ofile, &val);`

Each of these routines returns the same status **FREAD** or **FWRITE** would: 1 for single item reads and writes, and the number of items transferred for array types. Currently defined type codes are as follows:

char Characters. Signed convention is undefined. Canonical form in the file is a single 8 bit byte.

uchar Unsigned characters. Used for utility 8 bit data. Canonical form in the file is a single 8 bit byte.

short Signed 16 bit integers. Canonical form in the file is two's complement, least significant byte first, most significant byte last, two total bytes.

long Signed 32 bit integers. Canonical form in the file is 4 bytes, starting with the least significant byte and ending with the most significant byte. Two's complement.

real Double precision floating point numbers. 8 bytes in a file. Canonical form in the file is an 8 byte IEEE double precision number, stored with the least significant byte first and the most significant byte last.

string An array of **char** items. The third argument specifies the number of characters to be read or written. Canonical form in the file is one byte per item, written in ascending order as they would be addressed by a subscript.

If the binary I/O package is to do its job, you must be honest with it: only pass the functions pointers of exactly the type they are intended to process. If you use **b_wstring** to write a structure, you're going to generate files just as incompatible as if you used **fwrite**. And you must never, never use an **INT** as an argument to one of these routines.

When using the binary I/O package, you must explicitly read and write every datum: there is no way to read composite data types with one I/O. Bob Elman's code in **EREAD** solves this problem by packing data into a buffer, then writing it with one call. Since this handles the entity data, which is by far the largest volume of data that AutoCAD reads and writes, I felt that taking a simpler approach in the binary I/O package would have no measurable impact on performance. I felt that the complexity of the mechanism in **EREAD** was not required for handling the other files.

On a system such as MS-DOS, whose native internal data representation agrees with the canonical format of the database file, the various read and write functions are simply **#define**s to the equivalent calls on **FREAD** or **FWRITE**. The variable **TRANSFIO** in **SYSTEM.H** controls this. If it is not defined, all of the binary I/O routines generate in-line calls on **FREAD** and **FWRITE**. If **TRANSFIO** is defined, machine specific definitions in **BINIO.H** are used to define the I/O routines. Compatible types such as **char** may still generate direct I/O calls, but incompatible types should be defined as external **int**-returning functions.

If a machine uses a non-IEEE floating point format, the **b_rreal** and **b_wreal** functions must convert the IEEE format in the file to and from the machine's internal representation. In addition, because the entity data I/O code in **EREAD.C** does not use the Binary I/O package, you must tell it to perform the conversion. You do this by adding the statement:

#define REALTRAN

in the **SYSTEM.H** entry for the machine. This will generate code within **EREAD.C** which calls two new functions your binary I/O driver must supply. Whenever a real number is being written to a file, **EREAD** will call:

realenc(*bufptr, rvalue*);

where *bufptr* is a "**char ***" pointing to an 8 byte buffer in which the canonical IEEE value should be stored (remember, lsb first), and *rvalue* is the real number value to be stored, passed in the machine's internal type for **double**. When a number is being read, a call is made to:

rvalue = **realdec**(*bufptr*);

in which *bufptr* points to an 8 byte area containing the IEEE number. **Realdec** must return the corresponding internal value as a **double**.

Each machine architecture must define a binary I/O driver providing the non-defaulted I/O routines, and if real number conversion is required, **realenc** and **realdec**. Examine the driver for the Motorola 68000 family (**BIO68K.C**) for an example of such a driver.

Modifying AutoCAD

Utilising the binary I/O package within AutoCAD to implement portable databases involved modifications in several areas. The changes are large, numerous, widespread, and significant, despite their limited impact on what gets written into the file. Installing them and debugging database compatibility was not a difficult design task; it was simply a matter of hacking, slashing, slogging, and bashing until every place where a nonportable assumption was made was found, and then fixing them all. "That's what you were always best at," Galt interjected. I said that I hoped so, for I know of no single project I've done within AutoCAD which is so likely to destabilise the product as this one. The following paragraphs cover the highlights of each section.

The Drawing Database

Making drawing databases compatible consisted of several subprojects. The result of all of this is that an AutoCAD with the new code installed can read existing drawing databases written by the machine on which it is executing, old MS-DOS databases, and new portable databases. It writes new portable databases, which can be read by any AutoCAD with this code installed.

The ability to read both formats of databases is implemented via the flag **rstructs**. When a drawing database header is read by **MVALID**, if it is an old, nonportable database, **rstructs** is set to **TRUE** and the file pointer used to read the file is saved. Subsequent reads from that file will use the old code to read aggregate data. At the end of every database reading operation, such as **INSERT** or **PLOT**, **rstructs** is cleared.

The drawing header. The drawing header is managed by code in **MASTREC.C**. The header is defined, for I/O purposes, by a table called **MTAB**. This table previously contained pointers and lengths for all the items in the header, and each was written or read with an individual call on **FREAD** or **FWRITE**. Compatibility problems were created by the fact that the header contained several kinds of composite objects: symbol table descriptors, transformation matrices, the "header header", a view direction array, Julian dates, and calendar dates. I modified the table to contain an item type and implemented a switch to read and write each item with the correct calls on the Binary I/O package. Special code had to be added for each composite type to read and write it; just adding entries to the table for the components of the composite types falls afoul of the mechanism that allows addition of new fields to the header. I tried it; it doesn't work. The symbol table descriptors have a several unique problems: first, their definition contains a "**FILE ***" item. The length of this item varies depending on the system's pointer length, so the structure changes based on this length. On MS-DOS systems, data in the structure totals 37 bytes, and different compilers pad this structure differently. The file pointer field means nothing in a drawing database, but it is present in all existing databases and it varies in length. But if you think that it never uses a pointer read from a file, you haven't looked at the code in **WBLOCK.C** that saves and restores the header around its diddling with it. Look and see the horror I had to install to fix that one.

The symbol tables. The symbol tables, managed by **SMIO.C**, were an utter catastrophe from the standpoint of portability. The problems encountered in **MASTREC** with their headers was only a faint shadow of the beast lurking within **SMIO**. To refresh your memory, each symbol table has a descriptor which is usually in the drawing header (another symbol table is used for active font and shape files, but it is not saved with the drawing and does not enter this discussion). The descriptor for the symbol table contains its length, the number of items in the table, the file descriptor used to read and write it, and the address within the file where it starts. There is no type field in a symbol table. Symbol tables are read and written by the routines **GETSM** and **PUTSM**, which are passed the descriptor. Each symbol table entry consists of a structure containing several fields of various types.

Previously, **GETSM** and **PUTSM** did not care about the content of the symbol table record; they just read and wrote the structure as one monolithic block. That, of course, won't work if you want the tables to be portable: each field has to be handled separately with the Binary I/O package. So in order to do this, **GETSM** and **PUTSM** must know the type of table they are processing.

"So," said Galt, "add a type field to the table."

"Heh, heh, heh," I said, walking over to the Sun and bringing up all the references to the block symbol table descriptor in **CSCOPE**. There are few data structures within any program that are chopped, diced, sliced, shuffled, and maimed as much as an AutoCAD symbol table descriptor. Most (but not all) live within the drawing header. They can point to their own file or be part of a monolithic database. They contain that ghastly variable length file pointer which gets written in the drawing header. They get copied, created dynamically in allocated buffers, and in **WBLOCK**, saved to a file, modified to refer to another file, then read back in. And that "length" field I mentioned, **sm_eln**. Well, it may include a trailing pad byte on the disc depending on which compiler and options made your MS-DOS database. And it gets used both to seek into the file and to dynamically allocate symbol table descriptors except in the places where it uses `sizeof(struct whatever)` instead. One week into this project, I had the feeling that I had not stuck my head into the lion's mouth — I had climbed into the lion's stomach.

The most severe fundamental problem was that I had to both decouple the symbol table descriptor on disc from the one in memory, and also introduce separate lengths for the symbol table as stored on disc (used to seek to records) and in memory (used to allocate buffers, copy tables, and so on). I ended up adding two fields to the symbol table item in memory, **sm_typeid** and **sm_dlen**, which specify the type of the symbol table (mnemonics are defined in **SMIO.H**) and its length as stored on the disc. When a symbol table is in memory, **sm_eln** specifies the length of the structure in memory. When a symbol table is written out, the two new fields are not written: instead the disc length is written into the **sm_eln** field and the type is expressed implicitly in the symbol table's position in the drawing header.

By the way, the lack of a type code in symbol tables has been felt before: there is some marvelous to behold code in **WBLOCK.C** that figures out which symbol table it is working on by testing the pointer against the descriptor address. I did not fix these to use my new type codes. Somebody should some day. Once the type codes and disc lengths were present, the changes to process the symbol tables separately were straightforward to install in **SMIO.C**.

Because the code to process the symbol tables field by field is substantially larger and also somewhat slower than reading a single structure, I set up conditional compilation to use the old code on MS-DOS. Since MS-DOS already writes the tables in canonical form and has the most severe memory constraints, there's no reason it should have to pay the price of compatibility code it doesn't need. Note that if you remove the `#ifdef`s on **MSDOS** from the file, it will still work fine: it will just be bigger and slower.

The entity headers. There is a fixed set of fields which precedes every entity in the drawing database to specify its type, flags, length of the packed data which follows, and a pointer. When Bob made the entity data compatible, he could not use his scatter/gather mechanism for these fields because they *control* the scatter/gather process. I modified **EREAD.C** to use the Binary I/O package for these fields. In addition, if **REALTRAN** has been defined on this system, the **gathreal** and **scatreal** functions call **realenc** and **realdec** routines to translate floating point formats. If **REALTRAN** is not defined, no additional code is compiled or executed, so IEEE-compatible systems pay no price for the possibility of floating point format conversion. *The floating point conversion mechanism has never been tested.*

Shape and text font files

Compiled text font and shape files were made compatible by using the Binary I/O package within **SHCOMP.C** when compiling a shape file and in **SHLOAD.C** when loading it. The shape files written by the modified code are identical to those generated by an MS-DOS AutoCAD but are incompatible with other systems. All **.SHX** files on non-MS-DOS systems must be recompiled when converting to this release of AutoCAD. Attempting to load an old format file results in an I/O error message. It was my judgement that considering the tiny installed base of non-MS-DOS systems, it just wasn't worth putting in some form of level indicator and generating a special message. This code has never been tested with "big fonts" (e.g., Kanji).

DXB files

Binary drawing interchange files were just plain busted on non-MS-DOS systems. The problems were:

1. Type codes greater than 127 did not work due to some code incorrectly copied from **SLIDE.C**.

2. An **fread** was done into an **int**, resulting in failure on any machine whose **ints** are not 16 bits.

3. The AutoCAD manual documented **.DXB** files as being in Intel byte order, but the code did not perform the required reversals.

I modified all I/O within **DXBIN.C** to use the Binary I/O package, and corrected these problems. All systems now read **DXB** files which are compatible with existing MS-DOS files. Since the existing code in non-MS-DOS systems could never have worked, compatibility with existing non-MS-DOS **DXB** files is not a consideration since none exist.

Slide files

I corrected a problem in my earlier submission of code to make slide files portable which was found by the regression test. A null slide file created by MS-DOS (or the new portable code) would get an I/O error if you attempted to view it on a

Sun. **SLIDE.C** was reading the in-memory length of the slide file header when it validated the header. I changed it to read the portable length in the file.

Compatibility status summary

The following is a summary of AutoCAD file portability as of the integration of this code.

Drawing files	Fixed to be compatible. All systems read both their own old-format files and the new portable files. All systems emit portable files.
ASCII files	Fixed to be compatible. Note that this causes the following file types to become compatible: **HLP, HDX, SHP, DXF, DXX, MNU, PAT, LIN, PGP, MSG, LSP**.
ACADVS	The virtual string file is compatible by design.
Filmrolls	Compatible by design.
Slides	Fixed to be compatible. Systems can read their own old files and portable files. All write portable files.
Slide libraries	Compatible by design.
SHX files	Fixed to be compatible. Old MS-DOS files are portable. Old non-MS-DOS files must be recompiled.
IGES files	Compatible by design.
DXB files	Fixed to be compatible. Previously worked only on MS-DOS. Old MS-DOS files work without modification.
MNX files	Incompatible. A system must use menus compiled by its own AutoCAD.

Upper and lower case

I have done nothing in this project to resolve the issue of case conventions for file names. I consider this issue so controversial and politically charged that I'm not yet ready to step into it. I hereby submit my recommendations for comment. Each system will define a tag in **SYSTEM.H** called **CASECONV**. It shall be set to one of four values:

CCMONOU System is monocase and uses upper.
CCMONOL System is monocase and uses lower.
CCULU   System uses both cases and prefers upper.
CCULL   System uses both cases and prefers lower.

When a system writes a drawing database, it stores its **CASECONV** setting in the drawing header. This is referred to as the "case convention of the sending system". When a system reads a drawing, if it was created on a system with a different case convention, it processes file names in symbol table entries based upon a matrix of the sending system's case convention and its own. If the receiving system is monocase, file names in symbol tables are not translated, but **FFOPEN** and its clones translate all file names to the receiving system's case convention before submitting them to the system. If the receiving system uses both cases and the sending system was monocase, names in symbol tables are *translated at read-in time* to the preferred case of the receiving system. The names are then used as modified, without further modification by **FFOPEN**. This is asymmetrical and impossible to justify except by convincing yourself that this is the best approximation to what's best for the user.

My throat was feeling a little dry after such a lengthy dissertation. I got up to refill my glass. When I walked back to my chair, Galt was flipping through the listing of **SMIO.C** next to the Sun. He turned to me and said, "Why do you do this? Here you are in the middle of the night struggling trying to trick this megalith of software into threading its way around incompatibilities between computers that aren't even of your making."

I replied, "Differences in products are a consequence of their rapid evolution in a free market. Incompatibility is the price of progress". John Galt was speechless for at least 12 seconds.

He rose and said, "Join us. You weren't ready in 1967. Now, in 1987 you should see that you're struggling to make money in a world where the money you make is taxed away and handed to defence contractors like Lockheed and McDonnell-Douglas, who turn around and compete against you with products your taxes paid to develop. While so many others are sleeping, you labour to produce intellectual property, then you listen to others lecture you on their "right" to steal it. Can't you feel the circle closing? Can't you see that this can't go on? Why not hasten the inevitable and pave the way for a brighter day? You should drop out, or work to hasten the collapse."

I looked at the **DIFF**s of my portable database code. I said, "After this project, I can't help but feel that hastening the collapse would be an exercise in supererogation."

Galt shrugged. He sat back down and said, "Your time hasn't yet come. I try to talk to people when they'll see the issues most clearly. I try to find the times when they see what they're doing and begin to wonder why. I'll be back. It may be in two days, two years, or maybe twenty years."

We talked for an hour or so about old times, common friends, and shared interests. He left as the sun was rising.

Jeremiad — A Little Autodesk Philosophy

Every now and then I get my fill of arrogance, smugness, yuppies, blithering airheads, carpeted walls, opulent furniture, "departmental priorities", and "finalizing the game plan". Here's what happens shortly thereafter.

Remarks for the April Company Meeting

by John Walker — April 3rd, 1987

I was looking at some comparisons between companies a couple of days ago, and they set me to thinking.

Today, the market value of Autodesk, the number of shares of stock times the price per share, is about 610 million dollars. The market value of Computervision, for over a decade the colossus of the CAD industry, is now about 520 million dollars. In the minds of those who back their opinions with their money, Autodesk is worth more than Computervision.

How did that happen?

It happened because we were aggressive, hard-scrabble, hungry rats, responsive to our customers, and able to turn on a dime — while they were complacent, smug, arrogant, arthritic, and hubristic.

While we were working by day to tell our story, sign up dealers, help our users, convince OEMs, and manufacture quality products and ship them on time, and toiling by night designing, developing, testing, and innovating products, they were sitting around their fancy conference tables in their tasteful executive offices writing and reading their five year strategic plans, their market segmentation analyses, their technology forecasts, and their slick promotional brochures.

And while the dinosaurs congratulated each other on their success, we rats were eating their eggs. According to Charles Foundyller of Daratech, in 1982 every one of the top 10 CAD vendors was profitable, and they collectively forecast continued steady growth in unit sales, revenues, and profits. Today, five years later, more than four times as many CAD workstations have been sold as their forecasts predicted. Despite this, only 3 of the top 10 CAD vendors are profitable, and several are effectively leaving the business.

What happened?

Autodesk happened. In the space of 60 months, we plucked the technology of CAD from the clenched fists of the elitists and handed it to the tens of thousands of individuals they disdained. And the results are destroying the companies run by those complacent administrators in their serene office towers.

And what were those mandarins of CAD writing in their strategic overviews five years ago? What were they telling each other at their endless product planning meetings? Well, I'll bet they didn't even mention PC CAD or the low end of the market. I expect they were reassuring each other with those comforting phrases, "Now that we're a big company we can't react as fast as we did in the old days". "You can't expect people to work as hard now that we've made it as when we were struggling". "The low end of the market isn't viable — value will always command a premium price". "We have to protect our installed base — we can't afford the risk of new products to our sales". "The user can't adapt to new technology as fast as it is developed — we must deliver change to users at a moderate rate, one they can absorb".

We sold a hundred AutoCADs, then a thousand, then five thousand, and more. In 1984 AutoCAD became the most widely used CAD system in the world. And still they sat in their fancy chairs, skimming their executive summaries while dozing off to the drone of the projector fan. "The low end of the market may be high volume, but there's no revenue or profit there". "The serious end-user will demand more power.". "Our reputation and position in the market will always distinguish us from the little guys".

We twisted, we turned, we changed course, we took chances; we won and lost bets in the marketplace, we reacted to technological opportunities and user requests, and even though we told everybody exactly what we were doing, we managed to saw off the entire low end of the market pyramid before those statesmen of the CAD millennium got their minds off their Mercedeses, their stock bonus plans, their new office layouts, and their corporate image development programs and realised that we had rendered them impotent and obsolete.

Every quote I have put in the mouths of the big CAD people is a paraphrase of something I've heard in this building in the last two months.

I look at how our architects and interior decorators have betrayed, subverted, and sold out the low-rent surroundings which were not this company's image, but its very soul, and it makes me want to puke.

When we went to AutoCAD Expo in Europe, we went business class. I guess it's expected these days. The wide seats, the free booze, and the quiet surroundings cost our company a total of $27,000 more than the plebeian seats in the back of the plane. That's just a little less than half the cash it took to start this company.

Charles Foundyller showed another slide in his talk. It was a unit market share chart of the CAD industry, and Autodesk was in the usual number one position. Number two was Generic CADD, with half our market share. In the last year they have gone from zero to half as many units as us, and at the present shipping rates, we will end this year as number two.

Of all of the companies who sell products in the price category of AutoCAD, only Autodesk lacks a true 3D product. And we decline to even estimate a date for delivering one. "The customers have to understand, AutoCAD is a big, complicated program and … blah blah blah".

Why is this company successful?

Because more than 80,000 individuals and businesses have parted with thousands of dollars of their hard earned money to buy our products. They bought our products and the hardware to run them because they believed us when we told them that what we had to sell would do the job and repay their investment. Everything else flows from this simple act of trust and our keeping the promises we make when we sell a product.

If I hear one more comment about "end-user perceptions" I may be moved to homicide. What the hell is an end-user anyway? The last guy on a dull needle? I suggest that we ditch this yuppie-babble and call the people whose dollars and trust support our company by the old-fashioned term of respect they are due. Customers. They deserve the very best we can do for them. Little else matters very much.

Now I'm sure that after sharing these thoughts with you — these thoughts that keep me awake night after night — some people will tell me that I've created an "atmosphere of crisis", and that they feel "insecure". Well they should. This is a high technology business, and the only thing we have to sell is the quality of our products and our service to the customer. Doze off, get smug, bet the wrong way, and it can turn on you overnight and wreck all of your well-crafted plans. Lose that ineffable edge that comes from dedication, concentration, and maximum effort, and the flaming knife of retribution will flense the extravagance, the triviality, and the arrogance from the carcass of a company on the way down. All of the Cross pens, all the conference tables, all the business class airfares, the volleyball leagues, and the carpeted walls in the world won't buy us a second chance if we forget and abandon the things that brought our great success. The risk today is no less and no more than it was when we started the company. It's been that way throughout the company's history. The big rewards come from the big risk, and if you can't accept that, you might be happier working for the phone company or the government.

I have here a relic of the founding of Autodesk — a sheet of our original stationery, which Roxie and I designed on our dining room table. Below the company name, it said "Excellence in Computer Software". That is what this company is about. Excellence in design, implementation, testing, documentation, training, marketing, sales, support, manufacturing, shipping, customer service, dealer support, finance, administration, and everything else we do. That is what got us here. That is what can keep us growing, changing, and continuing to create challenges, opportunities, and rewards for all of us involved in this venture.

This is about more than just making money. I think that what we are doing here is right. I believe that the rewards we have reaped so far stem from that rightness as much as from hard work and luck. Responsiveness to our customers, aggressiveness in developing our products and promoting them in the marketplace — excellence in everything we do. We owe our best efforts to continuing the development of this industry we have created in the last five years. We owe it to our customers. We owe it to our dealers. We owe it to ourselves.

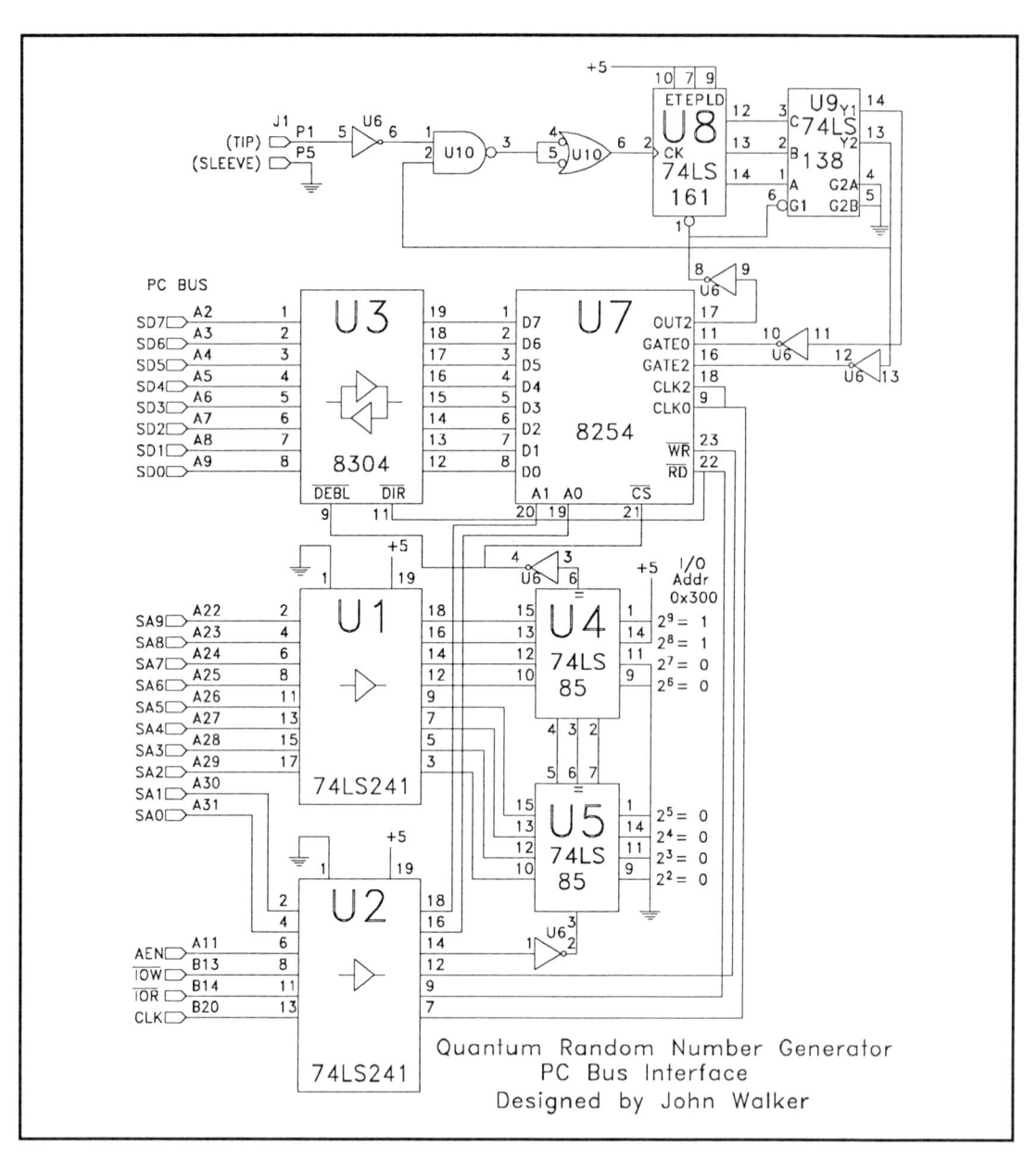

Quantum Random Number Generator
PC Bus Interface
Designed by John Walker

Even though Autodesk taught me that selling software works much better than selling hardware, I've learned that success with software doesn't assuage the compulsion to build a gizmo every now and then. In 1986 I built this card that plugs into the IBM PC bus and attaches to a trivially-modified Heathkit RM–4 Geiger tube radiation monitor. I use a 10 µCurie [137]Cesium source to generate radioactive decay events. Along with a little software, this generates true random numbers, as opposed to computer-generated pseudorandom numbers. I drew the schematics using a development version of AutoCAD Release 9 in an attempt to find AutoCAD bugs. I didn't find a one.

The Golden Age of Engineering

In mid-1987, after we had completed the second public offering, I came to believe that Autodesk should adopt a higher public profile. As the unquestioned market leader in CAD, with close to $100 million in cash, and a market valuation over half a billion dollars, increasing awareness of the company and what it was doing would, I felt, greatly benefit our ability to sell into large corporations and the government.

However, I was afraid that if we unleased an advertising agency on "corporate communications" we'd end up with something just as bad as all of our previous experiences with ad agencies. Who knows, they might come with something out of a Japanese monster movie, "It is invading your company as you sleep. It is extending its tendrils into your engineering department. It is coming back from the ocean floor and it is mad as Hell!".

But I digress. I wrote this in June to attempt to define an overall communications campaign that we could organise all of our efforts around. I believe that this initial message best sums up the potential Autodesk has in the markets in which it is the leader.

The Golden Age of Engineering

by John Walker — June 19th, 1987

In the lifetime and recent memory of currently practicing engineers a revolution has occurred; a revolution so profound, so widespread, and so rapidly advancing on so many fronts that the enormity of it and its consequences are often unappreciated. But they are real, and they are remaking the world.

The past thirty years have seen an unparalleled advance in our understanding of all of the basic sciences. New materials, such as polymers, titanium, semiconductors, and advanced composites have moved from the laboratory into manufacturing. Microelectronics has grown exponentially since its inception in the 1960's, and has not only made enormously complicated systems possible, as many predicted, it has made them extremely inexpensive, as few expected. This, in turn, has driven the growth of computing technology, placing personal computers in the hands of all who want them, while simultaneously allowing the development of the supercomputers which are becoming key research tools in their own right.

We live in the space age. Since 1962, we have dispatched robots to explore all the major planets, expanding our knowledge from one world to dozens. Men and women routinely fly into space, and space stations are being built by many countries. Our telephone calls and television broadcasts are routinely relayed by satellites a tenth of the way to the moon.

We carry calculators no larger than a credit card that contain more computing power than existed in the world in 1950. We routinely fly to the other side of the globe for a business meeting. And we are thinking about airplanes that fly from San Francisco to Tokyo in 90 minutes, superconducting power distribution systems, fusion power stations, portable telephones that work worldwide, and most of the other stuff of the science fiction of our youth.

Almost without noticing, we have entered an era where the fundamental question is not "What *can* be done" but "What *should* be done".

Truly, this is the golden age of engineering.

But even more, it is a golden age for the individual engineer. Driven by technology, design is not dominated by the all-encompassing government design bureaus many imagined in the 1930's, nor by an oligopoly of giant companies as many saw in the 1960's. Instead, the basic tools to invent, design, and manufacture have become so inexpensive and widespread that "downsizing" has become at least as much an imperative in management as in design.

We are entering the age where we are limited primarily by our creativity. Our ability to imagine, and the courage to make our dreams into reality will be our most precious resource. In this age, the designer has a resource that most designers of the past could hardly imagine — the computer. Engineers who, less than twenty years ago, toiled into the night with log tables, slide rule, and pencils, making parts, then breaking them on testing machines, or designing circuits and struggling to get them to work can now design on their desktops with productivity hundreds to thousands of times greater. And the products of their minds in turn accelerate the process.

Anybody who attempts to predict what we can do in our lifetimes should first reread predictions made in 1960. Anybody who draws a limit to what our children can achieve is a fool.

Autodesk designs, develops, manufactures, sells, and supports key computer-aided-design tools. We are working as hard as we can to make them worthy of the tasks to which they are put by the designers of this golden age.

Autodesk, Inc.
Sausalito, California
Tools for the golden age of engineering ™

AutoCAD • The Engineer Works • CAD/camera • AutoSketch • AutoShade
AutoCAD AEC Architectural • AutoCAD AEC Mechanical

Cosmic Perspective

Nobody can resist the temptation to ask, every now and then, "what does it all mean"? At least I can't.

Cosmic Perspective

At attempt to gain perspective in various domains at several different orders of magnitude. In three parts.

by John Walker
June 29th, 1987

Cosmic Perspective — A

Autodesk recently announced the shipment of the 100,000th copy of AutoCAD. Let's do some calculations of the size of the industry this represents. Throughout this paper, the numbers I calculate will be expressed in "astronomical units", precise to 10 decimal places but probably accurate to 1 or 2.

Since Autodesk's sales curve is reasonably approximated by an exponential, it's reasonable to assume an average retail price for AutoCAD of about $2,000, factoring in discounting at retail, earlier sales at lower prices, and sales of base, ADE-1, and ADE-2, all corrected for sales of foreign language versions which carry a premium over the English version and have recently benefited by the fall of the dollar.

This means that, at retail, total sales of AutoCAD to date are about $200 million. But we just sell the software. Charles Foundyller estimates that software accounts for about 15% of the revenue in the PC CAD business. If this is accurate, the total retail sales generated to date by AutoCAD is approximately $1.3 billion. If you discount the obscene wealth extracted from this market by a few people, assume that half the business has been done in the last year, assume an industry-wide living wage of $40,000 per year (remember overhead), and attribute a negligible materials cost to AutoCAD-related products, this means that roughly 15,000 people earn their living from the AutoCAD industry (this is, of course, an abstraction for a much larger number of people partially supported by the industry).

None of this existed in 1982.

Cosmic Perspective — B

An instrumentality of the federal government of the United States of America bought the 100,000th copy of AutoCAD. In its 1987 fiscal year, the federal government spent $1.3 billion, equal to the total five-year market for AutoCAD related products, about every twelve hours.

Roughly half of Autodesk's profits during the last five years have been paid as taxes.

Cosmic Perspective — C

At 07:35:35 UTC on February 23, 1987, neutrinos and photons from the exploding star Sanduleak -69°202 reached the Earth. Roughly 10 billion neutrinos from the supernova passed through every square centimetre of the Earth's surface. In approximately five seconds, 10^{58} neutrinos were emitted — equivalent to the total conversion into energy of one tenth of the mass of the Sun.[158]

Over 99% of the energy of the supernova was carried away by the neutrinos; the visible manifestation in the sky is caused by much less than 1% of the energy released. The energy emitted in five seconds by the supernova is roughly equal to the output of the Milky Way galaxy for a period of several years. So great was the neutrino flux that, despite the fact a beam of neutrinos is attenuated only 50% by passing through six light-years of lead, approximately one million people on Earth experienced a neutrino interaction in their bodies as a result of the supernova.[159]

The star that exploded is 160,000 light-years from Earth.

---

[158] A survey of SN 1987A results in *Science*, Vol. 240, Page 754, offered additional perspective on the neutrino burst. The neutrino luminosity in the first second was 10^{53} erg/sec. Using consensus numbers for the density of luminous matter and the size of the observable universe, the luminosity of the *entire universe* is approximately 5×10^{52} erg/sec. Thus, during the explosion the supernova was brighter than the entire rest of the universe, yet generated all of its energy in a region about 50 km across. By comparison, if the Sun shines for another 10 billion years its total energy output over that entire period will be about 10^{51} erg. The supernova released 100 times that energy *each second* of the collapse.

[159] The neutrino flux through the Earth was 50 billion neutrinos per square centimetre.

External Tanks

Many aerospace experts believe that the most cost-effective way to build a large orbital facility is to convert the External Tanks currently discarded on every Space Shuttle mission into habitable space. External Tanks Corporation, 80% owned by a consortium of universities and staffed and advised by a distinguished group of space statesmen and Washington hands, was first to do the extensive groundwork to bring this about.

When I learned they were seeking funding, it seemed to me a natural opportunity for Autodesk. Here was a group trying to do with the very highest of high technology, manned space operations, precisely what Autodesk had done to CAD — reduce the cost by one or two orders of magnitude and thereby increase the market size by an even larger factor.

In addition, the External Tank engineering project seemed a natural to apply Autodesk's engineering tools in environments outside the traditional, heavily funded, aerospace sector.

When we made the investment in External Tanks in July of 1987, negotiations were underway with NASA. Since then, commercialisation of the External Tank has become part of the official U.S. national space policy, External Tanks has received an official NASA Memorandum of Understanding to develop the tanks, and NASA has undertaken preliminary work to study External Tanks Corporation's proposal to convert the tank into a Gamma Ray Imaging Telescope. This is the second draft of the press release, expressing our joint intent; the actual press release sent out was watered down somewhat to avoid offending certain parties.

Autodesk Invests in External Tanks Corporation

Sausalito, California, July 8, 1987.

Autodesk, Inc. and External Tanks Corporation jointly announced today that Autodesk will purchase approximately 5% of the common stock of External Tanks Corporation for $225,000.

External Tanks Corporation's aim is the development of an orbiting research and manufacturing facility called Labitat™, based on the External Tank (ET) which is launched as part of every Space Transportation System (Space Shuttle) mission and is currently discarded. External Tanks Corporation is 80% owned by the University Consortium for Atmospheric Research (UCAR), a group of 57 universities who have administered research programs and facilities for over 25 years.

NASA is presently in the final stages of negotiating a Memorandum of Understanding with UCAR and External Tanks Corporation under which title for tanks lifted into orbit by STS missions will be transferred to UCAR and administered by External Tanks Corporation. External Tanks Corporation will transform these tanks into orbiting facilities which will then be leased to government, academic, and commercial customers at prices which are potentially one thousandth that of comparable orbiting facilities.

Alvar Green, President of Autodesk, Inc. said, "The phenomenal success of Autodesk has been based on taking computer aided design technology, which was previously thought to be priced out of the reach of all but a very few large users, and making it available to millions of people at costs a fraction of what was previously imagined. We hope, through our investment in External Tanks Corporation, to spark a similar reduction in the price of space research, observation, and manufacturing. We believe that as the computer revolution has shown and as the success of AutoCAD has demonstrated, every time you radically reduce the price of a product, a far, far larger market emerges. External Tanks Corporation can do for space research and development what silicon technology has done in the computer industry, and we're positioning ourselves to promote this and reap the benefits as it happens. We're also looking forward to applying our expertise as the world leader in computer aided design, and the pioneer in bringing solid modeling to the desktop to this challenging venture. Our participation in this venture will help demonstrate PC-based design tools in a space age, man rated project."

Dr. Randolph Ware, President of External Tanks Corporation said, "As the United States strives to regain the momentum of its space program and resume its leadership in space science and commercialization, the need for a low cost, large volume research and manufacturing facility in space will become manifest. As the National Commission on Space has recommended and numerous previous studies have shown, commercialization of the External Tank provides the lowest cost, nearest term solution. At a time of growing concern over our space program, NASA's provision of the previously discarded External Tank resource via a Space Grant to UCAR will parallel the Land Grant program of the 1800s in paving the way for research, development, and near-term industrial opportunities on the unlimited frontier of space. We're proud that Autodesk, Inc. will be joining us in developing and exploiting this enormous opportunity."

Source Distribution

Developing a program as large as AutoCAD on personal computers, with most programmers working off-site, presents some interesting logistical problems — mainly, how do you distribute the source code which presently occupies over twenty megabytes. The source has outgrown every medium we have chosen, and at times we've even handed out paper bags with twenty or more floppy discs.

We finally settled on Iomega Bernoulli Boxes, with twenty megabytes per cartridge. Naturally, the source grew to fill them. This is a modest proposal to buy some time before the inevitable happened. It wasn't implemented.

Source Distribution

Combining the files in a source distribution into a composite archive file can enormously speed up the process of copying source distribution media. Benchmarks, recommendations, and a moral are presented.

by Kelvin R. Throop
September 29th, 1987l

On the morning of July 18th, Liberty, New Hampshire became the first town to vanish. Many residents of New Providence, over a wooded ridge from Liberty, were awakened at about 3:30 A.M. by a clap of thunder. Those who looked outside saw clear sky and a glow in the direction of Liberty. Volunteer firemen called friends in Liberty to ask what had happened, but none of the calls were answered. Most people went back to sleep.

By midday, all the world knew what had happened, but nobody knew how or why. The town of Liberty was *gone*. Gone to a meter below the ground. Gone right to the town limits, where some branches had fallen on undisturbed grass after their trees had vanished.

There has never been a truly satisfactory way of distributing full source releases of AutoCAD. The product has grown so rapidly that it rapidly outgrew each medium selected for distribution and became a large burden to copy and maintain.

Largely at my urging, Autodesk spent a large sum of money to equip all AutoCAD developers with Iomega Bernoulli 20 megabyte drives and has purchased an seemingly endless supply of cartridges for these drives. On the face of it, the Bernoulli is an ideal source distribution medium.

- It is fast. Average access time is comparable to a high performance Winchester hard disc drive.
- It supports a true DOS file system. Files can be extracted with normal DOS commands. No special archiving tools are required.
- It is a high-density medium. Each cartridge stores over 20 megabytes formatted. This is enough for an entire AutoCAD source and object distribution.

In practice, several disadvantages have become apparent.

- They don't work very well. Cartridges which verify one day may prove unreadable the next.
- Software support is shaky. Several bugs which can cause loss of *all* data on a cartridge have only recently been fixed.
- Image copy is untrustworthy. Binary image copy from one cartridge to another seems to frequently result in undetected data errors. There is no confidence that image copy correctly intercalates the bad track maps of the cartridges involved.
- The alternative, MS-DOS copy of entire directory trees, is painfully slow.

But hey, what do you want, it's from Utah, right?

Right.

The president appointed an investigating panel chaired by the secretary of defense and made up of the secretary of the interior, the chairman of the National Academy of Sciences, and the president of M.I.T. On the 20th, the group held a press conference in Manchester and announced that no probable cause had yet been found. The defense secretary said that hostile action had been ruled out "for the time being", since no aircraft were in the area at the time, nor were any satellites tracked by NORAD overhead. "In any case", the secretary concluded, "we possess no technology which could do this, and we don't believe our adversaries do either".

Well, I got us into this, so I decided to spend some time seeing if I could get us out. The first thing I did is make some measurements of the AutoCAD X.0.60 (8/2/87) full distribution Bernoulli. I copied the directory tree from this cartridge to a Unix file system over NFS. I then made a **tar** file of the entire directory tree copied from the Bernoulli. The total size of the data on the Bernoulli was 19,786,240 bytes.

All of the measurements presented herein were made on an IBM PC/AT, 6 Mhz version, with an Iomega 2010 or 2020 removable cartridge disc system. In all of the following timings, I assume that the Bernoulli cartridges being written have been previously formatted. Formatting takes approximately 4 minutes per cartridge. Since all operations require a formatted cartridge, this is invariant under the options we're exploring and can be added to all the numbers presented below.

Over the next week ten more towns vanished: two in Massachusetts, another in New Hampshire, three in California (including one suburb of San Francisco), one in New Mexico, two in England, and one in the Netherlands. Data began to accumulate about the phenomenon. One of the California towns vanished during a Landsat pass; the multispectral camera recorded only the glow of ionized air molecules recombining. The nuclear test detectors on the remaining Vela satellite and the monitors on the Navstar constellation observed four light flashes coincident with disappearances. Nothing like the double flash of a nuclear detonation was seen, just slow airglow decay. No prompt radiation was detected at the time of the disappearances, nor was residual radiation found at the sites. Electromagnetic transients similar to a very large lightning strike were detected, and underground solar neutrino experiments reported six neutrino events near the time of the flashes, but gave only a 60% chance that this was correlated. *Aviation Week* reported that some at Los Alamos believed the flash spectrum similar to a free electron laser, but they had no idea how this could occur spontaneously.

First I measured the time to perform a file-by-file copy of all files on the distribution using Metaware's **FIND**. The file by file copy from one Bernoulli cartridge to another took a mind-numbing 63 minutes: one hour and 3 minutes!

The discrepancy between this and the time required to simply transfer the data from one cartridge to the next was elucidated by performing an image copy from one cartridge to another. The Iomega **RCD** utility copied the entire cartridge in a tad less than 5 minutes: more than twelve times faster.

As in time of war or natural disaster, the population surprised the politicians with its equanimity. Certainly there was uneasiness, and frustration grew as days passed without any explanation or plans to deal with the crisis, but no real signs of panic emerged. If scientists had no theories (as one physicist put it, "nothing even deserving of the term wild guess"), explanations nonetheless abounded. Television evangelists seized on the crisis as demonstrating God's wrath on sinful man (though none understood why Las Vegas was still around). The *National Star* interviewed 75 prophets and psychics who had predicted the disappearances, but was silent on which cities the "UFO Aliens" would kidnap next. Sinister rumors of Soviet secret weapons circulated, supported by the fact that no Eastern Bloc city had vanished.

Clearly, something odd is going on here. While one expects a hard-coded device-specific image copy utility to run faster than the operating system's copy facility, a factor of two is more than one typically gains. But *twelve times faster*? Hmmm....

Next I decided to try copying the 19.7 megabyte **tar** file I made from the distribution onto a Bernoulli across NFS. The entire copy operation took 6.4 minutes. Note that this was a DOS copy across an Ethernet link from a Unix file system, yet it was only 28% slower than Iomega's much-vaunted image copy facility. As all of those who have studied at the feet of the legendary masters of gonzo programming (especially those who did their studying in Cleveland) know, factors of ten percent may stem from sloppiness, but factors of ten invariably indicate idiocy. It was clear that somewhere deep within the sanctum sanctorum, the very nucleus of the operating system, there was some really major league *evil*.

By September 1st, over one hundred villages, towns, and cities in the United States, Western Europe, Latin America, Japan, and Australia had evaporated into the dead of night and the world was beginning to go truly crazy. Not one Soviet or Eastern European town had been affected; NATO moved to alert status "as a precautionary measure". Still, no pattern emerged. Mostly small and medium sized towns and suburbs were vanishing. In the U.S. most were on the East and

West coasts. Most of the mid-continent disappearances were university towns. No large cities nor unincorporated areas had yet gone, and people began to flow to the cities. Squatter camps appeared in state and national parks.

So, back into the Honda and down the hill to Duff's machine (which, unlike my humble configuration, has a gen-u-wine two-holer Bernoulli). I took the Bernoulli onto which I had copied the 19.7 megabyte **tar** file and tried copying it to an empty cartridge with a simple DOS **COPY** command. The entire copy completed in 5 minutes and 43 seconds.

At this point it's worth recapping the timings in these experiments. All timings in this table are in seconds.

Function	Time
Format cartridge.	240
Metaware **FIND** copy entire cartridge file by file.	3815
Iomega **RCD** image copy entire cartridge.	298
Copy **tar** file over **NFS** to cartridge.	386
Copy **tar** file cartridge to cartridge.	343

What can we conclude? Clearly the enormous difference between the time required to copy the **tar** file and the time to reproduce the entire file structure on the target Bernoulli is simply the time that the operating system required to create all of the directories and files in the source distribution. Since the inefficiency is in the nucleus of the operating system itself, there is only one way to get around it.

For perhaps the very first time, a librarian came to the rescue of civilization. Todd Murphy was a researcher for the Library of Congress project to build a computer database on the vanishing towns in the hope of finding some common thread or pattern. But the brain is still the best computer when it comes to finding patterns. The answer came not from the database, but to Murphy's mind as he was entering data in the middle of the night.

Clearly, since the problem is in the operating system, the only way to overcome it is to bypass the operating system. Hence, we should prepare our source distributions as **tar** archives which can be copied more than ten times faster than fully elaborated MS-DOS directory structures. Fortunately, the Metaware **FIND** utility (licensed to all AutoCAD developers as part of the High C distribution) can write Unix-compatible **tar** files. Using Unix **tar** format allows Unix systems to process the distribution without format conversion. If the current directory contains a complete AutoCAD source distribution, you can prepare a Unix **tar** format Bernoulli on drive **L** with file name **DIST.TAR** with the command:

find *.* -utarc L:DIST.TAR -t

Having prepared a Bernoulli containing a **tar** distribution, you can extract the entire directory tree into the current directory with the command:

find -utarx L:DIST.TAR -cp .

If you have access to a Unix system, you can copy the **tar** file from the Bernoulli to Unix as a single binary file and extract the component files under Unix with the command:

tar xfv *tarfile*

where *tarfile* is the name of the file you've copied the entire distribution **tar** file into. Note that files are archived as they were originally stored; no end of line convention conversion is performed. Hence, even if you de-**tar** the archive on Unix, you will end up with source files in MS-DOS format.

That Murphy is forceful and persuasive as well as wise was evident when, after hurriedly checking his hypothesis against the list of cities and finding complete confirmation, he convinced the White House switchboard to awaken the vice president and the national security adviser and ended up at 4 A.M. declaiming to a small, bleary-eyed group in the Situation Room, "Congress has to act on federal overriding legislation today, and you must get the President back in town to sign it before we lose any more people. Get State to work contacting the Europeans right now — it's going to be night soon over there. And *call the prime minister of New Zealand!* Every town that vanished had declared itself a nuclear-free zone. And the nuclei are moving out."

So, Horatio, the problem lies not in the stars nor in Roy, Utah, but rather in the nucleus of MS-DOS. Consequently, only one solution is possible. We must move to a completely *nuclear-free* software distribution format — one which can be replicated without a single call to the inefficient heart of MS-DOS. The **tar** file mechanism suggested herein provides such a solution and allows creation of AutoCAD full distribution media more than ten times faster than previous techniques without compromising data integrity.

I also investigated compression techniques. Our distribution almost fills a cartridge at present, and already excludes some items which should probably included in a full distribution (e.g., the Kelvinator). My experiments indicated that compression can help us fit far more data on a cartridge (and commensurately decrease the effective time to copy the original, uncompressed, data), but the convenience costs of compression are fairly high. I started with the original 19.7 megabyte composite **tar** file and used the Unix **compress** program. This reduced the file size to 8,751,305 bytes, saving over 55%, but compressing this file required almost 9 minutes of elapsed time on a Sun 3/260. Since the Unix compress program runs only on Unix, and Unix cannot directly read a Bernoulli, compressing the entire distribution in this manner means one must copy the entire 8.7 megabyte compressed **tar** file to Unix, then decompress it, then extract files from the archive. At the instant that the compression or decompression is complete, the entire mess occupies over 28.5 megabytes on the Unix system — a very severe free space constraint on any system. Decompressing the file takes about four minutes of elapsed time.

Since a large part of the problems with the Unix compress program stem from its inability to run on MS-DOS, I tried Kern's **fsq** program, which runs on both Unix and DOS. I was about to glibly say, "and it's still running", but it just finished. I don't think we'll use **fsq**: it took 39 minutes of elapsed time to compress the composite **tar** file on the Sun 3/260 (27 minutes of CPU time), and it only reduced the file to 17,640,789 bytes, saving less than 11%.

Compression seems impractical when applied wholesale to the entire distribution, but can be useful for compressing smaller parts of the release. Duff has suggested that we **tar** the files directory-by-directory and compress at that level. This would drastically reduce the disc space required to decompress each part and only marginally increase the time needed to copy the cartridge.

Finally, I have been thinking about how to guard against undetected errors in these distributions, however copied. Neither Unix **tar** nor Metaware **FIND** in its native archive mode provide any form of file checksum. I am willing to write an external checksum utility to guarantee accurate distributions. If the following description seems a tool we will actually use, I will invest the day or so to write it.

To make a distribution, compress the directories of the distribution into one or more **tar** archives. After creating the archives on a trusted system and compressing them if you like, run the checksum program on each archive:

feathers -m *tarfile*

This program reads the named *tarfile* and checksums each block in the file with a highly reliably checksum. It creates a checksum file named **tarfile.cks**, and reversibly encrypts the first 128 bytes of the *tarfile* so that **tar** cannot unpack the file. All of the `tar` files and their corresponding `.cks` files are placed on a master Bernoulli and then copied for all recipients.

When a developer receives a Bernoulli, he verifies all of the files on it with the call:

`feathers tarfile`

This validates the file against the corresponding `.cks` file and, *only if it is correct*, decrypts the `tar` file so it may be de-archived. This absolutely guarantees that no developer can end up with corrupted data (unless an error sneaks past the checksum algorithm).

Nuclear Free

The Morning After

On October 19th, 1987, the stock market crashed. The Dow Jones Industrial Average plummeted more than 500 points, almost five times the previous record single-day drop (which occurred the previous week), and in percentage terms, almost twice the size of the Crash of 1929. This was part of, and in turn accelerated, a global collapse in equity markets. Autodesk's stock, which had hit a high of over 33 less than three weeks before, plunged to close below 13 on October 27th. This decline wiped out all the gains in the stock for the last year, and left almost everybody hired in the last year with above-market stock options.

In addition, dire predictions about the future, concern for the value of retirement plan investments, and business prospects in general contributed to a general climate of unease. I made the following remarks at a special company meeting on October 27th.

Remarks for the Stock Market Crash Meeting

by John Walker — October 27th, 1987

Welcome to the morning after.

It's hard to watch frenzy in the stock market, 500 point drops on the Dow Jones Industrials, Autodesk stock shedding almost 60% of its value in less than a month, and ponderous predictions of panic from pompous prognosticators without wondering, "what does this mean to me, and what effect will this have on our company".

I'll try to explain what's going on as I see it, the steps we took months ago to prepare for this inevitable occurrence, and what we can expect to happen next. Then I'll be glad to field any questions you may have on any subjects except the three I never discuss: politics, religion, and text editors.

I'd like to read a quote from a memo I wrote on February 3rd of this year:

> I'm beginning to get nervous, *really* nervous, about this stock market runup and the action in our stock.

I think we may be entering into the kind of wild speculative blowoff that ran technology stocks into multiples of a hundred times earnings in the 1960's.

And you know what happens on the morning after.

As I recall, I started worrying at about the point the stock passed 13 (correcting for the split) on the way up. As one who has seen the crash of '70 and the crash of '74, it was abundantly clear to me that we were in one of those rampaging bull markets in which common sense, fundamental values, and historical perspective are trampled in the wild rush to get rich quick.

This happens every decade or so, and every time it happens, there invariably comes a time when all the news is rosy, when business has never been better, and when every last person in the world who is inclined to buy has bought. Then the bottom drops out.

Why? Because prices rise when everybody wants to buy and they drop when everybody wants to sell. But when everybody has already bought, there aren't any buyers left. Then somebody looks around and notices that it's a long way down, and that those black clouds that everybody ignored last week are now casting cold shadows and beginning to drizzle.

Bull markets lead to bear markets lead to bull markets in a cycle as old as commerce and as inevitable as the changing of the seasons.

So what does the stock market crash mean to Autodesk? In terms of direct effects, essentially nothing. The market value of our company has been cut in half, but since the company has no plans to sell additional stock, that has no effect on our operation. Since Autodesk's stock has gone down about the same amount as other comparable companies, we're in the same relative position as we were before. A receding tide deposits all boats on the muddy bottom.

Autodesk's business is as good as it's ever been. Our sales are stronger than ever, we continue to be one of the most profitable companies in the world, and we're expanding our product line, our distribution channels, our presence in major accounts and government markets, and our international operations. None of this is affected in any way by gyrations in the financial markets. When the value of our stock doubled in the last year for no good reason, it didn't make our business grow any faster than we had predicted two years before. And when our stock falls by one half, there isn't any reason to think that will affect us either.

Now none of this is to minimise the impact of what is going on. When you hack a trillion dollars off the value of financial assets, it's bound to have some impact on business and the economy. And if we find ourselves in a deep recession, our sales may be hurt. But amid all the comparisons with 1929, let's remember that not every stock market crash leads to a recession. The stock market crash of 1929 was only part of the great depression, which devastated the economy primarily due to the collapse of the banking system, not the stock market. That type of collapse is much less likely to happen today. This may be more like the crash of 1962, where the stock market hit a speed bump and scared everybody to death, but there was almost no effect on the economy, which continued to roar ahead and eventually carried the stock market to record highs in 1966. We don't know what will happen this time, but we have carefully prepared for whatever the future may bring.

If you're inclined to worry about the future of Autodesk, keep this in mind. We have one hundred million dollars in cash. That cash is invested in risk-free short-term government securities whose value is not affected at all by the stock market and whose value could be at risk only if money became obsolete. One hundred million dollars. That's about five dollars per share of stock, and I sometimes wonder if some of the people who are dumping our stock at 13 know that there's a green five-spot behind every share. One hundred million dollars. That's about three hundred thousand dollars for every employee, so even if sales went to zero, we have a multi-year buffer to keep the company operating and progressing. Autodesk is one of the most financially strong companies around. We got that way by deliberately choosing a prudent and conservative path to growth, politely declining to play the financial games that got so many in trouble in the recent turbulence.

We have no debt at all. We do so much business overseas that when the dollar falls, it actually improves our sales and profits. If the United States goes into a downturn, we'll do plenty of business in the rest of the world while we wait for better times. We don't gamble the future of our company in the stock market or in other short term speculations. We're building this company to be a force in the market for twenty, fifty, a hundred years to come — and we're not going to crapshoot it for a quick buck.

But most of all, what we are doing is *right*. We are not just a good stock, we are a good business. We sell tools that individuals and companies use to make themselves more creative and productive. And productivity is more important than ever when the economy turns down.

A month ago, I wrote the copy for advertisement which I now wish we'd been running the last two weeks. It's only two sentences, and I'd like to read it to you now.

> "Everybody says America must increase its productivity or reduce its standard of living."

> "Autodesk sells products that increase the productivity of every manufacturer in America."

It's true, you know. And people who work hard, in companies that work well, who make and sell products that make a difference, that make people's jobs easier, their lives more productive, and enable them to do things they couldn't do before, do well regardless of the stock market, the economy, or the folly of politicians.

I have called this "The Golden Age of Engineering". Part of that golden age is a resurgence in interest in truly productive endeavours, designing, building, and manufacturing, rather than corporate takeovers, leveraged buyouts, stock index futures, and "financial services".

Not long ago half the pundits in the world were explaining how Americans could prosper by selling innovative financial products to one other while importing productive work from Europe and the Far East. Personally, I've always thought that was a lot of turbo. You know, turbo, that's a device that makes hot air and high pressure. Now, I think, people are awakening to the folly of this monumentally silly idea. And as they focus on productive work and tools for that work, they will continue to buy those tools from the world's leading supplier, Autodesk, and the company that we have built will continue to prosper.

All of this may seem small consolation if you own Autodesk stock and have watched its value plummet by one half, or if you have stock options whose exercise price is now well above the market price of the stock. For option holders, things are not as bad as they may seem. When I wind up in a minute or so I'm going to turn things over to Chris Record. He'll describe the Amazing Counter Parabolic New Options For Old Trade In Plan. Take note, it's very important.

If you're a stockholder, there's nothing for it but to come to terms with the fact that the stock isn't worth what it was two weeks ago. If you were looking at that stock as the down payment on a house, the kids' college fund, or some other economic goal, the adjustment can be tough to make. But it's important that we don't let regret paralyse us at a time when our efforts are vital to keeping the company growing and eventually restoring the value of the stock as investors come to their senses and realise that Autodesk is different from the many other companies they dumped in time of panic.

You've all heard me talk again and again about the fact that this is a high-technology, high-risk business and that great rewards flow from the assumption of large risks. For the last five years, and especially in the last year, we've all shared in those great rewards. Now we get to taste the risks. It's both gratifying and frustrating to have your stock dumped when you didn't do anything wrong. Most small companies get pummelled when they fail to get a product to market on time or they can't meet their sales forecasts. We do everything right, and still we get bashed. It's little comfort indeed to know that everybody else is getting clobbered also.

We may look back on this period as a time of trial from which much good flowed, a time which tempered the company for its next great surge of success. Good times are wonderful, but they can lead to a feeling of complacency which can sow the seeds of destruction for any company. As I've said repeatedly, Autodesk is just one small company in a dangerous, highly competitive world. If this gust of winter's chill makes us rededicate ourselves to making our products, our service, and our marketing and sales the very best in the world, then I continue to believe what I said at the annual meeting in 1986.

> Autodesk has always competed like a hungry rat. We will continue. And we will prevail.

Section Seven
Working Philosophy

Publisher's Notes
January 1988 — December 1988

During 1988, Autodesk sales exceeded $100 million, and revenues exceeded $30 million. The company continued to grow by 50% over the previous year. John Walker completed the transition to programming, turning the job of Chairman of the Board over to Al Green.

The documents in this section give a retrospective view of the company, both a European view from Lars Moureau, and John Walker's own final summing up.

Key Events

Here are the key events and the documents provided in Section Seven.

- February 20, 1988. — Glasnost. Discusses changing Autodesk's release policy on AutoCAD.

- March 4, 1988. — Where's It All Going. Assesses the hardware "rollercoaster" that the entire computer industry is riding.

April 1988. Autodesk acquires 80% interest in Xanadu, a Hypertext company.

- April 8, 1988. — Xanadu. Press statements on the acquisition.

- April 15, 1988. — Bored of Directors. Dan Drake's internal memo announcing that John Walker will retire as the Chairman of the Board.

June 10, 1988. Annual shareholders' meeting. John Walker relinquishes position as Chairman of the Board. Al Green assumes the Chairmanship.

- June 10, 1988. — Valedictory. Gives a six year retrospective on the company.

- June 1988. — The View from Sweden. Lars Moureau gives the European view of Autodesk.

- June 1988. — L'Envoi. A final summing up of the first six years.

Malcom Davies is VP of Marketing and Sales. Chris Record is VP and Counsel to the company. Ted Nelson invented the idea of "hypertext." He was a founder of Xanadu.

Key Product Events

By the end of the year the company had an installed base of over 200,000 units. It shipped AutoCAD Release 10 with full 3D. Here is the release schedule for the year.

March 1988. AutoFlix Release.

June 1988. AutoSolid Release. This is the release of the Cadetron software acquired in 1987.

October 1988. AutoCAD Release 10 Release with full 3D.

Financial Summary

Both sales and revenue dollars increased. Sales increased 50% (again) to $117 million; and revenues increased 60% to over $33 million. Autodesk was valued at close to $700 million at the end of the year.

Here are the quarterly figures for the year.

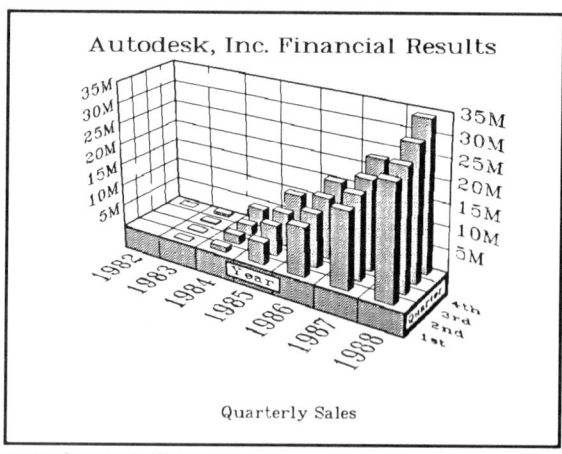

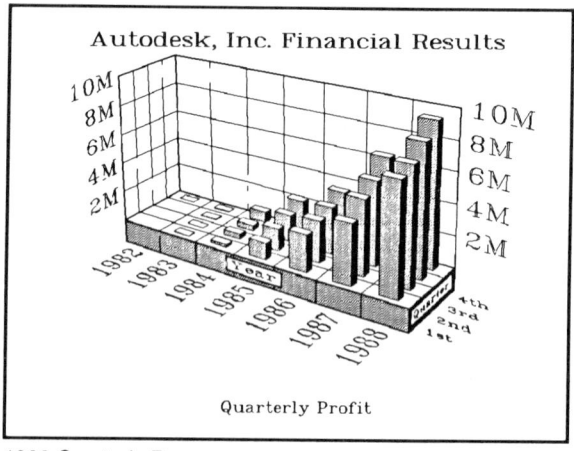

1988 Quarterly Sales

1988 Quarterly Revenues

Thoughts on Tight Security

Throughout 1987 I had been becoming increasingly convinced that Autodesk's long-standing policy of tight security regarding new product releases was growing counterproductive. My experience with Univac mainframes, where there was essentially full disclosure to the customers of Univac's software development plans, persuaded me that such an environment was far more conducive to developing products that met the customers' actual needs.

The question always was, "can we afford the financial risk of disclosure followed by a late shipment, and the competitive risk of laying out our development plans for all to see?". In this memo, I argue that we can. Pursuant to this proposal, for the first time we briefed our dealers and developers on the features to be announced in AutoCAD Release 10 (Abbey Road), well in advance of its official unveiling at AutoCAD Expo in May of 1988.

To: Al Green, Dan Drake, Malcolm Davies, Chris Record, Eric Lyons
From: John Walker
Date: 20th February 1988

Subject: Гласност

For some time I've felt that our policy of high security with regard to the features to be included in future releases of AutoCAD and general information concerning their release schedule, was growing increasingly outmoded in light of our dominance of the market and our desire to maintain a close cooperative relationship with our resellers and their customers. In this memorandum, I'd like to recap the reasons that caused us to originally adopt our policy of secrecy and then examine the changes in the competitive environment which have, in my opinion, caused this policy to become not only unnecessary, but actually damaging to our competitive position.

In this document, I will present the case for changing our policy to one of essentially complete openness and full disclosure regarding our plans for the future development of AutoCAD; moving toward a cooperative relationship with our user community more like that between a mainframe computer vendor and its user group, or MacNeal-Schwendler and the NASTRAN user group. I will present this case in the manner in which I communicate best: as an advocate. The fact that I present a strong argument here should not be taken as an indication that I harbour no doubts about the possibility of this policy backfiring, or that I am unaware of many equally strong arguments for continuing our current policy. My purpose in presenting this case is to make us reconsider what we are trying to accomplish with our current policy and then rationally decide what changes may be in order, instead of blindly maintaining the status quo.

The original rationale for maintaining security when a new release of AutoCAD impended was simple survival of the company. Since we never offered any formal inventory protection to our resellers, and because each release of AutoCAD contained a large collection of additional features, news of an upcoming release would cause dealers to defer orders until after the release became available. On several occasions when news of a forthcoming release leaked out, we saw our sales drop to half their previous level for the one or two months before shipment of the new version.

Since the company was so thinly capitalised, premature announcement of a new product followed by a shipment delay, for whatever reason, could place the company at risk of bankruptcy. Consequently, the prudent course was to maintain tight security about the content and schedule of upcoming releases. We even went so far as to try to eliminate notification clauses from OEM agreements we negotiated. Obviously, we had no desire to create ill-will by loading up resellers with soon-to-be obsolete product, but neither could we run the risk of sinking our company.

After the 1985 initial public offering, we had enough money that order deferral couldn't bankrupt us, but another imperative asserted itself — the need to report quarterly increases in sales and profits. Since we had experienced one- to two-month 50% sales fall-offs, followed by compensating sales bulges after shipment, it became essential that if one of these was to occur, it be totally contained within a fiscal quarter. Otherwise, the Wall Street isomorph of wind shear could buffet Autodesk's standing in the financial community.

So, our policy was total secrecy about what we were working on, and "no comment" regarding shipment dates. This policy was the product of the environment in which we operated at the time, and served us well. But I believe that it may have now become outdated, and may actually be working to our detriment.

At the time we adopted the policy of secrecy, we were a small, virtually unknown company attempting to establish itself in a market which was largely unrecognised by mainstream microcomputer analysts. Today, we command over 60% market share in a rapidly-growing market which is viewed as one of the primary applications for the high end of the desktop computer market. Autodesk's installed customer base dwarfs any competitor, our distribution network essentially controls the route of engineering software from producer to customer, and we have encouraged the development of a burgeoning market in third party software, hardware drivers, education, books, and consulting. Our goal was to become an industry standard, and I believe that we have achieved that goal. Now, I'd argue that it's time to start acting like an industry standard rather than a marginal producer, and that so doing can reinforce our position as the standard.

But enough generalities: let's look at AutoCAD Abbey Road, and examine the consequences of the two approaches on our market. First, it's worth noting that Autodesk took a totally unprecedented step when we announced, concurrent with the launch of Release 9, that Release 10 would contain full three dimensional capability and would be shipped in the first half of 1988. Never before had we so explicitly called our shots regarding the feature content of a release and its shipment date. The reasons we did this were obvious — we'd been assailed by every competitor (even those without a product, or those with somebody's else) for "not having 3D", and after a long hiatus during which we had no marketing presence whatsoever, we felt we had to respond with an explicit statement of when we would "have 3D".

This step was actually part of a series of liberalisations of our product secrecy which had occurred over the preceding two years. For releases 2.5, 2.6, and 9 we had formally briefed third party software vendors prior to the announcement, and given them pre-release copies of the product to adapt their products to. We did this even though many third party developers are also dealers, and hence could adjust their own ordering schedule based on the knowledge of the new release (yes, we never said when, but when you call in the developers 60 days before AutoCAD Expo, it isn't very hard to guess the launch date). In several OEM contracts we agreed to disclose new release dates in advance. Prior to the release of 2.6, we described the product in advance and demonstrated it to industry analysts. Since the White Album announcement, we've shown Abbey Road to selected subsets of our constituencies based on our feelings for the market. We've shown several customers in-depth previews of the product, and we've used their reactions to guide our development of features for inclusion in the final product. We've briefed book publishers about the features in Abbey Road. And most recently, of course, we have held a very successful pre-release disclosure to our ADI developers, notwithstanding the fact that many of these developers also support competitive CAD products.

What, precisely, are we gaining by withholding the details of what we are doing in Abbey Road from our general user community? I believe that the expectations for Abbey Road are much lower than the reality. I don't think that anybody really expects that we'll deliver multiple on-screen views, smooth surfaces, and database handles in addition to the already announced generalisation of AutoCAD to three dimensions. The total impact of the seamless growth of AutoCAD to 3D — the product of Scott's[160] genius — cannot be appreciated until seen, or better yet, used. If we're in a competitive environment where we've allowed our competitors to create the impression that they have 3D and we don't, then why in the world do we hide the wonder of our 3D release under a bushel? The mere announcement of the feature set for Abbey Road, which could consist of a pre-release of the manual supplement working document would, it seems to me, erect an insurmountable barrier in front of any competitor who based his sell on "AutoCAD lacks 3D". We've already said what, 3D; we've already said when, first half. Why clam up on the details when those details will end all uncertainty about our fully supporting 3D?

Now let's step back from the details of Abbey Road to the more general question of disclosure of our future plans for AutoCAD. And it's AutoCAD I'm talking about — I see nothing to be gained and much to be lost by talking about new products in advance. But if we really believe that AutoCAD has become an industry standard, almost by definition unassailable as long as its vendor maintains a technological lead, then shouldn't we make overt the partnership between the vendor, reseller, customer, and third-party value-adder community which is the essence of a de facto standard?

In one stroke, we'd be moving from the inherently adversarial relationship of those who know with those who must guess to a partnership — a partnership forged from common interest in the future of AutoCAD: those who make it, and those who have bet their companies on it. I think it would lift a veil of implicit conflict almost as obscurant as that of the hardware lock, and with no more consequences on our financial results than our expunging that particular bleeding sore. It would also be a brassy statement of self-confidence mixed with humility: we'll tell you where we're planning to go, and we're listening to you to hear if we're solving the problems you feel are important.

It would also give third party developers a clear message on what areas were safe from Autodesk's future development, and which areas had only a limited window of opportunity before Autodesk entered them. At the technical level, knowing the design of some forthcoming features might be very helpful to a developer in the midst of his own long-term project. For example, knowing how we're doing database handles would guide those who we expect to use them. This

---

160   Scott Heath, the chief architect of Release 10.

communication would not just benefit the developers, however. At every single developer briefing, we discover some oversight in what we've done that would have made the feature much more useful, but which it's too late to change and maintain the shipping schedule. Open, two-way communication would let us remedy these shortcomings before it was too late. After all, the very best guidance on the design of a product comes from the people who are actually using it, and by developing behind a wall, we insulate ourselves from much of the interchange of ideas which could help us provide the best solutions.

From a political standpoint (using "political" in the sense I define it "the means by which groups of three or more humans interact") this would be a golden opportunity to emerge from the marketing disarray and lack of clear strategy of the last two years with a turn that would leave our competitors without a card to play. I would envision Malcolm Davies walking onto the stage in Chicago at the opening session of AutoCAD Expo and saying something like:

"Up to now, Autodesk have been secretive about what we were doing. No more. At this show we are introducing AutoCAD Release 10, extending AutoCAD to fully general three-dimensional model creation. We are also showing AutoCAD on the Macintosh II, OS/2 Release 1, the Sun 386i, and Sun 4, providing a wide variety of hardware options for AutoCAD users who are presently limited by existing personal computer hardware and operating systems. In the sessions that follow we will describe the directions we see for the future development of Autodesk products, and invite your suggestions and comments. From here on, we'll talk openly with you about the composition and scheduling of Release 11, Release 12, and those that will follow. You, our customers, have defined the features we have included in AutoCAD ever since we started, and we seek a two-way dialogue with you."

"You have honoured us by choosing our products for your design work, and your choice has made AutoCAD the worldwide standard for computer aided design. Now it is time for all of us: Autodesk, the users, the resellers, the developers of applications, the manufacturers of hardware that supports AutoCAD, the user groups, the educational institutions that teach AutoCAD, and the authors and publishers of books about AutoCAD, to work together to continue to refine, expand, and develop this standard we have in common. We hope that by making our development plans public, we will stimulate the kind of two-way interchange with the rest of the AutoCAD community that will result in a better product which will serve us all well."

So that's the case for going public with the future of AutoCAD, and how much like "going public"[161] it is: full disclosure, high risk, and much greater visibility after you take the step. But we did pretty well by going public in the financial sense, and we might do just as well by taking that step in the product development arena as well.

If we end up adopting this path, we should immediately undertake the перестройка which will be required to roll out this policy at Expo.

---

161 Making the public stock offering, with all the disclosure in the prospectus.

Where's It All Going?

One of the hardest things for people who haven't been intimately involved in the computer business for at least a decade to grasp is the nature of the exponential growth underway in our industry, and the consequences of continued exponential growth. I believe that many technology-oriented companies fail because the financial or management-oriented executives who run them don't understand how rapidly the underlying technology is developing, and how quickly their companies must change to survive in such an environment.

Every now and then it's worth reminding ourselves that we're on a wild rollercoaster and that failing to aim high enough is as sure a prescription for disaster as falling off. Here's a view of the immediate future I presented at a company meeting in early 1988.

Remarks for the March Company Meeting

by John Walker — March 4th, 1988

Recently, a lot of people have been asking me "where's it all going?". Well, I've been spending some time thinking about that, both because if you get paid to design products, it's nice to know something about the world in which they'll be used, and also because it's embarrassing to have to answer that question "Beats me".

I guess you can't live in Marin County for 14 years without being prone to having "flashes". I was driving through San Rafael last Friday, and suddenly I flashed on this.

"Hey, this *is* the future."

As a typical 1950's technoid kid, I lived for the future. You know: *Mechanix Illustrated*, *Analog* science fiction, "Science Fiction Theatre", "The Outer Limits". Now you drive through San Rafael and what do you see? On this block there's a computer store. Around the corner, a software store. Down the street, there's a hologram store. And two blocks over there's a satellite ground station store.[162]

There's moon rocks in the museums, a space station in orbit, computers on our wrists, and telephones in our shoes. So now what? Would you believe ....

But first, what does this have to do with Autodesk? In thinking about starting Autodesk, I proceeded from two basic assumptions. One: it takes money to develop creative and innovative products and bring them to market. Two: it takes creative and innovative products to make money, or at least to have any fun making money. So when I thought about how to build a successful company, it seemed pretty obvious: hook up a creative engine to a cash machine and throw the switch. And hey, it not only works, there's money left over. Kind of like a high-tech cat and rat farm.

So what's going to be happening to this industry we're in? Things are going to get very weird, very fast. We all know what an IBM AT is, and what it feels like to use one. The current top end machines, such as the Compaq 20/20 and the Sun 3, run about ten times as fast as an AT, and it's that kind of performance that lets us go in for solid modeling, shading, and full 3D on a desktop. But it isn't going to stop there. A couple of weeks ago I took a little machine[163] home that runs *forty* times faster than an AT.[164] And let me tell you, that feels totally different from anything you've used before.

But it isn't going to stop there.

The two magazines I always read are "Aviation Leak"[165] and this one, *Electronics*. I'd just like to quote a few items from just the last two issues of *Electronics*.

"Stellar Computer to introduce $75,000 to $100,000 machine in the next few weeks. 20 – 30 million instructions per second, 40 million floating point operations per second." That will run floating point code like AutoCAD about eighty times faster than an AT.

"Motorola announces a totally new RISC chip for this spring. First shipment will be 17 MIPS, but we'll show our customers how they can hit 50 this year". That's about a hundred and fifty times faster than an AT for our kind of work.

---

162   And near the freeway, there's a store selling "clones — less than $1000". I assume they mean PC clones. I didn't go inside.
163   A Sun 4/260.
164   As measured by my floating point benchmark.
165   *Aviation Week and Space Technology*.

"Ardent launches first supercomputer on a desk. Runs up to 64 million floating point operations per second. Less than $150,000." Call it 200 times faster than an AT.

"Apollo unveils a desktop supercomputer. A true 64 bit workstation, it hits up to 140 million floating point operations per second. Priced below $80,000." Oh, say 450 times faster than an AT.

And where do *those* guys say they're going? After Cray, who's up there at about 3,000 times faster than an AT. And Cray's heading for 30,000, with IBM, ETA, Fujitsu, Hitachi, and NEC in hot pursuit.

And it isn't going to stop there.

Now you might ask, "What in the world do all of these $100,000 to 16 megabuck machines have to do with little ole Autodesk?" The answer lies in the fact that if you open up one of those gilded crunch-o-matics and look inside, you discover that there's really nothing in there but sand and profit.

We aren't running out of sand, and competition will take care of the profit.

So what this means is that the products that we start to develop today will, in the middle part of their life cycle, have machines available for less than ten thousand dollars, which run from one to five hundred times faster than the IBM AT — the platform that carried AutoCAD to its initial success, and from ten to fifty times faster than anything our customers have access to today.

Changes of that magnitude mean much more than nozzles appearing on the screen in 50 microseconds. They portend another qualitative shift in the kinds of products we can deliver to our customers, and those products will change the engineering design cycle at least as much as all of the computerisation to date.

Let's try to look at an Autodesk customer in two or three years. This person will be using a computer that looks little different from those we use today. It'll probably have a larger screen, and that screen will have higher resolution. But look at what's on that screen! All controlled from a common user interface, into which additional products can be plugged like chips into sockets, this user may be dragging the diameter of a weight-reducing hole in a mechanical link. In one window, the shaded image is updated in close to real time. In another, the weight and centre of gravity is being recalculated as the hole changes size, and in a third window, running a little behind, a stress analysis is being run on the part with the load displayed in colour. The design of the part may be overseen by a constraint manager that digests the design rules that bound the problem, and not only helps the designer move among acceptable designs, but even offers advice when a design limit is hit. In minutes, the designer can produce a photographic quality image of the part. And naturally, the manufacturing drawings are automatically updated as the design changes.

The designer will have access to a vast database of design data, will be able to track the design history of a project, and will be able to access large bodies of data and to work with others with the computer facilitating their collaborative endeavours, thus aiding in the evolution of knowledge and the development of sound designs.[166] All of this will shorten the design cycle, increase productivity, and feed back into the process of creating the tools. And, we get *paid* for it.

Autodesk is creating incentives that spawn vibrant, burgeoning, and highly competitive markets for add-on products, extensions to our product line, and new hardware platforms. This will continue to exponentially expand the armamentarium of tools the designer can apply to create better products and bring them to market faster. Those who attempt to define a "total solution", or "control the market" will continue to discover what Autodesk has been teaching them for the last half-decade: that an open system unleashes the talents of tens of thousands of creative people each motivated by their own self-interest, and that their energy and dedication will carry that open system to successes unimagined by those who think they can "plan for the future".

Variation, selection; replication, extinction; innovation, competition; it's been working for billions of years, and it isn't going to stop tomorrow.

I think that most great business successes are the result of somebody tripping over an exponential curve, driving a spike into it, and holding on for dear life. That's what we're doing now. And there's no sign that our curve is turning back down, or that we're losing our grip. Every part of that utopian dream system is the logical outgrowth of work which is already underway at Autodesk, and by the time it comes together in, say, two years, there's no doubt in my mind that the computer power it needs will be in the hands of our users.

And the beauty of it is, we don't have to disappear into a corner and make something new. We will evolve our way there, product by product, release by release, feature by feature, with the market we've created guiding us and everybody else in it toward the best solutions to the problems it faces.

Well, time's up. Enough of the distant blue-sky horizons 24 months from now. We have to get back to the future.

---

[166] Such as a Xanadu system, for example. The Xanadu deal was underway but not announced at this point.

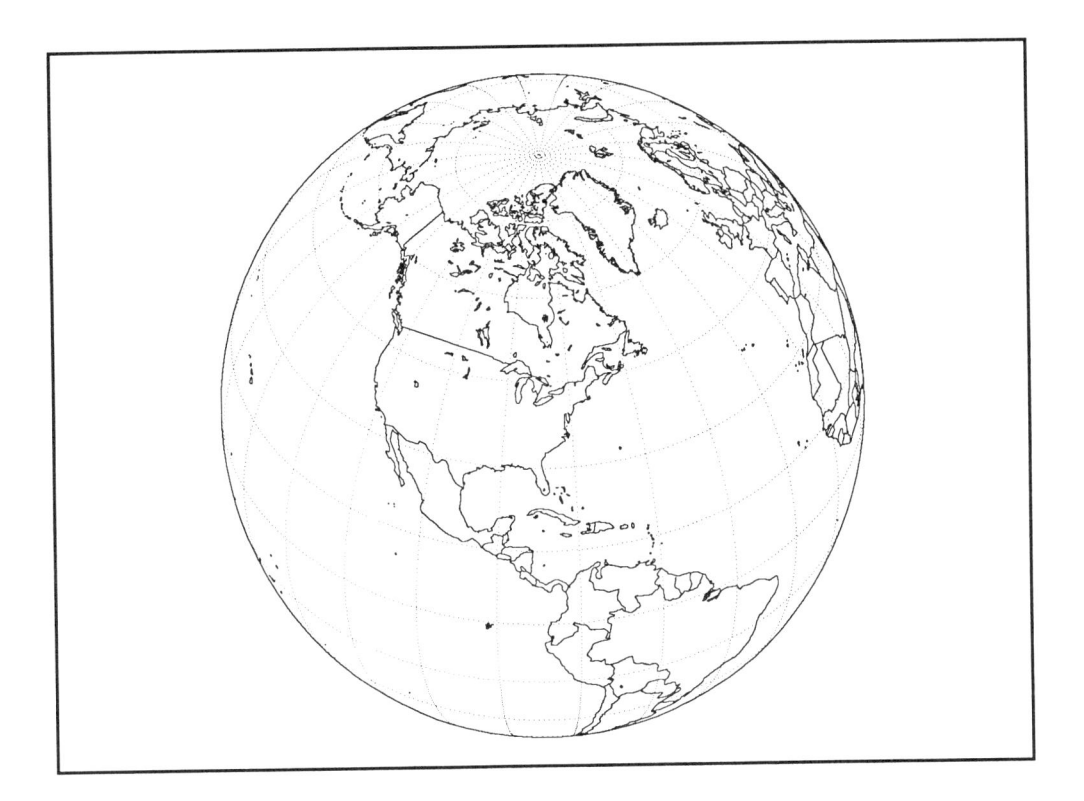

Every now and then I try to push a new feature of AutoCAD off the deep end to see if anything gives way. After adding three dimensional space polylines to the AutoCAD Release 10 development version, I used a map database to build a three dimensional model of the Earth's surface. This model, over 3.5 megabytes on disc, can be viewed from any point in space with an AutoLisp routine. This full-Earth view is centred on Cleveland, Ohio.

Xanadu

Many people within Autodesk have long been aware of Ted Nelson's work and the efforts to implement the Xanadu hypertext system. Before his involvement with Marinchip and later Autodesk, Lars Moureau met Ted Nelson in Stockholm and was instrumental in getting his books translated to Swedish and published in Sweden.

At the Hackers' Conference in October 1987 I spoke to Roger Gregory, President of Xanadu Operating Company, which was formed to implement Xanadu, about Autodesk acting as a beta site for a commercial Xanadu system. As we continued the discussion there and at several subsequent meetings, it became increasingly clear that a partnership between Xanadu and Autodesk might be beneficial to both parties; Autodesk had the financial resources and distribution to implement and launch the product and Xanadu had the technology and talented people who could build it. A Xanadu system could easily solve the data and project management tasks that Autodesk realised it needed to solve for users of its products, while offering them much more than just a drawing manager.

We eventually decided that Autodesk would purchase 80% of Xanadu and fund the development of the product. Ted Nelson came to Autodesk as a Distinguished Fellow, both to guide the development and promotion of Xanadu, and to explore other areas of research. What follows are the remarks I made at the press conference at the West Coast Computer Faire where the alliance between Autodesk and Xanadu was announced.

Statement for the Autodesk/Xanadu Press Conference

by John Walker
April 8th, 1988

The age we live in has been called many things: the Space Age, the Computer Age, the Atomic Age, the Age of the Microchip. But perhaps the most accurate appellation is "the Information Age".

Most of us have witnessed, in our own lifetimes, the unraveling of the genetic code, the uncovering of a new level of structure of matter which may, at last, prove "fundamental", cosmology transformed from a branch of philosophy into an experimental science, and through exploration by resourceful robots and brave men and women, our base of knowledge growing from one Earth to dozens of worlds.

As our fundamental knowledge has grown, so have our capacities to apply that knowledge through new technologies. It is now obvious to any thoughtful person that our powers are so great and our resources so large, that sound judgement based on accurate information is the most essential ingredient in the continuing progress of our technological civilisation. Yet often it seems that this unprecedented explosion of information has outstripped our ability to store, process, think about, distribute, and apply it. As our future becomes more dependent on making the right choices in highly complicated problem domains, the nineteenth-century means of communication we still largely use: professional journals, libraries, and mail, become increasingly inadequate as vehicles to store, transmit, and mediate the growth of human knowledge.

Over two decades ago, the idea that there might be a solution to the problem not yet named the "information explosion" began to form in the minds of a few technologists. The confluence of technological advancements in computers and communications, coupled with an understanding of how humans distill knowledge from a sea of information and the centuries-old literary tradition led these thinkers to imagine a new medium to represent knowledge. Theodor Nelson, one of the first to explore the potential of this medium, coined a name for it, "hypertext", and gave its realisation the name "Xanadu".

In 1964, Xanadu was a dream in a single mind. In 1980, it was the shared goal of a small group of brilliant technologists. By 1989, it will be a product. And by 1995 it will begin to change the world.

Much work remains to be done to realise the potential of Xanadu — it will take the Xanadu development team 18 months to field the first Xanadu system. This will be followed by a steady stream of releases bringing added power, capacity, and flexibility to Xanadu users. As these first users explore the potential of Xanadu, they will help define the market for true hypertext systems, a market which barely exists today. But as Autodesk has demonstrated, much can happen in five years.

Five years ago Autodesk began delivering computer-aided design technology to the desktops of designers around the world. Our first product, AutoCAD, has become the de facto standard for computer aided design, and has created a large market for computer aided design tools for personal computers. Autodesk's sales have grown from $17,000 in 1982 to more than $79 million in 1987, and Autodesk has been named the Number One Hot Growth Company in America by *Business Week* magazine in each of the last two years. Autodesk's success has come from identifying new ways the personal computer could be applied to solve the problems people encounter in getting their work done, then developing, marketing, distributing, and supporting products which solve those problems.

We believed in 1982 that the time was right to deliver computer aided design to any creative individual with a personal computer. Today, we believe it's time to place the dream and potential of hypertext in the hands of the millions of people whose productivity, creativity, and achievement can be amplified by such a tool.

We believe that Xanadu is not just the first hypertext system, but the only system that has the potential to serve the individual, the workgroup or small company, the large corporation, and eventually the entire world as a repository for information in all forms: text, graphics, sound, animation, scientific and engineering data, and more. Xanadu acts as a tool for the human minds which must find order among the chaotic barrage of information that inundates us. Xanadu allows people to work together more productively in ways that existing electronic mail, databases, and online services only hint at.

Xanadu has reached the point where theory must move into practice, design into implementation, and prototype into product. Autodesk and Xanadu are forming this alliance because we share the belief that Autodesk's financial, marketing, distribution, and manufacturing resources, coupled with the vision, concrete design, implementation experience, and the talent and energy of the Xanadu implementation team can bring an initial Xanadu system to the market within 18 months.

The Xanadu design is unique in that it rejects from the outset all limits on generality, capacity, and extensibility. Implementing it in its entirety will be difficult, protracted, and expensive, but no system less ambitious can be as useful, as powerful, or as important for the long term.

Following the first Xanadu product, we will, as with AutoCAD, follow the guidance of the market in delivering increasingly powerful Xanadu systems to an ever-widening community of users. Our near-term commitment to deliver small-scale Xanadu systems in no way signals a retreat from the dream of the Xanadu global library. Autodesk and Xanadu are embarking on this venture with the goal of expediting the achievement of Theodor Nelson's original vision, and to build a successful business which will continue the development of Xanadu to the global library and beyond. As with AutoCAD, every byte of information stored in the first Xanadu system we ship will be able to move onward to future systems, new computers, and growing networks, and will take its place in the ever-growing body of human knowledge stored in the Xanadu system.

As with AutoCAD, Xanadu is an open architecture system. Our access protocols will be fully disclosed and published. We will encourage others to invent innovative ways to encode, store, retrieve, and organise information stored in our ever-growing address space. We will rely on the judgement of customers in a free market to decide what are the best approaches, and we will heed that judgement as the best guide for the future development of the Xanadu system.

The promise of hypertext is self-evident. The visionary scope and technological soundness of the Xanadu design implements that promise in its fullness. The talent of the Xanadu team and the resources of Autodesk will bring that design to market in 1989. And the Xanadu era will begin.

Ted Nelson Joins Autodesk

This is the press release we issued on the event of Ted Nelson joining Autodesk.

Autodesk Announces New Fellowship

Sausalito, California, April 8, 1988 — Autodesk, Inc. announced today the appointment of Theodor Holm Nelson as a Distinguished Fellow. Ted will work in the Technology department at Autodesk's Sausalito office. Mr. Nelson, a world-famous visionary in computing, is one of the original developers of the hypertext concept and coined the term "hypertext" itself in the early 1960's. In 1979 Mr. Nelson joined with several others to found Xanadu Operating Company to develop hypertext as a commercial reality. Autodesk announced earlier this week that it had agreed to acquire an 80% interest in Xanadu.

Ted, a prolific author, has written numerous volumes, two of which are considered classics in the field: *Literary Machines* and *Computer Lib/Dream Machines* (recently re-issued by Microsoft Press). "Autodesk has always been committed to be the technological leader in the software industry," said Eric Lyons, Director of Technology at Autodesk. "We look forward to Ted's agile and prolific mind helping us to achieve that goal."

Ted Nelson — the man *Time* magazine called "[one of] the brightest stars in computerdom", the man Howard Rheingold, in *Tools for Thought*, called "the most outrageous and probably the funniest of the 'infonauts'", the man *Playgirl's* American Bachelor's Register called "the mad poet of computerdom" — Ted Nelson, maverick software designer, flamboyant legend, idealistic prognosticator, eloquent generalist, and now Distinguished Fellow at Autodesk.

Ted Nelson is where he belongs.

Bored of Directors

Having unloaded the job of President on Al Green in November of 1986, I was still left with the title of Chairman of the Board. As a consequence, I still ended up being asked to "say a few words" from time to time, to come up with comments for press releases (just try being pithy, quotable, and bland all at the same time), and I continued to be the recipient of letters and phone calls from virtually everybody who our company managed to annoy in the course of its business.

Since I am, by nature, about as gregarious as a moray eel, this began to take its toll on my ability to get productive work done. So, in early 1988, I decided to get rid of the silly Chairman title at the next annual meeting so I could program without being bothered. Since we are a public company and Everything Must Be Disclosed, we had to issue a press release bruiting this momentous announcement. Of course one must adhere to the standards of propriety on the financial wire, so we couldn't put anything interesting in the public release. That didn't stop Dan Drake from penning the following internal announcement, which was distributed within the company on April 15th, 1988.

Today or Monday we'll put out a press release, worded more or less respectably, to the same effect as what follows. What follows is the more truthful version for the benefit of Autodesk people. It speaks for itself; therefore, I'll stop speaking for it.

Autodesk, Inc. announced today that John Walker, a founder and Chairman of the Board, will not stand for re-election to its Board of Directors at its annual meeting on June 10. Alvar J. Green, the company's President and Chief Executive Officer, will assume the title of chairman. The board will be reduced from six members to five.

Mr. Walker remains with the company as a software developer, a role he has filled continuously since the company's inception in 1982.

Walker declaimed, "Ever since Autodesk was founded, my primary responsibility has been identifying product ideas, designing, implementing, and bringing products to market. This has been my most important contribution to Autodesk and it's what I do best. My goal in founding Autodesk was to build a large, profitable, financially strong, and professionally managed company that could turn product ideas into successful products that open new markets. When serving as president of Autodesk began to interfere with my ability to do these tasks, I stuck Al Green with the job. He's done it far better than I could have, and he's led Autodesk to its greatest successes. Now I find that far too many pithecanthropoids still think I 'call the shots' or want to use me as figurehead for a family of companies operating in six countries, made up of more than 400 independent, talented, and dedicated people. Consequently, far too much of the time I should be devoting to product development is being wasted on nonproductive tasks, merely because I'm Chairman."

"Now that Autodesk has achieved market leadership with AutoCAD, it is even more important that Autodesk introduce a wide variety of new products and enhancements to existing products, broadening the market for Autodesk products. By eliminating the distractions engendered by serving as Chairman, I can devote myself full time to these clamant tasks. Believing, as I do, that our industry progresses through innovation, not litigation, I will henceforth devote all my efforts to product development."

Daniel Drake, Executive Vice President, remarked, "While he was president and chairman, John invented the AutoSketch and AutoShade products and a number of other things, some of which aren't ready to be disclosed yet. That doesn't mean he wrote a spec in his spare time for some robot to implement; he wrote the first working version of the programs and worked with other programmers through the long process of product development and release. Since that's what he likes to do best, and giving dumb speeches, reading reams of legalese, and talking to boring people on the telephone is what he likes least, this change increases the likelihood that Mr. Walker will continue to effectively contribute to Autodesk's success in the coming years."

Mr. Drake deprecated the suggestion that Mr. Walker would "do a Mitch Kapor": sell all his stock and start a new company. "Whatever you say about John, he's quite bright enough to learn from experience. Besides, I'd kill him", said Mr. Drake in a paragraph he wishes he could include in the release.

Autodesk designs, manufactures, sells, etc. all the boilerplate that we put at the end of a press release.

Valedictory

The Autodesk annual shareholders' meeting on June 10th, 1988 marked the point where I relinquished the title of chairman (or as I usually put it, always afraid of offending, "chairbeing"). Since I had held that title since the inception of the company, and since my transition to total focus on the technological future of the company was now complete, the meeting seemed an apt time to sum up the first six years and comment on the perceived opportunities which compelled me to concentrate on software development as my best contribution to Autodesk's future.

Since this will be my last meeting as chairman, I'd like to take a few minutes to share with you my view of where the company is, how we got there, where we're going, and what I'm going to be doing in the future to see that we arrive safely.

When I was thinking about starting Autodesk in 1982, the local paper ran an article about software companies in Marin County. It said that the opportunity to start new ones had closed because "all the basic tools had been put on the computer".

This didn't make any sense to me. It seemed obvious that the new wave of mass-produced and mass-marketed personal computers would create ample opportunities for new products to perform tasks made possible, for the first time, by those new machines. In fact, the small group of people who founded Autodesk identified five such products, and we decided to work on all of them and see which one took off. One of our five products was AutoCAD — and its success in creating a new market for a new tool on the personal computer is what has brought us all here today.

Over the six-year history of Autodesk, technological progress in delivering affordable computer power to the mass market has, if anything, accelerated. The products we're developing today can expect, in the middle of their lifecycles, to run on computers 100 times faster than the computer that ran the first copy of AutoCAD — yet they'll cost no more than that first system. By the time Autodesk celebrates its first decade, we can expect to see affordable computers ten times faster than that entering the market, and there is no reason to believe it will stop there, either.

All of this computer power is pointless unless we can think of something to do with it. Who cares if you can recalculate your spreadsheet in 10 microseconds instead of 10 milliseconds? Fortunately, there is no shortage of tasks to which this kind of computational power can be applied — and Autodesk is superbly positioned to take advantage of this opportunity, which will create many entirely new product categories and markets, just as the IBM PC generation enabled us to create AutoCAD.

Let's think for a moment about what it is that Autodesk does — at the highest level. All of our products are basically in the business of putting models of real-world objects into a computer, and then letting you do things with them. This is a fundamentally different, and more interesting, business than twiddling numbers on a spreadsheet, shuffling text in a word processor, or whatever boring things a database does. It's different because every increment of computer power, graphics performance, large low-cost storage, or new computer architecture lets us get closer to a complete model of a real world system. As we continue to approach the ideal of a complete model, we're able to do more things with the computer model, and these things turn into products we can sell, to users who already understand the need for those new tools.

AutoCAD started out as a simple two dimensional drafting system. When we got computers with more memory and faster processors like the 80286, we were able to make AutoCAD programmable. This allowed us, and hundreds of third parties, to create applications that customise AutoCAD for vertical markets. Our own AutoCAD AEC Architectural has become the leading architectural design product in the United States, and we expect our recently-introduced AutoCAD AEC Mechanical to similarly dominate the heating, ventilation, and air conditioning market.

As AutoCAD was extended into a three-dimensional modeling system, we were able to use those models to generate realistic shaded pictures. The advent of low-cost, high-resolution, colour displays enabled us to introduce AutoShade, which is placing shaded rendering in the hands of thousands of customers who previously thought it far out of their reach. And recently, we've shipped AutoFlix, which adds animation to the list of things you can do with that model inside your computer.

And still our models continue to become more accurate. AutoCAD Release 10, announced at the recent AutoCAD Expo trade show, dramatically increases AutoCAD's three-dimensional capabilities, adding surface modeling and multiple views. AutoSolid, now shipping, delivers true solid modeling to the mechanical designer. From an AutoSolid model, you can calculate mass properties, perform finite element analysis, and begin to forge the direct links from design to manufacturing which are so essential to increasing manufacturing productivity.

We also recognised that many problems don't require a tool as powerful and complicated as AutoCAD, so we introduced AutoSketch for less than $100. It can put computer aided design in the hands of anybody who draws. And we've sold more than 60,000 of them.

But you know all that ... what about the future?

I believe that technological progress now underway is creating opportunities, as large or larger than the 1982 prospects for AutoCAD. Further, I believe that Autodesk is uniquely positioned to exploit these opportunities and thereby to prosper.

One of the great things about the CAD business is that you never run out of a desire for more powerful computers and more comprehensive modeling software. Extending the degree to which our products approximate reality, making models easier to build and manipulate, and enriching the ways in which one can interact with these models can easily consume all of the computer power we can envision, as far as we can foresee. This means that adding capabilities to all of our current products, adapting them to take advantage of developments in computer hardware, and extending our product line by adding additional modeling, rendering, and analysis tools will keep Autodesk's product family growing in size, and will open new markets and application areas for our products.

In addition, more powerful computers and networks will allow our customers to integrate the design, drafting, analysis, and manufacturing functions much more closely. Autodesk is the only software vendor whose products maintain complete compatibility across all computer hardware, and our commitment to open architecture makes our products the obvious choice for this integration. We are developing our products so they work equally well for the customer with one isolated desktop computer, and the customer with 10,000 workstations distributed around the world. Both are key to our success; both are central to our strategy; both deserve the best products we can design.

Most industries are founded on a single, simple idea, such as "cheap cars for everybody" or "machines to automate business". Autodesk remains the only software company committed to "putting the real world inside the computer", and we believe this idea has potential as great as those that spawned the great industries of the past.

There's a lot more to the real world than houses, turbine blades, and circuit boards.

The real world is also a world of words and ideas, images and information. When we recently acquired 80% of Xanadu Operating Company, we undertook the task of putting that world into the computer, as well. The dream of hypertext, and the ability to store, organise, retrieve, annotate, and present information in ways that do not mimic paper, but are fundamentally better, has inspired a generation of thinkers. We believe that Xanadu can benefit anyone who reads, writes, and thinks, and is applicable at scales ranging from an individual's personal computer to a global library storing all of human knowledge. We expect to ship the first commercial

Xanadu system in less than 18 months. And Theodor Nelson, who invented Xanadu and coined the word "hypertext", has joined Autodesk to help us do it.

Ideas are precious and rare. They should be immortal. Most ideas are lost, most discoveries ignored, most interrelationships unremarked upon because we have no effective way to store and then find them. Galileo observed Neptune, but nobody noticed until the 1980's. Most ideas are committed to bits of paper, obscure professional journals, or computer media made obsolete by the next wave of innovation and are lost forever. We can't afford to lose 90% of the products of our collective minds. Xanadu is intended to fix this, and we believe that in time it will become as universal a product for people who think as television is for people who don't. And if this happens, we will sell *lots* of them.

Autodesk's current products as well as Xanadu are converging to address another large opportunity — building tools that help people work together more effectively. We talk about personal computers. But how many people, even free-lancers, work in total isolation? The computer will come to play a role as fundamental in communication and collaboration among people as in facilitating the work of an individual. To succeed, it must enhance individual creativity, not stifle it.

Too many computer systems seem like one-lane roads where all must proceed at the pace of the slowest. We need instead to design freeways for the mind, where people can work together, each proceeding at his own pace, without impeding or imperiling others. Products that do this effectively will yield rapid and dramatic productivity gains, and create new product categories in the software industry.

As our computer models become richer, and the ways we can manipulate them increase, creativity in devising how we interact with these models will be rewarded by making them accessible to many more people, broadening the market for our products. The AutoCAD customer who, in 1982, squinted at a low-resolution screen while typing in commands from a keyboard, can today create animated colour movies of three dimensional models built largely by pointing to a screen. I believe that progress in user interfaces has only begun.

While the faltering leaders of the last technological revolution are suing each other over how their screens look, the pioneers of the next are developing tools that will take the user *through* the screen, and allow direct interaction with the data in the computer, whether as concrete as a connecting rod, or as abstract as the history of revisions to a document. Using a computer involves suspension of disbelief just as much as reading a novel. The ways people will use the tools and models we create will continue to evolve, just as styles in writing and filmmaking change with the times. Innovation spawns progress; litigation impedes it.

So what does the future look like for Autodesk? We're a software company. We build and sell tools. As long as there is demand for new tools, there will always be opportunities for great successes with software products. Anybody who thinks that all possible software tools have been invented is unimaginative, uninformed, or just stupid — man has been called the animal that creates tools — we've been at it for millions of years, and I don't think we're going to tire of it this quarter, this year, or this millennium. Autodesk has prospered so far from a tool that solves a fundamental problem — drawing and design. Autodesk will prosper in the future by continuing to develop that tool, and by creating and selling new ones that solve other problems as profound and fundamental.

The newspaper's claim in 1982 that "all the tools had been done" was actually profound as well as silly. The software that can be done at any point in time depends upon the computer power then available in the mass market. Computer power is now rising exponentially at constant price, and Autodesk is one of the few companies working seriously on products to take advantage of it.

Developing new products is difficult. I know — we've done 8 since 1982, but if we apply the same humility we had during the evolution of AutoCAD, I believe we'll continue to develop products which solve new problems and create new markets for the personal computer. In 1983 people used to ask us about "our vision of the future of CAD". We used to say in all candour, "we don't really know enough about CAD to have one". But we had a secret. We knew somebody who *did* know — our customers. No vendor in any market knows as much about his product, how it is being applied, where its shortcomings are, and what is needed to make it better, as the customers using it. And today, we have more CAD customers than any other company in the business, and they continue to guide the development of AutoCAD and all our other products. Hubris, borne of detachment from the real problems facing customers, has doomed many technology companies. That's not going to happen at Autodesk, because we still don't know enough to chart the future of anything. But we listen patiently, and we take lots of notes.

So we don't know what the future will bring, but we do think we know how to get there. This company was founded on the idea of developing 5 products and getting behind whichever one took off. I like to be able to be wrong 80% of the time and still do well. It worked, and we will continue to follow that evolutionary approach to the marketplace as we have for six years. Many things we try may not work, but we expect those that do to form the foundation of our future prosperity. This isn't all that unusual an approach — every investor with a diversified portfolio is doing the same thing. I think that companies don't like to admit they're being guided by the market because you get credit for being a brilliant planner, not for being a careful observer. Evolution looks like planning when you look back in time — that's why so many people have trouble understanding it. In fact, market-driven pragmatism not only works; it *pays* well.

Getting there won't be easy. But getting *here* wasn't easy. We've seen competitive products from IBM, CalComp, AT&T, and Computervision come and go. We've lived through the worst stock market crash in history. We've seen overt theft of our products, and we've discovered how hard it is to stop it. We've made misjudgements of the market and we've corrected our course. Sometimes we've been wrong, but we never stayed wrong too long. I'm not going to stand here and tell you that Autodesk will never have a bad quarter or never screw up. But I do believe that as long as Autodesk remains focused on the enormous opportunities we face, as long as we act prudently and responsibly to take advantage of them, what will be called Autodesk's period of great growth and success lies in the future, not in the past six years. And it is a measure of my confidence that the management and directors of Autodesk will achieve this that I have no hesitation whatsoever in entrusting the operation of our company to them.

Many of the things we need to do are obvious. But just because they're obvious doesn't mean they're easy. It is because I believe that the technical work ahead of us is so great, so important, and the benefits to Autodesk are so enormous, that I will be focusing all of my energies on these tasks, swearing off meetings with lawyers, giving speeches, signing checks, filling out forms, talking to analysts, and all of the other fun things that I got to do while chairman.

For whatever reasons, we've all wound up owning a company that's right in the middle of an exponentially growing technological revolution that's remaking our world. Many companies share this position with us. But we know where we are — and we think we know what to do about it.

Many companies have abandoned an optimistic view of the future. Starting a company out of thin air at the bottom of a recession with almost no money and seeing it grow into this in six years, largely as a result of simply plugging away day and night on the mundane, near-term tasks that had to be done, is a wonderful antidote for pessimism. It gives you great confidence in continuing to reach for further success and achievement that same way — getting all the details right, but never losing sight of where success can carry us. Without imagination we are all doomed to live in a grey world devoid of hope and excitement, fortune and glory. We talk about the Golden Age of Engineering. It's our age — if we work to build it. To achieve it, we must toil tirelessly at the gory details. If we invest that effort, our achievements will be unbounded, our horizons endless, and the potential for Autodesk incalculable.

Thank you for the confidence and trust you've placed in me the past six years.

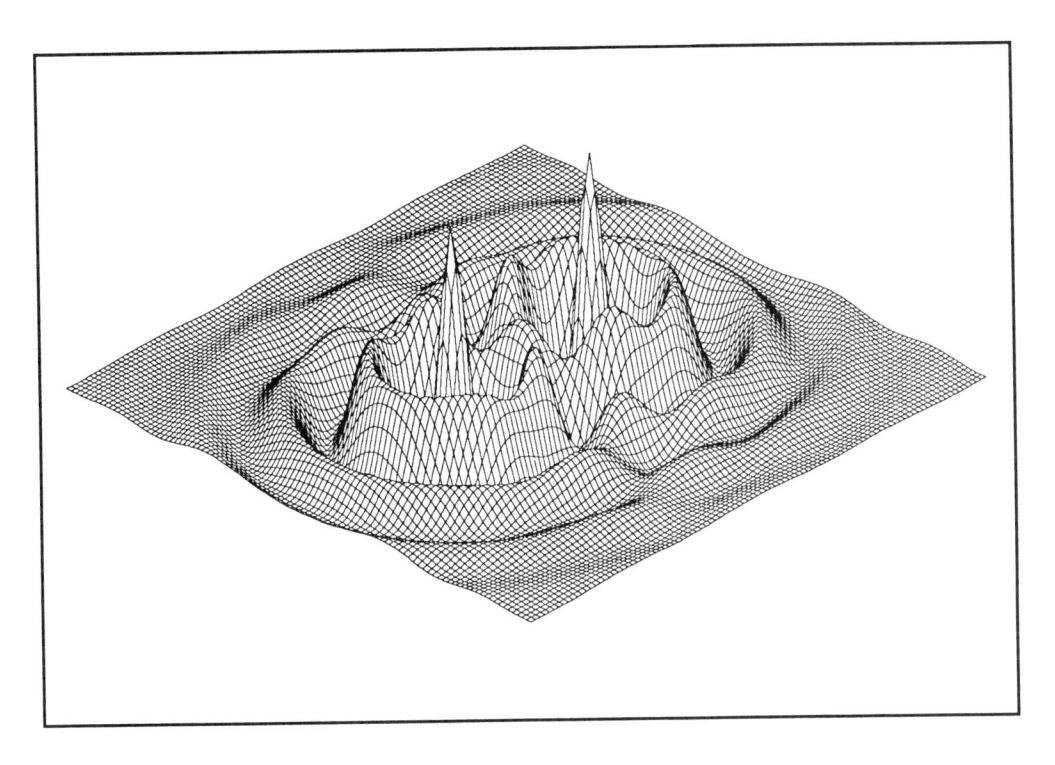

The ongoing development of AutoCAD is extending it into a general three-dimensional surface modeler. AutoCAD Release 10 adds polygon meshes, providing a general surface object. This allows new applications, such as modeling the surface defined by functions of two variables. Here's an interference pattern generated by two huge polygon meshes with interesting cases

The View From Sweden

Before the founding of Autodesk, Lars Åke Moureau was the proprietor of Smådatorinstitutet AB in Onsala, Sweden. Lars' company was one of Marinchip's very first dealers, and throughout Marinchip's history, one of the most successful. As few documents chronicling the growth of Autodesk outside the United States were available for this compilation, Lars contributed this view of Autodesk from the other side of the ocean. Unless otherwise identified, the footnotes are mine.

The notes I have from Autodesk and my participation in it are a mixture of business and personal matters. I am deliberately leaving out all personal (noninteresting) comments. The notes are written in a sort of diary form as virtually no meeting minutes were distributed. The goal is to give a viewpoint from overseas as I started to market Autodesk products in Scandinavia and later formed Autodesk AB, a wholly owned subsidiary of Autodesk, Inc.

Sweden, Fall 1981

This is it! People are now coming to *my* place to take a look at Interact, traveling 6 hours for a one hour demonstration. Never before in my computer career have I had a product that excites people like this. Interact is unusable as-is but with some extensions and new hardware it could make it.

Fortunately I only sold one Interact system to an existing Marinchip customer. He was never able to do any real work (PC-board) with it — but it sure was fun.

London, August 1982

Meeting in London with Rudolf Künzli and Richard Handyside. John Walker came later.[167] I read through a lot of material[168] for the company that later would be Autodesk Inc. John Walker brought with him his first version of MicroCAD (later renamed AutoCAD), written in PL/I (the listing could be carried in a briefcase then) and he was debugging the code as problems came up during the demonstration we had at Richard's office in London.

John Walker also brought with him some disks with a demo for a new super-machine called the Victor 9000. This was the first time I saw CAD on a "modern" PC.[169]

At the end of John Walker's stay in London, he and Richard went to a demonstration of a competing product, the Robocom BitStik.[170] It ran on an Apple II. The comment I later got was, "We drove to Dover to find the largest cliff from which to throw ourselves."[171] The BitStik was a superior product at that time. John Walker flew home and rewrote the whole code for better performance and enhancements.

---

167 This was the Autodesk/Marinchip dealers' meeting mentioned in Information Letter 7, which occurred on August 7–8th, 1982. Prior to this point I had not asked Lars about joining Autodesk because in all of my conversations with him he seemed totally focused on selling hardware systems based on Texas Instruments processors. At the London meeting it was clear that he was interested in a venture like Autodesk, and we asked him to join the company.

168 The Working Paper and Information Letters to date.

169 Well, kinda. The Victor demo was one of the sleaziest things I have ever done. We didn't have the 8086 version even close to running on the Victor, but we wanted to be able to show the "potential of CAD on the Victor", so I wrote a plot-to-file driver for Interact on the Marinchip 9900. This wrote what we would call slide files today. Then I wrote a BASIC program on the Victor that read these slides and drew them on the screen using a Victor-supplied graphics driver for BASIC. It worked well enough to convince Victor and many Victor dealers that CAD on a PC was real — even if it wasn't real quite yet.

170 The BitStik certainly was impressive, especially when you consider that it ran on a 64K Apple II. I brought one back from London and demonstrated it at the August 28th, 1982 meeting. Trivia lovers should note that the BitStik is also, to my knowledge, the only PC-based CAD product to ever appear in a James Bond movie *(For Your Eyes Only)*.

171 Hyperbole and exaggeration. After the demo, I merely asked Richard if the Post Office tower was the best place from which to hurl my humiliated body.

Göteborg Sweden, November 1982

This was the first time AutoCAD was shown in public in Scandinavia. I borrowed a Victor/Sirius[172] computer from the Scandinavian distributor Esselte, and had a set of drawings only to run on that machine. It was a 10' x 10' booth shared with an electrical utility product line. My strongest memory was when I came back to home at 4 A.M. after setting up the booth I was so exhausted I could not get out of the car. I fell asleep after pulling the handbrake.

London, January 1983

Rudolf, Richard, and I loaded Richard's Saab and drove from London to Birmingham to participate in the "Which Computer?" show. We had no booth of our own, just a desk in the Victor distributor's booth. We were now showing AutoCAD on the Victor with a touch-screen device[173] (looks like a light pen but acts nicer). We also brought a Hewlett-Packard plotter which we never got working during the show.

At this show Autodesk Europe took its first stumbling steps. Rudolf ran his business from his cellar, Richard from a combined computer/bookstore, and I from a 400 square foot garage in Sweden.

At this show in Birmingham, IBM made its first official appearance with the IBM PC made in Ireland. AutoCAD was about to be ported to IBM that time, but the Victor was superior to IBM in every respect.

The Victor computer pushed AutoCAD a lot in the first years. In Sweden a company called Esselte had the distributorship for Victor and they promoted AutoCAD enormously. I believe that Esselte laid one of the cornerstones for the success of AutoCAD in Sweden.

Hannover Germany, Spring 1983

Richard, Rudolf and I participated in the Victor booth at the Hannover Fair. Chuck Peddle (the wizard of Victor Computer) came one day into the booth and he was like a movie star with the usual courtiers surrounding him.

---

[172] The Victor 9000 was sold as the Sirius outside the United States. It was the same machine.
[173] This was the Sun-Flex Touch Pen.

Staying at a *gasthaus*[174] 30 miles from the show we had conversations with Autodesk in the USA at midnight. Autodesk proposed to give Sun-Flex (who made the touch-screen device) the exclusive right to sell AutoCAD on Victor worldwide. This was a slap in the face of all of us in Europe who were now building a dealer network. As we were all dealing directly with customers and dealers, we were developing a feeling for how AutoCAD should be sold and we knew that it was wrong to try to sell AutoCAD through hardware vendors. Sun-Flex got a contract excluding Europe and Autodesk probably survived at that point by large orders from Sun-Flex (100 systems/several times — wow!).

This has since been proven by our experience with all the big hardware manufacturers. Autodesk has had numerous OEM contracts, which helped us in the beginning as they endorsed our then-unknown product. It turned out, however, that selling CAD on a PC has its own difficulties, which require the support of a local dealer. Consequently, the OEM found himself with a big inventory of AutoCAD and decided to push hardware by discounting AutoCAD — thus upsetting the whole dealer network.

Visit to Autodesk, Inc., June 1983

This was my first visit to Autodesk Inc. Autodesk had no real office yet.[175] There was a condo with 3 IBM PCs for disc copying and a few people for distribution. We had a wishlist meeting[176] at John Walker's house and a technical meeting[177] in the South Bay.

One meeting was at Sun-Flex, a 20 minute trip north of the office. Nothing really came out of the meeting other than a wish list of features for AutoCAD. AutoCAD on the Victor was still outselling the IBM PC but its lead was shrinking.

Oslo Norway, June 1983

AutoCAD was shown by a Victor distributor. I met with a representative of a big, big company that wanted to sell AutoCAD. I began to realize what power there

---

174 Richard Handyside later described the amenities of this establishment as being as close to Fawlty Towers as he ever wishes to encounter. The conversation Lars describes was conducted on the U.S. end from Mike Ford's house in sunny California, and from the European end from a phone in an unheated corridor.
175 Hey, that *was* the real office. A month before that we were copying discs in Mike Ford's house.
176 Duff Kurland's notes from that meeting are presented in the AutoCAD Wish List in Appendix F.
177 See Kern Sibbald's notes from that meeting in the June 1983 Meeting.

was in AutoCAD as a sales tool for hardware, as this company was going to force the sales of their exclusive computer by limiting sales of AutoCAD to that machine only. I also received numerous threats and intimidation from them as I tried to straighten things out. That had never happened with any computer product I carried before.

Göteborg Sweden, July 1983

I had moved to Göteborg from the rural place in the countryside, but still was a one man show. The distribution organization was beginning to come together. There were no strategy guidelines from Autodesk, Inc. about marketing, distribution, and the like,[178] so I had to create my own.

Copenhagen Denmark, August 1983

First meeting with the Danish distributor — they seemed to be very concerned and took me for a ride around Copenhagen. At this time there was no money to fly so all traveling was done by car. (I wore out two engines and got two speeding tickets during 1982 – 1985.)

Göteborg Sweden, December 1983

European meeting at my office in Sweden. The idea of forming wholly owned subsidiaries was discussed on an initiative from Rudolf and Richard. The outline was discussed for budgets and marketing. The premises I had were too small so I was looking for a new place. I still did not have an IBM PC, and had only 2 Victor machines. The customer base was well over 100 systems and growing.[179]

London, January 1984

Richard had his own booth at the "Which Computer?" show and it was a success. Lots of items were discussed at nights in the hotel; all meetings were informal and more of an advisory type.

Onsala Sweden, March 1984

Back in the garage again. The distributor organization was getting bigger with Norway, Denmark, Finland, Iceland, and Sweden. The workload was beginning to become unbearable.

---

178   Autonomy through neglect — long an Autodesk tradition.
179   Lars notes that in January of 1988 Sweden sold their 10,000th copy of AutoCAD.

I was still doing everything myself: translating manuals, manufacturing, accounting, additional hardware sales, marketing, literature, negotiations, demonstrations, etc. Without the help from the distributors taking care of their territories this would have been impossible.

Basel Switzerland, May 1984

I visited Rudolf in Basel and made Swedish versions of AutoCAD 1.4. It took about 36 hours. After that I went to London and met with Al Green.[180] Al had just been hired, and coordinated the audit of the overseas offices which were going to become wholly-owned subsidiaries of Autodesk, Inc. At this time Autodesk, Inc. looked into getting capital from venture capitalists. Al was hired as Chief Financial Officer and opposed the plans of getting venture capital. The capital needed could, by better management, come from the cash flow. (Al Green, who later became president of Autodesk, Inc., managed the cash flow and later was instrumental in Autodesk's public stock offering.)

Sausalito USA, June 1984

Time for the yearly visit to Autodesk, Inc. It had now moved to bigger premises and was looking greater than ever. Sales were now beginning to ramp up and people were being hired for support, training, etc. In Europe we tried to establish some kind of policy and strategy. We still lacked guidelines from USA on how to attack the market and how to deal with OEMs and dealer networks, so we made our own policies and strategies for Europe. I was contacted by a Norwegian firm to make a port to a Scandinavian computer called Compis or Scandis. Seemed to be an easy task, but it almost got me killed. I finally got it done with help from the Swiss office.

---

180 When Al was hired as Chief Financial Officer, he spent his first week on the job in London, trying to figure out how we could get unified finance and accounting information, which we'd surely need in the future.

Onsala Sweden, August 1984

Autodesk AB[181] was finally constituted. I hired 2 more people but was still in the garage. We had about 300 customers at this point.

Onsala Sweden, September 1984

Visit from the USA to Europe. Mike Ford, VP of Marketing, visited every office and it felt fine to have direct communication and make the people at the main office understand what was going on at the rural offices.[182]

Sausalito USA, October 1984

One distributor was trying to bypass Autodesk AB by going to Autodesk, Inc. and making a direct agreement. At the same time a Scandis computer representative wanted to have an OEM agreement directly with Autodesk, Inc. This was disturbing, and some flak was thrown. Paradoxically, this was the kickoff for Autodesk AB's growth for the future.

Onsala Sweden, November 1984

Distributor meeting at the office. Gary Wells from Autodesk, Inc. came over with new versions and all distributors were gathered. Bullet-proof vest was recommended, worn, and needed.

Kungsbacka Sweden, December 1984

Autodesk AB moved into a new location six times bigger than the garage, and 5 employees were hired. We expected this big place to fit for the next 2 years. We outgrew it in 4 months.

---

181 The Swedish subsidiary of Autodesk. Prior to the organisation of the subsidiaries in 1984 we were operating in Europe through the businesses which had earlier been Marinchip dealers, with a complicated licensing and royalty scheme. This structure grew because we had better things to do than worry about incorporating new companies. We knew, however, that if we contemplated a public stock offering, we'd have to clean up all the details, so we formally organised the European companies in 1984.

182 When Mike Ford returned from this trip, his first to the overseas offices, he summarised it to me in the sentence, "We are very, very lucky to have those people over there".

London, Spring 1985

Dan Drake came and demonstrated the new features of AutoCAD 2.1. He also mentioned that Autodesk were going to take over the development and marketing of AE/CADD, paying a royalty to Archsoft. As usual when you buy a product, it seemed to have less quality and more flaws at a closer look.[183]

I never dreamed at the time that I would become the product manager for the AEC product line at Autodesk, Inc., 1987 – 88.

Mölndal Sweden, April 1985

A company that went bankrupt left an office ready to rent. Not only an office, but I was able to take over practically new furniture and a telephone system for a fraction of their original cost. The move was done within 2 weeks and we were now in a space of 5000 square feet, employing 7 people, and were soon to hire 3 more. The distribution organization was more or less set with distributors.

Mölndal Sweden, September 1985

The first cash flow crisis appeared. Taxes, royalty, and advertising added up to a point where we had to face going to the bank and begging for a loan. After straightening up the costs everyone in the office deeply understood how easy it is to create bad, expensive habits. The lesson was painful. Luckily it came in the beginning and became a part of the culture. The ad agency was cut off in 48 hours. Actually, I have not yet found an ad agency better able to convey our "message" than we can ourselves. The best luck I have had was with an ex-technical journalist working in a PR agency.

Sausalito USA, June 1985

Public offering of the company.

Mölndal Sweden, February 1986

Mike Ford, VP of Marketing, resigned. We heard the news over the fax machine the same day. Every fast growing company has its casualties and he was one of them. The company suffered a lot but Richard Handyside from the English office went in and acted as VP of Marketing until we found a replacement.

---

183   And as a result, Autodesk had to essentially re-implement the package before shipping it as an Autodesk product.

Mölndal Sweden, March 1986

The Swedish office closed for a conference in France. It sounds crazy but despite the costs and the outrageous criticism it was worth it. In a week the employees started to meld into a company team instead of a loosely formed group of individuals.

Chicago, June 1986

The first AutoCAD EXPO — a success. Autodesk, Inc. introduced the hardware lock to the American market.

Mölndal Sweden, August 1986

I decided to take the opportunity and follow the diluted part of me that has the blood of the Vikings. Go West. From the start of 1987 I would be Product Manager for AEC Architectural and Mechanical. The Swedish office was more or less prepared and the transition went extremely well.

Sausalito, May 1988

The Autodesk story as seen from an European viewpoint ... here is what I have learned from my experience being with Autodesk, almost from the beginning, taking the viewpoint that how we did the things we did contributed to the success we have had.

The group that started Autodesk, Inc. knew each other fairly well and shared very much the same values such as taking care of the customer.

In Europe we all had been selling hardware. (John Walker had even been manufacturing computer systems). Once we were a pure software company it was then easier to resist the temptation to start dealing with hardware again. If Autodesk, Inc. had been dealing with expensive computers and hardware, its growth pattern would have been impossible to finance.[184]

The first years, 1982 – 1984, were painful in terms of mistakes, dead ends, searching for a strategy, mis-communication, etc. We maybe did not know how to do it, but we sure learned what did *not* work, and as our business was loosely defined, casual, and under our fingertips, the course was easy to correct within the minutes it took to make a phone call. In 1988 it can take a week to send out a letter — for good reasons — if the wrong message sneaks in, it is enormously difficult to correct across our huge dealer and customer base.

---

[184] As so many of our competitors have learned.

When business started to take off late 1984 we all had been "trained internally".

When the Viking Red Serpent was heading for Miklagard (Constantinople) to do business, he came to a fork in the road. Asking an old native the best way, the answer was, "The road you don't take is the right one".

The message is: don't mourn the "bad" decisions made in the past — they were all part of the overall deal.

L'Envoi: The First Six Years

There you have it: six years of Autodesk. While the record is far from complete and, like all collections of raw sources, lacks the balance and perspective of a historical narrative, reading these documents can't help but recreate the excitement, the fear, the exhaustion, the tension, the uncertainty, the exhilaration, and the feeling of accomplishment that we all shared as we lived through the times that these papers bear witness to.

I certainly know that collecting and editing them reminded me of many things I had forgotten. It's always easy to believe that things were much easier in the good old days, or to wish that we could get things done as quickly and easily as we used to. These papers show that at every point in the company's evolution we faced difficult decisions whose effects could not be predicted but which had to be made immediately based on incomplete information. They show our constant struggle to be responsive to our customers, dealers, and stockholders. They show that the process of getting high-quality products into the hands of users in a timely manner can never be "easy". They prove beyond any possible dispute that the one asset that is responsible for the success of this company is the people in it: people who have always been willing to exert whatever effort was required to get the job done and to do that job to the best of their ability because they believed in what the company was doing and they believed they would be rewarded for their exertions.

Sometime in 1984, when the company had begun to make a mark in the industry, a reporter asked me if the company had a "philosophy". I hadn't really thought about it in those terms — it seemed to me that we were just doing what made sense. Like all reporters, this one pushed me for a pithy quote, so I said:

Make the best product.
No bullshit.
Reward the people that do the work.

A little more than six years ago Autodesk was all potential and no success. As the years have passed our efforts have brought us enormous success and have vaulted Autodesk into the first rank of small high-technology growth companies in the world. This success is both the well-deserved reward for what we've accomplished so far and the springboard that is creating new opportunities of unprecedented scale today.

It's easy to kick back and concentrate on meeting the sales and earnings projections on a quarter to quarter basis and to view our existing products as the centre of our business for all time, to be incrementally enhanced over the years. And we must do these things. But to remain true to the strategy that has brought us so far so fast we must also be constantly on the look-out for the next AutoCAD: the product that comes from nowhere, in an industry that doesn't exist yet, that all of the well-respected analysts say "can't be done", or "can't be done on a PC", or "won't sell". All of these things were said of AutoCAD.

In business you have to constantly try to expand the scope of your operations and move into new areas of opportunity. If you don't, your competitors will and you'll find yourself in a darkening corner of a market growing cold with obsolescence. If you run your business well and build the mainstream revenue sources while exploring the opportunities of the future, you can stay on the path to growth and success that dwarfs what we've achieved so far.

There was a day when General Electric, IBM, AT&T, Ford Motor Company — all of the Titans of industry, were the same size that Autodesk is now. Most of those companies took far longer to get to that point than we have, and few were in as strong a competitive and financial position when they got there. Like those companies, we're riding a technological wave which has been building for decades and whose limits cannot even be calculated today. If we continue to demonstrate the kind of creativity, productivity, and energy that we've shown so far, we can build Autodesk into a peer of these great industries. To take advantage of this opportunity we share will take vision, leadership, sound management, technological creativity, financial strength, a commitment to excellence in everything we do, and most importantly, the willingness to do the tedious work that turns opportunity into success.

Perhaps the greatest risk that faces Autodesk today is the tendency to think that our success to date is enough, or that now that we're a "large, established company" we can't afford the kinds of wild technological gambles we made in the early days. But it's those very gambles that will carry us from where we are today to the next plateau of success — and the next and the one after that. And there's one thing no reasonable person can doubt after reading this history: that the people who are Autodesk have what it takes to make it happen.

As Arthur C. Clarke said in 1963,[185]

"Despite the perils and problems we face, we should be glad we are here at this time. Every venture is like a surf rider, carried forward on the crest of a wave. The wave bearing us has scarcely started its run; those who thought it was already slackening spoke decades too soon. We are poised now, in the precarious but exhilarating balance that is the essence of real living, the antithesis of mere existence. Behind us lie the reefs we have already passed; beneath us the great wave, barely flecked with foam, humps its back still higher from the sea.

"And ahead?

"We cannot tell; we are too far out to see the unknown land. It is enough to ride the wave."

---

[185] In *Profiles of the Future* by Arthur C. Clarke, Harper & Row 1963 / Bantam 1964, 1967.

Section Eight

Appendices

Publisher's Notes
January 1982 — December 1988

For those who want to see how AutoCAD developed, particularly in its early formative stages, the following appendices include John Walker's development log for AutoCAD-80, and the Duff Kurland's first feature list put together to guide AutoCAD's development.

Documents

Here are the documents provided as Appendices in Section Eight.

- Appendix A. Financial History. January 1983 – December 1988. Shows Autodesk's stock performance, quarterly sales and profit history.

- Appendix B. AutoCAD Feature History. January 1983 – December 1987. Shows the features released in each AutoCAD release through Release 9 (1988).

- Appendix C. September 1981. — Before Autodesk. Gives a business strategy for Marinchip Systems.

- Appendix D. July 1982 — Auto Book Notes. An early product idea that still lives.

- Appendix E. August 1982. — AutoCAD-80 Development Log. This is a development log for AutoCAD's early software features for the CP/M version.

- Appendix F. June 1983. — AutoCAD Wish List. The first AutoCAD features' wish list compiled by Duff Kurland.

Appendix A — Financial Results

Autodesk Stock Price History

This stock chart was prepared by Kern Sibbald. Kern has developed software tools which process stock price information downloaded from CompuServe into an AutoCAD drawing of the stock price chart. Kern's stock chart generating program has become one of the standard "torture tests" for AutoLisp. This chart shows the stock price following the initial public offering, correcting for all stock splits to date.

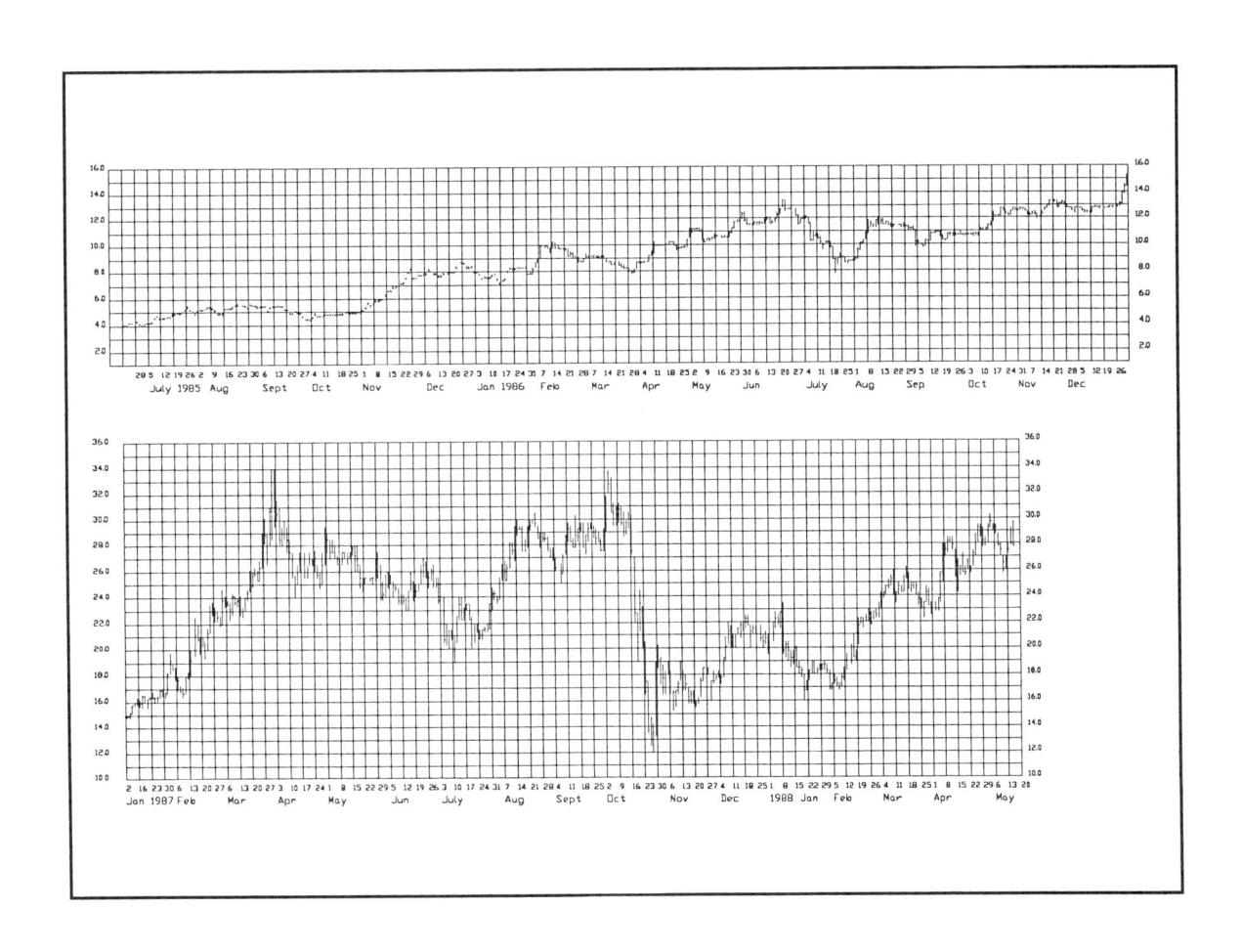

Pre-Public Offering Stock Valuation

Date range	Share price
4/29/82–11/8/83	$0.022222
11/9/83–8/21/84	$0.066667
8/22/84–4/14/85	$0.166667
4/15/85–6/10/85	$0.333333
6/11/85–6/27/85	$2.000000

Stock Splits

Date	Factor
July 1983	10 for 1
May 1985	3 for 2
March 1987	3 for 1

Quarterly Sales

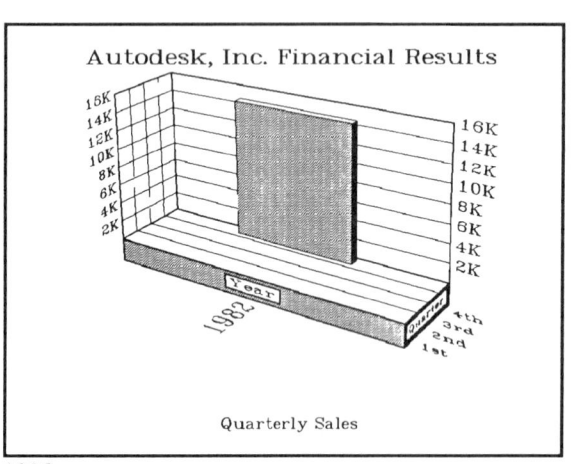

1982

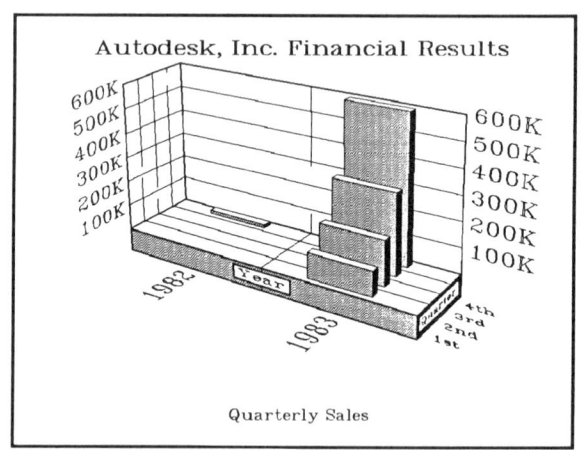

1983

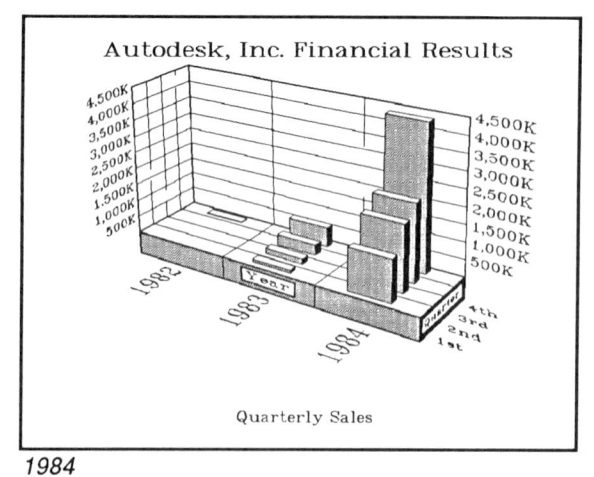

1984

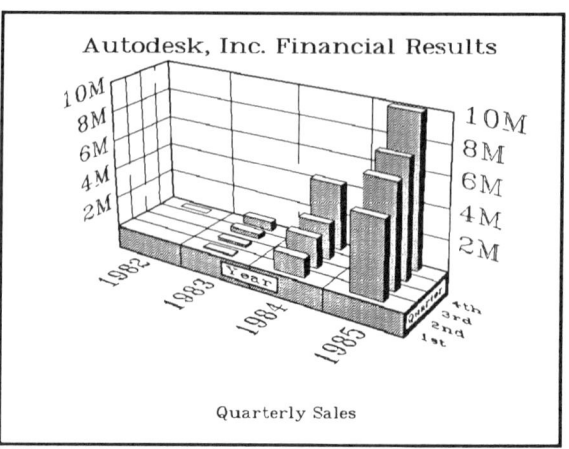

1985

Appendix A Financial Results 447

Quarterly Sales (continued)

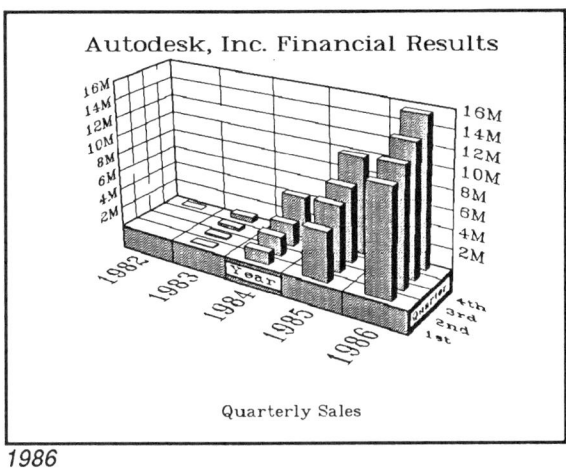

1986

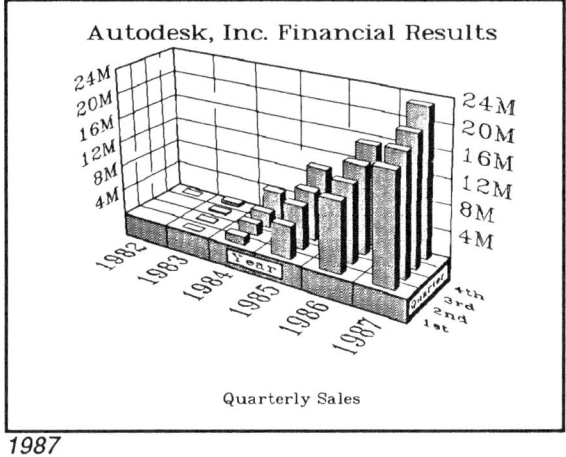

1987

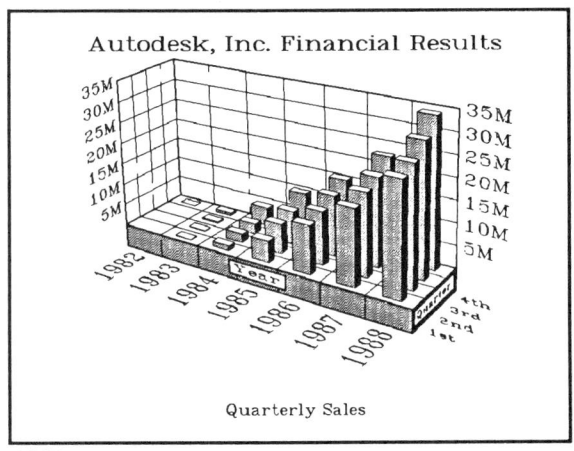

1988

Quarterly Profit/(Loss)

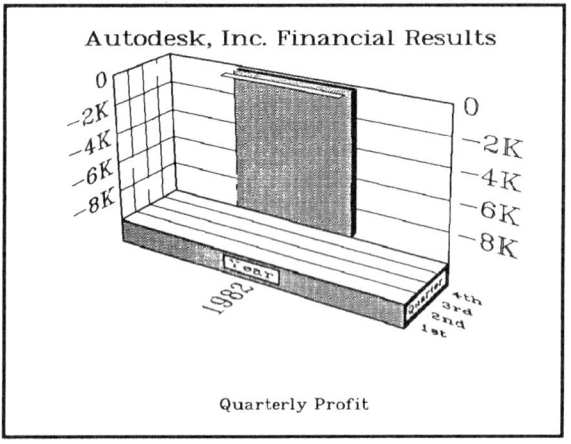

1982

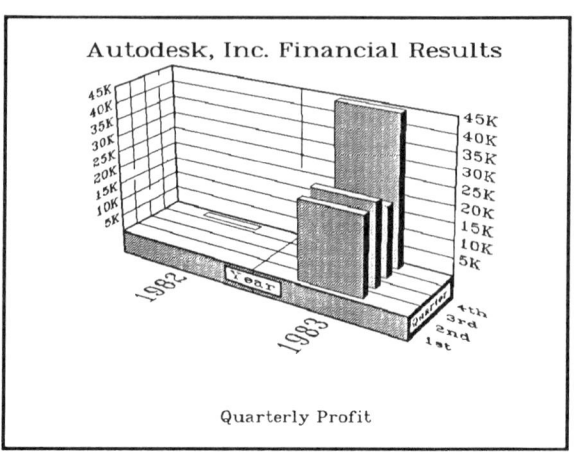

1983

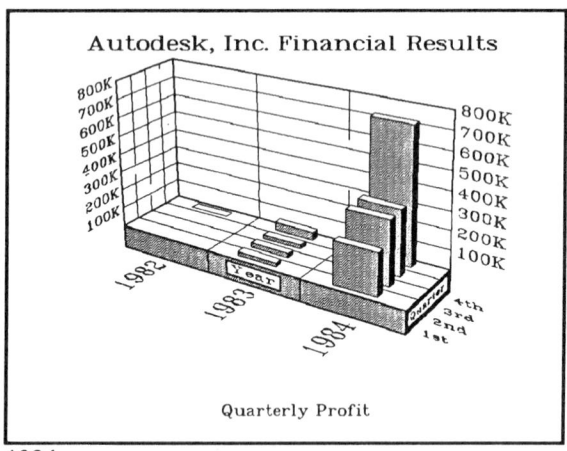

1984

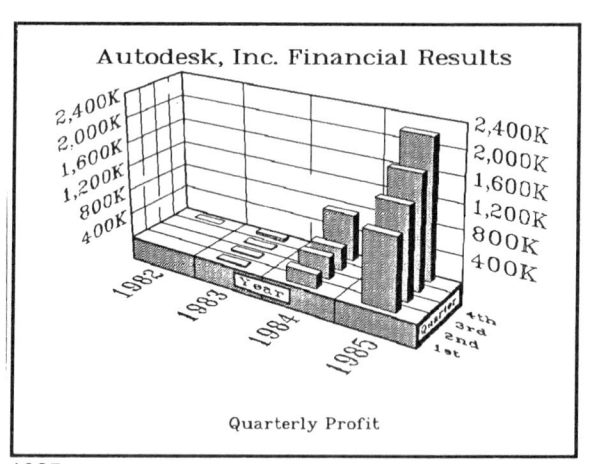

1985

Appendix A *Financial Results* 449

Quarterly Profits/Loss (Continued)

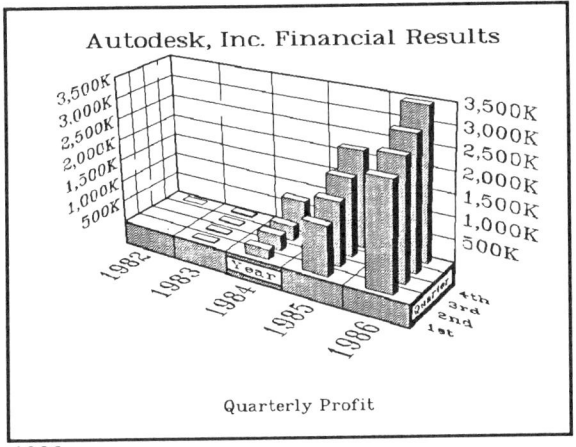

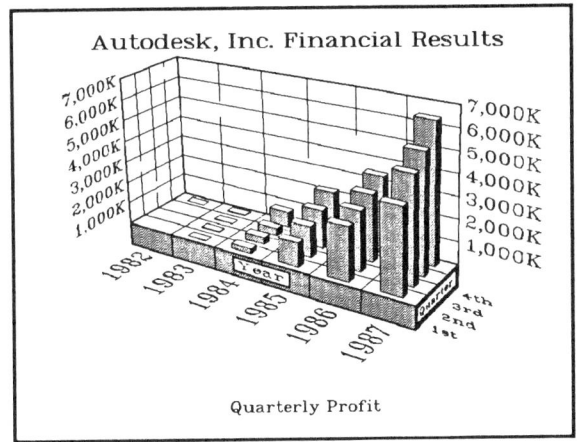

1986

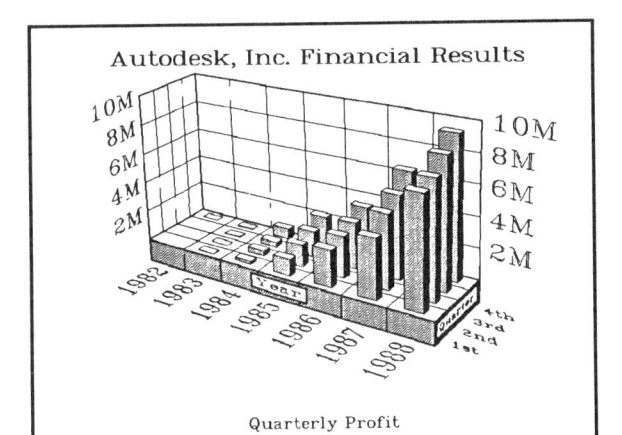

1987

1988

Appendix B — Product Release History

Autodesk Product Initial Shipment Dates

Product	First Shipped
AutoCAD-80	December 1982
AutoCAD-86	January 1983
AutoScreen	January 1983
AE/CADD / AEC Architectural	August 1985
CAD/camera	July 1985[186]
AutoSketch	October 1986
AutoShade	September 1987
AutoCAD AEC Mechanical	August 1987
AutoFlix	March 1988
AutoSolid	June 1988

AutoCAD Version Release Dates

Release	Version name	Release date
1	Version 1.0	December 1982
2	Version 1.2	April 1983
3	Version 1.3	August 1983
4	Version 1.4	October 1983
5	Version 2.0	October 1984
6	Version 2.1	May 1985
7	Version 2.5	June 1986
8	Version 2.6	April 1987
9	Release 9	September 1987
10	Release 10	October 1988

AutoCAD Major Feature Release History

Feature	Version	Date
ADE Package	1.4	October 1983
ADE–1	2.0	October 1984

Continued...

---

[186] CAD/camera was discontinued on December 9th, 1987.

Feature	Version	Date
Apollonius problem	2.5	June 1986
Arcs, alternate	1.4	October 1983
Array command	1.4	October 1983
Attributes	2.0	October 1984
AutoLisp	2.18	January 1986
AutoLisp entity access	2.5	June 1986
Axis command	1.4	October 1983
Blipmode command	2.1	May 1985
Break command	1.4	October 1983
Chamfer command	2.0	May 1985
Colour and linetype by entity	2.5	June 1986
Configuration	1.3	August 1983
Curve fitting	2.1	May 1985
Database, portable	9	September 1987
Dialogue boxes	9	September 1987
Dimensioning	1.2	April 1983
Dimensioning, associative	2.6	April 1987
Dimensioning, extended	2.0	October 1984
Divide command	2.5	June 1986
Doughnut command	2.5	June 1986
Dragging	2.0	October 1984
Dtext command	2.5	June 1986
DXB	2.1	May 1985
DXF	1.0	December 1982
DXF, new format	2.0	October 1984
Ellipse command	2.5	June 1986
Explode command	2.5	June 1986
Extend command	2.5	June 1986
External (shell) commands	2.1	May 1986
Files command	1.4	October 1983
Fillet command	1.4	October 1983
Filmroll command	2.6	April 1987
Grid, rotated, isometric	2.0	October 1984
Hardware lock, international	2.1	May 1985
Hardware lock, domestic	2.5	June 1986
Hatching	1.4	October 1983
Hide command	2.1	May 1985
Initial release	1.0	December 1982
Kanji font support	2.5	June 1986
Layer names	2.0	October 1984
Line types	2.0	October 1984
Measure command	2.5	June 1986

Continued...

Feature	Version	Date
Menus, icon	9	September 1987
Menus, pull-down	9	September 1987
Mirror command	2.0	October 1984
Object snap	2.0	October 1984
Offset command	2.5	June 1986
Pan reversed	1.0	December 1982
Pan reversed again	2.0	October 1984
Plot to file	2.5	June 1986
Point acquisition filters	2.6	April 1987
Points, fancy	2.5	June 1986
Polygon command	2.5	June 1986
Polylines	2.1	May 1985
Printer plotters	2.1	May 1985
Qtext command	2.0	October 1984
Repeat/Endrep removed	2.5	June1986
Rotate command	2.5	June 1986
Scale command	2.5	June 1986
Scripts	1.4	October 1983
Selection, interactive	2.1	May 1985
Shape compiler	2.0	October 1984
Sketch command	1.4	October 1983
Slides	2.0	October 1984
Slide libraries	9	September 1987
Spline curves	9	September 1987
Stretch command	2.5	June 1986
Style command	2.0	October 1984
Tablet configuration	2.0	October 1984
Text fonts, multiple	2.0	October 1984
3D Level 1	2.1	May 1985
3D Level 2	2.6	April 1987
Time command	2.5	June 1986
Transparent commands	2.6	April 1987
Trim command	2.5	June 1986
Undo and Redo	2.5	June 1986
Undefine/Redefine commands	9	September 1987
Units command	1.4	October 1983
Variables and Expressions	2.1	May 1985
View command	2.0	October 1984
Zoom and pan, fast	2.5	June 1986

Appendix C — Before Autodesk

Because Autodesk has been successful, there's a tendency to forget what a high-risk undertaking it was to start the company. Most of the founders of Autodesk were involved in preexisting ventures of their own, some while also holding down full-time jobs. Embarking on Autodesk meant abandoning these ventures, some of which looked quite promising at the time, for a new business in an untested market.

Starting Autodesk wasn't the only opportunity that beckoned at the time. I wrote this paper in late 1981 to plot the strategy of Marinchip and the people around it, who encompassed a large percentage of the Autodesk founders. This strategy represented the "safe evolutionary path" for Marinchip and would, had it been pursued, have led to utter failure.

It's worth keeping this in mind when evaluating new business opportunities that seem to diverge from Autodesk's traditional areas of success. Special thanks are in order to David Gari, who typed in this entire document from the only existing paper copy.

Product Development Strategy Working Paper

Revision 0 — September 29, 1981
by John Walker

This paper describes the background, plans, and goals for Marinchip Systems' hardware and software development projects. This paper is being prepared as a working document for Marinchip (MS), Evolution Computing (EC), Optimistic Systems (OS), and Pacific Software Associates (PSA), to identify how the plans will impact work in progress by each group, how work will be distributed among the organisations, and how the work must come together before goals can be met.

This is a working document. Nothing in here is final, decided, or immutable. It exists only to serve as a starting point for discussion and as a base for the development of a formal plan.

Basic Development Strategy

MS, EC, and PSA are engaged in marketing a dead horse. The time for the 9900 to establish itself as a contender in the microprocessor sweepstakes has come and gone. We are faced always with a selling job that T.I. should have done for us, not us for them. Our processor cannot compete in performance, address space, instruction set, or available software. No announced product from T.I., or any direction indicated in their product development holds out a hope for elimination of these problems.

Our selling point is our software. Our software is portable between processors. We should not consider ourselves tied to one processor or manufacturer because of a decision we made in the past.

We've discovered in converting the code to the Z8000 that conversion of even assembly language code poses no horrors. OS has developed the conversion tools for the Z8000, and we have learned how to best approach the problem. In addition, OS has made a native code MDEX, saving some work that would otherwise have to be done.

The Z8000 is not a good base for our future development because of the segmented memory addressing architecture, possible register set exhaustion when in segmented mode, and because the market perception seems to be that it is not the best product.

Based on our evaluation of the products available and the markets's perception of them, the Motorola 68000 seems to be the best really available, second sourced, processor. Its instruction set and register architecture promises an easy conversion of our code. Its memory architecture imposes no limits on future system growth.

There are no currently available boards, either S-100 or Multibus, which implement the 68000 in a general fashion including memory management. Without the memory management chip, the 68000 can not be used in a secure multi-user mode. The memory management chip is only available in samples now, so it will be some time until boards are available.

The best way for us to work with the 68000 is to design a "node board" exactly like the one contemplated for the 9995. This board (in its final PC implementation) will have a 68000 CPU, 256K RAM (depopulatable to 128K), 4 or 8K PROM, 2 SIO, 1 PIO ports, possibly a 9512 math chip, and an S-100 I/O bus interface. The 68000 will talk to the S-100 bus only as an I/O device.

Given this board, all those with 9900 systems can start working with the 68000 immediately. NOS will support the 68000 as a node processor, so all existing 9900 peripherals may be retained unchanged, and may be accessed through the 68000 as well as the 9900. The 68000 will then also be a straightforward upgrade for our existing customer base.

The software for the 68000 node board will request all I/O through the host system processor. NOS will, of course, support this protocol. We can write a CP/M program which talks this protocol and allow the 68000 to be added to a CP/M system using all our 68000 software. The only restriction is that file names on the 68000 would then have to conform to the CP/M standards (and that JSYS requests not supported by CP/M could not be performed). All the compilers should run with no difficulties. There might be a reasonably large market for such a product.

Once the software is converted to the 68000, we can shop around for an S-100 or Multibus 68000 to serve as the host processor. On finding one, NOS/MT will be converted to run on it, using memory management to support multiple users. Of course, node board users will also be supported (if Multibus, we would have to make a Multibus node board). This work would gain us an all-68000 system (easier to sell and maintain), a cheaper entry level system (no 9900 required, no processor per user, better memory utilisation=less memory), and the ability to run programs of any size, not limited to 256K.

Details — The 68000 Node Board

The 68000 Node Board will be designed and prototyped by EC. MS will take over manufacturing, testing, and service after the final testing of prototypes. The anticipated specifications of the 68000 node board will be:

    68000 CPU
    256K Dynamic RAM with Parity (40 x 4164)
    4K/8K/16K PROM (2 x [2716, 2732, 2764])
    2 Async RS-232 ports (header pin connectors)
    1 Parallel I/O port (header pin connector)
    9512 Math processor (if it fits)
    S-100 bus I/O interface

The node board will look like two I/O ports to the S-100 bus master. The base port address will be settable with a DIP switch. There will be a data port and a control port. Data written to the data port by port by the 68000 may be read by the S-100 bus master. The data port is bidirectional without restriction. The control port may be used by the S-100 bus master to:

    Hardware reset the 68000
    Interrupt the 68000
    Set a status bit the 68000 can read

Clear interrupt
Clear status bit

The control port may be used by the 68000 to:

Interrupt the S-100 master
Set a status bit the S-100 master can read
Clear interrupt
Clear status bit

In addition the control port may be read to determine the value of the status bit. This allows either interrupt or non-interrupt synchronisation of data transfer between the host and the node board.

Details — Software Conversion Plans

MS will write a 68000 assembler and linker in SPL. This will initially run on the 9900.

MS will develop an NOS support module for the 68000 which will allow programs to run as under NOS. It will make requests to the master CPU for I/O. This program will probably be put in PROM once stable. Marinchip will develop support code in NOS to handle these requests. This will probably initially be a user program (which will fit in space below the system). If demand seems to justify it, MS will develop a host support program for CP/M.

Somebody will convert META and its runtime system to the 68000.

Somebody will use 68000 META to convert QBASIC 2.x to the 68000.

Somebody will convert WINDOW and SPELL using the new QBASIC (not trivial because of assembly routines).

Somebody will convert Osborne packages, Selector, etc., to 68000 QBASIC.

Somebody will convert EDIT, WORD, and other 9900 assembly programs to the 68000, carefully considering whether they should be redone in QBASIC or SPL.

EC will convert SPL to the 68000. Using SPL, Interact may be converted.

Background — Why not the 9995/99000?

We will be abandoning the 9995 node board project and the plans to redesign the M9900 CPU with the 9995. There are two major reasons for this:

First, the major problem we are having with all 9900 work is exhaustion of the 64K address space of the 9900. Neither the 9995 nor the 99000 solve this problem. The 99000 allows larger memory, and could be used with a segmentation scheme, but this is not a general solution and could not be used by unsophisticated users. We have to have a system where we can simply let the user buy more memory when his program won't fit. Thus, the major advantages of both the 9995 and the 99000 are higher performance, but neither of them delivers enough extra performance to compete effectively with the newer processors from Zilog and Motorola.

Second, The 9900 family is a largely unknown product since T.I. has failed to effectively promote it. The 99/4, considered T.I.'s last chance to establish recognition for the processor, is widely considered a flop. There is nothing in the 9900 family and nothing expected to be added which would cause a designer today to design in the 9900. Thus, the future for the 9900 is not bright. T.I. has been dropping product lines (bubble memories, watches) in response to poor market response, and the 9900 may go that way. It seems clear that if T.I. is to become a contender in the high-end micro market, it will not be with the 9900, so we would have to convert anyway. Remember, this isn't the first time this happened. The TI-ASC, for years the fastest computer in the world, only sold 7 units, 5 to T.I. divisions. Most people were unaware it existed. They dropped the product.

Background — Why not the Z8001?

Since OS has converted most of our software to the Z8002, it would be far less painful to go to the Z8001 CPU. In addition, off the shelf Multibus systems exist with Z8001 CPU, memory management, and all the large memory and support boards at excellent prices. The basic problem with the Z8000 is that it is not a general large address space processor. The Z8000 addressing is split up into "segments" from 0 to 127, and "displacements" from 0 to 64K.[187] You can address 8 megabytes by concatenating the segment and displacement into one address. Segmented mode programs can do this in both direct address pointers and in index register pairs. The problem comes in how indexing and autoincrementation is handled. When addresses are added in the processor, only the displacements are added, and the carry is discarded. Thus, if you are indexing through an array and cross a segment boundary, you wind up back at the start of the segment you were in, not at the next one.

As a result, you can simulate large addressing only by manually computing addresses in software, bypassing the index hardware. This is grossly inefficient. You can ignore the problem if the linker never places a module across a segment boundary and dynamic allocation never splits a buffer across segment boundaries. This doesn't help you if the user simply declares an array larger than 64K.

---

187 Does this sound familiar...?

Further, it seems that most vendors who have looked at the Z8000 for our type of general purpose application have shied away from it and are now working with the 68000. We've had it with trying to push unpopular products.

Details — What about the Z8000 software?

OS has put a large amount of work into the Z8000 software project, and MS has supported this with hardware purchases and loans. We continue to feel that this is a valuable product, and that if properly marketed it can return not only its development costs, but also make a reasonable sum of money for both OS and MS. With the general slant of the industry being away from the Z8000, we have to target our marketing carefully, since we can't afford big splash advertising.

MS has contacted Central Data about putting QBASIC on their system. This would involve a Z8002 to Z8001 conversion as well, so we would have to work on their system to do this. They expect their operating system to be ready early next year so we should contact them then regarding that. Since we don't expect to buy one of their systems now, this may be a sticky matter to arrange.

I think we should send out new product announcements about the Z8000 QBASIC, emphasising that this is an OEM-tailorable product we want to put under customer's operating systems, and announce the development software the same way. Also, we should put together a catalogue, manual package, and OEM schedule for this and pass it on to Lifeboat so they can pitch it to OEM prospects.

There's nothing wrong with what we've done with the Z8000. It just doesn't look worth putting a lot more money and effort into unless we can generate some interest in it. If the Z8000 is going to bomb, we'd better be somewhere other than the target zone. If, say, Lifeboat uncovers a vast market for Z8000 software, we'd be happy to change our mind.

Details — What does this do to other projects?

This redirection will have remarkably little effect on the work in progress.

All work underway by PSA is conversion of QBASIC programs. These will be portable to the compatible QBASIC on the 68000. Obviously, assembly language routines should be avoided wherever possible. PSA's NOSMODEM will remain applicable as long as a 9900 host is retained, which will probably be for quite some time. Then they can convert it. Any development in SPL or QBASIC should be safe. The work on WORD will have to be carefully coordinated with the conversion. Maybe this is the time to rewrite WORD in QBASIC or SPL, or maybe PSA should convert WORD to the 68000 while adding the enhancements. Discussion is needed. PSA should avoid 9900 assembly programming like the plague.

EC will drop the 9995 node board project. The 9918A board will continue and Marinchip will market it as agreed. Marinchip's QBASIC drivers for the 9918A will not be converted to the 68000. This board will be offered primarily to existing customers who have expressed an interest in it. We won't advertise it heavily. EC will do the prototyping research on the 68000, hand wire a prototype node board, layout, tapeup, and prototype the actual node board. We anticipate a yield from the prototype run to supply MS, EC, PSA, and OS with all the 68000 node boards needed for development. EC will produce final separations, solder mask, etc., for MS to begin actual manufacture. MS will pay EC a per-board royalty on the 68000 node board, and will defray development and prototyping costs. The actual manufacturing of the node boards will be done with MS existing vendors and contractors and will not consume any EC resources, except for possible revisions and corrections as needed. EC may undertake the META conversion, and will convert SPL. FORTRAN should be developed with the large address space of the 68000 in mind. EC and MS should consult over features needed in the new linker to support FORTRAN.

OS can use a node board in the Z8002 system and work on 68000 code. Depending on the market we can stir up for the Z8000 code, OS will continue to develop and support that code. The Z8000 C should be evaluated for portability to the 68000, as that would be a very desirable product to have. Optimally, we could consider converting the OS machine to a native 68000 processor (when we can get one), and letting OS do the 68000 host support (NOS/MT conversion). This would not affect work with or use of the node board. We can lend OS a 9900 to bridge the conversion gap, if needed.

MS has no development work in progress, to speak of. We'll be busy enough converting code, we reckon, without taking on anything else.

Details — Whither the 9900 and its customer base?

With the emphasis on the 68000, Marinchip will cease to actively market the 9900 system to new customers. We will continue to support existing customers and OEM's, and we will continue to sell and service all our existing 9900 products. OEM's using our system will not be impacted by this change in direction, except if they anticipate future 9900 based products, which will not be forthcoming.

We will continue to market the 9900 software through Lifeboat, and if a new 9900 OEM walks in the door, we will not turn him away. However, we will be up-front about where we are going and what this means.

Our large-system OEM's will be encouraged to configure and expand systems by adding 68000 node boards. Our converted software should make this relatively painless and advantageous. We hope to keep these OEM's with Marinchip by offering them the same software, much better performance, less big system slowdown effects, better reliability, and a migration path which doesn't make them throw away either hardware or software.

We want to make it clear, though, that if an OEM is happy with the 9900, he can continue to get them for the foreseeable future.

We will announce all of this in the *Shifting Bit*[188] in a message for end users. We will basically say that support continues, sales continue, but most new products will be 68000 based. We'll explain the reasons and show how a user can upgrade at minimal hardware cost.

Details — Marketing strategy

As soon as we have the software on the node board, we will begin a multi-pronged marketing strategy.

We will market the 68000 utilities (QBASIC, SPL, WINDOW, WORD, etc.) under other operating systems by directly contacting other 68000 vendors and through Lifeboat. This would be sales on an OEM buyout or on a royalty basis.

We will announce a 68000 "system" and advertise it. This system will have a 9900 running NOS in 64K as the support processor.

We will announce the 68000 node board as an add-on to our existing customers and OEM's. We will emphasise its use in expanding or building large NOS configurations.

We will advertise the 68000 node board as a CP/M addition. We will supply CP/M program and disc so our software can be used on the 68000.

What we want to do is to sell the 68000 software to OEM's, and possibly (say under XENIX) to end users. We'll try lots of alternatives to get the visibility we need to find them.

---

188 The *Shifting Bit* was the independently-edited newsletter for Marinchip users. Marinchip subsidised its printing and mailing.

Details — Who pays and who gets what?

The current structure of the MS–OS–EC–PSA community is a complete mess. Before we all get into this stuff we should figure out exactly how everybody's going to be compensated for what they do.[189] MS intends to continue being the "shock troops" of the community. We'll do the manufacturing, testing, advertising, mailing, phone answering, shipping, and receiving.[190] OS, EC, and PSA will thus be freed to get development work done (although they are certainly welcome to do scuzz work if they wish!!). The cleanest arrangement for MS is to simply handle all work by OS–EC–PSA on a royalty basis, paid per item sold, credited upon sale. We would define the royalty as a percentage of the payment received by MS for the item sold, so discounted OEM sales would be attractive to MS to negotiate for.

MS will pay for the hardware and other out of pocket expenses involved in getting into the 68000. We will provide node boards to OS and PSA at cost, with payment deferred until offset by royalties. (EC, of course, will just keep a prototype of the node board).

MS would like to renegotiate the agreements for MIDAS software from PSA to the standard percentage royalty. This isn't to grab more money, it's to remove the ambiguity in OEM sales (e.g., if the royalty is a fixed price and we discount the package to 50% off to sell 20,000 of them, we'd end up losing money on the deal, so we can't pursue it). Also, we could promote those packages more aggressively.

Further, we must normalise the status of those packages initially developed and nominally owned by MS, which others have or are planning to enhance. We need to somehow make work on those packages pay off via a royalty or upgrade charge from sales of the package. We can't afford to let sidelines build up for these packages, especially if we're going to be moving them between processors.

We can help all these goals by unbundling the 68000 software as much as possible. If we eliminate the "free software" concept, we can at least handle royalty on a reasonable basis.[191]

---

189 It was precisely the messiness of this kind of issue that persuaded me that it was essential to start a new company with everything spelled out explicitly.
190 This idea was carried over, essentially unchanged, into the original organisation plan for Autodesk.
191 Because of the nonexistence of a microcomputer software market in 1977, and the prevalence of software piracy, Marinchip had adopted a strategy, then close to unique, of bundling most of the system software with its CPU board, thus funding the development of the software through hardware sales.

None of this implies that there's anything wrong with developing products and selling them directly. It's just that if we're going to go after large volume OEM sales, it's to the advantage of the developers of software to have it visible to all potential customers who may examine our software. We need to make something on the software we sell that way to defray the costs of learning it enough to answer questions and intelligently market it, to do the front line support, and to handle updates, etc.

Details — Things to be resolved

The following are things we need to pin down.

How much will it cost us to build the node board? How much should it sell for? What will be the problems making and testing it?

Who will do what in converting the software? What items are on the critical path? What other priorities are contending for the time of these people? What interest in the revenue from a piece of software will converting it earn?

How should the completed plans be best presented to dealers and OEM's? What is the best way to announce and advertise the products? What do we do about one-off user inquiries?

What exactly will be MS's role in selling Interact and PSA-developed software? Are EC and PSA prepared to provide full end user support? If not, how much will it cost MS to do so?

How can we use the conversion to the 68000 to make the next conversion easier? What should be rewritten in a higher level language now? What language?

Should we put OS's C on the 68000? Whitesmiths is supposed to have a C for the 68000 soon. Should we use it?

What about the INS16000? How about the IAPX432? Should we make node boards for them also? How real are they? Is software for them in demand? What pieces can we sell?

What is the maximum capital drawdown we can expect before we find out if this was a good idea or not? How long should it be until we know? If MS is putting up all the development money (and hence taking all the risk), what is reasonable compensation for that? What do we do if it doesn't work?

Appendix D — Auto Book Notes

I also included the original notes describing Auto Book in the Information Letter 7. Maybe someday we'll finish that product.

Auto Book Notes

by John Walker
Revision 6 — July 8, 1982
(Special IL7 Version)

Auto Book is an idea for an automated document retrieval and examination system. What exists today is a prototype intended to play around with the concepts and try out bright ideas without a lot of effort. It is implemented in QBASIC on the M9900, and no effort has been expended to make it transportable. I'd rather have the convenience of trying out ideas readily than always trying to maintain compatibility.

The Concept

Now that everybody has a computer, everybody will naturally write, edit, and print documents on the computer. As a result, more and more documents accumulate in machine readable form. Little has been done toward letting users *read* documents once they are written. If we have a computer between us and the document, we should be able to take more advantage of it than just having it print a hard copy that we later read. Why shouldn't we be able to:

- Ask questions about the document?
- Read sections based on content?
- Move between documents as they reference one another?
- Ask for explanations of terms the document uses?

The idea I'm exploring is "Computer Assisted Reading". It's a field I've seen little done with, and it's a far more universal need than even, say, VisiCalc. I'm calling the program "Auto Book" because it implements an automatic intelligent book. It also might be called the "Reader's Workbench".

READ – Reading an Auto Book

To get started, you should edit the file "ADI.CFG" on the Auto Book disc and change the "TERM" statement to specify your terminal type. The terminal type specified must be one listed in a "*" line in the file "WINDOW.TRM" on the disc. This is exactly like the CP/M Window configuration, and you may use the notes for that product to aid in configuring new terminals. Put the Auto Book disc in Drive 1. Call the read utility with the command:

READ

When you are asked for a document name, answer:

USC

If you're about to ask me about the plus signs, it's because the terminal definition defaults to plus signs for "flagged" lines. They're reverse video on my terminal. If you have a special display mode, make the entries in WINDOW.TRM to use it on your terminal.

READ Commands

You will see a menu of commands. **READ** works in two major ways, by locating sections of a document by content, and by working with marks in the document set by the user while viewing it (just like attaching paper clips to pages, inserting bookmarks, or dog-earing pages). There is a list of all "referenced" sections known to **READ** at any time. Keep these ideas in mind as you read the explanations of the commands (it is a good idea to play around with the program as you read these sections).

Add word to references. You're asked for a word. All sections in which that word appears are added to the list of referenced sections. (That is, in the logical sense, they are OR'ed.)

And word with references. You're asked for a word. All sections in which that word appears, and which have been previously marked as being referenced are marked as referenced. Other previously marked references are cleared.

Subtract word from references. You're asked for a word. All sections in which that word appears are removed from the reference list (if present).

Clear references. All references are cleared from the reference list.

List references. The titles of all sections referenced are listed. If more than a screen full of titles are referenced, the user can type "M" to see the next screen-load. "C" returns to the command menu.

Show referenced text. The text from the document is displayed for referenced sections, starting with the first referenced. If the text is more than a screen full, typing "M" will show the next screen-load. Typing "N" shows the next reference, if any. Typing "C" gets back to the command menu. "+" advances to the next section in the document (referenced or not), and "-" backs up to the previous section. "S" sets a mark on the section, and "U" unsets (i.e., clears) the mark.

List section titles. All section titles are displayed. "M" gets the next screen full, and "C" gets back to the command menu.

Select marked sections. All sections which have been marked by the user (with the "S" key while viewing the text) are added to the list of referenced sections. To view just the marked sections, clear the reference list, then select marked sections.

New document. The user is asked for a new document name, and viewing of that document is begun.

Help facility

When viewing a screen other than the main command menu, pressing any illegal key ("?" is always illegal), will replace the display at the top of the screen with a list of the meaning of all the currently valid response keys. Entering a proper response will turn the help display back off.

SCAN — The preprocessor

Auto Book consists of a document processor which reads the formatted text generated by a word processing program. The preprocessor scans the document, and based either on information encoded in the document, or by user-selected heuristic rules, identifies logical sections of the document and assigns them names. It prepares a rapid-access file of the document text, and creates a file containing encoded references to words in the document with pointers to the sections of text in which each word appears. The preprocessor may also perform compression of the text, and encode it against access by programs other than the Auto Book retrieval program. Neither of these functions are currently implemented.

The preprocessor contains an algorithm called the "rooter" which extracts the root of words with prefixes and suffixes. This algorithm must be carefully defined, and will vary for each natural language supported. References are stored by the root of the words, so that asking for references to "test" will find references to "test", "tested", "tests", "tester", "retest", etc. This is not currently implemented.

Once a document has been "compiled" by the preprocessor, it may be read with the "**READ**" utility.

The preprocessor is invoked by calling the **SCAN** program. It presents a menu allowing only the options of preprocessing a document or exiting. Before calling **SCAN**, you should have put the **WORD** formatted output of the document into a file with a .TXT type. You should also create a file with the same name and a .RAT type with size about one sector per line of text in the .TXT file. You should also create a .REF file. There's no easy way to estimate the .REF file size, so make a huge file initially. **SCAN** will tell you how much it used after it's done. You should have a **TEMP1$** file on Drive 1 (MDEX) before calling **SCAN**.

Once you tell **SCAN** you want to process a document, all you have to do is enter the "root name" (less the .TXT) of the document, and **SCAN** will do the rest.

SCAN knows about various commands embedded in the document. These commands will be removed from the files created by **SCAN**. All commands are flagged with a plus sign (+) in column 1. Note that these commands are entered as text with **WORD**, and that care must be taken to insure that **WORD** will not format them into the middle of another line. See the file "USC.WRD" for an example of how the **SCAN** commands can be inserted in a document.

SCAN Commands

The following commands are recognised by **SCAN**.

+TITLE *text*

The *text* is saved as the document title. The title is always displayed while the document is being read.

+COPYRIGHT *text*

The *text*, which should be of the form "1980 Mud Slingers International" will be displayed as a copyright notice when the document is being viewed. This may, in the future, be used to control reproduction of an encrypted document.

+ *number text*

If a single digit number from 1 to 9 follows the plus sign, this specifies a section break in the document. Up to 9 levels of sections are allowed. The title for each section is the concatenation of all sections with numbers less than or equal to the last section number which appeared.

Important: If no +*number* item is used, **SCAN** will break the document into paragraphs separated by blank spaces. Each will be assigned a paragraph number. This allows unencoded documents to be processed reasonably.

Trying SCAN

To see the process involved in running **SCAN** at work, look at the original document text "USC.WRD" on the documents disc. This text is processed by **WORD** to form the text file "USC.TXT". When **SCAN** is run over this document, the files "USC.RAT" and "USC.REF" are generated. These files are then accessed by **READ**.

Ideas for the future

The list of commands in **READ** and the whole idea of the command menu is distasteful. I think maybe a simple command language or some form of directed prompting would be more in order. The current set of commands evolved largely out of a desire to test the various sections of the program in an orthogonal manner. I'm sure a more elegant set of ideas should underlie the commands.

You should be able to do a lot more with marks in the text. They should be saved when you sign off or view another document, and you should be able to clear them, easily display them, automatically set marks for all referenced sections, etc., etc.

There should be a +ALIAS command in **SCAN**. Sometimes you want a section to be selected when a word not used in it is referenced. For example, the "necessary and proper" clause in the U.S. Constitution might have a +ALIAS ELASTIC before it, as it is often known as the "elastic clause". It could be found by its common name, even if the user didn't know what it said.

There's another aspect to aliases. You might want to have an alternate word or words indexed every time a given word is used. This would let relevant sections be retrieved regardless of which synonym were used. For example: +ALIAS BONNEY=BILLY THE KID . would index "Billy the Kid" every time the desperado's real name was used in the text.

Inter-document references: A complete system should let you file all your documents and move freely between them. **SCAN** could implement this with a +KEYWORDS statement listing keywords in the document for the global dictionary. One could start at the global level and get a list of all documents with selected keywords, then move on to read them. References between documents would be handled by a +SEE statement. One might, for example, in a manual about the text editor, insert the statement:

`+SEE SYSTEM REBOOT,LOAD,CREATE,FILE,DELETE,...`

where the user would be given a reference to the manual "SYSTEM" when one of the listed words were asked for.

SCAN should also have a command called +EXPLAINS. Before a section, one should be able to insert a statement like:

+EXPLAINS CHANGE,ALTER

and have it flagged as the section which explains those terms. Then the user reading the document could ask for the explanation of a term (rather than just the references) and get the section providing the most basic definition of the term.

When you're reading a real document, you can make marginal notes. **READ** should allow this too. The master copy of the document remains unchanged, but a user can "annotate" any section by typing in text which gets saved in a special notes file belonging to that user. When the section of the document is viewed, the user can see that he's made notes, review the notes, and edit them as desired.

The format **SCAN** stores the text in is wasteful of space, and results in each document being stored as two files (.RAT and .REF). This is because I was lazy. Fixing it wouldn't contribute anything to evaluation of the product idea. In a production system, one file should contain all information for a document, and the document text should be compressed using the "polygram compression" algorithm used in SPELL. Also, a simple encryption should be done to protect documents from being ripped off by the honest and naive. Whether the user is allowed to make a hard copy or store decoded text in a file would be controlled by a flag on the copyright statement in the document. Compression is very important because the value of this system depends on how many documents you can keep on-line.

There should be a way in **READ** to locate text by section title as well as by word references. I'd suggest a command which lets you specify words from the section title. It scans the section titles and looks for a section title containing all the words you used in your specification (regardless of order). If more than 1 were selected, you could look at them and choose the right one.

More general facilities should be available for moving around in the text when looking at text with **READ**. You should be able to:

- Go to next reference (in already).
- Go to previous reference.
- Go to next marked section.
- Go to previous marked section.
- Show previous page of long section.
- Go to next reference of specified word.
- Go based on section title.

These facilities are why I think that a "command line" at the end might be better then the menu/view mode presently installed.

Also, should we encode the hierarchical structure of the document? We know the levels based on the encoding given to **SCAN**. We might want to say, "Go to the next chapter", or such.

One of the most complicated design tasks is the "rooter". I think the guts of the TeX hyphenation algorithm are a good start. We want to index the original word, then add the derivative forms, flagged as such. Then we can retrieve based on the exact form, or any derivative form.

I don't expect most people to make as much effort encoding a document as we might make in indexing manuals for distribution with this thing. Thus, **SCAN** should be far more intelligent in breaking up documents into sections based on heuristic rules. We'll need to learn what information there may be in a WordStar file, for example, which would help in this task. The utopian idea is that once any document is written (letters, etc.), in an office, the original text is archived, and the formatted text is run through **SCAN** and saved on-line. Anybody who refers to it does so with **READ**. This makes references more productive, saves disc space, aids in building a master document library, and allows readers to make annotations without either changing the original or copying it.

Don't be upset by how slowly **SCAN** runs. I used a stupid merge algorithm in sorting word references. It should be able to be speeded up to run faster than **WORD**. For evaluation, it serves.

Yes, **READ** is awfully fast, isn't it? The sneaky way it looks up indexed words remains fast even with very large documents.

You can also use **READ** to aid in access to paper documents. To do this, just make **WORD** crank out a:

+1 Page *number*

item in the HEADING macro. Then all sections will be flagged with the page number.

Appendix E — AutoCAD-80 Development Log

During the summer and early fall of 1982, I was working furiously on AutoCAD-80, the CP/M-80 version of AutoCAD. At the same time, Dan Drake and Greg Lutz were working on AutoCAD-86 for the IBM (Greg) and the Victor 9000 (Dan). Because AutoCAD-80 started to work earlier, largely because it used intelligent display devices and didn't require the extensive low-level drivers that the IBM and Victor needed (and still need), AutoCAD-80 took the lead on feature implementation through the introduction of the package at COMDEX in November of 1982 and into early 1983.

What follows are excerpts from the extensive development log that chronicled AutoCAD's earliest formative stages. I've tried to select sections that show the first appearance of key facets of AutoCAD, foreshadow features implemented much later, and give a general flavour of the initial development of the package. You can see that from the very start a major theme in AutoCAD development was figuring out how to make it fit in memory. The version described below had to run in a machine with a total memory of 64K bytes, of which only 52K was free for user programs.

The log was begun in July of 1982. The practice of dating entries did not begin until late August.

MicroCAD Notes

When you specify a length (e.g., circle radius, size for text), GDATA/GEDIT should allow you to specify two points (if the first arg was a point, it would ask for a second. Then it would take DIST of the two points and use that for the length. If the second point were null, it would use the origin of the object being entered (center of circle, base of text, etc.)).[192] Installed in GEDIT 8/19/82. Could also do the same thing in GORIENT for angles, but it's a lot less frequently used and I don't feel like doing it at the moment.

Text and shape sizes should be specified in terms of the basic size of the drawing, not as a scale factor.[193]

To compress the redraw file: if start point of current coordinates is same as end point of last, just output (X2+10000, Y2).[194]

Group designation. When you're asked to "digitise entities", you should be able (somehow) to specify one or more boxes, as for the SOLID entity. Then every item which has a vector within that box (or is totally within the box [which??]) should be selected. This will let you grab a group of stuff in a drawing and move it somewhere else, or delete a section. Current point selection is a special case of this.[195]

Speed up regen — for every entity we should be able to calculate an "enclosing box". This is a conservatively larger box which we know to contain all vectors generated by the entity. If the box is totally off the screen, we can skip regen of the entity entirely and avoid all the calls on CLIP. If the box maps into one pixel, just draw a dot and forget it. This should make large, complex, drawings viewed in small pieces much more efficient.[196]

We need an interactive shape editor.[197]

All versions of MicroCAD should be able to write an "entity interchange format" file. The utility which does this may not be actually in the main package, or may be called

---

192 Origin of "two points" specification. This was the first user-interface improvement in AutoCAD.
193 Text size was originally specified as a scale factor for the text definition size, which varied from font to font.
194 This type of compression was not actually implemented until release 2.5 in 1986, though it was used much earlier for slide files.
195 First mention of window object selection, and allusion to the distinction between window and crossing selection.
196 First suggestion of maintaining entity extents and using them for quick rejection. Not implemented until release 2.5, June 1986.
197 We still do, but not as much as when this was written, when blocks had not yet been invented.

as an overlay. All versions of MicroCAD, regardless of internal file representation, will be able to interchange drawings this way.[198] Installed in MicroCAD-80.

Design change: Made DBLIST quit list and return to command mode if you type Control C. Fixed to also pause on Control S. Document this & pass on to C version.[199]

Can we use a better algorithm for FILL? Maybe we should have an entry in the display driver for FILL, as some displays have that capability. In fact, maybe we want to totally rework the interface between the display driver and MCAD: displays are getting smarter and smarter, even the Microangelo can draw circles, and the NEC can do arbitrary arcs as well as fill. Maybe the display should be passed an entity clipped and scaled to screen coordinates. The display driver could either do it itself, or buck it back to a vectoriser mechanism which would call the display again with individual lines as at present. Note that this would seriously mess up the REDRAW file interface and in particular VRTST, which would now have to test any kind of entity the device can draw.[200]

Dimensioning drawings — one should be able to specify a default scale for the drawing, e.g., feet, angstroms, kiloparsecs, and have all MCAD communications in that scale. MCAD should come with a units database, so if the user appends a unit name to a number input, it will perform the conversion to the drawing scale. You should be able to have a drawing rescaled to different units, or just ask for any output (DIST, AREA) in other units (for example, your design is metric but you need to know how many square feet of aluminum plate to buy).[201]

At some point we're going to have to put in some kinds of macro command facility. It might be wise to do this sooner rather than later, since we might avoid lots of custom coding and application specific stuff we'd otherwise get asked for. Obviously, the boundaries between shapes, INSERTs, and command macros are fuzzy. Here's an example of a request from an architect which I'd like to write a macro for. After finishing a floor plan, they want to put in those little dimension lines that look like:

←—————————— 12' 4" ——————————→

---

198 Original suggestion of **DXF** files.
199 First cross-fertilisation of PL/I AutoCAD-80 and C AutoCAD-86.
200 Hardware solid filling was implemented in release 1.2, and the software fill algorithm was eventually rewritten in release 2.0 (October 1984). Passing high-level drawing functions to the display driver is still a dream at this writing in 1987, for the reasons mentioned herein.
201 Great idea. Never implemented.

and they'd very much like to do that just by designating the two end points of the dimension and where the legend was supposed to go. Try working out this example in your head, and you'll see that some form of "entity variable" is required in the macro facility as well as control structures.[202]

Digitiser menu. We should supply preprinted digitiser menu overlays that the user could Xerox & write in the legends for his menu. When you install the program, you would tape the menu to the digitiser & digitise the two corner points. MCAD would then figure out where it was & therefore where the subdivisions were. We might also put the number of vertical & horizontal divisions in the configuration file, so you could make as crowded or open menu as you liked.[203] We might want to provide the option of a screen menu as well. This would be essential for use with a light pen, and might make the digitiser menu work better as well (wouldn't have to take your eyes off the screen). Maybe this could be cleanly integrated with the split-screen work we'll have to do to support one-screen systems.[204] If you have a large digitiser, you could have a small digitiser menu you could move to the area you were working on. Any designation within the menu would indicate the menu. To hit a drawing point there, just move the menu first. I installed a position sense and auto-scale in MCAD-80. When you specify a MENU file, it looks for the file **MCADMENU.CFG**. If this file is present, the digitiser menu lower left corner & upper right corner are taken from it, along with the default menu file. The menu is then automatically loaded. If the file does not exist, the user is asked to digitise the menu corners and to specify the menu file name.

Terminology change: SHIFT has been renamed PAN.

Terminology change: ARRAY is now REPEAT. REPEAT is now ENDREP.[205]

Terminology change: ORIGIN (for INSERT) has been renamed BASE. The BASE command now sets it, and it is called the "Insertion base" in the STATUS display.

---

202 This suggestion foreshadowed the development of AutoLisp, released more than three years later.
203 At this writing, the digitiser menu was fixed at 40 boxes at an absolute position on the tablet. This feature was finally implemented in release 2.0 (October, 1984).
204 First suggestion of an on-screen menu.
205 When REPEAT/ENDREP was eventually retired in release 2.5 (June 1986), the command that replaced it was called ARRAY. It's all on the wheel; it all comes around.

Terminology change: SNAP is now RESOLUTION (which may be abbreviated to RES). It works just like it used to, but defaults ON at the start of a new drawing. The status display was changed to call it "Resolution".[206]

Implemented a new option on the GRID command. You can now say GRID 5X for example, and set the grid to 5 times the resolution (formerly snap value). You can still specify a number without the X and set the grid to anything you like. Should we have grids with different X & Y increments?

Installed the new LIMITS facility. Drawing limits may be changed by the new LIMITS command. GPOINT will reject any point outside the defined drawing limits. Extents have been redefined to be the corners of a box enclosing the actual data in the drawing. They are recomputed on every REGEN (note special handling in REGEN for aborted REGENs). In STATUS they are displayed, flagged if the drawing runs outside the limits. ZOOM ALL was changed to display the drawing limits, or the extents, whichever is larger.[207]

The LIMITS facility has repercussions that run through MCAD . ZOOM ALL was rewritten again to hopefully do what we want. It gives you a display with the lower left corner aligned at the X and Y coordinates of the left lower drawing limit or extent, whichever is less. The extents were changed again to be reset based on generation only for a ZOOM ALL which runs to a normal completion. That means that if you delete something which reduces the used space extents, they won't be updated until you do another ZOOM ALL. Any other approach I can think of has disastrous implications on any attempt we might make to optimise generation of entities. See the comments in DSCMDS and CSCALE which explain this change.

Removed the CENTER command. It has been superseded by the ZOOM C option.

Installed the ZOOM L option. This allows setting the screen window by the lower left corner point and the side width.

Made the LAYER command accept COLOUR as well as COLOR for our friends across the Atlantic.[208] Note that since we've replaced CENTER with ZOOM C, center/centre is no longer a problem. I may just change LAYER to look at the first 2 characters of the command, but I haven't yet.

---

206 This was one of Stephanie Nydell's suggestions. We changed it back to SNAP in release 1.3 (August 1983).
207 First appearance of LIMITS. Fascist limits ruled until release 2.1 (May 1985), when the ability to turn limits checking off was provided.
208 First zephyr foreshadowing the coming hurricane of language translation issues.

Added the OOPS command. Now whenever ERASE is erasing entities, it makes a list called OOPSLIST which records the entity database file location of each entity erased. OOPSLIST is cleared at the start of an ERASE command, so following an ERASE, OOPSLIST represents the entities deleted by the most recent ERASE. The OOPS command scans OOPSLIST and goes through the entity database "un-erasing" all the entities on the list (this is easy because we erase simply by negating the TCODE of the entity, to bring back, just negate again).

The problem of REPEAT/ENDREP accumulation in files could be eliminated by detecting a REPEAT immediately followed by an ENDREP and deleting both on the fly. Then if you delete all the items within the pair, the REPEAT block would go away as well. Not hard to do on a REGEN.

Might we want to install a MODIFY command? It would work just like a LIST, but would give you the chance to change entity properties. Or is the ability to edit the drawing interchange file enough (I vote no). Any suggestions on how to specify a MODIFY of an ENDREP?

I went at the digitiser interface with a chainsaw on 8/26/82. The changes are major in concept and scope, and will be described below:

First, to allow greater resolution for larger digitisers, the scale of coordinates returned by DGDRV was changed from 0–1023 to 0–20479. This twentyfold multiplication of scale allows us to lose no resolution on a digitiser which resolves 200 points per inch and has a longest dimension of 100 inches. So much for large digitisers.

Second, I changed the way DIG smooths samples from the digitiser. Previously, it waited until it had two samples and averaged them. I changed this to use an exponentially smoothed moving average with smoothing constant .10 (it can be changed in DIG [parameter SMOOTH]) . This technique (used to smooth radar samples when computing trajectories) enormously reduces the jitter caused by single random samples, and imparts a "buttery smooth" motion to the cursor on the screen regardless of how jerky the digitiser sampling rate or motion is. It also avoids the overflow which would result from adding two FIXED(15) numbers in the 20000 range.

Third, I installed a totally new mode where the digitiser is used as a true digitiser rather than a screen pointing device. When you enter MCAD-80, the digitiser works just as it does in INTERACT. If you enter the TABLET ON command, MCAD-80 asks you to digitise two points on the drawing on the digitiser and enter their drawing coordinates. From the digitiser coordinates and the coordinates entered, MCAD-80 computes the scaling, translation, and rotation of the coordinate system of the digitiser with respect to that of the drawing, and saves these parameters. It turns on TABLET mode.[209] In TABLET mode, whenever GDATA processes a digitised point, it will transform the digitiser coordinates into the drawing coordinates. This allows dimensioned material to be entered and the actual drawing coordinates to be stored in the entity database.

This is completely general: the full resolution of the digitiser is used in the calculation, and the drawing may be placed on the digitiser in any orientation; may have any desired coordinates (we assume the coordinates are rectangular), and any two points may be digitised to establish the transformation to digitiser space. Thus a small drawing may be placed anywhere on the digitiser, and a large drawing may be digitised in pieces.

When in TABLET mode (which is indicated on the status display), points from the drawing are mapped into drawing space without regard to what the screen displays. Points may be entered which are off the screen, and the screen resolution is of no import. In TABLET mode, the cursor on the screen will track the digitiser cursor as before, but the relationship between where it points on the screen and the drawing points is broken (see below for why this done). The menu may continue to be used while in TABLET mode. Entities entered will be displayed windowed to whatever the screen window is.

Those commands which use entity designation rather than coordinate specification (such as ERASE, MOVE, and LIST), may be used while in TABLET mode, as long as the entity being specified is on the screen. In this case the cursor is used to point to the item on the screen. (That's why it displays in screen coordinates even though TABLET mode is on). The normal mode one would use when entering data in TABLET mode is to set up the TABLET, then do a ZOOM W to put the area being entered on the screen (just point to the drawing areas, TABLET mode will worry about internal coordinates). I think this is reasonable, but it isn't hard to make the cursor track the drawing coordinates rather than the screen if that seems better. I just didn't want to give up the ease of entity designation while in TABLET mode for the common case of deleting a bad entity just entered. My feeling is that the cursor position doesn't matter in TABLET mode because the user is looking at the digitiser, not the cursor on the screen.

---

209   This was, to my knowledge, the first piece of totally general Euclidean geometry installed in AutoCAD . I woke up after four hours of restless sleep with the constructions for the TABLET command fully formed in my mind and a compulsion to implement it. Geometry does that to you.

The TABLET command has other subcommands. TABLET OFF turns off TABLET mode and restores normal digitiser operation. A subsequent TABLET ON command will turn TABLET mode back on with the same coordinate transformations as before. TABLET CAL (for CALIBRATE), forces a recalibration of the tablet, in case the drawing is moved. TABLET CAL turns on TABLET mode if completed successfully.

Changed the extension and nomenclature for interchange files. Previously they were "Entity Interchange Files", **EIF**. Now they are "Drawing Interchange Files", **.DIF**. There's a hundred people who know what a drawing is for every one who knows what an "entity" is.

On 8/27/82 I installed the following optimisation for text generation. If the text is less than 4 dots and more than 2 dots high, I just draw a dot for each character centered vertically in the text height, with each character using .6 of the text box width (who knows?). If the text is less than 2 dots high, I just draw a line where the text would go with length equal to 0.6 x *txsize* x *length_of_text_string*. If the text start point is above the top of the screen or to the right of the screen, all generation is skipped. If the start Y coordinate plus the size of the text is below the bottom of the screen, we skip generation. Also if the start X coordinate plus the string length times the height is less than the left of the screen. The rules for skipping generation entirely are pretty conservative and shouldn't lose text unless you're doing something funny. See EREGEN for full details on the horrors arbitrary text rotation introduce in implementing these tests.[210]

Here's an idea. We've all come up with the idea to optimise regen by calculating an "enclosing box" for every entity. The problem is how to calculate the bounds of the box for shapes and text (arcs don't come cheap either). 'Spose, however, that we add 4 cells to each entity record. When we EREGEN the entity the first time, we have CLIP calculate an entity extents & save them in the entity item. Once calculated, we can instantly see whether an entity is on the screen or not. The disadvantage of this is that it makes the entity file bigger by 4 reals per entity; this is significant, and I don't know enough to say whether the speed is worth the space. It wouldn't be horrible to "have it both ways" I guess. Note that this scheme also gives you a very cheap test for whether the entity contains enough detail to bother generating.[211]

---

210   This the first entity generation optimisation ever installed in AutoCAD.
211   When we finally installed the index file (cheat file) in release 2.5, this is almost precisely how we did it.

As you know, I have great plans for INSERTs. One of the dilemmas with INSERT is that it can be used both for combining drawings done in pieces and as a user-defined part facility. When combining drawings, you want the layer information in the INSERT to be preserved (which is what INTERACT currently does), but when you use an INSERT as a part from a library, you want the INSERTed entity to go onto the current drawing layer. Rather than muck things up with modes and commands, I have installed the following logic: entity layers are copied on an INSERT *unless* the layer number from the insert file is 127. Layer 127 will be replaced by the current layer of the drawing. Thus, you can have it either way you like, and you define how the INSERT works when you create it (which is probably the time that makes most sense).

Further work on INSERT . When you load an INSERT, I now allow you to specify an arbitrary rotation, X size, and Y size.[212] The X size and Y size are divided by difference in the high limit and low limit, respectively of the X and Y dimensions of the drawing being inserted, resulting in X and Y scale factors to be applied to the drawing inserted. The rotation is used to rotate the inserted entities around the insertion base of the drawing being inserted. The resulting transformed entities are then inserted in the working drawing as before, with the insertion base of the inserted drawing aligned above the insertion point designated. If the X and Y scale do not result in a rectangular coordinate system for the inserted drawing, the following restrictions apply:

- CIRCLEs will have the centre moved correctly, but will not be displayed as ellipses. The X scale will be used to change the radius.
- ARCs are totally messed up. I should turn the internal representation back into 3 points and generate a new arc from the points. Instead, I just move the centre, scale the radius by the X scale, and rotate the start and end angles. Doing it right is intended to be in the final release. It isn't hard, just complicated.
- The height of TEXT is always scaled by the Y scale.
- SHAPE size is scaled by the X scale.

Note that everything works correctly as long as the X and Y scale are equal. I envision the installation of a new entity called a SCALE FACTOR which handles aspect ratio changes and scaling at the CLIP level. Then an INSERT can just

---

212 As you'll see below, this implementation was discarded in less than two weeks in favour of the far more general INSERT mechanism still used today. I'm including this description of the initial implementation of INSERT to give the flavour of the many pieces of code implemented and then discarded in favour of more general solutions.

generate this item if required. That's why I didn't go to great lengths here. As long as the drawing contains only lines, points, and traces, it may be changed in aspect ratio without restriction. Anything may be rotated without restrictions. Note that you can rotate your whole drawing by starting a new drawing and INSERTing the old one with a rotation specified and unity scale factor.

I also threw some effort into civilising the LAYER command. Now when you say LAYER, it prompts you with "Layer (Layer no./ON/OFF/COLOR): ". If you say ON or OFF, it prompts you for the list of layers (see **LAYRCM.PLI** for exact messages). The LAYER command previously did a REDRAW on normal exit, because it may have changed the visibility or colour of the lines on the screen. If LAYER exited in error (for example because a bad number were entered after an ON, this REDRAW would be skipped). I changed it so that whenever you leave LAYER, you get a redraw regardless of what you've done. Thus if you say: LAYER ON 1,2 OFF 19 FOOEY, the screen gets updated to reflect the changes you've made before the error.[213]

Installation of the menu driver and associated sicknesses: now **MCAD.COM** is the program you call to enter MicroCAD. You can optionally specify a drawing name on the call. If you do, that will be the default drawing name for menu selections. LPROG was changed to accept an extension, and all the other actual main programs (**MCADE**, **MCADP**, etc.) were given extensions of "**.OVL**", which will prevent some gonzo calling them directly from the console. **MCADE** always works on a **.$$$** work file. This file is prepared for it by **MCAD**, and is converted back into a **.DWG** file or discarded after **MCADE** returns with its completion code in the command tail. I added a PLOT command in **MCADE**. This chains to the plotter driver, which produces a plot of the current state of the **.$$$** drawing file, and chains back to **MCADE** right where you left off. This is very handy for interim views of the drawing.[214]

On 9/6/82 GEDIT was enhanced to allow you to specify two points when an angle (GORIENT) is required. It takes the angle between the first and second point and uses that for the orientation. That way, you can "show it" which way you want to text etc. to run.

---

213   You might call this the first of the many rewrites of the LAYER command.
214   This marked the introduction of the "AutoCAD Main Menu" which has proved so durable. Up to this time, the drawing editor and plotting module were separate programs called from the operating system command line.

As suggested by Richard Handyside, I made entering just an "@" when a point is expected return the same point as last entered. This works out as a logical default, since @x,y is the relative point specification.

Totally re-did the INSERT mechanism. These changes supersede the INSERT enhancements mentioned above, offering all the capabilities with none of the restrictions (the previous INSERT was done as a test vehicle for parts of this implementation). Three new entity types have been added. Type 12 is "Block definition start" and has a name, and X and Y base as attributes. Type 13 is "Block end" and has no attributes. Type 14 is "Block reference" and has attributes of block name, X and Y position, X and Y scale, and rotation.[215]

When you do an INSERT, MCAD asks you for a block name. If this block is not already used in the drawing, it loads the block from a file with the same name (a different name may be used by saying *blockname = filename*). Drive specifiers will be stripped from the file name if it is used as the default block name. A block definition start entity will be placed in the file, with X and Y base drawn from the master record of the drawing being INSERTed (old terminology, origin). Then all the nondeleted entities will be copied into the current drawing, followed by a block end entity. Unlike the old insert, the coordinates of the drawing being loaded are not translated as the entities are loaded. They remain in their host coordinates forever. All transformations are done when the block is elaborated as a result of a block reference entity.

Regardless of whether the block was previously defined or just loaded, a reference to it will then be generated, with the user being prompted for insertion position, X and Y scale, and rotation. As X and Y scale default to 1, and rotation 0, the effect of the command defaults to the operation of the old INSERT.

After entering the entities, PREGEN is called as before to process them. EREGEN contains almost all the support for the new entities. A block definition not previously seen causes the block to be scanned to the matching end (oh yes, blocks can be nested without limit other than memory space). The block is then defined on the in-memory list, with the start and end entity locations saved. If a block definition is seen for a block already known, the block is immediately skipped by the expedient of plugging the already stored end entity location into the entity scan address. This means that having lots of long block definitions in your drawing doesn't slow you up on REGENs.

---

[215] This is essentially the block mechanism used today.

When EREGEN sees a block reference entity, it makes a logical subroutine call in the entity file, pushing the return entity address and continuing with the first entity of the block referenced. Based on the attributes of the block reference item, a transformation descriptor is constructed and stacked so that CXFORM will correctly map the internal coordinates of the block being elaborated into the location, scale, and orientation desired by the user. Since both the return and coordinate transformation items are stacked, block calls may be nested without bound. EREGEN will always treat the regen of a block reference item as primitive. Hence one call on EREGEN may actually draw hundreds of entities. NOTE that as a result, the entity in the entity record when you come back from EREGEN may not be the same one as when you called it. Hence, people like MOVE, and OOPS had better do their MODDR before, not after, the call on EREGEN.

When CLIP is drawing vectors and writing them in the refresh file, it tests whether any block elaboration is underway. If so, all the vectors in the refresh file are tagged with the entity location of the OUTERMOST block being elaborated at the time. Why outermost? Because if you INSERT a part with complex internal structure, and you happen to point to an internal part, you still want the whole thing to move (be deleted, etc.). This very simple trick makes INSERTed entities primitive to all MCAD operations.

But why, you ask, copy the INSERTed entities into the drawing? Why not just save the block name as a file reference? I decided to copy them for reasons of efficiency and maintainability. CP/M file opening is extremely slow — we cannot tolerate a file open for every block reference, so we'd have to open the files and leave them open — not attractive from the standpoint of buffer space! Also, I feel that it's a valuable feature that a drawing be self-contained. If INSERTs stored references to other files, the user couldn't just copy the drawing and be confident he had everything. It would also make user programs which process **.DIF** files much more complicated.[216] If the user wants to change the definition of the part, we can easily provide him the option when the temp copy of the drawing is made (in the menu driver) to replace one or more INSERT blocks in the drawing with new versions in files.[217] Thus, after long thought, it seems to me that the way I put it in is the correct way from a design standpoint, not considering implementation at all. It certainly would have been easier to make each INSERT scan a file! Also, the way I did it allows us to let the user define his own blocks in the drawing independent of INSERT files. This might be handy in certain drawing environments.

---

216 This is still the essence of the justification for copying block definitions into the drawing that uses them.
217 Block redefinition was eventually implemented in release 1.4 (October 1983).

Hence, with these changes to INSERT, the art of coding SHAPEs will become much less necessary for most users. This gives us every capability in accessing stored drawings that Robocom has, and more (as their system cannot store parts which contain other parts).

Here's a point of contention: should a GRID be drawn by setting the grid points on, or by inverting them? If you had a drawing with lots of SOLIDs, the grid might be hard to see. On the other hand, grid points would seem to break lines into separate segments. I've left it as always turning the points on, but I'd like comments on which it should do.

Freeze for stabilisation declared on 9/14/82 04:30. No additional features to be added until release of level 1.0. Only discrepancy resolution form[218] changes will be made.

DRF#1 9/15/82 1:17 Arcs and circles don't always regen if part of a block which has been scaled. Corrected by applying all scale factors to a point centerX+radius,centerY+radius, taking DIST of that, and using that for the test for on-screen. Some extremely bizarre cases may still fail, but no realistic ones. For example, X scale=20, Y scale=.1, angle=90. Is it worth calling CXFORM 4 times to fix this?[219]

DRF#2 9/18/82 2:09 No way to configure a system without digitiser without accessing I/O ports. Output ready mask for digitiser (otherwise unused) was defined as "digitiser present flag". If nonzero, digitiser port will be polled. If zero, digitiser read routine always returns "no sample" and no I/O port accesses will be made.

DRF#3 9/18/82 2:12 Bad test for drawing limits in GEDIT . Fixed.

DRF#4 9/18/82 2:04 Can't set high drawing limits to large (> 600) value. If an overflow happened in CVDTS in attempt to BLIP point, coordinates weren't returned. Changed in GEDIT to ignore overflows in attempt to BLIP (since it's off screen, BLIP wouldn't do anything anyway).

DRF#5 9/18/82 13:28 Setting resolution to zero in MICROCAD doesn't turn off resolution snap mode as documented. Changed to do so. Also, if resolution is set to zero, default GRID value to X limit/10 to avoid confusion if GRID ON is done.

---

218 Like a proper software company, we had to come up with a suitably pompous name for a bug report. Only years later did we actually start calling it a "bug form".
219 The very first AutoCAD bug ever reported, and the first fixed.

DRF#6 9/18/82 13:26 Mike Riddle points out that ".DIF" is used for VisiCalc interchange files. Changed drawing interchange file extension to ".DXF" to keep some gonzo from trying to load one into VisiCalc.[220]

DRF#7 9/20/82 16:16 Shape compiler wasn't closing output file before chaining back to the main menu. This caused the last block not be written out. Changed to close output file in every case. (Reported by Jamal Munshi).

AutoCAD-80 Release 1.1 Development Log

On 10/10/82, I changed ERASE and MOVE to remove the old item by drawing over it with dark vectors. This eliminates the pesky and time-consuming REDRAW which used to follow every ERASE or MOVE, and makes things run immensely faster.[221] The routine UNDRAW in REDRAW accomplishes the magic. Note that if you have overlapped entities, the process of undrawing an entity may turn off bits which should be set by other entities. If this happens, and you really need to see a cleaned-up screen, you can just type REDRAW and everything will be correct. As with the use of FLOOD, my feeling is that this is the correct choice as the full REDRAW was just intolerable for complex drawings. This code has been integrated with the flood code for TRACE and SOLID entities, so that completely filled TRACEs and SOLIDs will be flooded with zeroes to turn them off. The Microangelo provides no way to turn off a pattern-flooded area, so such an area will remain on the screen until you do a REDRAW (its boundary lines will be turned off, making it clear the entity has been deleted).

I went through the whole thing and changed it to AutoCAD . This took about 6 hours because all the MCAD segment names buried in more than half of the modules had to be changed, and the modules recompiled. I sure hope this is the last time! You now start it up with ACAD, and all the file names which previously contained MCAD now use ACAD instead.[222]

DRF#17 10/11/82 19:53 Some people thought PAN worked backward, so it was changed to work backwards. (Reported by Keith Marcelius).[223]

---

220   Thus, .DXF was chosen as the extension for drawing exchange files.
221   That's right, up to this point every command that erased something from the drawing completely redrew the screen rather than erasing the object with dark vectors. This was visual fidelity carried to the lunatic fringe.
222   The product becomes AutoCAD, and **ACAD** is used to call it for the first time.
223   And backwards it still was. After this change was panned by the critics, we changed it back yet again in release 2.0 (October 1984).

I revised the interaction of INSERTs and layers. Previously, INSERTed entities retained their original layer, except entities on layer 127 were statically moved to the current layer at original transcription time. This was not very useful. I changed it so that an INSERT's layers are preserved, except that any entity in a block with layer of 127 will be drawn on the layer of the outermost block active at the time the entity is drawn. This lets you define an insert and put it (or parts of it) on any desired layer at the time it is used.

All the new features contributed to memory growth which blew off our goal of running in a 52K user space. To free up more memory, EACQ, which was the longest overlay, was split up into two separate overlays (ACAD9=EACQ1, ACAD10=EACQ2). SHAPE, TEXT, TRACE, and SOLID acquisition were moved to EACQ2, and COMMAND was changed to call the correct overlay based on which entity type is being entered.[224]

On 10/29/82 I installed light pen support code. There are two new configuration variables for the Microangelo associated with the light pen. The first is called LPUSED, and should be set to **OFF** if the light pen is used and zero otherwise. The second is called LPDELAY, which controls the light pen selection logic. When the light pen is enabled, the screen is run in reverse video so that the tracking cross may be seen better. To designate a point with the light pen, you "pick up" the tracking cross, move it to the desired point, and let go of the tracking cross (by removing pressure from the light pen or taking your finger off the end region). After the delay specified by LPDELAY, the point will be selected. Be careful not to move the light pen too fast across dark regions of the screen, or you'll lose the tracking cross and incorrectly designate a point within that region. Both a light pen and digitiser may be used on the same system, but only one at a time. If both are connected, the digitiser has priority; to use the light pen, just remove the digitiser cursor from the tablet (or otherwise make it stop sending samples).

On 10/30/82 I installed code by Greg Lutz to correct a bug he found in the interaction between INSERTs and REPEAT/ENDREP loops. If an INSERT was invoked inside a REPEAT loop, the coordinates of the block invocation entity were transformed by ETRANS to the loop instance coordinates. When the contents of the block were read, ETRANS transformed them again, resulting in (in the simplest case) double translation of the entities. The new code makes block invocation push AXTRANS and AYTRANS and set them to zero before a block is elaborated. At the end of the block, they are restored from the block execution (BX_) item. This should make all combinations of blocks and repeats work correctly.

---

224   First restructuring of the program to make it fit in memory.

Corrected a bug in TRACE entry reported by Richard Handyside. While entering a continued TRACE, if a point outside the drawing limits is inadvertently entered, a bizarre last leg of the trace was drawn. The TRACE entry code was assuming that when GPOINT returns an NVALID result, the X and Y coordinates were unchanged. In the case of an out of limits point, this is untrue (so that ID can be used on out of limits points). As it turned out, TRACE had already copied the last point to separate variables, so all that was needed was to use them. Now entering an out of limits point will terminate a trace just like hitting the space bar (that is, putting a right angle end on the last segment of the trace).

If the drawing editor crashed while editing a drawing, all changes made in the editing session would be lost beyond hope of recovery. This is because CP/M only updates the file directory item for a file on the disc when the file is closed, and even though we were faithfully writing out the new entities and refreshing the drawing header on every REGEN, all this new information would be lost if the normal closeout code were not executed. I changed REGEN to close and re-open the drawing file at the end of every REGEN. This means that if ACAD crashes, all you have to do to get back to the point of the last REGEN (ZOOM, PAN, ENDREP, or anything else that causes a REGEN) is rename the **.DWG** file to **.BAK** and the **.$$$** file to **.DWG**. The **.$$$** file thus contains a valid drawing as of the last REGEN. If you're doing a long editing session and want to make sure you're protected, just do an explicit REGEN every now and then. In normal use of the package, the user will probably be doing enough REGEN inducing operations that loss in a crash will be minimised.[225]

On 11/1/82 I made the ZOOM and PAN commands in DSCMDS an overlay (**ACAD11**). This freed up about 1600 bytes of memory to waste on other features.

AutoCAD 1.2 Development Log

On 11/17/82 I installed an on-screen menu for the light pen. This works the following way: if configured, the right border of the screen is dedicated to a menu, with one line for each of the 40 menu items. When you point at a menu item, it flashes. You may move up and down the menu area and the flashing will follow

---

225 That's right, as of this point AutoCAD-80 had the ability to recover from a crash and restore the drawing to the last REGEN . Unfortunately, the in-memory paging of AutoCAD-86 precluded an efficient implementation of this capability and, to this day, AutoCAD-86 lacks an automatic crash recovery facility.

you to confirm the location. When you get to the desired menu item and release the light pen, the menu item will go to reverse video as it is executed. It will be restored to normal when the light pen is next pointed into the menu area. When the light pen menu is used, the aspect ratio of the screen is changed and XDAR and YDAR are adjusted to accommodate the space removed from the right of the screen.[226]

On 11/18/82, as requested by Lars Moureau and Keith Marcelius, I added a feature to INSERT which allows old-style pure transcription of the file being loaded, rather than copying it into a block. You select this mode by preceding the file name with an asterisk.[227] You may insert a file previously loaded as a block without any duplication or error. The block is ETRANS relocated to the desired insert point based on its insertion base, but scaling and rotation are not allowed and the prompts for them are not issued.

To allow clearer and more concise labeling of MENU items displayed on the on-screen menu, I added a "menu label" field to the menu file. If the first character of a line in the .MNU file is "[", the text between the "[" and the next "]" will be displayed on the screen menu. The actual text sent to the input processor when that item is selected will be the text that follows the "]".

Often one wants to specify high-level commands using the menu facility but is thwarted by the inability to allow user-specified parameters in the midst of a canned input stream. No more. I installed a "menu macro" facility which allows the interpretation of the menu text to be suspended, a user input to be accepted (from the keyboard, digitiser, light pen, etc.), and then the menu text interpretation to be resumed. As the menu text is scanned, if a "\" character is hit, the next user input is accepted via GDATA(0) (that is, terminated by space, semicolon, or return), and logically inserted in the menu string at that point. After the user entry is processed, the scan of the menu text resumes after the "\".[228]

For example, suppose we've defined an INSERT file called **NANDGATE** and we want to be able to insert it at 1 x 1 scale with no rotation simply by pointing to the location. We would define a menu item as follows:

---

226 This marked the initial implementation of the screen menu at the right side of the screen. It was initially intended as a convenience for light pen users, but rapidly became the primary means by which users interacted with AutoCAD.
227 Thus, **INSERT ***.
228 Menu macros are born. Until the release of AutoLisp in with release 2.1 in May of 1985, this was the primary means of extending AutoCAD . The initial implementation of AutoCAD AEC (AE/CADD) was done entirely with menu macros.

`[NAND]insert nandgate \1 1 0`

This would do the INSERT command and supply the file name. Then a user input would be requested to supply the insertion location. The scale and rotation queries would be supplied by the menu text automatically. If that's not esoteric enough, define an insert called **BOX** which is a square with side of 1. You can then define a menu item as follows:

`[BOX]insert box \@ \@ \0` *Obsolete — see below.*

To use this menu item, you select it, and then digitise the location you want the box to go. Then the "@" forces a "2 points" entry form for the X scale. You supply the second point from the digitiser which sets the X scale to make the box as wide as the distance from the box origin to the second digitise. The second "@" forces "2 points" for the Y scale also, and you enter the second point specifying the height. Since the box has side of 1, the scaling makes it as big as the lengths you've specified. The angle is forced to zero. Thus you point to BOX, point to where you want it to go, point to where you want the right edge to go, and point to where you want the top to go, and there's your box. And all without adding any new entities to ACAD! Yes, I know it would be nicer to just point to the upper right of the box, and I'm working on that.

Note that in defining these menu items, the placement of spaces to force execution of commands is critical. I'm downright embarrassed at how little code it took to put this in. It's all in GDATA and it's not much.

On 11/19/82 I added the ability to specify both the X and Y scale factors of an INSERT by simply entering one point. If you respond to the "X scale factor" query for an INSERT with "CORNER" ("C" is enough), then it prompts you for the "upper right corner". You digitise a point, and the $|\Delta X|$ becomes the X scale factor and the $|\Delta Y|$ becomes the Y scale factor. Thus if you've defined the INSERT to be 1 by 1 you can insert it and scale it to the screen just by digitising two points.

Thus, with the changes made today, the BOX macro defined above becomes:

`[Box]insert box \center \0`

To use it, you just point to the BOX menu item, the left lower corner of the box, and the upper right corner point. A box is then inserted to the scale you selected. To make the rotation variable, replace the last "`0`" with a "`\F21M`", and you'll then be able to point to the angle you want the box to go on.

On 11/20/82 I finally got around to installing a buffering routine in LOAD. This cut the time needed to load the text shapes (**TXT.SHP**) by a factor of four. This reduces the annoying delay during the initial drawing of a picture while

AutoCAD loads the text definition. I also cleaned up the carriage return/line feed logic of error messages in LOAD, which had a bad case of conceptual acne.

I made some minor changes in the format of the on-screen menu which allow the menu to be overwritten with a new menu without confusing the light pen logic. This lets you have items in your main menu which select subsidiary menus. (Previously if you did this, it confused the logic which inverted the last-selected item, and you wound up with two items inverted. These fixes correct this bug.)

As suggested by Mike Ford, I changed the "Digitise entities" message to "Select objects".

I installed the long-awaited "window designation" facility to EID . The EID prompt message was further changed to "Select objects or window:", and EID was changed to recognise the letter "W" as a response before the first point is entered. Upon receiving the "W" it prompts for a left lower corner point and a right upper corner point (actually, you can enter them in any order). It then scans the refresh file and selects all entities which have at least one visible vector within the window, and from those only the ones which have no visible vectors outside the window. Read that over again and think about it for a while; it's not easy to comprehend, but it's easy to use and meets the most logical user assumption, I think.[229]

If you're using a light pen, often you want to move the tracking cross somewhere else on the screen to unclutter an area you're examining. Since the tracking cross only moves when the light pen is selected, and deselecting it designates a point, this generated an error message when the point was input to the command prompt. I changed COMMAND to just ignore points input at the command prompt, so you can move the tracking cross at will. Yes, I know, but this is the kind of little thing that users appreciate.

I added a "Last entity" selection option in EID . If you reply to the EID "Select objects" prompt with "L", EID will choose the most recently entity (whether visible or not). This is very, very handy especially for deleting the last thing you entered by mistake. Note that with ERASE you can step back through the file entity by entity by entering multiple ERASE L commands.

I installed Dan Drake's analytically correct code for calculating the number of segments to draw in a circle. This makes small circles smoother and big circles

---

[229] Window selection is implemented. Its complement, Crossing selection, was not implemented until release 2.5 (June 1986).

faster. It also optimises circles too small to see into a dot, speeding up REGEN of circles when you've zoomed way out. *Note to myself*: Dan's code uses ACOS, which pulled in 500 bytes of library. I must change it and define ACOS in terms of ATAN which ANG already pulls in. If you don't see a note below which says I did it, please remind me.

On 11/21/82 I looked up ACOS and redefined my own in EREGEN in terms of ATAN and SQRT. It gets the same answer as the one in the library and gets rid of 500 bytes (n.b., I wonder how much more can be saved with tricks like this — look at the library some time).

I installed a new BLOCK command. This command lets you create a block "on the fly" from parts of an existing drawing. This makes for more spontaneity while drawing, as you don't have to define all your parts ahead of time so you can insert them from files. When you enter the BLOCK command, you will first be asked "Insertion base:". Supply the point which is to become the insertion base of the new part (point to it on the screen). This has exactly the same effect as the BASE command when making an INSERT file. Next the standard "Select objects" prompt will appear, and you may use any of the entity designation options to choose the entities which are to make up the new part. To confirm that the entities you've selected are the right ones, they will disappear from the screen. Next the prompt "Block name:" will appear. Simply enter the name you want the new block to have (as no file name is relevant here, no equal sign should appear in the prompt). AutoCAD will then construct a block with that name containing the designated entities with the specified insertion base. You may then immediately use that block just like it was INSERTed from a file. The entities which were placed into the block are deleted from the drawing. If you don't want them to be deleted, just say "OOPS" after the BLOCK command finishes, and they will be restored to the drawing.

I installed a CHANGE command. This command is not the same as Mike Riddle's, and I don't know whether it is what we want. It is what I wanted to clean up drawings, and I'm convinced that something like it is a valuable addition to AutoCAD. I'm equally sure that what we really want isn't exactly this command, so maybe we don't want to document it until we come up with a final design. It is, however, awfully doggone handy. But on to the facts. When you say CHANGE, the first thing that appears is the standard "Select objects" prompt. You designate the objects that you want to change. Only lines and circles can be changed. Any other objects pointed to will not be changed (but they will disappear from the screen, only to reappear on the next regen — this is what we call "el buggo"). Assuming you've selected one or more entities, you will next be asked for an "Intersection point". If the object is a line, its endpoint closest to the intersection point will be changed to meet the intersection point. If ORTHO mode is on, the line's new coordinate in the direction of its longest run will be forced to the value of the corresponding coordinate of the other end. Thus, in ORTHO mode, only orthogonal lines will result from a CHANGE (this sounds clunky, but just wait until you use it to make a horizontal line meet a circle while zoomed way in, then you'll stand up and applaud). If the entity being changed is a circle, its radius will be adjusted so that the circumference of the circle passes through the intersection point. We all know that we need a much more general EDIT command which can talk about any property of an entity, plus modify entities based on properties of other entities (e.g., "Run this line in this direction until it hits that arc"[230] or "Make this circle pass through the endpoint of that line,"[231] and so on), but until we get one, this thing makes cleaning up perspective drawings and hybrid digitised stuff like the shuttle drawing about ten times faster than before.[232]

On 11/23/82 I fixed a bug in EREGEN. If we were generating a circle or arc which was very large with respect to the screen, the code which calculated the number of segments to draw could divide by zero. Since in this case we want to restrict the number of segments to the maximum anyway, I just changed it to catch the ON condition and set the number of segments to the maximum, which is shorter in code and less complex than testing for zero everywhere in this fairly involved code.

The code which decides how many segments to use to approximate an arc or circle was basing the number of segments drawn on the relative sizes of circle and screen, but did not reduce the number of segments when drawing an arc. Hence, a 5° arc would be drawn with as many segments as a 360° circle. This made for very beautiful arcs, but very slow drawing! I changed it to first calculate the number of segments it would be drawing were the circle complete, then reduce the count by the expression max(2, $NS \times TINCR/2\pi$), which guarantees that no arc will be compressed to a straight line, but proportionally decreases the sector count for arcs.

I made another speedup change in EREGEN: previously I drew text as dots if it was too small to read and just as a line if it was smaller than a dot. I changed this to always draw text too small to read as a line the approximate length of the generated text. This makes display of small text about 5 times faster, as only one entity is generated per text entity rather than one per character. I find the result just as aesthetic. Comments are welcome.

---

230   Finally provided in the EXTEND command in release 2.5 (June 1986).
231   Provided by object snap in release 2.0 (October 1984).
232   The CHANGE command was initially implemented to clean up drawings before Comdex 1982. I always viewed it as a short-term stopgap until a better editing command was developed. It's still with us.

> ## Comdex 1982
>
> "Strange memories on this nervous night in Las Vegas. It seems like a lifetime, or at least a Main Era — the kind of peak that never comes again. Maybe it *meant something*. Maybe not in the long run... but no explanation, no mix of words or music or memories can touch that sense of knowing that you were there and alive in that corner of time and the world. Whatever it meant... .
>
> "There was madness in any direction, at any hour. You could strike sparks anywhere. There was a fantastic universal sense that whatever we were doing was *right*, that we were winning.
>
> "That, I think, was the handle — that sense of inevitable victory over the forces of Old and Evil. Not in any mean or military sense; we didn't need that. Our energy would simply *prevail*. There was no sense in fighting — on our side or theirs. We had all the momentum; we were riding the crest of a high and beautiful wave."
>
> Hunter S. Thompson, *Fear and Loathing in Las Vegas*

AutoCAD-80 Release 1.3 Development Notes

On 12/16/82 I installed a centered text option in EACQ2. When the "Insertion point" prompt is issued, you may now enter "C". This will cause a "Center point" prompt to appear — a point is supplied as for the insertion point, but the text will be centered both vertically and horizontally around this point. This is accomplished by making a dummy run through SHDRAW for the text with a new flag set which causes SHDRAW simply to update a max and min X and Y area used by the text. This area is then used to adjust the insertion point so that the text will be centered around it. Implementation note: we assume in this code that the text font has already been loaded before the first text entity is entered. Because earlier logic only loaded the text font the first time EREGEN encountered a text entity, this assumption was not always true. As a result, COMMAND was fixed to check whether the text font was loaded when a TEXT entity command is encountered. If it is not (TXGRID=0), then LOAD is called to load **TXT.SHP** before EACQ2 is called. This guarantees that EACQ will be able to calculate the size of the text if required for centering. The centered text is very handy for labeling macros for things such as flowcharting packages, and will play an important part in the dimensioning facility.

The centered text mode is "remembered" and if more text is entered by just pressing return at the next command prompt, subsequent lines will be centered under (in the logical sense, depending on orientation) the original line.

On 12/19/82 I completed the installation of "simple dimensioning". This is a form of automatic dimensioning derived from a description of how Computervision does it as described by Jamal Munshi. Some changes and additional features were added in this implementation. The facility is controlled by the DIM command. The entire facility is in an overlay, and if the feature is not purchased with the package, the overlay can simply be deleted from the release disc. COMMAND will catch the overlay not found error and print the message "Optional feature not installed." and return to the command prompt.[233]

First some background and terminology: a dimension consists of two "extension lines" (referred to as "witness lines" in some texts) which lead from the points being dimensioned to the specification of the dimension, a "dimension line" which has arrows on the end and which points to the extension lines, and the "dimension text", which gives the actual dimension between the two extension lines. If there is sufficient room between the extension lines, the dimension line will be within the extension lines, as in:

If there isn't room between the extension lines, the dimension line will be split and point to the extension lines from outside, as in:

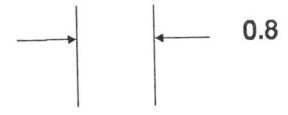

---

[233] Dimensioning was the first new feature installed in AutoCAD after COMDEX 1982, and the first deliberately intended as an extra cost add-on. The complete design of the initial dimensioning facility is presented here as an example of the developer documentation of the period.

In my implementation, dimension lines always run either horizontally or vertically. You can dimension a diagonal with a horizontal or vertical dimension line simply by running the extension lines to the ends of the diagonal line. To create a dimension, enter the DIM command. The first prompt to appear will be "First extension line origin:". You should designate the point near the item being dimensioned where you want the first extension line to appear. Next the prompt "Dimension line intersection:" will be given. You should then designate where the dimension line should be placed relative to the first extension line point (i.e., where the arrow will hit the first extension line). If the line between the first extension line origin and the dimension line intersection is more horizontal than vertical, the dimension line will run vertically, if more vertical, the dimension line will run horizontally. (Draw a couple and you'll understand.) Finally, you will be asked "Second extension line origin:" which requests you to designate the point near the object where the other extension line is to go. Before moving on to the rest of the command and its action, let me explain how these three points are used to define the dimension.

The first extension line will always start at the point designated for the first extension line origin. It will run either vertically or horizontally depending on the predominant direction between the origin point and the dimension line intersection. Any displacement of the dimension line intersection point from a true vertical or horizontal is ignored — it supplies only the direction and distance between the extension line end and the dimension line (or in other words, the dimension is taken from the extension line, not the dimension line, which is what you want). The second extension line is then drawn from the second extension line origin point, in the same direction as the first extension line, as far out as the first extension line went (note that the ends of the extension line at the dimension line always line up, but the ends nearest the item being dimensioned may appear anywhere, to accommodate strangely shaped objects). The dimension line will then be run either vertically or horizontally from the first extension line to the second.

There is a value called "arrow size" which influences many parts of dimensioning. The ANSI drafting standard specifies that drawn arrows should be 1/8 inch in size. Since we don't know the scale of the final drawing, we don't initially know how big to make the arrows. Thus we have a variable called arrow size which controls this. If no arrow size is specified, we will guess and use 1/64'th of the smallest dimension of the drawing. The arrow size controls the size of the arrows themselves, which are drawn with solid fill at the ANSI-specified aspect ratio of 1 to 3. It also controls how far the extension lines extend past the dimension line (1 arrow length), how much spacing will be placed between the dimension text and the dimension lines (1 arrow length), and the initial size of the dimension text (1.5

arrow length). Further, if the arrows must be moved outside the extension lines, their shafts will have a length of one arrow length. The arrow size can be explicitly specified by the "DIM A" command, and will be saved in the drawing header. ANSI specifies that all arrows in a drawing shall have the same size.

Now we come to the matter of the text that specifies the dimension. The user will be prompted with "Dimension text:". If just a carriage return is given as the response, the distance in the direction of the dimension line will be measured and edited as a decimal number with four significant digits. Trailing zeroes and decimal points will be suppressed. If text is entered, the text will be used as-is. Since the text is terminated by a carriage return, spaces may be used within it.

Now that all of the components of the dimension have been acquired, the dimension is assembled on the screen. The first test is whether the dimension lines should be drawn inside or outside the extension lines. Our criterion for this decision is that if we have less than 8 times the arrow size between the lines, we'll draw the arrows outside, otherwise we'll try them inside. The text within the dimension is always drawn with angle 0 (that is, horizontally). This is in conformance with the ANSI standard, which specifies "unidirectional" dimensioning as the preferable technique. As a result, there are two cases depending on whether the dimension line runs horizontally or vertically. If it runs horizontally, we have to squeeze the text between the arrows so that the arrows run from the first and last characters of text. If it runs vertically, the lines run from the top and bottom of the letter area. In the horizontal case it's obvious that the length of the text is an important consideration in composing the dimension. In the vertical case we might just ignore the length (as only the height matters in fitting the arrows), but this isn't wise as we might overlay the object being dimensioned with the text. Consequently, for both the horizontal and vertical dimension line cases we compute a length in which the dimension text must be forced to fit; if horizontal, this is the total dimension line less 6 arrow lengths (2 for arrows, 2 for minimum length dimension lines, 2 for clearance between text and lines). If vertical, the fit length is two times the least distance between the dimension line and the extension line origin (this guarantees that the text won't overlap a straight figure; if the figure is convex, it may still overlap, and the user will have to move the dimension line further out).

Now that we know the space we have to work with for the text, we calculate the actual size needed to draw the text with its initial size of 1.5 x *Arrow_size* (taken by measuring characters in ANSI-standard drawings). If the text fits at that size, it is drawn centered in the dimension line, and the lines extend to within 1 arrow size of the text. If the text doesn't fit, it will be reduced in size until it just fits in the space available. In the case where the arrows are drawn outside the extension lines and the dimension line runs horizontal, the text will be fit within 8 arrow lengths.

The extension lines and dimension line may have any geometrical relationship you desire; you may draw vertical dimensions top to bottom, bottom to top, and with the dimension line to the left or right of the extension line origins, and of course the equivalent for horizontal dimensions. The order you specify the ends makes a difference only when the arrows are drawn outside the extension lines, as the text will always be placed on the end of the second-specified dimension line (affording user control of placement), and when continuing dimensions.

At the point the "First extension line origin:" prompt appears, you may enter "B" or "C" to continue the last dimension. Either reply immediately advances you to the "Second extension line origin:" prompt, and draws a new dimension based on the last one. "B" adds a dimension relative to the *first* point of the last dimension, drawing the dimension above (or whatever) the last one. This is what you do when you want a set of dimensions all relative to the same base line. Multiple "B" DIM commands will all reference the same base line. The "C" response draws a dimension relative to the second extension line of the last dimension, with the dimension line colinear with the last one drawn (unless the last one was outside the extension lines, in which case the new dimension line will be moved to clear it). This is what you do when you could care less about cumulative tolerances and want all the dimensions in a chain.

All the items that make up the dimension (lines, solids, text) are drawn as primitive entities, so they may be manipulated individually. The dimension facility is simply a tool to make these entities for the user, there is no special support in AutoCAD for dimensioning per se. The dimension code is split between DIM1 and DIM2 so as not to constitute the largest overlay and hence consume more memory — for logical purposes you can consider the two to be one piece of code.

On 12/24/82 I fixed a bug in ERASE reported by Jamal Munshi. This is one of the more humorous bugs I've seen so far in AutoCAD . Suppose you had a REPEAT/ENDREP loop with more than 1 entity in it. If you did an ERASE W and pointed to the entire bounds of the array elaboration, the scan of the refresh file would find each entity once for every array instance. Since there was more than one item in the array, the refresh file will contain a new entity header for each instance in the array. If the operation was an ERASE, and the total number of array items was even, ERASE which just inverts the entity type to delete the entity, would flip the sign an even number of times, leaving the entity not deleted. Since the UNDRAW was driven from the REDRAW file, the items would disappear on the screen, but come back on the next REGEN . I fixed this by making ERASE test whether the entity it's about to delete is already deleted. If so, it just leaves it alone. It's then also necessary to fix OOPS, since OOPS will also see duplicate entities and may re-delete something it shouldn't. Note that other entity designation commands can still be messed up by this case. I think that the real solution is to make EID scan the select list as it chooses each entity and guarantee that any given entity is selected only once. Maybe I'll change it to do that someday.

On 12/25/82 I installed support alternate forms of cursors, as available in the Aurora 1000 board, whose driver I am finishing up. The Aurora 1000 offers a software-selectable set of cursor types. I installed code in various places to support them, if available in a display device, in a de-vice-in-de-pen-dent manner. If the display device handles multiple cursor types, it should reference the external **fixed(7)** variable CURSEL . When DSMARK is called, if CURSEL is 0, the normal cursor should be displayed. If 1, then a box or window cursor should be displayed. If 2, a rubberband cursor should be displayed (i.e. crosshairs "pulling" a line). If CURSEL is nonzero, the other point (other box corner, origin of rubberband line) is given by the external fixed variables CURSLX and CURSLY . These variables are set to the screen coordinates of the last point returned normally by DIG — thus they are normally set to the origin point of the last point entered. Commands may set them (remember to use screen coordinates!) to other points if desired. Code installed to use this new feature is: EID uses a box cursor for the "W" form of designation; DSCMDS uses a box cursor for ZOOM W selection; EACQ1 uses a rubberband cursor for LINE acquisition, and EACQ2 uses a rubberband for TRACE acquisition. Note that if the display device doesn't support alternate cursor types, it may just ignore CURSEL, CURSLX, and CURSLY .[234]

I decided to go ahead and fix the multiple designation bug mentioned above correctly. I removed the kludge code installed yesterday in EDIT for the ERASE and OOPS commands. Then I installed code in EID which, for every point selected, scans the list of already selected entities and if it finds that the designated entity is already on the list, doesn't add it. Instead, it adds the entity to a duplicate selection list, DUPLST . This is necessary because if EID is going to delete the found entities

---

234   The Graphics Development Laboratory A-1000 (Aurora-1000) was the first true high performance graphics board AutoCAD supported. The A-1000 was a high resolution (512 x 480) 16 colour board with a high-level command set including true polygon fill, multiple cursor types, and window and viewport support on-board. Its capabilities encouraged implementation of congruent facilities in AutoCAD, and exerted an influence on the design of the package still felt today.

from the refresh file (as for an ERASE or MOVE), it has to save all refresh file finds, even if for duplicate entities. After preparing the unique list and the duplicate list, if UNDRAW is requested, it undraws all refresh file entries in both lists. Otherwise, it just flushes the duplicate list and returns the unique list. This fixes all confusions known to exist when selecting entities within REPEAT/ENDREP loops.

On 1/1/83 I went back to work on the DataType 150 driver.[235] First some words about the design and history of this unfortunate device. It attempts to emulate a Tektronix 4010, but since its internal resolution is only 512 x 250, it translates the Tektronix coordinate space of 1024 x 780 into this raster matrix. This has a number of painful side effects. First, of course, the resolution is low to start with (vertical is the bad direction). Next, since we have to send Tektronix coordinates to the beast, AutoCAD believes that it has more resolution than is really available, so it draws things (text and circles) which aren't really visible on the screen. This makes things runs a lot slower than if the terminal were "honest". Since the Tektronix is a direct view storage tube, there were no commands defined in its command set for erase. Data Type extended the command set to include a dark vector, but did not include a complement vector. This has a horrible impact on the digitiser support, to be discussed below.

The DT150 driver, as currently implemented, uses the top 21 lines of alphanumeric space on the screen for the graphics display. The bottom 3 lines are used as a scrolling region for communication of commands. This is achieved by using the Televideo lock line command for the blank lines that overlay the graphics area, and leaving the bottom lines as a scrolling text area. Thus, the addressable graphics area is 1024 x 656. The terminal lacks any kind of area fill, so this is done with vectors as the AutoCAD default. Since there is no complement draw, implementing the screen cursor is basically impossible. I fixed it to draw a 3 x 3 (in Tek coordinates) cross. It draws this cross, then erases it whenever it moves and redraws it at the new location. Since there's no complement screen function, this means that the cross *erases whatever it passes over*! This means that as you use the digitiser, you slowly wipe the screen, until you're forced to do an explicit REDRAW to see where you are. I made the cursor small deliberately so that it wipes as little as possible.

---

235 In the early days of AutoCAD, we attempted to support some truly awful hardware in the hopes that its manufacturers would help us promote AutoCAD . To give you a flavour of some of the things we tried, I'm including a description of the attempt to get AutoCAD-80 running on the DataType 150, an RS-232 graphics terminal. The DataType 150 was neither the best nor the worst device we attempted to support. It shared with the best and the worst one common attribute: we never sold a single AutoCAD configured for it.

Another offshoot of supporting terminals which "lie" about their resolution is that the BLIPs drawn for selected points may not look right. In the case of the DT150, they are so small that sometimes they look like "T"s. (Sometimes because it depends on where the center point maps into the modularity of the logical and physical resolution.) I made the variable in BLIP which determines the size of blip external and named it BLIPPO. A display driver is now free to redefine the size of the BLIP in its initialisation routine to be whatever displays correctly on the screen (n.b., should we change the closeness criterion in EID to equal BLIPPO? I think so, but I haven't done so).

In the process of working on the DT150 driver I discovered a "facet" of PL/I which I should warn other potential ploners about. Suppose you have a procedure which you want to pass different text strings for processing. You might declare that procedure as:

```
ZONK: PROCEDURE(PSTR);
      DECLARE PSTR CHARACTER(128) VARYING;
```

then call it as **ZONK('Booga')**. Be warned, the strong typing rules will force all the string constants you use as arguments to be 128 characters long, with the first as the length flag. Of course it will work fine, and the only way you'll notice you've been had is when you wonder where 30K of memory went. The most obvious way out is to make **PSTR** a global variable and assign the strings to it. Assignment doesn't force conformance on the right side, so the right side string will retain its attribute of **CHARACTER(n)**, and be converted to the variable string on the left hand side. This little change knocked 2K of wasted data space out of the DT150 driver, and I suspect that I can find similar savings throughout AutoCAD (in particular the PROMPT routine).

On 1/5/83 I "completed" the driver for the DataType 150. This terminal is such a pig that should we really wish to sell AutoCAD on it, a literally endless amount of work can be poured into its gullet without yielding a usable product. What I ended up with was a driver with no on-screen menu, a graphics area at the top, and a 3 line scrolling region at the bottom. Several days were wasted trying to get an on screen menu to work using the cursor positioning keys to make the menu selection. I abandoned this after it became clear that there were fatal flaws in the firmware in the terminal which precluded using this strategy. In order to implement the separate scrolling region and graphics area, I take advantage of the fact that the graphics and alphanumeric displays are separate and logically ORed to create the CRT drive. I use the Televideo lock line function to make the top 21 lines not scroll. Since they are cleared to blanks and don't scroll, they don't interfere with the graphics drawn in the same space. The bottom lines, being unlocked, scroll. I attempted to put a menu on the right side of the screen, but discovered that the cursor address function refuses to go to a line that's locked. It will only address lines in the scrolling region. To circumvent this, I tried unlocking the screen, updating the menu, then locking it again. Because of the way the line lock command works, this takes about 60 characters to do, so moving the cursor up and down the menu took an extremely long time to do. Furthermore, when running this sequence, the terminal would randomly get confused about its scrolling and insert blank lines in the menu area, transpose lines from the bottom 3 into the middle of the screen, and even scroll up the status line from the bottom of the screen. As this behaviour was completely random and not related to XON–XOFF handshaking what was previously checked out, I just decided to pitch the whole idea of an on screen menu and let this porker trot along without.

That left the issue of how to handle commands with lengthy output, such as STATUS and DBLIST . I installed a new procedure in the terminal driver, called DSLONG. (This was put in all the other drivers, but is null in them, as they are two screen versions.) Any command which generates lengthy output should call DSLONG(TRUE) before the first line of the output and DSLONG(FALSE) at the end. It must not exit without calling DSLONG(FALSE). The DT150 DSLONG procedure, on TRUE, clears the graphics and alphanumeric screens and unlocks the scrolling region so the whole screen can scroll. On FALSE, it displays the prompt "Press any key to continue:" and waits for an input character. When it gets one, it clears the screen, re-locks the graphics area, and calls REDRAW to put the picture back up. This kind of trick should work on any reasonable graphics terminal (I hope). The commands which activate DSLONG are STATUS, DBLIST, LAYER ?, and LIST.

On 1/7/83 I fixed some bugs in the shape compiler. First, SHCOMP was failing to test whether the shape number was between 0 and 255. Since the shape number is used to subscript a number of arrays, a bad shape number could lead to disaster. I installed an error message and made the compiler terminate with a syntax error. (Reported by Lars Moureau).

On 1/14/83 I installed code to aid in the use of devices whose support of colors is truly heroic (such as the Vectrix 384). The LAYER COLOR subcommand now accepts "*" as an argument. LAYER COLOR * will set all layers colors equal to their layer numbers (layer 1 color=1, ... layer 127 color=127). Thus, drawings with many colors may be created simply by assigning the layer number equal to the desired color.[236]

---

[236] This was the first device we supported with a large colour gamut. It supported 512 colours from a palette of 16 million. It was five years ahead of its time.

On 2/12/83 I completed support of the Hitachi "Tiger Tablet", HDG-1111. This is an RS-232 tablet very similar in general specifications to the HI-PAD from Houston Instrument. It offers either a 12 button cursor or a stylus as the digitising instrument. The driver, in file DSDRVTG, is very similar to the HI-PAD driver. The Tiger Tablet offers many protocol options, and the modes in which I chose to run it were chosen for similarity to the HI-PAD. Should we choose to recommend this device, we can switch to the more efficient and faster-to-track binary mode.

The stylus works like the cursor on the HI-PAD. Moving it on the tablet moves the crosshairs, and pressing it down selects a point. The 12 button cursor is implemented in the following way: moving the cursor on the pad moves the crosshairs. The zero button selects a point. Buttons 1 through 9 select the first 9 menu items immediately, regardless of the position of the cursor. Thus, very commonly used menu items may be set up for instant access through the cursor. Note that with either the stylus or the cursor, conventional menu selections may be made either by pointing to the screen menu and doing a point select (stylus press or zero button), or by making a point select within the digitiser menu.

On 2/21/83 I implemented a driver for the USI Optomouse.[237] This is a four button optical mouse which talks a protocol very close to the Summagraphics Bit Pad. The Optomouse driver (in file DGDRVOM) replaces the digitiser driver in AutoCAD. Assuming that the "tail" of the mouse is at the top, the buttons are numbered with the top row 2–1 and the bottom row 3–4. (The buttons are activated by pressing one end or the other of a bar on the mouse.) Button 1 is the "hit" button and selects a pointed to menu item or a point on the screen. Buttons 2 through 4 select the first 3 menu items regardless of the position of the mouse, and thus may be used for very frequently used commands, obviating the need to move the mouse to point at the main menu. (Note: if this doesn't work for you, it's because whoever generated ACAD forgot to turn on the KEYPAD compile time variable in DIG — just a word to the perplexed.) The Optomouse can be configured by output commands for various modes. Currently, the only configuration done is to program it for 10 ms between samples in order to speed up sampling rate and smooth cursor motion. Note that this driver was developed and tested with a prototype Optomouse and will have to be modified when the production mice with auto-baud rate sensing are delivered. Note that the mouse driver differs from a standard digitiser driver in that DGACOR isn't enabled, and that the output coordinates are clipped to prevent returning a sample in the digitiser menu area, which we can't use with a relative positioning device like a mouse.

---

237 This was the first mouse ever supported by AutoCAD.

On 2/23/83 I blind-implemented a driver for the Summagraphics Bit Pad to solve a customer requirement.[238] The driver was created by modifying the Optomouse driver and tested with the Optomouse. It differs from the Optomouse driver only in that it doesn't send the command string to send sample rate, it turns on DGACOR, and enables the digitiser menu as for the HI-Pad and Tiger Tablet. The driver was tested with the Optomouse and works, but customer comment will be required before the driver can be considered operational.

On 3/11/83 I completed a complete rewrite of the plotter driver, encompassing both the device-independent part and the Houston Instrument driver. The rewritten driver is now compatible with the version in AutoCAD-86, the offshoot of the Plotter Integrity Project. The changes between the old and new drivers are massive, and will be discussed in something approaching order of importance.

First, there is now a plot configuration file which saves all the parameters for the plot. **ACADPLOT.CFG** is written and updated by the plot driver, being created the first time a plot is made. It contains the plotter manufacturer name, the plot paper size (either a standard ANSI or DIN size, or a custom size specified by the user in inches or millimeters) the units the plot is in (again Inches or Millimeters, also selecting ANSI or DIN sheet size nomenclature), and the pen width (of the narrowest pen), which is used to calculate the number of vectors needed to FILL a solid and the accuracy required for true circles and arcs.

The file also contains a driver specific configuration section. For the Houston Instrument driver, this specifies the model number (DMP-?), the assignments of pens, line types, and velocities to each color in the drawing.

The plotter driver is now organised so that one master driver can be supplied which runs all plotters we support. The code has been written so that drivers for each manufacturer can be overlays, so there will be no limit on the number of different plotter protocols we can support in one driver.

Once the standards for a plot are specified, they need not be entered again unless the user wants to change the standards. If a change is desired, the user can go through the items, changing only those desired. A null entry to any configuration query leaves the old value unchanged. An interactive entry dialogue is provided in the HI driver to set up the assignment to drawing colors. "X" ends the dialogue. If the parameters are changed, they may be used in the changed form for just this plot or for all future plots, at the user's option.

---

238 QA ? What's that?

Handling of scale and windowing the plot onto the paper is totally different. If the SCALE query is answered with a null reply, what is plotted will be identical to the screen contents, nothing more and nothing less. The paper size will be adjusted automatically to accomplish this (and a message will inform the user of the adjustment). Scale may now be answered with a number (specifying a scale greater than 1 to 1 (optionally followed by an "X")), or by a scale less than 1 in the form "1:n" or "1/n". This scale will map the drawing units to physical units on the paper according to the units in effect. If the plot is in English units, a scale of 1 will map 1 drawing unit to 1 inch. If metric, 1 drawing unit will become 1 millimeter on the paper. A scale of 2 will make things twice as big on the paper, and a scale of 1:10 or 1/10 will make things ten times smaller.

All input to the plot driver is now handled with a data input routine like that in the drawing editor. Thus space, CR, or ";" may now be used to terminate input, and ↑H and ↑X work as local editing keys normally. ↑C will now abort the plot during configuration, not return the user back to CP/M unexpectedly.

The Houston Instrument driver supports only 15 logical colors (1 to 15). Colors greater than 15 will be wrapped around modulo 15 (e.g., color 16 becomes 1, 17 becomes 2, etc.). This corrects a previous bug where out of range colors would result in the ridiculous action of faithfully drawing with no pen.

On 3/13/83 I made a large number of changes in the main menu module, **AUTOCAD**. If ACAD is serialised with dealer number 97, our code for an evaluation version, the main menu will now print "**EVALUATION VERSION—NOT FOR SALE**" in the drawing header for all displays.

I fixed a bug in ZOOM W. A null or line window would cause ACAD to ZOOM into hyperspace. I fixed it to reject a window without area. (Reported by Greg Lutz).

Aaaaah yes, the HI-Pad... . Well, the scum also rises, and it's time to resolve the issue of HI-Pad jitter once and for all. I spent about 2 hours looking at the character stream sent by the HI-Pad as I subjected it to various "stimuli" such as static electricity (thanks to a cooperative (?) cat), magnets, and proximity to the RGB designs "Big Mutha" monitor and a Hazeltine terminal. Except in cases of extreme and unreasonable abuse (25 KV kitty dragged across the pad), the jitter consisted of a random ± 10 in the HI-PAD sample. This jitter was completely random, exhibiting no periodicity or pattern that old "Random" Walker could detect. Run lengths varied randomly from 1 to 100! There is *no* smoothing technique which can compensate for this. The only answer is resolution reduction. So I fixed DGDRVHI to check the sample about to be returned against the last sample returned. If the absolute value of the difference between the current sample and the last sample is

10 or less, the last sample is returned. This results in a pad which is highly responsive to fast moves (as the JITTER averaging code can be disabled), but which settles to rock-steady stability when the cursor stops. But where's the catch? Well, it's very simple. Ignoring ± 10 excursions from the pad makes only movements of 20 points or more meaningful. With a pad resolution of 11000 in X and Y, this means that the pad can't address every pixel in a display with more than 512 dots in any direction. But then, with its jitter it would never succeed if it were to try! So, the HI-Pad has been bashed into acceptable performance for those applications for which it is usable.

I further changed the HI-Pad driver to automatically re-sync if synchronisation has been lost with the data stream. This prevents cursor flashing if an exogenous delay causes loss of sync with the data from the pad (such as a long cursor draw time).

I also changed the HI-Pad driver to lock its output coordinates within the 0 to 22000 limits by forcing out of range coordinates to the extreme limits rather than rejecting samples outside the range. This makes it much easier to select menu items and points near the edges of the screen. This mode is clearly preferable and will be the standard for all digitiser drivers in the future.

On 3/15/83 I hunted down the "8080/8085" bug and installed a workaround in ACAD. For certain values of X, Y and Z, the expression: $(X + Y) < Z$ yields incorrect logical values on an 8080 or 8085 processor, but the correct value on a Z-80 processor. In general, it appears that the use of an expression as an argument to a relational operator can lead to the ambiguity. This caused circles, arcs, text, and traces/solids not to generate in certain cases. The basic bug is in PL/I-80 and an 8 line program was prepared which gets different answers on a Z-80 and 8085. A bug report was submitted to Digital Research. By "Captain Empirical" techniques, it was determined that assigning the expression part of the relational to a temporary variable eliminated the error in evaluation of the relational expression. The code which used such expressions for the off-screen tests in EREGEN (ARC, CIRCLE, and TEXT), and FILL (TRACE, SOLID) was rewritten to bypass the bug until DR supplies a fix.

On 3/23/83 I was foolish enough to try to implement a driver for the Mouse Systems M-1 mouse. I'm not sure if "mouse" is the correct designation for the position of this little bugger within Rodentia. The main problem is that, unlike the USI mouse, the MSC mouse only sends data to the host when something changes. This means that motion of the mouse when the computer is off doing something else is lost, since the samples just pile up in the UART and get lost. Worse, the sample format is 5 bytes per sample, without parity, and with no unique synchronisation code for the first byte (it's a pattern "unlikely" to be used in the 4 binary data bytes which follow). So, you can fix it to time out when out of sync and know that it will re-sync on the next sample, and you can put up with not being able to move the cursor except when the computer is tracking, because that's the way most mice work anyway. But, now for the catch: when you push a button, if the mouse isn't moving, it sends just one sample on the push and one on the release. If you happen to miss the push because you're out of sync or off updating the cursor or checking the console, then the button push is lost forever. I consider this device only to be useful if supported with an interrupt driven driver. Since that's not practical in AutoCAD-80 with its universal configuration requirements, I don't consider this mouse to be usable. And it's a damn pity. The thing has a microcomputer in it, and could have been programmed to work reasonably.[239]

On 3/25/83 I implemented a driver for the Strobe model 100 plotter. This is a small A size plotter which talks a subset of the Hewlett-Packard protocol. The driver was added to the universal plot driver and is selected by answering STROBE to the manufacturer query. As this is a single pen plotter with no dashed line or variable speed support, there is no plotter-specific configuration at all. The plotter works magnificently, and no programming nor mechanical quirks were encountered in bringing it up or developing the driver for it. Since this is an RS-232 device, the port is configured in INSTALL exactly as for the Houston Instrument plotter.[240]

I also took Richard Handyside's HP driver and created a universal HP driver and installed it in the plotter driver. I suspect that it will do something vaguely reasonable, but won't work right until I understand a bit more about the family of HP plotters. It is accessed with the HP manufacturer specification, and has a configuration dialogue almost identical to the HI plotters. Configuration at the INSTALL level is identical, as the HP plotters are RS-232.[241]

On 4/1/83 I installed a CHANGE LAYER command. This command works on any entity type, and allows objects to be easily moved from layer to layer. To use it, give the CHANGE command. The usual prompt to select objects will be given.

---

239 The Mouse Systems mouse was an interesting device. To my knowledge, this is the first peripheral we encountered which was designed assuming the IBM PC as its primary host machine. CP/M machines usually didn't run their serial ports on interrupts, but IBM PC's did, and the Mouse Systems mouse lived long and prospered in that environment. I am editing this document on a Sun workstation equipped with a Mouse Systems mouse.

240 This was a remarkable device. You wrapped the glossy paper around a drum and screwed the nib end of a Pilot razor point pen into an 8-32 nut brazed onto the pen-down actuator, and away it went. It produced such good plots that we used it to make the illustrations for the first AutoCAD manual we printed.

241 Hewlett-Packard plotters are supported. Up to this point, we only drove Houston Instrument plotters.

Then designate the objects to be moved between layers by any of the standard methods. When the prompt "New location" is given, answer "LAYER" (actually, anything beginning with "L" is OK). The prompt "New layer:" will then be issued, and you should respond with the new layer number. The selected objects will then be redrawn on the new layer (if visible).

I extended the CHANGE command to work on TEXT. The location, size, angle, and content of text may now be modified by CHANGE. A null response to any of the queries will cause the selected modification to be ignored.

On 4/19/83 I installed code to allow a demo version of AutoCAD-80 to be generated. The demo version is identical to the regular version, except that it will not write out an output file, nor will it make a plot from within the drawing editor (plots from the main menu are OK). This results in the user being able to try all commands on the sample drawings supplied with the package, and to make new drawings, but since no output may be saved on disc, no real work can be done.[242]

On 1/12/84 I installed a gimmick in DSDRVAUR to provide support for the A-1030 colour mapping board. This option provides a user-loadable palette which can map any of the 16 color numbers generated by the A-1000 into any arbitrary analogue RGB value. Since if this board is present, the colour assignments are up to the user, we do not want AutoCAD's normal colour translation before the codes are sent to the A-1000. The configuration variable LPUSED, previously not used for the A-1000 (it is the light pen present flag for the Scion), is used as the A-1030 present flag. If zero (the default value if not specified) the A-1030 is assumed not to be present and colours are translated into the standard values as before. If LPUSED is set to **OFF** in the **.INP** file, then the A-1030 will be assumed to be configured and colours will be sent to the A-1000 without translation (modulo 16, of course). Thus, the user can set up any mapping he wishes by loading the translation tables in the A-1030 and AutoCAD will not stand in the way.[243]

---

242 Nobody ever imagined that there would be a need for a demo version of AutoCAD-80. But there was, anyway.
243 This was the last work done on AutoCAD-80. Additional copies of the final product were sold in 1984, but the development of the product ceased and effort was focused entirely on AutoCAD-86.

Appendix F — AutoCAD Wish List

We'd always hoped that once we got a product into the market, our customers would direct our development efforts through their requests for enhancements to the product. We couldn't have wished for a more energetic, imaginative, or vocal community of users. After six months of shipping AutoCAD, the lists of requests for new features were growing so long that we decided to get together, merge all of our private lists, and try to sort them by size of the job and importance of the feature. Duff Kurland prepared this first-ever AutoCAD Wish List from his notes of this meeting. Duff continued to be the keeper of the wish list for several years thereafter.

Any doubts about the veracity of our claim "our development agenda is taken directly from the list of user-requested features" can easily be dispelled by comparing the wish list with the features in AutoCAD releases up to the present day. I've added annotations in italics listing the release in which each item was eventually implemented.

AutoCAD Wish List

by Duff Kurland
Revision 0 — June 10, 1983

Introduction

An AutoCAD enhancement technical session was held on Monday, June 6, 1983, at John Walker's home. Present were Dan Drake, Richard Handyside, Rudolf Künzli, Duff Kurland, Greg Lutz, Lars Moureau, Mike Riddle, and John Walker.

A list of desirable features was compiled and discussed with varying degrees of detail. An attempt was made to prioritize these items, and some were assigned to individuals for implementation. This document has been prepared so that those who were not at the meeting (and those who were) will have a basic understanding of what's going on, and what the project names mean.

A few general notes are in order before presenting the list of features. First of all, AutoCAD-80 is *not* expected to be enhanced at all. Secondly, the priorities were set based on a combination of factors:

- Are we losing sales because we don't have this feature?
- Is this a "snazzy" gimmick feature which could attract additional sales?
- Does this feature reduce user confusion and our support burden?
- Could this feature be easily implemented?
- Would implementation of this feature make it easier to implement some of the other features?

Lastly, strict priorities have not been set. Some of the low priority items may actually be among the first done, if they're in areas where we're already poking around.

I have included notes on the discussion of most items, but they are by no means complete. I would welcome comments, clarifications, and additions; this list will be continually updated, and published at reasonable intervals.

High priority "quick kills"

Alternate arc specification

The ability to draw an arc by specifying its center, radius, and start/end angles has been requested by users. This is somewhat embarrassing; that's the way we encode arcs internally, but the user cannot specify them that way. Other combinations, such as endpoints and included angle have been requested, also. *1.4.*[244]

Text size by length

This is the ability to select the text size based on the length of the field in which it is to fit. *1.4.*

Layer-to-layer move

AutoCAD-80 now has a **"CHANGE LAYER"** command to allow selected entities' assigned layers to be changed. A similar capability is needed in AutoCAD-86. *1.3.*

Standard drawing config setup

This item was discussed briefly, and I'm not sure what it encompasses. Discussion included the ability to select the size and resolution of a new drawing without prompting the user for the details each time. Two methods were proposed; selecting defaults via the new "Configure AutoCAD" main menu item, or allowing the user to specify the size using ANSI or DIN sizes with a default

---

244   1.4 refers to the release for the feature. Here the feature was released in Release 1.4.

resolution. A more elaborate "drawing type" scheme was also proposed (see "Questionable items" below). *Prototype drawings in 2.1.*

Drawing header to DXF file

Drawing interchange files do not currently contain certain information about the drawing (insertion base point, etc.). This information is in the drawing file header, and should be added to the DXF file. *1.3.*

XOR grids when possible

This would be a change to the display drivers ("**dsdot**") to invert the pixel at each grid point, rather than simply set it. The idea is to ensure that the grid is visible even on a filled solid area. (Note: "**GRID ON**" will currently write a grid even if the grid is already on. This will have to be fixed first.) *1.3.*

Change "REDRAW ON/OFF" to "FILL ON/OFF"

This will avoid two areas of confusion, since "**FILL**" is a better description of the command's effect, and "**REDRAW**" won't perform different tasks depending on which key (space/return) is used to terminate it. *1.3.*

Change "RES" to "SNAP"

This should also eliminate some user confusion. *1.3.*

Change "P1, P2" point prompts

The "**SOLID**" command should prompt with "**1st point:**", "**2nd point:**", etc. as documented. *1.3.*

Change "Cmd:" to "Command:"

User friendliness (eschew obfuscation). *1.3.*

Enhanced HELP facility

I forgot to bring this up at the meeting, but feel it belongs in this category. First, "**HELP**" should be a synonym for "**?**". Second, we should support requests such as "**HELP CIRCLE**", which would display information about the **CIRCLE** command. I've already written an extended **HELP** file to support this capability. *1.3.*

INSERT angle governed by ORTHO

If **ORTHO** mode is on when an object is **INSERT**ed, the insertion angle should be constrained to 0, 90, 180, or 270 degrees. *1.4.*

Stop using square brackets

Several AutoCAD prompts display the current value within square brackets. Unfortunately, these character codes are used for foreign language letters. We will change to angle brackets. *1.3.*

High priority larger items

Polylines

A polyline is a group of lines, gaps, and arcs (?) which are associated with one another. They can be edited to add, delete, or move a vertex, move a line segment, etc. A width should be associated with the polyline; perhaps double walls could be special polylines. Assigned to Duff Kurland. *Done by Dan Drake in 2.1.*

Cross-hatch/pattern-fill

John Walker has been experimenting with a cross-hatching technique which seems to work. We should implement the standard hatching patterns for various structural materials (concrete, steel, mud, etc.), and should consider a general user-defined pattern fill capability. Would be an extra-cost option. The project has been assigned to Mike Riddle. *Done by John Walker in 1.4.*

Splines

John Walker has also been researching various spline drawing methods. We had hoped that IGES would point us in the right direction here, but it doesn't point anywhere. *Release 9.*

Double walls

Architects require this feature. A center line capability is also needed. Polylines might do the job here. *Provided in AEC.*

Line types & color

Several topics are covered by this item. First, we need to standardize on our color representations. For instance, the first eight colors should be:

0	black (erase)
1	red
2	green
3	blue
4	cyan
5	yellow
6	magenta
7	white (black on plotter?)

On monochrome devices, 0 means black (off), and any nonzero value means white (on).

Up until now, some AutoCAD implementations have used various bits of the "color" number to select the dotted/dashed line features of hardware devices (Scion Microangelo, NEC APC, plotters). While this has the desirable effect of allowing monochrome displays to differentiate between colors, it has two undesirable effects and must be avoided. First, it tends to make the color numbers difficult to work with (red + dashed line = 1 + 32 = 33). Second, it conflicts with the need for standardized line types.

One area which was not discussed at the meeting was the choice of colors for things AutoCAD (not the user) draws, like crosshairs and grids. My feeling is that the crosshairs should always be white, while the grid might be best in green. *1.3.*

Geometric snap

This is the ability to draw a line which intersects another entity in some specified manner (tangent to arc, perpendicular to line, etc.). *2.0.*

Breaking walls/partial delete

It should be possible to select two points on a line, and split the line into two segments with a gap spanning the two selected points. This should not be limited to simple lines, however. Polylines, walls, traces, circles, and arcs should be breakable. *2.0. Polylines: 2.5.*

Fillets

Fillets are arcs which smoothly connect two lines. We should have a method of applying fillets after the lines have been drawn, and a method (FLINE command, or POLY command) of drawing them on the fly. *1.4.*

IGES support

Creation and reading of IGES-format interchange files should be implemented. Could be an extra-cost option. Seen as large design project with quick implementation involving adaptation of **DIFIN** and **DIFOUT** functions.[245]

Block output

Currently, our **BLOCK** command allows dynamic creation of a new block, but the new block is **INSERT**able only in the current drawing. We need a way to write the

---

245 Later renamed **DXFIN** and **DXFOUT**. Assigned to Peter Goldmann. *Done by Ben Halpern and John Walker in 2.5.*

block to a new drawing file, so that it may be **INSERT**ed in other drawings as well. *1.4.*

Redefining blocks

Once a block has been **INSERT**ed in a drawing or created via a **BLOCK** command, its definition rides around in the drawing file. In one respect, this is nice; the drawing file for the **INSERT**ed part need not be present after the initial **INSERT** is done. However, it makes it difficult to update the part definition in all the drawings which include it. Even if all references to the block are erased from the drawing, the definition remains; the only way to delete it is to write a DXF file, edit it to remove the block definition, and load the DXF file back in. This is awkward. We need a way to delete or redefine an existing block definition. *1.4.*

Complete dimensioning

Our dimensioning facility can only draw horizontal and vertical dimensions. Several additional capabilities have been requested:

- Angular dimensions
- Arc length
- Circle/arc radius
- Circle center lines

2.0.

Large plotters (32K problem)

Our internal coordinate system uses 16-bit integers, giving a range of 0–32767 points in the X and Y directions. We are now seeing large (48-inch) plotters with 0.001 inch resolution. We need to support them, but they exceed our limits. A workaround might be to use only half of the plotter's resolution for the time being. *1.3.*

Generic user manual

So far, we've been producing a custom user manual for each machine implementation. This probably cannot continue. The basic reasons for separate manuals up to this point have been:

- Differing operating systems.
- Differing cursor control and function keys.
- Commands (**QPLOT**, **PALETTE**), which operate only on some machines.

It might be best for us to produce a generic AutoCAD-86 manual, documenting all the commands, and control keys which will work on *every* machine. I would suggest the following keys:

Cursor left	CTRL-H
Cursor right	CTRL-L
Cursor up	CTRL-K
Cursor down	CTRL-J
Flip screens	ESC 1
Select graphic cursor	ESC 2
Select menu cursor	ESC 3
Return to keyboard	ESC 4
Slow cursor	ESC 5
Fast cursor	ESC 6

A note such as "on some machines, the CTRL key is marked ALT; see the AutoCAD installation/user guide for your machine" could be added. Operating system differences would be noted, as well. A separate installation/user guide and reference card would be associated with each machine, and would include exceptions from the main user manual and a list of alternate function keys if applicable. *1.4.*

Function keys on reference card
The AutoCAD reference card for each machine should include a list of the function keys available on that machine.

Foreign language versions
Rudolf Künzli has been working on various foreign language versions of AutoCAD, translating not only the user manual, but also the messages generated by the program. As things stand, he must re-apply his changes each time we send him new source disks.

We decided to use compile-time tests for each language, so that the text of each message could be provided once and maintained in the master source files. *1.3, later redone using the automatic translation utility.*

Lower priority items

Point variables
This is the ability to attach a name to a designated point, and to use that name in subsequent relative coordinate specifications, geometric snaps, etc. *2.1, via Variables and Expressions, later AutoLisp.*

Extended entity selection
This is the ability to more finely describe the entities to be selected. Possible additional criteria would be layer, color, entity tag (see below), and entity type.

Mike Riddle has already done some work in this area. *Done by Kern Sibbald in Release 9.*

Entity tags

These are text items which would be carried around with each entity drawn. They could be used to construct a bill of materials. *2.0 Attributes.*

"Toy" bill of materials

A sample program was suggested to demonstrate the capabilities of DXF files (or was it for entity tags?). *2.0.*

EDIT command

This would be an extended **CHANGE** command, to allow modification of any of the properties of an existing entity. *Extension of the* **CHANGE** *command from 1.3 to Release 9.*

Extended OOPS (UNDO)

The **OOPS** command restores the last thing(s) which were erased. We need a more general ability to "undo" the previous command (e.g., **MOVE**). *2.5.*

Rejecting added entities

In some systems, the user can try drawing an entity; if it doesn't turn out as desired, he can reject it and try again. For continue commands like **LINE**, this seems like a nice approach. *2.0 for lines, 2.5* **UNDO** *for everything else.*

Repeat last selection

Currently, the "**L**" modifier allows the user to select the last entity in the redraw file. A more general ability to select the same set of entities as most recently selected would be useful. *2.5.*

New LAYER command

The current **LAYER** command, with its embedded **COLOR** option, is confusing to users and should be reworked. *Ongoing process. Dialogue box introduced in Release 9.*

GRID enhancements

Our current **GRID** command produces a square grid with specified spacing (within certain limits), with the grid origin at (0,0). We haven been asked to provide grids with differing X and Y spacing, isometric grids, offset and rotation capabilities, and something better than the "5 to 50" dot limits. *2.0.*

SNAP enhancements

Similar to the above **GRID** enhancements. Differing X and Y spacing, isometric snaps (or is that isometric **ORTHO**?), offset, rotation. Also, the ability to snap to the nearest of a list of arbitrary points. *2.0.*

Parts library

Some systems can display not only a list of the available drawing parts, but a sample of each one. This is desirable. *Release 9.*

File system interface

To list a disk directory or delete a file, it is first necessary to exit AutoCAD. These facilities should be provided while in the Drawing Editor. *1.4.*

Global coordinate transform

This would allow the user to rotate the display to work on a section of his drawing which is not easily visualized horizontally.

ELLIPSE command

Currently, the only way to draw an ellipse is to create a **CIRCLE** block and **INSERT** it with adjusted X and Y scales. *2.5.*

Direct commands vs. INSERT

Anything which can be done via **INSERT** should be possible via ordinary commands (see **ELLIPSE,** above).

Transformations and INSERT *

Allow scale factors and rotation to be applied to the individual entities in an "**INSERT ***". *2.5.*

Right-justified text

We can now left-justify and center text fields. Right-justification would complete the set. *1.3.*

Feet & inches

Architects like to work with feet and inches. We should be able to handle them in input, and display them in **STATUS, LIMITS, DIST,** and **DIM** command outputs. *1.4.*

Names for internal variables

Names should be assigned to many of AutoCAD's internal variables, and commands implemented to display and change their values. Some of the names could be documented for users, while others would remain secret for development and debugging. *2.1.*

Menu/keyboard macros

Discussion here included "smart parts" and "parametric entities", which would prompt the user for any needed parameters and use those parameters in expressions. It was also felt that a good macro feature would enable us to create all sorts of new entities easily. Perhaps more importantly, the users could create them also, taking some of the burden off us. *AutoLisp in 2.1.*

Redefine machine interface

Now that we've done a few conversions and have the package running on a variety of machines, we should take a careful look at the device driver routines, with an eye toward restructuring them. Some new common service routines might reduce the work needed for future conversions. *Ongoing process.*

Mode status display

Users sometimes forget what layer they're on, and whether or not **SNAP** or **ORTHO** is in effect. Use of the bottom right-hand corner of the display to indicate mode settings was proposed. *1.3, improved in 1.4.*

Asynchronous mode switches

When drawing something like a continued sequence of lines, it is sometimes necessary to **SNAP** or **ORTHO** only some of the segments. Currently, the user must end the **LINE** command, issue the appropriate mode command, and begin a new **LINE** command. We could provide control keys to allow mode switching during a command. *1.4.*

Arc traces — doughnuts

Again, this might fall under the general polyline-with-width implementation. *2.1. Doughnut command in 2.5.*

Various cross-hair types

Some hardware displays can draw "rubber band" lines and rectangles very quickly. A rubber band could be used along with the cross-hair when entering the "to" point of a line or trace, and when pointing to indicate a rotation angle. A rectangle could be used when selecting the objects in a window. The core program could indicate the preferred cross-hair type, and the base point, to the "**DSMARK**" outline, which would draw a normal cross-hair if it couldn't do the preferred type.

"**DSMARK**" would save the necessary information so that "**DSCMRK**" could clear the previous cross-hair when needed. *1.3.*

Enhanced text fonts

An ability to add a slant of a specified angle to an existing text font would be useful, but we should avoid prompting the user for too many things; the **TEXT** command already asks for insertion point, height, and angle as well as for the text string. *2.0.*

Some design work has been done on a new capability for text font definitions (to support more than just 16 vector directions), and some fancier text fonts, including italic, have been constructed and are waiting for this feature. *1.4.*

Multiple text fonts

The **LOAD** command permits the user to load a new text font at any time. What we don't tell him in the manual is that the next time he **REGEN**s the drawing, all his old text will now appear in the new font. Only one font at a time is actually supported. We should look into adding a multi-font capability. Again, we should be careful not to overload the user with prompts from the **TEXT** command. *2.0.*

ZOOM/LIMITS confusion

Our numeric **ZOOM** factors are confusing to users. "**ZOOM 2**" does not necessarily mean "double the size"; it is relative to the original drawing size, not the current display.

Also, "**ZOOM 0.1**" might result in a small drawing in the lower left corner of the screen, and a subsequent "**ZOOM 1**" might leave you with a blank screen. *1.4.*

Views

It was proposed that the user could assign "view" numbers to various portions of his drawing (with associated zoom, etc.). This would allow switching from one area to another rapidly, without the need for several **PAN** or **ZOOM** commands. This might fit in nicely with the "point variable" feature (e.g., "**VIEW KITCHEN**"). *2.0.*

Don't regen invisible layers

Performance optimization. *Freeze and thaw in 2.1.*

Rework REPEAT

The **REPEAT/ENDREP** facility is limited, and can cause confusing results. A capability to form a radial array would be useful. *Array command in 1.4* **REPEAT/ENDREP** *removed in 2.5.*

Generalize redraw files

Currently, our redraw file contains only vectors. Circles, for example, are composed of many small vectors, and cannot utilize the circle-drawing capabilities of various displays and plotters. Even if we could use these hardware features, we'd still need a way to identify such an object when it is pointed to; this currently depends on the vector approach.

Area and perimeter

This is the ability to simply select a polygon (polyline) and compute its area or perimeter. Our present **AREA** command requires the user to specify the polygon vertex by vertex. *2.6.*

QPLOT for additional printers

Currently, **QPLOT** operates only on Epson printers. Other dot matrix printers are popular as well, and could conceivably be used. This might require additional code in the new Configurator. *General printer plotter support added in 2.1.*

3D

A three-dimensional capability is desirable. It appears that an "extrusion" feature might be relatively simple to implement and sufficient for some users. Could be an extra-cost option. *2.1.*

Questionable items

These are items whose value to the program is questionable, or for which additional research is needed before we decide to implement them.

Should entities have colors?

Should color be associated with an entity rather than with a layer? *2.5.*

Aligned dimensions

Although the ANSI standard specifies that unidirectional dimension text is preferable, we have been asked for the ability to have the dimension text aligned with the dimension lines. *1.4.*

Ex post facto SNAP

This would allow the user to "sketch" his drawing just as he would on paper, without regard to precision. Once the sketch is done, it could be **SNAP**ped (or even **ORTHO**ed) into a precise drawing.

Display snapped crosshair

When **SNAP** mode is on, some systems only move the crosshairs from one snap point to the next. This makes it very evident that **SNAP** mode is on. *1.4.*

Relational entities

???

Display axes

??? We might not have known what it was, but that didn't stop us from putting it in 1.4.

Drawing types

A general "drawing type" facility was proposed. A drawing type could have an associated default drawing size, resolution, menu file, and even a skeleton drawing (such as ANSI title boxes). *2.1.*

Alignment of entities

Some systems allow you to draw several boxes, for example, and then adjust them so that their top lines align horizontally.

Shape dragging

This is the ability to move an object across the screen with the cross-hairs in real time, as opposed to erasing it and redrawing it in its new location, as we do now. "If it can be done on an Apple, we should be able to do it on our machines." *2.0.*

DXF to CalComp program

This wasn't discussed at the meeting, but I've had a couple of user requests for it. These guys have large mainframe systems with large CalComp plotters, and don't want to buy another plotter to hook up to their AutoCAD system. We tell them about DXF files, and they ask if we have a program (or know of one) to do the job. The CalComp subroutine package is used widely enough that it might make sense for us to provide a "sample" FORTRAN program, but we'd have to supply the source, and support could become a problem.

Index

A

Acquisitions
    Cadetron – 351
    Xanadu – 416
Ad copy
    Golden Age of Engineering – 381
    Number One – 235
    Super Programmers – 305
Advertising
    First budget – 140
    Lessons – 194, 237
AE/CADD description – 250
Agenda
    First founders meeting – 24
Alvar Green
    Assumes chairmanship – 421
    Assumes presidency – 344
Alan Kay
    Ideas on simulation – 310
Alternative minimum tax
    IRS rules – 227
Arrogance
    Remarks about – 376
Articles of Incorporation – 61, 66
Assumptions
    in starting Autodesk – 411
Auto Book
    Document retieval system – 465
    Potential product – 99
AutoBits
    Autodesk humor – 323
    Autodesk Technical Seminars – 325
    Autodesk Transportation – 333
    AutoSketch Announcement – 324
    CAD — The Final Frontier – 327
    Explaining 3D – 332
    Intergraph's Accuracy – 329
    Marinchip Defeats IBM – 328
    Progammers' Titles – 323
    Spine Police – 330
    VHSIC Project – 331

AutoCAD – 75
    as industry standard – 407
    Changing security on releases – 405
    Development Log – 473
    Drawing data base – 369
    Enhancement with 3D – 181
    First price at $1,000 – 101, 107
    First ship date – 112
    in IPO Prospectus – 248
    Major features history – 451
    Portable data base – 363
    Version for IBM PC – 107
    Version release dates – 451
    Wish List – 509
AutoCAD Applications
    AutoLISP interface – 233
    Program description – 253
AutoCAD Lite
    Ideas for AutoSketch – 219
AutoCAD-80
    Development – 137, 153, 179
    Development Log – 473
AutoCAD-86
    Development – 137, 153, 178
    Transcript facility – 185
Autodesk, Inc.
    as number one CAD company – 235
    Buying shares – 34
    Competitive edges – 45
    Filing Articles of Incorporation – 61, 66
    First Board of Directors – 67
    First expense report form – 193
    First full time employee – 128
    First IBM PC – 85
    First officers – 67
    First stockholders' meeting – 117
    Incorporating – 29, 43, 61, 66
    Initial liabilities – 57
    International participants – 45
    Issuance of shares – 50
    Issue of liability – 30

524   Index   The Autodesk File

      Liabilities – 57
      Naming company – 48
      Organization plan – 59
      Philosophy – 38
      Potential products – 39, 75
      Promise of venture – 36
      Profit history – 448
      Sales history – 446
      Stock options – 52
      Turning point – 156
      Warrants – 52
      Work commitments – 56, 79
      Working capital – 52
Autodesk Reorganization
      Kern Sibbald's plan – 166
AutoLISP – 233
AutoSketch
      Ideas for AutoCAD Lite – 219

B

Binary I/O – 365
Bonds
      Investment advice – 266
Bug reports – 131
Building go do programs – 320
Business before Autodesk
      Marinchip Systems – 455
Business philosophy
      Challenge of success – 208
Business plan – 49
      Changes in plan – 59, 76
      John Walker's plan – 162

C

C Language
      Importance – 96
      Potential product – 40
      Source code for AutoCAD – 295
CAD
      Modeling physical systems – 308, 425
CAD/camera description – 251
Cadetron acquisition
      Recommendation – 351
Capital gains

      IRS rules – 225
Capitalizing the company – 60
Changes in management
      John Walker leaves presidency – 336, 344
      Mike Ford resigns – 285
Chris Record
      VP and Counsel to company – 404
Code
      C source for AutoCAD – 295
      Source distribution – 389
COMDEX 1982
      AutoCAD shown – 125
Common stock
      Issuance of securities – 55
Communicator product idea – 80
Company success
      Based on software excellence – 378
Computer assisted reading
      with Auto Book – 465
Computer Faire 1982
      Products shown – 61
Computer industry
      Exponential growth – 411
      General trends – 294
Computer program design
      vs service economy – 313
Computer revolution
      Think Piece – 313
Computer simulation
      What CAD should do – 308
Conflicts of interest – 53
Copy protection
      Hardware lock – 338
      Removing hardware lock – 357
CP/M version
      of AutoCAD – 473
Crisis letter – 156

D

Dan Drake
      Taxes and Such – 224
Data base
      Portability – 363
dBASE II –41, 77

Debater's Guide
    to hardware lock – 338
Developer's Tool Kit
    Description – 252
Development Log
    AutoCAD-80 – 473
Diff product – 76
Document retrieval system
    Auto Book notes – 465
Drawing data base – 369
Duff Kurland
    Features Wish List – 509

E

Early
    AutoCAD development – 473
    Potential products – 5, 75
    Work distribution – 79
Electric Malcolm – 185
Endless miasma syndrome – 94
Earnings Per Share (EPS) – 273
Equity
    IRS and SEC rules – 224
Eric Lyons
    Joins Autodesk – 286
    on Solid Modeling – 351
European view
    of Autodesk – 430
Evolution
    of computer interfaces – 315
Excellence
    in computer software – 378
Expanding product line
    with AutoCAD Lite – 219
External Tanks
    Investment announcement – 386

F

Financial history
    Share price – 445
    Stock splits – 445
Financial low point – 127
Financial results – 445
    For 1982 – 5

For 1983 – 123
For 1984 – 204
For 1985 – 232
For 1986 – 284
For 1987 – 362
For 1988 – 404
First
    Annual stockholders' meeting – 117
    Board of Directors – 67
    Full time employee – 128
    Million in sales – 206
Founders
    First meeting agenda – 24
    List of – 5
    Marinchip Systems Ltd. – 59
    Meeting after IPO – 269
    Participation – 59, 64
    Warrant and options – 65
    Work distribution – 79
Frank Chambers
    Venture capital – 213
Future of company
    Remarks about – 423

G

Getting equity out
    IRS and SEC rules – 224
Go do programs – 317
Golden Age of Engineering
    Ad copy – 381
Guerrilla programming – 19

H

Hardware lock
    Debater's Guide – 338
    Reasons for removal – 357
How to develop
    Quality control – 130
Hunter S. Thompson – 205
Hypertext
    Ted Nelson – 416
    Xanadu – 416

I

Importance
  of staying competitive – 441
Incorporation
  as Autodesk, Inc. – 61, 66
  Initial stock distribution letter – 64
Industry standard
  AutoCAD as – 407
InfoCorp Speech – 292
Information
  Letter #1 – 28
  Letter #2 – 43
  Letter #3 – 49
  Letter #4 – 59
  Letter #5 – 66
  Letter #6 – 84
  Letter #7 – 94
  Letter #8 – 105
  Letter #10 – 196
  Letter #11 – 206
  Letter #12 – 269
  Letter #13 – 344
Initial Public Offering (IPO) – 245
  Products – 248
  Results for company – 232
  Sales and Marketing – 255
Insiders and Rule16(b) – 229
Intel 8086
  Understanding architecture – 87
Interact product – 39
International sales
  Importance of – 45
Investment
  Advice after IPO – 264
  in External Tanks Corporation – 386
Invitation to organize company – 7
IRS and SEC
  Stock options and warrants – 225
Issuance of securities – 55

J

Jeremiad
  Remarks about arrogance – 376
Job Descriptions
  Reorganization plan – 170

John Walker
  President of Autodesk – 67
  Relinquishes chairmanship – 421
  Relinquishes presidency – 344
  Transition to programming – 336
JPLDIS product idea – 77
  Availability – 111

K

Kelvin R. Throop
  High performance bicycles – 333
  Programmer's titles – 323
  Prospectus – 258
  Source distribution – 389
  Spine police – 330
  VHSIC project – 331
Kern Sibbald
  Reorganization plan – 166
Key Events
  In 1982 – 3
  In 1983 – 121
  In 1984 – 203
  In 1985 – 231
  In 1986 – 283
  In 1987 – 361
  In 1988 – 403
Key product events
  In 1983 – 123
  In 1984 – 204
  In 1985 – 232
  In 1986 – 284
  In 1987 – 362
  In 1988 – 404

L

Lars Moureau
  European view of Autodesk – 430
  Joins Autodesk – 122
Lens product idea – 40
Lessons
  in advertising – 194, 237
Liabilities
  Initial – 57

Lifeboat Associates
   as distributor – 9, 90
Lisp language
   Interface in AutoCAD – 233
List of founders – 5
Lock-up agreement
   after IPO – 267
Low rent 3D – 181

M

Mainframe CAD Interfaces
   Description – 250
Major features of AutoCAD – 451
Malcom Davies
   VP of Marketing and Sales – 404
Management issues
   Allocating manpower – 79
   Dealing with rapid growth – 154, 205
   Effective management – 133
   Organizational problems – 162
   Quality control – 144
   Reorganization – 166
   Seeking venture capital – 196
Marinchip hardware
   Based on TI9900 – 456
Marinchip Systems
   Background – 8, 455
   Role in founding – 36
Marketing
   after Mike Ford's resignation – 286
   Mike Ford – 84
   Sales commissions – 126
   Strategy – 233, 255
Martin Newell
   Teapot rendering test – 322
Meetings
   First annual stockholders' – 117
   First quarterly meeting – 190
   Regular monthly meetings – 69
MicroCAD – 75
   Development – 62, 70
   First name for AutoCAD – 5
Mike Ford
   Establishes marketing – 84
   Resigns – 285
   Sales commissions – 126
MJK
   Teleconferencing system – 114
Money management
   Budgeting – 163
   Cash flow – 127, 149
   First expense form – 193
   Purchasing equipment – 69
   Salary scales – 165
   Sales commissions – 126
   Seeking outside financing – 190, 196
Monthly meeting
   Agenda – 115
   Algorithm explained – 103
   First minutes – 100
   Last meeting – 175
   Odd job report – 142

N

Naming company
   Autodesk, Inc. – 61, 66
   List of names – 48
Need for programmers – 305
Number One
   Ad copy – 235

O

Odd job reports – 142
Opti-Calc product idea – 62
Options
   SEC and IRS rules – 226
Organizational problems
   Overcoming – 162
Organizing the company – 49
   Changes in plan – 59, 67
   Crisis – 156
   First report from Europeans – 151
   Impact of rapid growth – 154
   Initial liabilities – 57
   Overcoming problems – 162
   Paperwork – 54
   Progress after incorporation – 66
   Quality department priorities – 130

Regular monthly meetings – 69
Reorganization plan – 166
Shares – 56
Software control – 142
Task lists – 97
Work commitments – 56, 79
Working capital – 51

P

Price/Earnings (P/E) – 273
Paperwork in organizing – 54
Perils
    in computer technology – 411
Personal
    Holding companies – 53
Philosophy
    of software business – 38
Portability
    Between machine architectures – 363
    Between operating systems – 363
Press announcements
    External Tanks Corporation – 386
    Ted Nelson's Fellowshp – 420
    Xanadu acquisition – 416
Private corporations
    Agreements – 60
Product
    History ship dates – 451
    Ideas – 40, 75
    Release security – 405
    Style strategy – 277
Profit history – 448
Progress
    after incorporation – 66
    Monthly reports – 108
Prospectus
    Initial Public Offering – 245
Prospectus Descriptions
    AE/CADD – 250
    AutoCAD – 248
    AutoCAD Applications Program – 253
    CAD/camera – 251
    Developer's Tool Kit – 252
    General Background – 245
    Mainframe CAD Interfaces – 250

Product Strategy – 247
    Sales and Marketing – 255
Protecting your money
    Advice after IPO – 262
Public company – 273
Public Offering
    Initial – 245
    Second – 361
Putting real world
    inside computer – 425

Q

QBASIC product – 39, 78
Quality control policies – 144
Quality department priorities – 130
    Bug reports – 131
    Regression testing – 131
Quarterly meetings
    Shift from monthly meetings – 190

R

Recommendation
    for venture capital – 196
Regression testing – 131
Regular monthly meetings
    Structure of – 94
Remarks
    about company arrogance – 376
    about computer industry growth – 411
    after 1987 stock crash – 397
    Relinquishing chairman's title – 423
Reorganization
    Problems – 162
    Proposal by Kern Sibbald – 166
Resignation
    Mike Ford – 285
Retrospective
    European view – 430
    Six years – 440
    Valedictory – 423
Roger Gregory
    Principal in Xanadu – 416
Rule 16(b)
    Trading on inside information – 229

S

Sales
    and EPS – 273
    and Profit history – 445
    Over one million – 206
    Slingshot growth – 211
Saving company
    Crisis letter – 157
Scott Heath
    AutoCAD Release 10 – 408
Second public offering – 361
Securities
    Initial issuance of – 55
Security on product release
    Changing – 405
Selector product – 40
Selling your stock – 262
Service economy
    and computers – 315
Share price history – 445
Shares – 56
    Issuance of – 50
    Participation – 59, 64
Simulation
    as future of CAD – 310
Sleazy Motel Roach
    Hammer Awards – 259
Slingshot success – 211
Software company
    What business is – 276
Solid modeling
    Importance in CAD/CAM – 351
Sort product – 40
Source code distribution
    Media – 389
    Problem evaluation – 389
Speech at Silverado – 292
Stock market crash
    Remarks to company – 397
Stock options – 52
    How they worked – 191
    Question of transfer – 191
    SEC and IRS rules – 225
Stock splits
    First split – 178
    History – 445
Stock valuation
    History – 445
Stocks
    Investment advice – 266
    Publicly traded – 228
Strategy for company – 292, 423
    after IPO – 271
    What to do next – 278
Subchapter S
    Alternative to incorporation – 72
Summing up
    Autodesk's six years – 440
Sun-Flex
    as AutoCAD distributor – 152
Super Programmers
    Ad copy – 305
Surplus Value
    Protecting Your Money – 262
Sweat equity – 52

T

Task lists
    at monthly meetings – 97
Taxes
    after IPO – 263
    Alternative minimum tax – 227
    IRS and SEC rules – 224
    Laws – 52
Taxes and such
    Dan Drake's advice – 224
Technical seminars
    Proposal – 325
Ted Nelson
    Inventor of hypertext – 416
    Joins Autodesk – 420
Teleconference system
    MJK – 97
    Usage – 114

Texas Instrument 9900
    Processor used by Marinchip – 456
Toilet Announcement – 254

Trade shows
    CADCON and CPM-83 – 138
    COMDEX 1982 – 125
    Evaluating performance – 138
Trading
    on inside information – 229
Transcript facility – 185
Travel expenses
    Sleazy Motel Awards – 259
Trends
    in computer industry – 294

U

Users' wishes
    Shape AutoCAD design – 509

V

Valedictory – 423
Venture
    Business prospects – 36
Venture capital
    Deal on the table – 213
    Deal options – 214
    First offer – 213
    Frank Chambers – 213
    John Walker's recommendation – 196
    Turning down deal – 217
Version release dates
    AutoCAD – 451
Victor computer
    Early platform for AutoCAD – 97

W

Warrants – 52
Warrants and options
    Founders – 64
What happened
    to computer revolution? – 314
What is CAD?
    Think Piece – 309

What it means
    to be public company – 273
What you see is what you get
    (WYSIWYG) – 314
Window product – 40, 76
Wish List
    AutoCAD features – 509
Work commitments – 56, 79
    Monthly progress reports – 102
Work distribution
    Founders – 79
Working capital – 52
    Capitalizing the company – 60
    Sources – 127
Working paper to organize company – 7
    Agenda – 24
    Commitments of time – 18
    Mode of operation – 12
    Money and management – 16, 17
    Partnership organization – 10
    Potential products – 19
    Product development – 13
WYSIWYG – 314

X

Xanadu
    Acquisition – 416

New Riders Library

The Autodesk File
The Story of Autodesk, Inc., the Company Behind AutoCAD
Written and Edited by John Walker
532 pages
ISBN: 0-934035-63-6 **$24.95**

The unvarnished history of Autodesk, Inc., the company behind AutoCAD. Read the original memos, letters, and reports that trace the rise of Autodesk, from start-up to their present position as the number one CAD software company in the world. Learn the secrets of success behind Autodesk and AutoCAD. Must reading for any AutoCAD user or entrepreneur!

INSIDE AutoCAD   Over 250,000 sold
The Complete AutoCAD Guide   Fifth Edition — Release 10
D. Raker and H. Rice
864 pages, over 400 illustrations
ISBN 0-934035-49-0 **$29.95**

INSIDE AutoCAD, the best selling book on AutoCAD, is entirely new and rewritten for AutoCAD's 3D Release 10. This easy-to-understand book serves as both a tutorial and a lasting reference guide. Learn to use every single AutoCAD command as well as time saving drawing techniques and tips. Includes coverage of new 3D graphics features, AutoShade, and AutoLISP. This is the book that lets you keep up and stay in control with AutoCAD.

CUSTOMIZING AutoCAD   Second Edition — Release 10
A Complete Guide to AutoCAD Menus, Macros and More!
J. Smith and R. Gesner
480 Pages, 100 illustrations
ISBN 0-934035-45-8, **$27.95**

Uncover the hidden secrets of AutoCAD's 3D Release 10 in this all new edition. Discover the anatomy of an AutoCAD menu and build a custom menu from start to finish. Manipulate distance, angles, points, and hatches — ALL in 3D! Customize hatches, text fonts and dimensioning for increased productivity. Buy CUSTOMIZING AutoCAD today and start customizing AutoCAD tomorrow!

For fast service, call a New Riders Sales Representative
at (818) 991-5392

New Riders Library

INSIDE AutoLISP Release 10
The Complete Guide to Using AutoLISP for AutoCAD Applications
J. Smith and R. Gesner
736 pages, over 150 illustrations
ISBN: 0-934035-47-4, **$29.95**

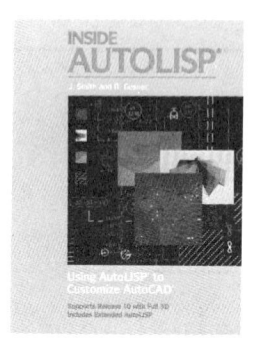

Introducing the most comprehensive book on AutoLISP for AutoCAD Release 10. Learn AutoLISP commands and functions and write your own custom AutoLISP programs. Numerous tips and tricks for using AutoLISP for routine drawing tasks. Import and export critical drawing information to/from Lotus 1-2-3 and dBASE. Automate the creation of scripts for unattended drawing processing. *INSIDE AutoLISP* is the book that will give you the inside track to using AutoLISP.

STEPPING INTO AutoCAD Fourth Edition—Release 10
A Guide to Technical Drafting Using AutoCAD
By Mark Merickel
380 pages, over 140 illustrations
ISBN: 0-934035-51-2, **$29.95**

This popular tutorial has been completely rewritten with new exercises for Release 10. The book is organized to lead you step by step from the basics to practical tips on customizing AutoCAD for technical drafting. Handy references provide quick set-up of the AutoCAD environment. Improve your drawing accuracy through AutoCAD's dimensioning commands. It also includes extensive support for ANSI Y14.5 level drafting.

AutoCAD Reference Guide
Everything You Want to Know About AutoCAD — *FAST!*
By Dorothy Kent
256 pages, over 50 illustrations
ISBN: 0-934035-57-1, **$11.95**

All essential AutoCAD functions and commands are arranged alphabetically and described in just a few paragraphs. Includes tips and warnings from experienced users for each command. Extensive cross-indexing make this the instant answer guide to AutoCAD.

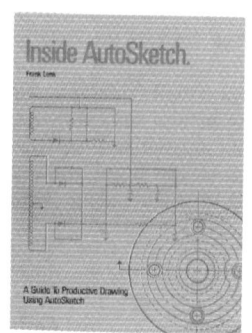

INSIDE AutoSketch
A Guide to Productive Drawing Using AutoSketch
By Frank Lenk
240 pages, over 120 illustrations
ISBN: 0-934035-20-2, **$17.95**

INSIDE AutoSketch gives you real-life mechanical parts, drawing schematics, and architectural drawings. Start by learning to draw simple shapes such as points, lines and curves, then edit shapes by moving, copying, rotating, and distorting them. Explore higher-level features to complete technical drawing jobs using reference grids, snap, drawing layers and creating parts.

For fast service, call a New Riders Sales Representative
at (818) 991-5392

AutoCAD Software Solutions

New Riders AutoLISP Utilities

Disk 1 — Release 10
ISBN 0-934035-79-2 **$29.95**

This disk contains several valuable programs and utilities and subroutines. You will find these useful to any AutoCAD drawing application. They include:

CATCH.LSP CATCH is great for selecting the new entities created by exploding blocks, polylines, 3D meshes, and dimensions.

HEX-INT.LSP is a set of hexadecimal arithmetic tools that make dealing with entity handles easier.

SHELL.LSP contains the SHELL function that executes and verifies multiple DOS commands with a single AutoCAD SHELL command execution (DOS only).

MERGE-V.LSP contains MERGE-V, which combines two files and verifies the copy procedure (DOS only).

PVAR.LSP provides functions for creating a personal variable system which can retain up to 254 variable values in a drawing's LTYPE table.

ISODIM.MNU implements an isometric dimensioning system as a TABLET1 menu. Using a tablet menu makes iso-dimensioning more intuitive.

GROUP.LSP contains functions to create and select *groups* of entities in AutoCAD drawings.

GRPT.LSP contains GRPT, a function that draws GRDRAW temporary points with any PDSIZE or PDMODE system variable setting.

FLATPAT.LSP is a program to generate flat pattern drawings of pipe end conditions.

XINSERT.LSP contains XINSERT, an external block extraction and insertion program.

STACK.LSP is a function loading program to minimize memory conflicts in using several moderate to large AutoLISP functions at once.

These AutoLISP programs and subroutines are not encrypted and are well documented by comments in the *filename*.LSP files.

Watch for or call New Riders Publishing for information on additions to the New Riders Utilities Disk family.

For fast service, call a New Riders Sales Representative
at (818) 991-5392

For fast service, call a New Riders Sales Representative
at (818) 991-5392

Order from New Riders Publishing Today!

Please indicate which release of AutoCAD you are using.

☐ AutoCAD Release _____

Yes, please send me the productivity-boosting material I have checked below. Make check payable to New Riders Publishing.

☐ Check enclosed.

Charge to my credit card:

☐ Visa # _____

☐ Mastercard # _____

Expiration date: _____

Signature: _____

Name: _____

Company: _____

Address: _____

City: _____

State: _____ Zip: _____

Phone: _____

The easiest way to order is to pick up the phone and call (818) 991-5392 between 9:00 AM and 5:00 PM PST. Please have your credit card available and your order can be placed in a snap!

Quantity	Description of Item	Unit Cost	Total Cost
	The Autodesk File	$24.95	
	Inside AutoLISP	$29.95	
	Inside AutoLISP Disk	$14.95	
	AutoLISP Utilities — Disk 1	$29.95	
	Inside AutoCAD 5th Edition	$29.95	
	Inside AutoCAD 5th Edition Disk	$14.95	
	Customizing AutoCAD 2nd Edition	$27.95	
	Customizing AutoCAD 2nd Edition Disk	$14.95	
	AutoCAD Reference Guide	$11.95	
	AutoCAD Reference Guide Disk	$14.95	
	Stepping into AutoCAD 4th Edition	$29.95	
	Stepping into AutoCAD 4th Edition Disk	$14.95	
	Inside AutoSketch	$17.95	
	Inside AutoSketch Drawing Disk	$ 7.95	
	COOKIES (Put the fun back in your computer)	$ 6.95	

Send to:

New Riders Publishing
P.O. Box 4846
Thousand Oaks, CA 91360
(818) 991-5392

Shipping and Handling: see information below.		
SalesTax: California please add 6.5% sales tax.		
TOTAL:		

Shipping and Handling: $4.00 for the first book and $1.75 for each additional book. Floppy disk: add $1.75 for shipping and handling. If you have to have it NOW, we can ship product to you in 24 to 48 hours for an additional charge and you will receive your item overnight or in 2 days.

New Riders Publishing P.O. Box 4846 Thousand Oaks, CA 91360   (818) 991-5392
FAX (818) 991-9263

TAF

NO POST
NECESS
IF MAIL
IN TH
UNITED S

BUSINESS REPLY MAIL
FIRST CLASS   PERMIT NO. 53   THOUSAND OAKS, CA

POSTAGE WILL BE PAID BY ADDRESSEE

New Riders Publishing
P.O. Box 4846
Thousand Oaks, CA 91359-9968